McCall's
CROCHET TREASURY

by The Editors of
McCall's Needlework & Crafts Publications

SIMON AND SCHUSTER/THE McCALL PATTERN COMPANY
New York

Published by Simon and Schuster
A Gulf+Western Company
Rockefeller Center, 630 Fifth Avenue
New York, New York 10020

Designed by Beri Greenwald

Manufactured in the United States of America

1 2 3 4 5 6 7 8 9 10

Library of Congress Cataloging in Publication Data

Main entry under title:

The McCall's crochet treasury.

1. Crocheting.   I. McCall's needlework & crafts.
TT820.M16   1976   746.4'34   76-17130
ISBN 0-671-22317-8

FOREWORD

WHAT A WORLD OF PLEASURE *there is in crochet, the most versatile of all the needlework arts! Crochet began as a lacemaking technique, to simulate the delicate needle laces used in accessories for the home. Because of its origin, for many years crochet was worked almost exclusively in fine threads with fine hooks.*

Today, crochet encompasses a whole range of fashion items for women, men and children, in yarns of every weight, from thinnest cotton to bulkiest wool and machine-washable acrylics. Home fashions still include lacy tablecloths and gossamer curtains, but also comprise thick, warm afghans and brightly patterned pillows. The variety of stitches and combinations of stitches in crochet is almost without limit and can produce openwork or thickset patterns, smooth or textured surfaces.

This book offers you more than 200 things to crochet, some simple, others more difficult and challenging, with complete directions for making them. For those who have never crocheted, an illustrated step-by-step lesson is included for right-handed and for left-handed persons. All the information you need to become a crocheter is given in Section V. Here is your key to a fascinating hobby, a creative craft to enjoy today and for many years to come.

The Editors of McCall's Needlework & Crafts

CONTENTS

1
FOR WOMEN

2
FOR MEN

3
FOR INFANTS, TODDLERS AND CHILDREN

4
CROCHET FOR THE HOME

5
COMPLETE INSTRUCTIONS FOR CROCHET

McCall's
CROCHET TREASURY

1

FOR WOMEN

INDIAN JACKET

This Aztec-patterned jacket glows in the colors of Indian pottery. Easy to make in rows of double and single crochet, and quick to work in knitting worsted or orlon yarn of same thickness, it has the casual fit of straight sides, loose sleeves and dropped shoulder line.

SIZES: Directions for small size (8-10). Changes for medium size (12-14) and large size (16) are in parentheses.

Body Bust Size: 31½"-32½" (34"-36"; 38").

Blocked Bust Size: 36" (40"-44").

MATERIALS: Knitting worsted, 3 (3-4) 4-oz. skeins orange (O); 1 (2-2) skeins brown (B); 1 skein each of light rust (LR), rust (R), turquoise (T). Crochet hook size I.

GAUGE: 3 sts = 1"; 1 row sc, 1 row dc = 1".

GENERAL DIRECTIONS: Design Note: When a row has more than one color, start extra color at beg of row; work over colors not being used to hide them. When changing colors, work last sc or dc of one color until there are 2 lps on hook, drop strand to wrong side, pick up new color and finish st. Cut and join colors as needed.

To Bind Off: At beg of a row, sl st across specified sts; **at end of a row,** leave specified number of sts unworked.

To Dec 1 St: Pull up a lp in each of 2 sts, (yo and through 2 lps on hook) twice.

VEST: BACK: Beg at lower edge, with B, ch 56 (62-68).

Row 1 (right side): Sc in 2nd ch from hook and in each ch across—55 (61-67) sc. Work off last 2 lps with R (see General Directions). With R, ch 1, turn.

Row 2: With R, sc in each st across, change to B in last sc. Ch 1, turn.

Row 3: With B, repeat row 2, change to R in last sc. Ch 1, turn.

Row 4: With R, repeat row 2, change to B in last sc. Ch 3, turn.

Row 5: With B, sk first st (ch 3 counts as first dc), dc in each st across, change to O in last dc. Ch 3, turn.

Row 6: With O, repeat row 5, working last dc in top of turning ch; change to T. Ch 3, turn.

Row 7: With T, repeat row 5.

Row 8: With O, repeat row 2.

Rows 9 and 10: With B, repeat row 5.

Row 11: With O, repeat row 2.

First Pattern Band: Rows 12-14: Following chart 1 from right to left, work 3 rows in sc.

Rows 15-33: With R, work 1 row sc. Working in dc, work 1 row B, 1 row T, 1 row B. With R, work 1 row sc. (With O, work 1 row dc, 1 row sc) 6 times. With R, work 1 row dc. With O, work 1 row sc, end right side, dec 1 st (see To Dec 1 St) at end of last row—54 (60-66) sts.

2nd Pattern Band: Following chart 2 from right to left, work 5 rows in dc. With O, work 1 row sc.

Shape Armholes: With R, bind off (see To Bind Off) 2 (3-4) sts each side of next row, work in dc across—50 (54-58) sts. Working in dc, work 2 rows B, 1 row LR. With T, work 1 row sc. Working in dc, work 1 row LR, 1 row B. With O, work 1 row sc. Working in dc, work 1 row T, 1 row B, 1 row R, 1 row O, 1 row LR. With T, work 1 row sc. With LR, work 1 row dc.

For Medium Size Only: Work another dc row with any desired color.

For Large Size: Work 2 more dc rows with any desired color.

Shape Shoulders: Working in sc, work 1 row B, 3 rows R; binding off 4 (5-6) sts each side once, 4 sts each side every row 3 times—18 (20-22) sts. End off.

RIGHT FRONT (Left-handed crocheters: This will be your left front): Beg at lower edge, with B, ch 26 (29-32).

Rows 1-11: Work same as for back on 25 (28-31) sts, end right side. Mark beg of last row for center edge.

First Pattern Band: Row 12: Following chart 3, working in sc, work from A to B.

Row 13: Working in sc, work from B to A.

Row 14: Repeat row 12.

Rows 15-33: Work same as for back, end side edge; do not dec on last row—25 (28-31) sts.

2nd Pattern Band: Row 34: Following chart 4, working in dc, work from A to B.

Row 35: Working in dc, work from B to A, dec 1 st at center edge—24 (27-30) sts. Working in dc, work to top of chart. With O, work 1 row sc.

Shape Armhole: Working in dc, with R, dec 1 st a center edge and bind off 2 (3-4) sts at arm side—21 (23-25) sts. Work to shoulder same as for back; **at the same time,** dec 1 st at center edge every 3rd row 5 (6-7) times; **at the same time,** when armhole measures same as back, working sc in same color sequence, bind off 4 (5-6) sts at arm side once, 4 sts at same edge every row 3 times.

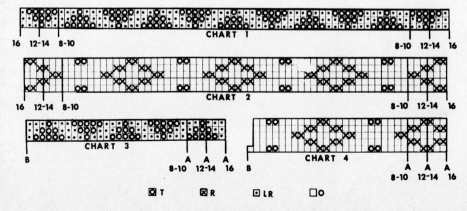

CHART 1
16 12-14 8-10   8-10 12-14 16

CHART 2
16 12-14 8-10   8-10 12-14 16

CHART 3
B   A A A
                  8-10 12-14 16

CHART 4
B   A A A
                  8-10 12-14 16

⊡ T   ⊠ R   ⊡ LR   □ O

LEFT FRONT: Work same as for right front to end of row 11, end right side. Mark end of last row for center edge.

First Pattern Band: Row 12: Following chart 3, working in sc, work from B to A. Complete same as for right front, reversing shaping (A on chart is center front).

SLEEVES: Beg at lower edge, with B, ch 37 (40-43).

Row 1: Sc in 2nd ch from hook and in each ch across—36 (39-42) sc. Ch 3, turn.

Row 2: Dc in each st across, change to T in last dc. Ch 3, turn.

Row 3: With T, repeat row 2, change to R. Ch 3, turn.

Row 4: With R, repeat row 2, change to O. Ch 1, turn.

Row 5: With O, sc in each st,

change to R. Ch 3, turn. Repeating row 2, work 1 row R, 1 row T, 2 rows B, 1 row O.

Next Row: With R, repeat row 5, inc 1 st each side, then every 4th row 6 times more. With O, repeat row 2. With B, repeat row 5. Working 1 row sc, 1 row dc alternately, work 11 rows O, 2 rows T, 2 rows O, 2 rows R, 1 row B, 1 row O, 2 rows B—50 (53-56) sts. End off.

FINISHING: Sew shoulder seams. Sew last row of sleeves to side edge of armholes. Sew underarm of back and fronts to side edge of sleeves. Sew side and sleeve seams.

Right Center Band: Beg at lower edge, with O, ch 5. Sc in 2nd ch from hook and in each ch across—4 sc. Ch 1, turn. Working

in sc, work 3 more rows O, 2 rows R, 4 rows B, 2 rows R, 4 rows O, 2 rows T, 4 rows B, 2 rows T. Repeat these 24 rows until piece is long enough to fit from lower right front to center back neck edge. End off.

Left Center Band: Work same as right center band. Sew bands to fronts and back neck edges. Weave ends tog at back of neck. From right side, with R, work 1 row sl st around front and neck edges. Run in yarn ends on wrong side. Steam-press lightly.

BELT: With R, ch 5. Sc in 2nd ch from hook and in each ch across—4 sc. Ch 1, turn. Work in sc until piece measures 80″ or desired length.

CANDY-STRIPED CARDIGAN

Shown on page 16

A simple single crochet and chain-one pattern forms the solid yoke and sleeves, the candy-striped bands and, with slight variations, the chevron-striped design on the front and back of this colorful cardigan.

SIZES: Directions for small size (8-10). Changes for medium size (12-14) and large size (16-18) are in parentheses.

Body Bust Size: 31½″-32½″ (34″-36″; 38″-40″).

Blocked Bust Size (closed): 38″ (40″-43″).

MATERIALS: Knitting worsted, 3 (4-4) 4-oz. skeins red (R); 2 skeins white (W). Crochet hook size I. Four buttons.

GAUGE: 4 sts = 1″.

Note: When changing colors, pull new color through last 2 lps to

complete sc. Cut and join colors as needed.

To Bind Off: At beg of a row, sl st loosely across specified sts; **at end of a row,** leave specified number of sts unworked.

To Dec 1 St: At beg of a row, ch 1, pull up a lp in each of first 2 sts, yo and through 3 lps on hook; **at end of a row,** pull up a lp in each of last 2 sts, yo and through 3 lps on hook. **Next Row:** Work in pat as established (sc over each sc, ch 1 over ch-1 sp).

To Inc 1 St: At beg of a row, ch

1 loosely, 2 sc in first st; **at end of a row,** 2 sc in last st. **Next Row:** Work in pat as established; when there are 3 sc tog, work into sc, ch 1 pat.

CARDIGAN: BACK: Beg at lower edge, with W, ch 63 (71-71); drop W. Do not turn.

Border: Row 1: With R, make lp on hook, sc in first ch, * ch 1, sk next ch, sc in next ch, repeat from * across—32 (36-36) sc. Work off last sc with W (see Note). With W, ch 1, turn.

Row 2: With W, sc in first sc, *

CANDY-STRIPED CARDIGAN

ch 1, sc in next sc, repeat from * across. Drop W. Do not turn. Pick up R at beg of row. Repeat row 2 for border pat, working 1 row R, 1 row W alternately and turning every other row, until 15 rows from start, end R row. Check gauge; piece should measure 16" (18"-18") wide.

Body Pattern: Row 1 (shell row): With W, sc in first sc, * sk next ch-1 sp, work shell of 5 dc in next ch-1 sp, sk next sc, sc in each of next 2 sc, repeat from * across, end last repeat sc in last sc—8 (9-9) shells.

Row 2: With R, sc in first sc, * sc in each of next 2 dc, 3 sc in next dc, sc in each of next 2 dc, sc in each of next 2 sc, repeat from * across, end sc in last sc—72 (81-81) sc. With W, ch 1, turn.

Row 3: With W, sk first sc, * sc in each of next 3 sc, 3 sc in next sc, sc in each of next 3 sc, sk next 2 sc, repeat from * across, end last repeat sk last sc instead of last 2 sc. Repeat last row for pat, working 1 row R, 1 row W, 3 rows R, (1 row W, 1 row R) twice, 3 rows W, (1 row R, 1 row W) twice, 3 rows R, (1 row W, 1 row R) twice.

Next Row (cluster row): With W, ch 3, sk first sc; holding back last lp of each dc on hook, make dc in each of next 3 sc, yo and through 4 lps on hook (½ cluster made), ch 2, * sc in next sc, ch 2, holding back last lp of each dc on hook, dc in each of next 2 sc, (sk next sc, dc in each of next 2 dc) twice, yo and through 7 lps on hook (cluster made), ch 2, repeat from * across, end ½ cluster across next 3 sc—7 (8-8) clusters, plus ½ cluster each side. Cut W.

Next Row: With R, sc in ½ cluster, ch 1, sc in ch-2 sp, ch 1, * (sc, ch 1) twice in next ch-2 sp, repeat from * across, end sc, ch 1 in last ch-2 sp, sc in ½ cluster—32 (36-36) sc.

Shape Armholes: Keeping to pat as established, bind off (see To

Bind Off) 4 sts each side of next row, 2 sts each side of next 1 (2-1) rows—26 (28-30) sc. Work even until armholes measure 7″ (7½″-8″) above first row of armhole shaping.

Shape Shoulders: Keeping to pat, bind off 6 sts each side of next 2 rows, 4 (6-6) sts each side of next row—10 (10-12) sc. End off.

RIGHT FRONT: Beg at lower edge, with W, ch 31 (31-39). Drop W; do not turn.

Row 1: With R, make lp on hook, sc in first ch, * ch 1, sk next ch, sc in next ch, repeat from * across—16 (16-20) sc. Work off last sc with W. With W, ch 1, turn. Work same as back border. Work body pat same as back, having 4 (4-5) shells on first shell row; 3 (3-4) clusters plus ½ cluster each side on cluster row.

Next Row: With R, work same as on back—16 (16-20) sc. Mark beg of right side row for center edge.

Shape V-Neck and Armhole: With R, keeping to sc, ch 1 pat, bind off 4 sts at arm side of next row, 2 sts at same edge of next 1 (1-2) rows; **at the same time,** dec 1 st (see To Dec 1 St) at center edge

every 3rd (3rd-2nd) row 9 (7-13) times. Work even, if necessary, on remaining 16 (18-18) sts until armhole measures same as back. Bind off 6 sts at arm side of next 2 rows. End off.

LEFT FRONT: Work same as for right front, reversing shaping (mark end of right side row for center edge).

SLEEVES: Beg at lower edge, with W, ch 29 (31-33). Work border same as for back until 8 R rows are completed—15 (16-17) sc. Cut W.

Next Row (inc row): With R, work in sc, ch 1 pat across, working (sc, ch 1) twice in 4 ch-1 sps evenly spaced across—19 (20-21) sc. Work in pat as established, inc 1 st (see To Inc 1 St) each side every 1½″ 6 times—25 (26-27) sc. Work even until piece measures 17½″ from start or desired length to underarm. Check gauge; piece above last inc row should measure 12½″ (13″-13½″) wide.

Shape Cap: Keeping to pat, bind off 4 sts each side of next row. Dec 1 st each side every row 16 (17-18) times—9 sts. End off.

LEFT CENTER BAND AND LAPEL: With W, ch 87 (89-91).

Work in border pat as for back on 44 (45-46) sc for 4 rows, end W row.

Shape Lapel: Mark beg of next row for top edge. With R, work in pat across 24 (25-26) sc only. Turn. Working 1 row W, 1 row R alternately, work in pat, dec 2 sts (1 pat) at lower edge every row until 7 (8-9) sc remain. End off.

RIGHT CENTER BAND AND LAPEL: Work same as for left center band for 4 rows, end W row. Mark end of last row for top edge. Cut R and W.

Shape Lapel: Beg at lower edge, sk 20 sc; with R, sc in next sc, work in pat to upper edge—24 (25-26) sc. Complete same as for first lapel.

FINISHING: Run in yarn ends on wrong side. Block pieces. Sew shoulder seams. Sew in sleeves; sew side and sleeve seams. With upper edge of lapels at shoulder seam, sew shaped edge of center band and lapel to front edges. With R, work 1 row sc across top of lapel and back of neck. Steam lightly. Sew buttons to left center band; spaces between sts form buttonholes.

LACED-UP PULL

Shown on page 18

Muted tones of yarn are doubled for tweed striping in this hooded sweater. The yoke is crocheted in one piece from top down, forming the raglan.

SIZES: Directions for small size (6-8). Changes for medium size (10-12) and large size (14-16) are in parentheses.

Body Bust Size: 30½″-31½″ (32½″-34″; 36″-38″).

Blocked Bust Size: 34″ (37″-39½″).

MATERIALS: Yarn of knitting worsted weight, 3 (3-4) 4-oz. skeins each of winter white (A), parch-

ment (B) and beige (C). Mohair-type yarn, 2 1-oz. balls mink brown (D). Crochet hook size J.

GAUGE: 9 dc = 4″; 4 rows = 3″ (double strand of yarn).

Note 1: Entire pullover is worked with 2 strands of yarn from neck to lower edge. When changing color, pull new color through last 2 lps to complete st. Cut and join colors as needed.

Note 2: Ch 3 at beg of row is counted as 1 dc.

PULLOVER: YOKE: Beg at neck edge with 1 strand of A and B (see Note 1), ch 48 (48-51).

Row 1: Dc in 4th ch from hook (counts as 2 dc), dc in each of next 6 (6-7) ch (front), (2 dc, ch 1, 2 dc) in next ch, dc in each of next 6 ch (sleeve), (2 dc, ch 1, 2 dc) in next ch, dc in each of next 14 (14-15) ch

front—76 (84-87) dc. Turn each row.

Row 2: Ch 3, sk first dc, dc in each dc and ch across—77 (85-89) dc. Working in dc, work 2 rows A and C, 2 rows A and B, 3 rows A and C, inc 2 dc evenly spaced across 3rd A and C row—79 (87-91) dc. Working in dc, work 2 rows B and C, 2 rows A and B, 3 rows B and C, 6 rows C and D or as many rows as needed for desired length. End off.

Weave side seam.

SLEEVES: Join 1 strand of A and C in ch-1 sp at underarm, ch 3, dc in each dc around—32 (35-35) dc. Turn each row.

Row 2: Ch 3, sk first dc, dc in each dc. Working in dc, work 4 rows A and B, 2 rows A and C, 2 rows A and B, 5 rows B and C, 5 rows C and D; **at the same time,** dec 1 dc (**to dec 1 dc,** pull up a lp in each of 2 dc, (yo hook and through 2 lps) twice) each side every 4th row 2 (3-3) times—28 (29-29) dc. End off.

FINISHING: Steam-press garment lightly. Weave sleeve seams. With 1 strand C and D, work 1 rnd dc around neck edge, dec 5 dc evenly spaced. End off.

From right side, with 1 strand C and D, work 1 row sl st around front opening. End off. Beg at left front neck edge, with 1 strand C and D, sc in back lp of each sl st around neck opening. End off.

HOOD: Beg at back edge, with 1 strand A and B, ch 50 (52-54).

Row 1: Dc in 4th ch from hook and in each ch—48 (50-52) dc. Turn.

Rows 2 and 3: Ch 3, sk first dc, dc in each dc. Working in dc, work 5 rows B and C, 4 rows C and D; **at the same time,** inc 1 dc each side every other row 4 times—56 (58-60) dc. End off. Weave back seam; weave to neck edge.

CORD: With 1 strand C and D, make chain 50″ long. End off; knot ends. Lace up opening.

(back), (2 dc, ch 1, 2 dc) in next ch, dc in each of next 6 ch (sleeve), (2 dc, ch 1, 2 dc) in next ch, dc in each of next 8 (8-9) ch (front)—58 (58-61) dc (see Note 2). Turn each row.

Row 2: Ch 3, sk first dc, dc in each dc across, work (dc, ch 1, dc) in each ch-1 sp—66 (66-69) dc.

Row 3: Ch 3, sk first dc, dc in each dc across, work (2 dc, ch 1, 2 dc) in each ch-1 sp—82 (82-85) dc.

Row 4: Repeat row 2, inc 1 dc (**to inc 1 dc,** work 2 dc in same st) in center of each sleeve—92 (92-95) dc.

Rows 5-7: Repeat row 2—116 (116-119) dc.

Row 8: With 1 strand of A and C, repeat 4 (3-3)—126 (132-135) dc.

Row 9: With 1 strand of A and C, repeat row 4—136 (142-145) dc.

For Medium and Large Sizes Only: With 1 strand of A and C, repeat row 2—(150-153) dc.

For All Sizes: End off.

Divide Work: Body: Join 1 strand of A and B in ch-1 sp at underarm. Ch 3, dc in each of 36 (40-41) dc across back, dc in ch-1 sp, sk next 31 (34-34) dc for left sleeve, dc in each of 19 (21-22) dc across front, ch 1 (1-2), continue across the 19 (21-22) dc on other

ARAN-PATTERN CARDIGAN

Popular fisherman's knit patterns are adapted in crochet for this unusual cardigan, worked in panels of raised stitches. For a more authentic look, make it in natural wool color.

SIZES: Directions for small size (8-10). Changes for medium size (12-14) and large size (16-18) are in parentheses.

Body Bust Size: 31½"-32½" (34"-36"; 38"-40").

Blocked Bust Size (closed): 33" (37"-41").

MATERIALS: Knitting worsted, 7 (8-9) 4-oz. skeins. Crochet hook size H. Six ¾" plastic rings for buttons.

GAUGE: 7 sts = 2"; 7 rows = 2".

To Bind Off: At beg of a row, ch 1, sl st loosely across specified number of sts; **at end of a row,** leave specified number of sts unworked.

To Dec 1 St: At beg of a row, ch 1, pull up a lp in each of 2 sts, yo hook and through 3 lps on hook; **at end of a row,** work to within last 2 sts, pull up a lp in each of 2 sts, yo hook and through 3 lps on hook.

To Inc 1 St: Work 2 sc in same st.

STITCH PATTERN: Note: Do not work in st directly behind raised dc or double raised dc, or in eye of a cluster.

CLUSTER: (Yo hook, draw up a lp in st) 4 times, yo and draw through all 9 lps on hook. Ch 1 tightly to form eye. (Cluster is worked from wrong side but appears on right side.)

RAISED DC: Dc around upright bar of dc 1 row below, inserting hook behind dc from front to back to front, for ridge on right side.

DOUBLED RAISED DC: Holding back last lp of each dc on hook, make 2 dc around upright bar of st 1 row below, yo and through all 3 lps on hook.

POPCORN: 4 dc in st, drop lp off hook, insert hook in top of first dc, pick up dropped lp and pull through.

CARDIGAN: BACK: Beg at lower edge, ch 58 (64-70).

Row 1: Sc in 2nd ch from hook and in each ch across—57 (63-69) sc. Ch 1, turn each row. .

Row 2 (wrong side): Sc in each of first 4 (7-10) sts, (cluster in next sc, sc in each of next 15 sts) 3 times, end cluster in next st, sc in each of last 4 (7-10) sts.

Row 3 (right side): Sc in each of first 2 (5-8) sc, * work dc around post of next sc 1 row below (row 1), sk next sc on row 2 (see Stitch Pattern: Note), sc in each of next 3 sts, dc around post of next sc 1 row below, sk next sc on row 2, sc in each of next 4 sc; holding back last lp of each dc on hook, make 2 dc around next sc 1 row below, yo and through 3 lps on hook, sk next sc on row 2, sc in next sc, sk 1 sc on row 1, make 2 dc around next sc as before, sk next sc on row 2, sc in each of next 4 sc, repeat from * twice, end dc around post of next sc 1 row below, sc in each of next 3 sts, dc around post of next sc 1 row below, sc in each of next 2 (5-8) sc.

Row 4: Sc in each of first 3 (6-9) sts, (cluster in next sc, sc in next sc, cluster in next sc, sc in each of next 13 sts) 3 times; end cluster in next sc, sc in next sc, cluster in next sc, sc in each of last 3 (6-9) sts.

Row 5: Sc in each of first 2 (5-8) sc, (raised dc in raised dc, sc in each of next 3 sts, raised dc in raised dc, sc in each of next 3 sts, double raised dc in double raised dc, sc in each of next 3 sc, double raised dc in double raised dc, sc in each of next 3 sc) 3 times, end raised dc in raised dc, sc in each of next 3 sts, raised dc in raised dc, sc in each of last 2 (5-8) sc.

Row 6: Repeat row 2.

Row 7: Sc in each of first 2 (5-8) sc, (raised dc in raised dc, sc in each of next 3 sts, raised dc in raised dc, sc in each of next 2 sc, double raised dc in double raised dc, sc in each of next 5 sc, double raised dc in double raised dc, sc in each of next 2 sc) 3 times, end raised dc in raised dc, sc in each of next 3 sts, raised dc in raised dc, sc in each of last 2 (5-8) sts.

Row 8: Repeat row 4.

Row 9: Sc in each of first 2 (5-8) sc, (raised dc in raised dc, sc in each of next 3 sts, raised dc in raised dc, sc in next sc, double raised dc in double raised dc, sc in each of next 3 sc, popcorn in next sc, sc in each of next 3 sc, double raised dc in double raised dc, sc in next sc) 3 times, end raised dc in raised dc, sc in each of next 3 sts, raised dc in raised dc, sc in each of last 2 (5-8) sc.

Row 10: Repeat row 2.
Row 11: Repeat row 7.
Row 12: Repeat row 4.
Row 13: Repeat row 5.
Row 14: Repeat row 2.

Row 15: Sc in each of first 2 (5-8) sc, (raised dc in raised dc, sc in each of next 3 sts, raised dc in raised dc, sc in each of next 4 sc, double raised dc in double raised dc, sc in next sc, double raised dc in double raised dc, sc in each of next 4 sc) 3 times, end raised dc in raised dc, sc in each of next 3 sts, raised dc in raised dc, sc in each of last 2 (5-8) sc. Repeat rows 4-15 for pat until piece measures 18" from start or desired length to underarm. Check gauge; piece should measure 16" (18"-20") wide.

Shape Raglan Armholes: Keeping to pat, bind off (see To Bind Off and To Dec 1 St) 4 sts each side of next row, then dc 1 st each side every other row 15 (17-19) times—19 (21-23) sts. End off.

RIGHT FRONT (Left-handed crocheters: This will be your left front): Beg at lower edge, ch 27 (30-33).

Row 1: Sc in 2nd ch from hook and in each ch across—26 (29-32) sc. Ch 1, turn each row.

Row 2 (wrong side): Sc in each of first 4 (7-10) sts, cluster in next sc, sc in each of next 15 sts, cluster in next st, sc in each of last 5 sts.

Mark end of last row for center edge.

Row 3 (right side): Sc in each of first 3 sc, work dc around post of next st 1 row below (row 1), sk next sc on row 2, sc in each of next 3 sts, dc around post of next sc 1 row below, sk next sc on row 2, sc in each of next 4 sc, double raised dc around next sc 1 row below, sk next sc on row 2, sc in next sc, sk 1 sc on row 1, double raised dc around next sc as before, sk next sc on row 2, sc in each of next 4 sc, dc around post of next sc 1 row below, sc in each of next 3 sts, dc around post of next sc 1 row below, sc in each of last 2 (5-8) sc.

Row 4: Sc in each of first 3 (6-9) sts, cluster in next sc, sc in next sc, cluster in next sc, sc in each of next 13 sts, cluster in next sc, sc in next sc, cluster in next sc, sc in each of last 4 sts. Continue in pat as established until piece measures same as back to underarm. Check gauge; piece should measure 7" (8"-9") wide.

Shape Raglan Armhole and Neck: Keeping to pat, bind off 4 sts at side edge of next row. Dec 1 st at same edge every other row 9 (11-13) times. Bind off 3 sts at center edge of next row, then dec 1 st at center edge every other row 3 (4-5) times; **at the same time,** continue to dec 1 st at arm side every other row 6 times more—1 st remains. End off.

LEFT FRONT: Work same as for right front to end of row 1. Mark end of row for center front.

Row 2 (wrong side): Sc in each of 5 sts, cluster in next st, sc in each of next 15 sts, cluster in next sc, sc in each of last 4 (7-10) sc.

Row 3 (right side): Sc in each of first 2 (5-8) sc; dc around post of next sc 1 row below (row 1), sk next sc on row 2, sc in each of next 3 sts, dc around post of next sc 1 row below, sk next sc on row 2, sc in each of next 4 sc, double raised dc around next sc 1 row below, sk next sc on row 2, sc in next sc, sk 1 sc on row 1, double raised dc around next sc as before, sk next sc on row 2, sc in each of next 4 sc, dc around post of next sc 1 row below, sc in each of next 3 sts, dc around post of next sc 1 row below, sc in each of last 3 sc. Work in pat as established; complete same as for right front, reversing shaping.

SLEEVES: Beg at lower edge, ch 28 (30-32).

Row 1: Sc in 2nd ch from hook and in each ch across—27 (29-31) sc. Ch 1, turn each row.

Row 2 (wrong side): Sc in each of first 5 (6-7) sc, cluster in next sc, sc in each of next 15 sc, cluster in next sc, sc in each of last 5 (6-7) sc.

Row 3: Work same as row 3 on right front, having 3 (4-5) sc at beg and end of row. Continue in pat as established, inc 1 sc (see To Inc 1 St) each side every 6th row 7 (8-9) times, working added sts in sc—41 (45-49) sts. Work even until piece measures 17" from start. Check gauge; piece above last inc row should measure 11¾" (12¾"-14") wide.

Shape Raglan Cap: Keeping to pat, bind off 4 sts each side of next row. Dec 1 st each side every other row 14 (16-18) times, then every row twice—1 st remains. End off.

FINISHING: Block pieces; do not flatten pat. Sew caps of sleeves to back and front armholes. Sew side and sleeve seams.

Left Front Border: Work 6 rows sc on left front edge. End off.

Right Front Border: Work 3 rows sc on right front edge, having same number of sc as left front edge.

With pins, mark position of 6 buttonholes evenly spaced on right front edge; first pin in 3rd sc from lower edge; last pin in 3rd sc below neck edge.

Row 4: * Work sc to within 1 sc of pin, ch 2, sk next 2 sc, repeat from * 5 times, sc in next sc, sc in last sc. Ch 1, turn.

Row 5: Sc in each sc and in each ch of buttonholes. Ch 1, turn. Work 1 more row in sc. End off.

Neck Border: From right side, beg 3 rows in from center edge, work 1 row sc around neck edge, ending within 3 rows of center front edge. Ch 1, turn. Work in sc for 6 rows, decreasing to desired fit. Do not turn at end of last row.

Next Row: Working from left to right, sc in each sc. End off.

From right side, beg at neck edge, work 1 row sc down front edge, around lower edge, up other front edge, ending at neck edge. End off.

Sleeve Border: From right side, work 5 rnds sc around lower edge of each sleeve, easing in to desired fit.

BUTTONS (make 6): Work sc tightly around plastic ring. Join in first sc. End off, leaving a long end for sewing. Thread needle, gather sts tog at center. Sew on buttons.

SHAWL-COLLARED JACKET

SIZES: Directions for small size (8-10). Changes for medium size (12-14) and large size (16) are in parentheses.

Body Bust Size: 31½"-32½" (34"-36"; 38").

Blocked Bust Size (closed): 34" (37"-40").

MATERIALS: Knitting worsted, 6 (7-7) 4-oz. skeins. Crochet hook size I. Four buttons.

GAUGE: 11 sts = 4".

To Bind Off: At beg of a row, ch 1, sl st loosely across specified number of sts; **at end of a row,** leave specified number of sts unworked.

To Dec 1 St: At beg of a row, ch 2, pull up a lp in sp between first 2 hdc, pull up a lp in next st, yo hook and through 3 lps on hook; **at end of a row,** pull up a lp in each of last 2 sps, yo hook and through 3 lps on hook.

JACKET: BACK: Waistband Ribbing (worked from side seam to side seam): Ch 16.

Row 1: Hdc in 3rd ch from hook and in each ch across—14 hdc. Ch 2, turn.

Row 2 (right side): Hdc in back lp of each hdc across. Ch 2, turn.

Row 3: Hdc in horizontal bar in front of top 2 lps of each st across. Ch 2, turn. Repeat last 2 rows for ribbing until 28 (32-36) rows from start, end right side. Check gauge; piece when slightly stretched should measure about 14½" (15½"-16½") from start; 5" wide. Ch 1; working along side edge from right side, work 48 (52-56) sl sts across. End off.

Bodice: Row 1: From right side, join yarn in first sl st, ch 2, hdc in same sl st and in each sl st across—48 (52-56) hdc. Ch 2, turn.

Row 2: Hdc in sp between first 2 hdc, * hdc in next sp between hdc, repeat from * across, end hdc in sp between last hdc and ch 2. Ch 2, turn. Repeat last row for pat until piece measures 7" above waistband ribbing.

Shape Armholes: Bind off 2 sts each side of next row (see To Bind Off and To Dec 1 St). Dec 1 st each side every row 2 (3-4) times—40 (42-44) sts. Work even until armholes measure 7½" (8"-8½") above first bound-off sts.

Shape Shoulders: Bind off 4 sts each side of next 2 rows, 3 (3-4) sts next row—18 (20-20) sts. End off.

Lower Back: From right side, work 51 (55-59) sl sts across lower edge of waistband ribbing. End off. Repeat rows 1 and 2 same as on bodice on 51 (55-59) hdc for 9". End off.

LEFT FRONT (Left-handed crocheters: This will be your right front): **Waistband Ribbing:** Work same as for back ribbing for 16 (18-20) rows, end right side. Check gauge; piece when slightly stretched should measure 7½" (8"-8½") from start. Ch 1; working along side edge, from right side, work 26 (28-30) sl sts across. End off.

Bodice: Row 1: Work same as for back on 26 (28-30) hdc for 11 rows. Mark end of last row for center edge. Ch 2, turn.

Shape Collar: Row 1: Work 2 hdc in back lp of first st (collar), hdc in each sp between sts across—27 (29-31) sts. Ch 2, turn.

Row 2: Work in pat to within last 3 sts, (hdc in horizontal bar in front of top 2 lps of next st) 3 times. Ch 2, turn.

Row 3: Work in rib pat as established across first 4 sts, hdc in sp between sts across.

Row 4: Work in pat to within last 5 sts, work in rib pat across last 5 sts.

Row 5: Work in rib pat across first 4 sts, work 2 hdc in back lp of next st (1 st inc in collar), finish row in pat. Continue to work 1 st more in rib pat every row until 16 sts are worked in rib pat; **at the same time,** inc 1 st at inner edge of collar every 4th row 3 times more; **at the same time,** when piece measures same as back to underarm, bind off 2 sts at side edge once. Dec 1 st at same edge every row 2 (3-4) times—27 (28-29) sts. Keeping 16 sts at center edge in rib pat, work even until armhole measures 7½" (8"-8½") above first row of armhole shaping.

Shape Shoulder: Keeping collar in rib pat, bind off 4 sts at arm side of next 2 rows, 3 (4-5) sts next row—16 sts. Work in rib pat for 3" (3½"-3½"). End off.

Lower Front: From right side, work 26 (28-30) sl sts across lower edge of waistband ribbing. End off. Repeat rows 1 and 2 same as on back bodice on 26 (28-30) hdc for 2". Inc 1 hdc (to inc, work 2 hdc in same sp) at side edge of next row—27 (29-31) hdc. Work even until piece measures same as back. End off.

RIGHT FRONT: Waistband Ribbing: Work same as for left front.

Bodice: Work same as for left front for 11 rows. Mark beg of last row for center edge. Ch 2, turn.

Shape Collar: Work hdc in each sp between sts across to within last st, end 2 hdc in back lp of next st—27 (29-31) sts. Ch 2, turn.

Next Row: Hdc in horizontal bar in front of top 2 lps of next 3 sts, work hdc in each sp between sts across. Ch 2, turn. Complete same as left front, reversing shaping.

SLEEVES: Ribbing: Ch 14. Work in ribbing same as for waistband on 12 hdc for 7" (7½"-7½"), end right side. Ch 1; working

The shawl-collared jacket, worked entirely in half double crochet, has an unusual ribbing pattern nipping in the waist, forming the cuffs and patch pockets, and decorating the collar.

along side edge, work 24 (26-28) sl sts across. End off. From right side, work hdc in each sl st across. Ch 2, turn.

Next Row: Hdc in each sp between sts across—24 (26-28) hdc. Work in pat as established, inc 1 st each side of next row, then every 2" 4 times more—34 (36-38) hdc. Work even until piece measures 17½" from start.

Shape Cap: Bind off 2 sts each side of next row. Dec 1 st each side every other row 3 times, then every row 5 (6-7) times—14 sts. End off.

POCKETS (make 2): Beg at side edge, ch 26. Work ribbing as for waistband on 24 sts for 7". Ch 1; sl st along side edge. Ch 1, turn. Sc in each sl st across. End off.

FINISHING: Block pieces. Sew shoulder seams. Weave ends of collar tog at back of neck. Weave collar to back neck edge. Sew in sleeves; sew side and sleeve seams. From right side, work 1 row sl st loosely around outer edge of collar. Join yarn in lower side seam. From right side, work 1 row sc around entire outer edge of jacket; join with a sl st in first sc. End off. Work 1 rnd sc around lower edge of each sleeve. Sew a pocket to each front as pictured. Sew buttons on left front edge, first button at start of collar, one button at beg and end of waistband ribbing, last button at center of lower front. Spaces between sts on right front edge form buttonholes.

LACE CARDIGAN

In white or in pastels, this shell stitch cardigan will see you through every hour of the day, every month of the year.

SIZES: Directions for small size (6-8). Changes for medium size (10-12) and large size (14) are in parentheses.

Body Bust Size: 30½"-31½" (32½"-34"; 36).

Blocked Bust Size (closed): 32" (34"-36").

MATERIALS: 3-ply fingering yarn, 7 (8-9) 1-oz. balls. Aluminum crochet hook size G. Steel crochet hook No. 1. Six beads for button molds.

GAUGE: 11 sts = 2"; 3 rows = 1".

SHELL PATTERN: Row 1: Dec in 4th ch from hook, * ch 1, sk next ch, sc in next sc, ch 1, sk next ch, dc in each of next 3 ch, repeat from * across, end ch 1, sk next ch, sc in last ch. Turn each row.

Row 2: Half shell of ch 3, dc in first sc, * ch 1, sc in center dc of 3-dc shell, ch 1, shell of 3 dc in next sc, repeat from * across, end ch 1, sc in top of turning ch. Repeat row 2 for shell pat.

CARDIGAN: BACK: Beg at lower edge, with size G hook, ch 90 (102-114). Work in shell pat on 14½ (16½-18½) pats until piece measures 14" from start or desired length to underarm. Check gauge; piece should measure 16" (18"-20") wide. Ch 1, turn.

Shape Armholes: Row 1: Sl st loosely across 6 sts; work ½ shell of ch 3, dc in next sc, work in pat across. Ch 1, turn.

Row 2: Repeat last row—12½ (14½-16½) shells. Ch 1, turn.

Row 3: Sl st loosely across 3 sts; work ch 1, sc in center dc of next shell, ch 1, 3 dc in next sc, work in pat across—12 (14-16) shells. Ch 1, turn.

Row 4: Repeat last row, end last repeat ½ shell of 2 dc in last sc—11½ (13½-15½) shells. Ch 1, turn.

Row 5: Sl st loosely across 3 sts; work ½ shell of ch 3, dc in next sc, work in pat across, end ½ shell of 2 dc in last sc—10 (12-14) shells, plus two ½ shells. Ch 1, turn.

Row 6: Repeat last row, end last repeat sc in top of ch 3—10½ (12½-14½) shells.

For Medium Size Only: Repeat rows 3 and 4.

For Large Size Only: Repeat rows 3-6.

For All Sizes: Work even on 10½ (11½-12½) shells until armholes measure 7" (7½"-8") above first row of armhole shaping.

Shape Shoulders: Bind off 1 shell at beg of next 4 rows, 1½ (1½-2) shells at beg of next 2 rows—3½ (4½-4½) shells. End off.

LEFT FRONT (Left-handed crocheters: This will be your right front): Beg at lower edge, with size G hook, ch 48 (54-60). Work in shell pat on 7½ (8½-9½) pats until piece measures same as back to underarm. Mark end of last row for side edge. Ch 1, turn.

Shape Armhole and V-Neck: Sl st loosely across 6 sts; work ½ shell of ch 3, dc in next sc, work in pat across—6½ (7½-8½) shells. Turn. Work 1 row even. Ch 1, turn.

Next Row: Sl st loosely across first 3 sts; ch 1, sc in next dc, ch 1, 3 dc in next sc, work in pat across—½ pat dec at arm side.

Next Row: Repeat last row, end last repeat ½ shell of 2 dc in last sc—½ pat dec at neck and arm side. Continue to dec ½ pat at arm side every other row 1 (2-3) times more; **at the same time,** dec ½ pat at neck edge every 4th row until

3½ (3½-4½) shells remain. Work even until armhole measures same as back, end arm side.

Shape Shoulder: Bind off 1 shell at beg of arm side twice. End off.

RIGHT FRONT: Work same as for left front; pat is reversible.

SLEEVES: Beg at lower edge, with size G hook, ch 54 loosely. Work in shell pat on 8½ pats for 6 rows.

Row 7: Work in pat across, end (ch 1, sc, ch 1, dc) in top of ch 3. Ch 1, turn.

Row 8: Sc in first dc, ch 1, shell of 3 dc in next sc, work in pat across, end (ch 1, sc, ch 1, dc) in top of ch 3. Ch 1, turn.

Row 9: Sc in first dc, ch 1, shell of 3 dc in next sc, work in pat across, end ½ shell of 2 dc in sc—9½ shells.

Rows 10-12: Repeat row 9.

Row 13: Work in pat across, end shell of 3 dc in sc. Turn.

Row 14: Ch 3, sk first dc, sc in next dc, ch 1, shell of 3 dc in next sc, work in pat across, end 3 dc in sc. Turn.

Row 15: Ch 3, sk first dc, sc in next dc, ch 1, shell of 3 dc in next sc, work in pat across, end shell of 3 dc in sc, ch 1, sc in ch-3 sp. Turn.

Row 16: ½ shell of ch 3, dc in first sc, work in pat across, end sc in ch-3 sp—10½ shells.

Rows 17 and 18: Repeat row 16, end sc in top of ch 3. Repeat rows 7-18 1 (1-2) times—12½ (12½-14½) shells.

For Medium Size Only: Repeat rows 7-9—13½ shells. Work even on 12½ (13½-14½) shells until piece measures 16″ from start or ½″ less (border allowance) than desired length to underarm. Check gauge; piece above last inc row should measure 13½″ (14½″-15½″) wide.

Shape Cap: Work back armhole shaping rows 1-6. Continue to dec ½ shell at beg of every row until 5 shells remain. End off.

FINISHING: Block pieces. Sew shoulder seams. Sew in sleeves; sew side and sleeve seams.

Sleeve Border: Join yarn in seam.

Rnd 1: From right side, with steel crochet hook, sc in each st around lower edge of sleeve. Join with a sl st in first sc. Ch 1, turn.

Rnd 2: Sc in each sc around. Join; ch 1, turn.

Rnds 3 and 4: Repeat rnd 2.

Rnd 5 (shell rnd): * Sc in first sc, ch 1, sk next sc, shell of 3 dc in next sc, ch 1, sk next sc, repeat from * around. Join; end off.

Outer Border: Rnd 1: Beg at lower right side seam, with steel crochet hook, sc in each st around entire outer edge of cardigan, working 3 sc in each lower front corner to keep work flat. Join; ch 1, turn.

Rnd 2: Repeat rnd 1.

With pins, mark position of 6 buttonholes evenly spaced on right front edge, first buttonhole 1½″ above lower edge, last buttonhole 2 sts before start of neck shaping.

Rnd 3: * Sc in each sc to within 1 st of pin, ch 2, sk next 2 sts, sc in next st, repeat from * 5 times, continue to work sc to end of rnd. Join; ch 1, turn.

Rnd 4: Sc in each sc and ch-2 sp around. Join; ch 1, turn.

Rnd 5: Sc in each sc around. Join; do not turn.

Rnd 6 (shell row): Work same as rnd 5 on sleeve border. End off.

BUTTONS (make 6): With steel crochet hook, ch 2, 5 sc in first ch.

Rnd 2: 2 sc in each sc—10 sc.

Rnd 3: Working over button mold, (draw up a lp in each of next 2 sc, yo and through 3 lps on hook, sc in next sc) 3 times. If necessary, sc in each sc until button mold is covered. Cut yarn, leaving a long end. Thread needle; draw sts tog; sew to left front border opposite buttonholes.

SWEATER TWINS

Matching bands of bright color meet at chest level on these sweater twins, crocheted in an easy single crochet, chain-one pattern. The sleeveless vest underneath can double as a top layer, too.

SIZES: Directions for small size (6-8). Changes for medium size (10-12) and large size (14-16) are in parentheses.

Body Bust Size: 30½″-31½″ (32½″-34″; 36″-38″).

Blocked Bust Size: Shell: 32″ (35″-39″). Cardigan (closed): 34″ (38″-42″).

MATERIALS: Yarn of knitting worsted weight, 3 (4-4) 4-oz. skeins winter white, main color (MC); 1 skein each of magenta (A), light blue (B), purple (C) and shocking pink (D) for cardigan; 2 (3-3) skeins MC and 1 skein each of A, B, C and D for shell. Crochet hooks sizes G and H. Six buttons for cardigan.

GAUGE: 15 sts = 4″; 4 rows = 1″ (pat, size H hook).

To Bind Off: At beg of a row, sl st loosely across specified number of sts; **at end of a row,** leave specified number of sts unworked.

SHELL: BACK: Band: Beg at side edge, with MC and size G hook, ch 9 (11-13).

Row 1: Sc in 2nd ch from hook and in each ch across—8 (10-12) sc. Ch 1, turn.

Row 2: Sc in back lp of each sc across. Ch 1, turn. Repeat last row until piece when slightly stretched measures 13″ (14″-15½″) from start. Working along side edge of band, * ch 1, sc in edge of row, repeat from * spacing 30 (34-38) sc across. Drop MC; do not turn. Change to size H hook.

Pattern: Row 1 (right side): With A, sc in first sc at beg of last row, * sc in next ch-1 sp, ch 1, repeat from * across, end sc in last ch-1 sp, sc in last sc—31 (35-39) sc. Cut A; pick up MC. Ch 1, turn.

Row 2: With MC, sc in first sc, * ch 1, sc in next ch-1 sp, repeat from * across, end ch 1, sk next sc, sc in last sc—30 (34-38) sc. Ch 1, turn.

Rows 3-5: With MC, * sc in sc, ch 1, repeat from * across, end sc in last sc. Ch 1, turn. Drop MC at end of row 5.

Row 6: With B, sc in first sc, * sc in ch-1 sp, ch 1, repeat from * across, end sc in ch-1 sp, sc in last sc—31 (35-39) sc. Drop B; pick up MC at beg of row.

Row 7: With MC, sc in first sc, * ch 1, sc in ch-1 sp, repeat from * across, end ch 1, sc in last sc—30 (34-38) sc. Ch 1, turn.

Rows 8 and 9: With MC, repeat row 3. Ch 1, turn. Drop MC. Repeat rows 6-9, 5 (5-6) times. Cut B. Check gauge; piece above band should measure 16″ (18″-20¼″) wide.

Pattern Stripe: Repeating row 3, work 2 rows A, 2 rows MC, 1 row C. Repeating row 6, work 1 row D.

Shape Armholes: Bind off 2 sts (see To Bind Off) each side every row 3 (4-5) times, working in following color and pat sequence: With C, repeat rows 6 and 3; with D, repeat row 6; with C, repeat row 6; with MC, repeat row 3 twice—24 (26-28) sc. With A, repeat row 3 twice; with MC, repeat row 3, 3 times. Repeat pat rows 6-9, 4 (4-5) times. Repeat row 6.

Shape Neck and Shoulders: With MC, repeat row 3 until 6 (7-8) sc are completed. Ch 1, turn.

Next Row: Repeat row 3 until 3 (4-5) sc are completed. End off. With MC, sc in 6th (7th-8th) sc from end on last long row. Work pat row 3 across. Ch 1, turn.

Next Row: Bind off first 6 sts; working pat row 3, finish row. End off.

FRONT: Work same as for back until 1 B row and 3 MC rows above armhole are completed.

Shape Neck: Keeping to pat, work until 9 (10-11) sc are completed. Working on one side, bind off 2 sts at neck edge every other row 3 times—6 (7-8) sc. Work even until armhole measures same as back. Shape shoulder same as for back. Join B in 9th (10th-11th) sc from end on last long row, finish row. Complete same as other side of neck, reversing shaping.

FINISHING: Run in yarn ends on wrong side. Block pieces. Sew side and shoulder seams.

Armhole Edging: With size G hook and MC, sc in underarm seam, work ch 1, sc around armhole edge, easing in slightly. Join with a sl st in first sc. End off.

Neck Edging: With size G hook and MC, work same edging around neck edge. Join; drop MC.

Next Rnd: With A, * sc in ch-1 sp, ch 1, repeat from * around. Join; end off. With MC, repeat last rnd.

Steam-press edgings lightly.

CARDIGAN: BACK: Band: Work same as for shell. Working along side edge of band, * ch 1, sc in edge of row, repeat from * spacing 31 (35-39) sc across. Work in pat as for shell, repeat pat rows 6-9, 6 (6-7) times before start of pat stripe, then continue as for shell until armholes measure 1 row more than back—25 (27-29) sc.

Shape Neck and Shoulders: With MC, repeat row 3 until 7 (8-9) sc are completed. Ch 1, turn.

Next Row: Repeat row 3 until 4 (5-6) sc are completed. End off. With MC, sc in 7th (8th-9th) sc from end of last long row. Work pat row 3 across. Ch 1, turn.

Next Row: Bind off first 6 sts; working pat row 3, finish row. End off.

LEFT FRONT (Left-handed crocheters: This will be your right front): Work band same as for back until piece measures 6½″ (7″-8″). Working along side edge of band, * ch 1, sc in edge of row, repeat from * spacing 15 (17-19) sc across. Mark end of pat row 1 for center edge. (On right front, mark beg of pat row 1 for center edge.) Work in pat as for back until piece measures same as back to underarm.

Shape Neck and Armhole: Keeping to pat, bind off 2 sts at center edge of next row, then bind off 2 sts at same edge every 5th row until 7 (8-9) sc remain; **at the same time,** bind off 2 sts at side edge every row 3 (4-5) times. Work even until armhole measures same as back.

Shape Shoulder: Bind off 6 sts at arm side once. End off.

RIGHT FRONT: Work same as for left front, noting changes and reversing shaping.

SLEEVES: Band: Beg at seam edge, with size G hook, ch 11 (12-13). Work same as for back until piece when slightly stretched measures 7½″ (7¾″-8″) from start. Working along side edge of band, * ch 1, sc in edge of row, repeat from * spacing 20 (21-22) sc across. Change to size H hook. Work in pat as for back (do not work pat stripe), inc 2 sts each side **(to inc,** work (sc, ch 1, sc) in first and last st on pat rows 7, 8 or 9) every 5″ (4″-3″) 2 (3-4) times—24 (27-30) sc. Work even until piece measures 17″ from start or desired length to underarm. Check gauge;

piece above last inc row should measure 12½″ (14¼″-16″) wide.

Shape Cap: Keeping to pat, bind off 4 (4-6) sts each side of next row, then bind off 2 sts each side every 8th row once, every 4th row twice, every row 3 (4-5) times. End off.

FINISHING: Run in yarn ends on wrong side. Block pieces. Sew shoulder seams; sew in sleeves. Sew side and sleeve seams.

Center Band: With MC and size G hook, make chain to fit up right front edge, around neck, down left front edge.

Row 1: Sc in 2nd ch from hook and in each ch across. Ch 1, turn.

Row 2: Sc in each sc across. Drop MC. Sew foundation ch around front and neck edges of cardigan. With pins, mark position of 6 buttonholes evenly spaced on right center edge of band; first buttonhole 3 sts above lower edge, 6th buttonhole at start of neck dec. Pick up MC.

Row 3: * Sc in each sc to within 1 st of pin, ch 2, sk next 2 sc, sc in next sc, repeat from * 5 times, sc in each sc across. Ch 1, turn.

Row 4: Sc in each sc, working 2 sc in each ch-2 sp. Ch 1, turn.

Row 5: Sc in each sc. End off.

Steam-press seams and bands. Sew on buttons.

RIPPLE SET

The ripple of chevrons in a short-sleeved jacket glides over a long-sleeved V-necked pullover striped in matching colors. The ribbed borders on the sleeves and bottom of the sweater are worked in slipper stitch.

SIZES: Directions for small size (6-8). Changes for medium size (10-12) are in parentheses.

Body Bust Size: 30½″-31½″ (32½″-34″).

Blocked Bust Size: Pullover: 32″ (34″). Cardigan: 33″ (39″).

MATERIALS: Sport yarn, 2-oz. skeins. Pullover: 3 (4) balls white (W); 2 skeins each of yellow (Y), pink (P) and turquoise (T). Cardigan: 2 skeins each of Y and P; 1 skein each of W and T. Crochet hook size G.

GAUGE: Cardigan: 11 (13) dc (1 scallop) = 2¾″ (3¼″); 2 rows = 1″. Pullover: 4 sts = 1″; 6 rows = 2″.

PULLOVER: To Bind Off: At beg of a row, ch 1, sl st loosely across specified number of sts; **at end of a row,** leave specified number of sts unworked.

To Dec 1 Dc: At beg of a row, ch 3 (counts as 1 dc), sk first st, yo hook, draw up a lp in each of next 2 sts, yo hook and through 2 lps, yo and through 3 lps, work in pat across; **at end of a row,** work to last 2 sts, yo hook, draw up a lp in each of next 2 sts, yo and through 2 lps, yo and through 3 lps.

To Dec 1 Sc: Ch 1, draw up a lp in each of next 2 sts, yo and through 3 lps on hook.

To Inc 1 St: Work 2 sts in same st.

Note: Cut and join P, T and Y as needed. When changing colors, pull new color through last 2 lps to complete st.

STRIPED PATTERN: Row 1 (right side): With W, dc in 4th ch from hook and in each ch across. Ch 1, turn.

Row 2: With W, sc in each dc across, sc in top of turning ch. Turn.

Row 3: With P, ch 3 (counts as 1 dc), sk first sc, dc in next sc and in each sc across. Ch 1, turn.

Row 4: With P, repeat row 2. Repeat rows 3 and 4 for pat, working 2 rows W, 2 rows T, 2 rows W, 2 rows Y, 2 rows W. Repeat the 12 rows from row 3 for striped pat.

BACK: Beg at lower edge above ribbing, with W, ch 64 (68). Work in striped pat on 62 (66) sts until piece measures 10″ (11″) or 2½″ less (ribbing allowance) than desired length to underarm, end wrong side. Check gauge; piece should measure 15½″ (16½″) wide.

Shape Armholes: Keeping to striped pat, bind off (see To Bind Off) 3 sts each side of next row. Work 1 row even. Bind off 2 sts each side of next row. Work 1 row even. Dec 0 (1) dc (see To Dec 1 Dc) each side of next row—52 (54) sts. Work even until armholes measure 7″ (7½″) above first row of armhole shaping, end wrong side.

Shape Shoulders: Keeping to color sequence, sc in each of 4 (5) sc, hdc in each of next 4 sts, dc in each of next 6 sts; cut yarn. Sk next 24 sts, join color yarn being used with a dc in next sc, dc in each of next 5 sts, hdc in each of next 4 sts, sc in each of next 4 (5) sts. End off.

FRONT: Work same as for back until piece measures 8″ (9″) or 2″ less than back to underarm, end wrong side.

Shape V-Neck and Armholes: Keeping to striped pat, work 31 (33) sts, drop yarn; join another strand of same color yarn with a dc in next sc, dc in each st across—31 (33) dc each side. Keeping to striped pat, dec 1 st each neck edge of next row, then every other row 11 times more; **at the same time,** when piece measures same as back to underarm, bind off 3 sts each arm side once, 2 sts at same edge of next row, 0 (1) st next row—14 (15) sts. Work even until armholes measure same as back.

Shape Shoulders: Work same as for back.

Sleeve Length Note: Sleeve is planned for 17″ (14½″ length from top of ribbing to underarm, plus 2½″ ribbing). Measure striped pat on back to determine starting row so that 14½″ (or desired sleeve length) will end with same pat row as back at start of underarm.

SLEEVES: Beg at lower edge above ribbing, with first row color (see Sleeve Length Note), ch 42 (44). Work in striped pat on 40 (42) sts for 2″. Inc 1 st (see To Inc 1 St) each side of next row, then every 2″ 5 (6) times—52 (56) sts. Work even until piece measures 14½″ from start or 2½″ (ribbing allowance) less than desired sleeve length, end same pat row as back underarm. Check gauge; piece above last inc row should measure 13″ (14″) wide.

Shape Cap: Keeping to striped pat, bind off 3 sts each side of next row. Work 1 row even. Bind off 2 sts each side of next row. Dec 1 st each side every other row 5 (6) times. Bind off 3 sts each side of next 3 rows—14 (16) sts. End off.

FINISHING: Block pieces to measurements. With backstitch, sew shoulder seams; sew in sleeves. Matching stripes, sew side and sleeve seams.

Body Ribbing (worked from seam to seam): With Y, ch 12 loosely.

Row 1: Sc in 2nd ch from hook and in each ch across—11 sc. Ch 1, turn.

Row 2: Sc in back lp of each sc across. Ch 1, turn. Repeat row 2 until piece when slightly stretched measures 23″ (25″) or desired waist measurement. End off. Weave ends tog. Easing in lower edge of body to fit, sew ribbing to body.

Sleeve Ribbing (make 2): Work

same as for body ribbing until piece measures 8″ (8½″). End off. Weave ends tog; sew to lower edge of sleeves.

Neck Border: Rnd 1: Join Y in shoulder seam. From right side, sl st around neck edge, being careful to keep work flat. Join; ch 1, turn.

Rnd 2: Sc in top lp of each sl st around. Join; ch 1, turn.

Rnd 3: Sc in each sc around, dec 2 sts at center front (to dec 2 sts, pull up a lp in each of 3 sc, yo hook and through 4 lps on hook). Join; ch 1, turn.

Rnd 4: Repeat rnd 3. Join; end off.

Steam-press seams and neck border lightly.

CARDIGAN: BODY: Beg at lower edge of fronts and back, with Y, ch 138 (162).

Row 1: Dc in 6th ch from hook, dc in each of next 3 (4) ch, * 3 dc in next ch, dc in each of next 4 (5) ch, sk next 2 ch, dc in each of next 4 (5) ch, repeat from * across, end last repeat sk next 2 ch, dc in last ch—12 scallops. Ch 1, turn.

Row 2: With Y, sc in first dc, sk

next dc, * sc in each of next 4 (5) dc, 3 sc in next dc, sc in each of next 4 (5) dc, sk next 2 dc, repeat from * across, end last repeat sk next dc, sc in top of turning ch. Cut Y; join P. Turn.

Row 3: Ch 3, sk first 2 sc, * dc in each of next 4 (5) sc, 3 dc in next sc (inc group), dc in each of next 4 (5) sc, sk next 2 sc, repeat from * across, end last repeat sk next sc, dc in last sc. Ch 1, turn.

Row 4: With P, repeat row 2. Repeat rows 3 and 4 for striped pat, working 2 rows W, 2 rows T. Repeat last 8 rows for color sequence until piece measures 14" from lower edge to top of point, end row 4. Check gauge; piece should measure 33" (39") wide.

RIGHT FRONT YOKE (Left-handed crocheters: This will be your left front yoke): **Next Row:** Keeping to color sequence, ch 3, sk first 2 sc, dec 1 dc over next 2 sc, work in pat to center sc on 3rd inc group (2½ scallops). Ch 1, turn.

Row 2: Work in pat across, dec 1 sc after last inc group.

Row 3: Repeat row 1.

Row 4: Work across, working 2 sts in last inc group. Continue to dec 1 st at center edge every row until 1½ scallops remain. Work even until armhole measures 7" (7½"), end center edge.

Shape Shoulder: With color to be used, dc in each of 2 (3) sts, hdc in each of next 2 sts, sc in each of next 3 sts, hdc in each of next 2 sts, dc in each of next 4 (6) sts, hdc in each of next 2 sts, sc in next 2 sts. Ch 1, turn.

Next Row: Sl st in each of next 4 sts, hdc in each of next 5 sts, dc in each remaining st. End off.

BACK: Join color to be used with a dc in center sc on 4th inc group from center edge (1 scallop for underarm), dc in same sc, work in pat to within 3½ scallops of end, work 2 dc in 4th inc group from center edge—4 scallops, plus ½ scallop each end. Ch 1, turn. Work striped pat until armhole measures same as front.

Shape Shoulders: Sc in each of first 2 sts, * hdc in each of next 2 sts, dc in each of next 4 (6) sts, hdc in each of next 2 sts, sc in each of next 3 sts, repeat from * across, end last repeat sc in each of last 2 sts.

Next Row: Sl st in each of 5 sts, hdc in each of next 5 sts, dc in each of next 7 (10) sts. End off. Sk next 2 scallops, join yarn in next st, work same as for first shoulder, reversing shaping. End off.

LEFT FRONT YOKE: Sk next scallop on last long row, join color to be used with a dc in center sc on 3rd inc group from center edge (1 scallop for underarm), dc in same sc, work across in pat, dec 1 dc before last dc. Complete same

as for right front yoke, reversing shaping.

SLEEVES: Beg at lower edge, with same color as 6th stripe below underarm of body, ch 61 (71) loosely. Work in striped pat on 5 scallops for 12 rows.

Shape Cap: With color to be used, sl st across first 6 (7) sts, ch 3, dc in next st, work to within last 6 (7) sts, work 2 dc in next st (center st of inc group)—3 scallops, plus ½ scallop each side. Work 2 rows even. Dec 1 st each side every row 6 (8) times. End off; turn.

Next Row: Keeping to color sequence, join yarn with sc in center st of next inc group, work same as back shoulder shaping row 1 to center st of last inc group. End off.

FINISHING: Run in yarn ends on wrong side. Block pieces. With backstitch, sew shoulder seams; sew sleeve seams. With top center of sleeve cap at shoulder seam, sew sleeves into armholes.

Front Border: Row 1: Join Y in lower front edge. From right side, sl st up front edge, across back of neck, down other front edge. Ch 1, turn.

Row 2: Sc in top lp of each sl st around, dec to desired fit. Ch 1, turn.

Rows 3 and 4: Sc in each sc. End off.

Steam-press seams and border lightly.

LACE BORDER SET

SIZES: Directions for small size (8-10). Changes for medium size (12-14) are in parentheses.

Body Bust Size: 31½"-32½" (34"-36").

Blocked Bust Size: Camisole: 32½" (36½"). Cardigan: 34" (38").

MATERIALS: Camisole: knitting worsted, 2 (3) 4-oz. skeins. Car-

digan: 4 (5) skeins. Crochet hook size H.

GAUGE: 4 sts (2 sc, 2 ch) = 1"; 7 rows = 2". Lace panel = 4" wide.

PATTERN STITCH: Row 1: Sc in 2nd ch from hook, * ch 1, sk 1 ch, sc in next ch, repeat from * across. Turn.

Row 2: Ch 1, sc in first sc, * ch 1,

sk ch-1 sp, sc in next sc, repeat from * across. Turn. Repeat row 2 for pat always working ch 1 over ch-1 sp and sc in sc.

To Bind Off: At beg of a row, sl st loosely across specified sts; **at end of a row,** leave specified number of sts unworked.

To Dec 1 St: At beg of a row, ch 1, pull up a lp in each of first 2 sts,

yo and through 3 lps on hook; **at end of a row,** pull up a lp in each of last 2 sts, yo and through 3 lps on hook. **Next Row:** Work in pat as established (sc over sc, ch 1 over ch-1 sp).

To Inc 1 St: At beg of a row, ch 1 loosely, 2 sc in first st; **at end of a row,** 2 sc in last st. **Next Row:** Work in pat as established; when there are 3 sc tog, work into sc, ch 1 pat.

LACE PANEL: Ch 17.

Row 1: Sc in 5th ch from hook, (ch 3, sk next 2 ch, sc in next ch) 4 times. Ch 4, turn.

Row 2: (Sc in next sp, ch 3) 4 times, sc in last sp. Ch 4, turn.

Rows 3 and 4: Repeat row 2.

Row 5: Sc in first sp, ch 2, 3-dc cluster st in each of next 2 sps (to make cluster st holding back last lp of each dc, work 3 dc, yo and through 4 lps on hook), ch 2, sc in next sp, ch 3, sc in last sp. Ch 4, turn.

Row 6: Sc in first sp, ch 3, sc in next ch-2 sp, ch 6, 2-dc cluster st in 4th ch from hook (to make 2-dc cluster st, holding back last lp of each dc, work 2 dc, yo and through 3 lps on hook), sc in sp between clusters, ch 4, 2-dc cluster st in 4th ch from hook, sc in next ch-2 sp, ch 3, sc in last sp. Ch 4, turn.

Row 7: Sc in first sp, ch 2, 3-dc cluster st in sc between clusters, ch 2, sc in next ch-2 sp, (ch 3, sc in next sp) twice. Ch 4, turn.

Row 8: Sc in first sp, (ch 3, sc in next sp) 4 times. Ch 4, turn. Repeat rows 2-8 for lace panel pat. When piece is desired length do not end off.

Picot Edging: Working along side edge, ch 4, sc in side of first sc, * ch 2, sc in 2nd ch from hook, sc in side of next sc, repeat from * along side edge. End off.

CAMISOLE: BACK: Beg at lower edge, ch 66 (74). Work in pat on 33 (37) sc for 12″. Check gauge; piece should measure 16¼″ (18¼″) wide. End off.

Yoke: Work lace panel pat for 11½″ (12½″). Work picot edging down one side. End off.

FRONT: Work same as for back.

FINISHING: With picot edging over edge, pin lace panel to top edge of front, leaving 2″ (2½″) free on each side for underarm. Sew side edge of lace panel to front. Sew lace panel to back in same manner. Block pieces. Sew side seams.

Upper Edging: Join yarn in upper left front corner; working around entire upper edge of camisole, work picot edge same as on side of lace panel, being careful to keep work flat. Join with a sl st in first sc. End off.

STRAPS (make 2): Ch 28 (30). Work pat row 1 across. End off. Try on camisole. Adjust straps to desired length; sew in place securely.

CARDIGAN: BACK: Beg at lower edge, ch 68 (76). Work in pat on 34 (38) sc for 15½″. Check gauge; piece should measure 17″ (19″) wide.

Shape Armholes: Keeping to pat, bind off (see To Bind Off) 4 sts each side of next row, then 2 sts each side every row twice—26 (30) sc or 51 (59) sts. Work even until armholes measure 7½″ (8″) above first row of armhole shaping.

Shape Neck and Shoulders: Bind off 4 (6) sts, ch 1, sc in sc, (ch 1, sc in next sc) 5 times, drop yarn, sk next 10 (12) sc, join another strand of yarn in next sc, ch 1, sc in same sc as joining, (ch 1, sc in next sc) 5 times. Turn. Working on both sides at once, with separate strands of yarn, bind off 4 sts at each arm side every row twice. End off.

LEFT FRONT: Beg at lower edge, ch 20 (24). Work in pat on 10 (12) sc until piece measures same as back to underarm. Mark end of last row for side edge.

Shape Armhole and Neck: Keeping to pat, bind off 4 sts at arm side of next row, then bind off 2 sts at same edge every row twice; **at the same time,** dec 1 st (see To Dec 1 St) at center edge every other row until 2 sc remain. Work even until armhole measures same as back. End off.

RIGHT FRONT: Work same as for left front; pat is reversible.

SLEEVES: Beg at lower edge, ch 40 (42). Work in pat on 20 (21) sc for 6″. Check gauge; piece should measure 10″ (10½″) wide. Inc 1 st (see To Inc 1 St) each side of next row, then every 6th row 4 (5) times—49 (53) sts. Work even until piece measures 13″ from start or 4″ less (lace panel allowance) than desired length to underarm.

Shape Cap: Bind off 4 sts each side of next row. Dec 1 st each side every row 12 (14) times. Bind off 2 sts each side of next row—13 sts. End off.

LACE PANEL: Work lace panel until piece fits from lower edge to shoulder on left front edge. Work picot edging on inner edge. Work same lace panel for right front edge. Work panel to fit around lower edge of each sleeve. Work picot edging on inner edge.

FINISHING: With picot edging over fronts, sew side edge of lace panels to fronts. Sew lace panel to lower edge of each sleeve. Block pieces. With edge of lace panel at neck edge of back, sew shoulder seams; sew in sleeves. Sew side and sleeve seams.

Join yarn in lower side seam. From right side work 1 rnd picot edging around entire outer edge of cardigan. Steam-press seams and edges lightly.

TIE: With double strand of yarn, make chain 80″ long or desired length. End off. Weave in ends of yarn.

REVERSE STRIPE SET

Pockets banded in pastels match the stripes of this jacket's short sleeves. The sleeveless pull-on underneath repeats the yellow and picks up the blue for its own striping. Both are worked in an easy pattern stitch.

SIZES: Directions for size 8. Changes for sizes 10, 12, 14, 16 in parentheses.

Blocked Bust Size: Shell: 31½″ (32½″-34¾″-37″-38¼″). Cardigan: 32¾″ (34½″-36¾″-39¼″-40¾″).

MATERIALS: Mohair-type yarn, 1-oz. balls. Shell: 5 (5-5-6-6) balls pink (A); 1 ball each of blue (B) and gold (C). Cardigan: 8 (8-8-9-9) balls B; 1 ball each of A and C. Crochet hook size H.

GAUGE: 7 sts = 2″; 2 rows (pat) = 1″.

Note: When changing colors, pull new colors through last 2 lps to complete st. Cut and join colors as needed.

PATTERN STITCH: Row 1: Sc in 2nd ch from hook, * ch 1, sk 1 ch, sc in next ch, repeat from * across. Turn.

Row 2 (right side): Ch 3 (counts as 1 dc), * dc in ch-1 sp, dc in sc, repeat from * across. Ch 1, turn.

Row 3: Sc in first dc, * ch 1, sk next dc, sc in next dc, repeat from * across. Turn. Repeat rows 2 and 3 for pat.

To Bind Off: At beg of a row, sl st loosely across specified sts; **at end of a row,** leave specified number of sts unworked.

To Dec 1 Dc: At beg of a row, ch 3 (counts as 1 dc), sk first sc, yo hook, draw up a lp in each of next 2 sts, yo hook and through 2 lps, yo and through 3 lps, work in pat across; **at end of a row,** work to within last 2 sts, yo hook, draw up a lp in each of next 2 sts, yo hook and through 2 lps, yo and through 3 lps.

SHELL: BACK: Beg at lower edge, with A, ch 56 (58-62-66-68). Work in pat on 55 (57-61-65-67) dc until piece measures 13″ from start, end pat row 2. Check gauge; piece should measure 15¾″ (16¼″-17¼″-18½″-19″) wide. Keeping to pat, work 2 rows B, 2 rows C, 2 rows B.

Shape Armholes: Keeping to pat, with B, bind off (see To Bind Off) 4 (4-4-5-5) sts; with C, work across, bind off 4 (4-4-5-5) sts. With C, work 1 row even. With B, dec 1 dc (see To Dec 1 Dc) each side of next row—45 (47-51-53-

55) sts. With B, work 1 row even. With A, work even until armholes measure 6″ (6″-6″-7″-7″) above first row of armhole shaping, end pat row 2.

Shape Neck and Shoulders: Next Row: Sc in first dc, (ch 1, sk next dc, sc in next dc) 7 (7-8-8-8) times, drop A, sk next 15 (17-17-17-19-21) dc, join another strand of A with a sc in next dc, (ch 1, sk next dc, sc in next dc) 7 (7-8-8-8) times—15 (15-17-17-17) sts each side. Keeping to pat, bind off 2 sts at each neck edge every row twice—11 (11-13-13-13) sts each side.

Next Row: Sl st across first 4 sts, sc in each of next 2 (2-3-3-3) sts, dc in each of next 5 (5-6-6-6) sts. End off. Working on 2nd shoulder, ch 3, sk first st, dc in each of next 4 (4-5-5-5) sts, sc in each of next 2 (2-3-3-3) sts. End off.

FRONT: Work as for back.

FINISHING: Block pieces. With backstitch, sew shoulder and side seams.

Edging: Join A in lower side seam. From right side, working from left to right (**left-handed crocheters:** from right to left), work 1 rnd sc loosely around lower edge of body. Work same edging around neck and each armhole edge.

CARDIGAN: BACK: Beg at lower edge, with B, ch 58 (60-64-68-70) sts. Work in pat on 57 (59-63-67-69) dc for 18″, end pat row 2. Check gauge; piece is 16¼″ (17″-18″-19¼″-19¾″) wide.

Shape Armholes: Keeping to pat, bind off 4 (4-4-5-5) sts each side of next row. Work 1 row even.

Bind off 2 sts each side of next row—45 (47-51-53-55) sts. Work even until armholes measure about 7¼″ (7¼″-7¾″-7¾″-7¾″) above first row of armhole shaping.

Shape Shoulders: Bind off 6 sts each side of next row, 9 (9-10-10-11) sts each side of next row. End off.

RIGHT FRONT (Left-handed crocheters: This will be your left front): Beg at lower edge, with B, ch 30 (32-34-36-38). Work in pat on 29 (31-33-35-37) dc for 14″ (14″-13″-13″-12″), end pat row 3. Mark end of last row for center edge. (On left front, mark beg of last row for center edge.) Check gauge; piece should measure 8¼″ (8¾″-9¼″-10″-10½″) wide.

Shape Neck and Armhole: Keeping to pat, dec 1 dc (see To Dec 1 Dc) at center edge on next row, then dec 1 dc at same edge every other row 7 (9-10-11-12) times more; **at the same time,** when piece measures same as back to underarm, bind off 4 (4-4-5-5) sts at arm side of next row, then 2 sts at same edge every other row once. Work even on remaining 15 (15-16-16-17) sts until armhole is same as back.

Shape Shoulder: Bind off 6 sts at arm side of next row, 5 sts next row. End off.

LEFT FRONT: Work same as for right front, noting changes in directions.

SLEEVES: Beg at lower edge, with A, ch 42 (42-44-44-46). Work in pat on 41 (41-43-43-45) dc, working (2 rows A, 2 rows C) twice, 2 rows A, 2 rows B. Check

gauge; piece should measure 11¾″ (11¾″-12¼″-12¼″-12¾″) wide.

Shape Cap: Working with B only, bind off 4 sts each side of next row. Work 5 rows even. Bind off 2 sts each side of next row, then bind off 2 sts each side every other row twice—21 (21-23-23-25) dc. End off.

POCKETS (make 2): Beg at lower edge, with A, ch 24 (24-24-26-26). Working in pat, work * 2 rows A, 2 rows C, repeat from * until 10 rows from start. End off.

Next Row (edging): From right side, join B in top left corner (**left-handed crocheters:** top right corner). Working from left to right (**left-handed crocheters:** from right to left), sc in each st across. End off.

FINISHING: Run in all yarn ends on wrong side. Block pieces. Sew shoulder seams; sew in sleeves. Matching stripes, sew side and sleeve seams.

Edging: Beg at one lower front corner, from right side, with B, sc around front and neck edges, end other front corner. Do not turn.

Next Row: Working from left to right (**left-handed crocheters:** from right to left), sc loosely in each sc. Continue to work in reverse sc across lower edge. Join with a sl st in first sc. End off. Work same edging around lower edge of each sleeve.

Sew a pocket to each front, placing pockets 2 rows above lower edge, about 1½″ in from front edges.

BELT: With A, make chain 50″ long. Dc in 4th ch from hook and in each ch.

CARDIGAN AND PULLOVER SET

Shown on page 36

A four-color cardigan, striped with bands of single crochet, has overlaid patterns of long single crochet. The sleeveless pullover alternates single crochet, chain-one pattern and double crochet. Instructions are given for a long, matching scarf, not shown.

CARDIGAN: SIZES: Directions for small size (6-8). Changes for medium size (10-12) and large size (14-16) are in parentheses.

Body Bust Size: 30½"-31½" (32½"-34"; 36"-38").

Blocked Bust Size (closed): 32" (36"-40").

MATERIALS: Knitting worsted, 2 (2-3) 4-oz. skeins each of teal blue (A), white (B), rust (C) and pale rust (D). Crochet hook size I. Five buttons.

GAUGE: 11 sc = 4"; 18 rows = 5".

Note: Cut and join colors as needed.

PATTERN (multiple of 5 sts plus 1):

Row 1 (right side): With A, sc in 2nd ch from hook and in each remaining ch. Ch 1, turn each row.

Rows 2-6: With A, sc in each sc across.

Row 7: With B, * sc in next sc, long sc in next sc on 2nd row below, long sc in next sc on 3rd row below, long sc in next sc on 4th row below, long sc in next sc on 5th row below, repeat from * across, end sc in last sc.

Rows 8-12: With B, sc in each sc across.

Row 13: With C, * long sc in next sc on 5th row below, long sc in next sc on 4th row below, long sc in next sc on 3rd row below, long sc in next sc on 2nd row below, sc in next sc, repeat from * across, end sc in last st.

Rows 14-18: With C, sc in each sc across.

Rows 19-24: With D, repeat rows 7-12.

Row 25: With A, repeat row 13. Repeat rows 2-25 for pat.

To Bind Off: At beg of a row, sl st across specified sts; **at end of a row,** leave specified number of sts unworked.

To Dec 1 St: Pull up a lp in each of 2 sts, yo and through 3 lps on hook.

To Inc 1 St: Work 2 sc in same st.

CARDIGAN: BACK: Beg at lower edge, with A, ch 47 (52-57). Work in pat on 46 (51-56) sts until piece measures 20" from start or desired length to underarm. Check gauge; piece should measure 16" (18"-20") wide.

Shape Armholes: Keeping to pat, bind off (see To Bind Off) 2 (3-3) sts each side of next row, then dec 1 st (see To Dec 1 St) each side every row 2 (2-3) times—38 (41-44) sts. Work even until armholes measure 7½" (8"-8½") above first row of armhole shaping.

Shape Shoulders: Keeping to pat, bind off 3 sts each side every row twice, 4 (5-6) sts once—18 (19-20) sts. End off.

POCKET LININGS (make 2): Beg at lower edge, with A, ch 15 (17-19).

Row 1: Sc in 2nd ch from hook and in each remaining ch—14 (16-18) sc. Ch 1, turn.

Row 2: Sc in each sc across. Ch 1, turn. Repeat row 2 until piece measures 5" from start. End off.

RIGHT FRONT (Left-handed crocheters: This will be your left front): Beg at lower edge, with A, ch 22 (27-32). Work in pat on 21

(26-31) sc for 26 rows, end pat row 2 (center edge).

Join Pocket: Next Row: With A, sc in each of next 6 (7-8) sc; with wrong side of last row on pocket facing wrong side of front, sc in each sc across pocket, sk next 14 (16-18) sc on front, sc in remaining 1 (3-5) sc on front—21 (26-31) sc. Keeping to pat, work even until piece measures 18" from start.

Shape Neck and Armhole: Dec 1 st at center edge of next row, then dec 1 st at same edge every 4th (4th-3rd) row 6 (9-12) times more; **at the same time,** when piece measures same as back to underarm, bind off 2 (3-3) sts at arm side of next row, then dec 1 st at arm side every row 2 (2-3) times— 10 (11-12) sts. Work even if necessary, until armhole measures same as back.

Shape Shoulder: Bind off 3 sts at arm side every row twice—4 (5-6) sts remain. End off.

LEFT FRONT: Work same as for right front for 26 rows, end pat row 2 (side edge).

Join Pocket: Next Row: Sc in each of 1 (3-5) sc; with wrong side of last row on pocket lining facing wrong side of front, sc in each sc across pocket, sk next 14 (16-18) sts on front, sc in remaining 6 (7-8) sc—21 (26-31) sc. Complete same as for right front, reversing shaping.

SLEEVES: Beg at lower edge, with C, ch 22 (22-27). Work in pat on 21 (21-26) sts, following same color sequence as back, inc 1 st each side (see To Inc 1 St) every 2½" (2"-2½") 6 (7-6) times, work-

ing added sts into pat—33 (35-38) sts. Work even until piece measures about 17″ from start, end same pat row as back underarm. Check gauge; piece above last inc row should measure 12″ (12½″-13½″) wide.

Shape Cap: Keeping to pat, bind off 2 (3-3) sts each side of next row, then dec 1 st each side every other row 6 (7-8) times, every row 3 times—11 (9-10) sc remain. End off.

FINISHING: Run in yarn ends on wrong side. Block pieces. With backstitch, sew shoulder seams. Sew in sleeves; sew side and sleeve seams. Sew pocket linings to wrong side.

From right side, with A, work 1 rnd sc around lower edge of each sleeve.

Front Edging: From right side, join A in lower front corner. Keeping work flat, work 1 row sc up front, around neck, down other front, end lower edge. Ch 1, turn each row.

Row 2: Sc in each sc.

With pins, mark position of 4 buttonholes evenly spaced on right front edge; first pin in 6th sc from lower edge, last pin in 3rd sc below start of neck shaping.

Row 3 (buttonholes): * Sc in each sc to within 1 sc of pin, ch 2, sk 2 sc, sc in next sc, repeat from * 4 times, complete row.

Row 4: Sc in each sc and ch across. End off.

Sew on buttons.

SCARF: SIZE: 8″ x 55″.

MATERIALS: 1 skein of each of cardigan colors. Crochet hook size I.

With A, ch 22. Work in pat as for cardigan until piece measures about 55″ from start, end pat row 6. End off. From right side, with A, work 1 row sc across each long edge, being careful to keep work flat.

FINISHING: Run in yarn ends on wrong side. Block.

PULLOVER: SIZES: Directions are for size 6-8. Changes for sizes 10, 12, 14 and 16 are in parentheses.

Body Bust Size: 30½"-31½" (32½"-34"-36"-38").

Blocked Bust Size: 32" (34"-36"-38"-40").

MATERIALS: Knitting worsted, 2 (2-3-3-3) 4-oz. skeins white, main color (MC); few yards teal blue, contrasting color (CC). Crochet hook size I.

GAUGE: 7 sts = 2"; 6 rows pat = 2".

To Bind Off: Work same as for cardigan. **Next Row:** Work in pat as established.

PULLOVER: BACK: With MC, ch 15 (15-16-16-16).

Ribbing (worked from side seam to side seam): **Row 1:** Sc in 2nd ch from hook and in each remaining ch—14 (14-15-15-15) sc. Ch 1, turn each row.

Row 2: Sc in back lp of each sc across. Repeat row 2 until piece when slightly stretched measures 14" (14½"-15"-15½"-16") from start. Ch 1, do not turn. Continuing along side edge of ribbing, work 55 (59-63-67-71) sc. Ch 1, turn.

PATTERN: Row 1: Sc in first sc, * ch 1, sk next sc, sc in next sc, repeat from * across—28 (30-32-34-36) sc. Ch 1, turn.

Rows 2-5: Sc in first sc, * ch 1, sc in next sc, repeat from * across. Ch 1, turn.

Row 6: Ch 3 (counts as 1 dc), sk first sc, * dc in ch-1 sp, dc in sc, repeat from * across—55 (59-63-67-71) dc. Ch 1, turn.

Row 7: Sc in first dc, * ch 1, sk next dc, repeat from * across—28 (30-32-34-36) sc. Repeat rows 2-7 for pat twice. Repeat row 2. Check gauge; piece above ribbing should measure 16" (17"-18"-19"-20") wide.

Shape Armholes: Keeping to pat, bind off (see To Bind Off) 4 (6-4-6-4) sts each side of next row, then 2 sts each side every row 1 (1-2-2-3) times—43 (43-47-47-51) sts. Work even until armholes measure 7" (7½"-7½"-8"-8") above first armhole shaping row.

Shape Shoulders and Neck: Keeping to pat, work across 11 (11-13-13-13) sts, turn. Bind off 4 sts at arm side of next 2 rows—3 (3-5-5-5) sts. End off. Join MC in 11th (11th-13th-13th-13th) st from arm side of last long row. Keeping to pat, work 1 row even, end arm side. Bind off 4 sts at arm side of next 2 rows. End off.

FRONT: Work ribbing same as for back. Work pat same as for back to end of pat row 7, repeat rows 2-7 once, then rows 2-5.

Divide for V-Neck: Ch 3 (counts as 1 dc), sk first sc, work in pat until 24 (26-28-30-32) dc from start; holding back last lp on hook, work dc in each of next 3 sts, yo and through 4 lps on hook (2 dc dec), drop yarn; with another strand of MC, make lp on hook, sk next st (center st); holding back last lp on hook, dc in each of next 3 sts, yo and through 4 lps on hook, dc in each st across— 25 (27-29-31-33) sts each side. Keeping to pat, work 1 row even. Bind off 2 sts at each neck edge of next row, then bind off 2 sts at same edge every 7th row 3 (3-3-3-4) times

more; **at the same time,** when piece measures same as back to underarm, bind off 4 (6-4-6-4) sts each arm side of next row, then bind off 2 sts each arm side every row 1 (1-2-2-3) times—11 (11-13-13-13) sts each side. Work even until armholes measure same as back.

Shape Shoulders: Keeping to pat, bind off 4 sts each arm side every row twice. End off.

FINISHING: Block pieces. With backstitch, sew shoulder and side seams. From right side, with MC, work 1 rnd sc around each armhole, holding in to desired fit.

Neck Edging: Join MC at center front.

Rnd 1: From right side, work 90 (90-95-95-100) sc around neck edge, end center front. Ch 1, turn.

Rnd 2: Pull up a lp in each of next 2 sc, yo and through 3 lps on hook (1 sc dec), sc in each sc to within last 2 sc, pull up a lp in each of next 2 sc, yo and through 3 lps on hook (1 sc dec). Ch 1, turn.

Rnds 3 and 4: Repeat rnd 2—84 (84-89-89-94) sc. Cut MC; join CC.

Rnd 5 (right side): * Sc in next sc, long sc in next sc on 2nd row below, long sc in next sc on 3rd row below, long sc in next sc on first row, repeat from * to left shoulder seam, ** long sc in next sc on 4th row below, long sc in next sc on 3rd row below, long sc in next sc on 2nd row below, sc in next sc, long sc in base of next sc on first row, repeat from ** to center front, end last repeat sc in last sc. Ch 1, turn.

Rnd 6: Sl st in each st. End off. Weave center front neckband tog.

SWEATER TWIN SET

Worked in ribby lines of easy double crochet, trimmed in darker single crochet. The sleeveless pull has a U neck offsetting the V-necked cardigan.

SIZES: Directions for size 8. Changes for sizes 10, 12, 14 and 16 are in parentheses.

Body Bust Size: 31½″ (32½″-34″-36″-38″).

Blocked Bust Size: Pullover: 32″ (34″-36″-38″-40″). Cardigan (closed): 34″ (36″-38″-40″-42″).

MATERIALS: Sport yarn, 2-oz. skeins. Pullover: 4 (4-5-5-6) skeins turquoise, main color (MC); 1 skein royal blue, contrasting color (CC). Cardigan: 6 (6-7-7-8) skeins MC; 1 skein CC. Crochet hook size E. Six buttons.

GAUGE: 4 dc = 1″; 12 rows = 5″.

Note: Always count turning ch as 1 dc.

To Bind Off: At beg of a row, ch 1, sl st loosely across specified sts; **at end of a row,** leave specified number of sts unworked.

To Dec 1 St: At beg of a row, ch 3 (counts as 1 dc), sk first dc, yo hook, draw up a lp in each of next 2 sts, yo hook and through 2 lps, yo and through 3 lps, work in pat across; **at end of a row,** work to last 2 sts, yo hook, draw up a lp in each of next 2 sts, yo and through 2 lps, yo and through 3 lps.

To Inc 1 Dc: A beg of a row, ch 3 (counts as 1 dc), dc in first dc; **at end of a row,** work 2 dc in top of turning ch.

PULLOVER: BACK: Beg at lower edge above border, with MC, ch 66 (70-74-78-82).

Row 1: Dc in 4th ch from hook, dc in next ch and in each ch across—64 (68-72-76-80) dc (see Note). Turn each row.

Row 2: Ch 3, sk first dc, dc in each dc across. Repeat row 2 until piece measures 12″ (12″-12½″-12½″-13″) or 1″ less (border allowance) than desired length to underarm.

Check gauge; piece should measure 16″ (17″-18″-19″-20″) wide.

Shape Armholes: Bind off (see To Bind Off) 4 (4-4-5-5) sts each side of next row. Dec 1 st (see To Dec 1 St) each side every row 3 (4-4-4-5) times—50 (52-56-58-60) sts. Work even until armholes measure 6½″ (6¾″-7″-7″-7½″) above first bound-off sts.

Shape Shoulders: Bind off 5 (5-6-6-7) sts each side of next row. End off.

FRONT: Work same as for back to underarm—64 (68-72-76-80) dc.

Shape Armholes and Neck: Bind off 4 (4-4-5-5) sts each side of next row. Dec 1 st each side of next row—54 (58-62-64-68) sts. Turn.

Next Row: Ch 3, sk first dc, dec 1 st over next 2 sts, dc in each of next 12 (14-15-16-18) dc, dec 1 dc over next 2 dc, dc in next dc, drop yarn; sk next 18 (18-20-20-20) dc, join another strand of MC in next dc, ch 3, dec 1 st over next 2 dc, dc in each of next 13 (15-16-17-19) dc, dec 1 st over next 2 sts. Working on both sides at once, dec 1 st each arm side every row 1 (2-2-2-3) times more; **at the same time,** dec 1 st at each neck edge every row 3 times—12 (13-14-15-16) sts each side. Work even until armholes measure same as back.

Shape Shoulders: Bind off 5 (5-6-6-7) sts at each arm side of next row. End off.

FINISHING: Block pieces. With backstitch, sew shoulder seams; sew side seams.

Lower Band: Join MC in lower side seam. From right side, working in sc, work 3 rnds MC, 3 rnds CC. End off.

Neckband: Join MC in right shoulder seam. Work same as for lower band, easing in to desired fit.

From right side, with MC, work 1 rnd sc around each armhole. Steam-press bands and seams lightly.

CARDIGAN: BACK: Beg at lower edge above border, with MC, ch 68 (72-76-80-84). Work same as for pullover back on 66 (70-74-78-82) sts for 15″ (15″-15½″-15½″-16″) or 1″ less (border allowance) than desired length to underarm. Check gauge; piece should measure 16½″ (17½″-18½″-19½″-20½″) wide.

Shape Armholes: Bind off 5 (5-5-6-6) sts each side of next row. Dec 1 st each side every row 2 (3-3-3-4) times—52 (54-58-60-62) sts. Work even until armholes measure 6¾″ (7″-7½″-7½″-8″) above first bound-off sts.

Shape Shoulders: Bind off 6 (6-7-7-8) sts each side of next row. End off.

RIGHT FRONT: Beg at lower edge above border, with MC, ch 35 (37-39-41-43) sts. Work same as for back on 33 (35-37-39-41) dc until piece measures 3″ less than back to underarm. Mark end of last row for center edge. Check gauge; piece should measure 8¼″ (8¾″-9¼″-9¾″-10¼″) wide.

Shape V-Neck, Armhole and Shoulder: Dec 1 st at center edge of next row, then dec 1 st at same edge every other row 13 (13-14-14-14) times; **at the same time,** when piece measures same as back to underarm, bind off 5 (5-5-6-6) sts at side edge of next row, then dec 1 st at same edge every row 2 (3-3-3-4) times—12 (13-14-15-16) sts. Work even until armhole measures same as back. Bind off 6 (6-7-7-8) sts at arm side of next row. End off.

LEFT FRONT: Work same as for right front; pat is reversible.

SLEEVES: Beg at lower edge above border, with MC, ch 40 (40-42-42-44). Work same as for back on 38 (38-40-40-42) dc for 3″. Check gauge; piece should measure 9½″ (9½″-10″-10″-10½″) wide. Inc 1 dc (see To Inc 1 Dc) each side of next row, then every 3rd row 8 (9-9-10-10) times more—56 (58-60-62-64) sts.

Shape Cap: Bind off 5 (5-5-6-6) sts each side of next row. Dec 1 st each side every row 4 (5-6-7-8) times.

Next Row: Ch 3, sk first dc, (dec 1 st over next 2 sts) twice, work to within last 5 sts, end (dec 1 st over next 2 sts) twice, dc in top of turning ch—4 sts dec. Repeat last row 3 times—22 (22-22-20-20) sts. End.

FINISHING: Block pieces. Sew shoulder seams; sew in sleeves. Sew side and sleeve seams.

Lower Border: Join MC in lower left front edge.

Row 1: Sc in each st across lower edge. Ch 1, turn. Working in sc, work 2 more rows MC, 3 rows CC. End off.

Front Border: Row 1: Join MC in lower right front edge. Sc up front edge, across back neck edge, down other front edge, having same number of sts on each front edge. Ch 1, turn.

With pins, mark position of 6 buttonholes on right front edge, first pin 1″ above lower edge, last pin ½″ below start of neck shaping.

Row 2 (buttonhole row): * Sc in each sc to within 1 sc of marker, ch 2, sk next 2 sc, sc in next sc, repeat from * 5 times, finish row. Ch 1, turn.

Row 3: Sc in each sc and ch across. Cut MC; join CC. With CC, ch 1, turn. Work 3 rows in sc. End off.

Sleeve Borders: Join MC in underarm seam. Working in sc, work 3 rnds MC, 3 rnds CC. End off.

Steam-press seams and borders lightly. Sew on buttons.

LACY TWINS

This sweater duet is trimmed with slipper stitch ribs, reverse crochet. The two-pattern cardigan has a band neck, turned-back front, squared sleeve caps. The button-up undershell repeats just one pattern.

SIZES: Directions are for small size (8-10). Changes for medium size (12-14) are in parentheses. **Note:** Size of hook and gauge determine size.

Body Bust Size: 31½″-32½″ (34″-36″).

Blocked Bust Size: Cardigan: 35″ (37″). Sleeveless sweater: 35″ (37″).

MATERIALS: Dress yarn of fingering weight, 1-oz. balls. Cardigan: 14 (16) balls. Sleeveless sweater: 6 (7) balls. Aluminum crochet hooks sizes C and E (C and F). Five buttons.

GAUGE: Cardigan: 3 V sts and 2 shells = 3″, size E hook (3¼″, size F hook). Sleeveless Sweater: 2 shells and 1 V st = 2″, size E hook (2¼″, size F hook).

CARDIGAN: Note: Body is worked in one piece to underarm.

With E (F) hook, ch 173 loosely.

Row 1: Dc in 4th ch from hook (turning ch counts as 1 dc), * sk 2 ch; in next ch work 5 dc for a shell, sk 2 ch; in next ch work 1 dc, ch 1 and 1 dc for a V st; repeat from * to last 7 ch, sk 2 ch, 5-dc shell in next ch, sk 2 ch, 1 dc in each of last 2 ch—28 shells, 27 V sts and 2 dc at each side. Ch 3, turn each row.

Row 2: Sk first dc (ch 3 counts as first dc), dc in next dc, dc in each of 5 dc of shell, * V st in ch-1 sp of next V st, dc in each of 5 dc of next shell, repeat from * across, end dc in each of last 2 dc.

Rows 3 and 4: Sk first dc, dc in each of next 6 dc, * V st in next V st, dc in each of next 5 dc, repeat from * across, end dc in each of last 2 dc. Check gauge; piece should measure 35″ (37″) across.

Row 5: Sk first dc, dc in next dc, * sk 2 dc, V st in next dc, sk 2 dc, 5-dc shell in ch-1 sp of next V st, repeat from * across, end sk 2 dc, V st in next dc, sk 2 dc, dc in each of last 2 dc.

Row 6: Sk first dc, dc in next dc, 5-dc shell in ch-1 sp of next V st, * V st in 3rd dc of next shell, 5-dc shell in next V st, repeat from * across, end dc in each of last 2 dc.

Row 7: Sk first dc, dc in next dc, V st in 3rd dc of next shell, * shell in next V st, V st in 3rd dc of next shell, repeat from * across, end dc in each of last 2 dc.

Rows 8 and 9: Repeat rows 6 and 7.

Row 10: Sk first dc, dc in next dc, V st in next V st, * dc in each of 5 dc of next shell, V st in next V st, repeat from * across, end dc in each of last 2 dc.

Rows 11 and 12: Sk first dc, dc in next dc, V st in next V st, * dc in each of next 5 dc, V st in next V st, repeat from * across, end dc in each of last 2 dc.

Row 13: Sk first dc, dc in next dc, shell in next V st, sk 2 dc, * V st in next dc, shell in next V st, repeat from * across, end dc in each of last 2 dc.

Row 14: Repeat row 7.

Row 15: Repeat row 13.

Rows 16 and 17: Repeat rows 7 and 13. Repeat rows 2-17 for pat working to about 14″ (15″) from beg, end with row 10.

Stitch Detail for Cardigan

Divide for Back and Fronts:
Right Front: Sk first dc, dc in next dc, * V st in next V st, dc in each of next 5 dc, repeat from * 5 more times, end with dc in first dc of next V st. Ch 3, turn.

Continue in pat on right front sts until armhole measures 4½″ (5″) above underarm, end at armhole edge with row 9. Ch 3, turn.

Shape Neck and Shoulder: Sk first dc, * dc in each of next 5 dc, V st in next V st, repeat from * twice more. Ch 3, turn. Continue in pat until armhole measures 7″ (7½″) above underarm. End off.

Left Front: Join yarn in 7th V st from left front edge, ch 3 for first dc, work pat as on row 11 to front edge. Work to correspond to right front.

Back: Leaving 1 shell, 1 V st and 1 shell free at right underarm, join yarn in 2nd st of next V st, work pat as on row 11 to left underarm, leaving 1 shell, 1 V st and 1 shell free for underarm. Ch 3, turn. Work in pat on back sts until armholes measure same as on fronts. Fasten off.

SLEEVES: With E (F) hook, ch 65 loosely. Work in pat same as on back with 10 shells, 11 V sts and 2 dc at each side. Work to about 16″ (17″) from start. End.

CUFFS (make 2): With C hook, ch 25.

Row 1: Sc in 2nd ch from hook and in each ch across—24 sc. Ch 1, turn.

Row 2: Working in back lps only, work sc in each sc. Ch 1, turn. Repeat row 2 to 7″ (8″) from beg. End off.

FRONT BANDS (make 2): With C hook, ch 10. Work as for cuffs until band when slightly stretched fits front edge to neck. End off. Weave bands to front edges.

FINISHING: Sew shoulder seams. Sew last row of sleeve to straight edge of armhole. Sew about 2″ at each side edge of sleeve to underarm edge of body, then

sew sleeve seams. Join cuff ends. Gather lower edge of sleeve to fit cuff and sew in place. Turn back front bands to right side and tack in place about ½″ in from edge of band.

Collar: With C hook, from right side, beg after front band, work in sc around neck edge to front band. Ch 1, turn. Work 2 more rows in sc. Working in back lps as for cuff, work 1 row even. Continue to work in back lps, inc 1 st in every 10th st across. Work 1 row even. On next row, inc in every 12th st. Work 2 rows even. On next row, inc in every 14th st. Work 2 rows even. End off. Fold collar in half to right side and tack in place about 1 inch from outer edge. From right side, working backwards from left to right on side edges and across lower edge of collar, work ch 1, hdc in first st, * ch 1, sk 1 sc, hdc in next st, repeat from * around, working through double thickness

at side edges. End off. Work same edging on front bands and across top of bands through double thickness. Work edging around bottom of cuffs.

SLEEVELESS SWEATER:
Note: Body is worked in one piece to underarm. With E (F) hook, ch 165 loosely.

Row 1: (right side): Dc in 4th ch from hook (turning ch counts as 1 dc), * sk 2 ch; in next ch work 5 dc for a shell, sk 3 ch, 5-dc shell in next ch, sk 2 ch; in next ch work dc, ch 1 and dc for a V st; repeat from * across, end sk 2 ch, 5-dc shell in next ch, sk 3 ch, 5-dc shell in next ch, sk 2 ch, dc in each of last 2 ch—16 double shell pats. Ch 3, turn each row.

Row 2: Sk first dc (ch 3 counts as first dc), dc in next dc, * (work V st in 2nd dc of next shell, V st in 4th dc of same shell) twice, V st in ch-1 sp of next V st, repeat from * across, end (V st in 2nd dc of next shell, V st in 4th dc of same shell) twice, dc in each of last 2 dc.

Row 3: Sk first dc, dc in next dc, 5-dc shell in sp between next 2 V sts, 5-dc shell in sp between next 2 V sts, (these shells are above shells of row 1), * V st in next V st (shell in sp between next 2 V sts) twice, repeat from * across, end dc in each of last 2 dc. Check gauge; piece should measure 32″ (36″) across. Repeat rows 2 and 3 for pat until piece is 11″ from beg, end with row 2.

Divide for Back and Fronts: Right Front: Work until there are 7 shells from front edge, dc in first dc of next V st. Ch 3, turn.

Shape Armhole and Neck: Row 1: Sk first dc, dc in 2nd dc of shell for armhole dec, V st in 4th dc of same shell, work to end. Ch 3, turn.

Row 2: Sk first dc, dc in next dc, 3 dc between next 2 V sts for a ½ shell (neck dec), work across row, end with ½ shell in last V st, dc in each of last 2 dc. Ch 3, turn each row.

Row 3: Sk first dc, dc in next dc, dc in center dc of ½ shell, work across row, end with dc in center dc of ½ shell, dc in each of last 2 dc.

Row 4: Sk first dc, dc in next dc, sk next dc, work across row, end with V st in last V st, sk next dc, dc in each of last 2 dc.

Row 5: Sk first dc, dc in next dc, work across row to last shell at front edge, work V st in 2nd dc of shell, dc in 4th dc of shell for neck dec, dc in each of last 2 dc.

Row 6: Sk first dc, dc in next dc, 3 dc for ½ shell in next V st, work pat to end.

Row 7: Work to last ½ shell, dc in center dc of ½ shell, dc in each of last 2 dc.

Row 8: Sk first dc, dc in next dc, sk next dc, work to end.

Row 9: Work to last V st, work dc in last V st, dc in each of last 2 dc.

Row 10: Sk first dc, dc in next dc, sk next dc, work to end.

Row 11: Work to last shell, V st in 2nd dc of shell, dc in 4th dc of same shell, dc in each of last 2 dc.

Row 12: Sk first dc, dc in next dc, ½ shell between next dc and V st, work to end.

Row 13: Work to ½ shell, dc in center dc of ½ shell, dc in each of last 2 dc.

Row 14: Sk first dc, dc in next dc, sk next dc, shell between next 2 V sts, work to end.

Row 15: Work to last shell, V st in 2nd dc of shell, dc in 4th dc of shell, dc in last 2 dc.

Row 16: Sk first dc, dc in next dc, sk 1 dc, dc in first dc of next V st, work to end.

Row 17: Work to last 3 dc, sk 1 dc, dc in each of last 2 dc.

If necessary, work in established pat until armhole measures 6¾″ (7¼″), end at armhole edge with a shell row. Ch 1, turn.

Shape Shoulder: Work sc in each of first 2 dc, sc in dc, ch 1 and next dc of V st, hdc in each dc of next 2 shell pats, dc in dc, ch 1 and dc of next V st, dc in each of last 2 dc. End off.

Left Front: Join yarn in the V st before the 7th shell from left front edge, ch 3 for first dc, work to front edge. Work to correspond to right front, reversing shaping.

Back: Leaving 3 V sts with ½ V st at each side free for underarm, join yarn in 2nd dc of 4th V st, ch 3 for first dc, dc in next V st, shell between next 2 V sts, work across until there are 14 shell pats across back, dc in next V st, dc in first dc of next V st. Ch 3, turn each row.

Row 2: Sk first dc, dc in next dc, dc in 2nd dc of shell, V st in 4th dc of shell, work to last shell, V st in 2nd dc of shell, dc in 4th dc of shell, dc in last 2 sts.

Row 3: Sk first dc, dc in next dc, ½ shell between next dc and V st, work to last 2 V sts, V st in next V st, ½ shell between last V st and next dc, dc in last 2 sts.

Row 4: Sk first dc, dc in next dc, dc in center dc of ½ shell, work pat to last ½ shell, dc in center dc of ½ shell, dc in each of last 2 dc.

Row 5: Sk first dc, dc in next dc, sk next dc, work to last 3 dc, sk 1 dc, dc in each of last 2 dc.

Continue in established pat until armholes are same length as front armholes.

Shape shoulders same as on fronts. End off.

WAISTBAND: With size C hook, ch 19. Work same as cuff of cardigan to 28″ (30″) or desired waist size. End off. Sew to lower edge of body, easing in fullness.

FINISHING: Sew shoulder seams.

Left Front Band: With size C hook, ch 9. Work same as waistband until band when slightly stretched fits front edge from lower edge to center back of neck. End off. Weave to left front edge and to center back of neck. Place markers on band for 5 buttons, having first one ½″ from lower edge and 5th about ½″ below start of neck shaping.

Right Front Band: Work same as left front band, forming buttonholes opposite markers as follows: Work 3 sts, ch 2, sk 2 sc, work to end. On next row, work sc in each of 2 ch. Weave band to right front edge and to back of neck. Join band at center back. Work edging around front band and neck edges same as on cardigan.

Armholes: With size C hook, from right side, beg at underarm, work 1 row of sc around armholes, holding in to fit if necessary. Sl st in first sc. Ch 1, turn.

Rnds 2 and 3: Working in back lps only, sc in each sc. Join, ch 1, turn at end of rnd 2. Do not turn at end of rnd 3.

Rnd 4: Work edging same as on front neck. End off.

TOPS
GRANNY HALTERS

The scarf-shaped halter has twenty-one colorful grannies sewn together to form a triangle. The top square is turned under for neck-tie insertion; bottom is edged by double crochet shells. V'd halter ties slightly above the waist to show just a touch of midriff. Follow chart to sew squares in place.

SIZE: One size fits all.
MATERIALS: Sport yarn, small amounts of any desired colors, about 4 ozs. for each halter. Crochet hook size H.

GAUGE: Each motif = 3″.
Notes: Join each rnd with a sl st in top of ch 3. Cut yarn, pull end through lp on hook. Join new color with sl st. Work over ends of

previous color and new color to hide them.
TRIANGLE HALTER: MOTIF (make 21): With first color, ch 4, sl st in first ch to form ring.

Rnd 1: Ch 3, 2 dc in ring, (ch 1, 3 dc in ring) 3 times, ch 1; join; end off (see Notes).

Rnd 2: Join 2nd color in any ch-1 sp, ch 3, 2 dc in same sp, ch 1, 3 dc in same sp, ch 1, (3 dc, ch 1, 3 dc, ch 1 in next sp) 3 times; join; end off.

Rnd 3: Join 3rd color in any corner sp (center of 6-dc group), ch 3, 2 dc in same sp, ch 1, 3 dc in same sp, ch 1, (3 dc in next sp; ch 1, 3 dc, ch 1, 3 dc, ch 1 in next sp) 3 times, 3 dc in next sp, ch 1; join; end off.

JOINING: Following chart, using colors to match one edge to be joined, sew motifs tog through back lps, forming triangle.

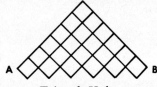

Triangle Halter

EDGING: Row 1: Join any desired color yarn in ch-1 corner sp (A on chart); working across lower edge, ch 3, * (3 dc in next ch-1 sp between 3-dc groups) twice, ch 2, sc in ch-1 corner sp, ch 2, (3 dc in next ch-1 sp) twice, dc in joining of motifs, repeat from * across lower edge, end dc in last ch-1 corner sp (B on chart); end off; do not turn.

Next Rnd: With any desired color yarn, dc in top of starting ch 3 at beg of last row, ch 2, * shell of 3 dc in next ch-1 sp between shells, (ch 2, sc in next ch-2 sp) twice, ch 2, 3 dc in next ch-1 sp between shells, dc in dc between shells, repeat from * across lower edge, end last repeat dc in last dc, ch 1; do not end off. Work sc, ch 1 evenly spaced across each side edge, end sl st in first dc; end off; do not turn.

Next Rnd: Join another color in first dc; (ch 2, sc in next ch-2 sp) 4 times, * 4 dc in dc between motifs, sc in next ch-2 sp, (ch 2, sc in next ch-2 sp) twice, repeat from * across lower edge, end last repeat ch 2, sc in last dc; end off.

FINISHING: Steam-press halter lightly. Fold top motif in half to wrong side; weave outer edge of motif in place.

TIES: With double strand of any color yarn, make ch 44″ long. Run through top edge of halter. Make two ties 20″ long; sew a tie to each point at lower edge.

V-NECK HALTER: Make 17 motifs as for Triangle Halter.

JOINING: Following chart, using colors to match one edge to be joined, sew motifs tog.

EDGING: Join any desired color yarn in ch-1 corner sp (A on chart); working across lower edge, * ch 3; holding back last lp on hook, work dc in next sp between 3-dc groups, tr in next sp between 3-dc groups, yo hook and through 3 lps on hook, ch 1; holding back last lp on hook, work tr in sp last worked in, dtr in joining of motifs (B on chart), tr in next sp between 3-dc groups, yo hook and through 4 lps on hook, ch 1; holding back last lp on hook, work tr in sp last worked in, dc in next sp between 3-dc groups, dc in corner ch-1 sp, yo hook and through 4 lps on hook, ch 3, sc in same corner ch-1 sp, repeat from * across lower edge, end at C on chart, ** ch 1, sk next st, sc in next st, repeat from ** around, end sl st in first st. End off.

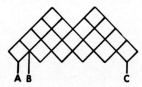

V-Neck Halter

FINISHING: Steam-press halter lightly.

TIES (make 4): With double strand of any color yarn, make chains 20″ long. Sew a tie to each point at neck and lower edge.

SURPLICE VEST

This surplice vest is a pretty summer top in double crochet, and easy enough for the beginner to make. Right front folds over left front and ties to the side for surplice effect. Front edging bands continue across shoulders and form the straps.

SIZES: Directions for small size (6-8). Changes for medium size (10-12) and large size (14-16) are in parentheses.

Fits Bust Size: 30½″-31½″ (32½″-34″; 36″-38″).

MATERIALS: Sport yarn, 2 2-oz. skeins white (W); 1 skein each of rose (R) and green (G). Steel crochet hook No. 1. One-half yd. 1″-wide green ribbon.

GAUGE: 5 dc = 1″; 2 rows = 1″.

Note: Halter is worked from top to lower edge. Cut and join colors as needed.

To Inc 2 Dc: At beg of a row, ch 3 (counts as 1 dc), 2 dc in first dc; **at end of a row,** 3 dc in top of ch 3.

To Inc 1 Dc: At beg of a row, ch 3 (counts as 1 dc), dc in first dc; **at end of a row,** 2 dc in top of ch 3.

VEST: BACK: First Half: Beg at upper edge (see Note), with W, ch 4.

Row 1: Dc in 4th ch from hook. Turn each row.

Row 2: Ch 3 (counts as 1 dc), dc in first dc, 2 dc in top of turning ch—4 dc.

Row 3: Inc 2 dc (see To Inc 2 Dc) at beg and end of row—8 dc.

Row 4: Inc 1 dc (see To Inc 1 Dc) at beg and end of row—10 dc. Repeat last 2 rows 3 (4-4) times—28 (34-34) dc.

For Small Size Only: Repeat row 4—30 dc.

For Large Size Only: Repeat row 3—38 dc. Check gauge; last row should measure 6″ (6¾″-7½″) wide. Cut yarn.

2nd Half: Work same as for first half; do not cut yarn at end of last row. Turn.

Join Work: Next Row: Ch 3, 2 dc in first dc, dc in each dc across, dc in top of turning ch; working across first half, dc in each dc across, 3 dc in top of turning ch—64 (72-80) dc. Turn. Working in dc, inc 2 dc each side every row 3 times— 76 (84-92) dc.

Next Row: With W, ch 3, sk first dc, dc in each dc across, dc in top of ch 3—76 (84-92) dc. Repeating last row, work 4 more rows of W, 2 rows G, 3 rows W, 3 rows R. End off.

FRONT: First Half: Beg at upper edge, ch 6.

Row 1: Dc in 4th ch from hook, ch 1, 2 dc in last ch—4 dc, counting 3 ch as 1 dc. Turn each row.

Row 2: Ch 3 (counts as 1 dc), dc in first dc, dc in next dc, (dc, ch 1, dc) in ch-1 sp, dc in next dc, dc in top of ch 3—7 dc.

Row 3: Ch 3, dc in first dc, dc in each dc across, working (dc, ch 1, dc) in center ch-1 sp—10 dc.

Rows 4-8: Repeat row 3—25 dc.

Row 9: Ch 3, dc in first dc, dc in each st across, working dc in ch-1 sp, 2 dc in top of ch 3—28 dc. Working in dc, inc 1 dc each side every row 6 (7-8) times—40 (42-44) dc. Mark beg of last row for center edge. On 2nd half, mark end of last row for center edge. Inc 1 st at center edge of next row, then every row 4 times—45 (47-49) dc. Continuing to inc 1 st at center edge every row, work 2 rows G, 3 rows W, 3 rows R—53 (55-57) dc. End off.

2nd Half: Work same as for first half, reversing shaping.

FINISHING: Run in yarn ends on wrong side. Block pieces.

Armhole Edging: From right side, with R, work 2 rows dc on each armhole edge of back and fronts. Sew side seams.

Beg at lower right front edge **(left-handed crocheters:** beg at lower left front edge), with R, sl st up right front edge, ch 28 for strap, sl st in top of right back edge, sl st around back neck edge, ch 28 for strap, sl st in top of left front edge, sl st down left front edge. End off.

Right Band: Join R with a dc in back lp of first sl st at lower right front edge **(left-handed crocheters:** lower left front edge); dc in back lp of each sl st and ch up

front edge, strap ch and down back edge, end center back. Turn.

Next Row: Ch 3, sk first 2 dc, dc in each dc. End off. Join R with a dc in back lp of first sl st at center back neck edge, sk next sl st, dc in back lp of each sl st and ch, end lower left front edge. Turn.

Next Row: Ch 3, sk first dc, dc in each dc to within last 2 dc, sk next dc, dc in last dc. End off, leaving a long end for sewing. Thread

needle; lap left back band over right back band; tack in place.

Cut ribbon to fit back waistband. Face back G rows with ribbon.

TIES (make 2): With G, ch 50 (52-54). Dc in 3rd ch from hook and in each ch across. Ch 3, turn.

Next Row: Dc in each dc across. End off.

Sew a tie to green stripe at right front edge. Sew 2nd tie to green stripe at left side seam.

SHELL-YOKE BLOUSE

Beginners can make this pretty blouse, all in one piece and all in double crochet. The front and back are the same except for a change to bright variegated yarn for the top rows of the front yoke.

SIZES: Directions for small size (6-8). Changes for medium size (10-12) and large size (14) are in parentheses.

Body Bust Size: 30½"-31½" (32½"-34"; 36").

Blocked Bust Size: 32" (34"-36½").

MATERIALS: Knitting worsted, 2 4-oz. skeins coral (A); 1 skein variegated (B). Crochet hook size I.

GAUGE: 5 dc = 2"; 4 rows = 3".

Note: Blouse is worked in one piece to underarm. Pull up each dc to height of ¾".

BLOUSE: BODY: Beg at lower edge of back and front, with A, ch 80 (86-92). Being careful not to twist chain, join with a sl st in first ch, forming circle.

Rnd 1: Ch 3 (counts as 1 dc), dc in each ch around—80 (86-92) dc. Join with a sl st in top of ch 3; do not turn.

Rnd 2: Ch 3 (counts as 1 dc), sk joining st, dc in each dc around. Join with a sl st in top of ch 3; do not turn. Check gauge; piece should measure 32″ (34″-36½″) around.

Rnds 3-9: Repeat rnd 2. End off.

SLEEVES AND BACK YOKE: With A, ch 18 (21-23); from right side, dc in joining st on body, dc in each of next 39 (41-45) dc, ch 20 (23-25). Turn.

Next Row: Dc in 4th ch from hook (counts as 2 dc), dc in each ch and dc across—76 (84-92) dc. Turn.

Next Row: Ch 3, sk first dc, dc in each dc across—76 (84-92) dc. Ch 3, turn.

Next Row: Sk 2 dc, shell of 4 dc in sp between dc's, * sk 4 dc, shell of 4 dc in sp between dc's, repeat from * across, end sk next dc, dc in top of turning ch—19 (21-23) shells. Ch 3, turn.

Next Row: Sk first dc, shell of 4 dc in sp before first shell, * shell of 4 dc in next sp between shells, repeat from * across, end dc in top of turning ch—19 (21-23) shells. Ch 3, turn. Repeat last row 4 (5-5) times.

Shape Neck and Shoulders: Work 7 (8-9) shells, sk next 2 dc, dc in next dc of shell. End off. Sk next 3 shells, work dc in 3rd dc of next shell, work shell in sp between each remaining shell across, end dc in top of turning ch. End off—7 (8-9) shells each side.

FRONT YOKE AND SLEEVES: From right side, with A, working into foundation ch of sleeve, work dc in first ch, 2 dc in each of next 2 (1-2) ch, dc in each remaining ch of first sleeve, work dc in each dc across front, dc in each ch of 2nd sleeve, working 2 dc in each of last 2 (1-2) ch—80 (88-96) dc. Turn.

Next Row: Ch 3, sk first dc, dc in each dc across—80 (88-96) dc. Work same as for back yoke and sleeves on 20 (22-24) 4-dc shells until 4 (5-5) shell rows are completed. Cut A; join B. With B, complete same as for back, leaving 4 shells free for front of neck. Sew tops of sleeves tog.

FINISHING: From right side, with B, work 1 rnd sc around neck edge, being careful to keep work flat. Join with a sl st in first sc. End off. Steam-press lightly.

ROSE SHELL
Shown at left on page 49

A bloom of roses patterns the front of an airy shell. Tiny scallops decorate neck and hem; tasseled drawstrings pull in the waist.

SIZES: Directions for size 8. Changes for sizes 10, 12 and 14 are in parentheses.

Body Bust Size: 31½″ (32½″-34″-36″).

Blocked Bust Size: 32½″ (33½″-35″-37″).

MATERIALS: Mercerized knitting and crochet cotton, 4 (5-5-6) 250-yd. balls. Steel crochet hook No. 8.

GAUGE: 10 meshes = 3″; 4 rows = 1″.

To Bind Off: At beg of a row, sl st loosely across each st to be bound off, then ch 5 and continue across row; **at end of a row,** work in pat to within specified number of meshes to be bound off.

To Dec 1 Mesh: At beg of a row, ch 3, sk first mesh, dc in next dc (counts as 1 dc), ch 2, dc in next dc (1 mesh); **at end of a row,** work to last dc, ch 2, yo, pull up a lp in last dc, yo and through 2 lps on hook, yo, pull up a lp in 3rd ch of turning ch, yo and through 2 lps on hook, yo and through 3 lps on hook.

To Inc 1 Mesh: At beg of a row, ch 4, dc in first dc; **at end of a row,** (ch 2, dc in 3rd ch of turning ch) twice.

To Make Meshes: Dc in dc, ch 2, sk 2 sts, dc in next dc (1 mesh), ch 2, sk 2 sts, dc in next dc for each additional mesh.

To Make Blocks: Dc in each of 4 sts (1 block); dc in each of next 3 sts for each additional block.

Chart Notes: Meshes are shown on chart as open squares, blocks by × squares.

BLOUSE: BACK: Beg at lower edge, ch 167 (173-179-191).

Row 1: Dc in 8th ch from hook (1 mesh), * ch 2, sk next 2 ch, dc in next dc, repeat from * across—54 (56-58-62) meshes. Ch 5, turn.

Rows 2 and 3: Sk first dc and ch-2 sp, dc in next dc (1 mesh), * ch 2, dc in next dc, repeat from * across, end ch 2, sk next 2 ch of turning ch, dc in next ch. Ch 5, turn. Check gauge; piece should measure 16¼″ (16¾″-17½″-18½″) wide.

Pattern: Row 4: Following chart 1, work from right to left (see Chart Notes). Ch 5, turn.

Row 5: Following chart 1, work from left to right. Ch 5, turn.

Rows 6-13: Repeat last 2 rows 4 times, dec 1 mesh (see To Dec 1 Mesh) each side of row 11—52 (54-56-60) meshes. Ch 5, turn.

Rows 14-16: Work in mesh pat. Ch 3, turn.

Waistband: Row 1 (eyelet row): Sk first dc, * dc in each of next 5 sts, ch 1, sk next st, repeat from * across, end last repeat dc in last dc, dc in each of next 3 ch of turning ch. Ch 5, turn.

Row 2: Work in mesh pat across—52 (54-56-60) meshes. Ch 3, turn.

Row 3: Sk first dc, dc in each st across, end dc in last dc, dc in each of next 3 ch of turning ch. Ch 5, turn.

Bodice: Rows 1-6: Work in mesh pat—52 (54-56-60) meshes.

Row 7: Keeping to mesh pat, inc 1 mesh (see To Inc 1 Mesh) each side—54 (56-58-62) meshes.

Rows 8-34: Work in mesh pat. Ch 1, turn.

Shape Armholes: Row 1: Sl st across 10 (10-10-13) sts, ch 3, * dc in each of next 2 ch, dc in next dc, repeat from * to within last 3 (3-3-4) meshes—145 (151-157-163) dc, counting ch 3 as 1 dc. Ch 3, turn.

Row 2: Sk first 3 dc, dc in next dc, * ch 2, sk next 2 dc, dc in next dc, repeat from * to within last 2 dc and turning ch, sk 2 dc, dc in top of ch 3. Ch 5, turn.

Row 3: Work in mesh pat across—46 (48-50-52) meshes. Dec

1 mesh each side of next row—44 (46-48-50) meshes. Work even until armholes measure 5½" (5¾"-6¼"-6¾") above first row of armhole shaping.

Shape Neck and Shoulders: Row 1: Work 12 (13-13-14) meshes; ch 3, turn.

Next Row: Sk first dc, dc in next dc, finish row. Ch 1, turn. Dec 1 mesh at neck edge every row twice; **at the same time,** bind off (see To Bind Off) 3 meshes at arm side every row twice. End off.

Sk next 20 (20-22-22) meshes on last long row, join another strand of yarn in next dc, ch 5, dc in next dc, finish row—12 (13-13-14) meshes. Complete same as first shoulder, reversing shaping.

FRONT: Work same as back to end of bodice row 13. Ch 5, turn.

Row 14: Following chart 2, work from right to left. Ch 5, turn.

Row 15: Following chart 2, work from left to right. Ch 5, turn. Repeating last 2 rows, work to top of chart (16 rows). Work 5 rows in mesh pat.

Shape Armholes: Work same as for back until armhole measures 2¾" (3"-3¼"-3½") above first row

of armhole shaping—44 (46-48-50) meshes.

Shape Neck: Next Row: Work 17 (18-18-19) meshes. Ch 1, turn. Bind off 2 meshes at neck edge every row twice, then dec 1 mesh at same edge every row 4 times—9 (10-10-11) meshes. Work even until armhole measures same as back.

Shape Shoulder: Bind off 3 meshes at arm side every row twice. End off.

Sk 10 (10-12-12) meshes on last long row, join another strand of yarn in next dc, ch 5, dc in next dc, finish row—17 (18-18-19) meshes. Complete same as for first shoulder.

FINISHING: Block pieces. Weave shoulder seams; sew side seams.

Armhole Edging: Join yarn in underarm seam. From right side, work 1 rnd dc around armhole, being careful to keep work flat. Join with a sl st in first dc. End off.

Lower Edging: Join yarn in underarm seam. From right side, * work 6 dc in next ch-2 sp, sc in next sp, repeat from * around; join. End off.

Neck Edging: Join yarn in shoulder seam. From right side, work same as lower edging around neck edge.

DRAWSTRING: Make chain 48" (52"-54"-58") long. Sl st in 2nd ch from hook and in each ch across. End off.

Weave drawstring through eyelet row (first waistband row).

TASSELS (make 2): Wind yarn 34 times around a 1½" strip of cardboard. Tie one end; cut other end. Wind yarn around tassel ¼" below tied end. Attach a tassel to each end of drawstring. Trim ends.

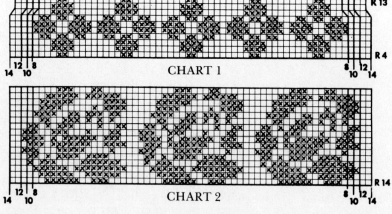

Charts for Rose Shell

SCROLL BLOUSE

Marvelous scrollwork accents the front of a little-sleeved blouse (right) that's plain filet crochet in the back.

SIZES: Directions for size 8. Changes for sizes 10, 12 and 14 are in parentheses.

Body Bust Size: 31½″ (32½″-34″-36″).

Blocked Bust Size: 32½″ (33½″-35″-37″).

MATERIALS: Mercerized knitting and crochet cotton, 4 (5-5-6) 250-yd. balls. Steel crochet hook No. 8.

GAUGE: 10 meshes = 3″; 4 rows = 1″.

To Bind Off: At beg of a row, sl st loosely across each mesh to be bound off, then ch 4 and continue across row; **at end of a row,** work in pat to within specified number of meshes to be bound off.

To Dec 1 Mesh: At beg of a row, ch 3, sk first mesh, dc in next dc

ROSE SHELL AND SCROLL BLOUSE

(counts as 1 dc), ch 2, dc in next dc (1 mesh); **at end of a row,** work to last dc, ch 2, yo, pull up a lp in last dc, yo and through 2 lps on hook, yo, pull up a lp in 3rd ch of turning ch, yo and through 2 lps on hook, yo and through 3 lps on hook.

To Inc 1 Mesh: At beg of a row, ch 4, dc in first dc; **at end of a row,** (ch 2, dc in 3rd ch of turning ch) twice.

To Make Meshes: Dc in dc, ch 2, sk 2 sts, dc in next dc (1 mesh); ch 2, sk 2 sts, dc in next dc for each additional mesh.

To Make Blocks: Dc in each of 4 sts (1 block); dc in each of next 3 sts for each additional block.

Chart Notes: Meshes are shown on chart as open squares, blocks by dotted squares.

BLOUSE: BACK: Beg at lower edge, ch 147 (153-159-171).

Row 1 (right side): Dc in 4th ch from hook and in each ch across—145 (151-157-169) dc, counting ch 3 at beg of row as 1 dc. Ch 5, turn.

Row 2: Sk first 3 dc, * dc in next dc, ch 2, sk next 2 dc, repeat from * across, end dc in top of turning ch—48 (50-52-56) meshes. Ch 5, turn. Check gauge; piece should measure 14½″ (15″-15¾″-16¾″) wide.

Row 3: Sk first dc and ch-2 sp, dc in next dc (1 mesh), * ch 2, dc in next dc, repeat from * across, end ch 2, dc in 3rd ch of turning ch. Ch 5, turn. Repeat row 3 for mesh pat until piece measures 5″ from start. Working in mesh pat, inc 1 mesh (see To Inc 1 Mesh) each side of next row, then every 6th row twice—54 (56-58-62) meshes. Work even until piece measures 12″ (12″-12½″-12½″) from start.

Shape Armholes: Keeping to mesh pat, bind off (see To Bind Off) 3 (3-4-4) meshes each side of next row. Dec 1 mesh (see To Dec 1 Mesh) each side every other row

twice—44 (46-46-50) meshes. Work even until armholes measure 6½″ (7″-7½″-8″) above first row of armhole shaping.

Shape Neck and Shoulders: Bind off 4 meshes, ch 3, dc in next dc, work 9 (10-10-11) meshes. Ch 5, turn.

Next Row: Sk first dc, dc in next dc, work 3 meshes, dc in next dc. End off.

Sk next 16 (16-16-18) meshes, join another strand of yarn in next dc, ch 5, dc in next dc, work 8 (9-9-10) meshes, dc in next dc. Ch 1, turn.

Next Row: Sl st in each st to within last 5 meshes, ch 3, dc in next dc, work in mesh pat across. End off.

FRONT: Work same as for back for 2 rows. Ch 5, turn.

Row 3: Sk first dc and ch-2 sp, dc in next dc (1 mesh), * ch 2, dc in next dc, repeat from * 1 (2-3-5) times, put a marker in last dc; following row 3 of chart (see Chart Notes), work from right to left, put a marker in last dc worked, work in mesh pat across remaining 3 (4-5-7) meshes. Ch 5, turn.

Row 4: Work in mesh pat to marked st, work chart, finish row

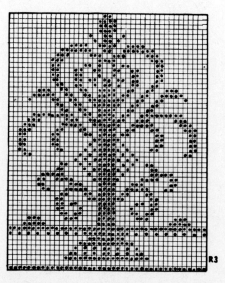

in mesh pat. Ch 5, turn. Repeat last row to top of chart; **at the same time,** when piece measures 5″ from start, inc 1 mesh each side of next row, then every 6th row twice—54 (56-58-62) meshes. When piece measures same as back to underarm, shape armholes same as back—44 (46-46-50) meshes. When chart is completed, work in mesh pat until armholes measure 1¼″ (1¼″-1½″-1¾″) above first row of armhole shaping—44 (46-46-50) meshes.

Shape Neck: Next Row: Work 19 (20-20-21) meshes, drop yarn; sk next 6 (6-6-8) meshes for center neck; join another strand of yarn in next dc, ch 5, dc in next dc, work in mesh pat across—19 (20-20-21) meshes each side. Working on both sides at once, with separate strands of yarn, dec 1 mesh at each neck edge every row 5 times—14 (15-15-16) meshes each side. Work even until armholes measure same as back.

Shape Shoulders: Working on both sides at once, shape shoulders same as back.

SLEEVES: Beg at lower edge, ch 114 (120-129-135).

Row 1: Dc in 4th ch from hook and in each ch across—112 (118-127-133) dc. Ch 5, turn.

Row 2: Sk first 3 dc, * dc in next dc, ch 2, sk next 2 dc, repeat from * across—37 (39-42-44) meshes. Work even until piece measures 2½″ (2½″-3″-3″) from start.

Shape Cap: Keeping to mesh pat, bind off 3 (3-4-4) meshes each side of next row. Dec 1 mesh each side every other row 1 (2-3-4) times, then every 3rd row 4 times—21 (21-20-20) meshes. End off.

FINISHING: Block pieces. Weave shoulder seams; sew in sleeves. Sew side and sleeve seams. From right side, work 1 rnd dc around neck edge, being careful to keep work flat.

FLOWERED FILET SHIRT

This filet crochet shirt is simple to make with a double strand of cotton, easy to fit with dropped shoulders that need no armhole shaping. Garlands of flowers are made separately and sewed on.

SIZES: Directions for small size (6-8). Changes for medium size (10-12) and large size (14-16) are in parentheses.

Body Bust Size: 30½"-31½" (32½"-34"; 36"-38").

Finished Bust Size: 36½" (39"-42").

MATERIALS: Mercerized knitting and crochet cotton, 14 (15-16) 175-yd. balls cream (A); 1 ball each of pink (B), vivid pink (C) and kelly green (D). Steel crochet hooks Nos. 0 and 3. 6 (7-8) ½" buttons.

GAUGE: 3 meshes = 1"; 2 rows = 1".

SHIRT: BACK: Beg at lower edge, with double strand A and size 0 hook, ch 110 (118-126).

Row 1: Sc in 2nd ch from hook and in each ch across—109 (117-125) sc. Ch 4, turn.

Row 2: Sk first 2 sc, dc in next sc, * ch 1, sk next sc, dc in next sc, repeat from * across. Ch 4, turn.

Row 3: Sk first dc, * ch 1, dc in next dc, repeat from * across, end dc in 3rd ch of turning ch—54 (58-62) meshes. Ch 4, turn. Piece should measure 18¼" (19½"-21") wide. Repeat row 3 for pat until 46 (48-50) rows from start. Piece should measure about 23" (24"-25") from start. End.

FRONT: Work same as for back until 34 rows from start, about 17". Ch 4, turn.

Divide for Neck Opening: Work in pat until 26 (28-30) meshes are completed. Ch 4, turn. Work even until piece measures same as back. End off. Sk center dc on last long row, attach double strand A in next dc, ch 4, work in pat across—26 (28-30) meshes. Complete as for first half. End off.

SLEEVES: Beg at lower edge, with double strand A and No. 0 hook, ch 86 (94-102).

Row 1: Sc in 2nd ch from hook and in each ch across—85 (93-101) sc. Ch 4, turn. Work as for back on 42 (46-50) meshes until 38 rows from start. Check gauge; piece should measure 14" (15½"-17") wide, about 19" from start. End off.

FINISHING: Sew 17 (18-19) dc tog at each shoulder edge for

shoulders. Placing center dc on sleeve at shoulder seam, sew in sleeves.

FLOWER TRIM: Make 3 small flowers with B and 2 large flowers with C for each sleeve. Make 4 small flowers with B and 3 large flowers with C for each shoulder. Trim is worked with 1 strand of thread.

Small Flower (make 14): **Note:** Small flowers measure 1¼" in diameter. With No. 3 hook, ch 6, join with sl st to form ring.

Rnd 1 : Ch 1, 16 sc in ring; join with sl st in first sc.

Rnd 2: * Ch 4, sk next sc, sl st in next sc, repeat from * 6 times, end ch 4, sl st in base of first ch 4.

Rnd 3: * Ch 1, 4 sc in ch-4 lp, sl st in same lp, repeat from * around. End off.

Large Flower (make 10): **Note:** Large flowers measure 1¾″ in diameter. With No. 3 hook, ch 6, join with sl st to form ring.

Rnd 1: Ch 1, 16 sc in ring, join with sl st in first sc.

Rnd 2: * Ch 6, sk next sc, sl st in next sc, repeat from * 6 times, end ch 6, sl st in base of first ch 6.

Rnd 3: Ch 1, * (sc, hdc, 2 dc, hdc, sc) in ch-6 lp, ch 1, repeat from * 6 times, (sc, hdc, 2 dc, hdc, sc) in last ch-6 lp, sl st in same lp. End off.

Vine: Leave 4″ end at beg and end for joining. Join D in ch-1 sp between any 2 petals; with No. 3 hook, ch 1, sc in back lp of each st around the edge of 4 petals on each flower. End off.

Join Flowers: Join 7 flowers for each shoulder, 5 flowers for each sleeve with 4″ D lengths, beg and ending with small flowers, alternating with large flowers, having vine edge of small flowers pointing down, large flowers pointing up.

Leaves (make 2 for each strip of flowers): Join D in first sc of vine at end of flower strip; with No. 3 hook, ch 7.

Row 1: Sc in 2nd ch from hook, hdc in next ch, dc in each of next 2 ch, hdc in next ch, sc in next ch, sl st in base of last ch. Ch 1, turn.

Row 2: Sc in sc, hdc in hdc, dc in each of next 2 dc, hdc in hdc, sl st in sc. End off. Make 2nd leaf in same sc. Make 2 leaves on other end of flower strip.

Pin center flower of shoulder flower strip over shoulder seam, vine edge of small flowers on 3rd row of dc from armhole seam; sew in place. Pin center flower of sleeve flower strip over center dc of sleeve, line edge of small flower on 3rd mesh row at lower edge of sleeve; sew in place. Sew side and sleeve seams.

NECK OPENING EDGING: Right Side: Beg at lower edge of right side of neck opening (**left-handed crocheters:** beg at top edge), join double strand A in base of first dc.

Row 1: With No. 0 hook, work 24 (28-32) sc up right side of opening. Ch 1, turn.

Row 2: Sc in each sc across. End off. Turn.

Row 3: Join single strand C in first sc, with No. 3 hook, ch 1, 2 sc in same sc, * 2 sc in next sc, repeat

from * across—48 (56-64) sc. Turn.

Row 4 (buttonhole row): Sl st in first sc (**left-handed crocheters:** sc in each of first 4 sc), ch 5, sk next 2 sc, sl st in next sc, * sc in each of next 4 sc, sl st in next sc, ch 5, sk next 2 sc, sl st in next sc, repeat from * to last 4 sc, sc in each of last 4 sc (**left-handed crocheters:** end ch 5, sl st in last sc)—6 (7-8) ch-5 lps. Turn.

Row 5: * Sl st in each of 4 sc, 7 sc in ch-5 lp, repeat from * 5 (6-7) times. End.

Left Side: Beg at top edge of left side of neck opening, join double strand A in side of first dc.

Row 1: With No. 0 hook, work 24 (28-32) sc down left side of opening. Ch 1, turn.

Rows 2-4: Sc in each sc across. Ch 1, turn. Do not turn at end of row 4.

Row 5: Sc around neck edge, working 1 sc in each st. End off.

EDGING: Join double strand C at front neck edge, with No. 3 hook, * ch 3, sk next st, sl st in next st, repeat from * around neck edge. End off. Work same edging around each sleeve edge and lower edge of back and front, working sl st in line with dc. Sew lower edge of right front neck edging over left edging.

Sew buttons on left neck edging.

HOODED PULLOVER

Open-air bands stripe a pull worked in double crochet and filet mesh. The hood is made separately and sewn on.

SIZES: Directions for small size (8-10). Changes for medium size (12-14) and large size (16) are in parentheses.

Body Bust Size: 31½″-32½″ (34″-36″; 38″).

Blocked Bust Size: 34″ (37½″-40″).

MATERIALS: Mercerized knitting and crochet cotton, 12 (12-14) 250-yd. balls. Steel crochet hook No. 0.

GAUGE: 11 sts = 2″; 3 rows = 1″.

Note: Entire jacket is worked with 2 strands of yarn throughout.

To Dec 2 Dc: At beg of a row, ch 3, sk first ch-1 sp; keeping last lp of

each dc on hook, dc in next dc and ch, yo and through 3 lps on hook; work in pat across; **at end of a row,** work to within last ch-1 sp; keeping last lp of each dc on hook, dc in ch and dc, yo and through 3 lps on hook, sk next ch, dc in next ch.

PULLOVER: BACK: Beg at lower edge, with 2 strands of yarn (see Note), ch 107 (117-123).

Row 1 (right side): Dc in 4th ch from hook and in each ch across—105 (115-121) dc, counting turning ch as 1 dc. Turn each row. Row is 19″ (21″-22″) wide.

Row 2: Ch 4, sk first 2 dc, dc in next dc, * ch 1, sk next dc, dc in next dc (mesh made), repeat from * across, end ch 1, sk next dc, dc in top of turning ch—52 (57-60) meshes.

Row 3: Ch 3 (counts as 1 dc), sk first dc, dc in each ch and in each dc across, end dc in each of first 2 ch on turning ch—105 (115-121) dc.

Rows 4 and 5: Ch 3 (counts as 1 dc), dc in next dc and in each dc across—105 (115-121) dc.

Rows 6-11: Repeat rows 2-5, then repeat rows 2 and 3.

Row 12: Ch 4, sk first 2 dc, * dc in next dc, ch 1, sk next dc, repeat from * across, end dc in top of turning ch.

Rows 13-16: Ch 4, sk first dc, dc in next dc, * ch 1, dc in next dc, repeat from * across, end ch 1, sk next ch, dc in next ch.

Row 17: Repeat row 3. Repeat rows 12-17 for pat until piece measures about 9″ from start, end pat row 16. Keeping to pat, dec 2 dc (see To Dec 2 Dc) each side of next row, then every 6th row twice—93 (103-109) dc. Work even until piece measures about 19″ (19″-21″) from start, end pat row 14.

Shape Armholes: Row 1: Sl st in each of first 7 (9-11) sts, ch 3, dc in next dc, work in pat to within last 4 (5-6) meshes, sk next ch-1 sp, dc in next dc.

Row 2: Ch 3, sk first 2 dc, dc in

next dc, work in pat across to within last ch-1 sp, sk last ch-1 sp, dc in next dc (do not work in ch 3)—1 mesh dec each side.

Row 3: Ch 3, sk first 2 dc, dc in next ch, dc in each dc and ch to within last dc and ch 3, sk dc, dc in top of ch 3.

Row 4: Ch 4, sk first 2 dc, dc in next dc, work in pat to within last dc and ch 3, ch 1, sk next dc, dc in top of turning ch—36 (39-40) meshes. Work in pat until armholes measure 6½″ (7½″-8″) above first row of armhole shaping, end with a mesh row.

Shape Shoulders and Neck: Row 1: Sl st in each of first 5 (7-7) sts, ch 2, dc in next dc, (ch 1, dc in next dc) 8 times, dc in next dc. Turn.

Row 2: Ch 3, sk first 2 dc, dc in next dc, (ch 1, dc in next dc) 3 times, hdc in next dc. End off.

Sk center 12 (13-14) meshes on last long row; join double strand of yarn in next dc, ch 3, work dc in next dc, (ch 1, dc in next dc) 8 times, hdc in next dc. Turn.

Next Row: Sl st in each of first 8 sts, ch 2, dc in next dc, (ch 1, dc in next dc) 3 times, dc in last dc. End off.

FRONT: Work same as for back until piece measures about 15½″ (15½″-17½″) from start, end pat row 16.

Divide Work: Ch 3 (counts as 1 dc), sk first dc, dc in next st and in each of next 33 (37-39) sts, drop yarn, sk next 12 (13-14) meshes, join double strand of yarn in next dc, ch 3, dc in next st and in each st across—35 (39-41) dc each side. Working on both sides at once, with separate strands of yarn, work even until piece measures

same as back to underarm.

Shape Armholes: Working on both sides, keeping center edges straight, shape armholes same as for back—12 (13-13) meshes each side. Work even until armholes measure same as back.

Shape Neck and Shoulders: Work same as for back.

SLEEVES: Beg at lower edge, with 2 strands of yarn, ch 83 (89-95). Work in pat same as for back for 16 rows, having 81 (87-93) dc on row 1 and 40 (43-46) meshes on row 2. Check gauge; piece should measure 15″ (16″-17″) wide. Keeping to pat as established, dec 2 dc each side of next row, then every 6th row twice—34 (37-40) meshes. Work even until piece measures about 18″ from start, end pat row 14.

Shape Cap: Rows 1-3: Work same as back armhole shaping rows 1-3.

Row 4: Ch 3, sk first 2 dc, dc in next dc, work in pat across, end ch 1, sk last dc, dc in top of ch 3.

Row 5: Ch 4, sk first 2 dc, dc in next dc, work in pat to within last dc, end ch 1, sk last dc, dc in top of ch 3.

Row 6: Ch 3, sk first ch-1 sp, dc in next dc, work in pat to within turning ch, sk first ch, dc in next ch.

Rows 7 and 8: Ch 3, sk first 2 dc, dc in next dc, work in pat to within last ch-1 sp, dc in last dc.

Row 9: Ch 3, sk first 2 dc, dc in next ch, dc in each dc and ch across to within last dc, sk dc, dc in top of ch 3. Repeat rows 4-9 once.

For Medium and Large Sizes Only: Repeat rows 4-6.

For Large Size Only: Work in pat for 2 rows.

For All Sizes: End off.

HOOD: Beg at center back, with 2 strands of yarn, ch 132 (136-140).

Row 1: Dc in 6th ch from hook, * ch 1, sk next ch, dc in next ch, repeat from * across—64 (66-68) meshes.

Row 2: Ch 4, sk first dc, dc in next dc, * ch 1, dc in next dc, repeat from * across, end ch 1, dc in 2nd ch of turning ch. Repeat last row until piece measures about 4″ from start.

Next Row (inc row): Ch 4, dc in first dc, * ch 1, dc in next dc, repeat from * across, end (ch 1, dc in 2nd ch of turning ch) twice—2 meshes inc. Working in mesh pat as established, inc 1 mesh each side every 3rd row twice—70 (72-74) meshes. Work even until piece measures about 7″ (7½″-8″) from start. End off.

FINISHING: Block pieces. Sew shoulder seams. Matching dc, fold foundation ch of hood in half; weave foundation ch tog for back seam. Gather lower edge (row ends) to fit neck edge. Sew hood to neck edge.

Front Opening and Hood Border: From right side, join 2 strands of yarn in base of first st on lower right front opening. Ch 3; working in ends of rows, dc evenly on right side edge of opening to neck seam, work dc in each st around front edge of hood, work same number of dc on left side edge of opening to base of first st on lower left front opening, having an odd number of sts. Turn.

Rows 2-5: Work same as rows 2-5 on back. End off. Sew ends of border to front opening.

Sew in sleeves; sew seams.

WHITE ROSE SWEATER

A big rose patterns the front of this pullover, a simple silhouette made elegant with the "picture painting" of filet crochet.

SIZES: Directions for size 8. Changes for sizes 10, 12, 14, 16 and 18 are in parentheses.

Body Bust Size: 31½" (32½"-34"-36"-38"-40").

Blocked Bust Size: 33" (34"-36"-38"-40"-42").

MATERIALS: Fingering yarn, 3 ply, 8 (8-9-9-10-11) 1-oz. skeins. Crochet hook No. 3 or F. Lining material (optional). Matching sewing thread.

GAUGE: 4 meshes = 1", 7 rows = 2".

To Bind Off: At beg of a row, sl st loosely across each mesh to be bound off, then ch 3 and continue across row; **at end of a row,** work in pat to within specified number of meshes to be bound off.

To Dec 1 Mesh: At beg of a row, ch 2, sk first dc, dc in next dc (counts as 1 dc), ch 1, dc in next dc (one mesh); **at end of a row,** work to last dc, ch 1, pull up a lp in last dc, pull up a lp in 3rd ch of turning ch, (yo and through 2 lps on hook) twice.

To Inc 1 Mesh: At beg of a row, ch 3, dc in first dc; **at end of a row,** (ch 1, dc in 3rd ch of turning ch) twice.

To Make Meshes: Dc in dc, ch 1, sk 1 st, dc in next dc (1 mesh); ch 1, sk 1 st, dc in next st for each additional mesh.

To Make Blocks: Dc in each of 3 sts (1 block); dc in each of next 2 sts for each additional block.

Chart Notes: Meshes are shown on chart as open squares, blocks by black squares.

BLOUSE: BACK: Beg at lower edge, ch 137 (141-149-157-165-173).

Row 1: Dc in 4th ch from hook and in each ch across—134 (138-146-154-162-170) dc. Ch 4, turn.

Row 2: Sk first 2 dc, * dc in next dc, ch 1, sk next dc, repeat from * across, end dc in top of turning ch—67 (69-73-77-81-85) meshes. Ch 4, turn. Check gauge; piece should measure 16¾" (17¼"-18¼"-19¼"-20¼"-21¼") wide.

Row 3: Sk first dc and ch-1 sp, dc in next dc (1 mesh), * ch 1, dc in next dc, repeat from * across, end ch 1, dc in 3rd ch of turning ch. Ch 4, turn.

Rows 4-46: Repeat row 3. Piece should measure about 14" from start.

Shape Armholes: Keeping to mesh pat, bind off (see To Bind Off) 4 (4-5-5-6-6) meshes each side of next row. Dec 1 mesh (see To

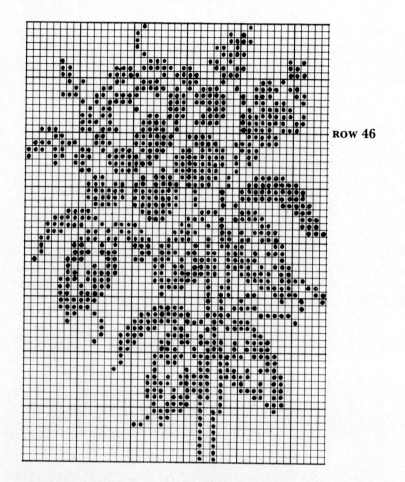

ROW 46

Dec 1 Mesh) each side every row 6 (6-6-7-7-8) times—47 (49-51-53-55-57) meshes. Work even until armholes measure 5″ (5″-5¼″-5½″-5½″-5¾″) above first row of armhole shaping.

Shape Neck and Shoulders: Work 13 (13-14-14-15-15) meshes, dc in next dc, drop yarn; sk next 19 (21-21-23-23-25) meshes for center neck; join another strand of yarn in next dc, ch 2, dc in next dc, work in mesh pat across—13 (13-14-14-15-15) meshes each side. Working on both sides at once, with separate strands of yarn, dec 1 mesh each neck edge every row 5 times—8 (8-9-9-10-10) meshes each side. Bind off 4 meshes each arm side once. End off.

FRONT: Work same as for back for 2 rows.

Row 3: Sk first dc and ch-1 sp, dc in next dc (1 mesh), * ch 1, dc in next dc, repeat from * 9 (10-12-14-16-18) times, put a marker in last dc; following chart (see Chart Notes), work from right to left **(left-handed crocheters: work from left to right)**, put a marker in last dc worked, work in mesh pat across remaining 11 (12-14-16-18-20) meshes. Ch 4, turn.

Row 4: Work in mesh pat to marked st, work chart from left to right **(left-handed crocheters: work chart from right to left)**, finish row in mesh pat. Ch 4, turn. Repeat last 2 rows to end of pat row 46.

Shape Armholes: Keeping to pat as established, shape armholes same as for back—47 (49-51-53-55-57) meshes. When the 61 rows of chart are completed, work in mesh pat until armholes measure 1 row less than back to start of neck shaping.

Shape Neck: Work same as for back—8 (8-9-9-10-10) meshes each side. Work 1 row even.

Shape Shoulders: Bind off 4 sts each arm side once. End off.

SLEEVES: Beg at lower edge, ch 51 (51-55-55-59-63).

Row 1: Dc in 4th ch from hook and in each ch across—48 (48-52-52-56-60) dc. Ch 4, turn.

Row 2: Sk first 2 dc, * dc in next dc, ch 1, sk next dc, repeat from * across, end dc in top of turning ch—24 (24-26-26-28-30) meshes. Work in mesh pat, inc 1 mesh (see To Inc 1 Mesh) each side every 4th row 13 (13-14-15-15-15) times—50 (50-54-56-58-60) meshes. Work even until piece measures 17″ (17″-17½″-17½″-18″-18″) from start or desired length to underarm. Check gauge; piece above last inc row should measure 12½″ (12½″-13½″-14″-14½″-15″) wide.

Shape Cap: Bind off 4 (4-5-5-6-6) meshes each side of next row. Dec 1 st each side every row 15 (15-16-17-17-18) times—12 meshes. End off.

FINISHING: Block pieces. Using back and front for patterns, cut lining, allowing ½″ on all edges for seams and 1″ for ½″ darts at waistline and bust; assemble lining. Weave shoulder seams; sew in sleeves. Sew side and sleeve seams. From right side, work 1 rnd dc around neck edge, being careful to keep work flat. Turn under ½″ on all edges of lining; slip-stitch in place to sweater.

SHELL-EDGED BLOUSE

This easy little sweater blouse is all double crochet to make the work go quickly. The back and fronts are worked in knitting-worsted-weight yarn; sleeves, collar, shell-edged trimming in frothy mohair-type yarn in two blending colors. Four crocheted buttons slip through the edging.

SIZES: Directions for size 8. Changes for sizes 10, 12 and 14 are in parentheses.

Body Bust Size: 31½" (32½"-34"-36").

Blocked Bust Size (closed): 32" (33"-35"-37½").

MATERIALS: Knitting worsted, 2 (2-3-3) 4-oz. skeins rust (A). Mohair, 1 (2-2-2) 1-oz. balls rust (B) and 1 ball peach (C). Crochet hook size H. Four ¾" button molds.

GAUGE: 3 dc = 1"; 3 rows = 2".

To Bind Off: At beg of a row, ch 1, sl st loosely across specified number of sts; **at end of a row,** leave specified number of sts unworked.

To Dec 1 St: Yo hook, pull up a lp in each of next 2 sts, (yo hook and through 2 lps) 3 times.

To Inc 1 St: At beg of a row, ch 3 (counts as 1 dc), dc in first dc; **at end of a row,** 2 dc in top of ch 3.

BLOUSE: BACK: Beg at lower edge, with A, ch 42 (44-46-49) loosely.

Row 1: Dc in 4th ch from hook (counts as 2 dc), dc in each ch across—40 (42-44-47) dc. Turn each row.

Row 2: Ch 3 (counts as 1 dc), sk first dc, dc in next dc and in each dc across. Repeat row 2 until piece measures 6" from start. Check gauge; piece should measure 13⅓" (14"-14⅔"-15⅔") wide. Inc 1 st (see To Inc 1 St) each side of next row, then inc 1 st each side every row 3 times more—48 (50-52-55) dc. Work even until piece measures 10" from start or desired length to underarm.

Shape Armholes: Bind off (see To Bind Off) 4 (4-5-6) sts each side of next row—40 (42-42-43) dc. Work even until armholes mea-

sure 6¾" (7"-7¼"-7½") above bound-off sts.

Shape Shoulders and Neck: Ch 3, sk first dc, dc in each of next 12 (13-13-13) dc; end off. Sk next 14 (14-14-15) sts, join yarn in next st, ch 3, dc in next dc and in each dc across. End off.

RIGHT FRONT: Beg at lower edge, with A, ch 22 (23-25-27) loosely. Work same as for back on 20 (21-23-25) dc until piece measures 6" from start. Mark end of last row for side edge. Check

gauge; piece should measure 6⅔" (7"-7⅔"-8⅓") wide. Inc 1 st at side edge of next row, then inc 1 st at same edge every row 3 times—24 (25-27-29) dc. Work even until piece measures same as back to underarm.

Shape Armhole: Bind off 4 (4-5-6) sts at arm side of next row—20 (21-22-23) sts. Work even until armhole measures 2 rows less than back to shoulder.

Shape Neck and Shoulder: Bind off 7 (7-8-9) sts at center edge of

next row—13 (14-14-14) dc. Work 1 row even. End off.

LEFT FRONT: Work same as for right front; pat is reversible.

SLEEVES: Beg at lower edge, with B, ch 34 (36-38-40). Work as for back on 32 (34-36-38) dc for 2″. Check gauge; piece should measure 10⅔″ (11⅓″-12″-12⅔″) wide.

Shape Cap: Bind off 4 (4-5-6) sts each side of next row. Dec 1 st (see To Dec 1 St) each side every row 5 (5-6-6) times—14 (16-14-14) sts. End off.

FINISHING: Block pieces. Weave shoulder seams tog; sew in sleeves. Sew side and sleeve seams.

Collar: With B, ch 36 (36-38-41) loosely to measure same as neck edge.

Row 1: Sc in 2nd ch from hook and in each ch across—35 (35-37-40) sc. Ch 3, turn.

Row 2: Dc in each of first 3 sc, * 2 dc in next sc, dc in next sc, repeat from * 14 (14-15-16) times, 2 dc in next sc, dc in each remaining sc— 52 (52-55-59) dc. Cut B; join C. Turn.

Row 3: With C, ch 3, sk first dc, dc in each dc across. End off. Weave foundation ch of collar to neck edge.

Front and Collar Edging: Join C in lower right front edge, ch 3, shell of 3 dc in same st as joining, * sc in edge of next row, ch 2, shell of 3 dc in edge of next row, repeat from * on right front edge, around collar edge, down left front edge, end lower front edge. End.

Join B in top of ch 3 at lower right front edge, ch 3, 3 dc in same st as joining, sk 1 dc, sc in next dc, ch 2, shell of 3 dc in next dc, * sk next dc, sc in next dc, ch 2, shell of 3 dc in next dc, repeat from * to neck edge, end sc in center dc of last shell, sc to neck edge. End off. Join B in top of ch 2 at left front neck edge. Work same as for right front edge; end off.

BUTTONS (make 4): With A, ch 2.

Rnd 1: 6 sc in 2nd ch from hook. Do not join rnds.

Rnd 2: 2 sc in each sc—12 sc.

Rnd 3: Sc in each sc around.

Next Rnd: Working over button mold, * pull up a lp in each of next 2 sts, yo and through 3 lps on hook, sc in next sc, repeat from * around until back of mold is covered. End off, leaving an end for sewing.

Sew buttons on left front edge, first button 1″ above lower edge, 4th button 5″ below neck edge, and remaining 2 buttons evenly spaced between. The spaces between shells on right front form buttonholes.

MEDALLION BLOUSE

Lacy medallions form a see-through midriff for this party blouse. The motifs are sewn together and joined to double-crochet top. Two yarns, one metallic gold, are combined.

SIZES: Directions for small size (8-10). Changes for medium size (12-14) are in parentheses.

Body Bust Size: 31½″-32½″ (34″-36″).

Finished Bust Size: 36″ (40″).

MATERIALS: Yarn of sport yarn weight, 10 (12) ozs. aqua (A). Metallic yarn, 9 (11) 100-yd. balls gold (B). Plastic or aluminum crochet hook size G or 6. Matching sewing thread. Large-eyed tapestry needle.

GAUGE: Each medallion = 3½″ diameter; 3 dc = 1″; 5 rows = 3″.

Note: Entire blouse is worked with 2 strands of yarn—1 strand each of A and B.

To Dec 1 Dc: At beg of a row, ch 3, sk next dc, dc in next dc; **at end of a row,** work to within last 2 sts, sk next dc, dc in last dc. Turn.

BLOUSE: BACK: Beg at lower edge, with 1 strand each of A and B (see Note), ch 52 (62) loosely.

Row 1: Dc in 4th ch from hook (counts as 2 dc), dc in each ch across—54 (60) dc. Turn.

Row 2: Ch 3 (counts as 1 dc), sk first dc, dc in next dc and in each dc across. Repeat row 2 until piece measures 6″ (6½″) from start. Ch 1, turn. Check gauge; piece should measure 18″ (20″) wide.

Shape Armholes: Sc in each of 3 (4) dc, ch 3, sk next dc, dc in next dc and in each dc to within last 3 (4) dc—48 (52) dc. Work even until armholes measure 7″ (7½″) above first bound-off sts. Ch 1, turn.

Shape Shoulders: Next Row: Sl st across first 5 sts, ch 1, sc in each st to within last 5 sts. Ch 1, turn. Repeat last row twice—18 (22) sc. End off.

FRONT: Work same as back until piece measures 6″ (6½″) from start.

Shape Armholes and V Neck: Sc in each of 4 (5) dc, ch 3, sk next dc, dc in each of next 22 (24) dc, drop yarn; join another strand of A and B with a dc in next dc, work to within last 4 (5) dc—23 (25) dc each side. Working on both sides at once, dec 1 dc (see To Dec 1 Dc) at each neck edge every row 8 (10) times—15 sts each side. Work even until armholes measure same as back.

Shape Shoulders: Working on both sides at once, work 1 row sc. Ch 1, turn.

Next Row: Sl st across 5 sts at beg of one arm side, sc across both shoulders, end sc to within 5 sts of other arm side—10 sts each side. Repeat last row once—5 sts each side. End off.

SLEEVES: Beg at lower edge, with 1 strand each of A and B, ch 42 (46). Work as for back on 40 (44) dc for 3 rows.

Row 4: Ch 3, dc in first dc, dc in each dc across, 2 dc in last dc—42 (46) dc. Work even for 1 (2) rows. Turn.

Shape Cap: Row 1: Sc in each of 3 (4) dc, ch 3, sk next dc, dc in each dc to within last 3 (4) dc—36 (38) dc. Turn.

Rows 2 and 3: Ch 3, sk first dc, dc in each dc to within last 2 dc—32 (34) dc.

Rows 4 and 5: Ch 3, sk first dc, dc in each dc to within last 3 dc. Turn. Repeat rows 4 and 5 2 (3) times—14 (10) dc. End off.

MEDALLION: Beg at center, with 1 strand of A and B, ch 9. Sl st in first ch to form ring.

Rnd 1: 12 sc in ring. Join with a sl st in first sc. Do not turn.

Rnd 2: Ch 2, holding back on hook last lp, work 1 dc in each of next 2 sts, yo and through 3 lps on hook, * ch 4, holding back on hook last lp, work dc in st last worked in and in each of next 2 sts, yo and through 4 lps on hook, repeat from * 4 times, ch 4, sl st in top of first st.

Rnd 3: * Sc in next ch-4 sp, ch 2, sc in top of last sc made (picot made), 2 sc in same ch-4 sp, ch 2, sc in top of last sc made (picot made), sc in same ch-4 sp, repeat from * around, end sl st in first sc—12 picots. End off. Make 36 (42) medallions.

FINISHING: Run in yarn ends on wrong side. Weave shoulder seams. Sew in sleeves. Sew side and sleeve seams. From wrong side, with 1 strand of A and B, work 1 row sc around neck edge, keeping work flat.

Lower Border: With matching sewing thread, join 2 picots of a medallion to 2 picots on 2nd medallion. Join 2 picots on opposite side of 2nd medallion to 2 picots on 3rd medallion. Continue in this manner until 10 (11) medallions are joined. Join 2 picots on the first medallion to 2 picots on the last medallion, forming a circle. There will be 4 free picots on each side of each medallion. Make 2nd circle in same manner. Join first circle to 2nd circle, having lower medallions between upper medallions as pictured. Join border to lower edge of blouse by sewing center 2 free picots of each medallion to starting ch of blouse. Join 1 strand of A and B to a free picot on upper edge of medallion, draw through ch on starting ch, join to free picot on next medallion. Join remaining free picots at top of border in this manner to starting ch.

Sleeve Border: Join 2 circles of 4 (5) medallions for each sleeve. Join to lower edge of sleeve as for lower edge of blouse.

TWO-TONE VEST

Quick-to-make laced-up vest in rust and apricot mohair can also be made of knitting worsted. Rib portion is worked vertically; top triangles that tie at the shoulders, horizontally.

SIZES: Directions for small size (6-8). Changes for medium size (10-12) are in parentheses.

Fits Bust Sizes: 30½"-31½" (32½"-34").

MATERIALS: Knitting worsted, 1 4-oz. skein each, or mohair, 2 1-oz. balls each, of rust (A) and apricot (B). Crochet hook size H.

GAUGE: 4 dc = 1"; 3 rows = 2".

Note: Rib portion of vest is worked vertically; top portion is worked horizontally.

VEST: RIB PORTION (worked vertically): Beg at left front edge (see Note), with A, ch 26.

Row 1: Dc in 4th ch from hook and in each ch across—24 dc, counting turning ch as 1 dc. Turn each row.

Row 2: Ch 3 (counts as 1 dc), sk first dc, dc in each of next 10 dc, ch 4, sk next 2 dc, dc in next dc and in each of next 9 dc, dc in top of ch 3.

Row 3: Ch 3, sk first dc, dc in each of next 8 dc, ch 4, sl st in ch-4 sp, ch 4, sk next 2 dc, dc in next dc and in each of next 7 dc, dc in top of ch 3.

Row 4: Ch 3, sk first dc, dc in each of next 6 dc, (ch 4, sl st in next ch-4 sp) twice, ch 4, sk next 2 dc, dc in each of next 6 dc, dc in top of ch 3.

Row 5: Ch 3, sk first dc, dc in each of next 4 dc, (ch 4, sl st in next ch-4 sp) 3 times, ch 4, sk next 2 dc, dc in each of next 4 dc, dc in top of ch 3.

Row 6: Ch 3, sk first dc, dc in each of next 2 dc, (ch 4, sl st in next ch-4 sp) 4 times, ch 4, sk next 2 dc, dc in each of next 2 dc, dc in top of ch 3.

Row 7: Ch 3, sk first dc, dc in

each of next 2 dc, dc in each of next 2 ch, (ch 4, sl st in next ch-4 sp) 3 times, ch 4, sk first 2 ch of next ch-4 sp, dc in each of next 2 ch, dc in each of next 2 dc, dc in top of ch 3.

Row 8: Ch 3, sk first dc, dc in each of next 4 dc, dc in each of next 2 ch, (ch 4, sl st in next ch-4 sp) twice, ch 4, sk first 2 ch of next ch-4 sp, dc in each of next 2 ch, dc in each of next 4 dc, dc in top of ch 3.

Row 9: Ch 3, sk first dc, dc in each of next 6 dc, dc in each of next 2 ch, ch 4, sl st in next ch-4 sp, ch 4, sk first 2 ch of next ch-4 sp, dc in each of next 2 ch, dc in each of next 6 dc, dc in top of ch 3.

Row 10: Ch 3, sk first dc, dc in each of next 8 dc, dc in each of next 2 ch, ch 2, sk first 2 ch of next ch-4 sp, dc in each of next 2 ch, dc in each of next 8 dc, dc in top of ch 3.

Row 11: Ch 3, sk first dc, dc in each dc and ch across, end dc in top of ch 3—24 dc,

For Medium Size Only: Row 12: Ch 3, sk first dc, dc in each dc across, end dc in top of ch 3. Repeat rows 2-12 twice, rows 2-11 once—44 rows.

For Small Size Only: Repeat rows 2-11 3 times—41 rows.

Check gauge; piece should measure about 27¼" (29¼") from start.

YOKE (worked horizontally): Join B in top edge of last row.

Row 1 (mark for right side): Ch 1, sc in corner, 2 sc in end of each row across—83 (89) sc. Ch 2, turn.

First Front Triangle: Sk first sc,

(yo hook, pull up a lp in next sc, yo and through 2 lps on hook) twice, yo and through 3 lps on hook, * ch 1, yo hook, pull up a lp in last sc worked in, yo and through 2 lps on hook, (yo hook, pull up a lp in next sc, yo and through 2 lps on hook) twice, yo and through 4 lps on hook, repeat from * 7 (8) times —9 (10) cluster dc. Ch 2, turn.

Row 2: Yo hook, pull up a lp in ch-1 sp, yo and through 2 lps on hook, yo hook, pull up a lp in top of cluster dc, yo and through 2 lps on hook, yo and through 3 lps on hook, * ch 1, yo hook, pull up a lp in st last worked in, yo and through 2 lps on hook, yo hook, pull up a lp in ch-1 sp, yo and through 2 lps on hook, yo hook, pull up a lp in next cluster dc, yo and through 2 lps on hook, yo and through remaining 4 lps on hook, repeat from * 6 (7) times—8 (9) cluster dc. Ch 2, turn.

Row 3: Repeat row 2 having 1 cluster dc less—7 (8) cluster dc. Ch 2, turn.

Rows 4-10 (11): Repeat row 3—1 cluster dc remains. Ch 52 at end of last row for tie.

Tie: Sc in 2nd ch from hook and in each ch across. End off.

Back Yoke: Sk 2 sc on last long row; join B in next sc, ch 2, (yo hook, pull up a lp in next sc, yo and through 2 lps on hook) twice, yo and through 3 lps on hook, * ch 1, yo hook, pull up a lp in last sc worked in, yo and through 2 lps on hook, (yo hook, pull up a lp in next sc, yo and through 2 lps on hook) twice, yo and through 4 lps on hook, repeat from * 18 (19)

times—20 (21) cluster dc. Ch 2, turn.

Rows 2 and 3: Work same as for rows 2 and 3 on front triangle—18 (19) cluster dc. Ch 2, turn.

First Back Triangle: Next Row: Work 6 cluster dc. Ch 2, turn. Work in pat having 1 cluster dc less each row until 1 cluster dc remains. Ch 52 at end of last row for tie.

Tie: Sc in 2nd ch from hook and in each ch across. End off.

2nd Back Triangle: Join B in 7th cluster dc from end on last back yoke long row. Ch 2, work in pat across—6 cluster dc. Complete same as for first back triangle.

2nd Front Triangle: Sk 2 sc on last long sc row, join B in next sc, work in pat across—9 (10) cluster dc. Complete same as for first front triangle.

EDGING: From right side, join A in lower edge of one front triangle. Working around triangles, being careful to keep work flat, * work 3 sl sts, ch 3, sl st in 3rd ch from hook (picot made), repeat from * across yoke, end lower edge of other front triangle. End off.

FRONT TIE: With B, make chain 44" long; sc in 2nd ch from hook and in each ch across. End off. Beg at lower edge of front, lace tie through front rib portion as pictured.

TASSELS (make 2): Wind B 20 times around a 3" strip of cardboard. Tie one end; cut other end. Wind B around tassel, ½" below tied end. Attach a tassel to each end of front tie.

POCAHONTAS VEST

This leather-brown fringed vest has American Indian motifs in yellow, orange and turquoise cross-stitched on afghan-stitch bands around vest. Alternating pattern bands are in long loops crocheted over a strip and a lacy openwork design.

SIZES: Directions for small size (10-12). Changes for medium size (14-16) are in parentheses.

Fits Bust Size: 32½″-34″ (36″-38″).

MATERIALS: Knitting worsted, 3 (4) 4-oz. skeins light brown, main color (MC); 1 oz. each of dark yellow (A), orange (B) and turquoise (C) for embroidery. Afghan hook size H; aluminum crochet hook size H. Strip of cardboard or plastic 2¾″ wide, 10″ to 12″ long. Tapestry needle.

GAUGE: 4 sts = 1″; 9 rows = 2″ (afghan st).

VEST: BACK: Beg at lower edge, with MC and afghan hook, ch 77 (85).

Pattern 1: Row 1: With afghan hook, keeping all lps on hook, sk first ch from hook (lp on hook is first st), pull up a lp in each ch across—77 (85) lps.

To Work Lps Off: Yo hook, pull through first lp, * yo hook, pull through next 2 lps, repeat from * across until 1 lp remains. (Lp that remains always counts as first st of next row.)

Row 2: Keeping all lps on hook, sk first vertical bar, pull up a lp under next vertical bar and under each vertical bar across. Work off as before.

Rows 3-10: Repeat row 2.

Pattern 2: Change to crochet hook.

Row 1: Ch 2, dc in first vertical bar (**Note:** Always work dc in vertical bar and horizontal lp next to bar for added strength), * sk next 3 vertical bars, dc in next vertical bar, ch 2, sl st in same bar (pat made), ch 2, dc in same bar, repeat from * across, end sk next 3 bars, dc in last vertical bar, ch 2, sl st in same vertical bar. Ch 4, turn.

Row 2: Dc in next sp between dcs, * ch 2, sl st in same sp, ch 2, dc in same sp, dc in next sp, repeat from * across, end last repeat dc in last sp, ch 2, sl st in same sp, ch 2, dc in same sp. Ch 1, turn.

Row 3: Sc in first dc, * ch 3, sc in sp between next 2 dc, repeat from * across, end ch 3, sc in last sp. Ch 1, turn.

Row 4: Sc in first sc, * 3 sc in ch-3 sp, sc in next sc, repeat from * across—77 (85) sc. Turn.

Pattern 3: Row 1: Place cardboard strip along top edge of last row. Pull lp on hook up in back of strip, * insert hook from front of strip in next sc, pull up lp to top of strip, yo hook and through 2 lps on hook (lp sc made), ch 1, sk next sc, repeat from * across, end lp sc in last sc. Remove strip. Ch 1, turn.

Detail for Making Pattern 3

Row 2: * Sc through lp of lp sc, sc in ch-1 sp, repeat from * across, end sc through lp of lp sc—77 (85) sc. Turn. Check gauge; piece should measure 19″ (21″) wide. Work pat 1 for 10 rows, dec 1 st each side every 4th row twice (to dec 1 afghan st: **at beg of a row,** insert hook under 2nd and 3rd vertical bars and pull up a lp; keep lp on hook; **at end of a row,** insert hook under 3rd and 2nd vertical

bars from end and pull up a lp, then make last st)—73 (81) sts. Work the 4 rows of pat 2, 2 rows of pat 3. Work the 10 rows of pat 1, dec 1 st each side every 4th row twice—69 (77) sts.

Shape Armholes: With crochet hook, sk first vertical bar, * pull up a lp under next vertical bar and through lp on hook (1 st bound off), repeat from * 7 times (8 sts bound off), ch 2, work from * on row 1 of pat 2 to within last 12 vertical bars, ch 2, sk next 3 vertical bars, sl st in next vertical bar. Turn.

Row 2: Sl st in each of 2 ch, ch 2, dc in same sp, dc in next sp, work from * on row 2 to within last sp, end dc in last sp. Ch 1, turn.

Rows 3 and 4: Work same as rows 3 and 4 of pat 2—45 (53) sc. Work the 2 rows of pat 3, then the 10 rows of pat 1. End off.

RIGHT FRONT (Left-handed crocheters: This will be your left front): Beg at lower edge, ch 33 (37). Mark beg of first row for center edge. Work in pats 1, 2 and 3 until piece measures same as back to underarm, end 10th row of pat 1 (center edge).

Shape Armhole: Work pat 2 to within last 12 vertical bars, end ch 2, sk next 3 vertical bars, sl st in next vertical bar. Turn.

Row 2: Sl st in each of 2 ch, ch 2, dc in same sp, dc in next sp, work in pat across.

Row 3: Work same as row 3 of pat 2.

Row 4: Sc in first sc, sc in next ch-3 sp, sc in next sc, * 3 sc in next ch-3 sp, sc in next sc, repeat from * to within last ch-3 sp, sc in last ch-3 sp, sc in last sc—17 (21) sc. Work the 2 rows of pat 3. Work the 10 rows of pat 1.

Next Row: Work row 1 of pat 2, skipping 4 vertical bars instead of 3.

Next Row: Work same as row 2 of pat 2. End off.

LEFT FRONT: Work same as right front to start of armhole shaping. Beg of first row is arm side.

Shape Armhole: With crochet hook, sk first vertical bar, * pull up a lp under next vertical bar and through lp on hook, repeat from * 7 times (8 sts bound off), ch 2, work from * on row 1 of pat 2 across.

Row 2: Work row 2 of pat to within last sp, end dc in last sp. Turn. Complete same as right front.

FINISHING: Steam-press pieces. Weave side seams tog, matching pats. Tack the points of front shoulder to every 4th vertical bar on back shoulders. From right side, work 1 row sc around each armhole and entire outer edge of

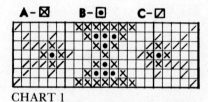

CHART 1

CHART 2   CHART 3

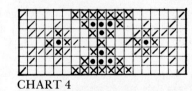

CHART 4

Charts for Pocahontas Vest

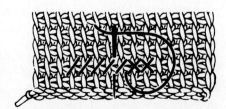

Cross-Stitch on Afghan Stitch

vest, working 9 ch on edge of pat 3. Cut yarn into 6″ lengths for fringe. Knot 2 strands into every other sc around outer edge of vest.

Embroidery: Embroider afghan-stitch bands in cross-stitch, working 1 cross-stitch over vertical bar of 1 afghan st. Each square on charts represents 1 cross-stitch. Motifs, 7 rows high, are worked on rows 2-8 of afghan-stitch bands. Following chart 1, embroider motif on center 21 sts of four bands of back. Skip 3 (5) sts each side of center motif on first (lowest) band, embroider motif each side, following chart 2. Repeat on next two bands, skipping 2 (4) sts. Repeat on top band, skipping 1 (3) sts. Skip 3 (5) sts on each side of

second motif on first band, embroider motif each side, following chart 3. (Motif may extend onto fronts.)

Skip 2 (4) sts from front edges, embroider motif on each of first three bands, following chart 3. Skip 1 (3) sts, embroider motif, following chart 4. On top band, embroider motif, following chart 2.

BIG APPLE VEST

A big red apple in front, a game of tick-tack-toe in back, decorate a young-and-fun fashion shown opposite, top left and bottom. Two black patches are made in afghan crochet, the perfect background for cross-stitch designs. Shoulders and sides are filet mesh; bottom banding is a combination of stitches.

SIZES: Directions for small size (8-10). Any changes for medium size (12-14) are in parentheses. **Note:** Both sizes are made the same. Hook size and gauge determine size.

Body Bust Size: 31½″-32½″ (34″-36″).

Blocked Bust Size: 33″ (37″).

MATERIALS: Knitting worsted, 2 2-oz. balls each black, main color (MC), and red (R); 1 ball green (G). Afghan hook size J (K); crochet hook size I (J). Yarn needle.

GAUGE: 4 sts = 1″ (size J afghan hook); 7 sts = 2″ (size K afghan hook).

AFGHAN STITCH: Row 1: Keeping all lps on hook, draw up a lp in 2nd ch from hook and in each ch across.

To Work Lps Off: Yo hook and through first lp, * yo hook, pull through next 2 lps, repeat from * across until 1 lp remains. Lp that remains on hook always counts as first st of next row.

Row 2: Keeping all lps on hook, sk first vertical bar, pull up a lp

under next vertical bar and each vertical bar across. Work lps off as before. Repeat row 2 for afghan stitch.

VEST: FRONT: Square: With afghan hook size J (K) and MC, ch 41 loosely. Work in afghan st on 41 sts for 31 rows. Check gauge; square should measure 10¼″ (11¾″) wide. Do not end off. Using crochet hook size I (J) sl st across last row, working under vertical bars.

Edging: Rnd 1: Ch 3 (counts as 1 dc); working down side of square, dc in end st of each row; in corner work dc, ch 1, dc, ch 1, dc; working across bottom of square, dc in first st, * sk 1 st, dc in each of next 3 sts, repeat from * to next corner; in corner dc, ch 1, dc, ch 1, dc; working up side of square, dc in end st of each row to top; in corner work dc, ch 1, dc, ch 1, dc; repeat from first * to 2nd * across top, dc, ch 1, dc in last corner, ch 1, sl st to top of ch 3. End off.

Rnd 2: Join R in sp before ch 3, ch 4, dc in same sp, * sk next 2 dc,

dc in next dc, ch 1, dc in same dc (V st), repeat from * 9 times, V st in first ch-1 sp at corner, ch 2, V st in next ch-1 sp; repeat from first * to 2nd * 10 times, V st in first ch-1 sp at corner, ch 2, V st in next ch-1 sp; repeat from first * to 2nd * 10 times, V st in first ch-1 sp at corner, ch 2, V st in next ch-1 sp; repeat from first * to 2nd * 10 times, V st in ch-1 sp at corner, ch 2, sl st in 3rd ch of ch 4. End off.

Rnd 3: Join G in ch-2 sp at corner, sc in same sp, * 2 sc in next ch-1 sp, sc in sp between V sts, repeat from * around making 3 sc in each corner ch-2 sp, end 2 sc in last corner, sl st in first sc. End off.

RIGHT SIDE PANEL (Left-handed crocheters: This will be your left side panel): **Row 1:** Sk first 7 sc of rnd 3, join R in next sc, ch 4, sk 1 sc, dc in next sc, (ch 1, sk 1 sc, dc in next sc) 14 times. Ch 4, turn.

Row 2: Sk first dc, dc in next dc, (ch 1, dc in next dc) 12 times, ch 1, sk next dc, dc in ch-4 sp. Ch 4, turn.

Row 3: Sk first 2 dc, dc in next

dc, (ch 1, dc in next dc) 11 times, ch 1, sk 1 ch, dc in 3rd ch of ch 4. Ch 4, turn.

Row 4: Sk first dc, dc in next dc, (ch 1, dc in next dc) 11 times, ch 1, sk 1 ch, dc in 3rd ch of ch 4. End off.

LEFT SIDE PANEL (Left-handed crocheters: This will be your right side panel; join R at lower right corner): **Row 1:** Join R in center sc at lower left corner, ch 4, sk 1 sc, dc in next sc, (ch 1, sk 1 sc, dc in next sc) 14 times. Ch 4, turn.

Row 2: Sk first 2 dc, dc in next dc, (ch 1, dc in next dc) 12 times, ch 1, sk 1 ch, dc in 3rd ch of ch 4. Ch 4, turn.

Row 3: Sk first dc, dc in next dc, (ch 1, dc in next dc) 11 times, ch 1, sk 1 dc and ch, dc in 3rd ch of ch 4. Ch 4, turn.

Row 4: Sk first dc, dc in next dc, (ch 1, dc in next dc) 11 times, ch 1, dc in 3rd ch of ch 4. End off.

SHOULDER STRAP: From right side, join R in center sc at top right corner. **(Left-handed crocheters:** Join R at top left corner.)

Row 1: Ch 4, sk 1 sc on top edge, dc in next sc, (ch 1, sk 1 sc, dc in next sc) 4 times. Ch 4, turn.

Row 2: Sk first dc, dc in next dc, (ch 1, dc in next dc) 3 times, ch 1, sk 1 ch, dc in 3rd ch of ch 4. Ch 4, turn. Repeat row 2, 7 times more. End off. Turn square to wrong side. Join R in center sc at top left corner, work 2nd shoulder strap the same.

Work another piece the same for back. Sew shoulder seams.

SHOULDER STRAP EDGING: From right side, with G, work 2 sc in each sp along armhole and neck edges of shoulder straps.

SIDE EDGING: From right side, with G, work 2 sc in each sp on lower side and top edges of side panels, 5 sc in lower corner. Sew side seams.

NECK AND ARMHOLE EDGING: From right side, with R, sc in

BIG APPLE VEST AND FLOWER APPLIQUÉ TOP

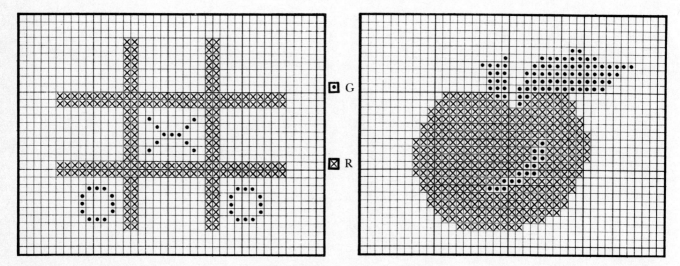

each st around neck and armhole edges.

WAISTBAND: Rnd 1: From right side, join R at side seam, ch 3, dc in each st around lower edge, sl st in top of ch 3. Ch 3, turn.

Rnd 2: Dc in each dc around, sl st in top of ch 3. Ch 3, turn.

Rnd 3: Repeat rnd 2. End off. Do not turn.

Rnd 4: With G, sc in each dc around. Sl st in first st. End off. Do not turn.

Rnd 5: Join R in first sc, ch 4, dc in same sc, * sk 2 sc, V st in next sc, repeat from * around, end V st, sl st in 3rd ch of ch 4. End off. Do not turn.

Rnd 6: With G, work 2 sc in each ch-1 sp of V st, 1 sc in sp between V sts. Sl st in first sc. End off.

Rnds 7-9: Repeat rnds 1-3. Work 1 rnd sc around lower edge.

EMBROIDERY: Embroider designs in cross-stitch, following charts. See page 320 for embroidery detail.

Each square on charts is one stitch; each row on charts is one row of afghan st.

FLOWER APPLIQUÉ TOP

Shown top right, on page 65

A medallion flower blooms bright on a blue skimp, made in V-stitch mesh. Blue front and back are framed with bands of color (one side is green, one coral!) and lacy scallops. The flowers—one on back too—are crocheted separately, to sew on.

SIZES: Directions for small size (8-10). Any changes for medium size (12-14) are in parentheses. **Note:** Crochet hook and gauge determine size.

Body Bust Size: 31½"-32½" (34"-36").

Blocked Bust Size: 32" (36").

MATERIALS: Knitting worsted, 2 2-oz. balls royal (R); 1 ball each of olive (O) and coral (C). For size 8-10: Crochet hook size J. For size 12-14: Crochet hook size K. Yarn needle.

GAUGE: 5 V sts = 4" (size J hook); 1 V st = 1" (size K hook).

TOP: BACK: Beg at lower edge, with R, ch 35 loosely.

Row 1 (right side): (Dc, ch 1, dc) in 4th ch from hook (V st made), * sk next 2 ch, V st of dc, ch 1, dc in next ch, repeat from * across, end dc in last ch. Turn each row.

Row 2: Ch 3 (counts as 1 dc), V st of dc, ch 1, dc in each ch-1 sp of each V st across, end dc in top of turning ch—11 V sts plus 1 dc each side. Turn. Repeat row 2, 18 times. Check gauge; piece should measure 9½" (11½") wide.

First Strap: Row 1: Ch 3, V st in ch-1 sp of first 2 V sts, 1 dc in next ch-1 sp. Turn.

Row 2: Ch 3, V st in ch-1 sp of each V st, dc in top of turning ch—2 V sts plus 1 dc each side. Turn. Repeat row 2, 7 times. End off.

2nd Strap: Sk 5 V sts on last long row. Join R in ch-1 sp of next V st. Ch 3, V st in ch-1 sp of next 2 V sts, dc in top of turning ch. Turn. Complete as for first strap.

RIGHT SIDE PANEL: Row 1: Right side facing, join O in lower right corner. **(Left-handed crocheters:** Join O in lower left corner.) Working up side edge, ch 3, sk first row, cluster of 3 dc in next row, * sk next row, cluster of 3 dc in next row, repeat from * 6 times—8 clusters. Turn.

Row 2: Ch 3, (cluster of 3 dc in sp between next 2 clusters) 7 times, end cluster in sp between last cluster and turning ch. Turn.

Row 3: Ch 3, (cluster of 3 dc in sp between next 2 clusters) 7 times, end dc in top of turning ch. End off O; join C in first dc. Turn.

Row 4: With C, ch 3, (cluster between next 2 clusters) 6 times, end cluster in sp between last cluster and turning ch—7 clusters. End off C; join R. Turn.

Row 5: With R, ch 1, sc in each dc across, end sc in top of turning ch. End off.

LEFT SIDE PANEL: Wrong side facing, join C in lower left corner. **(Left-handed crocheters:** Join C in lower right corner.) Work as for right side panel, working rows 1-3 with C, row 4 with O. End off O. Do not turn.

Row 5: From right side, join R in top of turning ch at beg of last row. Ch 1, sc in same place as joining, sc in each dc across. End off.

FRONT: Work same as for back.

FINISHING: Block front and back to measure 16″ (18″) each. With R, sew shoulder and side seams.

Left Armhole Edging: Join C at underarm seam. From right side, work 1 row sc around entire armhole, keeping work flat. End off; do not turn.

Next Rnd: Join R; work 1 sc in each sc. Join; end off.

Right Armhole Edging: Work same as for left armhole, working 1 row O, 1 row R.

Neck Edging: With R, work 1 row sc around neck edge.

Lower Edging: Rnd 1: Right side facing, join O at underarm seam. Ch 3, dc in R sc, * 2 dc in end of each of next 4 rows, dc in each ch of starting ch, 2 dc in end of each of next 4 rows *, 1 dc in each R sc, repeat from * to * once, join with sl st to top of ch 3. Turn.

Rnd 2: Ch 4, * sk 1 dc, dc in next dc, ch 1, repeat from * around, join with sl st to 3rd ch of ch 4. Turn.

Rnd 3: Ch 4, * dc under next ch-1 sp, ch 1, repeat from * around, join with sl st to 3rd ch of ch 4. End off. Do not turn.

Rnd 4: Join C in any ch-1 sp. Ch 3, 1 dc in same sp, 2 dc under each ch-1 sp around, join with sl st to top of ch 3.

Rnd 5: Ch 6, * sk 3 dc, sc in next dc, ch 5, repeat from * around. Join with sl st to first ch of ch 5.

Rnd 6: Work sc, hdc, 3 dc, hdc, sc in each ch-5 lp around. End off.

FLOWER (make 2): With O, ch 6, join with sl st to form ring.

Rnd 1: Ch 6, * dc in ring, ch 3, repeat from * 6 times, join with sl st to 3rd ch of ch 6—8 sps.

Rnd 2: Ch 3, * 3 dc under next sp, dc in next dc, repeat from * around, end 3 dc under last sp, join with sl st to 3rd ch of ch 3. Cut O.

Rnd 3: With C, make lp on hook, sc in sl st, ch 10, * sk 3 dc, sc in next dc, ch 10, repeat from * 6 times, join with sl st to first sc—8 ch-10 lps.

Rnd 4: Work sc, 2 hdc, 2 dc, 3 tr, 2 dc, 2 hdc, sc in each ch-10 lp. Join; end off.

Sew a flower to center front and back of the sweater.

TWO-PIECE DRESS

At left, crimson bands, in pattern and double crochet, stripe front and back of raglan-styled top, worked from the neck down. Solid flared skirt has elasticized waist. Note: For sizes 18, 38-42, see page 70.

SIZES: Directions for size 8. Changes for sizes 10, 12, 14 and 16 are in parentheses.

Body Bust Size: 31½" (32½"-34"-36"-38").

Blocked Bust Size: 32" (34"-36"-38"-40").

MATERIALS: Knitting worsted, 8 (9-9-9-9) 4-oz. skeins. Crochet hook size G. One yard ½"-wide elastic for skirt.

GAUGE: 7 dc = 2"; 2 rows = 1".

Note 1: Skirt is worked from waist to lower edge; blouse is worked from neck to lower edge.

Note 2: Ch 3 at beg of row is counted as 1 dc.

To Inc 1 Dc: Work 2 dc in same st.

SKIRT: BACK: Beg at waist (see Note 1), ch 54 (56-58-60-62).

Row 1: Dc in 4th ch from hook (counts as 2 dc), dc in each ch across—52 (54-56-58-60) dc (see Note 2). Turn each row.

Row 2: Ch 3, sk first dc, dc in each dc across. Check gauge; piece should measure 14¾" (15¼"-16"-16½"-17") wide. Work 1 row even. Inc 4 dc (see To Inc 1 Dc) evenly spaced across next row, then every 4th row 3 times—68 (70-72-74-76) dc. Work 1 row even. Inc 4 (4-5-5-5) dc evenly spaced across next row, then every 4th row 3 times more, 6 sts every 4th row twice, 8 sts every 4th row twice—112 (114-120-122-124) dc. Work even until piece measures 26" from start or 1½" less than desired skirt length.

Next Row: Ch 3, sk first dc, (dc, ch 1, dc) in next dc, * sk next 2 dc, (dc, ch 1, dc) in next dc, repeat from * across, end dc in top of turning ch. Turn.

Next Row: Ch 3, dc in each dc

and ch-1 across, end dc in top of ch 3. End off.

FRONT: Work same as for back.

FINISHING: Block pieces. With backstitch, sew side seams.

Picot Edging: Join yarn in lower side seam; from right side, * sc in next st, ch 3, sl st in 3rd ch from hook, sk next st, repeat from * around lower edge. Join with a sl st in first sc. End off.

Casing: With wrong side facing you, join yarn at top edge, * make ch ¾", sl st in st ½" to left in row ½" below, make ch ¾", sl st at top of skirt ½" to left of last st, repeat from * around, working a zigzag casing. Join; end off. Cut elastic to waist measurement. Thread through casing; sew ends tog securely.

Steam-press seams and edging lightly.

BLOUSE: Beg at neck edge, ch 70 (72-72-74-76). Being careful not to twist ch, sl st in first ch.

Rnd 1: Ch 4 (counts as dc, ch 1), dc in same ch as joining, dc in each of next 10 (11-11-11-11) ch (sleeve), (dc, ch 1, dc) in next ch, dc in each of next 23 (23-23-24-25) ch (front), (dc, ch 1, dc) in next ch, dc in each of next 10 (11-11-11-11) ch (sleeve), (dc, ch 1, dc) in next ch, dc in each of next 23 (23-23-24-25) ch (back)—4 ch-1 sps; 74 (76-76-78-80) dc. Join with a sl st in 3rd ch of starting ch, sl st in next ch. Turn each rnd.

Rnd 2: Ch 4 (counts as dc, ch 1), dc in same sp, dc in each dc around, working (dc, ch 1, dc) in each ch-1 sp—8 dc inc. Join with a sl st in 3rd ch of starting ch, sl st in next ch each rnd.

Rnd 3: Repeat rnd 2—90 (92-92-94-96) dc.

Rnd 4: Repeat rnd 2, inc 2 dc evenly spaced on each sleeve, back and front—16 dc inc—106 (108-108-110-112) dc. * Repeat rnd 2, 3 (2-2-2-2) times—130 (124-124-126-128) dc. Repeat rnd 4—146 (140-140-140-142-144) dc. Repeat from * 1 (2-2-3-3) times—186 (204-204-238-240) dc. Repeat rnd 2, 2 (1-1-0-1) times—202 (212-212-238-248) dc.

For Size 12 Only: Repeat rnd 4—228 dc. There will be 44 (47-51-53-55) dc on each sleeve; 57 (59-63-66-69) dc on back and front. End off.

BACK: Row 1: Make lp on hook; from wrong side, dc in ch-1 raglan sp at beg of back, sk next dc, work V st of (dc, ch 1, dc) in next dc, * sk next 2 dc, V st of (dc, ch 1, dc) in next dc, repeat from * across, end dc in ch-1 raglan sp—19 (20-21-22-23) V sts. Ch 3, turn.

Row 2: V st of (dc, ch 1, dc) in ch-1 sp of each V st across, end dc in top of last dc. Ch 3, turn.

Rows 3-5: Repeat row 2, end dc in top of turning ch. Ch 3, turn.

Row 6: Dc in each dc and ch-1 sp of each V st across, end dc in top of turning ch.

Rows 7-11: Ch 3, sk first dc, dc in each dc across.

Row 12: Ch 3, * sk 2 dc, V st in next dc, repeat from * across, end dc in top of turning ch.

Rows 13-20: Repeat row 2.

Row 21: Repeat row 6. Repeating row 7, inc 1 dc each side every 3rd row twice. Work even until piece measures 15" from underarm or desired length, end wrong side.

Next Row (picot row): Sc in first

TWO-PIECE DRESS AND PICOT-EDGED DRESS

dc, * ch 3, sl st in 3rd ch from hook, sk next dc, sc in next dc, repeat from * across. End off.

FRONT: Make lp on hook; from wrong side, dc in ch-1 raglan sp at beg of front. Work same as for back.

SLEEVES: Make lp on hook from wrong side, dc in ch-1 raglan sp at beg of sleeve. Work same as row 1 on back—14 (15-16-17-18) V sts.

Rows 2-11: Work same as for back. Continue to work in dc until piece measures 17″ from underarm or desired sleeve length, end wrong side.

Next Row: Work same as picot row on lower edge of back. End off. Work other sleeve in same manner.

FINISHING: Block. Sew side and sleeve seams.

DRAWSTRING: With double strand of yarn, make chain 60″. End off. Draw through center of lower V-st band. Tie ends at center front.

TWO-PIECE DRESS, LARGER SIZES

Shown on page 69

SIZES: Directions for size 18. Changes for sizes 38, 40 and 42 are in parentheses.

Body Bust Size: 40″ (42″-44″-46″).

Blocked Bust Size: 42″ (44″-46″-48″).

MATERIALS: Knitting worsted, 10 (10-11-11) 4-oz. skeins. Crochet hook size G. One (1-1¼-1¼) yards ½″-wide elastic for skirt.

GAUGE: 7 dc = 2″; 2 rows = 1″.

Note 1: Skirt is worked from waist to lower edge; blouse is worked from neck to lower edge.

Note 2: Ch 3 at beg of row is counted as 1 dc.

To Inc 1 Dc: Work 2 dc in same st.

SKIRT: BACK: Beg at waist (see Note 1), ch 64 (66-68-70).

Row 1: Dc in 4th ch from hook (counts as 2 dc), dc in each ch across—62 (64-66-68) dc (see Note 2). Turn each row.

Row 2: Ch 3, sk first dc, dc in each dc across. Check gauge; piece should measure 17½″ (18¼″-18¾″-19¾″) wide. Work 1 row even. Inc 4 dc (see To Inc 1 Dc) evenly spaced across next row, then every 4th row 3 times—78 (80-82-84) dc. Work 1 row even. Inc 5 dc evenly spaced across next row, then every 4th row 3 times more, 6 sts every

4th row twice, 8 sts every 4th row twice—126 (128-130-132) dc. Work even until piece measures 26″ from start or 1½″ less than desired skirt length.

Next Row: Ch 3, sk first dc, (dc, ch 1, dc) in next dc, * sk next 2 dc, (dc, ch 1, dc) in next dc, repeat from * across, end dc in top of turning ch. Turn.

Next Row: Ch 3, dc in each dc and ch-1 across, end dc in top of ch 3. End off.

FRONT: Work same as for back.

FINISHING: Block pieces. With backstitch, sew side seams.

Picot Edging: Join yarn in lower side seam; from right side, * sc in next st, ch 3, sl st in 3rd ch from hook, sk next st, repeat from * around lower edge. Join with a sl st in first sc. End off.

Casing: With wrong side facing you, join yarn at top edge, * make ch ¾″, sl st in st ½″ to left in row ½″ below, make ch ¾″, sl st at top of skirt ½″ to left of last st, repeat from * around inner edge of skirt, working a zigzag casing. Join; end off. Cut elastic to waist measurement. Thread through casing; sew ends tog securely.

Steam-press seams and edging lightly.

BLOUSE: Beg at neck edge, ch

76 (76-78-78). Being careful not to twist ch, sl st in first ch.

Rnd 1: Ch 4 (counts as dc, ch 1), dc in same ch as joining, dc in each of next 11 ch (sleeve), (dc, ch 1, dc) in next ch, dc in each of next 25 (25-26-26) ch (front), (dc, ch 1, dc) in next ch, dc in each of next 11 ch (sleeve), (dc, ch 1, dc) in next ch, dc in each of next 25 (25-26-26) ch (back)—4 ch-1 sps, 80 (80-82-82) dc. Join with a sl st in 3rd ch of starting ch, sl st in next ch. Turn each rnd.

Rnd 2: Ch 4 (counts as dc, ch 1), dc in same sp, dc in each dc around, working (dc, ch 1, dc) in each ch-1 sp—8 dc inc. Join with a sl st in 3rd ch of starting ch, sl st in next ch each rnd.

Rnd 3: Repeat rnd 2—96 (96-98-98) dc.

Rnd 4: Repeat rnd 2, inc 2 dc evenly spaced on each sleeve, back and front (16 dc inc)—112 (112-114-114) dc. Repeat rnds 3 and 4, 6 (6-7-8) times—256 (256-282-306) dc. Repeat rnd 3 (4-3-0) once—264 (272-290-306) dc. There will be 59 (61-65-69) dc on each sleeve; 73 (75-80-84) dc on back and front. End off.

BACK: Row 1: Make lp on hook; from wrong side, dc in ch-1 raglan sp at beg of back, sk next dc, work V st of (dc, ch 1, dc) in next dc, * sk next 2 dc, V st of (dc, ch 1, dc) in next dc, repeat from * across, end dc in ch-1 raglan sp—24 (25-27-28) V sts. Ch 3, turn.

Row 2: V st of (dc, ch 1, dc) in ch-1 sp of each V st across, end dc in top of last dc. Ch 3, turn.

Rows 3-5: Repeat row 2, end dc in top of turning ch. Ch 3, turn.

Row 6: Dc in each dc and ch-1 sp of each V st across, end dc in top of turning ch.

Rows 7-11: Ch 3, sk first dc, dc in each dc across.

Row 12: Ch 3, * sk 2 dc, V st in next dc, repeat from * across, end dc in top of turning ch.

Rows 13-20: Repeat row 2.

Row 21: Repeat row 6. Repeating row 7, inc 1 st each side every 3rd row twice. Work even until piece measures 16″ from underarm or desired length, end wrong side.

Next Row (picot row): Sc in first dc, * ch 3, sl st in 3rd ch from hook, sk next dc, sc in next dc, repeat from * across. End off.

FRONT: Make lp on hook; from wrong side, dc in ch-1 raglan sp at beg of front. Work same as for back.

SLEEVES: Make lp on hook; from wrong side, dc in ch-1 raglan sp at beg of sleeve. Work same as row 1 on back—20 (21-22-23) V sts.

Rows 2-11: Work same as for back. Continue to work in dc until piece measures 18″ from start or desired sleeve length, end wrong side.

Next Row: Work same as picot row on lower edge of back. End off. Work other sleeve in same manner.

FINISHING: Block. Sew side and sleeve seams.

DRAWSTRING: With double strand of yarn, make chain 65″. End off. Draw through center of lower V-st band. Tie ends at center front.

PICOT-EDGED DRESS

Shown at right on page 69

A column of beige pulls over the head, draws in at the waist. Crocheted squares, in decreasing sizes, are sewn together; sleeves have plain row shaping.

SIZES: Directions for small size (8-10). Any changes for medium size (12-14) are in parentheses. **Note:** Both sizes are made the same. Hook size and gauge determine size.

Body Bust Size: 31½″-32½″ (34″-36″).

Blocked Bust Size: 33″ (36″).

MATERIALS: Dress yarn of fingering yarn weight, 21 (23) ozs. Crochet hooks sizes E (F) and G (H).

GAUGE: Each motif (4 rnds) = 3¼″ (size E hook); 3½″ (size F hook); 3¾″ (size G hook); 4″ (size H hook).

GENERAL DIRECTIONS: Motifs: Ch 5, join with a sl st to form ring.

Rnd 1: Ch 1, 8 sc in ring; join with a sl st in first sc.

Rnd 2: Ch 3 (counts as 1 dc), dc in same st as joining, 2 dc in next sc, (ch 3, 2 dc in each of next 2 sc) 3 times, ch 3, join with a sl st to top of ch 3.

Rnd 3: Ch 3 (counts as 1 dc), dc in each of next 3 dc, (2 dc, ch 3, 2 dc) in ch-3 sp, * dc in each of next 4 dc, (2 dc, ch 3, 2 dc) in ch-3 sp, repeat from * twice, join with a sl st to top of ch 3 (4 corners).

Rnd 4: Ch 3 (counts as 1 dc), dc in each of next 5 dc, (2 dc, ch 3, 2 dc) in ch-3 sp, * dc in each of next 8 dc, (2 dc, ch 3, 2 dc) in ch-3 sp, repeat from * twice, dc in each of next 2 dc, join with a sl st to top of ch 3.

Rnd 5: Work same as rnd 4, having 12 dc between corners. Join; end off.

SKIRT: Following general directions, with size G (H) hook, make 48 4-rnd motifs, 24 5-rnd motifs. Sew 12 4-rnd motifs tog forming a ring. Check gauge; ring should measure 37½″ (40″) around. Make 3 more 4-rnd rings. Sew rings tog. Sew 12 5-rnd motifs tog forming a ring. Sew this ring to lower edge of 4-rnd rings, easing in to 4-rnd rings. Make another 12 5-rnd motif ring; sew to lower edge.

BODICE: Following general directions, with size E (F) hook, make 48 4-rnd motifs. Following chart 1, sew motifs tog.

Underarm Motifs (make 2): With size E (F) hook, ch 2.

Row 1: 4 sc in 2nd ch from hook. Ch 3, turn.

Row 2: Dc in first sc, ch 3, 2 dc in each of next 2 sc, ch 3, 2 dc in last sc. End off; do not turn.

Row 3: Make lp on hook, 2 dc in top of turning ch at beg of last row, dc in next dc, (2 dc, ch 3, 2 dc) in ch-3 sp, dc in each of next 4 dc, (2 dc, ch 3, 2 dc) in ch-3 sp, dc in next dc, 2 dc in last dc. End off; do not turn.

Row 4: Make lp on hook, 2 dc in first dc, dc in each of next 4 dc, (2 dc, ch 3, 2 dc) in ch-3 sp, dc in each of next 8 dc, (2 dc, ch 3, 2 dc) in ch-3 sp, dc in each of next 4 dc, 2 dc in last dc. End off.

Sew underarm motifs in place. Sew shoulder motifs (A) to back. Sew side seam, forming circle. Sew upper edge of skirt to lower edge of bodice, easing in skirt to fit.

SLEEVES (make 2): Make 16 motifs same as for bodice. Sew tog, forming a 3 by 5 motif strip for each sleeve. Weave 1 motif to top center motif.

Cap Motif (make 2): With size E (F) hook, ch 2.

Row 1: 4 sc in 2nd ch from hook. Ch 4, turn.

Row 2: 2 dc in each of first 2 sc, ch 3, 2 dc in next sc, (2 dc, ch 1, dc)

in last sc. End off; do not turn.

Row 3: Make lp on hook, (dc, ch 1, 2 dc) in first sp at start of last row, dc in each dc to ch-3 sp, (2 dc, ch 3, 2 dc) in ch-3 sp, dc in each dc to ch-1 sp, (2 dc, ch 1, dc) in ch-1 sp. End off; do not turn.

Row 4: Repeat row 3.

Sew to sleeve as shown on chart 2.

Sleeve Gusset: Join yarn in first sp on 3rd motif on right side edge of sleeve (X on chart), sc in sp, sc in each of next 6 dc, hdc in each of next 6 dc, 2 dc in sp, * 2 dc in sp of next motif, dc in each dc, 2 dc in sp, repeat from * once. End off; do not turn.

Next Row: Sk sc and hdc; join yarn in 5th dc on last row, sc in each of next 3 dc, hdc in each of next 3 dc, dc in each remaining dc. End off. Beg at underarm, work other side of sleeve in same manner, reversing shaping (beg with dc, end with hdc, then sc).

Sew sleeve seam. With sleeve seam at center of underarm motif, sew in sleeve.

Block to measurements.

CORD: With 2 strands of yarn and size G (H) hook, make chain about 50″ long. Beg at center front, weave through motifs about 9″ below underarm. Coil ends into flat disks; tack securely.

PICOT EDGING: Join yarn in lower side edge. With size E (F) hook, * sc in next st, ch 2, sl st in 2nd ch from hook, sk next st, repeat from * around. Join; end off. Work same edging around neck and sleeve edges.

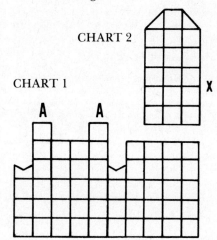

SHELL DINNER DRESS

A heathery apricot dress is worked in an all-over pattern of tight little shells.
All the edges are finished with a narrow ruffling of more little shells.

SIZES: Directions for small size (8). Changes for medium size (10-12) and large size (14) are in parentheses.

Body Bust Size: 31½″ (32½″-34″; 36″).

Blocked Bust Size: 32½″ (35″-37½″).

MATERIALS: Sport yarn, 8 (8-9) 2-oz. skeins. Aluminum or plastic crochet hook size F. 2½ yards round elastic cord.

GAUGE: 2 shells, 2 sc = 2½″; 3 rows = 1″.

PATTERN (worked on a multiple of 6 sts plus 2): **Row 1:** Sc in 2nd ch from hook, * sk next 2 ch, shell of 5 dc in next ch, sk next 2 ch, sc in next ch, repeat from * across. Turn each row.

Row 2: Ch 3 (counts as 1 dc), 2 dc in first sc (½ shell made), sk next 2 dc, sc in next dc, * sk next 2 dc, shell of 5 dc in next sc, sk next

2 dc, sc in next dc, repeat from * across, end sk next 2 dc, ½ shell of 3 dc in next sc.

Row 3: Ch 1, sc in first dc, * sk next 2 dc, 5 dc in next sc, sk next 2 dc, sc in next dc, repeat from * across. Repeat rows 2 and 3 for pat.

DRESS: BACK: Beg at lower edge, ch 122 (128-134).

Rows 1-13 (13-15): Work in pat, end pat row 3—20 (21-22) shells.

Check gauge; piece should measure 25″ (26¼″-27½″) wide; about 4½″ (4½″-5″) from start.

Row 14 (14-16) (dec row): Ch 3, dc in first sc, sk next 2 dc, sc in next dc, work in pat across, end sc in center dc of last shell, sk next 2 dc, 2 dc in last sc—2 sts dec.

Row 15 (15-17) (dec row): Sl st in first 2 dc, ch 3, 2 dc in next sc, sk next 2 dc, sc in next dc, work in pat to last shell, sk next 2 dc, 3 dc in next sc—4 sts dec. Turn. Work 5 rows even.

Row 21 (21-23) (dec row): Sl st in first sc and in each of next 2 dc, ch 1, sc in next dc, work in pat to center of last shell—6 sts dec.

Rows 22-25 (22-25; 24-27): Work 4 rows even.

Rows 26-61 (26-61; 28-63): Repeat rows 14-25 (14-25; 16-27) 3 times—12 (13-14) shells. Work 8 rows even.

Row 70 (70-72) (inc row): Ch 3, 4 dc in first sc, sk next 2 dc, sc in next dc, work in pat to center of last shell, end sk next 2 dc, 5 dc in last sc—4 sts inc.

Row 71 (71-73) (inc row): Ch 3, 2 dc in first dc, sk next dc, sc in next dc, sk next 2 dc, 5 dc in next sc, work in pat to center of last shell, sk next dc, 3 dc in last dc—2 sts inc, 12 (13-14) shells plus ½ shell each side. Work 5 rows even. End off. Turn. Check gauge; piece should measure about 25½″ (25½″-26½″) from start.

Shape Armhole: Row 77 (77-79): Join yarn in center dc of 2nd shell, ch 1, sc in same st, work in pat to center of 2nd shell from end. Turn.

Row 78 (78-80): Sl st across first sc and in each of next 2 dc, ch 1, sc in next dc, work in pat to center of last shell.

Rows 79-83 (79-83; 81-85): Repeat last row 5 times. Work even in pat on 4 (5-6) shells for 10 (12-14) rows.

Row 94 (96-100): Ch 3, 4 dc in

first sc, sk next 2 dc, sc in next dc, work in pat to center of last shell, sk next 2 dc, work 5 dc in last sc.

Row 95 (97-101): Ch 3, 2 dc in first dc, sk next dc, sc in next dc, sk next 2 dc, 5 dc in next sc, work in pat to center of last shell, sk next dc, 3 dc in last dc.

Row 96 (98-102): Work even in pat.

Rows 97-99 (99-101; 103-105): Repeat rows 94-96 (96-98; 100-102).

Rows 100-101 (102-103; 106-107): Repeat rows 94 and 95 (96 and 97; 100 and 101)—6 (7-8) shells plus ½ shell each side.

Shape Shoulders and Neck: Left Shoulder: Row 102 (104-108): Ch 1, work in pat to center of 2nd full shell. Turn.

Row 103 (105-109): Sl st across first sc and next 2 dc, ch 1, sc in next dc, work in pat across. End off.

Right Shoulder: Row 102 (104-108): Sk 2 (3-4) shells on last long row for back of neck, attach yarn in center dc of next shell, ch 1, sc in same st, work in pat across. Turn.

Row 103 (105-109): Ch 3, 2 dc in first sc, work in pat to center dc of 2nd full shell. End off. Armhole should measure about 9″ (9¾″-10¼″) above first row of armhole shaping.

FRONT: Work same as for back through row 76 (76-78)—13 (14-15) shells.

Shape Armholes: Row 77 (77-79): Sl st across sc and in each of next 2 dc, ch 1, sc in next dc, work in pat to center dc of last shell. Turn.

Rows 78-79 (78-79; 80-81): Work even in pat.

Rows 80-88 (80-88; 82-90): Repeat rows 77-79 (77-79; 79-81) 3 times.

Shape Neck and Shoulders: Left Shoulder: Row 89 (89-91): Sl st across sc and in each of next 2 dc, ch 1, sc in next dc, work in pat across next shell, end sc in center dc of next shell. Turn.

Row 90 (90-92): Sl st across first sc and in each of next 2 dc, ch 1, sc in next dc, work in pat across 1 shell. Turn.

Rows 91-103 (91-105; 93-109): Work in pat on 1 shell. End off.

Right Shoulder: Row 89 (89-91): Sk center 3 (4-5) full shells, attach yarn in center dc of next shell, ch 1, sc in same st, work in pat to center dc of last shell. Turn.

Rows 90-103 (90-105; 92-109): Work in pat on 1 shell. End off.

FINISHING: Block piece to desired measurements. Sew shoulder and side seams.

Neck Edging: From right side, join yarn in shoulder seam; ch 3, 5 dc in same st, work shells of 6 dc around neck edge, working a shell in each sc and in center dc of shells on horizontal edges and working 1 shell between rows on vertical and curved edges; join with a sl st in top of ch 3. End off. Work same edging around armholes.

Lower Edging: From right side, work 1 rnd of 6-dc shells around lower edge, working a shell in each sc and center of each shell; join with a sl st in first shell.

Thread large-eyed needle with elastic cord; from wrong side, run cord around each armhole and neck edge along base of edging. Draw elastic to desired fit; fasten ends securely.

AT-HOME GOWN

Granny afghan squares in red, white and blue are sewn together to form yoke, straps and sides of this white patio gown, crocheted in an easy pattern of trebles. Sides are left open at bottom for easy motion. To make of knitting worsted or Orlon yarn of same thickness.

SIZES: Directions for small size (6-8). Changes for medium size (10-12) and large size (14-16) are in parentheses. **Note:** Crochet hook and gauge determine size.

Body Bust Size: 30½″-31½″ (32½″-34″; 36″-38″).

Blocked Bust Size: 32½″ (35″-38″).

MATERIALS: Knitting wor- sted, 5 (6-6) 4-oz. skeins white, main color (MC); 2 skeins sapphire (S); 1 skein crimson (C). For size 6-8, crochet hook size F; for size 10-12, crochet hook size G; for size 14-16, crochet hook size H. Large-eyed needle.

GAUGE: Each square = 3¼″ (3½″-3¾″).

Note: Gown is worked from top to lower edge. Squares are sewn on later.

GOWN: BACK: Beg at upper edge, with MC and size F (G-H) crochet hook, ch 38 to measure 9¾″ (10½″-11½″).

Row 1: Sc in 2nd ch from hook and in each ch across—37 sc. Turn each row.

Row 2: Ch 3, 3 tr in first sc, * sk

next 3 sc, shell of 4 tr in next sc, repeat from * across—10 shells.

Row 3: Ch 4, shell of 4 tr in sp between first 2 shells, * shell of 4 tr in sp between next 2 shells, repeat from * across, end tr in top of ch 3—9 shells.

Row 4: Ch 3, 3 tr in sp between first tr and first shell, * shell of 4 tr in sp between next 2 shells, repeat from * across, end shell of 4 tr in ch-4 sp—10 shells. Repeat rows 3 and 4 until piece measures 12" from start, end pat row 4.

Inc Rows: Row 1: Ch 3, tr in first tr (½ shell made), shell of 4 tr in sp between first 2 shells, * shell of 4 tr in sp between next 2 shells, repeat from * across, end ½ shell of 2 tr in top of ch 3.

Row 2: Ch 4, shell in sp between ½ shell and first shell, work in pat across, end shell in sp between last shell and ½ shell, tr in top of ch 3—10 shells.

Row 3: Repeat row 4—11 shells. Work even until piece measures 20" from start, end pat row 4. Repeat inc rows 1-3—12 shells. Work even until piece measures 28" from start, end pat row 4. Repeat inc rows 1-3, 5 times—17 shells. Work even until piece measures 43" from start or about 3¼" (3½"-3¾") (top border allowance) less than desired length.

FRONT: Work same as for back.

SQUARES: Center Front Square: With S, ch 4, join with a sl st to form ring.

Rnd 1: Ch 3 (counts as 1 dc), make 2 dc in ring, ch 1, * 3 dc in ring, ch 1, repeat from * twice, join last ch 1 to top of ch 3 with a sl st (4 groups of 3 dc in rnd). End off.

Rnd 2: Join MC in a ch-1 sp, ch 3, 2 dc in same sp, ch 1, * 3 dc in next ch-1 sp, ch 1, 3 dc in same sp, ch 1, repeat from * twice, 3 dc in same sp with first 3 dc, ch 1, join with a sl st to top of ch 3. End off.

Rnd 3: Join C in a corner ch-1 sp, ch 3, 2 dc in same sp, ch 1, * 3

dc in next ch-1 sp, ch 1, (3 dc, ch 1, 3 dc) in corner ch-1 sp, ch 1, repeat from * around, end 3 dc in same sp with first 3 dc, ch 1, join with a sl st to top of ch 3. End off.

A Square: Make 36 (34-32) squares same as center front square, working rnd 1 with C, rnd 2 with MC, rnd 3 with S.

B Square: Make 37 (35-33) squares same as center front square, working rnd 1 with MC, rnd 2 with C, rnd 3 with S.

FINISHING: Front: With center front square at center, arrange 5 squares across top, 14 (13-12) squares down each side, alternating A and B squares. With S, sew squares tog. Pin top and side edges of front to inner edges of squares; sew tog.

Back: Work same as front, using a B square for center top square.

Block pieces to measurements. Weave side seams 20″ down, leaving lower edges open for slits. Sew 4 squares tog for each strap. Sew front end of straps to 2nd square in from side seams; cross straps, sew to back.

LACE-BORDERED DRESS

For cool days and nights at home, crochet yourself this charming dress, designed and made in Greece. Of medium-weight sport yarn, dress in double crochet has gentle shaping, deep lace bands forming bodice yoke and skirt border, and thick shell edgings.

SIZES: Directions for small size (6-8). Changes for medium size (10-12) and large size (14-16) are in parentheses.

Body Bust Size: 30½″-31½″ (32½″-34″; 36″-38″).

Blocked Bust Size: 33″ (35″-39″).

MATERIALS: Sport yarn, 22 (24-26) ozs. Aluminum crochet hooks sizes F and H.

GAUGE: 4 dc = 1″; 5 rows dc = 3″ (size H hook).

To Inc 1 St: At beg of a row, ch 3 (counts as 1 dc), dc in first dc; **at end of a row,** work 2 dc in top of turning ch.

To Dec 1 St: At beg of a row, ch 3 (counts as 1 dc), sk first 2 dc, dc in next dc; **at end of a row,** work to last 2 sts, sk next dc, dc in top of turning ch.

To Bind Off: At beg of a row, ch 1, sl st across specified number of sts; **at end of a row,** leave specified number of sts unworked.

BORDER PATTERN: Row 1: Ch 3 (counts as 1 dc), sk first dc, dc in each of next 2 dc, * ch 1, sk next dc, dc in next dc, repeat from * to within last 3 dc, end ch 1, sk next dc, dc in next dc, dc in top of turning ch. Turn each row.

Row 2: Ch 3 (counts as 1 dc), sk first dc, dc in next dc, * ch 1, sk next ch 1, dc, and ch 1; work 4 dc in next dc, repeat from * to within last 3 dc, end sk ch 1, dc; work ch 1, dc in next dc, dc in top of ch 3.

Row 3: Ch 3 (counts as 1 dc), sk first dc, dc in next dc, ch 4, * holding back last lp of each dc, work dc in each of next 4 dc, yo and through 5 lps on hook (cluster dc or cl-dc made), ch 4, repeat from * across, end last repeat ch 4, dc in dc, dc in top of turning ch 3.

Row 4: Ch 3 (counts as 1 dc), sk first dc, dc in next dc, ch 1, * dc in ch-4 sp, ch 1, dc in cl-dc, ch 1, repeat from * across, end dc in ch-4 sp, dc in next dc, dc in top of turning ch 3.

Row 5: Ch 3 (counts as 1 dc), sk first dc, dc in next dc and in each dc and ch-1 sp across, end dc in top of turning ch 3.

DRESS: Skirt is worked from top of waistband to lower edge of skirt; bodice is worked from waistband to shoulder.

SKIRT: BACK: Waistband: Beg at upper edge, with size F hook, ch loosely 57 (63-71).

Row 1: Sc in 2nd ch from hook and in each ch across—56 (62-70) sc. Ch 1, turn each row.

Row 2: Sc in each sc across. Work even in sc for 1½″. Change to size H hook. Turn.

Skirt: Row 1: Ch 3 (always count ch 3 as 1 dc), sk first dc, * dc in each of next 5 (6-7) sc, 2 dc in next sc, repeat from * 7 times, dc in each sc to end of row—64 (70-78) dc. Turn each row.

Row 2: Ch 3, sk first dc, dc in each dc across, dc in top of turning ch. Check gauge: last row should measure 16″ (17½″-19½″) wide. Work in dc, inc 1 dc (see To Inc 1 St) each side of next row, then every 5th row 6 (5-5) times—78 (82-90) dc. Work even until piece measures 25″ from start or 8″ less (border allowance) than desired skirt length. Work border rows 1-5 twice, inc 6 dc evenly spaced across last row—84 (88-96) dc. Work in dc for 3 rows. End off.

FRONT: Work same as for back.

BODICE: BACK: Working across starting ch of back skirt, with size H hook, dc in each st across—56 (62-70) dc. Work in dc, inc 1 dc each side every other row 5 (4-4) times—66 (70-78) dc. Work even until piece measures 7″ above waistband. Check gauge; piece above last inc row should measure 16½″ (17½″-19½″) wide.

Shape Armholes: Bind off (see To Bind Off) 4 (4-5) dc each side of next row. Dec 1 st (see To Dec 1 St) each side every row 4 (5-6) times—50 (52-56) dc. Work even until armholes measure 5½″ above first row of armhole shaping.

Shape Neck and Shoulders: Work 16 (17-19) dc, sk next dc, dc in next dc, drop yarn; sk center 14 dc, join another strand of yarn in next dc, ch 3, sk next dc, dc in each dc across. Working on both sides at once, dec 1 dc each neck edge every row 3 (3-4) times; **at the same time,** when armholes measure 7″ (7″-7½″) above first row of armhole shaping, bind off 7 dc at armhole edge of next row. End.

FRONT: Work same as for back until piece measures 2 rows less than back to underarm—66 (70-78) dc.

Pattern: Row 1: Ch 3, sk first dc, dc in each of next 4 (4-6) dc, (ch 1, sk next dc, dc in next dc) 28 (30-32) times, end ch 1, sk next dc, dc in each of next 3 (3-5) dc, dc in top of turning ch.

Row 2: Ch 3, sk first dc, dc in each of next 3 (3-5) dc, * ch 1, sk next ch 1, dc, and ch 1; work 4 dc in next dc, repeat from * to within

last 4 (4-6) dc and turning ch, end ch 1, sk ch 1, dc; work dc in each of next 3 (3-5) dc, dc in top of turning ch.

Row 3: Ch 1, sl st loosely across 4 (4-6) dc, ch 3, * cl-dc over next 4 dc, ch 4, repeat from * 12 (13-14) times, cl-dc over next 4 dc—14 (15-16) cl-dc. Turn.

Row 4: Ch 3, * dc in ch-4 sp, ch 1, dc in cl-dc, ch 1, repeat from * across, end last repeat dc in cl-dc.

Row 5: Ch 3, sk first dc, * dc in ch-1 sp, dc in dc, repeat from * across, end dc in top of ch 3—52 (56-60) dc. Work in dc, dec 1 dc each side every row 1 (2-2) times—50 (52-56) dc. Work even until armholes measure 4″ above first row of armhole shaping.

Shape Neck and Shoulders: Work 18 (19-21) dc, sk next dc, dc in next dc, drop yarn; sk center 10 dc, join another strand of yarn in next dc, ch 3, sk next dc, dc in each dc across. Working on both sides at once, dec 1 dc each neck edge every row 5 (5-6) times; **at the same time,** when armholes measure same as back, bind off 7 dc at armhole edge of next row. End off.

SLEEVES: Beg at lower edge, with size H hook, ch 32 loosely.

Row 1: Dc in 4th ch from hook and in each ch across—30 dc, counting turning ch as 1 dc. Work border pat rows 1-5. Work in dc, inc 1 dc each side of next row, then every 3rd (3rd-2nd) row 7 (8-9) times—46 (48-50) dc. Work even until piece measures 17″ from start or desired sleeve length. Check gauge; piece above last inc row should measure 11½″ (12″-12½″) wide.

Shape Cap: Bind off 4 dc each side of next row. Dec 1 dc each side every row 10 (11-12) times—18 dc. End off.

FINISHING: Block pieces. Sew shoulder seams; sew in sleeves. Sew side and sleeve seams.

Sleeve Edging: Join yarn in lower edge of sleeve seam. With size H hook, sc in same st as joining, * sk next 3 dc, shell of 8 dc in sp between dc, sk next 3 dc, sc in sp between dc, repeat from * around—5 shells. Join with a sl st in first sc; end off. Work same shell edging around lower edge of skirt. Work shell edging around neck edge, being careful to space shells to keep work flat.

Steam-press edges lightly.

FLOWER-COLOR GOWN

Circle medallions in bright flower colors are squared with white, joined by crochet. The bodice is in a simple pattern stitch; drawstring waist pulls in the dirndl skirt.

SIZES: Directions for small size (8-10). Changes for medium size (12-14) are in parentheses.

Body Bust Size: 31½″-32½″ (34″-36″).

Blocked Bust Size: 32½″ (36½″).

MATERIALS: Sport yarn, 9 (10) 2-oz. skeins winter white, main color (MC); 1 skein each of orange, turquoise, green, hot pink, magenta, blue or any desired colors. For both sizes, crochet hook size H; for medium size only, crochet hook size J.

GAUGE: Skirt and Sleeves: Motif = 6½″ (size H hook); motif = 6¾″ (size J hook). **Note:** Gauge and crochet hook determine size of skirt. Bodice: 4 sts (2 sc, 2 ch) = 1″ (size H hook).

To Bind Off: At beg of a row, sl st loosely across specified sts; **at end of a row,** leave specified number of sts unworked.

SKIRT: MOTIF: Beg at center, with any desired color and size H (J) hook, ch 4. Sl st in first ch to form ring.

Rnd 1: Ch 3 (counts as 1 dc), 11 dc in ring—12 dc. Sl st in top of ch 3.

Rnd 2: Ch 3 (counts as 1 dc), dc in same ch with sl st, 2 dc in each of next 11 dc—24 dc. Sl st in top of ch 3. End off.

Rnd 3: With 2nd color, make lp on hook, sc between any 2 dc, * ch 3, sk next 2 dc, sc in sp between dc, repeat from * around, end ch 3, sl st in first sc—12 ch-3 lps. End off.

Rnd 4: With 3rd color, make lp on hook, sc in any ch-3 sp, * ch 3, sc in next ch-3 sp, ch 3, (2 dc, ch 3, 2 dc) in next sp, ch 3, sc in next sp, repeat from * around, end last repeat sl st in first sc—4 corners. End off.

Rnd 5: With MC, make lp on

hook, * (3 dc, ch 3, 3 dc) in corner ch-3 sp, (3 dc in next ch-3 sp) 3 times, repeat from * around, end sl st in first dc.

Rnd 6: Sc in next dc, * ch 3, (sc, ch 3, sc) in corner ch-3 sp, (ch 3, sk next dc, sc in next dc) 7 times, repeat from * around, end last repeat sl st in first sc. End off. Check gauge; motif should measure 6½″ (6¾″) square.

2ND MOTIF: Using different colors for rnds 1-4, MC for rnd 5, work same as first motif for 5 rnds.

Joining Rnd: Rnd 6: Sc in next dc, ch 3, sc in corner sp, ch 1, sc in corner ch-3 sp on first motif, ch 1, sc in same corner sp on 2nd motif, * ch 1, sc in next ch-3 sp on first motif, ch 1, sk next dc on 2nd motif, sc in next dc, repeat from * 6 times, ch 1, sc in next ch-3 sp on first motif, ch 1, sc in corner ch-3 sp on 2nd motif, ch 1, sc in corner ch-3 sp on first motif, ch 1, sc in same corner sp on 2nd motif, ch 3, sk next dc, sc in next dc, complete same as first motif. End off. Make and join 7 more motifs in same manner for first strip at lower edge of skirt; join sides of first and last motifs tog, forming ring—9 motifs in ring. Make 9 motifs in same manner, joining to side as on first strip; **at the same time,** join lower edge of motifs of 2nd strip to top edge of first strip. Continue to work and join strips of 9 motif strips in this manner until 6 strips are joined—54 motifs.

FINISHING: Run in yarn ends on wrong side.

Upper Edging: With size H (J) hook and MC, sc in any ch-3 sp, * ch 1, sc in next sp, repeat from * around. Join; end off.

Lower Edging: With size H (J) hook and MC, dc in any ch-3 sp, * ch 1, dc in next sp, repeat from * around, working dc in each corner joining. Join; end off.

BODICE: BACK: With MC and size H hook, ch 66 (74).

Row 1: Sc in 2nd ch from hook, * ch 1, sk 1 ch, sc in next ch, repeat from * across—33 (37) sc—65 (73) sts. Ch 1, turn.

Row 2: Sc in first sc, * ch 1, sk ch-1 sp, sc in next sc, repeat from * across. Ch 1, turn. Repeat row 2 for pat, always working ch 1 over ch-1 sp and sc over sc. Work even until piece measures 3″ from start.

Check gauge; piece should measure 16¼″ (18¼″) wide. Drop MC. With orange or any desired color, work 1 row. Cut orange; join blue or any desired color, work 1 row. Cut blue. With MC, work even until piece measures 7½″ from start or desired length to underarm.

Shape Armholes: Keeping to pat, bind off (see To Bind Off) 4

sts each side of next row, then 2 (4) sts each side of next row—27 (29) sc, 53 (57) sts. Work even until armholes measure 5¾" (6") above first bound-off sts.

Shape Neck and Shoulders: Work in pat across 9 (10) sc, drop yarn; sk next 9 sc; with MC, make lp on hook, sc in next sc, finish row—9 (10) sc each side. Working on both sides at once, with separate strands of MC, bind off 2 sts at each neck edge every row 3 (4) times, then bind off 4 sts at each arm side every row twice. End off.

FRONT: Work same as back until armholes measure 2¾" (3") above first bound-off sts—27 (29) sc.

Shape Neck and Shoulders:

Work in pat across 9 (10) sc, drop yarn, sk next 9 sc; with MC, make lp on hook, sc in next sc, finish row—9 (10) sc each side. Working on both sides at once, with separate stands of MC, bind off 2 sts at each neck edge every row 3 (4) times—6 sc each side. Work even until armholes measure same as back. Bind off 4 sts at each arm side every row twice—3 sts remain. End off.

SLEEVES: Make and join 2 rings of 2 motifs.

Cap: Join 2 motifs to top of sleeve, omitting last rnd on sides and top.

FINISHING: Run in yarn ends. Block pieces. Sew shoulders; sew side seams. Sew in sleeves, gather-

ing top of sleeve to fit armhole if necessary. Gathering skirt to fit bodice, sew skirt to bodice.

Neck Edging: Join MC in right shoulder seam. With size H hook, work (sc, ch 1) around neck edge, keeping work flat. Join with a sl st in first sc.

Rnd 2: * Sc in next st, ch 4, sk next 2 sts, repeat from * around. Join; end off.

Work edging on lower edge of sleeve same as for lower edge of skirt.

BELT: With 3 strands of MC, make chain 100" long. End off. Weave in ends at beg and end of chain. Thread belt through last rnd at upper edge of skirt. Tie ends into bow at center front.

PATCHWORK SKIRT

Patchwork squares, striped and plain in poster-paint colors, are crocheted in an eyelet pattern and sewn together for a festive suspender skirt. Bands of color at bottom edge make the skirt the length you want.

SIZES: Directions for small size (6-8). Changes for medium size (10-12) and large size (14-16) are in parentheses.

Body Waist Size: 22"-23" (24"-25½"; 27"-29").

Blocked Waist Size: 23" (25½"-29").

MATERIALS: Knitting worsted, 4 (4-5) ozs. each of pink (A) and lilac (B); 3 (4-4) ozs. each of lime green (C), apple green (D), melon (E), yellow (F) and tangerine (G). Crochet hook size G/5. Six-inch skirt zipper. Two ⅝" buttons. One 1¼" button mold or button. Two hooks and eyes. Felt strip 2¼" x 31" of any desired color. Matching sewing thread.

GAUGE: 4 sts = 1"; 5 rows dc = 3". Large block = 7" (7¾"-8½") wide.

Note: Separate blocks of different colors and sizes are sewn together for skirt. Border is added after blocks are sewn together.

SKIRT: BLOCKS (30 blocks): **ONE-COLOR BLOCKS: Large Block** (make 2 each of B and D; 1 each of A, C, E, F and G—9 blocks): Beg at lower edge, ch 31 (34-37).

Row 1 (right side): Dc in 4th ch from hook, * ch 1, sk next ch, dc in each of next 2 ch, repeat from * across—20 (22-24) dc, counting turning ch at beg of row as 1 dc. Turn each row.

Row 2: Ch 3, sk first dc, dc in next dc, * ch 1, dc in each of next 2 dc, repeat from * across, end ch 1, dc in last dc, dc in top of turning ch.

Rows 3-12: Repeat row 2. Check

gauge; block should measure 7" (7¾"-8½") wide; 7" from start. End off.

Medium Block (make 1 each of E, F and A—3 blocks): Work same as for large one-color block for 3 rows—20 (22-24) dc.

Row 4: Ch 3, sk first 2 dc, * dc in each of next 2 dc, ch 1, repeat from * to within last ch-1 sp; do not ch 1, sk next dc, dc in top of turning ch—1 dc decreased each side.

Rows 5-7: Ch 3, sk first dc, * dc in each of next 2 dc, ch 1, repeat from * across, end dc in each of last 2 dc, dc in top of ch 3.

Row 8: Ch 3, sk first dc, (yo hook, pull up a lp in next dc, yo and through 2 lps on hook) twice, yo and through 3 lps on hook (1 dc dec), * ch 1, dc in each of next 2 dc, repeat from * across to within last 2 dc and turning ch, end ch 1, dec 1 dc over next 2 dc, dc in top of turning ch—16 (18-20) dc, counting turning ch as 1 dc.

Rows 9-12: Repeat row 2. End off.

Small Block (make 1 each of C, F, and G—3 blocks): Beg at lower edge, ch 25 (28-31). Work same as for medium block, having 16 (18-20) dc on row 1, 14 (16-18) dc on row 4 and 12 (14-16) dc on row 8.

TWO-COLOR BLOCKS: Large Block (make 2 blocks with F and G; 1 block each with B and E, A and F, B and D—5 blocks): Beg at lower edge, with first color, ch 28 (30-34).

Row 1 (right side): Sc in 2nd ch from hook, * ch 1, sk next ch, sc in next ch, repeat from * across—14 (15-17) sc. Turn each row.

Row 2: Ch 4 (counts as 1 dc, ch 1), sk first sc, dc in next sc, * ch 1, dc in next sc, repeat from * across. End off; join next color.

Row 3: Ch 1, sc in first dc, * ch 1, sc in next dc, repeat from * across, end ch 1, sk next ch on turning ch, sc in next ch—14 (15-17) sc.

Row 4: Repeat row 2. End off; join first color.

Row 5: With first color, repeat row 3.

Row 6: With first color, repeat row 2. End off; join 2nd color. Repeat rows 3-6 until 16 rows from start, end row 4. End off.

Medium Biock (make 1 with F and G—1 blcck): Work same as for large two-color block for 4 rows. End off; join first color.

Row 5: Ch 1, sc in each of first 2 dc (dec made), * ch 1, sc in next dc, repeat from * to within last dc and turning ch, end ch 1, sc in next dc, sk next ch, sc in next ch of turning ch (dec made.).

Row 6: Ch 4, sk first 2 sc, dc in next sc, * ch 1, dc in next sc, repeat from * to within last 2 sc, end ch 1, sk next sc, dc in last sc. End off; join 2nd color.

Rows 7-16: Work even in pat as for large two-color block. End off.

Small Block (make 1 each of B and E, D and B, F and E—3 blocks): With first color, ch 22 (24-28).

Rows 1-4: Work same as for large two-color block, having 11 (12-14) sc on row 1. End off; join first color.

Rows 5-16: Work same as rows 5-16 of medium two-color block, having 9 (10-12) sc on last sc row. End off.

THREE-COLOR BLOCKS: Large Block (make 2 blocks with A, G, B; 1 block with C, A, D; 1 block with E, F, C—4 blocks).

Rows 1-4: Using 2 colors, work same as for first 4 rows of large two-color block. End off; join 3rd color.

Rows 5 and 6: With 3rd color, work same as for rows 3 and 4. End off; join first color. Working 2 rows with each of the 3 colors, work same as for rows 3 and 4 until 16 rows from start. End off.

Medium Block (make 1 block with F, E, C; 1 block with A, C, D—2 blocks).

Rows 1-4: Using 2 colors, work same as for first 4 rows of large two-color block. End off; join 3rd color.

Rows 5 and 6: With 3rd color, work same as rows 5 and 6 of medium two-color block. End off; join first color. Working 2 rows with each of 3 colors, work even in pat until 16 rows from start. End off.

JOIN BLOCKS: Following chart, sew blocks together, matching colors of the one-color blocks to chart. Sew back and front tog, leaving a 6″ opening at upper left side seam for zipper.

LOWER BAND: From right side, join G in lower side seam.

Rnd 1: Working in starting ch of blocks, sc in next ch, * ch 1, sk next ch, sc in next ch, repeat from *

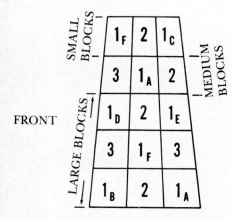

FRONT

1 = ONE-COLOR BLOCK
2 = TWO-COLOR BLOCK
(any combination)

BACK

3 = THREE-COLOR BLOCK
(any combination)

around, end ch 1, join with a sl st to first sc. Turn each rnd.

Rnd 2: Ch 4, * sk next ch-1 sp, dc in next sc, ch 1, repeat from * around, join with a sl st in 3rd ch of starting ch 4. End off; join B.

Rnd 3: Sc in joining st, * ch 1, sc in next dc, repeat from * around, end ch 1, join with a sl st in first sc.

Rnd 4: With B, repeat rnd 2. End off; join A. Using a different color for each 2-row stripe, repeat rnds 3 and 4 until skirt measures 39″ (40″-40″) from start or desired length, end rnd 4.

Next Rnd: With last color used, repeat rnd 3. End off.

WAISTBAND: Beg at lower edge of waistband with A, make ch 25″ (28″-31″) long or 2″ longer than desired waist measurement.

Row 1: 3 dc in 4th ch from hook (inc made at front edge of waistband), dc in each ch across. End off; join G. Turn each row.

Row 2: Ch 3, sk first dc, dc in each dc across, dc in top of turning ch. End off; join B.

Row 3: Repeat row 2. End; join C.

Row 4: Repeat row 2 to within last 3 sts, (yo hook, pull up a lp in next st, yo and through 2 lps on hook) 3 times, yo and through 4 lps on hook, ch 1. End off.

BUTTON LOOP: Join A to top of ch at beg of first row of waistband, ch 8, sk next 2 rows, sl st in base of end st on 4th row, ch 1, turn; sl st in each ch, sl st in end of first row. End off.

BUTTON (make 1): Beg at center with A, ch 4, join with a sl st, forming ring.

Rnd 1: 6 sc in ring; do not join.

Rnd 2: 2 sc in each sc around—12 sc.

Rnd 3: (Sc in next sc, 2 sc in next sc) 6 times—18 sc.

Rnd 4: Sc in each sc around. Insert button mold.

Rnd 5: Working over button mold, (sk next sc, sc in each of next 2 sc) 6 times—12 sc.

Rnd 6: (Sk next sc, sc in next sc) 6 times—6 sc. Cut yarn, leaving a long end. Run yarn through all sts and draw up tightly; sew button to back end of waistband.

SHOULDER STRAPS (make 2): With A, make ch about 32″ (34″-35″) long, having an even number of sts. Work same as for large two-color block until end of row 4, using B for rows 3 and 4. With B, repeat row 3. End off.

FINISHING: Steam-press garment lightly. Face waistband with felt strip, cut to measurement. Sew top edge of skirt to lower edge of waistband, leaving 1½″ waistband extension at back and easing in skirt to waist measurement. Close underlap of band with hooks and eyes. Sew ends of shoulder straps to wrong side of front waistband about 4½″ apart. Sew 2 buttons to wrong side of back waistband about 4″ apart. Spaces between sc on shoulder straps form buttonholes. Cross straps in back and button to back buttons.

CROCHETED COLORS SKIRT

This skirt of many colors, accented by black, is made of clusters, granny squares, and triangles and has a drawstring waist.

SIZES: Directions for small size (6-8-10). Any changes for medium size (12-14-16) are in parentheses.

Fits Body Hip Size: 32½″-33½″-34½″ (36″-38″-40″).

MATERIALS: Yarn of knitting worsted weight, 4-oz. skeins: 2 skeins black, main color (MC); 1 skein each of turquoise, orange, light green, purple, rose, light brown, dark rose, yellow, light orange, cranberry, lavender, winter white, medium green or any desired colors. Crochet hook size G.

GAUGE: Each square = 3½". 1 shell (3 dc) = 1"; 3 rnds = 2".

SKIRT: SQUARES (make 29 (32)): With any desired color, ch 4, join with a sl st to form ring.

Rnd 1: Ch 3 (counts as 1 dc), make 2 dc in ring, ch 2, (3 dc in ring, ch 2) 3 times, join last ch 2 to top of ch 3 with a sl st (4 groups of 3 dc in rnd). End off.

Rnd 2: Join another color in a ch-2 sp, ch 3, 2 dc in same sp, ch 1, (3 dc in next ch-2 sp, ch 2, 3 dc in same sp, ch 1) 3 times, 3 dc in same sp with first 3 dc, ch 2, join with a sl st to top of ch 3. End off.

Rnd 3: Join another color in a ch-2 sp, ch 3, 2 dc in same sp, ch 1, * 3 dc in next ch-1 sp, ch 1, (3 dc, ch 2, 3 dc) in corner ch-2 sp, ch 1, repeat from * around, end 3 dc in same sp with first 3 dc, ch 2, join with a sl st to top of ch 3. End off.

TRIANGLES (make 58 (64)): With any desired color, ch 4, join with a sl st to form ring.

Rnd 1: Ch 3 (counts as 1 dc), make 2 dc in ring, ch 2, (3 dc in ring, ch 2) twice, join last ch 2 to top of ch 3 with a sl st (3 groups of 3 dc in rnd). End off.

Rnd 2: Join another color in a ch-2 sp, ch 3, 2 dc in same sp, ch 1, (3 dc in next ch-2 sp, ch 2, 3 dc in same sp, ch 1) twice, 3 dc in same sp with first 3 dc, ch 2, join with a sl st to top of ch 3. End off.

Rnd 3: Join another color in a ch-2 sp, ch 3, 2 dc in same sp, ch 1, * 3 dc in next ch-1 sp, ch 1, (3 dc, ch 2, 3 dc) in corner ch-2 sp, ch 1, repeat from * around, end 3 dc in same sp with first 3 dc, ch 2, join with a sl st to top of ch 3. End off. Triangle cups slightly; will flatten after blocking.

JOINING: Following diagram below, make three strips by sewing

squares and triangles tog, sewing through back lps of edge sts only; do not join corner ch-2 sps at bottom and top edges of strips. Form circle with each strip; sew back seam.

UPPER BAND: Lower Edging: Rnd 1: With MC, make lp on hook, work tr in point of any square (between triangles), * shell of 3 dc in corner ch-2 sp on next triangle, (ch 2, 3 sc in next ch-1 sp) twice, ch 2, shell of 3 dc in corner ch-2 sp of same triangle, tr in point of square (between triangles), repeat from * around. Join with sl st in top of tr.

Rnd 2: Ch 3, 2 dc in sp between tr and shell, * (shell of 3 dc in next ch-2 sp) 3 times, shell in sp before next tr, shell in sp after tr, repeat from * around, end last repeat shell in sp before tr, sl st in top of ch 3—40 (45) shells.

Rnd 3: Sl st in each of next 2 dc, sl st in sp between shells, ch 3, 2 dc in same sp, shell in each sp between shells around, end sl st in top of ch 3.

Rnd 4: Repeat rnd 3.

Rnd 5: Repeat rnd 3, inc 5 shells evenly spaced around (**to inc 1 shell,** work 2 shells (6 dc) in same sp)—45 (50) shells.

Rnds 6 and 7: Repeat rnds 4 and 5—50 (55) shells. End off. Put aside to be joined later.

CENTER BAND: Top Edging:

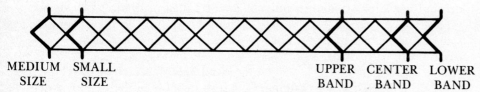

MEDIUM SMALL   UPPER CENTER LOWER
SIZE   SIZE   BAND BAND BAND

Piecing Diagram for Crocheted Colors

Rnds 1 and 2: Work as for lower edging on upper band—50 (55) shells. End off. Sew to lower edge of upper band.

Lower Edging: Rnds 1 and 2: Work as for upper band—50 (55) shells. End off.

Rnds 3-10: Work same as rnd 3, working each rnd with another color, inc 2 shells every other rnd twice, one shell once—55 (60) shells.

LOWER BAND: Top edging: Rnds 1 and 2: Work as for lower edge on upper band—55 (60) shells. End off. Sew to lower edge of center band.

Lower Edging: Rnds 1 and 2: Work as for upper band —55 (60) shells. Cut yarn.

Rnd 3: With any desired color, dc in each dc around, changing colors as desired for patchwork design. Repeat rnd 3, 4 times or until desired skirt length, allowing 2″ for top edging.

TOP EDGING: Rnd 1: Working around upper edge of skirt, with MC, work same as for lower edge.

Rnd 2: Ch 3, 2 dc in tr, * sk next shell, (shell in next ch-2 sp) 3 times, shell in tr, repeat from * around—32 (36) shells. Join with a sl st in top of ch 3.

Rnds 3-5: Work shell in each sp. End off.

CORD: With 2 strands of MC, make chain 60″ long. End off; knot ends. Weave through spaces between shells around top rnd.

PLAID SHORTCOAT

Pink and green crisscross this cream-white shortcoat for all-year-round wear. Colors are carried across the rows and worked into stripes.

SIZES: Directions for small size (8-10). Changes for medium size (12-14) and large size (16) are in parentheses.

Body Bust Size: 31½"-32½" (34"-36"; 38").

Blocked Bust Size (closed): 33" (36"-40").

MATERIALS: Knitting worsted, 6 (6-7) 4-oz. skeins winter white (W); 2 skeins each pink (P) and green (G). Crochet hook size H.

GAUGE: 7 dc = 2"; 3 rows (1 pat) = 1½".

To Bind Off: At beg of a row, ch 1, sl st loosely across specified number of sts; **at end of a row,** leave specified number of sts unworked.

To Dec 1 Dc: At beg of a row, ch 3 (counts as 1 dc), sk first st, yo hook, draw up a lp in each of next 2 sts, yo hook and through 2 lps, yo and through 3 lps, work in pat across; **at end of a row,** work to last 2 sts, yo hook, draw up a lp in each of next 2 sts, yo and through 2 lps, yo and through 3 lps.

To Dec 1 Sc: At beg of a row, ch 1, draw up a lp in each of next 2 sts, yo hook and through 3 lps on hook, work in pat across; **at end of a row,** work to last 2 sts, draw up a lp in each of next 2 sts, yo and through 3 lps.

Note: When changing colors, pull new color through last 2 lps to complete st. On dc rows, work over colors not being used to hide them in work. No strands must show on wrong side of work.

TOPPER: BACK: Beg at lower edge, with W, ch 85 (91-97). Join P and G in last ch. **(Left-handed crocheters:** Work back as directed.)

For Small and Large Sizes

Only: Row 1 (right side): With W, dc in 4th ch from hook and in each of next 3 ch; * with P, dc in next ch; with W, dc in each of next 5 ch; with G, dc in next ch; with W, dc in each of next 5 ch, repeat from * across, end last repeat, with P, dc in next ch; with W, dc in each of last 5 ch—83 (95)dc, counting turning ch as 1 dc. Turn.

Row 2: With W, ch 3 (counts as 1 dc), sk first st, dc in each of next 4 sts; keeping to colors as established, dc in each st across. Turn.

For Medium Size Only: Row 1 (right side): With W, dc in 4th ch from hook, * with P, dc in next ch; with W, dc in each of next 5 ch; with G, dc in next ch; with W, dc in each of next 5 ch, repeat from * across, end last repeat, with W, dc in each of last 2 ch—89 dc, counting turning ch as 1 dc. Turn.

Row 2: With W, ch 3 (counts as 1 dc), sk first st, dc in next st; keeping to colors as established, dc in each dc across. Turn.

For All Sizes: Check gauge; piece should measure 24″ (25½″-27″) wide.

Row 3: Drop all colors but P. From right side, working with P only, dec 1 sc each side (see To Dec 1 Sc), sc in each st across. Cut P; do not turn.

Row 4 (right side): Join another strand of P; with W, ch 3 (counts as 1 dc); keeping to colors as established, dc in each sc across. Turn.

Row 5: Keeping to colors as established, dc in each dc across. Turn.

Row 6: Drop all colors but G. From right side, working with G only, dec 1 sc each side, sc in each st across. Cut G; do not turn.

Row 7 (right side): Join another strand of G; keeping to colors as established, ch 3 for first dc, dc in each st across, making each P dc in top of P dc of row 5. Turn.

Row 8: Repeat row 5. Repeat rows 3-8 for pat. Working in pat as established, dec 1 st each side of next row, then every 3rd row 10 times—57 (63-69) sts. Work even (do not dec on rows 3 and 6) until piece measures about 21″ from start, end pat row 3 or 6.

Shape Armholes: Keeping to pat as established, bind off (see To Bind Off) 3 sts each side of next row. Dec 1 st each side (see To Dec 1 Dc) every row 3 (4-5) times—45 (49-53) sts. Work even until armholes measure 7½″ (8″-8½″) above bound-off sts.

Shape Shoulders: Bind off 4 sts each side of next 2 rows, 4 (5-6) sts next row—21 (23-25) sts. End off.

LEFT FRONT (Left-handed crocheters: This will be your right front): Beg at lower edge with W, ch 49 (55-61). Work in pat as for back on 47 (53-59) sts for 2 rows. Mark end of last row for side edge. Check gauge; piece should measure 13½″ (15″-17″) wide across last row.

Row 3: From right side, working with P only, sc in each st across. Cut P; do not turn.

Rows 4 and 5: Work as for back.

Row 6: From right side, working with G only, sc in each st across. Cut G; do not turn.

Rows 7 and 8: Work as for back. Repeat rows 3-8 for pat. Dec 1 st at side edge of next row, then dec 1 st at same edge every 4th row 8 times—38 (44-50) sts. Work even until piece measures same as back to underarm, end same pat row as back.

Shape Armhole and Neck: Bind off 4 sts at side edge of next row. Dec 1 st at same edge every row 3 (4-5) times; **at the same time,** dec 1 st at center edge every 3rd (2nd-2nd) row 5 (7-9) times—26 (29-32) sts. Work even if necessary until armhole measures same as back. If decs are not completed, continue to dec at front edge while shaping shoulder.

Shape Shoulder: Bind off 4 sts at beg of arm side twice, 4 (5-6) sts once—14 (16-18) sts remain for back collar. Mark shoulder edge of beg of collar.

Collar: Keeping to pat, inc 1 st at shoulder edge and dec 1 st at front edge every row until collar measures about 2¾″ (3″-3¼″) above marked row.

Shape Back of Collar: Keeping to pat, dec 2 sts at front edge, 1 st at shoulder edge every row for 4 (5-5) rows. End off.

RIGHT FRONT (Left-handed crocheters: This will be your left front): Work same as left front, but mark **beg** of row 2 for side edge.

SLEEVES: Beg at lower edge with W, ch 43. Work rows 1 and 2 as for medium size on back, having 41 sts. Check gauge; piece should measure 12″ wide. Work in pat as for fronts, inc 1 st each side every 6th row 4 (5-6) times—49 (51-53) sts. Work even until piece measures about 20″ from start or 2″ longer (cuff) than desired sleeve length, end same pat row as back underarm.

Shape Cap: Bind off 4 sts each side of next row. Dec 2 sts each side every dc row and 1 st each side every sc row for 9 (10-11) rows. End off.

FINISHING: Run in all yarn ends on wrong side. Block pieces. With backstitch, sew shoulder seams. Weave ends of collar tog; sew back neck to collar. Sew in sleeves; sew side and sleeve seams.

Front Band (make 2): With P, make chain to measure from lower front corner to center back of collar.

Row 1: Sc in 2nd ch from hook, * ch 1, sk next ch, sc in next ch, repeat from * across. Ch 1, turn.

Rows 2 and 3: * Sc in sc, ch 1, repeat from * across, end sc in sc. End off.

Pin foundation ch of band to

wrong side of front and collar, ¼" in from edge. Sew band in place. Fold band over edge to right side; sew in place.

From right side, with P, work 1 row sc across lower edge of topper. Fold 2" at lower edge of sleeve to right side for cuff; with P, work 1 rnd sc around edge of cuff.

BELT: With P, ch 180 (186-192). Sc in 2nd ch from hook and in each ch across—179 (185-191) sc. End off. Do not turn; join W, P and G at beg of row. Work in dc

pat as for back: 5 (2-5) W, * 1 P, 5 W, 1 G, 5 W, repeat from * across, end last repeat 1 P, 5 (2-5) W. Turn; work another dc row. End off W and P. Turn. Work 1 row of G sc. End off.

Steam-press belt lightly.

IRISH ROSE JACKET

Shown on page 88

Irish crochet jacket combines large and small squares of lacy picot pattern, each motif centered with a raised rose. Front buttons up to low V; jacket may be worn with high back neckline in front.

SIZES: Directions for small size (6-8). Any changes for medium size (10-12) are in parentheses.

Body Bust Size: 30½"-31½" (32½"-34").

Blocked Bust Size (closed): 32" (36").

MATERIALS: Mercerized knitting and crochet cotton, 6 250-yd. balls white. Steel crochet hook No. 7 (No. 4). About 18 small pearl buttons.

GAUGE: 1 small square = 4" (4½"); 1 large square = 8" (9").

Note: Directions are the same for both sizes. Gauge determines size. For medium size, use No. 4 hook, or whatever hook is needed to obtain gauge given.

JACKET: LARGE SQUARE (make 7): With No. 7 (No. 4) hook, ch 6, sl st in first ch to form ring.

Rnd 1: Ch 6, (dc in ring, ch 3) 5 times, sl st in 3rd ch of ch 6—6 sps.

Rnd 2: In each sp around work sc, 3 dc, sc—6 petals.

Rnd 3: (Ch 4; working behind petal, sc around next dc of rnd 1) 6 times.

Rnd 4: In each sp around work sc, 5 dc, sc—6 petals.

Rnd 5: * Ch 5; working behind petals, sc in ch-4 lp of rnd 3 about halfway across next petal, (ch 5, sc around next sc between petals) 3 times, repeat from * once—8 lps.

Rnd 6: Repeat rnd 4—8 petals. Sl st in first sc.

Rnd 7: Sl st in first dc, ch 5, sl st in 3rd ch from hook for picot, ch 3, sc in last dc of same petal, * ch 5, sl st in 3rd ch from hook for picot, ch 3 (picot-lp), sc in first dc of next petal, picot-lp, sc in last dc of same petal, repeat from * around, end picot-lp, sl st in sl st at beg of rnd.

Rnd 8: Sl st in 2 ch, sc in picot-lp before picot, * dtr in next picot-lp before picot, ch 1; in sp made by dtr work 1 sc, 8 dc and 1 sc, (ch 5, sl st in 3rd ch from hook for picot) twice, ch 2, sc in next picot-lp before picot (2-picot-lp made), 2-picot-lp in each of next 2 lps, repeat from * 3 times, end sl st in first sc.

Rnd 9: * 2-picot-lp, sc in 4th dc of scallop, 2-picot-lp, sc in 8th dc of scallop, (2-picot-lp, sc in center of next lp) 3 times, 2-picot-lp, sc in first dc of next scallop, repeat from * 3 times, end sl st in sl st.

Rnd 10: Sl st to center of picot-lp, sc in picot-lp, * dtr in center of next picot-lp, ch 1; in sp made by dtr work 1 sc, 8 dc and 1 sc, (2-picot-lp, sc in center of next lp) 5 times, repeat from * 3 times, end sl st in first sc of scallop.

Rnd 11: Sc in first dc, * 2-picot-lp, sc in 4th dc of scallop, 2-picot-lp, sc in 8th dc of scallop, (2-picot-lp, sc in center of next lp) 5 times, 2-picot-lp, sc in first dc of next scallop, repeat from * 3 times, end sl st in first sc.

Rnd 12: Repeat rnd 10, making 7 2-picot-lps between scallops.

Rnd 13: Repeat rnd 11, making 8 2-picot-lps between scallops and 2 2-picot-lps over scallops.

Rnd 14: Repeat rnd 10, making 9 2-picot-lps between scallops.

Rnd 15: Repeat rnd 11, making 10 2-picot-lps between scallops and 2 2-picot-lps over scallops. End off.

SMALL SQUARE (make 30): Work as for large square through rnd 9. End off.

FINISHING: See diagram for placement of squares.

Joining Squares: Join thread in center of 2nd lp over scallop in any corner of small square; make ch-3 picot, drop lp off hook; insert hook in center ch of corresponding lp over scallop (first lp) of another small square, draw dropped

IRISH ROSE JACKET

lp through; * make picot, join to next lp of first square, make picot, join to next lp of 2nd square, repeat from * until first lp of next corner on first square is joined to corresponding lp on 2nd square. End off. Join all squares in this manner. When joining small squares to large squares, join only as far as small squares will permit.

Do not join 4 small squares each side at top, as shown, for armholes. Join edges marked with short arrows for shoulders, then join edges marked with long arrows.

Fill-in Motifs: Fill in spaces at corners between 4 motifs as follows: Ch 6, sl st in first ch to form ring; * ch 4, sl st in first corner lp over a scallop, ch 4, drop lp off hook, insert hook in ring, pull lp through; ch 5, sl st in sc between corner lps, ch 5, join in ring as before; ch 4, sl st in 2nd corner lp over same scallop, ch 4, join in ring, repeat from * around, working each repeat in next square.

Where 2 small squares join 1 large square, join thread in center sc on last rnd of large square, work ch-lps, joining to corner lps of small squares.

At shoulders, where 4 small squares and 1 large square come

Diagram for Assembling Squares

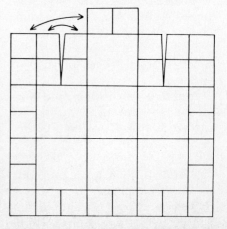

tog, work extra ch-lps to fill in space.

Front Edging: Join thread in lower front corner lp, * (make 1-picot-lp, sc in next lp on front edge) 5 times, make 1-picot-lp; holding back last lp of each tr, make tr in corner sc between corner lps, tr in next corner lp of same square, tr in corner lp of next square, tr in corner sc between corner lps, yo and through all lps on hook, make 1-picot-lp, sc in next corner lp, repeat from * 4 times (5 tr cluster joinings between squares for front edge), work in 1-picot-lps around 6 neck squares, work picot edging and tr cluster joinings down other front edge to correspond to first front.

On front edges only, work 2 more rows of 1-picot-lp edging.

Armhole Edging: Work 1-picot-lp edging around each armhole.

Sew buttons evenly spaced to left front edge. Picot-lps are buttonholes.

BLOUSON JACKET SUIT

Shown on page 90

A trim battle jacket, precisely buttoned in silver, just grazes the top of a slightly flared skirt. Suit is worked in alternating panels of plain afghan stitch crochet and purl afghan stitch.

SIZES: Directions for small size (8-10). Changes for medium size (12-14) are in parentheses.

Body Bust Size: 31½"-32½" (34"-36").

Blocked Bust Size (closed): 37" (40").

MATERIALS: Yarn of knitting worsted weight, 10 (11) 4-oz. skeins. Aluminum afghan hooks sizes G and I. Round elastic cord. Seven plastic rings and 7 buttons.

GAUGE: 4 sts = 1"; 3 rows = 1" (size I hook).

PLAIN AFGHAN STITCH:
Row 1: Keeping all lps on hook, sk first ch from hook (lp on hook is first st), pull up a lp in each ch across.

To Work Lps Off: Yo hook, pull through first lp, * yo hook, pull through next 2 lps, repeat from * across until 1 lp remains. Lp that remains on hook always counts as first st of next row.

Row 2: Keeping all lps on hook, sk first vertical bar, pull up a lp under next vertical bar and under each vertical bar across. Work lps off as before. Repeat row 2 for plain st.

PURL AFGHAN STITCH: Holding yarn with thumb in front and below hook, pull up a lp under vertical bar. Work off lp same as for plain st.

To Bind Off (work loosely): **At beg of a row,** start with 2nd vertical bar; work first part of st, pull lp through lp on hook thus making a sl st (1 st bound off). Continue in this manner for specified number of sts. **At end of a row,** leave specified number of sts unworked. Work lps off as before. As each section of garment is completed, with afghan hook, work sl st across unworked bound-off sts, keeping to pat as established.

To Dec 1 St: Keeping to pat, insert hook under each of 2 vertical bars and pull up 1 plain lp for plain st or 1 purl lp for purl st; keep lp on hook.

Skirt Length Note: Skirt is planned for 20" length from lower edge to waistband. For longer or shorter skirt, add or subtract desired number of inches before first dec row. More yarn may be needed for longer skirt.

SKIRT: BACK: Beg at lower edge, with size I hook, ch 81 (85) loosely.

Row 1: Work same as for row 1 of plain afghan st—81 (85) lps. Work lps off in same manner.

Row 2: Keeping all lps on hook, sk first vertical bar (lp on hook is first st); **for small size only,** make 3 plain sts, * make 7 purl sts, 4 plain sts, repeat from * across; **for medium size only,** make 1 purl st, * make 4 plain sts, 7 purl sts, repeat from * across, end make 4 plain sts, 2 purl sts. Work lps off as before. Repeat row 2 for pat until piece measures 10" from start (see Skirt Length Note). Check gauge; piece should measure 20" (21") wide. Dec 1 purl st (see To Dec 1 St) in each of the 7-st purl panels—74 (78) lps. Work lps off as before. Having 1 purl st less every dec row, repeat dec row every 4" twice more—60 (64) lps. Work even in pat, having 4 purl sts in each of the 7 purl st panels, plus 2 purl sts each side of medium size. Work even until piece measures 20" from start or desired length to waist. Bind off (see To Bind Off).

BLOUSON JACKET SUIT

FRONT: Work same as for back.

FINISHING: Steam lightly; do not press. Sew side seams. With size G hook, work 4 rnds sc around upper edge of skirt, working 2nd and 4th rnds over elastic. End off. Draw elastic in to desired fit; fasten.

JACKET: BACK: Beg at lower edge, above border, with size I hook, ch 76 (80) loosely.

Row 1: Work same as for row 1 of plain afghan st—76 (80) lps. Work lps off in same manner.

Row 2: Keeping all lps on hook, sk first vertical bar, make 0 (2) purl sts, * make 4 plain sts, 4 purl sts, repeat from * across, end make 4 plain sts, 0 (2) purl sts. Work lps off as before. Repeat row 2 until piece measures 11″ from start. Check gauge; piece should measure 19″ (20″) wide. Work remainder of back in plain st only.

Shape Armholes: Bind off 4 sts each side of next row. Work lps off. Dec 1 st each side every row 5 times—58 (62) sts. Work even until armholes measure 7½″ (8″) above first bound-off sts.

Shape Shoulders: Bind off 9 sts each side of next row, then 9 (10) sts each side of next row. Bind off remaining 22 (24) sts for back of neck.

Lower Border: Working across lower edge, from right side, with size G hook, pick up 1 st in each vertical bar across, dec 1 st in center of each 4-st purl and 4-st plain panel—57 (61) sts. Work in plain st for 3″. Bind off.

Note to Left-handed Crocheters: Follow directions for right front first, omitting buttonholes. This will be your left front. With pins, mark position of 7 buttons evenly spaced on center edge of left front; first one ¾″ above lower edge, last one ½″ below neck edge. Work right front following directions for left front, working buttonholes 3 sts in from center edge, opposite markers.

LEFT FRONT: Beg at lower edge, above border, with size I hook, ch 40 (42) loosely.

Row 1: Work same as for row 1 of plain afghan st—40 (42) lps. Work lps off in same manner.

Row 2: Keeping all lps on hook, sk first vertical bar, make 0 (1) purl st, make 3 (4) plain sts, * 4 purl sts, 4 plain sts, repeat from * to within last 8 sts, make 8 plain sts (center border). Work lps off as before. Repeat row 2 until piece measures 11″ from start. Complete in plain st.

Shape Armhole: Bind off 4 sts at arm side of next row, then dec 1 st at same edge every row 5 times—31 (33) sts. Work even until armhole measures 5″ (5½″) above first bound-off sts.

Shape Neck: Bind off 9 (10) sts at center edge of next row, then dec 1 st at same edge every row 4 times—18 (19) sts. Work even until armhole measures same as back.

Shape Shoulder: Bind off 9 sts at arm side once, 9 (10) sts once.

Lower Border: From right side, working across lower edge, with size G hook, pick up 1 st in each st, dec 1 st in center of each 4-purl-st panel and 4-plain-st panel—32 (34) lps. Work in plain st for 3″. Bind off.

With pins, mark position of 7 buttons evenly spaced on center edge of left front; first one ¾″ above lower edge, last one ½″ below neck edge.

BUTTONHOLES: Keeping to pat, work 2 sts at beg of center edge (3 lps on hook), bind off next 2 sts, finish row. When working lps off, ch 2 for buttonhole over the 2 bound-off sts. **Next Row:** Pull up a lp on each ch of buttonhole.

RIGHT FRONT: Work same as for left front to end of row 1.

Row 2: Keeping all lps on hook, sk first vertical bar, make 7 plain sts (center border), * make 4 purl sts, 4 plain sts, repeat from * across, end make 0 (2) purl sts. Working in pat as established, complete same as left front, forming buttonholes (see Buttonholes) opposite markers.

Lower Border: Work same as for left front border, forming buttonhole opposite marker.

SLEEVES: Beg at lower edge, above border, with size I hook, ch 52 (56). Work in plain st for 14″ or 3″ less (border allowance) than desired sleeve length. Check gauge; piece should be 13″ (14″) wide.

Shape Cap: Bind off 4 sts each side of next row. Dec 1 st each side every row 13 (15) times. Bind off 2 sts each side of next row. Bind off remaining 14 sts.

Border: From right side, with size G hook, pick up 33 (35) lps across lower edge of sleeve. Work in plain st for 3″. Bind off.

FINISHING: Steam pieces lightly. With backstitch, sew shoulder seams; sew in sleeves. Sew side and sleeve seams. From right side, with size G hook, work 1 rnd sc around each sleeve edge. From right side, work 1 rnd sc around outer edge of jacket, working 3 sc in each corner and easing in neck to desired fit.

COLLAR: Beg at outer edge, with size I hook, ch 84 loosely. Work in 4-plain-st, 4-purl-st pat for 1″.

Next Row: Dec 1 st in each purl-st panel. Keeping to pat, work 1″.

Next Row: Dec 1 st in each purl-st panel. Work even in 4-plain-st, 2-purl-st pat until piece measures 3½″ from start. Bind off. With size G hook, work 1 row sc around entire outer edge of collar, working 3 sc in each corner and easing in slightly across bound-off edge to fit neck edge of jacket. With ends of collar 1″ in from front edges, sew bound-off edge of collar to neck edge.

BUTTONS (make 7): With size G hook, work sc tightly around plastic ring. End off, leaving a long end. Thread needle; turn sts

to center of ring, gather sts tog at center. Sew a button to center of ring. Sew buttons on left center band.

PLAID SUIT

This Chanel-inspired suit is a contemporary classic, worked in a simple mesh pattern. Horizontal stripes of plaid are crocheted in; vertical stripes are woven.

SIZES: Directions for size 12. Changes for sizes 14, 16 and 18 are in parentheses.

Body Bust Size: 34″ (36″-38″-40″).

Blocked Bust Size (jacket closed): 36″ (38″-40″-42″).

MATERIALS: Yarn of sport yarn weight, 23 (24-26-27) ozs. beige (A); 16 (16-17-17) ozs. black (B); 7 (8-9-9) ozs. orange (C). Steel crochet hook No. 1. Seven-inch skirt zipper. Three-quarter yd. 1″ elastic. Eight round button molds. Large-eyed rug needle or bodkin. Lining material. Matching sewing thread. Hook and eye. Two snaps.

GAUGE: 3 meshes = 1″; 3 rows = 1″.

To Bind Off: At beg of a row, sl st loosely across each mesh to be bound off, then ch 4 and continue across row; **at end of a row,** work in pat to within specified number of meshes to be bound off.

To Dec 1 Mesh: At beg of a row, ch 2, sk first dc, dc in next dc (counts as 1 dc), ch 1, dc in next dc (one mesh); **at end of a row,** work to last dc, ch 1, yo, pull up a lp in last dc, yo and through 2 lps on hook, yo, pull up a lp in 2nd ch of turning ch, yo and through 2 lps on hook, yo and through 3 lps on hook.

To Inc 1 Mesh: At beg of a row,

ch 4, dc in first dc; **at end of a row,** work dc, ch 1, dc in 3rd ch of turning ch.

Note: Cut and join colors as needed. When changing colors, pull new color through last 2 lps to complete dc.

STRIPED MESH PATTERN: Row 1: Dc in 6th ch from hook, * ch 1, sk next ch, dc in next ch, repeat from * across. Ch 4, turn each row.

Row 2: Sk first dc, * dc in next dc, ch 1, repeat from * across, end dc in 3rd ch of turning ch.

Rows 3-8: With B, repeat row 2.

Rows 9-12: With A, repeat row 2.

Rows 13 and 14: With C, repeat row 2.

Rows 15-18: With A, repeat row 2.

Rows 19-22: With B, repeat row 2. Repeat rows 9-22 for striped mesh pat.

SKIRT: BACK: Beg at lower edge, with B, ch 144 (152-156-164). Work in striped mesh pat on 70 (74-76-80) meshes until piece measures 4″ from start. Check gauge; piece should measure 23⅓″ (24⅔″-25⅓″-26⅔″) wide. Dec 1 mesh (see To Dec 1 Mesh) each side of next row, then every 4th row 15 times more—38 (42-44-48) meshes. Work even until piece measures 25″ from start or 2″ more

(hem and waistline facing allowance) than desired skirt length. End off.

FRONT: Work same as for back.

FINISHING: Block.

Weaving: With basting thread, mark center back dc from lower edge to upper edge. Cut 2 strands C about 9″ longer than twice the length of skirt. Thread into rug needle or bodkin. Starting in first mesh to left of center, bring needle through to right side and draw strands through, leaving 2″ hanging at lower edge. Weave over first bar, under 2nd bar, over 3rd bar, etc. to top. Go over top edge, through first mesh on other side of center and continue to alternate weaving to lower edge.

* Weave 4 stripes of A to right of center stripe, then 4 stripes of B, 4 stripes of A, 2 stripes of C, repeat from * to side edge. Repeat from * to left side edge.

Using small backstitches, sew across all weaving ends. Trim ends to ½″; turn ends and tack to wrong side on first mesh row. Weave front in same manner.

Cut lining to fit pieces, allowing for seams. Assemble lining, leaving 8″ open at upper side edge. Cut elastic same as waist measurement. With backstitch, sew side seams, leaving 8″ opening at upper left side edge. Fold 4 rows at lower edge to wrong side; sew in place. Fold ½″ at upper edge to wrong side; sew in place. Sew in zipper 1″ below waistline so that it does not show. Insert lining; turn under raw edge at top, hem to waist and side opening. Hem lower edge 1″ shorter than skirt. Sew elastic inside top edge of skirt. Close top edge of skirt above zipper with hook and eye.

JACKET: BACK: Beg at lower edge, with B, ch 112 (118-124-130). Work in striped mesh pat on 54 (57-60-63) meshes until piece measures 4″ from start. Check gauge; piece should measure 18″ (19″-20″-21″) wide. Keeping to color sequence, dec 1 mesh each side of next row, then every 1″ once—50 (53-56-59) meshes. Work even until piece measures 8″ from start. Inc 1 mesh (see To Inc 1 Mesh) each side of next row, then every 1½″ once—54 (57-60-63) meshes. Work even until piece measures 14″ (14½″-15″-15½″) from start or 1″ longer than desired length to underarm.

Shape Armholes: Bind off (see To Bind Off) 3 meshes each side of next row. Dec 1 mesh each side every row 3 times—42 (45-48-51) meshes. Work even until armholes measure 8½″ (8½″-9″-9½″) above bound-off sts.

Shape Shoulders: Bind off 4 meshes each side of next 2 rows, 3 (4-5-6) meshes each side of next row—20 (21-22-23) meshes. End off.

LEFT FRONT: Beg at lower edge, with B, ch 64 (68-72-76). Work in striped mesh pat on 30 (32-34-36) meshes until piece measures 4″ from start. Mark end of last row for side edge. Check gauge; piece should measure 10″ (10⅔″-11⅓″-12″) wide. Dec 1 mesh at side edge of next row, then dec 1 mesh at same edge

every 1″ once—28 (30-32-34) meshes. Work even until piece measures 8″ from start. Inc 1 mesh at side edge of next row, then inc 1 mesh at same edge every 1½″ once—30 (32-34-36) meshes. Work even until piece measures same as back to underarm.

Shape Armhole: Bind off 3 meshes at side edge of next row. Dec 1 mesh at same edge every row 3 times—24 (26-28-30) meshes. Work even until armhole measures 6½″ (6½″-7″-7½″) above bound-off sts.

Shape Neck and Shoulder: Bind off 6 (7-8-9) meshes at front edge of next row. Dec 1 mesh at same edge every row 7 times—11 (12-13-14) meshes. Work even until armhole measures same as back.

Bind off 4 meshes at arm side twice—3 (4-5-6) meshes remain. End off.

RIGHT FRONT: Work same as for left front; pat is reversible.

SLEEVES: Beg at lower edge, with B, ch 62 (66-70-74). Work in striped pat on 29 (31-33-35) meshes for 4″. Keeping to color sequence, inc 1 mesh each side every 2″ 5 times—39 (41-43-45) meshes. Work even until piece measures 17″ (17½″-18¼″-18½″) from start or 1″ longer (hem allowance) than desired length to underarm.

Shape Cap: Keeping to color sequence, bind off 3 meshes each side of next row. Dec 1 mesh each side every other row 10 (11-12-13) times—13 meshes. End off.

COLLAR: Beg at neck edge, with B, ch 136 (140-144-148). Work in striped mesh pat, working 4 rows B, 4 rows A, 4 rows C.

FINISHING: Block pieces.

Weaving: Weave back, sleeves and collar same as for skirt. Weave fronts as follows: Beg at center front edge, weave 1 stripe of C, * 4 stripes of A, 4 stripes of B, 4 stripes of A, 2 stripes of C, repeat from * to side edge. Cut lining to fit pieces, allowing for shoulder darts and center back pleat; assemble lining. Sew shoulder seams; sew in sleeves. Sew side and sleeve seams. Turn 4 rows at lower edge of sleeves and jacket to wrong side; hem in place. Turn last 2 rows and 2 sts on each side edge of collar to wrong side; hem in place. Sew collar to neck edge with sides of collar 1″ in from front edges. Line collar. With A, work 4 rows of sc across each front edge. Fold to wrong side; hem in place. Steam-press seams and hems. Insert lining; hem to jacket.

Make 4 machine buttonholes evenly spaced on right center front, first buttonhole 5″ above lower edge, last buttonhole 1″ below neck edge.

BUTTONS (make 8): With C, ch 2.

Rnd 1: 6 sc in 2nd ch from hook. Do not join rnds.

Rnd 2: 2 sc in each sc—12 sc.

Rnd 3: * Sc in next sc, 2 sc in next sc, repeat from * around—18 sc.

Rnd 4: Sc in each sc around.

Next Rnd: * Pull up a lp in each of next 2 sts, yo and through 3 lps on hook (dec made), sc in next sc, repeat from * around. Insert button mold. Continue to dec 1 st every other st until back of mold is covered. End off, leaving an end for sewing.

Sew buttons on left front edge, opposite buttonholes. Sew 2 buttons to side of each sleeve for trim. Sew a snap fastener to neck and lower edge of jacket.

TWEED SUIT

Classic tweed suit, softened with scallops, is simpler than you think to crochet. Jacket has set-in sleeves, sewn-on collar. Scallops on collar, front closing, pockets, and cuffs are worked in colors picked up from the tweed.

SIZES: Directions for size 12. Changes for sizes 14, 16 and 18 are in parentheses.

Body Bust Size: 34″ (36″-38″-40″).

Blocked Bust Size (closed): 36″ (38″-40″-42″).

MATERIALS: Tweed dress yarn of sport yarn weight, 26 (28-30-32) 40-gram balls main color (MC); fingering yarn, 1 1-oz. skein each of yellow (A), orange (B) and purple (C). Steel crochet hook No. 0. Seventeen buttons. Lining fabric, if desired. Seven-inch skirt zipper. One yard ¾″-wide grosgrain ribbon. One hook and eye. Matching sewing thread.

GAUGE: 7 sts = 1″; 7 rows = 1″.

PATTERN (worked on multiple of 2 sts plus 1): **Row 1:** Sc in 2nd ch from hook, * ch 1, sk next ch, sc in next ch, repeat from * across. Ch 1, turn.

Row 2: Sc in first sc, * ch 1, sk ch-1 sp, sc in next sc, repeat from * across. Ch 1, turn. Repeat row 2 for pat, always working ch 1 over ch-1 sp and sc over sc.

To Bind Off: At beg of a row, sl st loosely across specified sts; **at end of a row,** leave specified number of sts unworked.

To Dec 1 St: At beg of a row, ch 1, pull up a lp in each of first 2 sts, yo and through 3 lps on hook; **at end of a row,** pull up a lp in each of last 2 sts, yo and through 3 lps on hook. **Next Row:** Work in pat as established (sc over each sc, ch 1 over ch-1 sp).

To Inc 1 St: At beg of a row, ch 1 loosely, 2 sc in first st; **at end of a row,** 2 sc in last st. **Next Row:** Work in pat as established; when there are 3 sc tog, work into sc, ch 1 pat.

Note: Always count sc as 1 st, ch 1 as 1 st.

Skirt Length Note: Skirt is planned for 23″ length from lower edge to waistband. For longer or shorter skirt, add or subtract desired number of inches before first dec row. More yarn may be needed for longer skirt.

SKIRT: BACK: Beg at lower edge, with MC, ch 142 (150-156-164). Work in pat on 141 (149-155-163) sts for 3″. (see Skirt Length Note.) Check gauge; piece should measure 20″ (21¼″-22″-23¼″) wide. Keeping to pat as established, dec 1 st (see To Dec

1 St) each side of next row, then every 1″ 13 times more, every ¾″ 9 times—95 (103-109-117) sts. Work even until piece measures 23″ from start. End off.

FRONT: Work same as for back.

FINISHING: Steam-press pieces lightly. Using pieces for pattern, cut lining allowing ½″ on all edges for seams and 2″ for waist darts on each of back and front. Sew side seams and darts of lining leaving a 7″ opening on upper left side seam. With back-stitch, sew skirt side seams leaving a 7″ opening on upper left side seam.

Waistband: From right side, work 1 row sc around upper edge of skirt, dec to desired fit. Ch 1, turn.

Rows 2-7: Sc in each sc. Ch 1, turn each row. End off.

Face waistband with grosgrain ribbon. Sew in skirt zipper below waistband. Insert lining. Turn raw edges to wrong side at lower edge of skirt, lower edge of grosgrain ribbon and side opening edge; hem in place. Close waistband with hook and eye.

JACKET: BACK: Beg at lower edge, with MC, ch 126 (134-140-148). Work in pat on 125 (133-139-147) sts for 1″. Check gauge; piece should measure 18″ (19″-20″-21″) wide. Dec 1 st each side of next row, then every 1″ 5 times more—113 (121-127-135) sts. Work even until piece measures 7″ from start. Inc 1 st (see To Inc 1 St) each side of next row, then every 1″ 5 times more—125 (133-139-147) sts. Work even until piece measures 14½″ (15″-15″-15½″) from start or desired length to underarm.

Shape Armholes: Bind off (see To Bind Off) 6 (7-7-8) sts each side of next row. Dec 1 st each side every other row 8 times—97 (103-109-115) sts. Work even

until armholes measure 7½″ (8″-8″-8½″) above first armhole shaping row.

Shape Shoulders: Work 40 (42-44-46) sts, drop yarn; sk next 17 (19-21-23) sts; with another strand of MC, sc in next st, finish row—40 (42-44-46) sts each side. Working on both sides at once, with separate strands of yarn, dec 1 st at each neck edge every row 10 times; **at the same time,** bind off 8 sts at each arm side every other row 3 times, 6 (8-10-12) sts once.

LEFT FRONT: Beg at lower edge, with MC, ch 64 (68-72-76). Work in pat on 63 (67-71-75) sts for 1″. Mark end of last row for side edge. Check gauge; piece should measure 9″ (9½″-10¼″-10¾″) wide. Keeping to pat, dec 1 st at side edge of next row, then dec 1 st at same edge every 1″ 5 times more—57 (61-65-69) sts. Work even until piece measures 7″ from start. Inc 1 st at side edge of next row, then inc 1 st at same edge every 1″ 5 times more—63 (67-71-75) sts. Work even until piece measures 14½″ (15″-15″-15½″) from start.

Shape Armhole: Keeping to pat, bind off 6 (7-7-8) sts at arm side of next row, then dec 1 st at same edge every other row 8 times—49 (52-56-59) sts. Work even until armhole measures 5″ (5½″-5½″-6″) above first armhole shaping row.

Shape Neck: Bind off 10 sts at center edge of next row. Dec 1 st at neck edge every row 9 (10-12-13) times—30 (32-34-36) sts. Work even if necessary until armhole measures same as back.

Shape Shoulder: Bind off 8 sts at arm side every row 3 times, 6 (8-10-12) sts once. End off.

RIGHT FRONT: Work same as for left front; pat is reversible.

SLEEVES: Beg at lower edge, with MC, ch 62 (66-68-72). Work in pat on 61 (65-67-71) sts for 2″. Check gauge; piece should measure 8¾″ (9¼″-9½″-10″) wide. Inc 1 st each side of next row, then every 1″ 10 times, working added sts into pat—83 (87-89-93) sts. Work even until piece measures 16″ (16½″-16½″-17″) from start or desired length to underarm.

Shape Cap: Bind off 6 (7-7-8) sts each side of next row. Dec 1 st each side every other row 17 (18-18-19) times, every row 12 times—13 (13-15-15) sts. End off.

POCKETS (make 2): Beg at lower edge, with MC, ch 32. Work in pat on 31 sts for 4½″; do not end off. Work 1 rnd sc around outer edge of pocket, working 3 sc in each corner. Join with a sl st in first sc. End off.

COLLAR: Beg at neck edge, with MC, ch 102 (106-110-114). Work in pat on 101 (105-109-113) sts for 1½″. End off.

FINISHING: Steam-press pieces lightly. Using crocheted pieces for patterns, cut lining for back, fronts and sleeves allowing for waistline darts on back and fronts, bustline darts on fronts, and ½″ on all edges for seams and hems. Stitch darts. Sew side and shoulder seams of lining; sew side and sleeve seams.

Sew shoulder seams; sew in sleeves. Sew side and sleeve seams. Sew collar to back and front neck edges.

Left Front Border: From wrong side, beg at lower edge, with MC, work 101 sc up left front edge, end 4½″ below collar seam. **(Left-handed crocheters:** Start 4½″ below collar seam, work to lower edge.) Ch 1, turn.

Row 2: * Sc in each of next 2 sc, sk next 3 sc, work scallops of 8 dc in next sc, sk next 3 sc, repeat from * across, end sk next 3 sc, sc in each of last 2 sc—11 scallops. Cut MC; join A. With A, ch 1, turn.

Row 3: With A, * sc in sp between the 2 sc, sc in each of first 3 dc, 2 sc in each of next 2 dc, sc in each of next 3 dc, repeat from * across, end sc between last 2 sc. Cut A; join B. With B, ch 1, turn.

Row 4: With B, * sk next sc, sc in each of next 3 sc, 2 sc in next sc, sc in each of next 2 sc, 2 sc in next sc, sc in each of next 3 sc, repeat from * across, end sc in last sc. Cut B; do not turn. Join C at beg of row 4.

Row 5: With C, * sc in sc on row 3, sl st in next 12 sc on row 4, repeat from * across, end sc in sc on row 3. End off.

Right Front Border: From right side, beg at lower right front edge, with MC, work 101 sc up right front edge, end 4½″ below collar seam. **(Left-handed crocheters:** Start 4½″ below collar seam, work to lower edge.) Ch 1, turn.

Row 2 (buttonhole row): With MC, sc in each of next 4 sc, * ch 4, sk next 3 sc (buttonhole), sc in each of next 6 sc, repeat from * across, end ch 4, sk next 3 sc, sc in each of last 4 sc—11 buttonholes. Ch 1, turn.

Row 3: With MC, sc in each of first 2 sc, * sk next 2 sc, work a scallop of 8 dc in ch-4 sp, sk next 2 sc, sc in each of next 2 sc, repeat from * across, end sk next 2 sc, sc in last 2 sc. Cut MC; join A. With A, ch 1, turn. Repeat rows 3-5 on left front border. End off.

Lapel and Collar Border: From right side, join MC in sc on row 1 of right front border **(left-handed crocheters:** left front border); work 40 sc to corner of collar, 3 sc in collar corner, 87 sc across outer edge of collar, 3 sc in collar corner, 40 sc down front lapel, end last sc in sc on row 1 of front border—173 sc. Ch 1, turn. Work rows 2-5 same as for left front border—19 scallops. End off.

Pocket Border: With MC, work 29 sc evenly spaced across top of pocket. Work rows 2-5 same as for left front border—3 scallops. Work same border on other pocket. Sew a pocket to each front, 2½″ above lower edge, 3½″ in from front edge.

Sleeve Border: With thread, baste a line up center of sleeve for about 4½″ up from lower edge. Beg at top of basting line on left sleeve (**left-handed crocheters:** on right sleeve), work 28 sc down basting line; working on wrong side, work 55 sc around lower edge of sleeve—83 sc. Ch 1, turn. Work rows 2-5 same as for left front border on 9 scallops. End off. From wrong side, beg at lower edge of basting line on right sleeve (**left-handed crochet-ers:** on left sleeve), work 58 sc around lower edge, 28 sc up basting line. Ch 1, turn. Complete same as for left sleeve.

With MC, work 1 row sc around lower edge of jacket. Insert lining; sew in place. Sew 3 buttons in center of each sleeve scallop; remove basting line. Sew 11 buttons on left front edge.

LACY CLASSIC

Shown on page 98

A classic cardigan and skirt become a costume for special occasions with rich and airy lace forming its pattern. Shells, clusters, and V stitches combine to make the spun-sugar effect of this white ensemble. Jacket has closing of little round crocheted buttons; skirt has drawstring waistline.

SIZES: Directions for small size (8-10). Changes for medium size (12-14) are in parentheses. **Note:** Needles and measurements determine size.

Body Bust Size: 31½″-32½″ (34″-36″).

Blocked Bust Size (closed): 35″ (36½″).

MATERIALS: Dress yarn of sport yarn weight, 7 2-oz. skeins each for jacket and skirt. Aluminum crochet hook size E for small size; size F for medium size. Thirteen round button molds.

GAUGE: Be sure to follow measurements given in instructions.

JACKET: BODY: Beg at lower edge of back and fronts, ch 130 to measure 34½″ (36″).

Row 1: Sc in 2nd ch from hook and in each ch across—129 sc. Turn each row.

Row 2: Ch 4 (counts as 1 dc), sk first sc, dc in next sc, sk next 2 sc, * shell of 2 dc, ch 1, 2 dc in next sc, ch 3, sk next 4 sc, dc, ch 5, dc all in next sc (V st), ch 3, sk next 4 sc, repeat from * across, end shell in next sc, sk next 2 sc, dc in each of last 2 sc.

Row 3: Ch 4 (counts as 1 dc), sk first dc, dc in next dc, * shell of 2 dc, ch 1, 2 dc in ch-1 sp of next shell, ch 3, cluster st in ch-5 sp (to make cluster st, yo hook twice, pull up a lp in ch-5 sp, yo hook and through 1 lp, yo hook and through 2 lps, yo hook, pull up a lp in same ch-5 sp, yo hook and through 1 lp, (yo hook and through 2 lps) twice, yo hook and through 3 lps on hook); work (ch 1, cluster st in same ch-5 sp) 4 times, ch 3, repeat from * across, end shell in ch-1 sp of last shell, dc in last dc, dc in top of turning ch.

Row 4: Ch 4 (counts as 1 dc), sk first dc, dc in next dc, * shell in ch-1 sp of next shell, ch 3, sc in ch-3 sp, (ch 2, sc in next ch-1 sp) 4 times, ch 2, sc in next ch-3 sp, ch 3, repeat from * across, end shell in ch-1 sp of last shell, dc in last dc and in top of turning ch.

Row 5: Ch 4 (counts as 1 dc), sk first dc, dc in next dc, * shell in ch-1 sp of next shell, ch 3, sk next ch-3 and ch-2 sps, work (cluster st, ch 1) in each of next 2 ch-2 sps, cluster st in next ch-2 sp, ch 3, sk next 2 sps, repeat from * across, end shell in ch-1 sp of last shell, dc in last dc and in top of turning ch.

Row 6: Ch 4 (counts as 1 dc), sk first dc, dc in next dc, * shell in ch-1 sp of next shell, (ch 3, sc in next sp) 4 times, ch 3, repeat from * across, end shell in ch-1 sp of last shell, dc in last dc and in top of turning ch.

Row 7: Ch 4 (counts as 1 dc), sk first dc, dc in next dc, * shell in ch-1 sp of next shell, (sk next ch-3 sp, shell in next ch-3 sp) twice, sk next ch-3 sp, repeat from * across, end shell in ch-1 sp of last shell, dc in last dc and in top of turning ch.

Row 8: Ch 4 (counts as 1 dc), sk first dc, dc in next dc, * shell in ch-1 sp of next shell, repeat from * across, end dc in last dc and top of turning ch.

Row 9: Ch 4 (counts as 1 dc), sk

LACY CLASSIC

first dc, dc in next dc, * shell in ch-1 sp of next shell, ch 3, V st of dc, ch 5, dc in sp between next 2 shells, ch 3, repeat from * across, end shell in ch-1 sp of last shell, dc in last dc and in top of turning ch. Check gauge; piece should measure 34″ (35½″) wide. Repeat rows 3-9 for pat 3 times. Repeat pat rows 3-7. Check gauge; piece should measure about 15″ (16″) from start.

Divide Work: Right Front Yoke: Working row 8 of pat, ch 4, sk next dc, dc in next dc, work 8 shell pats and 2 dc (½ shell) in ch-1 sp of next shell. Turn.

Next Row: Ch 4 (counts as 1 dc), sk first dc, dc in next dc, (shell in ch-1 sp of next shell) twice, * ch 3, V st between next 2 shells, ch 3, shell in ch-1 sp of next shell, repeat from * across, end dc in last dc and in top of turning ch. Work in pat as established, keeping 2 shell pats and 2 dc at armhole edge for 6 rows more, end pat row 8. End off.

Shape Neck: Beg at center edge, sk first 2 dc and 3½ shells; make lp on hook, work 1 dc in each of next 2 dc of 4th shell pat, work in pat across. Work even in pat for 5 (6) rows, end pat row 7 (8). Ch 1, turn.

Next Row: Sc in each st across. End off.

Back Yoke: Working on last long row, beg at right front armhole edge, sk ½ shell, 1 complete shell and ½ shell for right underarm, join yarn in ch-1 sp, ch 4 (counts as 1 dc), sk next dc, dc in next dc of ½ shell, work shell in ch-1 sp of next 15 shell pats, end dc in each of 2 dc of next shell. Turn. Work in pat, keeping 2 dc and 2 shell pats at each armhole edge. Work even until armhole measures same as right front armhole, end pat row 7 (8). Ch 1, turn.

Next Row: Sc in each st. End off.

Left Front Yoke: Working on last long row, beg at back armhole edge, sk ½ shell, 1 complete shell and ½ shell for left underarm, join yarn in ch-1 sp, ch 4 (counts as 1 dc), sk next dc, dc in next dc of ½ shell, work in pat across. Complete same as right front yoke, reversing shaping.

SLEEVES: Beg at lower edge, ch 40 loosely to measure 8½″ (9″).

Row 1: Sc in 2nd ch from hook and in each ch across—39 sc. Beg with pat row 2, work in pat, inc 1 dc each side (**to inc 1 dc,** work 2 dc in same st) every 2½″ 5 (6) times, working inc sts in dc—7 (8) dc each side. Work even until piece measures same as back to underarm, end pat row 7. Check gauge; piece should measure about 15″ (16″) from start. Ch 1, turn.

Shape Cap: Sl st across first 3 sts, work to within last 3 sts. Turn. Work 1 row even. Dec 1 st each side of next 2 (3) rows (**to dec 1 st,** yo hook, pull up a lp in each of 2 sts, yo hook and through 2 lps, yo hook and through 3 remaining lps)—2 dc each side. Work 1 row even.

Next Row: Ch 4 (counts as 1 dc), sk first 2 dc (dec), work in pat across, end sk 1 dc, dc in top of turning ch. Leave off a ½ shell each side of every row for 2 (1) rows, end pat row 8. Repeat shell pat row 1 (2) times, leaving off half a shell each side every row. End off.

FINISHING: Sew shoulder seams.

Edging: Work 2 rows dc around neck edge, holding in to desired fit. Work 1 row dc on each front edge, being careful to keep work flat and having same number of sts on each edge. Join yarn in lower left front edge; working from left to right, sc in each dc around fronts, neck and lower edge. (**Left-handed crocheters:** Join yarn in lower right front edge and work from right to left.) End off.

Sew sleeve seams; sew in sleeve, placing sleeve seam at center underarm.

Edging: From right side, work 1 rnd dc around lower edge of sleeve. Do not turn.

Next Rnd: From right side, working from left to right, sc in each dc around. (**Left-handed crocheters:** Work from right to left.) End off.

BUTTONS (make 11): Ch 3, work 6 sc in 2nd ch from hook.

Rnd 2: 2 sc in each sc around. Insert button mold or scraps of yarn.

Rnd 3: (Sk next sc, sc in next sc) 6 times. Cut yarn, leaving a 10″ end. Thread needle, draw sts tog.

Sew buttons on left front edge evenly spaced, first button 1″ above lower edge, last button ½″ below neck edge. Spaces between dc on right front edge form buttonholes. Steam very lightly; do not press.

SKIRT: Beg at upper edge of back and front, ch 131 loosely to measure 34″ (35½″).

Row 1: Sc in 2nd ch from hook and in each ch across—130 sc. Join with a sl st to form a ring, being careful not to twist row.

Rnd 1: Ch 4 (counts as 1 dc), dc in first sc (½ shell), * ch 3, sk next 4 sc, dc, ch 5, dc all in next sc (V st made), ch 3, sk next 4 sc, shell of 2 dc, ch 1, 2 dc in next sc, repeat from * around, end sk next 4 sc, 2 dc in joining st, ch 1, join with a sl st to top of starting ch. Do not turn each rnd.

Rnd 2: Ch 4, dc in ch-1 sp before joining (½ shell), * ch 3, (cluster st, ch 1) 4 times in ch-5 sp of V st, cluster st in same ch-5 sp, ch 3, shell of 2 dc, ch 1, 2 dc in ch-1 sp of next shell, repeat from * around, end ½ shell of 2 dc in ch-1 sp between ½ shells, ch 1, join with a sl st to top of starting ch.

Rnd 3: Half shell of ch 4, dc in ch-1 sp before joining, * ch 3, sc in next sp, (ch 2, sc in next sp) 5 times, ch 3, shell in ch-1 sp of next shell, repeat from * around, end ½ shell of 2 dc in ch-1 sp between ½ shells, ch 1, join with a sl st to top of starting ch.

Rnd 4: Half shell of ch 4, dc in ch-1 sp before joining, * ch 3, sk 2 sps, (cluster st in next sp, ch 2) twice, cluster st in next sp, ch 3, sk 2 sps, shell in ch-1 sp of next shell, repeat from * around, end ½ shell of 2 dc in ch-1 sp between ½ shells, ch 1, join with a sl st to top of starting ch.

Rnd 5: Half shell of ch 4, dc in ch-1 sp before joining, * (ch 3, sc in next sp) 4 times, ch 3, shell in ch-1 sp of next shell, repeat from * around, end ½ shell of 2 dc in ch-1 sp between ½ shells, ch 1, join with a sl st to top of starting ch.

Rnd 6: Half shell of ch 4, dc in ch-1 sp before joining, * (sk next sp, shell in next sp) twice, sk next sp, shell in ch-1 sp of next shell, repeat from * around, end ½ shell of 2 dc in ch-1 sp between ½ shells, ch 1, join with a sl st to top of starting ch.

Rnd 7: Half shell of ch 4, dc in ch-1 sp before joining, * shell in ch-1 sp of next shell, repeat from * around, end ½ shell of 2 dc in ch-1 sp between ½ shells, ch 1, join with a sl st to top of starting ch.

Rnd 8: Half shell of ch 4, dc in ch-1 sp before joining, * ch 3, V st of dc, ch 5, dc in sp between next 2 shell pats, ch 3, shell in ch-1 sp of next shell, repeat from * around, end ½ shell of 2 dc in ch-1 sp between ½ shells, ch 1, join with a sl st to top of starting ch. Repeat rnds 2-8 for pat. Work even until 11 rnds of pat have been completed, end pat rnd 4.

Next Rnd (inc rnd): Work pat rnd 5, work ½ shell of ch 4, 2 dc in ch-1 sp before joining, and shell of 3 dc, ch 1, 3 dc for shell in each ch-1 sp of shell, ending ½ shell of 3 dc in ch-1 sp between ½ shells, ch 1, join with a sl st to top of starting ch. Continue in pat as established, working shell of 3 dc, ch 1, 3 dc instead of 2 dc, ch 1, 2 dc where established and shell of 2 dc, ch 1, 2 dc for all other shell pats, for 16 rnds, end pat rnd 7.

Next Rnd (inc rnd): Work pat rnd 8, working shell of 4 dc, ch 1, 4 dc for shell in each ch-1 sp of

shell and ½ shell of 4 dc at beg and end of rnd. Continue in pat as established, working shell of 4 dc, ch 1, 4 dc instead of 3 dc, ch 1, 3 dc where established and shell of 2 dc, ch 1, 2 dc for all other pats for 13 rnds, end pat rnd 7. Repeat last rnd once. Check gauge; piece should measure about 21″ in length. If longer skirt is desired, repeat last rnd for desired length.

Next Rnd: Working from left to right, from right side, sc in each st

around. End off. **(Left-handed crocheters:** Work from right to left.)

FINISHING: Work 1 rnd dc around upper edge. Join with a sl st in first dc. End off.

DRAWSTRING: With double strand of yarn, make ch 52″ long. Crochet 2 buttons as for jacket. Draw string through rnd of dc at waistline. Sew a button to each end of string. Steam very lightly.

"WOVEN" COAT

A slim button-free coat is crocheted in a pattern that looks woven. Sleeves are set in; rib stitch pockets are sewn on.

SIZES: Directions for size 10. Changes for sizes 12, 14 and 16 are in parentheses.

Body Bust Size: 32½″ (34″-36″-38″).

Blocked Bust Size: 34″ (36″-38⅔″-41⅓″).

MATERIALS: Knitting worsted, 9 (9-10-11) 4-oz. skeins. Crochet hook size I.

GAUGE: 3 sts = 1″; 3 rows = 2″.

To Bind Off: At beg of a row, sl st loosely across specified sts plus 1, ch 3, work in pat across; **at end of a row,** leave specified number of sts unworked.

To Dec 1 St: At beg of a row, ch 3, sk first 2 sts, work in pat across; **at end of a row,** work to within last 2 sts, sk next st, dc in top of turning ch.

COAT: BACK: Beg at lower edge, ch 70 (74-78-82) loosely.

Row 1: Dc in 4th ch from hook and in each ch across—68 (72-76-80) dc counting turning ch as 1 dc. Turn.

Row 2: Ch 3 (counts as 1 dc), sk first dc, * front raised dc in each of

next 2 sts (**to make front raised dc,** dc around upright bar of dc, inserting hook from front to back to front), back raised dc in each of next 2 sts (**to make back raised dc,** dc around upright bar of dc, inserting hook from back to front to back), repeat from * across, end front raised dc in each of next 2 dc, dc in last dc. Turn. Repeat row 2 for pat until piece measures 3″ from start. Check gauge; piece should measure 22⅔″ (24″-25⅓″-26⅔″) wide. Keeping to pat, dec 1 st each side (see To Dec 1 St) of next row, then every 3″ 7 (8-8-8) times more—52 (54-58-62) sts. Work even until piece measures 33″ from start or desired length to underarm.

Shape Armholes: Bind off (see To Bind Off) 3 sts each side of next row. Dec 1 st each side every row 3 (3-4-5) times—40 (42-44-46) sts. Keeping to pat, work even until armholes measure 7½″ (7½″-8″-8½″) above first row of armhole shaping. Ch 1, turn.

Shape Shoulders: Row 1: Sc in

each of 4 (4-5-6) sts, work in pat to within last 4 (4-5-6) sts, sc in each st across. Ch 1, turn.

Row 2: Sl st loosely in each of 4 (4-5-6) sc, sc in each of next 4 dc, work in pat to within last 4 dc, sc in each of last 4 dc. Ch 1, turn.

Row 3: Sl st loosely in each of next 4 sc, sc in each of next 4 dc, work in pat to within last 4 dc, sc in each of last 4 dc—16 (18-18-18) dc for back of neck. End off.

LEFT FRONT: Beg at lower edge, ch 34 (38-38-42) loosely. Mark beg of first row for side edge. **(Left-handed crocheters:** Mark end of first row for side edge.) Work in pat on 32 (36-36-40) sts for 3″. Check gauge; piece should measure 10⅔″ (12″-12″-13⅓″) wide. Dec 1 st at side edge of next row, then every 3″ 6 (8-6-8) times more—25 (27-29-31) sts. Work even until piece measures same as back to underarm.

Shape Neck and Armhole: Dec 1 st at center edge of next row, then dec 1 st at same edge every other row 6 (8-8-8) times more; **at**

the same time, bind off 3 sts at arm side of next row, then dec 1 st at same edge every row 3 (3-4-5) times—12 (12-13-14) sts. Work even until armhole measures same as back, end arm side.

Shape Shoulder: Row 1: Sc in each of 4 (4-5-6) sts, work in pat across.

Row 2: Work in pat to within last 4 dc, sc in each of next 4 dc. Ch 1, turn.

Row 3: Sl st in each of 4 sc, sc in each of next 4 dc. End off.

RIGHT FRONT: Work same as for left front; pat is reversible.

SLEEVE: Beg at lower edge, ch 30 (30-34-34) loosely. Work in pat on 28 (28-32-32) sts for 2". Inc 1 st (**to inc 1 st,** work 2 dc in same st) each side of next row, then every 3" 3 (4-4-5) times more, working added sts into pat—36 (38-42-44) sts. Work even until piece measures 17" (17"-18"-18") from start or desired length to underarm. Check gauge; piece above last inc row should measure 12" (12⅔"-14"-14⅔") wide.

Shape Cap: Bind off 2 sts each side of next row. Dec 1 st each side every row 7 (8-9-10) times. Bind off 2 sts each side of next row—14 (14-16-16) dc. End off.

POCKETS (make 2): Beg at side edge, ch 21 loosely.

Row 1: Sc in 2nd ch from hook and in each ch across—20 sc. Ch 1, turn.

Row 2: Sc in back lp of each sc across—20 sc. Ch 1, turn. Repeat row 2 until 24 rows (12 ridges) from start. Do not end off; working across side edge (top of pocket) sc across. End off.

FINISHING: Block pieces; do not flatten pattern. With backstitch, sew shoulder seams; sew in sleeves. Sew side and sleeve seams.

Edging: Row 1: From right side, beg at lower front corner, sc up front edge, across back of neck, down other front edge, end at

lower front corner. Ch 1, turn each row.

Row 2: Sc in back lp of each sc.

Rows 3 and 4: Repeat row 2. End off.

Row 5: From wrong side, beg in first sc of row 4, sl st in front lp of each sc around. End off. From right side, work 1 row sc across lower edge of fronts and back.

Work sleeve edge in same manner as front edging. Sew pockets to each front edge, placing pocket 6 sts in from front edge, about 13″ above lower edge.

TWEEDED COAT SET

A classic coat is crocheted with two yarns, mohair and fingering yarn, in a simple two-stitch pattern. Lapels are part of coat front; separate collar and patch pockets are sewn on. A rolled-brim hat completes the set.

SIZES: Directions for small size (8-10). Changes for medium size (12-14) are in parentheses.

Body Bust Size: 31½″-32½″ (34″-36″).

Blocked Bust (closed): 36″ (40″).

MATERIALS: Mohair, 25 (26) 40-gram balls cream (A). Fingering yarn, 14 (15) 1-oz. balls scarlet (B). Aluminum crochet hooks sizes G/5 and J/9. Four buttons. Four yds. lining material. Matching sewing thread.

GAUGE: Coat: 8 sts = 3″; 2 rows = 1″ (pat, size J hook). Hat: 3 sc = 1″.

Length Note: Directions are for coat 30″ (32″) from lower edge to underarm. For longer or shorter coat, add or subtract desired number of inches before first dec row. More yarn may be needed for longer coat.

Note: Work coat with 1 strand of A and B held together throughout.

To Bind Off: At beg of a row, sl st loosely across specified number of pats, ch 2, work in pat across; **at end of a row,** leave specified pats unworked, sc in next st.

To Dec 1 Pat: At beg of a row, sl st loosely across 1 pat, ch 2, work in pat across; **at end of a row,** leave 1 pat unworked, sc in next st.

To Inc 1 Pat: At beg of a row, ch 2, (dc, sc) in each of first 2 sc, work in pat across; **at end of a row,** work (dc, 2 sc) in top of turning ch.

COAT: RIGHT BACK: Beg at lower edge with 2 strands of yarn (see Note) and size J hook, ch 52 (55).

Row 1: Work (dc, sc) in 3rd ch from hook (pat made), * sk next 2 ch, (dc, sc) in next ch, repeat from * across, end sc in last ch—17 (18) pats plus sc at end of row. Mark end of row for side edge. Ch 2, turn.

Row 2: Sk first sc, * (dc, sc) in next sc, sk next dc, repeat from * across, end sk dc, work sc in top of turning ch. Ch 2, turn. Repeat row 2 for pat until piece measures 7″ from start, end side edge. Check gauge; piece should measure 12¾″ (13½″) wide. Dec 1 pat at beg of next row (see To Dec 1 Pat)—16 (17) pats. Work even until piece measures 14″ from start. Dec 1 pat at side edge of next row—15 (16) pats. Work even for 2″. Dec 1 pat at side edge of next row—14 (15) pats. Work even until piece measures 25″ (27″) from start or 5″ less than desired length to underarm, end side edge. Inc 1 pat (see To Inc 1 Pat) at beg of next row. Work 3 rows even. Inc 1 pat at beg of next row—16 (17) pats. Work even until piece measures 30″ (32″)

from start or desired length to underarm, end side edge.

Shape Armhole: Bind off (see To Bind Off) 2 pats at beg of next row. Dec 1 pat at same edge every other row 4 times—10 (11) pats. Work even until armhole measures 8″ (9″) above first bound-off sts.

Shape Shoulder: Bind off 1 pat at arm side every row 6 times —4 (5) pats. End off.

LEFT BACK: Work same as for right back; pat is reversible.

LEFT FRONT: Beg at lower edge, with 2 strands of yarn and size J hook, ch 55 (58). Work same as for right back, having 1 pat more until armhole measures 5″ (6″) above first bound-off sts—11 (12) pats.

Shape Neck: Bind off 5 (6) pats at center edge of next row—6 pats. Work even until armhole measures 8″ (9″) above first bound-off sts.

Shape Shoulder: Bind off 2 pats at arm side every row twice—2 pats. End off.

With pins, mark position of 4 buttons evenly spaced on left center front edge; first button 17″ above lower edge, last button 5″ below neck edge.

BUTTONHOLES: Beg at center edge, ch 2, sk first sc, dc in next

sc, ch 3, sk next 3 sts, (dc, sc) in next sc, work in pat across. **Next Row:** Work in pat across, end pat of (dc, sc) in sc before ch-3 sp, dc in first ch, sc in next ch, dc in next ch, sc in dc, sc in top of turning ch. Ch 2, turn.

RIGHT FRONT: Work same as for left front, forming buttonholes (see Buttonholes) opposite markers.

SLEEVES: Beg at lower edge, with 2 strands of yarn and size J hook, ch 49 (55). Work in pat as for back on 16 (18) pats for 6″. Check gauge; piece should measure 12″ (13½″) wide. Inc 1 pat each side of next row, then every 6″ once more—20 (22) pats. Work even until piece measures 18″ (19″) from start or desired length to underarm.

Shape Cap: Bind off 2 pats each side of next row. Dec 1 pat each side every other row 6 (7) times—4 pats. End off.

POCKETS (make 2): Beg at lower edge, with 2 strands of yarn and size J hook, ch 31 (34). Work in pat as for back on 10 (11) pats for 10″. End off.

COLLAR: Beg at neck edge, with 2 strands of yarn and size J hook, ch 64 (70). Work in pat as for back, inc 1 pat each side every other row 5 times—31 (33) pats. End off.

FINISHING: Block pieces. Using crocheted pieces for pattern, cut lining to fit backs, fronts and sleeves, allowing for 1″ pleat at center back, 1″ for ½″ darts at back waistline, front waistline and bust, ½″ on all edges. Put aside.

Baste shoulders and side seams; try on coat. Adjust seams. With backstitch or machine stitch, sew shoulder seams; sew in sleeves. Sew back, side and sleeve seams. From right side, beg at top of lapel, 5 (6) pats in from center front edge, with 2 strands of yarn and size J hook, working over sts of top row, work in sc across lapel sts, work 3 sc in corner; working over edge st of each row, sc down front, 3 sc in lower corner; working over bottom row, sc across lower edge of coat, 3 sc in lower front corner; up other front edge, 3 sc in upper corner; sc across 5 (6) pats on front lapel. End off. From right side, working over first row, work 1 row sc around each sleeve edge. Fold 2″ at top of pocket to right side for cuff. Line pocket; sew in place, placing pocket 1 pat in from side edge, top edge of pocket 9″ below armhole.

Sew lining; adjust seams. Pin lining to body of coat; tack at seams. Turning in raw edges, sew lining in place inside of edging. Fold lapels to right side; do not line lapels. Slit lining under button-holes; hem lining around button-holes. Work buttonhole stitch around buttonholes. With 2 strands of yarn, work 1 row sc around side and outer edges of collar, working over 1 row or stitch. Sew starting ch of collar to neck edge of coat about 4″ in from front edges. Sew on buttons.

HAT: Beg at top center, with 2 strands of yarn and size G hook, ch 3.

Rnd 1: 8 sc in 3rd ch from hook. Do not join rnds; mark end of each rnd.

Rnd 2: 2 sc in each sc around—16 sc.

Rnd 3: (Sc in next sc, 2 sc in next sc) 8 times—24 sc.

Rnd 4: (Sc in each of next 2 sc, 2 sc in next sc) 8 times—32 sc.

Rnd 5: (Sc in each of next 7 sc, 2 sc in next sc) 4 times—36 sc.

Rnd 6: (Sc in each of next 5 sc, 2 sc in next sc) 6 times—42 sc.

Rnd 7: (Sc in each of next 6 sc, 2 sc in next sc) 6 times—48 sc.

Rnds 8-11: Inc 4 sc evenly spaced every rnd—64 sc. Work even until piece measures 6″ from center top. Change to size J hook.

Brim: Next Rnd: Dc in next sc, ch 1, dc in same sc (V st made), * sk next sc, V st of (dc, ch 1, dc) in next sc, repeat from * around—32 V sts.

Next Rnd: V st of (dc, ch 1, dc) in ch-1 sp of each V st around. Repeat last rnd 3 times.

Next Rnd: Sc in each dc around; join with a sl st in first sc. End off.

Roll brim to right side.

QUICK PONCHO

A cozy "afghan" poncho is easy to make in double crochet. Two "granny" squares are made for front and back; the V neck is created by adding more rows on two sides of one square.

SIZE: 30″ long at center back and front, plus fringe.

MATERIALS: Bulky yarn, 1 100-gram (3.6 ozs.) skein each of natural (A), light oxford (B), dark oxford (C), brown heather (D), heather white (E) and charcoal brown (F). Fingering yarn or other fine yarn, 4 ozs. brown or gray heather, for fringe. Aluminum crochet hook size J.

GAUGE: 16 sts (4 groups of 3 dc, ch 1) = 6″; 6 rows = 5″.

PONCHO: FRONT: Beg at center of square, with A, ch 3, work 2 dc in 3rd ch from hook (counts as 3 dc), ch 2, * 3 dc in same ch, ch 2, repeat from * twice, join with a sl st in top of starting ch—4 groups of 3 dc.

Rnd 2: Ch 3, 2 dc in joining sl st (½ corner), ch 1, * 3 dc, ch 2, 3 dc in next sp (corner), ch 1, repeat from * twice, ½ corner of 3 dc in last sp, ch 2, sl st in top of starting ch 3—8 groups of 3 dc (4 corners).

Rnd 3: Ch 3, 2 dc in joining sl st, ch 1 (½ corner), * 3 dc in next ch-1 sp, ch 1, corner of 3 dc, ch 2, 3 dc in next corner sp, ch 1, repeat from * twice, 3 dc in next ch-1 sp, ch 1, ½ corner of 3 dc in last sp, ch 2, sl st in top of starting ch 3. End off.

Rnd 4: With B, make lp on hook, work ½ corner of 3 dc in any corner sp, ch 1, * 3 dc in next ch-1 sp, ch 1, repeat from * to corner sp, work corner of 3 dc, ch 2, 3 dc in corner sp, ch 1, repeat from first * twice, work 3 dc, ch 1 in each ch-1 sp to next corner sp, work ½ corner of 3 dc, ch 2, join with sl st in top of first st.

Rnd 5: Ch 3, 2 dc in joining sl st

(½ corner), ch 1, work from first * on rnd 4. End off.

Rnd 6: With C, repeat rnd 4. End off.

Rnd 7: With D, repeat rnd 4.

Rnd 8: With D, repeat rnd 5; do not end off.

Rnd 9: With D, repeat rnd 5.

Rnds 10 and 11: With E, repeat rnds 4 and 5.

Rnds 12 and 13: With F, repeat rnds 4 and 5.

Rnd 14: With C, repeat rnd 4. End off.

BACK: Work same as for front; do not end off at end of rnd 14.

Side Panel: Row 1: With C, ch 3 (counts as 1 dc), work 2 dc in sl st, ch 1, * 3 dc in next ch-1 sp, ch 1, repeat from * to next corner, work 3 dc in corner sp—15 3-dc groups. Cut C; join A. Turn.

Row 2: With A, ch 3, * 3 dc in next ch-1 sp, ch 1, repeat from * across, end last repeat ch 1, dc in last dc—14 3-dc groups. Turn.

Row 3: Ch 3 (counts as 1 dc), 2 dc in first ch-1 sp, ch 1, * 3 dc in next ch-1 sp, ch 1, repeat from * across, end 3 dc in turning ch—15 3-dc groups. Cut A; join D, turn. Repeating rows 2 and 3 alternately, work 1 row D, 2 rows B, 1 row F, 2 rows B, 1 row C, 2 rows A, 1 row D, 2 rows B, 1 row E. End off.

2nd Side Panel: Join C in same corner of rnd 14 with end of row 1 of side panel. Work another side panel same as for first side panel, making 13th row F instead of D.

FINISHING: Run in all yarn ends on wrong side. Weave side panels to corresponding sides of front square, leaving two lower sides free. From right side, with E, work 1 row sc around neck edge.

FRINGE: Cut fine yarn into 12" strands. Using 20 to 25 strands for each fringe, knot fringe in each sp around lower edge of poncho. Trim ends of fringe evenly.

FAN-PATTERN SHAWL

Shown at right on page 107

Delicate fans and mesh borders of a graceful openwork wrap are of double crochet and chain stitch. Finished size is 33" deep, then add a generous fringe. In knitting and crochet cotton.

SIZE: 56″ wide; 33″ deep at center back, plus fringe.

MATERIALS: About 1,400 yds. of mercerized knitting and crochet cotton. Steel crochet hook No. 1.

GAUGE: 3 meshes (ch 2, dc) = 1″.

SHAWL: Beg at lower center back, ch 19.

Row 1: Dc in 7th ch from hook, (ch 2, sk next 2 ch, dc in next ch) 4 times. Ch 5, turn each row.

Row 2: (Dc, ch 2, dc) in first ch-2 sp, (ch 2, dc in next ch-2 sp) 3 times, ch 2, (dc, ch 2, dc) in last sp—7 dc.

Row 3: (Dc, ch 2, dc) in first ch-2 sp, * ch 2, dc in next ch-2 sp, repeat from * across, end ch 2, (dc, ch 2, dc) in last ch-2 sp (do not work in turning ch)—8 dc.

Rows 4-9: Repeat row 3—14 dc.

Row 10: * (Dc, ch 2, dc) in first ch-2 sp, (ch 2, dc in next ch-2 sp) 5 times, ch 2 *, 5 dc in next ch-2 sp, ch 2, # (dc in next ch-2 sp, ch 2) 5 times, (dc, ch 2, dc) in last ch-2 sp #.

Row 11: Work from first * to 2nd * on row 10, dc in next ch-2 sp, dc in each of next 5 dc, dc in next ch-2 sp, ch 2, work from first # to 2nd # on row 10.

Row 12: Work from first * to 2nd * on row 10, dc in next ch-2 sp, dc in each of next 7 dc, dc in next ch-2 sp, ch 2, work from first # to 2nd # on row 10.

Row 13: Work from first * to 2nd * on row 10, 5 dc in next sp, ch 4, sk next 3 dc, sc in next dc, ch 4, sk next dc, sc in next dc, ch 4, 5 dc in next sp, ch 2, work from first # to 2nd # on row 10.

Row 14: Work from first * to 2nd * on row 10, dc in next sp, dc in each of next 5 dc, dc in next sp, ch 4, sc in next sp, ch 4, dc in next sp, dc in each of next 5 dc, dc in next sp, ch 2, work from first # to 2nd # on row 10.

Row 15: Work from first * to 2nd * on row 10, (dc in next sp, dc in each of next 7 dc, dc in next sp, ch 2) twice, work from first # to 2nd # on row 10.

Row 16: Work from first * to 2nd * on row 10, (5 dc in next sp, ch 4, sk next 3 dc, sc in next dc, ch 4, sk next dc, sc in next dc, ch 4) twice, 5 dc in next sp, ch 2, work from first # to 2nd # on row 10.

Row 17: Work from first * to 2nd * on row 10, (dc in next sp, dc in each of next 5 dc, dc in next sp, ch 4, sc in next sp, ch 4) twice, dc in next sp, dc in each of next 5 dc, dc in next sp, ch 2, work from first # to 2nd # on row 10.

Row 18: Work from first * to 2nd * on row 10, (dc in next sp, dc in each of next 7 dc, dc in next sp, ch 2) 3 times, work from first # to 2nd # on row 10—3 pats.

Rows 19-99: Repeat rows 16-18 having 1 more pat every 3 rows. Ch 1, turn at end of last row.

Row 100: Sc in each st across. End off.

FINISHING: Steam lightly.

FRINGE: Wind yarn around 8″ cardboard. Cut one end. With 8 strands tog, fold strands in half, pull lp through ch-5 turning ch, pull end through lp; tighten knot. Knot a fringe in each turning ch on sides of shawl. Trim ends evenly.

SPIDER-WEB SHAWL

Shown at left on page 107

A lacy spider-web shawl drapes gently over cool shoulders for just the right amount of summer cover. The triangle is made in one piece from bottom point to 56"-wide top. Of knitting and crochet cotton.

SIZE: 56″ wide; 28″ deep at center back, plus fringe.

MATERIALS: About 1,200 yds. of mercerized knitting and crochet cotton. Steel crochet hook No. 1.

GAUGE: 3 meshes (ch 2, dc) = 1″.

SHAWL: Beg at lower center back, ch 10; join with a sl st to form ring.

Row 1: Ch 5, dc in ring, (ch 2,

dc in ring) 9 times. Ch 5, turn each row.

Row 2: (Dc, ch 2, dc) in first ch-2 sp,. * (ch 2, dc in next ch-2 sp) 3 times, (ch 2, dc) twice in next ch-2 sp, repeat from * once—12 dc, plus turning ch.

Row 3: (Dc, ch 2, dc) in first ch-2 sp, ch 2, dc in next ch-2 sp, (ch 2, dc) twice in next ch-2 sp, ch 2, dc in next ch-2 sp, ch 2, 3 dc in next ch-2 sp, ch 3, dc in next ch-2 sp, ch 3, 3 dc in next ch-2 sp, ch 2, dc in next ch-2 sp, (ch 2, dc) twice in next ch-2 sp, ch 2, dc in next ch-2 sp, (ch 2, dc) twice in next ch-2 sp.

Row 4: * (Dc, ch 2, dc) in first ch-2 sp, (ch 2, dc in next ch-2 sp) 4 times, ch 2, 2 dc in next ch-2 sp, dc in dc *, ch 3, sc in next ch-3 sp, sc in dc, sc in next ch-3 sp, ch 3, sk next 2 dc, # dc in next dc, 2 dc in ch-2 sp, (ch 2, dc in next ch-2 sp) 4 times, (ch 2, dc) twice in next ch-2 sp #.

Row 5: Work from first * to 2nd * on row 4, ch 3, sc in next ch-3 sp, sc in each of next 3 sc, sc in next ch-3 sp, ch 3, sk next 2 dc, work from first # to 2nd # on row 4.

Row 6: Work from first * to 2nd * on row 4, ch 2, sk next dc, dc in next dc, 2 dc in next sp, ch 3, sk next sc, sc in each of next 3 sc, ch 3, 2 dc in next sp, dc in next dc, ch 2, sk next dc, work from first # to 2nd # on row 4.

Row 7: Work from first * to 2nd * on row 4, ch 3, dc in next ch-2 sp, ch 3, sk next 2 dc, dc in next dc, 2 dc in next ch-3 sp, ch 3, sk next sc, dc in next sc, ch 3, 2 dc in next ch-3 sp, dc in next dc, ch 3, dc in next ch-2 sp, ch 2, sk next 2 dc, work from first # to 2nd # on row 4.

Row 8: Work from first * to 2nd * on row 4, ch 3, sc in next sp, sc in dc, sc in next sp, ch 3, sk next 2 dc, dc in next dc, 2 dc in next sp, ch 2, 2 dc in next sp, dc in first dc, ch 3, sc in next sp, sc in dc, sc in next sp, ch 3, sk next 2 dc, work from first # to 2nd # on row 4.

Row 9: Work from first * to 2nd * on row 4, ch 3, sc in next sp, sc in each of next 3 sc, sc in next sp, ch 3, sk next 2 dc, dc in next dc, dc in sp, dc in next dc, ch 3, sc in next sp, sc in each of next 3 sc, sc in next sp, ch 3, sk next 2 dc, work from first # to 2nd # on row 4.

Row 10: Work from first * to 2nd * on row 4, (ch 3, sk next dc, dc in next dc, 2 dc in sp, ch 3, sk next sc, sc in each of next 3 sc, ch 3, 2 dc in next sp, dc in first dc) twice, ch 2, sk next dc, work from first # to 2nd # on row 4.

Row 11: Work from first * to 2nd * on row 4, (ch 3, dc in next sp, ch 3, sk next 2 dc, dc in next dc, 2 dc in sp, ch 3, sk next sc, dc in next sc, ch 3, 2 dc in next sp, dc in next dc) twice, ch 3, dc in next sp, ch 3, sk next 2 dc, work from first # to 2nd # on row 4.

Row 12: Work from first * to 2nd * on row 4, (ch 3, sc in next sp, sc in next dc, sc in next sp, ch 3, sk next 2 dc, dc in next dc, 2 dc in next sp, ch 2, 2 dc in next sp, dc in next dc) twice, ch 3, sc in next sp, sc in next dc, sc in next sp, ch 3, sk next 2 dc, work from first # to 2nd # on row 4.

Row 13: Work from first * to 2nd * on row 4, (ch 3, sc in next sp, sc in each of next 3 sc, sc in next sp, ch 3, sk next 2 dc, dc in next dc, dc in next sp, dc in next dc) twice, ch 3, sc in next sp, sc in each of next 3 sc, sc in next sp, ch 3, sk next 2 dc, work from first # to 2nd # on row 4.

Row 14: Work from first * to 2nd * on row 4, (ch 2, sk next dc, dc in next dc, 2 dc in next sp, ch 3, sk next sc, sc in each of next 3 sc, ch 3, 2 dc in next sp, dc in next dc) 3 times, ch 2, sk next dc, work from first # to 2nd # on row 4.

Row 15: Work from first * to 2nd * on row 4, (ch 3, dc in next sp, ch 3, sk next 2 dc, dc in next dc, 2 dc in sp, ch 3, sk next sc, dc in next sc, ch 3, 2 dc in next sp, dc in next dc) 3 times, ch 3, dc in next sp, ch 3, sk next 2 dc, work from first # to 2nd # on row 4—3 pats.

Rows 16-101: Repeat rows 12-15 having 1 more pat every 4 rows—25 pats. Ch 1, turn at end of last row.

Row 102: Sc in each st across. End off.

FINISHING: Steam lightly.

FRINGE: Wind yarn around 9″ cardboard. Cut one end. With 7 strands tog, fold strands in half, pull lp through ch-5 turning ch, pull end through lp; tighten knot. Knot a fringe in each turning ch on sides of shawl. Trim ends evenly.

LACY SHAWL

A circle in a square creates a pretty pattern for a shawl that is quick to make.
Each 5"-square motif is worked in chain loops and double crochet.
Size: 30" deep to point.

SIZE: 58" wide across top.

MATERIALS: Sport yarn, 4 2-oz. skeins. Crochet hook size H.

GAUGE: One motif = 5" square.

SHAWL: FIRST MOTIF: Ch 8; sl st in first ch to form ring.

Rnd 1: Ch 3, 23 dc in ring. Join with sl st in top of ch 3.

Rnd 2: Ch 4, dc in next dc, * ch 1, dc in next dc, repeat from * around, end ch 1, sl st in 3rd ch of ch 4.

Rnd 3: Sl st in next ch-1 sp, ch 7, dc in same sp, * ch 4, sk 3 dc, dc in next ch-1 sp, ch 4, dc in same sp, repeat from * around, end ch 4, sl st in 3rd ch of ch 7.

Rnd 4: Sl st in next ch-4 sp, ch 3, 2 dc in same sp, dc in dc, 4 dc in ch-4 sp, dc in dc, 3 dc in next ch-4 sp, * ch 9, sk next ch-4 sp, 3 dc in next sp, dc in dc, 4 dc in next sp, dc in dc, 3 dc in next sp, repeat from * twice, ch 9, sl st in top of ch 3. End off.

2ND MOTIF: Work as for first motif through rnd 3.

Rnd 4: Sl st in next ch-4 sp, ch 3, 2 dc in same sp, dc in dc, 2 dc in ch-4 sp; drop lp off hook; insert hook from front through 7th dc on one side of previous motif, pull lp through; 2 more dc in ch-4 sp, dc in dc, 3 dc in next ch-4 sp, * ch 4, drop lp off hook; insert hook through corner ch-9 lp of previous motif, pull lp through; ch 5, sk next ch-4 sp, 3 dc in next sp, dc in dc, 4 dc in next sp, dc in dc, 3 dc in next sp, repeat from * once, finish motif as for first motif, end ch 4, join to corresponding ch-9 lp of previous motif, ch 5, sl st in top of ch 3. End off.

Work and join motifs at corners and center of side as follows:

1st Row: 6 motifs.

2nd Row: 5 motifs. In working 2nd row of motifs, join first motif to first motif of first row, join 2nd motif to first motif of 2nd row and to 2nd motif of first row.

3rd Row: 4 motifs. Join to 2nd row.

4th Row: 3 motifs. Join to 3rd row.

5th Row: 2 motifs. Join to 4th row.

6th Row: 1 motif. Join to first motif of 5th row.

HALF MOTIF (used at top of shawl at ends of 2nd to 6th rows): Ch 8. Sl st in first ch to form ring.

Row 1: Ch 3, 10 dc in ring. Ch 4, turn.

Row 2: Sk first dc, dc in next dc, (ch 1, dc in next dc) 8 times, ch 1, dc in top of ch 3. Ch 7, turn.

Row 3: Dc in first sp, (ch 4, sk 3 dc, dc, ch 4, dc in next sp) 3 times. Ch 4, turn.

Row 4: Drop lp from hook, insert hook through ch-9 lp of motif at top of shawl, draw lp through, ch 5, work 3 dc in ch-4 lp, dc in dc, 2 dc in next ch-4 lp, join to side of adjoining motif, 2 dc in same ch-4 lp, dc in dc, 3 dc in next lp, ch 4, join half motif to corner where 3 motifs meet, ch 5, work 2nd side to correspond to first side, end 3 dc in last lp, ch 4, join to corresponding ch-9 lp of next motif at top of shawl, ch 5, sl st in last lp. End off.

EDGING: Row 1: From right side, join in ch-9 lp at side top edge of shawl. Working along side of shawl, ch 5, dc in same ch-9 lp, * ch 2, dc in next dc, (ch 2, sk 1 dc, dc in next dc) 5 times, (ch 2, dc in next corner lp, ch 2, dc in same corner lp) twice, repeat from * across side to back point; in ch-9 lp at point work ch 2, 3 dc, ch 3, 3 dc, repeat from first * to 2nd * across other side, end ch 2, dc in corner lp, ch 2, dc in same corner lp. Ch 5, turn.

Row 2: Dc in first sp, * ch 2, dc in next sp, repeat from * to back point, ch 3; in ch-3 lp work 3 dc, ch 3, 3 dc, ch 3, repeat from first * to 2nd * across other side. Ch 5, turn.

Row 3: Repeat row 2.

Row 4: * Yo hook, pull up a lp in next sp, yo hook, pull up a lp in same sp, yo and through 4 lps on hook, yo and through 2 lps on hook, ch 1, repeat from * to back point, ch 3; in ch-3 lp work 3 dc, ch 3, 3 dc, ch 3; repeat from first * to

2nd * across other side. Ch 5, turn.

Rows 5 and 6: Repeat row 2. At end of row 6, ch 1. Do not turn.

TOP EDGING: Working across top of shawl, 5 dc in first sp, sc in next sp, 5 dc in side of next row, sc in next sp, 5 dc in next sp, sc in next sp, 5 dc, sc in next lp, (sk 2 dc, 5 dc in next dc, sk 2 dc, sc in next dc) twice, (5 dc, sc in next lp) twice, 5 dc in next sp, sc in next sp, * 5 dc, sc in next lp (center of half motif), sk first row of motif, 5 dc in end of next row, sc in next sp, 5 dc, sc in next lp, 5 dc, sc in first lp of next half motif, 5 dc in next sp, sc in next sp, repeat from * across to last motif, 5 dc, sc in ch-9 lp, (sk 2 dc, 5 dc in next dc, sk 2 dc, sc in next dc) twice, 5 dc, sc in next ch-9 lp, (5 dc in next sp, sc in next sp) 3 times. End off.

FINISHING: Steam lightly. For fringe, cut strands 14″ long. Knot 3 strands tog in every other sp on side edges.

SCALLOPED SHAWL

Soft scallops, descending layer on layer, form a deep semicircle of luxuriant warmth. The shawl is crocheted in panels; the scallops are worked in simple chain stitch and double crochet.

SIZE: 56″ wide x 32″ deep, plus fringe.

MATERIALS: Sport yarn, 7 2-oz. skeins. Aluminum crochet hook size H.

GAUGE: 4 dc = 1″; 2 rows = 1″.

SHAWL: FIRST STRIP (make 2): **First Scallop:** Ch 12.

Row 1: Dc in 8th ch from hook, ch 4, sl st in last ch of ch 12. Ch 3, turn.

Row 2: 10 dc in lp just formed, 10 dc in next lp. Ch 5, turn.

Row 3: Sk first dc, dc in next dc, (ch 2, sk 1 dc, dc in next dc) 9

times, ch 2, dc in top of ch 3—11 sps. Ch 3, turn.

Row 4: 3 dc in each sp across. Ch 4, turn.

Row 5: Sk first dc, dc in next dc, (ch 2, sk 1 dc, dc in next dc) 15 times, ch 2, dc in top of ch 3—17 sps. This is end of first scallop. Ch 6, turn.

2nd Scallop: Row 6: Sk first dc, dc in next dc, ch 4, sl st in next dc, ch 3, sl st in next dc. Ch 1, turn.

Row 7: 10 dc in ch-4 lp, 10 dc in ch-6 lp. Ch 5, turn.

Row 8: Sk first dc, dc in next dc,

(ch 2, sk 1 dc, dc in next dc) 9 times, ch 2, dc in sl st at top of ch 3, sl st in next dc on previous scallop, ch 3, sl st in next dc on same scallop—11 sps. Ch 1, turn.

Row 9: 3 dc in each sp across. Ch 4, turn.

Row 10: Sk first dc, dc in next dc, (ch 2, sk 1 dc, dc in next dc) 15 times, ch 2, dc in top of ch 3—17 sps. Sl st in next dc of previous scallop. Ch 6, turn.

Next Scallop: Row 11: Repeat row 6.

Row 12: 10 dc in ch-4 lp, 10 dc

in ch-6 lp, sl st in next free dc on scallop below, ch 3, sl st in next dc of same scallop, ch 2, turn.

Row 13: Repeat row 8.

Row 14: 3 dc in each sp across, sl st in next free dc on scallop below, ch 3, sl st in next dc of same scallop, ch 2, turn.

Row 15: Repeat row 10.

Repeat rows 11-15 until there are 12 scallops (6 on each side). End off.

Note: There should be only 7 sps free on first scallop after 3rd scallop is made, and only 7 sps free on 2nd scallop after 4th scallop is made. There will be only 7 sps free on all scallops but the 2 end ones at the bottom of the shawl if strips are made correctly.

2ND STRIP (make 2): Work as for first strip until there are 14 scallops (7 on each side).

3RD STRIP (make 2): Work as for first strip until there are 16 scallops (8 on each side).

FINISHING: Place the two 3rd strips side by side, 7 sps on 2nd scallop of each strip tog. Sew strips tog, matching 7 free sps on corresponding scallops to last scallops. On last scallops, join 6 sps only. Sew a 2nd strip each side of joined strips, joining 2nd scallop of 2nd strip to first scallop of 3rd strip, to last scallops. On last scallops, join 5 sps only. Sew a first strip each side of joined strips, joining 2nd scallop of first strip to first scallop of 2nd strip, to last scallops. On last scallops, join 4 sps only.

Edging: Row 1: Working across top edge only, from right side, join yarn in sp at outside edge of first scallop of first strip, ch 4, dc in side of next dc row, * ch 3, dc in next sp, ch 3, dc in side of next dc row, ch 3, dc in bottom of next dc (center of scallop), (ch 3, dc in next sp,

ch 3, dc in side of next dc row) 3 times, ch 3, sk next sp, 2 sc in side of next dc row, 2 sc in next sp, working in next strip, 2 sc in next sp, 2 sc in side of next dc row, repeat from * twice; work 2nd half to correspond to first half, ending ch 4, sl st in last sp. Ch 1, turn.

Row 2: 2 sc in each sp, sc in each sc across. Ch 2, turn.

Row 3: Sk first 2 sc, 3 dc in next sc, * sk 2 sc, sc and 3 dc in next sc, repeat from * across, end sk 2 sc, sc in last sc. End off.

FRINGE: Cut strands 18″ long. Hold 4 strands tog, fold in half; insert hook in sp on scalloped edge, pull lp of yarn through, pull 8 ends through lp; tighten knot. Knot a fringe in each sp around sides and bottom of shawl.

Trim fringe evenly.

"TATTED" SHAWL

Dazzling white shawl, luxuriously fringed, alternates bands of double crochet with "tatting crochet" (a series of loops put on the hook and joined to look like tatting). Shawl is semicircular for a super wrap-up.

SIZE: 40″ long at center back, plus fringe.

MATERIALS: Mohair-type yarn, lightweight, 10 1½-oz. balls. Aluminum crochet hooks sizes G and J.

GAUGE: 7 dc = 2″ (G hook).

Note: Shawl is semicircular; it is begun at top center back and worked out from there.

To Inc 1 St: Work 2 dc in 1 dc.

SHAWL: Beg at top center, with G hook, ch 4.

Row 1: 4 dc in 4th ch from hook—5 dc counting turning ch. Ch 3, turn.

Row 2: Dc in first st, 2 dc in each dc across, 2 dc in turning ch—10 dc counting ch 3 as 1 dc. Ch 3, turn.

Row 3: Dc in first st, inc 3 dc evenly spaced across next 8 sts, 2 dc in turning ch—15 dc. Ch 3, turn.

Row 4: Dc in first st, inc 3 dc evenly spaced across, 2 dc in turning ch—20 dc. Ch 3, turn.

Rows 5-7: Repeat row 4—35 dc.

Row 8: Dc in first st, inc 4 dc evenly across, 2 dc in turning ch—41 dc. Change to J hook. Turn.

Note: In doing the Tatting Pattern, it may help you to think of the loops put on the crochet hook as looping stitches onto a knitting needle (or casting on stitches in the simplest way). When you wrap yarn from front to back, turn your index finger away from you and insert your needle as if to knit. When you wrap yarn from back to front, turn your index finger toward you and insert hook from the back.

Tatting Pattern: Row 9: Ch 4, tr in first st, ** wrap yarn over index finger of left hand (**left-handed crocheters,** right hand), from front to back, forming a lp. Insert hook from front to back through front thread of lp, slip lp on hook (front lp). Wrap yarn from back to front over index finger, forming a

lp. Insert hook from back to front through back thread of lp, slip lp on hook (back lp) ** ; repeat between **'s 3 times (9 lps on hook); sk 1 dc, draw up a lp in next dc;

repeat between **'s 4 times (18 lps on hook), yo and through all 18 lps, ch 1 (1 rosette), * ch 2, repeat between **'s 4 times, sk 2 dc, draw up a lp in next dc, repeat between **'s 4 times (18 lps), yo and through all lps on hook, ch 1 (1 rosette); repeat from * across, end 2 tr in turning ch—13 rosettes. Ch 4, turn.

Row 10: Tr in first st, ch 1, work a rosette, attaching to ch-1 sp of first rosette of previous row, * ch 3, work a rosette, attaching to ch-1 sp of next rosette, repeat from * across, end ch 1, 2 tr in turning ch. Ch 4, turn.

Row 11: Tr in first st, ch 2, work a rosette, attaching to ch-1 sp of first rosette of previous row, work as for row 10, making ch 4 between rosettes, end ch 2, 2 tr in turning ch. Ch 4, turn.

Row 12: Tr in first st, ch 2, work as for row 10, making ch 5 between rosettes, end ch 2, 2 tr in turning ch. Change to G hook. Ch 3, turn.

Row 13: Dc in first st, dc in next tr, dc in next 2 ch, * dc in ch-1 sp of rosette, dc in next 5 ch, repeat from * across, end dc in last rosette, dc in 2 ch, dc in next tr, 2 dc in turning ch—83 dc. Ch 3, turn.

Rows 14-16: Work in dc, inc 1 st (see To Inc 1 St) each end and 8 sts evenly spaced on row, ch 3, turn on rows 14 and 15—113 dc. Change to J hook.

Row 17: Ch 4, tr in first st, work 8 lps of rosette, sk 1 dc, draw up a lp in next dc, complete rosette, * ch 2, work 8 lps of rosette, sk 3 dc, draw up a lp in next dc, complete rosette; repeat from * across, end 2 tr in turning ch—28 rosettes. Ch 4, turn.

Rows 18-20: Repeat rows 10-12. Change to G hook. Ch 3, turn.

Row 21: Repeat row 13—173 dc.

Rows 22-24: Work in dc, inc 1 st each end and 6 sts evenly spaced on row. Ch 3, turn on rows 22 and 23—197 dc. Change to J hook.

Row 25: Work as for row 17—49 rosettes. Ch 4, turn.

Row 26: Repeat row 10.

Row 27: Repeat row 10.

Row 28: Repeat row 11. Change to G hook.

Row 29: Work as for row 13, making dc in each of 4 ch between rosettes—251 dc.

Rows 30-32: Work in dc, inc 1 st each end and 3 sts evenly spaced on row. Ch 3, turn on rows 30 and 31—266 dc. Change to J hook.

Row 33: Repeat row 17—66 rosettes.

Row 34: Repeat row 10.

Row 35: Repeat row 10.

Row 36: Repeat row 11. Change to G hook.

Row 37: Work as for row 13, making dc in each of 4 ch between rosettes—335 dc.

Rows 38 and 39: Work in dc, inc 1 st each end and 3 sts evenly spaced on row. Ch 3, turn each row.

Row 40: Work in dc, inc 1 st each end and 2 sts evenly spaced on row—349 dc. Change to J hook. Ch 4, turn.

Row 41: Repeat row 17.

Rows 42-44: Repeat row 10. Change to G hook.

Row 45: Repeat row 13. End off.

FINISHING: With G hook, work 1 row hdc along entire straight edge, keeping work flat.

FRINGE: Cut 20″ strands. Fold 3 strands in half to form lp, insert hook in st from wrong side, pull lp through st, bring all ends through lp and pull to tighten knot. Work 1 fringe in every other dc on curved edge. Trim fringe. Steam lightly. Do not block.

PASTEL-SQUARES SHAWL

Shown at left on page 114

Big and beautiful shawl of pastel patches, joined in the crocheting, is soft and frothy in mohair yarn.

SIZE: 80″ x 40″.

MATERIALS: Mohair or mohair blend yarn, 2 40-gram balls each of light blue (A), white (B), pink (C) and yellow (D). Aluminum crochet hook size F.

Note: Following chart, shawl is worked from 1 to 63 in colors as noted.

SHAWL: TRIANGLE 1: With A (see chart), ch 5.

Row 1: Work 2 dc, ch 2, 2 dc, ch 1, dc in 5th ch from hook. Ch 4, turn.

Row 2: 2 dc in next ch-1 sp, ch 1, corner of 2 dc, ch 2, 2 dc in next ch-2 sp, ch 1, 2 dc in top of turning ch, ch 1, dc in next ch of turning ch. Ch 4, turn.

Row 3: (2 dc in next ch-1 sp, ch 1) twice, corner of 2 dc, ch 2, 2 dc in next ch-2 sp, ch 1, 2 dc in next ch-1 sp, ch 1, 2 dc in top of turning ch, ch 1, dc in 3rd ch of turning ch. Ch 4, turn.

Row 4: Work same as row 3, having 1 more group of 2 dc before and after corner.

Row 5: Repeat row 4. End off.

SQUARE 2: With B, ch 4, join with a sl st to form ring.

Rnd 1: Ch 3 (counts as 1 dc), dc in ring, ch 2, * 2 dc in ring, ch 2, repeat from * twice, join last ch 2 to top of ch 3 with a sl st (4 groups of 2 dc in ring).

Rnd 2: Ch 3, dc in last ch-2 sp of rnd 1 (half corner), ch 1, * 2 dc, ch 2, 2 dc in next ch-2 sp (corner), ch 1, repeat from * twice, half corner of 2 dc in last sp, ch 2, sl st in top of starting ch—8 groups of 2 dc (4 corners).

Rnd 3: Ch 3, dc in last ch-2 sp of previous rnd (half corner), ch 1, * 2 dc in next ch-1 sp, ch 1, corner of 2 dc, ch 2, 2 dc in next corner sp, ch 1, repeat from * twice, 2 dc in next ch-1 sp, ch 1, half corner of 2 dc in last sp, ch 2, sl st in top of starting ch 3.

Rnd 4: Repeat rnd 3, having 1 more group of 2 dc between corners.

Rnd 5: Ch 3, dc in last ch-2 sp of previous rnd (half corner), ch 1, (2 dc in next ch-1 sp, ch 1) 3 times. **Joining:** 2 dc in corner ch-2 sp, ch 1; with wrong sides facing, sc in ch-2 sp of corner of triangle, ch 1.

PASTEL-SQUARES SHAWL AND FLOWER-PETAL SHAWL

2 dc in same corner ch-2 sp on square, sc in next ch-1 sp on triangle, (2 dc in next ch-1 sp on triangle) 3 times, 2 dc in corner ch-2 sp of square, sc in next sp of triangle, ch 1, 2 dc in same corner ch-2 sp of square. Complete rnd as for rnd 4, having 1 more group of 2 dc between corners. End off. Join one side of squares 3, 4, 5, 6, 7, 8, 9, 10, 11, 12, 13, 14 in sequence as shown on chart in same manner as square 2 was joined to triangle 1. Work triangle 15 to corner on row 5; join to one side of square 14 to correspond to opposite side.

TRIANGLE 16: With D, work rows 1-4 same as for triangle 1.

Row 5: Work to corner; work 2 dc, ch 1 in corner ch-2 sp; with wrong sides facing, sc in corner ch-2 sp of square 2, ch 1, 2 dc in same ch-2 sp on triangle, continue to join same as other squares. End off.

SQUARE 17: With A, work rnds 1-4 same as for square 2.

Rnd 5: Work to corner; work 2 dc, ch 1 in corner ch-2 sp; with wrong sides facing, sc in corner ch-

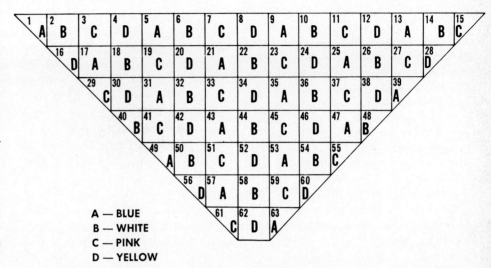

A — BLUE
B — WHITE
C — PINK
D — YELLOW

2 sp of square 3, ch 1, 2 dc in same ch-2 sp on square 17. Continue to join to one side of square 3 and one side of triangle 16. Finish rnd. End off.

SQUARE 18: With B, work rnds 1-4 same as for square 2.

Rnd 5: Work to corner; work 2 dc, ch 1 in corner ch-2 sp; join to one side of square 4 and one side of square 17. Continue in this manner, following chart for placement and color sequence of squares and triangles.

FINISHING: Run in yarn ends on wrong side. Work 1 row sc across long edge of shawl, working same colors as squares. **Note:** When changing colors, work off last 2 lps of sc with new color.

FRINGE: Cut A, B, C and D into 20″ lengths. Using 4 strands tog, fold strands in half, pull lp through sp, pull 8 ends through loop; tighten knot. Knot a fringe in each sp on sides and bottom of shawl, using same color yarn as triangles.

FLOWER-PETAL SHAWL

Shown at right on page 114

Rose-pink triangle combines six-sided motifs to form flower pattern.

SIZE: 45″ wide; 25″ deep at center back, plus fringe.

MATERIALS: Lightweight yarn (fingering yarn weight), 13 ozs. Aluminum crochet hook size F or 5. Tapestry needle.

GAUGE: Each motif = 5″ diameter.

SHAWL: MOTIF (make 39): Beg at center, ch 6, join with sl st to form ring.

Rnd 1: Ch 4 (counts as 1 dc), 8 dc in same ch as joining, drop lp off hook, insert hook in first dc, pull dropped lp through (popcorn made), ch 4, * 9 dc in next ch, drop lp off hook, insert hook in first dc, pull dropped lp through (popcorn made), ch 4, repeat from * 4 times, join with sl st in first popcorn—6 popcorns.

Rnd 2: Ch 5 (counts as 1 tr), 3 tr in first ch-4 sp, * ch 4, 4 tr in next ch-4 sp, repeat from * 4 times, ch 4, sl st in top of starting ch 5.

Rnd 3: Ch 5 (counts as 1 tr), tr in same st as joining, tr in each of next 2 tr, 2 tr in next tr, * ch 5, 2 tr in next tr, tr in each of next 2 tr, 2 tr in next tr, repeat from * 4 times, end ch 5, sl st in top of starting ch 5. End off.

JOINING: Sew 6 tr on one

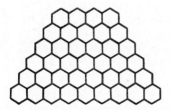

motif to 6 tr on 2nd motif. Sew 6 tr on opposite side of 2nd motif to 6 tr on 3rd motif. Continue to join motifs in this manner until 9 motifs are joined into a strip. Join 8, 7, 6, 5 and 4 motifs into strips—6 strips. Following chart, sew strips tog.

EDGING: From right side, join yarn in first free tr of first motif of top row; ch 5 (counts as 1 dc, ch 2), (sk next tr, dc in next tr, ch 2) twice, dc in next tr, * ch 2, dc in center ch of ch 5, ch 2, dc in next tr, (ch 2, sk next tr, dc in next tr) twice, ch 2, dc in next tr, repeat from * twice, ch 2, tr in center ch of next ch 5, tr in center ch of next ch 5 (2nd motif), ch 2 and continue around shawl in this manner, making 3 ch-2 sps over each group of 5 tr, 2 ch-2 sps over each ch 5 and 2 tr between motifs. Join last ch 2 in 3rd ch of ch 5 at beg of rnd.

Work 1 row of sc across top row of motifs only, working sc in each dc and tr, and 2 sc in each ch-2 sp. End off.

FRINGE: Cut yarn into 16″ strands. Hold 4 strands tog; fold in half. With crochet hook, draw folded lp through ch-2 sp on outer edge of shawl, pull strands through lp and tighten. Knot fringe in each ch-2 sp on side and bottom edges. Trim evenly.

CIRCULAR SHAWL

Crocheted mesh shawl, worked round and round in deep rows of treble crochet, folds in half for a double layer of fascination. Circle is edged with three rounds of lacy loops for a ruffled border.

SIZE: 40″ diameter.

MATERIALS: Mohair or mohair blend yarn, 7 1-oz. balls. Aluminum crochet hook size G.

GAUGE: 1 rnd tr = 1¼″. Be sure to pull up each tr high enough to get this gauge.

SHAWL: Beg at center, ch 4; join with sl st in first ch, forming ring.

Rnd 1: Ch 4 (counts as 1 dc, ch 1), (dc in ring, ch 1) 11 times; join with sl st in 3rd ch of ch 4.

Rnd 2: Ch 5 (counts as 1 tr, ch 1), tr in next ch-1 sp, * ch 1, (tr, ch 1, tr) in next ch-1 sp, repeat from * around, end ch 1, join with a sl st in 4th ch of starting ch—24 tr.

Rnd 3: Ch 5 (counts as 1 tr, ch 1), tr in first ch-1 sp, * ch 1, tr in next ch-1 sp, ch 1, (tr, ch 1, tr) in next ch-1 sp, repeat from * around, end ch 1, sl st in 4th ch of starting ch—36 tr.

Rnd 4: Ch 5 (counts as 1 tr, ch 1), tr in first ch-1 sp, * (ch 1, tr in next ch-1 sp) twice, ch 1, (tr, ch 1, tr) in next ch-1 sp, repeat from * around, end last repeat ch 1, sl st in 4th ch of starting ch—48 tr.

Rnd 5: Ch 5 (counts as 1 tr, ch 1), tr in first ch-1 sp, * (ch 1, tr in next ch-1 sp) 3 times, ch 1, (tr, ch 1, tr) in next ch-1 sp, repeat from * around, end last repeat ch 1, sl st in 4th ch of starting ch—60 tr.

Rnd 6: Repeat rnd 4—80 tr.

Rnd 7: Repeat rnd 5—100 tr.

Rnd 8: Ch 5 (counts as 1 tr, ch 1), tr in first ch-1 sp, * (ch 1, tr in next ch-1 sp) 4 times, ch 1, (tr, ch 1, tr) in next ch-1 sp, repeat from * around, end last repeat ch 1, sl st in 4th ch of starting ch—120 tr.

Rnd 9: Repeat rnd 8—144 tr.

Rnd 10: Ch 5 (counts as 1 tr, ch 1), tr in first ch-1 sp, * (ch 1, tr in next ch-1 sp) 5 times, ch 1, (tr, ch 1, tr) in next ch-1 sp, repeat from * around, end ch 1, sl st in 4th ch of starting ch—168 tr.

Rnd 11: Ch 5 (counts as 1 tr, ch 1), tr in first ch-1 sp, * (ch 1, tr in next ch-1 sp) 6 times, ch 1, (tr, ch 1, tr) in next ch-1 sp, repeat from * around—192 tr.

Rnd 12: Repeat rnd 10—224 tr.

Rnd 13: Repeat rnd 11—256 tr.
Edging: Rnd 14: * Ch 5, sc in next ch-1 sp, repeat from * around.

Rnd 15: * Ch 6, sc in next ch-5 sp, repeat from * around.
Rnd 16: * Ch 6, sc in next ch-6 sp, repeat from * around. End off.

FILET MESH SHAWL

Filet crochet shawl is a wrap for all seasons, for daytime or evening glamour. Worked from a chart in easy blocks and spaces, triangular shawl has raised shell edging added later to the two sides.

SIZE: 70″ x 35″.

MATERIALS: Wintuk baby yarn, 14 1-oz. skeins. Crochet hook size F.

GAUGE: 3 meshes = 1″; 3 rows = 1″.

Notes: Each square on chart represents 1 mesh or space (sp); each X represents 1 block (bl). 3 dc = 1 bl; each additional bl requires 2 dc. Shawl is worked from top edge to bottom point. Dec 1 mesh at beg and end of every row for triangular shaping. To follow chart, work from right edge (dec edge) to center, then work from center back to right edge on same row. At center of large flower, work 6 bls and sps for 5 rows as shown on chart.

To Dec 1 Sp: At beg of a row, sl st in ch-1 sp, sl st in next dc; **at end of a row,** leave last mesh unworked.

SHAWL: Ch 396 to measure about 65″.

Row 1 (right side): Dec in 6th ch from hook (1 sp), * ch 1, sk 1 ch, dc in next ch, repeat from * across—196 sps. Turn.

Row 2: Dc 1 sp (see To Dec 1 Sp), ch 4, dc in next dc, * ch 1, dc in next dc, repeat from * across to last sp, dec 1 sp. Turn.

Rows 3-97: Dec 1 sp at beg and end of each row, ch 4 for first sp at beg of each row, follow chart for pat—4 sps remain. End off.

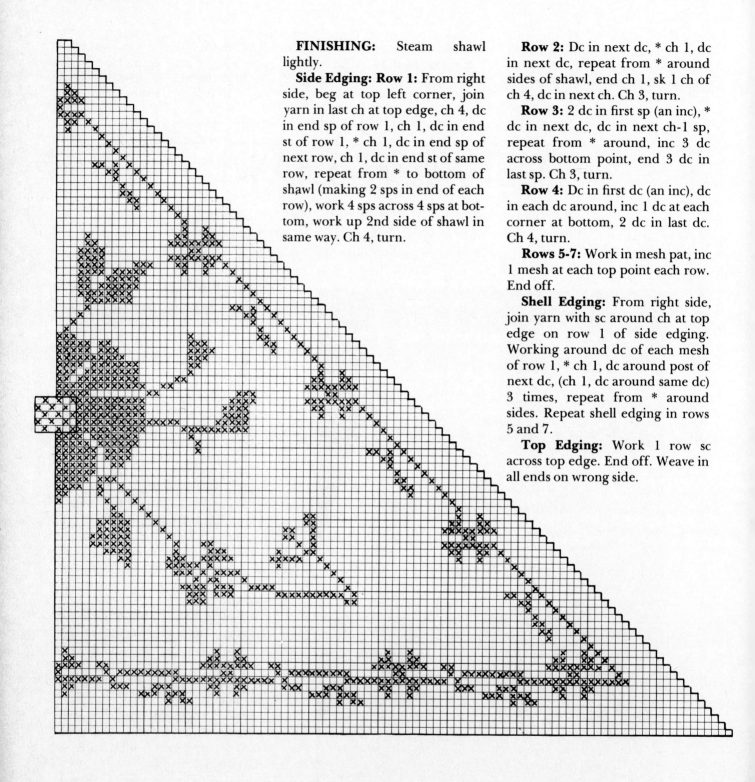

FINISHING: Steam shawl lightly.

Side Edging: Row 1: From right side, beg at top left corner, join yarn in last ch at top edge, ch 4, dc in end sp of row 1, ch 1, dc in end st of row 1, * ch 1, dc in end sp of next row, ch 1, dc in end st of same row, repeat from * to bottom of shawl (making 2 sps in end of each row), work 4 sps across 4 sps at bottom, work up 2nd side of shawl in same way. Ch 4, turn.

Row 2: Dc in next dc, * ch 1, dc in next dc, repeat from * around sides of shawl, end ch 1, sk 1 ch of ch 4, dc in next ch. Ch 3, turn.

Row 3: 2 dc in first sp (an inc), * dc in next dc, dc in next ch-1 sp, repeat from * around, inc 3 dc across bottom point, end 3 dc in last sp. Ch 3, turn.

Row 4: Dc in first dc (an inc), dc in each dc around, inc 1 dc at each corner at bottom, 2 dc in last dc. Ch 4, turn.

Rows 5-7: Work in mesh pat, inc 1 mesh at each top point each row. End off.

Shell Edging: From right side, join yarn with sc around ch at top edge on row 1 of side edging. Working around dc of each mesh of row 1, * ch 1, dc around post of next dc, (ch 1, dc around same dc) 3 times, repeat from * around sides. Repeat shell edging in rows 5 and 7.

Top Edging: Work 1 row sc across top edge. End off. Weave in all ends on wrong side.

FLOWER BEACH DRESS

A flower beach dress in a marvelous shade of deep rose is splashed with lilac blooms. The mesh stitch and straight shape make it easy to crochet.

SIZES: Directions for size 10. Changes for sizes 12, 14 and 16 are in parentheses.

Body Bust Size: 32½″ (34″-36″-38″).

Finished Bust Size: 36″ (38″-39½″-41″).

MATERIALS: Sport yarn, 7 (8-9-10) 40-gram balls hot pink, main color (MC); 2 balls lilac, contrasting color (CC). Aluminum or plastic crochet hook size F or 4. Tapestry needle.

GAUGE: 5 meshes = 2″; 2 rows = 1″.

DRESS: BACK: Beg at lower edge, with MC, ch 92 (96-100-104) loosely.

Row 1: Hdc in 3rd ch from hook and in each ch across—90 (94-98-102) hdc. Turn.

Row 2: Ch 4 (counts as dc, ch 1), sk first st, dc in next st, * ch 1, sk next st, dc in next st, repeat from * across—45 (47-49-51) meshes. Turn.

Row 3: Ch 4 (counts as dc, ch 1), dc in next ch-1 sp, * ch 1, dc in next ch-1 sp, repeat from * across—45 (47-49-51) meshes. Turn. Repeat row 3 until piece measures 20″ from start or desired length to underarm. Turn. Check gauge; piece should measure 18″ (19″-19¾″-20½″) wide.

Shape Armholes: Next Row: Sl st loosely across first 7 sts, ch 4, dc in next ch-1 sp (4th ch-1 sp), work in pat to within last 3 meshes—39 (41-43-45) meshes. Turn. Work in pat, working to within 1 mesh of end every row 4 times—35 (37-39-41) meshes. Work even until armholes measure 6½″ (7″-7½″-8″) above first bound-off sts.

Shape Shoulders and Neck: First Shoulder: Work across 12 (13-13-14) meshes, turn.

Next Row: Sl st across dc, ch 1;

work ch 4, dc in next ch-1 sp, work in pat across—11 (12-12-13) meshes. Turn. Work 1 row even. End off.

2nd Shoulder: Sk 11 (11-13-13) ch-1 sps on last long row, join MC in next dc, ch 4, dc in next ch-1 sp, finish row—12 (13-13-14) meshes. Turn.

Next Row: Work in pat to within last mesh—11 (12-12-13) meshes. Turn. Work 1 row even. End off.

FRONT: Work same as for back until armholes measure 5″ (5½″-6″-6½″) above first bound-off sts—35 (37-39-41) meshes. Turn.

Shape Neck and Shoulders: First Shoulder: Work across 13 (14-14-15) meshes. Turn.

Next Row: Sl st across dc, ch 1; work ch 4, dc in next ch-1 sp, finish row—12 (13-13-14) meshes. Turn.

Next Row: Work in pat to within last mesh—11 (12-12-13) meshes. Turn. Work even until armhole is same as back. End off.

2nd Shoulder: Sk 9 (9-11-11) ch-1 sps on last long row, join MC in next dc, ch 4, dc in next ch-1 sp, finish row—13 (14-14-15) meshes. Turn. Complete as for first shoulder, reversing shaping.

SLEEVES: Beg at lower edge, with MC, ch 62 (64-66-68) loosely.

Row 1: Hdc in 3rd ch from hook and in each ch across—60 (62-64-66) hdc. Turn. Work in pat as for back on 30 (31-32-33) meshes until piece measures 16½″ from start or desired length to underarm. Check gauge; piece should measure 12″ (12½″-13″-13¼″) wide.

Shape Cap: Sl st loosely across first 7 sts, ch 4, dc in next ch-1 sp (4th ch-1 sp), work in pat to within last 3 meshes—24 (25-26-27) meshes. Turn. Work in pat, working to within 1 mesh of end every row 12 (13-14-15) times—12 meshes. End.

FLOWERS (make 22): Beg at center with MC, ch 6. Join with a sl st to form ring.

Rnd 1: 12 sc in ring. Join with a sl st in first sc. End off. Join CC in same sc.

Petals: * Ch 9, turn.

Row 1: Sc in 2nd ch from hook and in each of next 7 ch—8 sc. Ch 1, turn.

Row 2: Sk first sc, sc in each of next 7 sc. Ch 1, turn.

Row 3: Sk first sc, sc in each of next 6 sc, sc in ch 1, sl st in each of next 2 MC sc on first rnd, repeat from * 5 times, end last repeat, join with a sl st in first rnd—6 petals. End off.

FINISHING: With MC, weave shoulder seams; sew in sleeves. Sew side and sleeve seams.

Neck Edging: From right side, with MC, work 1 rnd sc around neck edge, keeping work flat. Join with a sl st in first sc. Do not turn.

Next Rnd: Working from left to right * ch 1, sk next sc, sc in next sc, repeat from * around neck. End off.

With CC, tack 8 flowers to front and back, 3 flowers to each sleeve.

CHECKERED SUNDRESS

SIZES: Directions for small size (6-8). Changes for medium size (10-12) and large size (14-16) are in parentheses.

Fits Bust Size: 30½″-31½″ (32½″-34″; 36″-38″).

MATERIALS: Yarn of knitting worsted weight, 4 (5-5) 4-oz. skeins amber (A); 1 (2-2) skeins orange (B). Crochet hooks sizes H and I. Two yds. of round elastic.

GAUGE: 13 dc = 4″; 5 rows = 3″ (size H hook in pat, size I hook in solid color).

Notes: When working with 2 colors, hold color not in use along top of last row; work sts over unused color to conceal it. To change

colors, work last st to last 2 lps on hook; work off last 2 lps with new color. Carry unused color loosely along side edge.

To Inc 1 St: Work 2 sts in 1 st. Keep to checkered pat when increasing.

DRESS: BODICE: BACK: Beg at waist edge, with A and size H hook, ch 50 (54-58).

Row 1: Dc in 4th ch from hook (counts as 2 dc), dc in next 0 (2-0) ch, * change to B (see Notes), dc in next 4 ch, change to A, dc in next 4 ch, repeat from * across, end 2 (4-2) A dc—48 (52-56) dc. Ch 3, turn each row. Ch 3 always counts as first dc of next row.

Row 2: Sk first st, dc in next 1 (3-1) dc, * change to B, dc in next 4 dc, change to A, dc in next 4 dc, repeat from * across, end 2 (4-2) A dc, change to B.

Row 3: Sk first st, dc in next 1(3-1) dc, * change to A, dc in next 4 dc, change to B, dc in next 4 dc, repeat from * across, end 2 (4-2) B dc.

Row 4: Repeat row 3. Change to A.

Rows 5-9: Work even in checkered pat.

Row 10: Dc in first st (1 st inc), work in pat across, 2 dc in last st (1 st inc)—50 (54-58) dc.

Row 11: Work even in pat.

Simple-to-make sundress in warm colors is worked in rows of double crochet and is checkerboarded bottom and top. Waist and top of bodice are elasticized.

Row 12: Repeat row 10—52 (56-60) dc.

Rows 13 and 14: Work even in pat. End off.

BODICE: FRONT: Work as for back.

Note: Skirt is planned for 18″ length. For longer or shorter skirt, add or subtract an even number of rows before starting border.

SKIRT: Row 1: From right side, working along opposite side of starting ch for back bodice, with A and size I hook, join yarn in first ch, ch 3, dc in next 2 ch, * 2 dc in next ch, dc in next 3 ch, repeat from * across—60 (65-70) dc.

Rows 2-6: Work even in dc.

Row 7: Dc in first st, inc 2 (2-0) dc evenly spaced across, 2 dc in last st—64 (69-72) dc.

Rows 8-10: Work even.

Row 11: Dc in first st, inc 2 (4-2) dc evenly spaced across, 2 dc in last st.

Rows 12-14: Work even.

Row 15: Dc in first st, inc 2 (3-2) dc evenly spaced across, 2 dc in last st—72 (80-80) dc.

Rows 16-18: Work even.

Row 19: Dc in first st, inc 2 dc evenly spaced across, 2 dc in last st—76 (84-84) dc.

Rows 20-22: Work even.

Row 23: Repeat row 19—80 (88-88) dc.

Row 24: Work even.

Border: Row 1: Change to H hook. Sk first st, dc in next st, * change to B, dc in next 4 dc, change to A, dc in next 4 dc, repeat from * across, end 2 A dc.

Rows 2-6: Work even in pat.

End off. Work front skirt the same.

STRAPS (make 2): With A and size H hook, make a ch 13″ (14″-15″) long. Dc in 4th ch from hook and in each ch across, ch 3, sl st in first ch of starting ch, ch 3, dc in each ch on other side of starting ch. End off.

FINISHING: Steam-press pieces lightly. Sew side seams, matching pats. From right side, with A and size H hook, work 1 row sc around bottom edge. Work 1 row sc around top of bodice, working over elastic. Adjust elastic to fit; fasten securely. Cut elastic to waist measurement less 2″; run through first row on bodice. Fasten securely. Sew shoulder straps in place.

WHITE BEACH DRESS

A beach dress, dazzling in white, combines openwork crochet with a deep border of flowers and leaves. Matching bikini, to sew or buy, is encrusted with the same daisies and roses.

SIZES: Directions for small size (8-10). Changes for medium size (12-14) are in parentheses.

Body Bust Size: 31½″-32½″ (34″-36″).

Blocked Bust Size: Dress: 34″ (38″).

MATERIALS: Dress yarn of fingering yarn weight, 12 (15) 30-gram balls for dress; 4 (6) balls for bikini flowers. Steel crochet hook No. 0. White fabric bikini. Sixteen-inch neck zipper. Matching thread.

GAUGE: Pattern: 8 sts = 1″; 5 rows = 1″. Daisies: 2½″ diameter. Roses: 1½″ diameter. Leaves: ¾″ wide x 2″ long.

PATTERN (worked on a multiple of 4 ch): **Row 1:** Sc in 2nd ch from hook, * ch 1, sk next ch, dc in next ch, ch 1, sk next sc, sc in next ch, repeat from * across, end ch 1, sk next ch, dc in last ch. Ch 1, turn.

Row 2: Sc in first dc, * ch 1, dc in sc, ch 1, sc in dc, repeat from * across, end ch 1, dc in last sc. Ch 1, turn. Repeat row 2 for pat, always working sc over dc and dc over sc of previous row. Be sure to check your gauge frequently.

To Bind Off: At beg of a row, ch 1, sl st loosely across specified sts; **at end of a row,** leave specified number of sts unworked.

To Dec 1 St: On first dec row, omit ch 1 between first or last 2 sts; **on 2nd dec row,** pull up a lp in each of 2 sts, yo and through 3 lps on hook. If row starts with dc, work ch 2 to turn; do not work in this turning ch. Alternate these 2 dec rows when decreasing.

DRESS: BACK: Beg at lower edge, ch 144 (160). Work in pat on 143 (159) sts for 8 rows. Check gauge; piece should measure 18″ (20″) wide. Keeping to pat, dec 1 st (see To Dec 1 St) each side of next row, then every 6th row 7 times—127 (143) sts. Check gauge; last row should measure 16″ (18″) wide. Work even until piece measures 13½″ (14″) from start.

Shape Armholes: Bind off (see To Bind Off) 4 sts each side of next row. Dec 1 st each side every row 8 (12) times—103 (111) sts. Work even until armholes measure 7″ (7½″) above first bound-off sts.

Shape Neck and Shoulders: Bind off 2 sts each side every row 4 times—87 (95) sts.

Next Row: Bind off 2 sts at beg of row, work across 28 (30) sts, drop yarn, sk next 27 (31) sts; join another ball of yarn, work in pat across next 28 (30) sts. Working on both sides at once, with separate strands of yarn, bind off 2 sts each side of each shoulder every row 6 (7) times—4 (2) sts. End off.

LEFT FRONT: Beg at lower edge, ch 80 (88). Work in pat on 79 (87) sts for 8 rows. Mark beg of next row side edge. (**On right front,** mark end of next row side edge.) Check gauge; piece should measure 10″ (11″) wide. Dec 1 st at side edge of next row, then dec 1 st at same edge every 6th row 7 times—71 (79) sts. Check gauge; last row should measure 9″ (10″) wide. Work even until piece mea-

sures 12½″ (13″) from start, end center edge.

Shape Bustline Dart: * Work to within 8 sts of end of previous row, ch 1, turn, work to center edge. Repeat from * 2 (3) times, end center edge.

Next Row: Work in pat across all sts—71 (79) sts. Work even until side edge measures 13½″ (14″) from start.

Shape Armhole: Bind off 8 sts

at arm side of next row. Bind off 2 sts at same edge every row 6 (8) times—51 (55) sts. Work even until armhole measures 4″ (4½″) above first bound-off sts.

Shape Neck and Shoulder: Bind off 5 (7) sts at center edge of next row, then 2 sts at same edge every row 4 times. Dec 1 st at neck edge every row 12 times; **at the same time,** when armhole measures same as back, bind off 2 sts at arm side every row 12 (13) times—2 sts. End off.

RIGHT FRONT: Work same as left front, reversing shaping.

SLEEVES: Beg at lower edge, ch 96 (104). Work on 95 (103) sts for 8 (12) rows. Check gauge; piece should measure 12″ (13″) wide.

Shape Cap: Keeping to pat, bind off 6 sts each side of next row, 2 sts each side every row twice. Dec 1 st each side every row 20 (24) times—35 sts. Bind off 2 sts each side every row 4 times—19 sts. End off.

FINISHING: Block pieces. Sew shoulder seams; sew in sleeves. Sew side and sleeve seams. Beg at lower edge of right front, from right side, work 1 row sc up right front edge, around neck and down left front edge, working 3 sc in each neck corner and keeping work flat. Ch 1, turn. Work 2nd row sc. End off. Sew zipper to front edges, placing zipper at neck edge; sew fronts tog below zipper.

LACE BORDER: Roses: Ch 5; join with a sl st in first ch to form a ring.

Rnd 1: 10 sc in ring, join with a sl st in first sc.

Rnd 2: (Ch 3, sk 1 sc, sc in next sc) 5 times.

Rnd 3: (6 sc in ch-3 lp, sl st in sc) 5 times. End off. Make 66 (72) roses.

Daisies: Ch 4; join with a sl st in first ch to form a ring. Ch 1.

Rnd 1: 8 sc in ring; join with a sl st in first sc.

Rnd 2: * Ch 6, sc in 2nd ch from hook, dc in each of next 3 ch, sc in next ch, sc in next sc on rnd 1, repeat from * 7 times—8 petals. End off. Make 33 (36) daisies.

Leaves: Ch 12.

Row 1: Sc in 2nd ch from hook, (ch 1, sk next ch, dc in next ch) 3 times, ch 1, sk next ch, sc in next ch, ch 1, sk next ch, sl st in last ch. Ch 1, turn.

Row 2: 3 sc in each of next 4 ch-1 sps, 8 sc in end sp, * sc in base of next st, sc in next sp, repeat from * across starting ch, end 2 sc in last sp, sl st in first sc. End off. Make 88 (96) leaves.

Assemble 6 roses, 3 daisies and 8 leaves, as shown by solid lines on diagram. This forms one complete motif; sew them tog with sewing thread where they meet. Make 11 (12) motifs in this manner; each motif will fit against previous motif as shown by dotted lines. Join all motifs to form a circle. Steampress lightly and sew to lower edge of tunic using wrong side of motifs as right side.

BIKINI: TOP: Work daisies, roses and leaves as necessary. Use wrong side of motifs as right side. Cover straps with 1 daisy, 1 rose alternately. Beg at narrow end of back, use 1 daisy, then a leaf, a rose, a daisy, a leaf, a rose and a daisy. Sew 2 daisies vertically at center front, 1 rose and 1 daisy alternately across top, and 5 roses under each cup. Fill in spaces with leaves and daisies, pinning them in place and adjusting as necessary before sewing to top.

PANTS: Allowing for stretch, pin 1 daisy and 1 rose alternately, wrong side out, around waist edge, then add leaves and flowers to correspond with motifs on tunic until lace reaches leg edges. Sew in place.

TRICOLOR COVER-UP

Shown on page 126

Scarlet, navy and white band an airy, zippered cover-up, simple to make in mesh crochet. Short sleeves, side and front slits add ease.

SIZES: Directions for small size (8-10). Changes for medium size (12-14) are in parentheses.

Body Bust Size: 31½″-32½ (34″-36″).

Finished Bust Size: 33″ (37½″).

MATERIALS: Knitting worsted, 3 (4) 4-oz. skeins white (W); 2 skeins each of navy (N) and scarlet (S). Aluminum crochet hook size H or 8. Twenty-two-inch zipper.

GAUGE: 9 meshes = 5″; 7 rows = 4″.

Note to Left-handed Crocheters: Follow directions as printed.

To Bind Off: At beg of a row, sl st loosely across each mesh to be bound off, then ch 4 and continue across row, **at end of a row,** work in pat to within specified number of meshes to be bound off.

To Dec 1 Mesh: At beg of a row, ch 2, sk first dc, dc in next dc (counts as 1 dc), ch 1, dc in next dc (one mesh); **at end of a row,** work to last dc, ch 1, yo, pull up a lp in last dc, yo and through 2 lps on hook, yo and through 3 lps on hook.

Note: When changing colors, drop color being used, pull new color through last 2 lps to complete dc.

MESH PATTERN: Row 1: Dc in 6th ch from hook, * ch 1, sk next ch, dc in next ch, repeat from * across. Ch 4, turn.

Row 2: Sk first dc, * dc in next dc, ch 1, repeat from * across, end sk 1 ch of turning ch, dc in next ch. Ch 4, turn. Repeat row 2 for mesh pat.

COVER-UP: BACK: Left Half: Beg at lower edge, with N, ch 54 (58). Work in mesh pat on 25 (27) meshes, working 2 rows N, 2 rows W for 20 rows (5 W stripes completed). Check gauge; piece should measure 14″ (15″) wide. Dec 1 mesh (see To Dec 1 Mesh) at beg of next row (side edge), then dec 1 mesh at same edge every 6th row 5 times more—19 (21) meshes. Keeping to stripe pat, dec 1 mesh at side edge every 5th row 4 times—15 (17) meshes. Work even until 75 rows from start (1 row of 19th W stripe completed) or desired length to underarm.

Shape Armhole: Bind off (see To Bind Off) 2 meshes at side edge of next row. Dec 1 mesh at arm side every row 1 (2) times—12 (13) meshes. Work even until armhole measures 7½″ (8″) above first row of armhole shaping.

Shape Shoulder: Bind off 2 (3) meshes at arm side of next row. End off.

Right Half: Working with S instead of N, work same as for left half; pat is reversible.

FRONT: Left Front: Work same as for left back until armhole measures 4½″ (5″) above first row of armhole shaping—12 (13) meshes.

Shape Neck and Shoulder: Bind off 3 meshes at center edge of next row. Dec 1 mesh at same edge every row 3 times—6 (7) meshes.

Work even until armhole measures same as back. Bind off 2 (3) meshes at armhole edge of next row. End off.

Right Front: Work same as for left front, working with S instead of N.

SLEEVES: Right Sleeve: Beg at lower edge with S, ch 38 (42).

Row 1: Dc in 6th ch from hook, * ch 1, sk next ch, dc in next ch, repeat from * across—17 (19) meshes. Ch 4, turn.

Row 2: Sk first dc, dc in next dc, (ch 1, dc in next dc) twice, (ch 1, dc in ch-1 sp, ch 1, dc in dc) 11 (13) times, (ch 1, dc in next dc) twice, ch 1, sk 1 ch, dc in next ch of turning ch—28 (32) meshes. Working 2 rows W, 2 rows S, work until 7 rows from start, end first W row of 2nd W stripe.

Shape Cap: Keeping to color sequence, bind off 2 meshes each side of next row. Dec 1 mesh each side every row 1 (2) times—22 (24) meshes. Work even for 5 (6) rows. Dec 1 mesh each side of next 2 rows—18 (20) meshes. End off.

Left Sleeve: Work same as for right sleeve, working with N instead of S.

FINISHING: Weave center back seam, matching rows. Leaving 5 N or S stripes at lower side edges free for side slits, sew side seams. Sew shoulder and sleeve seams. Gathering top of sleeve, sew in sleeves. With W, from right side, work 1 row sc around neck edge, easing in to desired fit. With N, working 2 sc in each sp, work 1 row sc along left front edge; with S, work 1 row sc along right front edge. Beg at neck edge, sew in zipper. Sew fronts tog below zipper to top of 6th W stripe from bottom. With W, beg at lower front edge, work 1 row sc across lower edge of one front, around side slit, across back, around other side slit, across lower edge of 2nd front. End off. Steam-press lightly on wrong side. Steam-press seams open flat.

BIG BRIM HAT

Versatile cloche, with big brim to pull down or roll up, works up quickly with two strands of knitting worsted or three strands of sport yarn. Contrasting chains trim crown.

SIZE: Adjustable head size.

MATERIALS: Knitting worsted, 2 4-oz. skeins, or 4-ply sport yarn, 3 2-oz. skeins of main color; 1 oz. of contrasting color. Crochet hook size K.

GAUGE: 1 sc and ch 1 or 2 sc = 1″ (2 strands of knitting worsted or 3 strands of sport yarn).

HAT: With 2 strands of knitting worsted or 3 strands of sport yarn held tog, ch 3, sl st in first sc to form ring.

Rnd 1: * Ch 1, sc in ring, repeat from * 4 times—5 sc. Do not join rnds; mark end of rnds.

Rnd 2: * Ch 1, sc in next ch-1 sp, ch 1, sc in same ch-1 sp, repeat from * 4 times—10 sc.

Rnd 3: * (Ch 1, sc in next ch-1 sp) twice, ch 1, sc in ch-1 sp just worked in, repeat from * 4 times—15 sc.

Rnd 4: Ch 1, sc in next ch-1 sp, * ch 1, sc in same ch-1 sp, (ch 1, sc in next ch-1 sp) 3 times, repeat from * 4 times—21 sc.

Rnd 5: Ch 1, sc in same ch-1 sp, * ch 1, sc in next ch-1 sp, repeat from * around—22 sc.

Rnds 6-11: * Ch 1, sc in next ch-1 sp, repeat from * around.

Rnd 12: * Sc in next sc, sc in next ch-1 sp, repeat from * around—44 sc.

Rnd 13: * Sc in next sc, 2 sc in next sc, repeat from * around—66 sc.

Rnds 14-18: Sc in each sc around. At end of rnd 18, sl st in next st; end.

With contrasting color, using 2 strands of knitting worsted or 3 strands of sport yarn, make 3 chains about 1 yard long. Beg at side of hat, run chains through rnds 7, 9 and 11. Knot ends of each chain, adjusting chains to head size. Knot each end of each chain 5″ from tied knot; cut off extra chain.

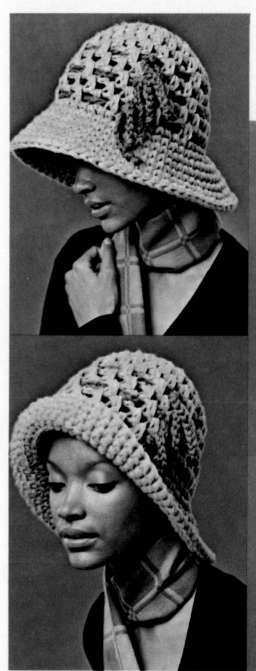

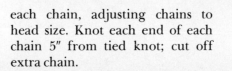

MOHAIR TAM

This easy-to-make mohair beret is all single crochet. To keep hat snug to the head, a narrow band at bottom is worked over elastic cord. Furry pompon trims top.

SIZE: Adjustable head size.
MATERIALS: Mohair, 2 40-gram (1½-oz.) balls. Crochet hook size J. Two yds. elastic cord.
GAUGE: 5 sc = 2"; 5 rnds = 2".
BERET: Ch 3, sl st in first ch to form ring.
Rnd 1: Ch 1, 10 sc in ring. Do not join rnds; mark end of rnds.
Rnd 2: 2 sc in each sc—20 sc.
Rnd 3: 2 sc in each sc—40 sc.
Rnd 4: 2 sc in each sc—80 sc.
Rnds 5-15: Work even in sc.
Rnd 16: Dec 5 sc evenly around—75 sc.
Rnds 17 and 18: Work even in sc. Cut 2 pieces of elastic cord 2"

longer than head size. Knot each piece 1" from ends.
Rnd 19: Working over one piece of elastic, * sk next sc, sc in each of next 4 sc, repeat from * around—60 sc.
Rnds 20 and 21: Work even in sc.
Rnd 22: Working over elastic, work even in sc. Sl st in next sc; end off.
POMPON: Wind mohair 100 to 150 times around 2" cardboard. Tie all windings securely tog at one edge with several strands of mohair. Cut lps at other edge. Trim pompon. Tie on.

GRANNY SQUARE CAP

Six granny afghan squares create a puffed pattern around this warm-toned hat (opposite page, top). Tapering sections are added to squares to form segments that are crocheted together. Size of hat is adjusted in the colorful band.

SIZE: Adjustable head size.
MATERIALS: Knitting worsted, 1 oz. each of light natural (N), orange (O), rust (R) and black (B). Crochet hook size H/6.
GAUGE: 3 sc = 1"; 4 sc rows = 1"; motif = 3" square.
Note: Cut and join colors as needed.

CAP: SECTION A (make 3): Beg at center of motif, with R, ch 4, join with a sl st to form ring.
Rnd 1: Ch 3 (counts as 1 dc), 2 dc in ring, ch 1, * 3 dc in ring, ch 1, repeat from * twice, join last ch 1 to top of ch 3 with a sl st (4 groups of 3 dc in rnd). End off.
Rnd 2: Join O in a ch-1 sp, sl st in

back lp of each ch 1 and dc around.
Rnd 3: Ch 3, 2 dc in first ch-1 sp, ch 1, * 3 dc in next sp, ch 1, 3 dc in same ch-1 sp, ch 1, repeat from * twice, 3 dc in same sp with first 3 dc, ch 1, join with a sl st to top of ch 3. End off; join B in corner sp.
Rnd 4: * (Sc, ch 1, sc) in ch-1 sp

for corner, sk next dc, sc in each of next 2 dc, sc in ch-1 sp, sk next dc, sc in each of the next 2 dc, repeat from * 3 times, join with a sl st in first sc—28 sc. End off.

Top: Row 1: Join N in any corner ch-1 sp, sc in same sp, sc in each of next 7 sc, sc in next ch-1 sp—9 sc. Ch 1, turn.

Row 2: Sk first sc, sc in each sc across—8 sc. Ch 1, turn. Repeat last row until 1 sc remains. Ch 1; do not turn.

Edging: Sc in top of last sc made; working along ends of rows, sc in end of next 8 rows, sc in corner sp on last rnd of motif, * sc in each sc to next corner sp, (sc, ch 1, sc) in corner sp, repeat from * once, sc in each sc to next corner sp, sc in corner sp, sc in end st of next 9 rows, join with a sl st in first sc. End off.

SECTION B (make 3): Work same as for section A, using O instead of R and R instead of O.

Steam-press motifs.

JOIN SECTIONS: With wrong sides of an A and B section tog, join B in top point; working through both sections, sc in each sc to lower edge of sections, end sl st through corner ch-1 sp of both sections. End off. Alternating A and B sections, join all 6 sections; join last section to first section forming cap. With B, sl st in each section around top point of cap, join with a sl st in first sl st. End off.

LOWER BAND: Rnd 1: From right side, join B in end of any joining row, work 10 sc loosely across each section—60 sc. Join with a sl st in first sc. End off; turn.

Rnd 2: With R, sc in each sc around, join with a sl st in first sc. Ch 2, turn.

Rnd 3: Hdc in each st around, join with a sl st to top of ch 2. End off; join O. Do not turn.

Rnds 4 and 5: Ch 1, sc in back lp of each sc around. End off.

GRANNY SQUARE CAP AND RAINBOW HAT

RAINBOW HAT

Shown on page 129

Wear a rainbow to suit your mood: brim up, down, slouched! Six softly merging colors cover the spectrum from crown to brim. Hat is made with double yarn, alternating two strands of one color with one each of two colors.

SIZE: Adjustable head size.

MATERIALS: Knitting worsted, 1 oz. each of yellow (A), green (B), blue (C), purple (D), red or purple-red (E) and orange or melon (F). Crochet hook size J.

GAUGE: 5 dc = 2″ (double strand of yarn).

Note: Hat is worked with double strand of yarn throughout with colors in the order of the spectrum. Each color is used solid then combined with the next color. Hat can be started with any color.

HAT: Beg at top of hat, with 2 strands of A, ch 4, sl st in first ch to form ring.

Rnd 1: Ch 3 (counts as 1 dc), 11 dc in ring. Join each rnd with sl st in top of ch 3. Cut 1 strand of A. Join 1 strand of B.

Rnd 2: With AB, ch 3, dc in same ch with sl st, 2 dc in each dc around—24 dc. Cut A. Join another strand of B.

Rnd 3: With BB, ch 3, 2 dc in next dc, * dc in next dc, 2 dc in next dc, repeat from * around—36 dc. Cut 1 strand of B. Join 1 strand of C.

Rnd 4: With BC, ch 3, dc in each dc around. Cut B. Join another strand of C.

Rnd 5: With CC, ch 3, dc in same ch with sl st, * dc in each of next 2 dc, 2 dc in next dc, repeat from * around, end dc in each of last 2 dc—48 dc. Cut 1 strand of C. Join 1 strand of D.

Rnd 6: With CD, work even—48 dc. Cut C. Join another strand of D.

Rnd 7: With DD, work even.

Cut 1 strand of D. Join 1 strand of E.

Rnd 8: With DE, work even. Cut D. Join another strand of E.

Rnd 9: With EE, work even.

Rnd 10: With EE, sc in each dc around, working loosely or tightly for proper head size.

Brim: Rnd 11: With EE, * ch 4, sk 3 sc, sc in next sc, ch 3, sk 3 sc, sc in next sc, repeat from * around—12 lps. Sl st in first ch. Cut 1 strand of E. Join 1 strand of F.

Rnd 12: With EF, ch 3, * 6 dc in next lp, dc in sc, repeat from * around. Cut E. Join another strand of F.

Rnd 13: With FF, ch 3, dc in each dc around. Cut 1 strand of F. Join 1 strand of A.

Rnd 14: With FA, ch 3, dc in each dc around. End off.

WINTER DENIM SET

Denim blues are great for cold-weather dressing, too! Shown on opposite page, top, brimmed hat is worked in single crochet rounds; over-six-foot muffler has stripes in different stitches.

SIZE: Hat: Adjustable head size. Scarf: 10″ wide x 75″ long, plus fringe.

MATERIALS: Knitting-worsted-weight yarn. Hat: 2 ozs. dark denim (DD); 1 oz. each of medium denim (MD), light denim (LD) and cranberry (C). Scarf: 4 ozs.

dark denim (DD); 1 oz. medium denim (MD); 3 ozs. light denim (LD); and 2 ozs. cranberry (C). Crochet hooks size F for hat, size J for scarf.

GAUGE: 4 sc = 1″ (size F hook, hat); 5 sts = 2″ (size J hook, scarf).

HAT: With LD and size F hook,

ch 4. Sl st in first ch to form ring.

Rnd 1: Ch 1, 8 sc in ring.

Rnd 2: 2 sc in each sc around—16 sc. Mark ends of rnds.

Rnd 3: Repeat rnd 2—32 sc.

Rnd 4: * Working over strand of DD, with LD, sc in each of next 2 sc, pull up a lp in next sc, drop LD, finish sc with DD, pull up a lp of DD in next sc, finish sc with LD, repeat from * around—32 sc. Always change colors in this way, finishing last sc of one color with new color and working over unused color.

Rnd 5: (LD sc in next sc, DD sc in next sc, LD sc in next sc, DD sc and LD sc in next sc, DD sc in next sc, LD sc in next sc, DD sc in next sc, LD sc and DD sc in next sc) 4 times—40 sc. Cut LD.

Rnd 6: With DD, sc around, inc 1 sc in every 5th st—48 sc.

Rnd 7: Sc around, inc 1 sc in every 8th st—54 sc.

Rnds 8 and 9: Sc around, inc 12 sc evenly spaced each rnd—78 sc.

Rnd 10: Working over strand of C, (DD sc in each of next 3 sc, C sc in next sc, DD sc in next sc, 2 DD sc in next sc, C sc in next sc) 10 times, (DD sc in each of next 3 sc, C sc in next sc) twice—88 sc.

Rnd 11: (DD sc in next sc, C sc in next sc) 44 times. Drop DD.

Rnd 12: With C, sc around. Cut C.

Rnds 13-18: With DD, sc around.

Rnd 19: * Working over strand of MD, DD sc in each of 3 sc, MD sc in next sc, repeat from * around.

Rnd 20: * DD sc in next sc, MD sc in next sc, repeat from * around. Drop DD.

Rnd 21: With MD, sc around.

Rnd 22: * Working over strand of LD, MD sc in each of 3 sc, LD sc in next sc, repeat from * around.

Rnd 23: * MD sc in next sc, LD sc in next sc, repeat from * around. Drop MD.

Rnd 24: With LD, sc around. Drop LD.

Rnd 25: With MD, sc around. Drop MD.

Rnd 26: With DD, sc around. Drop DD.

Rnd 27: With C, sc around. Drop C.

WINTER DENIM SET AND WINTER TRIO

Rnd 28: With LD, sc around. Sl st in first sc. Ch 1, turn.

Rnd 29: From wrong side, * LD sc in next sc, MD sc in next sc, repeat from * around, always having both strands of yarn above hook when inserting hook in st. Sl st in first st. Ch 1, turn. Drop LD.

Rnd 30: * MD sc in LD sc, DD sc in MD sc, repeat from * around. Drop MD and DD.

Rnd 31: With C, sc around. Cut C.

Rnd 32: With DD, sc around, inc 1 sc in first st and every 5th st around—106 sc. Sl st in first st. Ch 1, turn.

Rnd 33: From wrong side, 2 DD sc in first sc, * (LD sc in next sc, DD sc in next sc) twice, LD sc and DD sc in next sc, repeat from * around—128 sc. Sl st in first st. Ch 1, turn. Drop LD.

Rnd 34: Working DD sc and MD sc alternately, inc in every 7th st around—146 sc. Drop MD.

Rnd 35: With DD, work even in sc. Cut DD.

Rnd 36: With MD, work even in sc. Drop MD.

Rnd 37: With LD, work even in sc. Sl st in first sc. Ch 1, turn.

Rnd 38: From wrong side, work LD sc and MD sc alternately around. Sl st in first st. Ch 1, turn.

Rnd 39: Work LD sc in MD sc and MD sc in LD sc around. Drop MD.

Rnd 40: With LD, work even in sc. Cut LD.

Rnd 41: Work MD sc and DD sc alternately around. End off.

SCARF: FIRST HALF: With LD and size J hook, ch 186 loosely.

Row 1 (wrong side): Sc in 2nd ch from hook and in each ch across—185 sc. Ch 1, turn.

Row 2 (right side): Sc in each sc across. Cut LD. Do not turn.

Row 3: Beg in first st of last row and working over strand of DD, LD sc in first sc, pull up a lp of LD in next st, finish sc with DD; * working over strand of LD, pull up a lp of DD in next st, finish sc with LD; working over strand of DD, work LD sc in each of next 3 sts changing to DD in last st, repeat from * across, end with 2 LD sc. End off LD. Cut both colors. Do not turn. **Note:** Always change colors in this way, finishing sc with new color to be used and working over unused color. Leave yarn ends hanging to be woven in later, or work over them on next row.

Row 4: Beg in first st of last row, work LD sc and DD sc alternately across. Cut LD and DD. Do not turn.

Row 5: Join DD in first st of last row, ch 3, dc in next st and in each st across. Ch 3, turn.

Row 6 (wrong side): Sk first dc, dc in each dc across, dc in top of ch 3. Ch 1, turn.

Row 7: Working over strand of C, work 2 DD sc, * C sc, 3 DD sc, repeat from * across, end 2 DD sc. End off. Do not turn.

Row 8: Work C sc and MD sc alternately across. End off. Do not turn.

Row 9: With C, work in sc across. Do not turn.

Row 10: With MD, work in sc across. Ch 1, turn.

Row 11 (wrong side): Work LD sc and MD sc alternately across, always having both strands of yarn above hook when inserting hook in st. Ch 1, turn.

Row 12: Repeat row 11. End off. Do not turn.

Row 13: With DD, sc across. End off.

2ND HALF: From right side, working on opposite side of starting ch, with LD, sc in each ch across. Cut LD. Do not turn. Beg with row 3, work as for first half.

FINISHING: Cut strands of yarn in 10″ lengths (or desired length) for fringe. Using 2 strands tog and matching colors of rows, knot fringe across both ends.

WINTER TRIO

Shown at bottom, page 131

Stained-glass colors of a variegated yarn stripe a long green scarf, form the tasseled hat and two-finger mittens, worked in half double crochet.

SCARF: SIZE: 6″ x 70″, plus fringe.

MATERIALS: Yarn of knitting-worsted weight, 2 4-oz. skeins dark green (A); 1 3½-oz. skein of variegated coloring (B). Crochet hook size H.

GAUGE: 7 sts = 2″. See page 317.

SCARF: With A, ch 249.

Row 1: Tr in 5th ch from hook (counts as 2 tr) and in each ch across—246 tr. Turn each row. Check gauge; row should measure 70″.

Row 2: Ch 2 (counts as 1 hdc), sk first st, hdc in next st and in each st across—246 hdc. Cut A. Measure enough B to make 4 hdc before color gold and join to beg of next row.

Row 3: With B, ch 2 (counts as 1 hdc), sk first st, hdc in next st and in each st across. Cut B; join A.

Row 4: With A, ch 2, hdc in each st across.

Row 5: With A, ch 4, tr in each st across.

Row 6: With A, repeat row 4. Cut A. Measure enough B to make 8 hdc before color gold and join at beg of next row.

Row 7: With B, repeat row 3. Cut B; join A.

Rows 8-10: Repeat rows 4-6. Measure enough B to make 4 hdc before color hot pink and join at beg of next row.

Row 11: With B, repeat row 3. Cut B; join A.

Rows 12-14: With A, repeat rows 4 and 5. Ch 1, turn. Work 1 row sc. End off. Mark last row for right side.

From right side, with A, work 1 row sc across foundation ch. End off.

FINISHING: Steam-press scarf lightly.

FRINGE: Wind B 56 times around a 5½″ cardboard. Cut one end. Hold two strands tog; knot a fringe in edge of each row on each end of scarf. Trim evenly.

HAT AND MITTENS: SIZE: Adjustable.

MATERIALS: Variegated yarn of knitting worsted weight, 2 3½-oz. skeins. Crochet hook size H.

GAUGE: 7 hdc = 2″.

HAT: Beg at lower edge, ch 72, Being careful not to twist ch, join with a sl st in first ch.

Rnd 1: Ch 2 (counts as 1 hdc), hdc in next ch and in each ch around. Join with a sl st in top of ch 2 each rnd; do not turn—72 hdc.

Rnd 2: Ch 2 (counts as 1 hdc), hdc in next hdc and in each hdc around.

Rnds 3-26: Repeat rnd 2.

Rnd 27: Ch 2 (counts as 1 hdc), sk next hdc, * yo hook, pull up a lp in each of next 2 sts, yo hook and through 4 lps on hook (1 hdc dec), repeat from * around. Join—36 hdc.

Rnd 28: Ch 2 (counts as 1 hdc), * dec 1 hdc over next 2 sts, hdc in next st, repeat from * around, end dec 1 hdc over last 2 sts—24 hdc.

Rnd 29: Repeat rnd 28—16 hdc.

Rnd 30: Repeat rnd 27—8 hdc. Cut yarn, leaving a long end for sewing. Thread needle; draw sts tog. Fasten securely on wrong side.

FINISHING: Fold 2 rows at lower edge of hat to wrong side; sew in place loosely.

POMPON: Wind yarn 100 times around cardboard 5″ wide. Tie tog tightly at one edge of cardboard, cut through lps at opposite edge. Trim pompon; sew to top of hat.

MITTENS: LEFT MITTEN: Beg at wrist, ch 28. Being careful not to twist ch, join with a sl st in first ch.

Rnd 1: Ch 2 (counts as 1 hdc), hdc in next ch and in each ch around—28 hdc. Join; do not turn.

Rnds 2-9: Ch 2 (counts as 1 hdc), hdc in next hdc and in each hdc around. Join.

Thumb Openings: Rnd 10: Ch 2 (counts as 1 hdc) hdc in each of next 21 hdc, ch 6, sk next 6 hdc. Join with a sl st in top of ch 2.

Rnd 11: Ch 2 (counts as 1 hdc), hdc in next hdc and in each hdc and ch around—28 hdc. Join.

Rnds 12-17: Repeat rnd 2. End off.

Finger Opening: Next Rnd: Sk first 4 sts, join yarn in next hdc, ch 2 (counts as 1 hdc), hdc in each of next 19 hdc, ch 2, sl st in top of ch 2.

Next Rnd: Ch 2, hdc in next hdc and in each hdc and ch around—22 hdc. Join. Work 2 rnds even.

Next Rnd: Ch 2, hdc in each of next 8 hdc, dec 1 hdc, hdc in each of next 9 hdc, dec 1 hdc—20 hdc. Join.

Next Rnd: Ch 2, hdc in each of next 7 hdc, dec 1 hdc, hdc in each of next 8 hdc, dec 1 hdc—18 hdc. Join.

Next Rnd: Ch 2, hdc in each of next 6 hdc, dec 1 hdc, hdc in each of next 7 hdc, dec 1 hdc—16 hdc. Join. Dec 1 hdc on outer edge of palm every rnd 3 times—13 hdc. End off, leaving a long end. Thread needle; weave sts tog.

Thumb: Join yarn in first ch at base of thumb; ch 2 (counts as 1 hdc), hdc in each ch and hdc around, working 2 hdc at each side of opening—14 hdc. Join. Work 1 rnd even.

Next Rnd: Dec 1 hdc each side of opening—12 hdc. Work 4 rnds even.

Next Rnd: Dec 2 hdc evenly spaced around—10 hdc. End off, leaving a long end. Draw sts tog; fasten securely on wrong side.

Finger: Join yarn in first ch, ch 2, hdc in next ch and in each hdc around—10 hdc. Join. Work 1 rnd even.

Next Rnd: Ch 2 (counts as 1 hdc), dec 1 hdc over next 2 sts, finish rnd—9 hdc. Work 3 rnds even.

Next Rnd: Ch 2 (counts as 1 hdc), hdc around, dec 1 hdc each side of finger—7 hdc. Join. End off, leaving a long end. Draw sts tog; fasten securely on wrong side.

RIGHT MITTEN: Work same as for left mitten, reversing shaping (ch 6 for thumb opening at beg of rnd).

Lower Edging: Join yarn at lower edge, * ch 1, sk next ch, sc in next ch, repeat from * around. Join.

Next Rnd: * Sc in sc, ch 1, sk next ch-1 sp, repeat from * around. Join. Repeat last rnd once. End off.

Steam lightly.

FRINGY SCARF SET

Greens and reds predominate on a winter twosome. Both are single crochet—cloche is circular, the two-yard-plus scarf is in rows worked from one side—but the motifs are not easy.

SIZE: Hat: Adjustable head size. Scarf: 9½″ wide x 76″ long, plus fringe.

MATERIALS: Knitting-worsted-weight yarn. Hat: 2 ozs. light olive (LO); ½ oz. each of black (B), dark olive (DO), hot pink (HP), cranberry (C), old rose (OR), wine (W) and dark green (DG). Scarf: 2 ozs. each of light olive (LO), black (B) and hot pink (HP); 1 oz. each of dark olive (DO), cranberry (C), old rose (OR), wine (W) and dark green (DG). Crochet hooks size F for hat, size J for scarf.

GAUGE: 4 sc = 1″ (size F hook, hat); 5 sc = 2″ (size J hook, scarf).

HAT: With B and size F hook, ch 4. Sl st in first ch to form ring.

Rnd 1: Ch 1, 12 sc in ring.

Rnd 2: 2 sc in each sc around—24 sc. Mark ends of rnds.

Rnd 3: Working over strand of LO, pull up a lp of B in first sc, finish sc with LO; working over strand of B, pull up a lp of LO in same sc, finish sc with B. Always changing colors in this way, finishing sc with new color and working over unused color, work (4 B sc, 1 LO sc in same st as last B sc) 5 times, B sc in each of last 3 sts—30 sc.

Rnd 4: B sc in next 3 sc, B sc and LO sc in next sc, (B sc in next 4 sc, B sc and LO sc in next sc) 5 times, B sc in last sc—36 sc.

Rnd 5: (Working over strands of DO and LO, B sc in next 3 sc, LO sc in next sc, 2 DO sc in next sc, LO sc in next sc) 6 times—42 sc.

Rnd 6: (Working over strands of DO, LO, and C, B sc in next 3 sc, LO sc in next sc, DO sc and C sc in next sc, DO sc in next sc, LO sc in next sc) 6 times—48 sc. With LO, sl st in first sc.

Rnd 7: Add a strand of HP. Working in each sc around, beg in first sc, ch 1, (work LO sc, 2 B sc in next sc, LO sc, DO sc, C sc, HP sc, C sc, DO sc) 6 times—54 sc. With DO, sl st in first sc.

Rnd 8: Ch 1, (DO sc in LO sc, LO sc and B sc in next sc, LO sc, DO sc, C sc, HP sc in each of 3 sc, C sc) 6 times—60 sc. With C, sl st in first sc. Cut B.

Rnd 9: Ch 1, (C sc in DO sc, DO sc, LO sc, DO sc, C sc, HP sc in each of 2 sc, 2 HP sc in next sc, HP sc in each of 2 sc) 6 times—66 sc. With HP, sl st in first sc. Cut LO.

Rnd 10: Ch 1, (HP sc in C sc, C sc, 2 DO sc in next sc, C sc, HP sc in 3 sc, HP sc and C sc in next sc, HP sc in 3 sc) 6 times—78 sc. Sl st in first sc. Cut DO.

Rnd 11: With HP, ch 1; add a strand of LO. (HP sc, C sc, LO sc in 2 sc, C sc, HP sc in 3 sc, C sc, LO sc, C sc, HP sc in 2 sc) 6 times—78 sc. With LO, sl st in first sc. Cut C and HP.

Rnd 12: With LO, ch 1, 2 sc in first sc, (sc in 6 sc, 2 sc in next sc) 11 times—90 sc.

Note: Cutting and joining colors as needed, work even in sc to last rnd of cap (90 sc each rnd), joining each rnd with sl st. Ch 1 at beg of each rnd.

Rnd 13: 3 LO sc, (3 OR sc, 3 W sc, 3 OR sc, 6 LO sc) 6 times, end last repeat 3 LO sc.

Rnd 14: LO sc, B sc, LO sc, * (W sc, OR sc) 4 times, W sc, (B sc, LO sc) 3 times, repeat from * around, end last repeat B sc, LO sc, B sc.

Rnd 15: Repeat rnd 13.

Rnd 16: With LO, work even.

Rnd 17: 3 DG sc, (LO sc, DG sc, LO sc, 3 DG sc, LO sc, DG sc, LO sc, 6 DG sc) 6 times, end last repeat 3 DG sc.

Rnd 18: (LO sc, DG sc) 45 times.

Rnd 19: 2 DG sc, (3 LO sc, 3 DG sc) 14 times, 3 LO sc, 1 DG sc.

Rnd 20: Repeat rnd 18.

Rnd 21: Repeat rnd 17.

Rnd 22: With LO, work even.

Rnd 23: Repeat rnd 13.

Rnd 24: LO sc, B sc, LO sc, * (OR sc, W sc) 4 times, OR sc, (B sc, LO sc) 3 times, (W sc, OR sc) 4 times, W sc, (B sc, LO sc) 3 times, repeat from * twice, end last repeat B sc, LO sc, B sc.

Rnd 25: Repeat rnd 13.

Rnd 26: With LO, ch 2, hdc in each sc around. Join; end off.

SCARF: FIRST HALF: With B and size J hook, ch 182.

Row 1: Sc in 2nd ch from hook and in each remaining ch—181 sc. End off. Do not turn.

Row 2: With LO, make lp on hook. Beg in first st of last row. Working over B strand, LO sc in first sc, completing sc with B; * with B, working over LO strand, sc in each of next 5 sc, completing last sc with LO; with LO, sc in next sc, completing sc with B, repeat from * across. End off. Do not turn.

Row 3: With DO, make lp on hook. Beg in first st of last row, working over B and LO strands, DO sc in first sc, changing to LO, * LO sc, changing to B, 3 B sc, changing to LO to complete last sc, DO sc, changing to LO, repeat from * across. End off. Do not turn.

Note: Work each row from right side, working sc in each sc across, always finishing last 2 lps of one color with next color to be used and always working over unused colors. End off colors each row.

Row 4: * C sc, DO sc, LO sc, B sc, LO sc, DO sc, repeat from * across, end C sc.

Row 5: * HP sc, C sc, DO sc, LO sc, DO sc, C sc, repeat from * across, end HP sc.

Row 6: 2 HP sc, * C sc, DO sc, C sc, 3 HP sc, repeat from * across, end 2 HP sc.

Row 7: * C sc, 2 HP sc, repeat from * across, end C sc.

Row 8: With HP, work in sc across.

Row 9: With LO, work in sc across.

Row 10: 2 OR sc, * 3 W sc, 3 OR sc, repeat from * across, end 2 OR sc.

Row 11: * LO sc, B sc, repeat from * across, end LO sc.

Row 12: * DG sc, LO sc, repeat from * across, end DG sc.

Row 13: With LO, work in sc across.

2ND HALF: Working on opposite side of starting ch, work rows 2-13.

FINISHING: Run in all yarn ends on wrong side. Cut a strand of DO longer than scarf. Thread in yarn needle, weave under 1 B lp of each st on row 1. Weave in DO ends.

With LO, from right side, work 1 row sc across end of scarf. Ch 3, turn. Work dc in each sc across. Work same edging on other end.

Fringe: Cut strands of LO about 12″ long. Knot 3 strands tog in each dc across each end.

GREEN-AND-GOLD HAT

Shown

Greens and golds go 'round and 'round on an intricate-patterned hat.
Single crochet can be a challenge to the crocheter!

SIZE: Adjustable head size.

MATERIALS: Knitting worsted, 3 ozs. dark green (DG); 1 oz. each of gold (G) and light green (LG). Crochet hook size F.

GAUGE: 5 sc = 1".

HAT: Beg at center, with DG, ch 4. Sl st in first ch to form ring.

Rnd 1: Ch 1, 10 sc in ring.

Rnd 2: (2 sc in next sc, sc in next sc) 5 times—15 sc. Mark end of rnds.

Rnd 3: (Sc in each of next 2 sc, 2 sc in next sc) 5 times—20 sc.

Rnd 4: * Pull up a DG lp in next sc, finish sc with G, work 1 G sc in same st, repeat from * around—40 sc.

Rnd 5: * Pull up a G lp in next sc, finish sc with DG, pull up a DG lp in next sc, finish sc, with G, repeat from * around—40 sc.

Rnd 6: With G, sc in each st around, inc 6 sc evenly spaced around, finish last sc with LG—46 sc.

Rnd 7: * Pull up a lp of LG in next sc, finish sc with G, pull up a lp of G in next sc, finish sc with LG, repeat from * around, finish last sc with DG—46 sc. Hereafter, always finish sc with color of next sc.

Rnd 8: * DG sc in next sc, LG sc in next sc, repeat from * around, finish last sc with DG.

Rnd 9: With DG, sc around, inc 8 sc evenly spaced around—54 sc.

Rnd 10: Repeat rnd 8, inc 10 sc evenly spaced around (work DG and LG sc in same st)—64 sc.

Rnd 11: * LG sc in DG sc, G sc in LG sc, repeat from * around. Cut LG.

Rnd 12: With G, sc around, inc in every 6th st—74 sc.

Rnd 13: * G sc in next sc, DG sc in next sc, repeat from * around, inc in every 6th st—86 sc.

Rnd 14: With DG, sc around, inc in every 6th st—100 sc.

Rnd 15: * 2 DG sc in next sc, DG sc in next sc, G sc in next sc, (DG sc in each of next 3 sc, G sc in next sc) 5 times, repeat from * 3 times, end last repeat (DG sc in each of next 3 sc, G sc in next sc) 7 times—104 sc.

Rnd 16: G sc in first sc, (DG sc in next sc, G sc in next 3 sc) 25 times, DG sc in next sc, G sc in last 2 sc.

Rnd 17: With G, sc in each st around.

Rnd 18: * G sc in next sc, DG sc in next sc, repeat from * around. Cut G.

Rnds 19-22: With DG, sc in each st around.

Rnd 23: DG sc in first sc, (LG sc in next sc, DG sc in next 3 sc) 25 times, end LG sc in next sc, DG sc in last 2 sc.

Rnd 24: (LG sc in next 3 sc, DG sc in next sc) 26 times. With LG, sl st in first st. Ch 1, turn.

Rnd 25: Note: When inserting hook, keep both color strands above hook. Working on wrong side, LG sc in first sc, * G sc in next sc, LG sc in next sc, repeat from * around, end G sc in last sc. Sl st in first sc. Ch 1, turn.

Rnd 26: Work G sc in G sc, LG sc in LG sc around. Cut G.

Rnd 27: (LG sc in next 3 sc, DG sc in next sc) 26 times.

Rnd 28: Repeat rnd 23.

Rnd 29: With DG, sc in each st around. Sl st in first sc. Ch 1, turn.

Rnd 30: Working on wrong side, DG sc in first sc, * LG sc in next sc, DG sc in next sc, repeat from * around, end LG sc in last sc. Sl st in first sc. Ch 1, turn.

Rnd 31: Work LG sc in LG sc, DG sc in DG sc around. Cut LG.

Rnd 32: With DG, 2 sc in first sc, * sc in 5 sc, 2 sc in next sc, repeat from * around, sc in last sc—122 sc. Sl st in next sc. Ch 1, turn.

Rnd 33: Working on wrong side, * (DG sc in next sc, G sc in next sc) twice, DG sc in next sc, G sc and DG sc in next sc, (G sc in next sc, DG sc in next sc) twice, G sc in next sc, DG sc and G sc in next sc, repeat from * around—142 sc. Sl st in first sc. Ch 1, turn.

Rnd 34: G sc and DG sc in first sc; alternating G sc and DG sc, work in sc, inc in every 6th st—166 sc. Cut G.

Rnd 35: With DG, sc around.

Rnd 36: With DG, hdc around.

Rnd 37: With DG, sc around. With LG, sl st in first sc. Ch 1, turn.

Rnds 38 and 39: Repeat rnds 25 and 26. At end of rnd 39, cut LG and G.

Rnd 40: With DG, sc around. Sl st in first sc. End off.

"FEATHER" PATTERN HAT

Shown at right on page 136

Autumn tones repeat and repeat on our peacock "feathered" cap. Colors are carried around as you crochet the design.

SIZE: Adjustable head size.

MATERIALS: Knitting worsted, 3 ozs. rust (R); 1 oz. each of gold (G) and olive green (O). Crochet hook size H.

GAUGE: 3 sc = 1".

HAT: Beg at top, with R, ch 4. Sl st in first ch to form ring.

Rnd 1: Ch 1, 8 sc in ring.

Rnd 2: 2 sc in each sc. Mark end of each rnd.

Rnd 3: (2 sc in next sc, sc in next sc) 8 times—24 sc.

Rnd 4: * Sc in 2 sc, pull up a lp in next sc, drop R; with G, finish sc, pull up a lp in same st; with R, finish sc, repeat from * 7 times—32 sc. Always change colors in this way, by completing sc with new color. Carry unused colors loosely across inside of hat.

Rnd 5: (R sc in each R sc, 2 G sc in G sc) 8 times—40 sc.

Rnd 6: (R sc in each R sc, 2 G sc in next G sc, G sc in next G sc) 8 times—48 sc.

Rnd 7: (R sc in each R sc, G sc in next G sc, 2 G sc in next G sc, G sc in next G sc) 8 times—56 sc.

Rnd 8: (R sc in each R sc, G sc in next G sc, 1 G and 1 R sc in next sc, G sc in each of next 2 G sc) 8 times—64 sc.

Rnd 9: (R sc in next R sc, O sc in next R sc, R sc in next R sc, G sc in next 2 G sc, 2 R sc in next R sc, G sc in next 2 G sc) 8 times—72 sc.

Rnd 10: (R sc in next 3 sc, G sc in next 2 G sc, R and O sc in next sc, R sc in next sc, G sc in next 2 G sc) 8 times—80 sc.

Rnd 11: (R sc in next R sc, O sc in next R sc, R sc in next R sc, G sc in next 2 G sc, R sc in next R sc, 2 O sc in next O sc, R sc in next R sc, G sc in next 2 G sc) 8 times—88 sc.

Rnd 12: Continue in this manner, working in each sc (R sc, O sc, R sc, 2 G sc, R sc, 2 O sc in next sc, O sc, R sc, 2 G sc) 8 times—96 sc.

Rnd 13: (O sc, R sc, O sc, 2 G sc, R sc, O sc, 2 O sc in next sc, O sc, R sc, 2 G sc) 8 times—104 sc.

Rnd 14: (O sc, R sc, O sc, 2 G sc, R sc, O sc, O and G sc in next sc, 2 O sc, R sc, 2 G sc) 8 times—112 sc.

Rnd 15: (O sc, R sc, O sc, 2 G sc, R sc, 2 O sc, sk G sc, 2 O sc, R sc, 2 G sc) 8 times—104 sc.

Rnd 16: (O sc, 2 R sc in next R sc, O sc, 2 G sc, R sc, 2 O sc, sk next sc, O sc, R sc, 2 G sc) 8 times—104 sc.

Rnd 17: (O sc, 2 R sc in next sc, R sc, O sc, 2 G sc, R sc, O sc, sk next sc, O sc, R sc, 2 G sc) 8 times—104 sc.

Rnd 18: (O sc, R sc, 2 R sc in next sc, R sc, O sc, 2 G sc, R sc, sk next sc, O sc, R sc, 2 G sc) 8 times—104 sc.

Rnd 19: (O sc, R sc, 2 R sc in next sc, 2 R sc, O sc, 2 G sc, R sc, sk next sc, R sc, 2 G sc) 8 times—104 sc.

Rnd 20: (O sc, 2 R sc, G sc, 2 R sc, O sc, 2 G sc, sk next sc, R sc, 2 G sc) 8 times—96 sc.

Rnd 21: (O sc, 2 R sc, sk next G sc, 2 R sc, O sc, 2 G sc, sk next R sc, 2 G sc) 8 times—80 sc.

Rnd 22: (O sc, 4 R sc, O sc, G sc, sk next sc, 2 G sc) 8 times—72 sc.

Rnd 23: (O sc, 4 R sc, O sc, G sc, sk next sc, G sc) 8 times—64 sc.

Rnd 24: (O sc, R sc, 2 R sc in next sc, 2 R sc, O sc, sk next sc, G sc) 8 times—64 sc.

Rnd 25: (O sc, 2 R sc, 2 R sc in next sc, 2 R sc, O sc, sk next sc) 8 times —64 sc.

Rnd 26: (O sc, 2 R sc, 2 R sc in next sc, 3 R sc, sk next sc) 8 times—64 sc.

Rnds 27-31: Work even in sc, working 2 rnds R, 1 rnd O, 1 rnd G, 1 rnd O. Sl st in next st. End off.

BEACH HAT AND BAG SET

The beach hat and bag are made of string in a natural tone. The flowers are formed on a Crazy Daisy Winder, petals are finished with crochet, then motifs are trimmed with beads and sewn together. Hat brim is wired to hold its pretty shape. Bag has chains for drawstrings, jaunty fringe for decoration.

SIZE: Hat: Adjustable head size. Bag: 15″ deep, plus fringe.

MATERIALS: Six balls medium-weight string. Sixty-six wooden beads. Matching sewing thread. Crazy Daisy Winder. Hero aluminum crochet hook size G. Wooden crochet hook No. 15. Four feet of galvanized wire.

GAUGE: 7 sc = 2″.

HAT: Following directions accompanying Crazy Daisy Winder, make 22 double-wrap daisies. Complete each daisy as follows:

Rnd 1: With G hook, sc in one double petal, * ch 2, sc in next double petal, repeat from * around, end ch 2, sl st in first sc.

Rnd 2: Sc in each sc and ch around—36 sc. End off. Sew a bead to center of each daisy with matching thread.

CROWN: Rnd 1: Using 1 daisy for top of crown, arrange 6 daisies around top one. Sewing through back lps of sc with twine, join 3 sc of a daisy in first rnd to 3 sc of top daisy. Sk 3 sc on top daisy and join next daisy in same way. Repeat until 6 daisies are joined to top daisy. Join these 6 daisies tog in same way, skipping 3 sc from top joinings. There will be 21 free sc on bottom edge of each daisy.

Rnd 2: Join 6 daisies tog for lower rnd of crown, joining 3 sc on opposite sides of daisies (there will be 15 free sc on top and bottom edges of these daisies). Join each daisy of lower rnd to 2 daisies of first rnd, skipping 3 sc between joinings on lower rnd and skipping 5 sc between joinings on first rnd.

BRIM: Rnd 1: With size G hook, sk 4 sc on lower edge of crown, * sc in back lp of each of next 7 sc, ch 6, sk 4 sc on lower edge of next daisy, repeat from * around.

Rnd 2: Sc in each sc and ch around—78 sc.

Rnd 3: * Sc in next sc, 2 sc in next sc, repeat from * around—117 sc. Sl st in first sc. End off.

Join 9 daisies in a ring, skipping 12 sc on top edge of each daisy. Place top edge of ring over 3 sc rnds of brim. Sew daisies over sc rnds.

BRIM EDGING: Rnd 1: Sk 6 sc on lower edge of brim, * sc in back lp of each of next 7 sc, ch 9, sk 6 sc on lower edge of next daisy, repeat from * around.

Rnd 2: Cut wire to fit around bottom of brim, allowing 2″ extra for overlapping. Working over wire, sc in each sc and ch around.

CORD: With No. 15 hook, using 5 strands of string tog, make a chain 36″ long. Knot each end. Sew cord around top of brim, leaving equal ends for tying at back of hat.

BAG: Make 44 daisies and complete each daisy as for hat. Using 22 daisies for front and 22 daisies for back, arrange each piece with 3 top rows of 4 daisies each and 2 bottom rows of 5 daisies each. With string, sew daisies tog through back lps of sc where they meet. Do not sew back and front tog. Line each piece if desired.

FINISHING: With No. 15 hook, using 5 strands of string tog, make a chain long enough to fit around sides and bottom of bag. Sew front and back of bag to sides of chain.

FRINGE: Cut string in 12″ lengths. Using 4 strands tog, starting and ending below top row of daisies, knot strands in each ch along sides and bottom of bag.

DRAWSTRINGS (make 2): Make a chain as for cord about 45″ long. Beg at side of bag, weave chain around bag through open spaces below top row of daisies. Sew ends tog. Beg at opposite side of bag, repeat with 2nd drawstring.

FISHLINE BAGS

Fishline was used to make these little bags, but other materials can be used. The bag with key closing and the bag with button closing are both made of two squares, the back squares extended to form the flap. Sides, bottom and handle are in one piece.

BAG WITH KEY CLOSING:

SIZE: About 8″ square.

MATERIALS: Nylon fishline, 200-lb. test, about 120 yds. Aluminum crochet hook size I or 8. Key. Lining material, 9″ x 18″. Matching sewing thread.

GAUGE: 3 sts = 1″; 5 rnds = 4″.

BAG: FRONT PIECE: Ch 5, sl st in first ch to form ring.

Rnd 1: Ch 3 (counts as 1 dc), 2 dc in ring, (ch 2, 3 dc in ring) 3 times, ch 2, join with sl st to top of ch 3.

Rnd 2: Ch 3, 2 dc in ch-2 sp just made, (ch 1, 3 dc, ch 2, 3 dc in next ch-2 sp) 3 times, end ch 1, 3 dc in first corner, ch 2, join to top of ch 3.

Rnd 3: Ch 3, 2 dc in ch-2 sp just made, (ch 1, 3 dc in next ch-1 sp, ch 1, 3 dc, ch 2, 3 dc in corner ch-2 sp) 3 times, ch 1, 3 dc in next ch-1 sp, ch 1, 3 dc in first corner, ch 2, join to top of ch 3.

Rnd 4: Ch 3, 2 dc in ch-2 sp just made, * (ch 1, 3 dc in next ch-1 sp) twice, ch 1, 3 dc, ch 2, 3 dc in corner sp, repeat from * twice, (ch 1, 3 dc in next ch-1 sp) twice, ch 1, 3 dc in first corner, ch 2, join to top of ch 3.

Rnd 5: Work as for rnd 4, having 1 more group of 3 dc between corners. End off.

BACK PIECE: Work as for front through rnd 5; do not end off.

Flap: Row 1: Ch 3, dc in each of next 2 dc, (dc in next ch, dc in each of next 3 dc) 4 times. Ch 3, turn.

Row 2: Sk first dc, dc in each dc across, dc in top of ch 3. Ch 3, turn.

Row 3: Sk first dc, dc in each of next 2 dc, (ch 1, sk 1 dc, dc in each of next 3 dc) 4 times. Ch 4, turn.

Row 4: (3 dc in next ch-1 sp, ch 1) 4 times, dc in top of ch 3. Ch 3, turn.

Row 5: 2 dc in ch-1 sp, (ch 1, 3 dc in next ch-1 sp) 3 times, ch 1, 2 dc in ch-4 sp, dc in 3rd ch of ch 4. Ch 4, turn.

Row 6: Repeat row 4.

Row 7: Repeat row 5. Do not ch 4. Turn.

Row 8: Sl st in each st across to center group of 3 dc, ch 6, sk center group of 3 dc, sl st in each st to end of row. End off.

SIDES, HANDLE, AND BOTTOM: Ch 100. Dc in 3rd ch from hook and in each ch across.

FINISHING: Hold strip for side, bottom and handle to wrong side of front piece. Beg at one corner, sc strip to side, bottom and opposite side of front piece, working through back lp only of each dc and ch of front piece and front lp only of each dc of strip. Join back piece to strip in same way. Remainder of strip is for handle. Sew end in place.

KEY CHAIN: Join cord securely to hole of key, ch 10, sl st in ch-1 sp at one end of ch-lp on flap. End off. (To close bag, key is inserted down through ch-lp on flap, under 3-dc group on first rnd of bag, and up through ch-lp on flap.)

LINING: Fold lining piece in half crosswise, stitch ½″ seam each side. Insert lining in bag, turn under ½″ around top edge, sew to bag.

BAG WITH BUTTON CLOSING:

SIZE: About 7″ square.

MATERIALS: Dacron fishline, 80-lb. test, about 250 yds. Steel crochet hook No. 4. Tapestry needle. Cotton for stuffing button. Lining fabric, 8″ x 16″. Matching sewing thread.

GAUGE: 6 dc = 1″; 3 rnds = 1″.

BAG: FRONT PANEL: Ch 5, sl st in first ch to form ring.

Rnd 1: Ch 3 (counts as 1 dc), 2 dc in ring, (ch 2, 3 dc in ring) 3 times, ch 2, sl st in top of ch 3.

Rnd 2: Ch 3, 2 dc in ch-2 sp just made, (ch 1, 3 dc, ch 2, 3 dc in next ch-2 sp) 3 times, ch 1, 3 dc in first ch-2 sp, ch 2, sl st in top of ch 3.

Rnd 3: Ch 3, 2 dc in ch-2 sp just made, (ch 1, 3 dc in next ch-1 sp, ch 1, 3 dc, ch 2, 3 dc in next ch-2 corner sp) 3 times, ch 1, 3 dc in next ch-1 sp, ch 1, 3 dc in first corner sp, ch 2, sl st in top of ch 3.

Rnds 4-9: Continue in this manner, having 1 more group of 3 dc between corners each rnd; end with 7 groups of dc between corners. End off.

BACK PANEL AND FLAP: Work back panel as for front panel through rnd 9. Do not end off.

Row 1: Ch 3, dc in each of next 2 dc, dc in next ch 1, * dc in each of next 3 dc, dc in next ch, repeat from * across first side, end dc in each of first 3 dc of corner—35 dc. Ch 3, turn.

Row 2: Sk first dc, dc in each dc across, dc in top of ch 3. Ch 3, turn.

Row 3: Sk first dc, dc in back lp of each of next 2 dc, * ch 1, sk 1 dc, dc in back lp of each of next 3 dc, repeat from * across, end dc in back lp of each of last 2 dc, dc in top of turning ch. Ch 4, turn.

Row 4: * 3 dc in next ch-1 sp, ch 1, repeat from * across, end ch 1, dc in top of turning ch. Ch 3, turn.

Row 5: 2 dc in ch-1 sp, * ch 1, 3 dc in next ch-1 sp, repeat from * across, end 2 dc in last sp, dc in 3rd ch of ch-4 turning ch. Ch 4, turn.

Rows 6-9: Repeat rows 4 and 5 twice. At end of row 9, ch 1, turn.

Row 10: * Sc in each of 3 dc, sc in next ch, repeat from * twice, sc in next dc, ch 14 for button loop, sk next 9 sts, sc in next dc, sc in next ch, sc in each of next 3 dc, continue across in sc, end sc in top of turning ch. End off.

SIDES, HANDLE, AND BOTTOM: Ch 185, or long enough to fit around sides and bottom of front panel and form handle. Dc in 3rd ch from hook, dc in each ch across, 7 dc in last ch. Working on opposite side of ch, dc in each ch across. Do not end off.

FINISHING: Hold strip just made along side edge of front panel. Beg at top corner of front panel, working down side, sc front panel to strip, working through back lp only of each dc and ch of front panel and front lp only of each dc of strip. Continue around bottom and opposite side of front panel to top. Working across top edge of front panel, work sc in back lp of each dc and ch across. Sc across top edge of strip. Join back panel below flap to opposite edge of strip in same way. Sew curved end of remaining strip over top edge of strip on opposite side, for handle.

From right side, join cord to corner st at top of back. Sc along side edge of flap, keeping work flat, 3 sc in corner, sc in each sc and each ch of button loop to opposite corner, 3 sc in corner, sc along side edge of flap. End off.

BUTTON: Ch 4, sl st in first ch to form ring.

Rnd 1: Ch 3, 10 dc in ring. Join to top of ch 3.

Rnd 2: Ch 3, 2 dc in each dc around. Join to top of ch 3.

Rnd 3: Ch 3; * working in back lps only, dec 1 dc over next 2 sts (**to dec 1 dc:** yo hook, pull up a lp in next dc, yo hook and through 2

lps, yo hook, pull up a lp in next dc, yo hook and through 2 lps, yo hook and through 3 lps on hook), repeat from * around—10 dc. Join to top of ch 3.

Rnd 4: Ch 3, dec to 5 dc, stuffing button with cotton during rnd. Cut cord, leaving end for sewing. Thread end in needle, pull sts tog; sew button to center of front.

LINING: Fold fabric in half crosswise, stitch ½″ seam each side. Slip lining into bag, turn under ½″ around top edge, sew to bag.

WATERMELON BAG

A slice of melon is the model for this shoulder bag. Quick to crochet of rug yarn in rows of double crochet. Seeds are cut from black felt, glued on. Lining is optional.

SIZE: 7½″ wide.
MATERIALS: Rug yarn, 1 70-yd. skein each of melon (M), light green (G) and dark green (DG). Aluminum crochet hook size I. Scrap of black felt. One large snap fastener.
GAUGE: 3 dc = 1″; 5 rnds = 3″.
BAG: FIRST HALF: With M, ch 4, sl st in first ch to form ring.

Rnd 1: Ch 3, 12 dc in ring. Sl st in top of ch 3.

Rnd 2: Ch 3, dc in same ch as sl st, 2 dc in each dc around—26 dc, counting ch 3 as 1 dc. Join with sl st in top of ch 3.

Rnd 3: Ch 3, * 2 dc in next dc, 1 dc in next dc, repeat from *

around, end 2 dc in last dc—39 dc. Join.

Rnd 4: Ch 3, dc in each of next 2 dc, * 2 dc in next dc, dc in each of next 3 dc, repeat from * around, end dc in 2 dc, 2 dc in last dc—49 dc. Join.

Rnd 5: Ch 3, dc in each of next 4 dc, 2 dc in next dc, * dc in each of next 5 dc, 2 dc in next dc, repeat from * 3 times, dc in each of next 5 dc—40 dc. Working across top of bag, ch 2, 2 hdc in side of last dc made, dc in same st with last dc made, hdc in each of next 3 dc, sl st in each of next 7 dc, hdc in each of next 3 dc, dc in next st, 3 hdc in side of ch 3. End off M.

Join G in last hdc, ch 3, dc around to opposite side of top edge, inc 1 dc every 8th st. End off.

Make another piece the same for 2nd half.
FINISHING: Steam-press pieces lightly. Hold pieces wrong side tog; with DG, sc pieces tog around sides and bottom, ch 36″ or desired length for strap, sl st twice in opposite corner, being careful not to twist ch. Sc in each ch to beg of ch. Sl st in edge. End off. Sew snap fastener inside top center of bag. Cut 12 or 14 "seeds" about ¾″ long from black felt. Glue or sew half to each side of bag.

STRAWBERRY BAG

A plump strawberry inspired teen's bag. Of two identical pieces, the bag is easy to make in double crochet of rayon and cotton rug yarn. The seeds are embroidered.

SIZE: 7½″ wide.
MATERIALS: Rug yarn, 1 70-yd. skein each of red (R) and avocado (A); small amount of black (B). Aluminum crochet hook

size I. Yarn needle. One large snap fastener.
GAUGE: 3 dc = 1″; 3 rows = 2″.
BAG: FIRST HALF: Beg at bottom, with R, ch 9.

Row 1: Dc in 3rd ch from hook and in each remaining ch. Ch 3, turn.

Row 2: Dc in first st, dc in each of next 5 dc, 2 dc in next dc, dc in

top of turning ch—10 dc counting turning ch as 1 dc. Ch 3, turn.

Row 3: Dc in first st, 2 dc in next st, dc in each of 6 dc, 2 dc in next dc, 2 dc in turning ch—14 dc. Ch 3, turn.

Rows 4-6: Dc in first st, dc in each dc across, 2 dc in turning ch, ch 3, turn.

Row 7: Sk first st, dc in each dc across, dc in turning ch—20 dc. Ch 3, turn.

Row 8: Repeat row 7. Ch 2, turn.

Row 9: Sk first st, hdc in next st, dc in 16 sts, hdc in last 2 sts. Ch 2, turn.

Row 10: Repeat row 9.

Row 11: Sk first st, hdc in next st, dc in next 6 sts, hdc in next st, sl st in next 2 sts, hdc in next st, dc in next 6 sts, hdc in last 2 sts. Ch 1, turn.

Row 12: Sc in 2nd st, hdc in next 6 sts, sc in next st, sl st in next 2 sts, sc in next st, hdc in next 6 sts, sc in last 2 sts. End off.

Make another piece the same for 2nd half.

FINISHING: Steam-press pieces lightly. With B, embroider V-shaped seeds on both halves. Hold pieces wrong sides tog; with R, sc pieces tog along side and bottom edges.

LEAVES: With A, make lp on hook, sc in first sc at center of row 12, * ch 7; sc in 2nd ch from hook and in next 5 ch, sc in next st on row 12, repeat from * 3 times—4 leaves. End off. Work leaves on both halves.

SHOULDER STRAP: Join A in top side edge of bag, make ch 36″ long or desired length, sl st twice in opposite side edge, being careful not to twist ch. Sc in each ch to opposite side. Sl st in edge. End off. Sew snap fastener inside top center of bag.

2
FOR MEN

CROCHETED "ARAN"

Rugged fisherman pullover is crocheted to look just like the knits from Aran!
Puffs and popcorns and other raised stitches are a challenge to the crocheter.
Neckline is V'd; raglan sleeves are sewn in.

SIZES: Directions for small size (36-38). Changes for medium size (40-42) are in parentheses.

Blocked Chest Size: 40" (44").

MATERIALS: Knitting worsted, 7 (8) 4-oz. skeins. Crochet hook size J.

GAUGE: 3 sc = 1"; 7 rows = 2".

To Dec 1 St: At beg of a row, ch 1, pull up a lp in each of 2 sts, yo hook and through 3 lps on hook; **at end of a row,** work to within last 2 sts, pull up a lp in each of 2 sts, yo hook and through 3 lps on hook.

To Inc 1 St: Work 2 sc in same st.

STITCH PATTERNS: Note: Do not work in st directly behind raised dc or double raised dc, or in eye of a cluster.

CLUSTER: (Yo hook, draw up a lp in st) 4 times, yo and draw through all 9 lps on hook. Ch 1 tightly to form eye. (Cluster is worked from wrong side but appears on right side.)

RAISED DC: Dc around upright bar of dc 1 row below, inserting hook behind dc from front to back to front, for ridge on right side.

DOUBLE RAISED DC: Holding back last lp of each dc on hook, make 2 dc around upright bar of st 1 row below, yo and through all 3 lps on hook.

POPCORN: 4 dc in st, drop lp off hook, insert hook in top of first dc, pick up dropped lp and pull through.

PULLOVER: BACK: Beg at lower edge, ch 52 (58).

Row 1: Sc in 2nd ch from hook

CROCHETED "ARAN" AND ARGYLE SOLO

and in each ch across—51 (57) sc. Ch 1, turn each row.

Row 2 (wrong side): Sc in each of first 7 (10) sts, (cluster in next sc, sc in each of next 17 sts) twice, end cluster in next st, sc in each of last 7 (10) sts.

Row 3 (right side): Sc in each of first 5 (8) sc, * work dc around post of next sc 1 row below (row 1), sk next sc on row 2 (see Stitch Patterns: Note), sc in each of next 3 sts, dc around post of next sc 1 row below, sk next sc on row 2, sc in each of next 5 sc; holding back last lp of each dc on hook, make 2 dc around next sc 1 row below, yo and through 3 lps on hook, sk next sc on row 2, sc in next sc, sk 1 sc on row 1, make 2 dc around next sc as before, sk next sc on row 2, sc in each of next 5 sc, repeat from * once, end dc around post of next sc 1 row below, sc in each of next 3 sts, dc around post of next sc 1 row below, sc in each of last 5 (8) sc.

Row 4: Sc in each of first 6 (9) sts, (cluster in next sc, sc in next sc, cluster in next sc, sc in each of next 15 sts) twice, end cluster in next sc, sc in next sc, cluster in next sc, sc in each of last 6 (9) sts.

Row 5: Sc in each of first 5 (8) sc, (raised dc in raised dc, sc in each of next 3 sts, raised dc in raised dc, sc in each of next 4 sts, double raised dc in double raised dc, sc in each of next 3 sc, double raised dc in double raised dc, sc in each of next 4 sc) twice, end raised dc in raised dc, sc in each of next 3 sts, raised dc in raised dc, sc in each of last 5 (8) sts.

Row 6: Repeat row 2.

Row 7: Sc in each of first 5 (8) sc, (raised dc in raised dc, sc in each of next 3 sts, raised dc in raised dc, sc in each of next 3 sc, double raised dc in double raised dc, sc in each of next 5 sc, double raised dc in double raised dc, sc in each of next 3 sc) twice, end raised dc in raised

dc, sc in each of next 3 sts, raised dc in raised dc, sc in each of last 5 (8) sts.

Row 8: Repeat row 4.

Row 9: Sc in each of first 5 (8) sc, (raised dc in raised dc, sc in each of next 3 sts, raised dc in raised dc, sc in each of next 2 sc, double raised dc in double raised dc, sc in each of next 3 sc, popcorn in next sc, sc in each of next 3 sc, double raised dc in double raised dc, sc in each of next 2 sc) twice, end raised dc in raised dc, sc in each of next 3 sts, raised dc in raised dc, sc in each of last 5 (7) sc.

Row 10: Repeat row 2.
Row 11: Repeat row 7.
Row 12: Repeat row 4.
Row 13: Repeat row 5.
Row 14: Repeat row 2.
Row 15: Sc in each of first 5 (8) sc, (raised dc in raised dc, sc in each of next 3 sts, raised dc in raised dc, sc in each of next 5 sc, double raised dc in double raised dc, sc in next sc, double raised dc in double raised dc, sc in each of next 5 sc) twice, end raised dc in raised dc, sc in each of next 3 sts, raised dc in raised dc, sc in each of last 5 (8) sc.

Repeat rows 4-15 until piece measures 19″ from start or desired length to underarm. Piece should measure 20″ (22″) wide.

Shape Raglan Armholes: Keeping to pat, dec 1 st each side (see To Dec 1 St) every other row 18 (20) times—15 (17) sts remain. End off.

FRONT: Work same as for back until piece measures 1 row less than back to underarm.

Divide Work: Work 25 (28) sts, drop yarn; sk center st, join another strand of yarn in next st, finish row.

Shape Raglan Armhole and V-Neck: Working on both sides at once, with separate strands of yarn, dec 1 st at each arm side

every other row 18 (20) times; **at the same time,** dec 1 st at each neck edge every 4th row 6 (7) times—1 st remains. End off.

SLEEVES: Beg at lower edge, ch 28 (30).

Row 1: Sc in 2nd ch from hook and in each ch across—27 (29) sc. Ch 1, turn each row.

Row 2 (wrong side): Sc in each of first 4 (5) sts, cluster in next sc, sc in each of next 17 sts, cluster in next st, sc in each of last 4 (5) sts.

Row 3 (right side): Sc in each of first 2 (3) sc, work dc around post of next sc 1 row below (row 1), sk next sc on row 2, sc in each of next 3 sts, dc around post of next sc 1 row below, sk next sc on row 2, sc in each of next 5 sc, double raised dc around next sc 1 row below, sk next sc on row 2, sc in next sc, sk 1 sc on row 1, double raised dc around next sc as before, sk next sc on row 2, sc in each of next 5 sc, dc around post of next sc 1 row below, sc in each of next 3 sts, dc around post of next sc 1 row below, sc in each of last 2 (3) sc. Continue in pat as established, inc 1 sc each side (see To Inc 1 St) every 6th row 7 (8) times, working added sts in sc—41 (45) sts. Work even until piece measures 19″ from start or desired length to underarm. Piece above last inc row should measure 15½″ (17″) wide.

Shape Raglan Cap: Keeping to pat, dec 1 st each side every other row 18 (20) times—5 sts remaining. End off.

FINISHING: Sew caps of sleeves to back and front armholes. Sew side and sleeve seams.

Neckband: Join yarn in shoulder seam. From right side, sc across back of neck, down front neck edge, sc in center front st, mark this st for center front, sc up other front neck edge having same number of sts on both edges and easing in to desired fit. Join with a sl st in first sc; do not turn.

Rnds 2-4: Sc in each sc around, dec 1 sc each side of center front st.

Rnd 5: From right side, working from left to right (**left-handed crocheters:** from right to left), sc in each sc around. End off.

From right side, work 3 rnds sc around lower edge of each sleeve, easing in to desired fit. Work 2 rnds sc around lower edge of body.

Steam lightly; do not flatten pattern.

ARGYLE SOLO

Shown at right on page 147

One bold argyle pattern emblazons the front of this sleeveless slip-on, worked in double crochet. The deep-blue bands on neck and armholes are knitted, then sewn on. The band at the waist is knitted on.

SIZES: Directions for small size (36-38). Changes for medium size (40-42) and large size (44-46) are in parentheses.

Body Chest Size: 36"-38" (40"-42"; 44"-46").

Blocked Chest Size: 38" (43"-46").

MATERIALS: Knitting worsted, 5 (5-6) 2-oz. skeins main color (MC); 2 skeins border color (A); 1 skein design color (B). Knitting needles No. 6. Crochet hook size H.

GAUGE: 7 dc = 2"; 5 rows = 3".

To Bind Off: At beg of a row, sl st loosely across specified number of sts, ch 3, work in dc across: **at end of a row,** leave specified number of sts unworked.

To Dec 1 Dc: At beg of a row, ch 3 (counts as 1 dc), sk first dc, * yo hook, pull up a lp in each of next 2 dc, yo hook and through 3 lps on hook, yo and through remaining 2 lps on hook *; **at end of a row,** work to last 3 sts, work from first * to 2nd * dc in top of turning ch.

SLIP-ON: BACK: With MC and crochet hook, ch 69 (77-83).

Row 1: Dc in 4th ch from hook (counts as 2 dc), dc in each remaining ch—67 (75-81) dc. Ch 3, turn.

Rows 2-20: Sk first dc, dc in each dc across, dc in top of turning ch. Ch 3, turn each row. Check gauge; piece should measure 19" (21½"-23") wide.

Shape Armholes: Bind off (see To Bind Off) 5 sts each side of next row. Dec 1 st (see To Dec 1 Dc) each side every row 4 (5-6) times. Work even on 49 (55-59) sts until armholes measure 8½" (9"-9½") from bound-off sts.

Shape Shoulders: Bind off 5 (7-8) sts each side of next row. On next row, bind off 5 sts, work 5 dc; end off. Sk 19 (21-23) dc for back of neck, join yarn in next dc, work 5 dc; end off.

Notes: When changing colors, always pull new color through last 2 lps of old color to complete dc. Carry yarn not used loosely across top of sts and work over it within design.

FRONT: Work as for back for 2 rows.

Row 3: Work 33 (37-40) dc, change to B (see Notes), work 1 B dc, change to MC, work 33 (37-40) dc. Following chart, work design on center front until 20 rows from start of front.

Shape Armholes and Neck: Continuing with chart, bind off 5 sts each side of next row. Dec 1 st each side every row 4 (5-6) times; **at the same time,** when top of chart is reached, cut B, work 1 row MC; begin V neck on next row: work to st before center st; drop MC. Sk center st, join another strand of MC in next st, ch 3, finish row. Working with separate balls of yarn, dec 1 st at neck edge every row 9 (10-11) times. Work even on 15 (17-18) dc until armholes measure same as back.

Shape Shoulders: Bind off 5 (7-8) sts each arm side on next row, 5 sts on next row. End off.

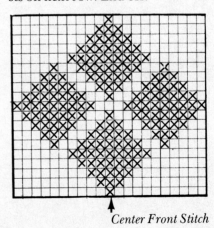

Center Front Stitch

FINISHING: Sew shoulder seams.

Ribbing: From right side, with A and knitting needles, pick up and k 86 (90-94) sts across lower back edge. Work in k 1, p 1 ribbing for 5″ or desired length. Bind off in ribbing. Work same ribbing on front. Sew side seams.

Neckband: With A, cast on 149 (155-161) sts. Work in k 1, p 1 ribbing, dec 1 st each end every row 4 times. Bind off. Sew ends tog to form a mitered point. Sew neckband over neck edge, mitered point at center front.

Armband (make 2): With A, cast on 101 (109-117) sts. Work as for neckband. Sew around armhole, mitered point at underarm seam.

PLAID PULLOVER

SIZES: Directions for boys' size 12. Changes for sizes 14 and 16 are in parentheses.

Body Chest Size: 30″ (32″-34″).

Blocked Chest Size: 31½″ (34″-36″).

MATERIALS: Knitting worsted, 5 (5-6) 4-oz. skeins yellow, main color (MC); 1 skein each of red (R) and gray (G). Aluminum crochet hooks sizes G and H.

GAUGE: 7 sts = 2″; 3 rows = 1″ (pat, size H hook).

To Bind Off: At beg of a row, ch 1, sl st loosely across specified sts, work in pat across; **at end of a row,** leave specified number of sts unworked.

To Dec 1 St: At beg of a row, ch 1 loosely, pull up a lp in each of first 2 sts, yo and through 3 lps on hook; **at end of a row,** pull up a lp in each of last 2 sts, yo and through 3 lps on hook.

To Inc 1 St: Make 2 sts in 1 st.

Note: Vertical stripes are crocheted after pieces are completed. Cut and join R and G as needed; carry MC loosely up sides when not being used.

PULLOVER: BACK: Beg at lower edge, with MC and size G hook, ch 57 (59-63) loosely.

Border Pattern: Row 1 (wrong side): Dc in 4th ch from hook and in each ch across—55 (57-61) dc, counting starting ch 3 as 1 dc.

Row 2: Ch 3 (counts as 1 dc), sk first dc, dc in each of next 1 (2-2) sts, * front raised dc in next st (**to make front raised dc,** dc around upright bar of dc 1 row below, inserting hook from front to back to front, for ridge on right side), dc in next dc, repeat from * across, end last repeat dc in each of last 2 (3-3) sts.

Row 3: Ch 3 (counts as 1 dc), sk first dc, dc in each of next 1 (2-2) dc, * back raised dc in next st (**to make back raised dc,** dc around upright bar of dc 1 row below, inserting hook from back to front to back, for ridge on right side), dc in next dc, repeat from * across, end last repeat dc in each of last 2 (3-3) sts. Repeat rows 2 and 3 for border pat until piece measures about 3″ from start, inc 0 (1-1) st (see To Inc 1 St) each side of last row, end wrong side—55 (59-63) sts. Change to size H hook.

Striped Pattern: Row 1 (right side): Ch 3 (counts as 1 dc), (sc in next st, dc in next st) 1 (2-3) times, * ch 1, sk next st, (dc in next st, sc in next st) 3 times, dc in next st, repeat from * across, end last repeat (dc in next st, sc in next st) 1 (2-3) times, dc in last st. Turn.

Row 2: Ch 1, (sc in next st, dc in next st) 1 (2-3) times, sc in next st, * ch 1, sk ch-1 sp, (sc in next st, dc in next st) 3 times, sc in next st, repeat from * across, end last repeat (sc in next st, dc in next st) 1 (2-3) times, sc in last st.

Rows 3-8: Repeat rows 1 and 2.

Row 9: With R, repeat row 1.

Row 10: With G, repeat row 2. Repeat rows 1-10 for striped pat, always working sc over dc, dc over sc and ch 1 over ch 1. Work even until piece measures 13″ (14″-15″) from start or desired length to underarm. Check gauge; piece above border should measure 15¾″ (17″-18″) wide.

Shape Armholes: Keeping to striped pat, bind off (see To Bind Off) 3 sts each side of next row. Dec 1 st (see To Dec 1 St) each side every row 2 (3-3) times—45 (47-51) sts. Work even until armholes measure 7″ (7½″-8″) above bound-off sts.

Shape Shoulders: Bind off 4 (5-6) sts, sc in each of next 5 sts, hdc in each of next 5 sts, end off. Sk next 16 (16-18) sts for neck edge, join color to be used in next st, hdc in each of next 5 sts, sc in each of next 5 sts, end off.

FRONT: Work same as for back until piece measures 1 row less than back to underarm shaping—55 (59-63) sts.

Shape Neck and Underarms: Next Row: Keeping to striped pat, work 27 (29-31) sts, drop yarn, sk next st, join same color yarn in next st, finish row—27 (29-31) sts

Sun-yellow pullover in boys' teen sizes is strongly plaided in a cardinal red and steel gray. Horizontal stripes are worked in the pattern stitch; vertical stripes are chain-stitched up.

each side. Working on both sides at once, with separate strands of yarn, bind off 3 sts each arm side of next row, then dec 1 st at each arm side every row 2 (3-3) times; **at the same time,** dec 1 st at each neck edge every 3rd row 6 (6-7) times, then every other row twice—14 (15-16) sts each side. Work even until armholes measure same as back.

Shape Shoulders: Working on first shoulder, beg at arm side, bind off 4 (5-6) sts, sc in each of next 5 sts, hdc in each of next 5 sts, end off. Working on other shoulder, beg at neck edge, hdc in each of 5 sts, sc in each of next 5 sts, end off.

SLEEVES: Beg at lower edge, with MC and size G hook, ch 29 (29-31) loosely.

Border Pattern: Row 1 (wrong side): Dc in 4th ch from hook and in each ch across—27 (27-29) dc, counting starting ch 3 as 1 dc.

Row 2: Ch 3 (counts as 1 dc), sk first dc, dc in each of next 1 (1-2) dc, * front raised dc in next st, dc in next st, repeat from * across, end last repeat dc in each of last 2 (2-3) sts. Work in border pat as established until piece measures 3″ from start, end right side.

Next Row (inc row): Ch 3, sk first dc, dc in each of next 1 (1-2) sts, back raised dc in next st, dc in next st, (back raised dc in next st, 2 dc in next st) 8 (10-10) times, (back raised dc in next dc, dc in next dc) 3 (1-1) times, end dc in each of last 2 (3-3) sts—35 (37-39) sts. Change to size H hook. To determine where to start striped pat on sleeves, so that you end at underarm with same pat row as back, measure down from back underarm for 13″ (14″-15″) or 3″ less than desired sleeve length (border allowance). Note striped pat row color.

Striped Pattern: Row 1 (right side): Beg with this color, **for size 12 only,** ch 3, (sc in next st, dc in next st) twice; **for size 14 only,** ch 1, sc in first st, dc in next st, (sc in next st, dc in next st) twice; **for size 16 only,** ch 3, (sc in next st, dc in next st) 3 times; **for all sizes,** * ch 1, sk next st, (dc in next st, sc in next st) 3 times, dc in next st, repeat from * across, end last repeat dc (sc-dc) in last st. Working striped pat as established, inc 1 st each side every 2″ 6 times, working added sts into pat—47 (49-51) sts. Work even until piece measures 16″ (17″-18″) from start or desired sleeve length, end same pat row as back at underarm. Check gauge; piece above last inc row should measure 13½″ (14″-14½″) wide.

Shape Cap: Keeping to pat, bind off 3 sts each side of next row. Dec 1 st each side every row 11 (12-13) times. Bind off 2 sts each side every row twice—11 sts. End off.

VERTICAL LINES (worked in each ch-1 sp): Beg at center lower edge of striped pat with right side of back facing you, hold double strand of G on wrong side of work; insert size H hook in first ch-1 sp, bring yarn through to right side (lp on hook), * insert hook in ch-1 sp above, bring yarn through work and through lp on hook at same time, repeat from * to top of back, end off. Work vertical R stripe in ch-1 sps on each side of G stripe. Continue to alternate R and G stripes to outer side edge. Alternate G and R stripes in ch-1 sps on each sleeve. Weave ends in on wrong side.

FINISHING: With backstitch, sew shoulder seams; sew in sleeves. Sew side and sleeve seams.

Neckband: Beg at shoulder seam, with MC and size H hook, work 32 (34-36) sl sts down front neck edge, sl st in center front st, work 32 (34-36) sl sts up other front neck edge, work 19 (21-23) sl sts across back of neck. Ch 3, do not turn.

Next Rnd: Dc in back lp of each sl st to within 2 sts of center front sl st, dec 1 dc, dc in center sl st, dec 1 dc, dc in back lp of each sl st around, join with a sl st in top of ch 3.

Next Rnd: Ch 3, * dc in next dc, front raised dc in next dc, repeat from * around, join with a sl st in first dc. End off.

Steam lightly; do not press.

CONTINENTAL JACKET

Man's side-zip jacket in golden beige wool has Continental styling in the high round neckline, leather-buttoned. Made in Switzerland, the sweater features a unique star stitch pattern, snug borders in single crochet.

SIZES: Directions for size 38. Changes for sizes 40, 42 and 44 are in parentheses.

Body Chest Size: 38″ (40″-42″-44″).

Blocked Chest Size (closed): 39″ (42″-45″-48″).

MATERIALS: Knitting worsted, 8 (8-9-9) 4-oz. skeins. Crochet hook size H. Separating zipper. Two buttons.

GAUGE: 5 star sts= 3″; 9 rows = 5″.

PATTERN: Row 1 (wrong side): Yo hook, pull up a lp in first dc, yo hook, pull up a lp in next dc, yo hook, pull up a lp in same dc, yo hook and through 7 lps on hook, ch 1 for eye (star st made), * (yo hook, pull up a lp in next dc) twice, yo hook, pull up a lp in dc just worked in, yo hook and through 7 lps on hook, ch 1 for eye, repeat from * across, end yo hook, pull up a lp in last dc, yo hook, pull up a lp in top of turning ch, yo hook, pull up a lp in same ch, yo hook and through 7 lps on hook, ch 1 for eye. Ch 3, turn.

Row 2: Dc in eye of first star st, * 2 dc in eye of next star st, repeat from * across, end dc in eye of last star st, dc in top of turning ch. Ch 3, turn. Repeat these 2 rows for pat.

JACKET: BACK: Beg at lower edge, ch 68 (72-76-82). Dc in 4th ch from hook and in each ch across—65 (69-73-79) dc plus turning ch. Ch 3, turn. Work in pat on 33 (35-37-40) star sts until piece measures 16″ from start or desired length to underarm, end pat row 2. Check gauge; piece should be 19½″ (21″-22½″-24″) wide.

Shape Armholes: Row 1 (wrong side): Sl st in each of 2 (2-2-4) dc, star st over next 2 dc, work in pat to within last 1 (1-1-3) dc and turning ch—31 (33-35-36) star sts. Ch 1, turn.

Row 2: Sl st in sp after first star st, ch 3, dc in eye of next star st, * 2 dc in eye of next star st, repeat from * to last star st, end sl st in sp before last star st—57 (61-65-67) dc plus turning ch. Ch 1, turn.

Row 3: Sl st in each of 2 dc, star st over next 2 dc, work in pat to within last dc and turning ch, sl st in next dc—27 (29-31-32) star sts. Work even in pat until piece measures 9½″ (9½″-10″-10½″) above first row of armhole shaping, end pat row 2. Ch 1, turn.

Shape Shoulders: Row 1 (wrong side): Sl st in each of 6 (6-8-8) dc, work in pat to within last 5 (5-7-7) dc and turning ch—21 (23-23-24) star sts. Ch 1, turn.

Row 2: (Sl st in eye of star st and in sp after star st) 3 times, sl st in eye of next star st, ch 3, dc in eye

of star st just worked in, work in pat to within last 3 star sts—29 (33-33-35) dc plus ch 3. Ch 1, turn.

Row 3: Sl st in each of 4 (6-6-8) dc, work in pat to within last 3 (5-5-7) dc and ch 3—11 (11-11-10) star sts. Ch 1, turn.

Row 4: Sc in each eye and in each sp between star sts. End off.

Note to Left-handed Crocheters: Right front will be your left front and left front your right front. Zipper will be on right side.

RIGHT FRONT: Beg at lower edge, ch 46 (48-50-52). Dc in 4th ch from hook and in each ch across—43 (45-47-49) dc plus turning ch. Ch 3, turn. Check gauge; row should measure 13″ (13½″-14¼″-15″) wide. Work in pat on 22 (23-24-25) star sts until piece measures same as back to underarm, end pat row 2. Ch 1, turn.

Shape Armhole: Row 1 (wrong side): Sl st in each of 2 (2-2-4) dc, star st over next 2 dc, work in pat across—21 (22-23-23) star sts. Ch 3, turn.

Row 2: Work in pat to last star st, end sl st in sp before last star st—39 (41-43-43) dc plus turning ch. Ch 1, turn.

Row 3: Sl st in each of 2 dc, star st over next 2 dc, work in pat across—19 (20-21-21) star sts. Work even until armhole measures 8″ (8½″-9″-9½″) above first row of armhole shaping, end pat row 2. Ch 3, turn.

Shape Neck and Shoulder: Row 1 (wrong side): Work 10 (11-12-13) star sts. Ch 3, turn.

Row 2: Sk first star st, 2 dc in eye of next star st, work in pat across—18 (20-22-24) dc. Ch 1, turn.

Row 3: Sl st in each of 6 (6-8-8) dc, ch 3, work in pat across—6 (7-7-8) star sts. Ch 3, turn.

Row 4: Sk first star st, 2 dc in eye of next star st, work in pat to within last 3 star sts—4 (6-6-8) dc. Ch 1, turn.

Row 5: Sl st in each st across.

End off. From wrong side, join yarn in 4th dc from end (center edge) of last long row.

Row 1: Ch 3, star st over next 2 dc, star st over next dc and turning ch. Ch 3, turn.

Row 2: Dc in eye of first star st, 2 dc in eye of next star st. Ch 3, turn.

Row 3: Sk first star st, star st over last dc and turning ch. Ch 3, turn.

Row 4: Dc in top of turning ch. End.

LEFT FRONT: Beg at lower edge, ch 24 (26-28-32). Dc in 4th ch from hook and in each ch across—21 (23-25-29) dc plus turning ch. Ch 3, turn. Check gauge; row should measure 6½″ (7¼″-8″-9″) wide. Work in pat on 11 (12-13-15) star sts until piece measures same as back to underarm, end pat row 2.

Shape Armhole: Row 1 (wrong side): Work in pat to within last 1 (1-1-3) dc and turning ch—10 (11-12-13) star sts. Ch 1, turn.

Row 2: Sl st in sp after first star st, ch 3, dc in eye of next star st, * 2 dc in eye of next star st, repeat from * across—17 (19-21-23) dc plus turning ch.

Row 3: Work in pat to within last dc and turning ch, sl st in next dc—8 (9-10-11) star sts. Work in pat until armhole measures same as right front armhole, end pat row 2.

Shape Shoulder: Row 1 (wrong side): Work in pat to within last 5 (5-7-7) dc and turning ch—5 (6-6-7) star sts. Ch 1, turn.

Row 2: (Sl st in eye of star st and in sp after star st) 3 times, sl st in eye of next star st, ch 3, dc in eye of star st just worked in, finish row—3 (5-5-7) dc plus ch 3. Ch 1, turn.

Row 3: Sl st in each st across. End off.

SLEEVES: Beg at lower edge, ch 36 (36-38-38). Dc in 4th ch from hook and in each ch across—

33 (33-35-35) dc plus turning ch. Ch 3, turn. Work in pat on 17 (17-18-18) star sts for 3 rows, end pat row 1. Ch 3, turn.

First Inc Row (right side): 2 dc in eye of first star st, dc in sp between first and 2nd star st (2 dc inc), 2 dc in eye of next star st, work in pat across. Ch 3, turn.

Next Row: Work in pat across—18 (18-19-19) star sts. Work 2 rows even, end pat row 1.

2nd Inc Row (right side): Work in pat to last star st, dc in sp between last 2 star sts, 2 dc in eye of last star st, dc in top of turning ch (2 dc inc). Ch 3, turn.

Next Row: Work in pat across—19 (19-20-20) star sts. Alternating inc rows, inc 2 dc every 4th row 3 times more, every other row 4 (5-5-6) times—26 (27-28-29) star sts. Work even until piece measures 18″ from start or 1″ less (border allowance) than desired length to underarm, end pat row 2. Check gauge; piece above last inc row should measure 16″ (16½″-17″-17½″) wide.

Shape Cap: Rows 1-3: Work same as for back armhole shaping—20 (21-22-21) star sts. Ch 3, turn.

Row 4: Work 1 row even—39 (41-43-41) dc plus turning ch. Ch 1, turn.

Row 5: Sl st in each of 2 dc, star st over next 2 dc, work in pat to within last dc and turning ch, sl st in next dc—18 (19-20-19) star sts. Ch 3, turn. Repeat last 2 rows 3 (3-4-4) times—12 (13-12-11) star sts.

On Sizes 40, 44 Only: Repeat row 4.

On All Sizes: Sc in each st across. End.

FINISHING: Block pieces. With backstitch, sew shoulder seams; sew in sleeves. Sew side and sleeve seams.

Lower Border: Join yarn in lower front edge. From right side, sc in sp between each dc across lower edge of fronts and back. Ch 1, turn.

Rows 2-5: Sc in each sc across. End off.

Neckband: From right side, beg at top of right front neck edge **(left-handed crocheters:** beg on left front neck edge, and at right shoulder seam), sc around neck edge, easing in to desired fit, end at left shoulder seam. Ch 1, turn each row.

Rows 2-5: Sc in each sc across. End off.

Reverse Sc Edging: From right side, join yarn in lower left front edge. Working from left to right **(left-handed crocheters:** work from right to left), sc up left front edge, edge of neckband, around neck, down right front edge and around lower edge. End off.

Sleeve Border: From right side, join yarn in underarm seam. Sc in

sp between each dc around sleeve edge. Join with a sl st in first sc. Ch 1, turn each rnd.

Rnds 2-5: Sc in each sc around. Join with a sl st in first sc. Do not turn at end of last rnd.

Rnd 6: Work reverse sc edging.

Sew zipper below neck border leaving 1¾" of lower jacket open. Sew buttons to back edge of neckband. Work button loops on front edge of neckband.

TENNIS PULL-ON

This tennis slip-on for man or ms. looks like a traditional knit sweater, with ribbing and cables, but it is made entirely in afghan crochet, using "knit" and "purl" stitches.

SIZES: Directions for small size (34-36). Changes for medium size (38-40) and large size (42-44) are in parentheses.

Body Chest Size: 34″-36″ (38″-40″; 42″-44″).

Blocked Chest Size: 38⅔″ (41⅓″-44″).

MATERIALS: Orlon yarn of knitting worsted weight, 3 (3-4) 4-oz. skeins white, main color (MC); 1 skein each of red (A) and blue (B). Afghan hooks sizes G and I. Double-pointed or cable needle.

GAUGE: 10 sts = 3″; 10 rows = 3″ (size G hook). 3 sts = 1″; 3 rows = 1″ (size I hook).

KNIT AFGHAN STITCH: Row 1: Keeping all lps on hook, draw up a lp in 2nd ch from hook and in each ch across.

To Work Lps Off: Yo hook and through first lp, * yo hook, pull through next 2 lps, repeat from * across until 1 lp remains. Lp that remains on hook always counts as first st of next row.

Row 2: Keeping all lps on hook, sk first vertical bar, * insert hook from front to back through center

of next lp (between vertical bar and strand behind it), yo hook and pull up a lp (knit st made), repeat from * across. Work off lps as before.

PURL STITCH: Holding yarn with thumb in front and below hook, pull up a lp under vertical bar of next st.

To Bind Off: At beg of a row, sk first vertical bar, pull up a lp in center of next st and pull lp through lp on hook making a sl st (1 st bound off), continue in this manner for specified number of sts; **at end of a row,** leave specified number of sts unworked. Work lps off as before.

To Dec 1 St: When working lps off, **at beg of a row,** yo hook and through first 2 lps; **at end of a row,** work until 3 lps remain on needle, yo hook and through last 3 lps.

PULL-ON: BACK: Beg at lower edge, with MC and size G hook, ch 56 (60-64).

Row 1: Work same as for row 1 of knit afghan st—56 (60-64) lps. Work lps off in same manner.

Ribbing: Row 2: Keeping all lps on hook, sk first st (lp on hook is first st), * make purl st, knit st, repeat from * across, end p st. Work lps off as before. Repeating row 2, work 1 more row MC, 3 rows A, 3 rows B, 3 rows MC. Change to size I hook.

Pattern: Row 1: With MC, sk first st (lp on hook is first st), (make 9 (10-11) k sts, 1 p st, 4 k sts (cable 4-st panel), 1 p st) 3 times, make 10 (11-12) k sts—3 cable panels. Work lps off as before.

Row 2: Repeat row 1.

Row 3 (cable row): Pick up lps as for pat row 1.

To Work Lps Off: Yo hook and through first lp, (yo hook, pull through next 2 lps) 10 (11-12) times, * drop first lp off hook and hold with left thumb **(left-handed crocheters:** with right thumb); with cable needle, sl next 2 lps and hold in front of work, pick up dropped lp and work off next 2 lps, drop first lp off hook and hold with thumb, sl lps from dp needle back to hook, pick up dropped lp and work off next 2 sts (cable made), (yo hook, pull through next 2 lps) 11 (12-13) times, repeat from * twice.

Rows 4 and 5: Repeat row 1. Repeat rows 1-5 for pat until piece measures 15″ (16″-17″) from start or desired length to underarm. Check gauge; piece above ribbing should measure 18⅔″ (20″-21⅓″) wide.

Shape Armholes: Bind off (see To Bind Off) 5 sts each side of next row. Keeping to pat, dec 1 st (see To Dec 1 St) each side every row 4 (5-6) times—38 (40-42) sts. Work even until armholes measure 9″ (9½″-10″) above first bound-off sts.

Shape Shoulders: Keeping to pat, bind off 3 sts each side every row twice, then 4 (5-6) sts each side of next row—18 sts for back of neck. End off.

FRONT: Beg at lower edge, with MC and size G hook, ch 60 (64-68). Work ribbing same as for back on 60 (64-68) sts. Change to size I hook.

Pattern: Row 1: With MC, sk first st (lp on hook is first st), (make 10 (11-12) k sts, 1 p st, 4 k sts (cable panel), 1 p st) 3 times, make 11 (12-13) k sts—3 cable panels. Work lps off as before.

Row 2: Repeat row 1.

Row 3 (cable row): Work in pat as established, working cable on each 4-st cable panel. Continue in pat until piece measures 1 row less than back to underarm.

Divide Work: Keeping to pat, work until 30 (32-34) lps on hook, drop MC; with another strand of MC, pull up a lp in next st, finish row. Working on both sides at once, with separate strands of MC, work off lps as before.

Shape V-Neck, Armholes and Shoulders: Bind off 6 sts each arm side of next row, then dec 1 st each arm side every row 4 (5-6) times; **at the same time,** dec 1 st at each neck edge of next row, then every 3rd row 9 times; **at the same time,** when armhole measures same as back, bind off 3 sts at each arm side every row twice, 4 (5-6) sts once.

FINISHING: Block pieces. With backstitch, sew left shoulder seam **(left-handed crocheters:** sew right shoulder seam).

Neckband: From right side, with MC and size G hook, pick up and k 1 st in each st across back of neck (18 sts), pick up and k 1 st in edge of each row down front neck edge, being sure to have an even number of lps on hook, put a marker on work for center front, pick up and k same number of sts up other front neck edge. Work lps off as before, dec 1 st each side of front marker—2 sts dec.

Row 2: K first st, * make p st, k st, repeat from * to front marker; beg with a k st, make k st, p st to end of row. Work lps as before, dec 1 st each side of front marker.

Row 3: Keeping to pat, repeat row 2. Bind off.

Sew shoulder and neckband seam.

Armbands: From right side, with MC and size G hook, pick up and k 1 st in each st at underarm and 1 st in edge of each row around armhole edge. Work off lps.

Rows 2 and 3: Work in ribbing of k 1 st, p 1 st. Bind off.

Sew side and armband seams. Steam-press seams and armbands lightly.

V-NECKED PULLOVER

Variegated yarn and easy single crochet make this dashing pullover. For a different effect, use any one of the other color combinations available in multicolored knitting worsted. Made entirely in the simplest crochet stitch of all, and styled in the simplest way, this V-necked sweater is a perfect beginner's project.

SIZES: Directions for small size (38-40). Changes for medium size (42-44) and large size (46-48) are in parentheses.

Body Chest Size: 38″-40″ (42″-44″; 46″-48″).

Blocked Chest Size: 42″ (46″-49″).

MATERIALS: Variegated knitting worsted, 8 (9-10) 3¾-oz. skeins main color (A); small amount edging color (B). Crochet hook size G.

GAUGE: 7 sc = 2″; 4 rows = 1″.

To Bind Off: At beg of a row, sl st loosely across specified number of sts, ch 1, work sc across; **at end of a row,** leave specified number of sts unworked. Ch 1, turn.

To Dec 1 Sc: Pull up a lp in each of 2 sc, yo and through 3 lps on hook.

To Inc 1 Sc: Work 2 sc in same sc.

PULLOVER: BACK: Beg at lower edge with A, ch loosely 75 (81-87).

Row 1: Sc in 2nd ch from hook and in each ch across—74 (80-86) sc. Ch 1, turn.

Row 2: Sc in each sc across. Ch 1, turn each row. Repeat last row until piece measures 17″ from start or desired length to underarm. Check gauge; piece should measure 21″ (23″-24½″) wide.

Shape Armholes: Bind off (see To Bind Off) 3 (4-5) sc each side of next row. Dec 1 sc (see To Dec 1 Sc) each side every other row 4 times—60 (64-68) sc. Work even until armholes measure 9″ (9½″-10″) above first bound-off sts.

Shape Shoulders: Bind off 4 sts

each side every row 4 times, 3 (4-5) sc once—22 (24-26) sc. End off.

FRONT: Work same as for back until piece measures same as back to underarm.

Shape Armholes and V Neck: Bind off 3 (4-5) sc each side of next row—68 (72-76) sc.

Next Row: Sc in each of next 34 (36-38) sc, drop yarn; join another

strand of A, finish row—34 (36-38) sc each side. Working on both sides at once, with separate strands of yarn, dec 1 sc at each arm side every other row 4 times; **at the same time,** dec 1 sc at each neck edge every 3rd row 11 (12-13) times—19 (20-21) sc each side. Work even until armholes measure same as back.

Shape Shoulders: Bind off 4 sts at each arm side every row 4 times, 3 (4-5) sts once.

SLEEVES: Beg at lower edge with A, ch 35 (37-39). Work as for back on 34 (36-38) sc for 2″. Check gauge; piece should measure 9¾″ (10¼″-10¾″) wide. Inc 1 sc (see To Inc 1 Sc) each side of next row, then every 6th row 11 (12-13) times—58 (62-66) sc. Work even until piece measures 19″ (19½″- 20″) from start or desired length to underarm.

Shape Cap: Bind off 3 (4-5) sc each side of next row. Dec 1 sc each side every other row 4 (5-6) times, every row 11 times. Bind off 2 sts each side every row 3 times— 10 sc. End off.

FINISHING: Block pieces. With backstitch, sew shoulder seams; sew in sleeves. Sew side and sleeve seams. From right side, with B, work 1 rnd sc around neck edge, easing in to desired fit. Join with a sl st in first sc. End off. From right side, with B, work 1 rnd sc around lower edge of each sleeve.

MEN'S PATTERNED VEST

SIZES: Directions for medium size (36-38). Changes for large size (40-42) are in parentheses. **Note:** Both sizes are made the same. Hook size and gauge determine size.

Body Chest Size: 36″-38″ (40″- 42″).

Blocked Chest Size: 40″ (44″).

MATERIALS: Knitting worsted, 3 4-oz. skeins each of olive green (A) and beige (B). Aluminum crochet hook size G (I).

GAUGE: 7 sts = 2″; 11 rows (1 pat) = 3½″ (size G hook). 13 sts = 4″; 11 rows (1 pat) = 4″ (size I hook).

Note 1: When B is to be used in design, start at beg of row. Always carry color not in use across wrong side of work. When changing colors, work last sc or reverse sc of one color until there are 2 lps on hook, drop strand to wrong side of work. Pick up new color and finish sc.

Note 2: Work right-side row in sc, wrong-side row in reverse sc.

Note 3: Vest is worked vertically.

Reverse Sc (r-sc): Holding yarn in front of work, insert hook under yarn from back to front in next st, pull lp through and complete sc.

To Bind Off: At beg of a row, sl st loosely across specified sts; **at end of a row,** leave specified sts unworked.

VEST: RIGHT BACK (Left-handed crocheters: This will be your left back): Beg at center back, with B, ch 92.

Pattern: Row 1 (right side): Sc in 2nd ch from hook and in each ch across—91 sc. Check gauge; row should measure 26″ (28″) long. Ch 1, turn. Mark beg of row 1 for lower edge.

Row 2 (wrong side): Working in r-sc (see Reverse Sc), * work 1 B, (2 A, 1 B) twice, repeat from * across. Change to A, ch 1, turn.

Row 3 (right side): Working in sc, work 3 A, * 1 B, 6 A, repeat from * across, end last repeat 3 A. Cut A and B; do not turn.

Row 4 (right side): With A, dc in first sc at beg of last row, dc in each sc across. Cut A; do not turn.

Row 5 (right side): Working in sc, work 1 B in first st at beg of last row, * work 5 A, 2 B, repeat from * across, end 1 B. With A, ch 1, turn.

Row 6 (wrong side): Working in r-sc, * work 1 A, (2 B, 1 A) twice, repeat from * across. Ch 1, turn.

Row 7 (right side): Working in sc, repeat row 6. With B, ch 1, turn.

Row 8 (wrong side): Working in r-sc, repeat row 5. Ch 1, turn.

Row 9 (right side): With A, dc in each sc across. Cut A; do not turn.

Row 10 (right side): Beg in first dc at beg of last row, repeat row 3. With B, ch 1, turn.

Row 11 (wrong side): Repeat row 2. With B, ch 1, turn.

Row 12 (right side): With B, sc in each sc across. Ch 1, turn. Repeat rows 2-4. Do not cut A at end of row 4. With A, ch 91 for right front. Cut A; do not turn.

Next Row (right side): Working in sc, work 1 B in first st at beg of last row, * work 5 A, 2 B, repeat from * across each dc and ch, end 1 B—182 sc. With A, ch 1, turn. Beg with row 6, work pat rows 6-12, then rows 2-8, end wrong side. Ch 1, turn.

Next Row (right side): With A, sc in each st across. Ch 1, turn.

Next Row (wrong side): With A, r-sc in each sc across. Turn.

Next Row (right side): With B, sc in each of next 52 sts, mark last st for underarm, hdc in each of next 20 sts, dc in each of next 38 sts, hdc in each of next 20 sts, mark last st for underarm, sc in each of next 52 sts. Ch 1, turn.

Side Slit Facing: Sc in each of next 22 sc. Ch 1, turn. Work 4 rows sc on these 22 sts. End off.

This sleeveless slip-on for men has many unusual features. Made vertically, back and front start at the center. The two-color patterns are worked in single crochet on right side, reverse single crochet on wrong side. Side vents make for easy fit.

Join B in first st on last long row; sc in each of next 22 sc. Ch 1, turn. Work 4 rows sc. End off.

Shape Right Front: From right side, join A in first ch at lower front edge. Ch 3, working along foundation ch, dc in each ch—91 dc. Cut A. Working on these 91 sts, work pat rows 10-12.

Shape Neck: Working pat rows 2-12, bind off (see To Bind Off) 7 sts at neck edge of next row, then bind off 2 sts at same edge every row 5 times. Work even to end of pat row 12. End off.

LEFT BACK: From wrong side, join A and B in first ch of foundation ch on lower right back. Work-

ing up foundation ch, work same as pat row 2 on right back. Work to end of pat row 12, then pat rows 2 and 3, end right side. Cut A and B. Join A in first st on last row (upper edge), ch 93 for left front.

Next Row (right side): Dc in 4th ch from hook (counts as 2 dc), and in each ch and st across—182 dc. Cut A; do not turn.

Next Row (right side): Beg with pat row 5, complete same as right back and slit facing.

Shape Front: From right side, join A and B in first ch at upper front edge, ch 1, work pat row 10 down foundation ch—91 sts. Ch 1, turn. Repeat rows 11 and 12.

Shape Neck: Working pat rows

2-12, work same as for right front, reversing shaping.

FINISHING: Run in yarn ends on wrong side. Block pieces. With B, weave center fronts tog. Sew shoulder seams. Fold slit facings to wrong side, sew in place. Weave side seams from top of slits to underarm markers.

Neck Border: Join A at neck edge of right shoulder. From right side, sc around neck edge, being careful to keep work flat. Join with a sl st in first st each rnd; do not turn. Cut A; join B. Work 1 rnd hdc, 2 rnds sc around neck edge. End off.

Steam seams and neck border lightly.

SUN GOLD VEST

Sunny gold for a man's vest that's easy to make. The raised double crochet pattern is airy in mohair-type yarn. Deep V neck and armholes are edged with single crochet.

SIZES: Directions for size 36. Changes for sizes 38, 40, 42, 44 and 46 are in parentheses.

Body Chest Size: 36" (38"-40"-42"-44"-46").

Blocked Chest Size: 38" (40"-42"-44"-46"-48").

MATERIALS: Mohair or mohair-type yarn, 8 (9-9-10-10-11) 1-oz. balls. Crochet hooks sizes G and H.

GAUGE: 3 sts = 1"; 3 rows = 2" (pat, size H hook).

To Bind Off: At beg of a row, sl st loosely across each st to be bound off, then ch 2 and continue across row; **at end of a row,** work in pat to within specified number of sts to be bound off.

To Dec 1 St: At beg of a row, ch 2, sk first st, (yo hook, pull up a lp

in next st, yo and through 2 lps on hook) twice, yo and through 3 lps on hook; **at end of a row,** work to within last 3 sts, (yo hook, pull up a lp in next st, yo and through 2 lps on hook) twice, yo and through 3 lps on hook, dc in top of turning ch.

VEST: BACK: Beg at lower edge, with size H hook, ch 58 (62-64-68-70-74).

Row 1 (right side): Sc in 2nd ch from hook and in each ch across—57 (61-63-67-69-73) sc. Ch 2, turn.

Row 2 (wrong side): Sk first sc, dc in each sc across. Turn each row.

Row 3 (right side): Ch 2 (counts as 1 dc), sk first st, * post dc (p-dc) around next st (**to make p-dc,** yo hook, insert hook from front to back to front around bar of next

dc, pull up a lp, yo hook, insert hook from front to back to front around bar of same dc, pull up a lp, yo and through 4 lps, yo and through remaining 2 lps on hook), dc in next dc, repeat from * across, end last repeat dc in top of turning ch.

Row 4: Ch 2 (counts as 1 dc), sk first dc, * dc in p-dc, dc in next dc, repeat from * across, end last repeat dc in top of turning ch.

Row 5: Ch 2 (counts as 1 dc), sk first dc, dc in next dc, * p-dc around next dc, dc in next dc, repeat from * across, end dc in top of turning ch.

Row 6: Ch 2 (counts as 1 dc), sk first dc, * dc in dc, dc in p-dc, repeat from * across, end last repeat dc in top of turning ch. Repeat rows 3-6 for pat until piece measures 15″ (15″-15½″-15½″-16″-16″) from start or desired length to underarm. Check gauge; piece should measure 19″ (20″-21″-22″-23″-24″) wide.

Shape Armholes: Keeping to pat, bind off (see To Bind Off) 5 (6-6-7-7-8) sts each side of next row. Dec 1 st (see To Dec 1 St) each side every row 3 times—41 (43-45-47-49-51) sts. Work even until armholes measure 9″ (9″-9½″-9½″-10″-10″) above first row of armhole shaping.

Shape Shoulders: Bind off 4 (5-6-7-7-8) sts each side of next row, 6 (6-6-6-7-7) sts each side of next row—21 sts. End off.

FRONT: Work same as for back until piece measures 1″ less than back to underarm.

Shape V-Neck: Keeping to pat, work 28 (30-31-33-34-36) sts, drop yarn, sk next st; join another strand of yarn, ch 2, work in pat across—28 (30-31-33-34-36) sts each side. Working on both sides at once, dec 1 st at each neck edge every row 10 times: **at the same time,** when piece measures same as back to underarm, bind off 5 (6-6-7-7-8) sts each arm side of next row, then dec 1 st each arm side every row 3 times—10 (11-12-13-14-15) sts each side. Work even until armholes measure same as back armholes.

Shape Shoulders: Keeping to pat, bind off 4 (5-6-7-7-8) sts each arm side of next row—6 (6-6-6-7-7) sts each side. End off.

FINISHING: With backstitch, sew shoulder and side seams.

Neckband: Rnd 1: Join yarn in shoulder seam; with size G hook, sc in each st across back neck edge; keeping work flat, sc down neck edge, sc in skipped center st (mark this st for center front), sc up other neck edge having same number of sts on each side of front neck, join with a sl st in first sc. Do not turn. Ch 1.

Rnd 2: Sc in each sc to within 2 sc of center front sc, pull up a lp in each of next 2 sc, yo hook and through 3 lps on hook (1 sc dec), sc in marked sc, dec 1 sc, finish rnd. Join. Repeat last rnd once. End off.

Armbands: Join yarn in underarm seam. Work 3 rnds sc around each armhole. End off.

PATCH-POCKET VEST

A spicy paprika vest in a shell pattern stitch has plain single crochet bands.
Low patch pockets are made separately, then sewn on.

SIZES: Directions for small size (34). Changes for medium (36-38), large (40-42) and extra-large (44-46) are in parentheses.

Blocked Chest Size (closed): 36″ (40″-44″-48″).

MATERIALS: Mohair or mohair- type yarn, 11 (11-12-13) 1-oz. balls. Crochet hooks sizes F and H. Five buttons.

GAUGE: Sc, 2 dc (gr-st) = 1″; 2 rows = 1″ (pat, size H hook).

VEST: BACK: Beg at lower edge, with size H hook, ch 56 (62-68-74).

Row 1: Work sc, 2 dc in 2nd ch from hook (group stitch (gr-st) made), * sk next 2 ch, work sc, 2 dc in next ch (gr-st made), repeat from * to last 3 ch, end sk next 2 ch, sc in last ch—18 (20-22-24) gr-sts. Check gauge; row should measure 18″ (20″-22″-24″) wide. Mark last row for wrong side. Ch 1, turn each row.

Row 2: Gr-st of sc, 2 dc in first sc, * gr-st in sc of next gr-st, repeat from * across, end sc in sc of last gr-st—18 (20-22-24) gr-sts. Repeat row 2 for pat until piece measures 15″ from start or desired length to underarm, end right side.

Shape Armholes: Row 1: Sl st in each of next 6 sts; work gr-st in next sc (sc of 2nd gr-st), work in pat to within last 3 gr-sts, end sc in sc of next gr-st, sl st in next dc—2 gr-sts bound off each side.

Row 2: Sk sl st, sl st in each of next 3 sts, gr-st in next sc, work in pat to last 2 gr-sts, sc in next sc, sl st in next st—12 (14-16-18) gr-sts. Work even until armholes measure 10″ (10½″-11″-11½″) above first row of armhole shaping. End off.

LEFT FRONT: Beg at lower edge, with size H hook, ch 29 (32-35-38). Work in pat on 9 (10-

11-12) gr-sts until piece measures 4 rows less than back to underarm. Mark beg of next row for center edge. Check gauge; piece should measure 9″ (10″-11″-12″) wide.

Shape Neck and Armhole: Row 1: Work sc, dc in first sc, work in pat across—1 st dec.

Row 2: Work in pat across, end sc in sc of last complete gr-st, sc in last sc.

Row 3: Sk first sc, gr-st in next sc, work in pat across.

Row 4: Work in pat—8 (9-10-11) gr-sts.

Row 5: Work sc, dc in first sc, work in pat to last 3 gr-sts, sc in sc of next gr-st, sl st in next dc—2 gr-sts bound off at arm side.

Row 6: Sk sl st, sl st in each of 3 sts, gr-st in next sc, work in pat across, end sc in sc of last complete gr-st, sc in last sc.

Row 7: Repeat row 3.

Row 8: Work in pat—4 (5-6-7) gr-sts. Repeat rows 1-4, 1 (2-2-3) times—3 (3-4-4) gr-sts. Work even until armhole measures same as back. End off.

RIGHT FRONT: Work same as for left front; pat is reversible.

BUTTONHOLES: Beg at center edge, sc in each of 2 sc, ch 2, sk next 2 sc, sc in each of next 3 sc. **Next Row:** Sc in each sc and ch across.

Weave shoulder seams.

FRONT AND NECK BAND: With size F hook, ch 8.

Row 1: Sc in 2nd ch from hook and in each ch across—7 sc. Row 1 should measure 2″ across. Ch 1, turn each row.

Row 2: Sc in each sc across. Repeat row 2 until piece when slightly stretched measures same as right front and back neck edge to left shoulder seam. Pin in place. Count number of rows from lower edge to right shoulder seam. With pins, mark position of 5 buttons evenly spaced on right front band, first one 3 rows above lower edge, 5th one 1″ below start of neck shaping. Continue to work in sc, working same number of rows as right front band and forming buttonholes (see Buttonholes) on same row as markers. End off. Sew band in place.

ARMBAND: From right side, with size F hook, work 1 row sc around armhole edge, easing in to desired fit. Ch 1, turn. Work 2 more rows sc; end off. Sew side seams.

POCKETS (make 2): Beg at lower edge, with size H hook, ch 17. Work in pat as for back on 5 gr-sts for 10 rows. Piece should measure 5″ wide. End off.

Pocket Bands (make 2): Bands are worked from side to side. Work same as for front band until piece measures 5″. End off. Sew band to top of pocket. With lower edge of pocket at lower front edge, sew to each front, 3″ in from center band.

Beg at lower front edge, with size H hook, work 1 row sc across lower edge; sl st around front and neck band. End off.

From right side, with size H hook, work 1 row sl st across upper edge of each pocket. Sew on buttons.

MEN'S SWEATER SET

SIZES: Directions for small size (36-38). Changes for medium size (40) and large size (42-44) are in parentheses.

Body Chest Size: 36″-38″ (40″; 42″-44″).

Blocked Chest Size: Cardigan (closed): 42″ (44″-47″). Slipover: 40″ (42″-45″).

MATERIALS: Cardigan: Knitting worsted, 7 (8-9) 4-oz. skeins variegated colors (A); 1 skein solid color (B). Five buttons. Slipover: 3 (3-4) skeins variegated colors (A); 2 skeins solid color (B). For both sweaters, crochet hook size H.

GAUGE: 4 sts = 1″; 7 rows = 2″.

CARDIGAN: Note: When changing colors, pull new color through last 2 lps to complete sc. Cut and join colors as needed.

PATTERN STITCH: Row 1: Sc in 2nd ch from hook, * ch 1, sk 1 ch, sc in next ch, repeat from * across. Turn.

Row 2: Ch 1, sc in first sc, * ch 1, sk ch-1 sp, sc in next sc, repeat from * across. Turn. Repeat row 2 for pat always working ch 1 over ch-1 sp and sc over sc.

To Bind Off: At beg of a row, sl st loosely across specified sts; **at end of a row,** leave specified number of sts unworked.

To Dec 1 St: At beg of a row, ch 1, pull up a lp in each of first 2 sts, yo and through 3 lps on hook; **at end of a row,** pull up a lp in each of last 2 sts, yo and through 3 lps on hook. **Next Row:** Work in pat as established (sc over each sc, ch 1 over ch-1 sp).

To Inc 1 St: At beg of a row, ch 1 loosely, 2 sc in first st; **at end of a row,** 2 sc in last st. **Next Row:** Work in pat as established; when there are 3 sc tog, work into sc, ch 1 pat.

CARDIGAN: BACK: Beg at lower edge, with A, ch loosely 84 (88-96). Work in sc, ch 1 pat on 42 (44-48) sc for 18½″ or desired length to underarm. Check gauge; piece should measure 20¾″ (21¾″-23¾″) wide.

Shape Armholes: Keeping to pat, bind off (see To Bind Off) 4 sts each side of next 2 rows, 2 sts each side of next 1 (1-2) rows—32 (34-36) sc. Work even until armholes measure 9″ (9½″-10″) above first bound-off sts.

Shape Shoulders: Bind off 6 (6-8) sts each side of next 2 (3-2) rows, 4 sts next 2 (1-2) rows—12 sc. End off.

POCKET LINING (make 2): Beg at lower edge, ch loosely 24. Work in pat on 12 sc for 5½″. End off.

LEFT FRONT: Beg at lower edge, with A, ch loosely 42 (44-48). Work in pat on 21 (22-24) sc for 6¼″. Ch 1, turn.

Pocket Opening (side edge): (Sc in sc, ch 1) 3 times, work across one pocket lining, sk next 12 sc on front for pocket opening, (sc in next sc, ch 1) 5 (6-8) times, sc in last sc—21 (22-24) sc. Work even until piece measures 1″ less than back to underarm. Check gauge; piece should measure 10¼″ (10¾″-11¾″) wide.

Shape V-Neck, Armhole and Shoulder: Keeping to pat, dec 1 st (see To Dec 1 St) at center edge every 3rd row, then dec 1 st at same edge every 3rd row 10 times more; **at the same time,** when piece measures same as back to underarm, bind off 4 sts at side edge of next 2 rows, 2 sts at same edge on next 1 (1-2) rows. Work even until armhole measures same as back. Bind off 6 (6-8) sts at arm side every row twice. End off.

RIGHT FRONT: Work same as for left front; pat is reversible.

SLEEVES: Ribbing (worked from seam to seam): With B, ch 12 loosely.

Row 1: Sc in 2nd ch from hook and in each ch across—11 sc. Ch 1, turn.

Row 2: Sc in back lp of each sc across. Ch 1, turn. Repeat row 2 until piece when slightly stretched measures 9″ (9½″-10″). Cut B; join A. Ch 1, do not turn. Working along side edge of ribbing, work (sc, ch 1) 22 (23-24) times across. Work in pat, inc 1 st (see To Inc 1 St) each side every 4th row 10 (11-12) times—32 (34-36) sc. Work even until piece measures 19″ from start or desired sleeve length. Check gauge; piece above last inc row should measure 16″ (17″-18″) wide.

Shape Cap: Keeping to pat, bind off 4 sts each side of next row, 2 sts each side every row twice. Dec 1 st each side every 3rd row 4 times, every row 6 (8-10) times. Bind off 2 sts each side every row twice. End off.

FINISHING: Block pieces. Sew shoulder seams; sew in sleeves. Sew side and sleeve seams. Sew pocket linings in place to wrong side of fronts.

Pocket Edging: With B, work 3 rows in pat across top of pocket opening. Sew side edges in place.

Center Band: Row 1: Beg at lower front edge, with B, sl st up front edge, across back neck edge, down other front edge, having same number of sts on each front edge. Ch 1, turn.

Row 2: Sc in front lp of first sl st, * ch 1, sk next st, sc in front lp of next sl st, repeat from * around. Ch 1, turn.

With pins, mark position of 5 buttonholes on left center front edge, first pin 2″ above lower edge, last pin in sc below start of neck shaping.

Row 3 (buttonhole row): * Work in pat to within ch-1 sp before pin, ch 3, sk ch-1 sp, sc, ch-1 sp, work sc

An easy-stitch sweater set combines variegated yarn and solid color in a tone to match. Classic cardigan in the shaded yarn has one-color bands and cuffs. Sleeveless vest is in alternating stripes of the two yarns.

in next sc, repeat from * 4 times, finish row. Ch 1, turn.

Row 4: Work in pat across, working ch 1, sc, ch 1 in each ch-3 buttonhole sp. Ch 1, turn.

Row 5: Work in pat across. End off.

Steam-press edges and pocket bands. Sew on buttons.

SLIPOVER: STRIPED PATTERN: Working pat st same as on cardigan, work 6 rows A, 6 rows B. Repeat these 12 rows for striped pat.

BACK: Beg at lower edge, with A, ch loosely 80 (84-92). Work in striped pat on 40 (42-46) sc for 17" or desired length to underarm. Check gauge; piece should measure 20" (21"-22½") wide.

Shape Armholes: Bind off (see To Bind Off, under Cardigan) 6 sts each side of next row, 4 sts each side of next row—30 (32-36) sc. Work even until armholes measure 9½" (10"-10½") above first bound-off sts.

Shape Shoulders: Bind off 6 (6-8) sts each side of next 2 rows, 8 sts each side of next row—10 (12-12) sc. End off.

FRONT: Work same as for back until piece measures 1 row less than back to underarm—40 (42-46) sc.

Divide Work: Sc in first sc, (ch 1, sc in next sc) 19 (20-22) times, drop yarn; sk next ch-1 sp, join another strand of color to be used with a sc in next sc, work in pat across—20 (21-23) sc each side.

Shape V-Neck and Armholes: Keeping to striped pat as established, working on both sides at once, with separate strands of yarn, dec 1 st (see To Dec 1 St, under Cardigan) at next edge of next row, then dec 1 st at neck edge every 3rd row 4 times, then every other row 5 (7-7) times more; **at the same time,** bind off 6 (6-8) sts

each arm side of next row, 4 st each arm side of next row. Work even on remaining 10 (10-11) s until armhole measures same a back.

Shape Shoulders: Bind off 6 (6 8) sts each arm side of next 2 rows End off.

FINISHING: Block pieces With backstitch, sew shoulder seams; sew side seams.

Neck Edging: Rnd 1: Join A in shoulder seam. From right side, work 1 rnd sl st around neck edge, being careful to keep work flat. Ch 1; do not turn.

Rnd 2: Working in back lp, work in pat around, skipping 1 st at point of V. Join with a sl st in first sc. Ch 1; do not turn.

Rnd 3: Work in pat around; dec at point of V. Join; end off.

Armhole Edging: Work same as for neck edging. End off.

Steam-press seams and edgings.

TWEED AND STRIPES

Powerful striping makes the perfect top layer for a man's sweater set. Sleeveless vest is worked in variegated yarn for a tweeded effect. Cardigan stripes pick up colors from the variegation.

SIZES: Directions for small size (36-38). Changes for medium size (40) and large size (42-44) are in parentheses.

Body Chest Size: 36"-38" (40"; 42"-44").

Blocked Chest Size: Cardigan (closed): 42" (44"-47"). Slipover: 40" (42"-45").

MATERIALS: Cardigan: Knitting worsted, 4 (5-5) 4-oz. skeins blue (A); 3 (3-4) skeins green (B); 1 skein white (C). Five buttons. Slip-

over: 3 (3-4) 4-oz. skeins blue-green ombré (A); 1 skein blue (B). For both sweaters, crochet hook size H.

GAUGE: 4 sts = 1"; 7 rows = 2".

CARDIGAN: Note: When changing colors, pull new color through last 2 lps to complete sc. Cut and join colors as needed.

PATTERN STITCH: Row 1: Sc in 2nd ch from hook, * ch 1, sk 1 ch, sc in next ch, repeat from * across. Turn.

Row 2: Ch 1, sc in first sc, * ch 1, sk ch-1 sp, sc in next sc, repeat from * across. Turn. Repeat row 2 for pat always working ch 1 over ch-1 sp and sc over sc.

STRIPED PATTERN: Working pat st, work 6 rows A, 6 rows B, 2 rows C. Repeat these 14 rows for striped pat.

To Bind Off: At beg of a row, sl st loosely across specified sts; **at end of a row,** leave specified number of sts unworked.

To Dec 1 St: At beg of a row, ch

1, pull up a lp in each of first 2 sts, yo and through 3 lps on hook; **at end of a row,** pull up a lp in each of last 2 sts, yo and through 3 lps on hook. **Next Row:** Work in pat as established (sc over each sc, ch 1 over ch-1 sp).

To Inc 1 St: At beg of a row, ch 1 loosely, 2 sc in first st; **at end of a row,** 2 sc in last st. **Next Row:** Work in pat as established; when there are 3 sc tog, work into sc, ch 1 pat.

CARDIGAN: BACK: Beg at lower edge, with A, ch loosely 84 (88-96). Work in striped pat on 42 (44-48) sc for 16½″ (17″-17½″) or desired length to underarm.

Shape Armholes: Keeping to striped pat, bind off (see To Bind Off) 4 sts each side of next 2 rows, 2 sts each side of next 1 (1-2) rows—32 (34-36) sc. Work even until armholes measure 9″ (9½″-10″) above first bound-off sts.

Shape Shoulders: Bind off 6 (6-8) sts each side of next 2 (3-2) rows, 4 sts next 2 (1-2) rows—11 (12-12) sc. End off.

LEFT FRONT: Beg at lower edge, with A, ch loosely 42 (44-48). Work in striped pat on 21 (22-24) sc until piece measures same as back to underarm. Mark end of last row for center edge.

Shape V-Neck, Armhole and Shoulder: Keeping to striped pat, dec 1 st (see To Dec 1 St) at center edge of next row, then dec 1 st at same edge every 3rd row 10 times more; **at the same time,** bind off 4 sts at side edge of next 2 rows, 2 sts at same edge on next 1 (1-2) rows; **at the same time,** when armhole measures same as back, bind off 6 (6-8) sts at arm side every row twice, 2 sts at arm side of 0 (0-1) row. End off.

RIGHT FRONT: Work same as for left front; pat is reversible.

Sleeve Length Note: Sleeve is planned for 19″ (17″ length from top of cuff to underarm, plus 2″

cuff). Measure striped pat on back to determine starting row so that 17″ (or desired sleeve length) will end with same pat row as back at start of underarm.

SLEEVES: Ribbing (worked from seam to seam): With A, ch 9 loosely.

Row 1: Sc in 2nd ch from hook and in each ch across—8 sc. Ch 1, turn.

Row 2: Sc in back lp of each sc across. Ch 1, turn. Repeat row 2 until piece when slightly stretched measures 9″ (9½″-9½″). Ch 1, do not turn. Continue along side edge of ribbing, work (sc, ch 1) 22 (23-24) times across. Work in striped pat (see Sleeve Length Note), inc 1 st (see To Inc 1 St) each side every 4th row 10 (11-12) times—32 (34-36) sc. Work even until piece measures 19″ or desired sleeve length. Check gauge; piece above last inc row should measure 16″ (17″-18″) wide.

Shape Cap: Keeping to striped pat, bind off 4 sts each side of next row, 2 sts each side every row twice. Dec 1 st each side every 3rd row 4 times, every row 6 (8-10) times. Bind off 2 sts each side every row twice. End off.

FINISHING: Block pieces. Sew shoulder seams; sew in sleeves. Matching stripes, sew side and sleeve seams.

Center Band: Row 1: Beg at lower front edge, with A, sl st up front edge, across back neck edge, down other front edge, having same number of sts on each front edge. End off.

Row 2: Join A with sc in back lp of first sl st made on lower front edge, sc in back lp of each sl st of band. Ch 1, turn.

With pins, mark position of 5 buttonholes on left center front edge, first pin 2″ above lower edge, last pin in 2nd sc below start of neck shaping.

Row 3 (buttonhole row): * Sc in each sc to within 1 st before pin, ch 3, sk next 2 sc, sc in next sc, repeat from * 4 times, finish row. Ch 1, turn.

Row 4: Sc in each sc across, work 2 sc in each ch-3 sp. Ch 1, turn.

Row 5: Sl st in each sc. End off.

Work 1 rnd sc around lower edge of each cuff.

Steam borders and seams. Sew on buttons.

SLIPOVER: BACK: Ribbing (worked from side seam to side seam): With B, ch 9.

Row 1: Sc in 2nd ch from hook and in each ch across—8 sc. Ch 1, turn.

Row 2: Sc in back lp of each sc across. Ch 1, turn. Repeat row 2 until 54 (56-60) rows from start. Cut B; join A. With A, ch 1, do not turn.

Pattern: Row 1: Work (sc, ch 1) 40 (42-46) times across side edge of ribbing (about 3 sts over every 2 rows). Turn.

Row 2: Sc in first sc, * ch 1, sk ch-1 sp, sc in next sc, repeat from * across—40 (42-46) sc. Ch 1, turn. Repeat row 2 for pat always working ch 1 over ch-1 sp and sc over sc until piece measures 15″ (15½″-16″) from start or desired length to underarm. Check gauge; piece above ribbing should measure 20″ (21″-22½″) wide.

Shape Armholes: Bind off (see To Bind Off, under Cardigan) 6 sts each side of next row, 4 sts each side of next row—30 (32-36) sc. Work even until armholes measure 9½″ (10″-10½″) above first bound-off sts.

Shape Shoulders: Bind off 6 (6-8) sts each side of next 2 rows, 8 sts each side of next row—10 (12-12) sc. End off.

FRONT: Work same as for back until piece measures 1 row less than back to underarm—40 (42-46) sc.

Divide Work: Sc in first sc, (ch 1, sc in next sc) 19 (20-22) times, drop yarn; sk next ch-1 sp, join another strand of A with sc in next sc, work in pat across—20 (21-23) sc each side.

Shape V-Neck and Armholes: Working on both sides at once, with separate strands of yarn, dec 1 st (see To Dec 1 St, under Cardigan) at neck edge of next row, then dec 1 st at each neck edge every other row 9 (11-11) times more: **at the same time,** bind off 6 (6-8) sts each arm side of next row, 4 sts each arm side of next row— 10 (10-11) sc each side. Work even until armholes measure same as back.

Shape Shoulders: Bind off 6 (6-8) sts each arm side of next 2 rows. End off.

FINISHING: Block pieces. With backstitch, sew shoulder seams; sew side seams.

Neck Edging: Rnd 1: Join B in shoulder seam. From right side, work ch 1, sc pat around neck edge, being careful to keep work flat.

Rnds 2 and 3: Work in pat around, dec 2 sts at center front each rnd (**to dec 2 sts,** pull up a lp in each of 3 sts, yo hook and through 4 lps on hook). End off.

Armhole Edging: Rnd 1: Join B in underarm seam. From right side, work ch 1, sc pat around armhole, easing in to desired fit.

Rnds 2 and 3: Repeat rnd 1. End off.

Steam-press seams and edgings.

3

FOR INFANTS, TODDLERS AND CHILDREN

INFANTS AND TODDLERS
BUNTING AND CAP

A special-occasion fashion for babies is an elongated sacque that gathers in at the bottom. Yoke and crown and cuff of bonnet are in cluster stitch, setting off main pattern of raised shells and crocheted "fagoting."

SIZE: Infants'.
Fits Chest Size: Up to 19″.

MATERIALS: 3-ply baby wool or fingering yarn, 6 1-oz. balls white (W); 1 ball yellow (Y). Yellow rayon crochet cord or pearl cotton for trim (T). Aluminum crochet hook size F. Steel crochet hook No. 1. Five yards ⅝″-wide double-faced satin ribbon.

GAUGE: 1 shell pat = 1″; 3 rows = 1″.
Note: Cut and join colors as needed.

BUNTING: YOKE: Beg at neck edge, with No. 1 hook and W, ch 57 loosely.

Row 1: Dc in 4th ch from hook and in each ch across—55 dc, counting turning ch as 1 dc. Turn each row.

Row 2: Ch 3 (counts as 1 dc), sk first dc, 2 dc in each dc to within last dc and turning ch, end sk next dc, dc in top of turning ch—106 dc.

Row 3: Ch 3 (counts as 1 dc), dc in sp between first 2 dc, * sk next 2 dc, 2 dc in next sp (cluster dc or cl-dc made), repeat from * to within last 2 dc and turning ch, end sk next 2 dc, dc in top of turning ch—52 cl-dc plus 1 dc at end of row.

Row 4: Ch 3, dc between first dc and cl-dc, (cl-dc of 2 dc in sp between next 2 cl-dc) 7 times (front), (cl-dc, ch 1, cl-dc) in sp between next 2 cl-dc, (cl-dc in sp between next 2 cl-dc) 8 times (sleeve), (cl-dc, ch 1, cl-dc) in sp between next 2 cl-dc, (cl-dc in sp between next 2 cl-dc) 16 times (back), (cl-dc, ch 1, cl-dc) in sp between next 2 cl-dc, (cl-dc in sp between next 2 cl-dc) 8 times (sleeve), (cl-dc, ch 1, cl-dc) in sp between next 2 cl-dc, (cl-dc in sp between next 2 cl-dc) 8 times, dc in top of turning ch (front)—4 cl-dc

inc, 56 cl-dc plus 1 dc at end of row.

Row 5: Ch 3, dc between first dc and cl-dc, work cl-dc in each sp be-

tween cl-dc across, working (cl-dc, ch 1, cl-dc) in each ch-1 sp, end dc in top of turning ch—4 cl-dc inc. Repeat row 5, 4 times—76 cl-dc plus 1 dc. Change to size F hook.

Edging: With Y, working up front edge, ch 3, ½ shell of 2 dc in last st worked in, * sk next row, sc in edge of next row, ch 3, sk next row, shell of 5 dc in edge of next row, repeat from * twice, sc in first ch of foundation ch, sc in each ch across neck edge; working down front edge, (shell of 5 dc in edge of next row, ch 3, sk next row, sc in edge of next row, sk next row) 3 times, ½ shell of 3 dc in last st. End off.

Next Row: With T and No. 1 hook, from right side, join yarn in first st, ch 1, * sc in next st, ch 1, repeat from * up front edge, across neck, down front edge. End off.

BODY: From right side, join W at center back of yoke, sc in each of 23 dc to ch-1 sp at underarm; work sc in ch-1 sp, ch 4 for underarm, sk 15 cl-dc for sleeve, sc in ch-1 sp, sc in each of 23 sts across front; work 3 sc in edge of Y row; continue across other front, working 3 sc in edge of Y row (fronts are joined), sc in each of 23 sts across front, sc in ch-1 sp at underarm, ch 4 for underarm, sk next 15 cl-dc for sleeve, sc in next ch-1 sp, sc in each of 23 sts across back, join with a sl st in top of first sc—110 sc. Ch 3, turn.

Shell Pattern: Rnd 1 (wrong side): 4 dc in same st as joining, sk next 2 sts, sc in next st, * ch 3, sk next st, 5 dc in next st, sk next 2 sts, sc in next st, repeat from * around, end ch 3, sc in top of turning ch. Turn.

Rnd 2: * Ch 3, sk ch 3, work shell of 5 dc in next sc, sk next 4 dc, sc in next dc, repeat from * around, end last repeat sc in joining. Turn.

Rnd 3: Ch 3 (counts as 1 dc), 4 dc in first sc, * sk next 4 dc, sc in next dc, ch 3, shell of 5 dc in next sc, repeat from * around, end ch 3, sc in top of starting ch 3. Turn. Repeat rnds 2 and 3 for shell pat until body measures 14" from start, end right side. Keeping to pat, work 1 rnd Y, 3 rnds W, 1 rnd Y.

Trim: From right side, with No. 1 hook and T, * ch 1, sc in next st, repeat from * around. End off.

SLEEVES: From right side, join W in center underarm ch. With size F hook, sc in each st around, join with sl st in first sc—36 sc. Turn. Work 6 shell pats around, spacing shells evenly. Work same as for body until 12 shell rnds from start, end right side. Work (1 rnd Y, 1 rnd W) twice, work 1 rnd Y.

Trim: From right side, with No. 1 hook and T, work same as for body. End off.

FINISHING: Run in all yarn ends on wrong side. Weave a 32" length of ribbon through center of W stripe around lower edge of body; a 16" length through center Y rnd around each sleeve; sew a 14" length to each side of neck opening. Tie ends into bow.

CAP: Crown: Beg at center with No. 1 hook and W, ch 6, join with sl st to form ring.

Rnd 1: Ch 3 (counts as 1 dc), 11 dc in ring, join with sl st to top of ch 3. Do not turn.

Rnd 2: Ch 3 (counts as 1 dc); work dc, ch 1, 2 dc in sp between first and 2nd dc (cl-dc inc made), * sk next 2 dc, 2 dc, ch 1, 2 dc in next sp between dc's, repeat from * 4 times—6 cl-dc inc. Mark end of rnd.

Rnd 3: * Cl-dc inc of 2 dc, ch 1, 2 dc in next ch-1 sp, cl-dc of 2 dc in sp between next cl-dc, repeat from * 5 times.

Rnd 4: * Cl-dc inc of 2 dc, ch 1, 2 dc in next ch-1 sp, (cl-dc of 2 dc in sp between next cl-dc) twice, repeat from * 5 times.

Rnds 5-7: Repeat rnd 4, having 1 more cl-dc between each cl-dc inc every row. End last rnd with sl st in next st.

Rnd 8: Sc in each st around—90 sc. Turn. Change to size F hook.

Shell Pattern: Row 1: Ch 3, 4 dc in next sc, * sk next 3 sc, sc in next sc, ch 3, sk next 3 sc, shell of 5 dc in next sc, repeat from * 7 times, end sk next 3 sc, sc in next sc—9 shells. Turn.

Row 2: Ch 3, 4 dc in first sc, * sk next 4 dc, sc in next dc, ch 3, shell of 5 dc in next sc, repeat from * across, end sc in top of turning ch. Turn. Repeat row 2 for pat 7 times. Change to No. 1 hook. Ch 1, turn.

Cuff: Row 1: Sc in each dc and ch across. Ch 3, turn.

Row 2: * Sk next sc, cl-dc of 2 dc in next sc, repeat from * across. Ch 3, turn.

Row 3: Cl-dc of 2 dc in sp between each cl-dc across. Ch 3, turn.

Row 4: Repeat row 3. End off.

Row 5: With Y, sc in each dc across.

Row 6: With T, sc in each sc across. End off.

FINISHING: Fold cuff to right side. With W and No. 1 hook, work 1 row sc across neck edge, working through both thicknesses at edge of cuff and holding in to desired fit. End off. Cut ribbon into two 24" lengths. Form 3 lps on one end of each length; sew to each side edge of cap.

With T, ch 6, sl st in first ch to form ring.

Rnd 1: 12 sc in ring.

Rnd 2: 2 sc in each sc around.

Rnd 3: * Sc in next sc, ch 3, sk 2 sc, sc in next sc, repeat from * around, sl st in first sc; end off. Sew to crown.

STRIPED BUNTING

Baby bunting in rainbow colors is easy to make in bands of single crochet. Long stitches worked one, two or three rows below create the interesting overlay pattern. Bunting has a zipper closing at center front for quick on-and-off. Matching cap is separate, ties on in front.

SIZE: Up to 1 year.

MATERIALS: Knitting worsted, 2 4-oz. skeins each of red, royal blue, kelly green and yellow. Crochet hook size I or J. Eighteen-inch red zipper.

GAUGE: 3 sc = 1"; 4 rows = 1".

To Bind Off: At beg of a row, sl st across specified number of sts; **at end of a row,** leave specified number of sts unworked.

BUNTING: BACK: With green, ch 56 loosely.

Row 1: Sc in 2nd ch from hook and in each ch across—55 sc. Ch 1, turn each row.

Rows 2-4: Sc in each sc. At end of row 4, drop green. Join red, ch 1, turn.

Row 5: * Sc in next sc, sc in next sc 1 row below (row 3), sc in next sc 2 rows below (row 2), sc in next sc 3 rows below (row 1), sc in next sc 2 rows below, sc in next sc 1 row below, repeat from * across, end sc in last sc.

Rows 6-8: Repeat rows 2-4. At end of row 8, drop red. Join yellow, ch 1, turn.

Rows 9-12: With yellow, repeat rows 5-8. At end of row 12, drop yellow. Join blue, ch 1, turn.

Row 13: With blue, repeat row 5.

Row 14: Dec 1 sc each end of row **(to dec 1 sc,** pull up a lp in each of 2 sc, yo hook and through 3 lps on hook).

Rows 15 and 16: Repeat row 2. At end of row 16, finish last sc with green picked up from row 4, ch 1, turn.

Row 17: Beg and ending with sc in sc 1 row below, work as for row 5. Keeping to pat and color stripes as established, dec 1 sc each end every 3" 3 times more, every 2" twice—43 sc. Work even in pat until 5th red stripe is completed,

changing to yellow in last sc. Turn.

Sleeves: With yellow, ch 10.

Row 1: Sc in 2nd ch from hook and in next 8 ch, work in pat across, ch 10, turn.

Rows 2-4: Repeat row 1. At end of row 4, omit ch. Cut yellow. Join blue, work even in pat on 79 sc until red stripe is completed. Continue in pat, bind off (see To Bind Off) 4 sts each side every other row 5 times, 5 sts every other row once, 6 sts every other row once, working last 2 rows in green sc—17 sc remain for back of neck. End off.

FRONT: Work as for back through row 17—53 sc. Mark center st.

Right Front (Left-handed crocheters: This will be your left front): Work in pat to marked st; do not work in center st. Ch 1, turn. Working in pat as established, dec 1 sc at side edge every 3″ 3 times more, every 2″ twice—21 sc. Work even in pat until 5th red stripe is completed, changing to yellow in last sc. Turn.

Sleeve: Row 1: Work in pat across. Ch 10, turn.

Row 2: Sc in 2nd ch from hook and in next 8 ch, sc in each sc across.

Rows 3 and 4: Repeat rows 1 and 2—39 sc. Work even in pat until red stripe is completed.

Shape Top of Sleeve and Neck: Continue in pat, bind off 4 sts at side edge every other row 5 times, 5 sts once, 6 sts once. **At the same time,** when first row of blue stripe has been completed, bind off 5 sts at neck edge once, then dec 1 st every row 3 times.

Left Front: Join green in st next to marked st, ch 1, sc in each sc to side edge. Dec as for right front, work until 5th red stripe is completed, changing to yellow in last sc. Turn.

Sleeve: With yellow, ch 10,

Row 1: Sc in 2nd ch from hook and in next 8 ch, work in pat across. Ch 1, turn.

Row 2: Sc in each sc across, ch 10, turn.

Row 3: Repeat row 1—39 sc. Finish as for right front.

FINISHING: Sew top of sleeves, underarm, side and bottom seams. With red, work 2 rows of sc around neck and front edges. Work 2 rows of sc around sleeve edges. Sew zipper in front opening. With red, make 2 chains 10″ long. Attach to neck edge each side of opening.

HOOD: Beg at front edge, with green, ch 44. Work in pat as for back of bunting on 43 sc until 26 rows have been completed. Working in yellow, bind off 5 sts each end of next 3 rows. End off.

FINISHING: Sew back seam.

Edging: Join red to front corner of neck edge. From right side, sc across neck edge, 2 sc in next front corner, sc in each st across front of hood, sl st in first sc. Ch 1.

Beading: Sc in first sc on neck edge, * ch 1, sk 1 sc, sc in next sc, repeat from * across neck edge. End off.

With red, make a chain 30″ long. Weave through ch-1 sps of beading.

GRANNY SQUARE BUNTING

Add dazzle to your baby's wardrobe with a cozy and colorful bunting. Easy and fun to crochet in afghan squares that "grow" for shaping!

SIZE: Infants'.
MATERIALS: Sport yarn, 3 ply, about 8 ozs. of desired colors. Crochet hook size F. Knitting needles No. 4. Five buttons.
GAUGE: Square No. 1 = 3¾″.
BUNTING: SQUARE NO. 1 (make 8): With any desired color, ch 4, join with a sl st to form ring.

Rnd 1: Ch 4 (counts as dc, ch 1), * dc in ring, ch 1, repeat from * 6 times, join last ch 1 to 3rd ch of ch 4. End off.

Rnd 2: Join another color in a ch-1 sp, ch 3, 2 dc in same sp, ch 1, * 3 dc in next ch-1 sp, ch 1, repeat from * around, join with a sl st to top of ch 3 (8 groups of 3 dc in rnd). End off.

Rnd 3: Join another color in a ch-1 sp, ch 3, 2 dc in same sp, * 3 dc in next ch-1 sp, (3 dc, ch 2, 3 dc) in next ch-1 sp, repeat from * around, end 3 dc in same sp with first 3 dc, ch 2, join with a sl st to top of ch 3. End off.

Rnd 4: Join another color in a ch-2 sp, ch 2, hdc in same sp, * hdc in each of next 9 dc, (2 hdc, ch 2, 2 hdc) in ch-2 sp, repeat from * around, end 2 hdc in same sp with first 2 hdc, ch 2, join with a sl st to top of ch 2. End off; leave end for sewing.

SQUARE NO. 2 (make 42): Work same as for square No. 1 to end rnd 3. Leave end for sewing.

SQUARE NO. 3 (make 26): With any desired color, ch 4, join with a sl st to form ring.

Rnd 1: Ch 3, 2 dc in ring, ch 2, * 3 dc in ring, ch 2, repeat from * twice, join last ch 2 to top of ch 3 with a sl st (4 groups of 3 dc in ring). End off.

Rnd 2: Join another color in a ch-2 sp, ch 3, dc in same sp, * dc in each of next 3 dc, (2 dc, ch 2, 2 dc)

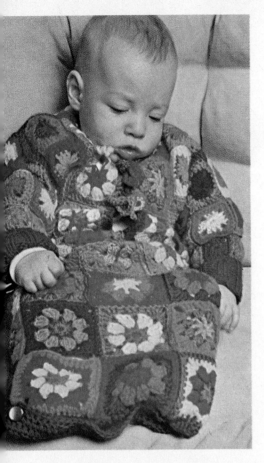

SQUARE NO. 5 (make 10): With any desired color, ch 4, join with a sl st to form ring.

Rnd 1: Ch 3, make 2 dc in ring, ch 3, * 3 dc in ring, repeat from * twice, join last ch 3 to top of first ch 3 with a sl st. End off; leave end for sewing.

HALF SQUARES (make 2): With any desired color, ch 4.

Row 1: Dc in 4th ch from hook, * ch 1, dc in same ch, repeat from * twice. End off; join another color. Ch 3, turn each row.

Row 2: 3 dc in first ch-1 sp, (ch 1, 3 dc in next ch-1 sp) twice, ch 1, 3 dc in last sp. End off; join another color.

Row 3: 3 dc in 3rd ch from hook, 3 dc in next ch-1 sp, (3 dc, ch 3, 3 dc) in next ch-1 sp, 3 dc in next ch-1 sp, 3 dc in top of ch 3. End off; leave end for sewing.

JOINING: Beg at lower edge of front, following chart, sew motifs tog catching back lps of sts only. Where larger motifs join smaller motifs, ease in larger motifs to fit. Do not join sleeves to body. Work 1 row dc across armhole edge of each sleeve; then join sleeves to body. Do not join side edges.

FINISHING: From right side, work 1 row hdc around neck and front opening edge.

Cuffs (make 2): With any desired color and No. 4 needles, cast on 28 sts. Work in ribbing of k 2, p 2 for 2″. Bind off loosely in ribbing. Sew bound-off edge of cuffs to sleeves. Fold work across shoulders; sew side and sleeve seams. From right side, beg at right side edge, work 1 row dc around lower edge. Join with a sl st to top of first dc. Ch 2, turn. Working across back sts only work 3 rows dc, then 1 row sc. End off. Sew five buttons evenly spaced across lower front edge; spaces between dc on back edge form buttonholes.

TIES (make 4): With 2 strands of any desired colors, make ch 10″ long. Sew 2 ties to each edge of front opening. Tie ends.

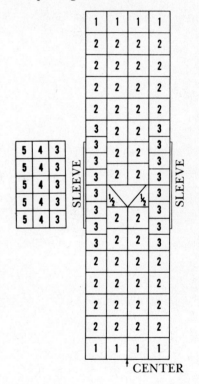

in ch-2 sp, repeat from * around, end 2 dc in same sp with first 2 dc, ch 3, join with a sl st to top of ch 3. End off; leave end for sewing.

SQUARE NO. 4 (make 10): Work same as rnd 1 on square No. 3. End off.

Rnd 2: Join another color in a ch-2 sp, ch 2, hdc in same sp, * hdc in each of next 3 dc, (2 hdc, ch 2, 2 hdc) in ch-2 sp, repeat from * around, end 2 hdc in same sp with first 2 hdc, ch 2, join with a sl st to top of ch 2. End off; leave end for sewing.

SHELL SET

Shown on page 176

An unusual but easy shell stitch is the pattern for this pink set; solid areas are single crochet. Picot edgings and tasseled cords accent all.

SIZE: Infants'.
Fits Chest: Up to 19″.
MATERIALS: Baby wool, 4 1-oz. balls. Steel crochet hook No. 1.
GAUGE: 1 shell pat = 1″.

SACQUE: YOKE: Beg at neck edge, ch 61 loosely.
Row 1: Sc in 2nd ch from hook

SHELL SET

and in each ch across—60 sc. Ch 1, turn each row.

Row 2: Sc in each of 12 sc (front), 3 sc in next sc, sc in each of 4 sc (sleeve), 3 sc in next sc, sc in each of 24 sc (back), 3 sc in next sc, sc in each of 4 sc (sleeve), 3 sc in next sc, sc in each of 12 sc (front)—8 sc inc.

Rows 3, 5, 7 and 9: Sc in each sc across.

Row 4: Sc in each of 13 sc, 3 sc in next sc, sc in each of 6 sc, 3 sc in next sc, sc in each of 26 sc, 3 sc in next sc, sc in each of 6 sc, 3 sc in next sc, sc in each of 13 sc—8 sc inc.

Row 6: Sc in each of 14 sc, 3 sc

in next sc, sc in each of 8 sc, 3 sc in next sc, sc in each of 28 sc, 3 sc in next sc, sc in each of 8 sc, 3 sc in next sc, sc in each of 14 sc.

Row 8: Sc in each of 15 sc, 3 sc in next sc, sc in each of 10 sc, 3 sc in next sc, sc in each of 30 sc, 3 sc in next sc, sc in each of 10 sc, 3 sc in next sc, sc in each of 15 sc.

Row 10: Sc in each of 16 sc, 3 sc in next sc, sc in each of 12 sc, 3 sc in next sc, sc in each of 32 sc, 3 sc in next sc, sc in each of 12 sc, 3 sc in next sc, sc in each of 16 sc—100 sc.

Row 11: Sc in each sc across. Turn.

Pattern: Row 1 (wrong side): * Ch 3, sk next sc, 4 dc in next sc, sk next sc, sl st in next sc (shell made), repeat from * across—25 shells. Turn.

Row 2: * Ch 3, 4 dc in sl st, sl st in next ch-3 sp, repeat from * across—25 shells. Turn.

Rows 3 and 4: Repeat row 2.

Divide Work: Right Front: Next Row: Work in pat across 4 shells, turn. Work in pat on 4 shells for 6 more rows. End off.

Back: Sk next 4 shells on yoke for right sleeve, join yarn with a sl st in sl st, ch 3, work 4 dc in same sl st, work in pat across next 8 shells. Turn. Work in pat on 9 shells for 6 more rows. End off.

Left Front: Sk next 4 shells on yoke for left sleeve, join yarn with a sl st in sl st, ch 3, work 4 dc in same sl st, work in pat across. Work in pat on 4 shells for 6 more rows; do not end off. Turn.

Join Body: Next Row: Work across 4 shells of left front, ch 3, sl st in first sl st of back, ch 3 and work in pat across 9 shells on back, ch 3, sl st in first sl st of right front, ch 3 and work in pat across 4 shells on right front. Turn.

Next Row: Work in pat across right front, ch 3, shell in first ch of ch-3 sp on underarm, sl st in 2nd ch of ch 3, ch 3, continue in pat

across back, work extra shell as before in left underarm, finish row—19 shells. Work even for 17 rows. End off.

SLEEVES: From wrong side, join yarn in center ch of ch 3 at right underarm. Working up armhole of right front, ch 3, work 2 shell pats to yoke, work across 4 shells on sleeve, work 2 shell pats down armhole of back—8 shells. Turn. Work even for 18 rows.

Border: Row 1: Ch 1, * sc in each of 2 dc, sk next dc, sc in next dc, sc in ch-3 sp, repeat from * across—32 sc. Ch 1, turn each row.

Rows 2-5: Sc in each sc across. End off. From wrong side, join yarn in center ch of ch 3 at left underarm, work left sleeve the same.

FINISHING: Steam-press lightly. Weave sleeve seams.

Beading and Edging: From right side, join yarn at neck edge. Ch 4, * sk 1 ch, dc in next ch, ch 1, repeat from * across neck edge. Working down front edge, * ch 3, sc in 3rd ch from hook (picot made), sk 1 row on edge, sc in edge of next row, repeat from * around outer edge of sacque, keeping work flat (work sc in every other row of pat on front edges, 2 picot pats in each shell across lower edge, sc in every other sp of beading). End off.

CORD: Make a 30″ twisted cord (see page 319), run through beading.

TASSELS (make 2): Wind yarn 20 times around a 1″ piece of cardboard. Cut one end, tie other end. Sew tassel to each end of cord.

BONNET: Crown: Ch 4, sl st in first ch to form ring.

Rnd 1: 8 sc in ring. Sl st in first sc, ch 1, turn each rnd.

Rnd 2: 2 sc in each sc—16 sc.

Rnd 3: * Sc in next sc, 2 sc in next sc, repeat from * around—24 sc.

Rnd 4: Sc in each sc around.

Rnd 5: Repeat rnd 3—36 sc.

Rnd 6: * Sc in each of next 2 sc, 2 sc in next sc, repeat from * around—48 sc.

Rnds 7 and 8: Sc in each sc around.

Rnd 9: * Sc in each of next 3 sc, 2 sc in next sc, repeat from * around—60 sc.

Rnd 10: Repeat rnd 9—75 sc.

Rnds 11 and 12: Sc in each sc around. At end of rnd 12, sl st in first sc, end off. Turn.

Front: Row 1 (right side): Sk 7 sc from end of rnd, join yarn in next sc, * ch 3, sk next sc, 4 dc in next sc, sk next sc, sl st in next sc, ch 3, sk next sc, 4 dc in next sc, sk next 2 sc, sl st in next sc, repeat from * 5 times, ch 3, sk next sc, 4 dc in next sc, sk next 2 sc, sl st in next sc—13 shells. Leave remaining sc for neck edge. Turn. Work in pat until 14 pat rows are completed, end wrong side. Turn.

Border: Row 1: Ch 1, * sc in each of 2 dc, sk next dc, sc in next dc, sc under ch-3 sp, repeat from * across. Turn.

Rows 2 and 3: Ch 1, sc in each sc across. Do not turn at end of row 3. Working on neck edge, work 2 rows sc, dec to desired fit. Turn.

Beading: Ch 4, * sk next sc, dc in next sc, repeat from * across neck edge. Working across front edge, * ch 3, sc in 3rd ch from hook (picot made), sk next sc, sc in next sc, repeat from * across, sc in each st across beading on neck edge. End off.

FINISHING: Steam-press lightly. Make a 26″ twisted cord; run through beading. Make two 1″ tassels; sew to ends of cord.

BOOTEES: Sole: Ch 14.

Rnd 1: 3 sc in 2nd ch from hook, sc in each of next 11 ch, 3 sc in last ch; working on other side of starting ch, sc in each of next 11 ch—28 sc. Do not join rnds; mark ends of rnds.

Rnd 2: (2 sc in each of next 3 sc, sc in each of 11 sc) twice—34 sc.

Rnd 3: (Sc in next sc, 2 sc in next sc) 3 times, sc in each of next 12 sc, 2 sc in next sc, (sc in next sc, 2 sc in next sc) twice, sc in each of next 11 sc—40 sc.

Rnds 4 and 5: Sc around, inc 3 sc evenly spaced on each end—52 sc.

Foot: Rnds 1-6: Sc in each sc around. At end of rnd 6, continue to center st at next end, work 4 sc beyond center st. Sl st in next st. Ch 1, turn.

Instep: Sc in each of next 9 sc. Sl st in next st on foot, ch 1, turn each row. Work in sc on these 9 sts for 9 more rows, joining sides of instep to foot each row. End off.

Top: Join yarn in sc at center back of foot. Work in shell pat around—7 shells. Do not join; turn. Work in pat for 5 more rows. Work a picot row same as on lower edge of sacque. End off.

FINISHING: Weave edges of top tog. Make two 18" twisted cords; run through first row of pat. Make two 1" tassels; sew to ends of cord. Tie ends into bow to fasten.

MULTICOLOR JACKET

Color-bright stripes go ring-around-baby in a jacket bordered with afghan squares. The jacket is worked in double crochet with a picot edging.

SIZES: Directions for size 6 mos. Changes for size 1 are in parentheses.

Body Chest Size: 19" (20").

Blocked Chest Size: 20" (22").

MATERIALS: Fingering yarn, 3 ply, about 3 (4) ozs. of desired colors. Steel crochet hook No. 1. Five buttons.

GAUGE: 9 dc = 2"; 5 rows = 2".

JACKET: BODY: Beg at lower edge of striped section for back and fronts, with any desired color, ch 82 (92). Cut yarn; join another color.

Row 1: Ch 3 (counts as 1 dc), dc in 4th ch from hook, dc in next ch and in each ch across—83 (93) dc. Cut yarn; join another color. Turn.

Row 2: Ch 3, sk first dc, dc in next dc and in each dc across. Cut yarn; join another color. Turn. Using desired colors, repeat row 2 until piece measures about 3¼" (4") from start or 3" less (border allowance) than desired length to underarm. Turn. Check gauge; piece should measure 18½" (20½") wide.

Divide Work: Right Front: Ch 3, sk first dc, dc in each of next 20

(22) dc. Cut yarn; join another color. Turn. Working on these 21 (23) dc, work 3″ (3½″). End off.

Shape Neck and Shoulder: Leaving 7 (8) dc free at front edge, work even on remaining 14 (15) dc until armhole measures 4″ (4½″) above start of armhole. End off.

Back: Keeping to same color sequence as right front, join yarn in next dc on last long row, ch 3, dc in next dc and in each of next 39 (45) dc. Turn. Work even until armhole measures same as right front. End off.

Left Front: Keeping to color sequence, join yarn in next dc on last long row, ch 3, dc in next dc and in each dc across. Complete same as right front.

Sew shoulders.

SLEEVE: Join any desired color at underarm, ch 3, work 2 dc in edge of each row around arm-hole, join with a sl st in top of starting ch 3. End off; join another color. Do not turn.

Next Rnd: Ch 3, dc in next dc and in each dc around, join with a sl st. End off; join another color. Repeat last rnd, dec 1 dc at underarm every 1″ 6 times. Work even until sleeve measures 7″ (8″) from start. Work other sleeve in same manner.

SQUARES: With any desired color, ch 4, join with a sl st to form ring.

Rnd 1: Ch 3 (counts as 1 dc), make 2 dc in ring, ch 2, * 3 dc in ring, ch 2, repeat from * twice, join last ch 2 to top of ch 3 with a sl st (4 groups of 3 dc in rnd). End off.

Rnd 2: Join another color in a ch-2 sp, ch 3, dc in same sp, ch 3, 2 dc in same sp, * dc in each of next 3 dc, 2 dc in next ch-2 sp, ch 3, 2 dc in same ch-2 sp, repeat from * twice, dc in each of next 3 dc, join with a sl st to top of starting ch 3. End off. Make 8 (9) squares.

Join Squares: Sew squares tog forming a strip 8 (9) squares long.

FINISHING: Sew edge of strip to lower edge of back and fronts.

Edging: Join any desired color at lower side edge.

Rnd 1: From right side, work hdc around outer edge, working 2 hdc in each lower front and neck corner; join with a sl st in first hdc. End off; join another color.

Rnd 2: Repeat rnd 1.

Rnd 3: * Sc in each of next 4 hdc, ch 3, sc in last sc (picot made), repeat from * around, join with a sl st in first sc. End off.

Block. Sew five buttons, evenly spaced, on left front edge for girl, right front edge for boy. Spaces between hdc on rnd 2 of edging form buttonholes.

BIB-SHORTS

Shown on page 180

Granny square bib in four colors tops shorts worked in an easy double crochet pattern. The back straps button in front.

SIZES: Directions for size 6 mos. Changes for sizes 1 and 2 are in parentheses.

Body Hip Size: 20″ (21″-22″).

Blocked Hip Size: 21″ (22½″-24″).

MATERIALS: Knitting worsted, 4 ply, 3 (4-5) ozs. of desired colors. Crochet hook size G. Two buttons.

GAUGE: Square = 4″; 7 dc = 2″.

SHORTS: BIB: Square: With any desired color, ch 4, join with a sl st to form ring.

Rnd 1: Ch 3 (counts as 1 dc), make 2 dc in ring, ch 1, * 3 dc in ring, ch 1, repeat from * twice, join last ch 1 to top of ch 3 with a sl st (4 groups of 3 dc in ring). End off.

Rnd 2: Join another color in a ch-1 sp, ch 3, 2 dc in same sp, ch 1, * 3 dc in next ch-1 sp, ch 2, 3 dc in same sp, ch 1, repeat from * twice, 3 dc in same sp with first 3 dc, ch 2, join with a sl st to top of ch 3. End off.

Rnd 3: Join another color in a ch-2 sp, ch 3, 2 dc in same sp, ch 1, * 3 dc in next ch-1 sp, ch 1, (3 dc, ch 2, 3 dc) in corner ch-2 sp, ch 1, repeat from * around, end 3 dc in same sp with first 3 dc, ch 2, join with a sl st to top of ch 3. End off.

Rnd 4: Work same as rnd 3, having 2 groups of 3 dc between corners. Join with a sl st to top of ch 3; do not end off.

PANTS: Ch 47 (53-59); being careful not to twist chain, join with a sl st in corner ch 2 of bib forming circle.

Rnd 1: Ch 3 (counts as 1 dc), (dc in each of 3 dc, dc in ch-1 sp) 4 times, dc in each ch around—64 (70-76) dc. Join with a sl st in top of ch 3. End off; do not turn.

Rnd 2: Sk next dc, join another color in next dc, ch 3 (counts as 1 dc), dc in next dc, ch 1, sk next dc, dc in each of next 2 dc, ch 1, sk next dc, 2 dc in next dc, ch 1 (mark

FOR INFANTS, TODDLERS AND CHILDREN

BIB-SHORTS

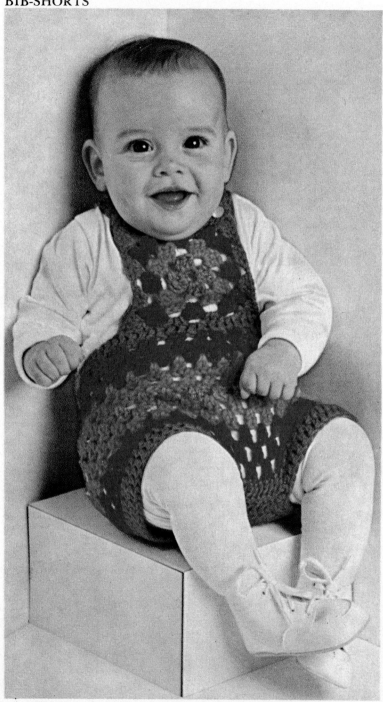

in ch-1 sp, (* ch 1, 2 dc in next ch-1 sp, repeat from * to marked ch-1 sp, work 2 dc, ch 1, 2 dc in marked ch-1 sp) twice, ch 1, 2 dc in each ch-1 sp around, end sl st in top of ch 3, sl st in next dc and in next sp.

Rnd 4: Repeat rnd 3. End off.

Rnd 5: With another color make lp on hook, * 2 dc in any ch-1 sp, ch 1, repeat from * around, join with sl st in top of first dc, sl st in next dc and in next sp.

Rnd 6: Ch 3, dc in ch-1 sp, * ch 1, 2 dc in next sp, repeat from * around, ch 1, sl st in top of ch 3, sl st in next dc and in next sp. End off. Repeat rnds 5 and 6 until piece measures 6½″ (7″-7½″) from starting ch. End off.

Next Rnd: With color used on rnd 1, dc in each st and ch-1 sp around. End off.

Shape Crotch: With last color used, dc in each of 8 dc across center back of pants.

FINISHING: Weave crotch to front. Work 1 rnd dc around each leg opening.

Straps (make 2): With color used on last row of bib, ch 6.

Row 1: Dc in 4th ch from hook and in each of next 2 ch. Turn.

Row 2: Ch 3, sk first dc, dc in each of next 2 dc, dc in top of ch 3. Turn. Repeat last row until strap measures 14″ (15″-16″). End off. Sew one end of each strap to back edge of pants, 4 sts each side of center back. Sew a button to other end of strap.

Front Edging: Join yarn with sc in top corner of bib, sc in first dc, ch 1 for buttonhole, sk next dc, sc in each st to within last 2 dc on top edge, ch 1 for buttonhole, sk next dc, sc in each of next 2 sts. Ch 1, turn.

Next Row: Sc in each st across. End off.

Steam-press lightly.

for center front), 2 dc in same dc, (ch 1, sk next dc, dc in each of next 2 dc) 10 (11-12) times, sk next dc, ch 1, 2 dc in next dc, ch 1 (mark for center back), 2 dc in same dc, (ch 1, sk next dc, dc in each of next 2 dc) 8 (9-10) times, ch 1, sl st in top of ch 3, sl st in next dc and in next sp.

Rnd 3: Ch 3 (counts as 1 dc), dc

BUTTERFLY SUNSUIT

A butterfly in baby colors is crocheted into bib of a charming summer fashion for babies. Simple to make, all in double crochet, the sunsuit is worked from top of bib down, like its Pentagon Sunsuit companion, in bands of white, yellow, pink and blue.

SIZE: Directions for sizes 1-2.
Fits Body Waist Size: 19½"-20".
Fits Body Hip Size: 21"-22".
MATERIALS: Sport yarn, 1 2-oz. skein each of light blue (B), light pink (P), yellow (Y) and white (W). Steel crochet hook No. 1. One yd. round elastic.

GAUGE: 11 dc = 2"; 5 rows = 2".

Note: When changing colors, pull new color through last 2 lps to complete dc. Use another strand of color for each color change.

SUNSUIT: BIB: Beg at upper edge with W, ch 33.

Row 1: Dc in 4th ch from hook and in each ch across—31 dc. Always count ch 3 at beg of row as first dc. Turn each row.

Row 2: Ch 3, sk first dc, 2 dc in next dc (1 dc inc), dc in each dc to within last dc and turning ch, end 2 dc in next dc (1 dc inc), dc in top of turning ch—33 dc.

Rows 3-11: Following chart, work in dc; **at the same time,** inc 1 dc each side of row 5, then every 3rd row twice more—39 dc. Working even in dc, work 2 rows W, 1 row B, 1 row P. With P, ch 12 at end of last row. End off; do not turn.

PANTS: FRONT: Join Y at beg of last row, ch 14, dc in 4th ch from hook and in each of next 10 ch, dc in each dc across bib, dc in each of last 12 ch—63 dc. Cut Y; join W. Work even in dc, working * 3 rows W, 1 row B, 1 row P, 1 row Y, repeat from * until pants measure about 8½" from start or desired length to crotch, end with a W row. End off; turn. Check gauge; pants should measure 11½" wide.

Crotch: Sk first 24 dc, join W in

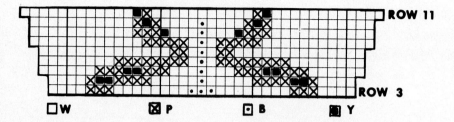

next dc, ch 3, dc in each of next 14 dc. Ch 3, turn. Work 2 rows even. End off.

STRAPS: Join Y in first ch of foundation ch at top of bib. Ch 3, dc in each of next 3 ch. Ch 3, turn. Work even until 22 rows from start. End off. Make other strap in same manner.

BACK: Beg at upper edge with Y, ch 65.

Row 1: Dc in 4th ch from hook and in each ch across—63 dc, counting starting ch as 1 dc. Cut Y; join W. Work even in dc in same color sequence as front until piece measures same as front to crotch.

Crotch: Work same as for front crotch for 2 rows. End off.

FINISHING: Run in yarn ends on wrong side. Steam-press pieces. Matching colors, sew side and crotch seams.

Leg Edging: From right side, with W, work 1 rnd sc around leg opening; join with a sl st in first sc.

Rnd 2: * Sc in next sc, ch 1, sk next sc, repeat from * around; join. End off. Cut elastic to thigh measurement; fasten ends securely.

Rnd 3: Working over elastic, sc in each st around. End off.

Bib and Waist Edging: From right side, with Y, sc in each st across top of bib. End off.

Beg at upper side edge of bib, with Y, * ch 1, sc in side of next row, repeat from * down side edge of bib; working over elastic, sc in each st across upper edge of pants; work from first * up right side edge of bib, end top of bib. End off. Draw up elastic to desired fit; fasten each end securely.

PENTAGON SUNSUIT

Shown on page 181

A five-sided motif in pretty pastels and white forms the bib for this little striped sunsuit. Worked mostly in double crochet of medium-weight yarn, the suit is easy to make. Elastic snugs back waist edge.

SIZE: Directions for size 1-2.
Fits Body Waist Size: 19½″-20″.
Fits Body Hip Size: 21″-22″.
MATERIALS: Sport yarn, 3 ply, 2 ozs. each of blue (B) and yellow (Y); 1 oz. each of white (W) and pink (P). Steel crochet hook No. 1. One yd. round elastic.
GAUGE: 11 dc = 2″; 5 rows = 2″.
Note: Cut and join colors as needed.
SUNSUIT: BIB: Beg at center with W, ch 5; join with sl st to form ring.

Rnd 1: Ch 4 (counts as 1 dc, ch 1), (dc, ch 1) 9 times in ring; join last ch 1 with a sl st in 3rd ch of ch 4. End off.

Rnd 2: Join P in a ch-1 sp, ch 3, dc in same sp, ch 1, * work 2 dc, ch 1, 2 dc in next ch-1 sp, ch 1, 2 dc in next ch-1 sp, ch 1, repeat from * 3 times, end 2 dc, ch 1, 2 dc in next ch-1 sp, ch 1, join with a sl st in top of ch 3. End off.

Rnd 3: Join Y in last ch-1 sp made, ch 3, dc in same sp, ch 1, 2 dc in next ch-1 sp, ch 1, * work 3 dc, ch 1, 3 dc in next ch-1 sp (corner made), ch 1, (2 dc in next ch-1 sp, ch 1) twice, repeat from * around, end last repeat 2 dc in next ch-1 sp, ch 1, join with a sl st to top of ch 3. End off; join B in ch-1 sp before ch-1 corner sp.

Rnd 4: Ch 3, dc in same sp, ch 1, work from * on rnd 3, having 3 groups of 2 dc between corners. Join with a sl st to top of ch 3. End off; join W in ch-1 sp before ch-1 corner sp.

Rnd 5: With W, repeat rnd 4, having 4 groups of 2 dc between corners. End off.

Rnd 6: Join P in any ch-1 corner sp, ch 1, 3 sc in ch-1 corner sp, * sc in each dc, 3 sc in ch-1 corner sp, repeat from * 3 times, sc in each remaining dc—85 sc. Join with a sl st in first sc; do not turn.

Rnd 7: Ch 3 (counts as 1 dc), dc in same sc as joining, ch 2, sk next sc, 2 dc in next sc, * dc in each sc to within next 3-sc group at corner; work 2 dc in next sc, ch 2, sk next sc, 2 dc in next sc, repeat from * 3 times, dc in each remaining sc—90 dc. Join; end off.

Rnd 8: Join Y in any ch-2 sp, ch 3, work dc, ch 2, 2 dc in same ch-2 sp as joining, * work dc in each dc, (2 dc, ch 2, 2 dc) in ch-2 sp, repeat from * 3 times, end dc in each remaining dc—110 dc. Join; end off.

Rnd 9: With B, repeat rnd 8—130 dc. Sl st to ch-2 sp. Ch 3, turn.

Straps: Row 1: Dc in each of 3 dc. Turn.

Rows 2-22: Ch 3, sk first dc, dc in next dc and in each of next 2 dc. Turn each row. End off. Work other strap in same manner.

PANTS: FRONT: Row 1: Join B in first ch-2 sp after strap, ch 3, dc in same sp, dc in each dc to next ch-2 sp, (2 dc, ch 2, 2 dc) in ch-2 sp, dc in each dc to next ch-2 sp, 2 dc in ch-2 sp—60 dc. Turn.

Row 2: Ch 3, sk first dc, dc in each dc to ch-2 sp, (2 dc, ch 2, 2 dc) in ch-2 sp, dc in each dc—64 dc. End off B. Turn.

Row 3: Join W, repeat row 2. Cut W; join P.

Rows 4-8: Repeat row 2, working 1 row P, 4 rows Y—92 dc.

Shape Sides: Row 1: Working with Y, ch 3, sk first dc, dec 1 dc (**to dec 1 dc,** yo hook, draw up a lp in each of next 2 sts, yo hook and through 2 lps, yo and through 3 lps), dc in each dc to within ch-2

sp, (2 dc, ch 2, 2 dc) in ch-2 sp, dc in each dc to within last 3 dc, end dec 1 dc over next 2 dc, dc in top of turning ch—1 dc dec each side—94 dc. Repeat last row, working 1 row Y, 1 row P, 1 row W, 1 row B—102 dc.

Shape Leg: With B, ch 3, sk first dc, dec 1 dc over next 2 dc, dc in each dc to 6 sts before ch-2 sp, hdc in each of next 2 dc, sc in each of next 3 dc, sl st in next dc. Ch 1, turn.

Row 2: Sk sl st, sl st loosely in each of next 2 sts, hdc in next st, dc in each st to within last 3 sts, end dec 1 dc over next 2 sts, dc in top of turning ch. Turn.

Row 3: Ch 3, sk first dc, dec 1 dc over next 2 dc, dc in each dc to within last 7 sts (do not count sl sts), end hdc in each of next 2 sts, sc in each of next 3 sts, sl st in next st. Ch 1, turn. Repeat last 2 rows 4 times.

Next Row: Sl st in each of next 4 sts, sc in each of next 3 sts, hdc in each of next 2 sts, dc in each st to within last 3 sts, end dec 1 dc over next 2 sts, dc in top of turning ch. Turn.

Next Row: Ch 3, sk first dc, dec 1 dc over next 2 dc, dc in next dc, hdc in next 2 sts, sc in next 3 sts, sl st in next st. End off.

Join B at side edge of last long row; shape leg same as other leg. End off.

Crotch: Join B in 9th st from center ch-2 sp (5th B row of leg), ch 3, dc in each st to ch-2 sp, dc in ch-2 sp, dc in each of next 9 sts—19 dc. Turn. Dec 1 dc each side of next 2 rows—15 dc. End off.

BACK: Beg at top edge, with B, ch 66.

Row 1: Dc in 4th ch from hook and in each ch across—63 dc, plus turning ch. Cut B. Turn.

Rows 2 and 3: Working in dc, work 1 row W, 1 row P. End off.

Rows 4-9: With Y, work 6 rows, inc 1 dc each side every other row (**to inc 1 dc,** work 2 sts in same st)—69 dc, plus turning ch.

Row 10: With P, work even.

Row 11: With W, inc 1 st each side.

Rows 12-24: With B, work even. End off.

Crotch: Sk 28 dc, join B in next dc, ch 3, dc in each of next 14 dc. Turn.

Next Row: Ch 3, sk first dc, dc in each dc. End off.

FINISHING: Run in yarn ends. Steam-press pieces. Sew side and crotch seams, easing in front side edges.

Leg Edging: From right side, with B, work 1 rnd sc around leg opening; join with a sl st in first sc. Cut B; join W.

Rnd 2: * Sc in next sc, ch 1, sk next sc, repeat from * around, drawing in leg opening. Join, end off.

Bib and Waist Edging: From right side, join W in upper side edge of bib, * ch 1, sc in side of next row, repeat from * down side edge of bib; working over elastic, sc in each st across upper edge of pants; work from * up side edge of bib, end top of bib. End off. Draw up elastic to desired fit; fasten ends securely at each side of pants.

BUTTERFLY PINAFORE

Two different yarns make the difference in twin back-buttoned pinafores. Yoke is worked in double crochet; ruffles and skirt are in shell stitch. Make them to wear all year 'round—alone in summer, over a dress when the days grow cool.

SIZES: Directions for size 6 mos. Changes for sizes 1 and 2 are in parentheses.

Fits Body Chest Size: 19″ (20″-21″).

MATERIALS: Acrylic yarn of knitting worsted weight, 1 4-oz. skein. Crochet hook size G. Three buttons.

GAUGE: 4 shells = 5″; 3 rows = 2″.

PINAFORE: YOKE: Beg at neck edge, ch 52 (60-60) to measure 13″ (15″-15″).

Row 1: Dc in 4th ch from hook, dc in each of next 4 (6-6) ch (back), 3 dc in next ch, dc in each of next 11 ch (sleeve), 3 dc in next ch, dc in each of next 12 (16-16) ch (front), 3 dc in next ch, dc in each of next 11 ch (sleeve), 3 dc in next ch, dc in each of next 6 (8-8) ch (back)—58 (66-66) dc (counting ch 3 as 1 dc). Turn each row.

Row 2: Ch 3, sk first dc, dc in each of 6 (8-8) dc, 3 dc in next dc, dc in each of next 13 dc, 3 dc in next dc, dc in each of next 14 (18-18) dc, 3 dc in next dc, dc in each of next 13 dc, 3 dc in next dc, dc in each of next 6 (8-8) dc, dc in top of ch 3—8 dc inc.

Row 3: Ch 3, sk first dc, dc in each of next 7 (9-9) dc, 3 dc in next dc, (sk next dc, shell of 5 dc in next dc) 7 times (sleeve ruffle), sk next dc, 3 dc in next dc, dc in each of next 16 (20-20) dc, 3 dc in next dc, (sk next dc, shell of 5 dc in next dc) 7 times (sleeve ruffle), sk next dc, 3 dc in next dc, dc in each of next 7 (9-9) dc, dc in top of ch 3.

Row 4: Ch 3, sk first dc, dc in each of next 8 (10-10) dc, 3 dc in next dc (center dc of 3-dc group), (shell of 5 dc in center dc of shell) 7 times, 3 dc in center dc of 3-dc group, dc in each of next 18 (22-22) dc, 3 dc in next dc (center dc of 3-dc group), (shell of 5 dc in center dc of shell) 7 times, 3 dc in center dc of 3-dc group, dc in each of next 8 (10-10) dc, dc in top of ch 3.

BODY: Row 5: Ch 3, sk first dc, dc in each of next 9 (11-11) dc, 3 dc in next dc, ch 2 (2-5), sk sleeve ruffle, 3 dc in center dc of next 3-dc group, dc in each of next 20 (24-24) dc, 3 dc in next dc, ch 2 (2-5), sk sleeve ruffle, 3 dc in center of dc of next 3-dc group, dc in each of next 9 (11-11) dc, dc in top of ch 3.

Row 6: Ch 3, 2 dc in first dc (½ shell made), * sk next 2 sts, shell of 5 dc in next st, repeat from * 16 (19-21) times, end ½ shell of 3 dc in last st—17 (20-22) shells plus ½ shell each side.

Row 7: Ch 3, 2 dc in first dc (½ shell made), shell of 5 dc in center dc of each shell across, end ½ shell of 3 dc in top of ch 3. Repeat last row 6 times or until desired length from underarm. Check gauge; shell row should measure 22″ (26″-29″) wide. End off.

FINISHING: Steam-press lightly. Sew 3 buttons evenly spaced to left back yoke. Space between dc forms buttonholes.

ADD-A-SQUARE SKIRT

A tiny girl will thrill to the zingy colors of her bibbed skirt. The afghan squares are crocheted in graduating sizes to give a gentle flare to the skirt; small squares make the bib. A great way to use your leftover sport yarn!

SIZES: Directions for size 6 mos. Changes for sizes 1 and 2 are in parentheses. **Note:** Crochet hook and gauge determine size.

Body Waist Size: 19″ (19½″-20″).

MATERIALS: Sport yarn, 3 ply, 3 (3-4) ozs. of desired colors. Crochet hook size D (E-F). Two buttons.

GAUGE: Square No. 1 = 3¼″ (3½″-3¾″).

SKIRT: FIRST RING: Square No. 1 (make 8): With any desired color, ch 4, join with a sl st to form ring.

Rnd 1: Ch 4 (counts as dc, ch 1), * dc in ring, ch 1, repeat from * 6 times, join last ch 1 to 3rd ch of ch 4. End off.

Rnd 2: Join another color in a ch-1 sp, ch 3, 2 dc in same sp, ch 1, * 3 dc in next ch-1 sp, ch 1, repeat from * around, join with a sl st to top of ch 3 (8 groups of 3 dc in rnd). End off.

Rnd 3: Join another color in a ch-1 sp, ch 3, 2 dc in same sp, * 3 dc in next ch-1 sp, (3 dc, ch 2, 3 dc) in next ch-1 sp, repeat from * around, end 3 dc in same sp with first 3 dc, ch 2, join with a sl st to top of ch 3. End off.

Rnd 4: Join another color in a ch-2 sp, ch 2, hdc in same sp, * hdc in each of next 9 dc, (2 hdc, ch 2, 2 hdc) in ch-2 sp, repeat from * around, end 2 hdc in same sp with first 2 hdc, ch 2, join with a sl st to top of ch 2. End off.

Joining: Sew squares tog forming a ring. Check gauge; strip should measure 26″ (28″-30″) around.

SECOND RING: Square No. 2 (make 8): Work same as for square No. 1 to end of rnd 3.

Joining: Sew squares tog forming a ring. Sew this ring to top of first ring, easing in first ring.

THIRD RING: Square No. 3 (make 8): With any desired color, ch 4, join with a sl st to form ring.

Rnd 1: Ch 3 (counts as 1 dc), make 2 dc in ring, ch 2, * 3 dc in ring, ch 2, repeat from * twice, join last ch 2 to top of ch 3 with a sl st (4 groups of 3 dc in ring). End off.

Rnd 2: Join another color in a ch-2 sp, ch 3, dc in same sp, * dc in each of next 3 dc, (2 dc, ch 2, 2 dc) in ch-2 sp, repeat from * twice, dc in each of next 3 dc, 2 dc in same sp with first 2 dc, ch 2, join with a sl st to top of ch 3. End off.

Joining: Sew squares tog forming a ring. Sew this ring to top of 2nd ring, easing in 2nd ring.

BIB: Square No. 4 (make 9):

Work same as for square No. 3 to end of rnd 1.

Joining: Sew squares tog forming a square 3 by 3.

STRAPS (make 2): With any desired color, ch 8.

Row 1: Dc in 4th ch from hook and in each of next 4 ch. Turn.

Row 2: Ch 3, sk first dc, dc in each of next 3 dc and in top of ch 3. Turn. Repeat row 2, changing colors as desired until strap measures 13" (14"-15") or desired

length. Work 2nd strap in same color sequence.

FINISHING: From right side, work 1 rnd hdc around upper edge of skirt. If necessary, work hdc around elastic cut to waist measurement. Sew bib across two squares of skirt. From right side, work 1 row hdc around bib. Sew straps to back of skirt; sew button to other end of straps. Ch-2 corner sps on bib form buttonholes. Steam-press.

HOLIDAY HELMET

A toddler will love a helmet in happy colors. Granny afghan squares and pentagons of variegated yarn are crocheted into four segments to join for snug hat.

SIZE: Fits 17"-21" head size.

MATERIALS: Knitting worsted, 1 oz. each of mixed rainbow colors (M), yellow (Y) and red (R). Crochet hook size G.

GAUGE: 7 sc = 1"; 4 rows = 1"; back motif = 3½" square.

Note: Cut and join colors as needed.

HELMET: BACK SECTION: Motif: Beg at center, with M, ch 4, join with a sl st to form ring.

Rnd 1: Ch 3 (counts as 1 dc), make 2 dc in ring, ch 1, * 3 dc in ring, ch 1, repeat from * twice, join last ch 1 to top of ch 3 with a sl st (4 groups of 3 dc in rnd).

Rnd 2: Sl st in back lp of each dc and ch around. End off.

Rnd 3: Join Y in a ch-1 sp, ch 3, 2 dc in same sp, ch 1, * 3 dc in next sp, ch 1, 3 dc in same ch-1 sp, ch 1, repeat from * twice, 3 dc in same sp with first 3 dc, ch 1, join with a sl st to top of ch 3. End off.

Rnd 4: Join R in a corner ch-1 sp, ch 3, 2 dc in same sp, ch 1, * 3 dc in next ch-1 sp, ch 1, (3 dc, ch 1, 3 dc) in corner ch-1 sp, ch 1, repeat from * around, end 3 dc in same sp with first 3 dc, ch 1, join with a sl st to top of ch 3. End off.

Top: Row 1: Join Y in any corner ch-1 sp, 2 sc in same sp, (sk next dc, sc in each of next 2 dc, sc in ch-1 sp) 3 times—11 sc. Ch 1, turn.

Row 2: Sk first sc, sc in each sc across—10 sc. Ch 1, turn. Repeat this row until 1 sc remains. Ch 1; do not turn.

Edging: Sc in top of last sc made; working along ends of rows, sc in end of next 10 rows, sc in corner sp of motif, * (sk next dc, sc in each of next 2 dc, sc in ch-1 sp) 3 times, ch 1, sc in same corner sp, repeat from * once, (sk next dc, sc in each of next 2 dc, sc in ch-1 sp) 3 times, sc in end of each of next 11 rows, join with a sl st in first sc. End off.

FRONT SECTION: Work same as back section.

SIDE SECTION (make 2): **Motif:** Beg at center with M, ch 5, join with a sl st to form ring.

Rnd 1: Ch 3 (counts as 1 dc), make 2 dc in ring, ch 1, * 3 dc in ring, ch 1, repeat from * 3 times, join last ch 1 to top of ch 3 with a sl st (5 groups of 3 dc in rnd).

Rnd 2: Sl st in back lp of each dc and ch around. End off.

Rnd 3: Join R in a ch-1 sp, ch 3, 2 dc in same sp, ch 1, * 3 dc in next sp, ch 1, 3 dc in same ch-1 sp, ch 1, repeat from * 3 times, 3 dc in same sp with first dc, ch 1, join with a sl st to top of ch 3. End off.

Rnd 4: Join Y in a corner ch-1 sp, ch 3, 2 dc in same sp, ch 1, * 3 dc in next sp, ch 1, (3 dc, ch 1, 3 dc) in corner ch-1 sp, ch 1, repeat from * around, end 3 dc in same sp with first 3 dc, ch 1, join with a sl st to top of ch 3. End off.

Top: With R, work same as for back section.

Edging: With R, work same as for back section, repeat from * twice.

JOIN SECTIONS: With wrong sides of back and side section tog, join M in top point; working through both sections, sc in each sc to lower edge of sections, end sl st through corner ch-1 sp of both sections. End off. Join other side of side section to front section. Join 2nd side section to front and back sections in same manner. With M, sl st around the 4 sts at top of sections; join with a sl st in first st. End off.

LOWER EDGING: With M, sc in each sc and ch around lower edge of helmet; join with a sl st in first sc. End off.

TOP TRIM: Work same as rnds 1 and 2 of motifs on side section. Tack to top of helmet.

TIES (make 2): With M, make ch 15″ long. End off. Sew a tie to lower corners of sides; make 1½″ tassels.

LITTLE PRINCESS DRESS

Angel-soft angora frosts the ruffles and skirt of our little princess dress. Crocheted in an easy pattern stitch, the dress is pulled in to an empire waist with matching angora drawstring.

SIZES: Directions for small size (6 mos.-1). Changes for medium size (2-3) and large size (4-6) are in parentheses.

Fits Waist Size: 19"-19½" (20"-20½"; 21"-22").

MATERIALS: Sport yarn, 2 (2-3) 2-oz. balls white (A); 1 ball angora (B). Crochet hook size H.

GAUGE: 9 sts = 2"; 9 rows = 2".

DRESS: SKIRT: Beg at lower edge of back and front, with A, ch 136 (140-148).

Row 1: Sc in 2nd ch from hook, * ch 1, sk next ch, sc in next ch, repeat from * across—68 (70-74) sc. Turn each row.

Row 2: Ch 1, sc in first sc, * ch 1, sk ch-1 sp, sc in next sc, repeat from * across. Repeating row 2 for pat, always working ch 1 over ch-1 sp and sc in sc, work 1 more row A, 1 row B, 2 rows A, 1 row B. Check gauge; piece should measure 30" (31"-33") wide. With A, work even until piece measures 9½" (10½"-12") from start or desired length to waistline.

Dec Row: Working in pat, dec 28 sc (**to dec 1 sc,** pull up a lp in each of 2 sc, yo hook and through 3 lps on hook) evenly spaced across—40 (42-46) sc. Work 1 row even. End off. Turn.

BACK YOKE: With A, make lp on hook, sk first 3 sc, join with sc in next sc, * ch 1, sc pat in each of next 13 (14-16) sc—14 (15-17) sc. Turn. Work even for 8 (10-12) rows more. Turn.

Shape Neck and Shoulders: (Ch 1, sc in next sc) 3 (3-4) times, drop yarn, sk next 8 (9-9) sc; with A, make lp on hook, join with sc in next sc, (ch 1, sc in next sc) 2 (2-3) times—3 (3-4) sc each side. Working on both sides at once, with separate strands of A, work 5 (6-8) rows. End off.

FRONT YOKE: Sk 6 sc on last long row, join MC with a sc in next sc, * ch 1, sc pat in each of next 13 (14-16) sc. Turn. Work same as for back yoke.

FINISHING: Weave side and shoulder seams.

Ruffle: From right side, join A with sc at start of right back yoke; work (ch 1, sc) 6 (7-9) times evenly spaced to shoulder seam, ch 1, sc in shoulder seam, (ch 1, sc) 7 (8-10) times to start of front yoke—15 (17-21) sc. End off. Turn.

Short Rows: Row 1: Sk first 5 (6-8) sc; join A with a sl st in next sc, * (ch 1, sc) twice in next sc (1 sc inc), repeat from * twice, ch 1, sl st in next dc—6 sc. Turn.

Row 2: Sk sl st, (ch 1, sc in next sc) 6 times, (ch 1, sc) twice (inc made) in base of sl st on previous row, (ch 1, sc) twice in each of next 2 sc, ch 1, sl st in next sc—12 sc. Turn.

Row 3: Sk sl st, (ch 1, sc in next sc) 12 times, (ch 1, sc) twice in base of sl st on previous row, (ch 1, sc) twice in each of next 2 sc, ch 1, sl st in next sc—18 sc. Turn.

Row 4: Sk sl st, (ch 1, sc in next sc) 18 times, (ch 1, sc) twice in base of sl st on previous row, (ch 1, sc) twice in each of next 1 (2-4) sc, sl st in next sc—22 (24-28) sc. Turn. Cut A; join B.

Row 5: With B, sk sl st, (ch 1, sc in next sc) 22 (24-28) times, (ch 1, sc) twice in base of sk sl st on previous row, (ch 1, sc) twice in each of next 1 (2-4) sc, sl st in next sc—26 (30-38) sc. Turn. Cut B; join A.

Row 6: With A, * ch 1, sc in next sc, repeat from * across. Cut A; join B. Turn.

Row 7: With B, repeat row 6. Cut B; join A.

Row 8: With A, repeat row 6. End off. Work same ruffle on left arm side edge.

Neck Edging: Join B in shoulder seam. Work in ch 1, sc pat around neck edge, keeping work flat, end sl st in first sc.

CORD: With B, make chain 34" (35"-37") long. End off. Weave through ch-1 sps above dec row at waistline. Tie ends into bow.

Turn 1 row at lower edge of skirt to wrong side; hem in place. Steam lightly.

SMOCK DRESS

Shown on page 190

Little girl's smock-style dress has snug yoke, full skirt in solid shells, puffy sleeves and collar in open shells.

SIZES: Directions for size 2. Changes for sizes 4, 6 and 8 are in parentheses.

Body Chest Sizes: 21" (23"-24"-26").

Width of Back or Front at Lower Edge of Yoke: 11¼" (12¾"-13½"-14¼").

MATERIALS: 2-ply sport yarn, 8 (8-9-10) ozs. red (A); 3 (4-4-5) ozs. white (B). Crochet hook size H. Four ⅝" buttons.

GAUGE: 5-dc shell, sc = 1½"; 5 rows = 2".

DRESS: YOKE: Beg at lower edge of back and front, with A, ch 92 (104-110-116).

Foundation Row: Sc in 2nd ch from hook, * sk next 2 ch, shell of 5 dc in next ch, sk next 2 ch, sc in next ch, repeat from * across—15 (17-18-19) shells. Check gauge; row should measure 22½" (25½"-27"-28½") wide. Turn.

Left Back: Row 1: Ch 3, 2 dc in first sc (½ shell), * sc in center dc of next shell, shell of 5 dc in next sc, repeat from * 2 (2-2-3) times, sc in center dc of next shell. Ch 3, turn.

Row 2: * Sc in center dc of next shell, shell in next sc, repeat from * 2 (2-2-3) times, sk next 2 dc, sc in top of ch 3. Turn.

Row 3: Ch 3, 2 dc in first sc (½ shell), * sc in center dc of next shell, shell in next sc, repeat from * 1 (1-1-2) times, sc in center dc of next shell, ½ shell of 3 dc in next sc. Ch 1, turn.

Row 4: Sc in first dc, * shell in next sc, sc in center dc of next shell, repeat from * across, end sc in top of ch 3—3 (3-3-4) shells. Turn. Repeat rows 3 and 4 for pat until piece measures 5" (5½"-6"-6½") above foundation row, end row 4. Ch 3, turn.

Shape Neck and Shoulder: Row 1: * Sc in center dc of next shell, shell in next sc, repeat from * across, end sc in center dc of last shell. Ch 3, turn.

Row 2: (Sc in center dc of next shell, shell in next sc) 1 (1-1-2) times, sc in center of last shell.

For Size 8 Only: Ch 3, turn. Sc in center of shell, shell in next sc, sc in center of last shell.

For All Sizes: End off.

Front: Sk next sc on foundation

row, join A in center dc of next shell, ch 1, sc in same dc, * shell in next sc, sc in center dc of next shell, repeat from * 5 (7-8-7) times—6 (8-9-8) shells. Ch 3, turn.

Row 2: * Sc in center dc of next shell, shell in next sc, repeat from * across, end sc in center dc of last shell, dc in last sc. Turn.

Row 3: Ch 3, 2 dc in sc (½ shell), * sc in center dc of next shell, shell in next sc, repeat from * across, end last repeat ½ shell of 3 dc in last sc. Ch 1, turn.

Row 4: Sc in first dc, * shell in next sc, sc in center dc of next shell, repeat from * across, end sc in top of ch 3—5 (7-8-7) shells. Turn. Repeat last 2 rows until piece measures about 3″ (3½″-4″-4½″) above foundation row, end row 4. Turn.

Shape Neck and Shoulder: Row 1: Ch 3, 2 dc in first sc (½ shell), * sc in center dc of next shell, shell in next sc, repeat from * 1 (2-2-2) times, end sc in 2nd dc of next shell. Ch 3, turn.

Row 2: Sc in center dc of next shell, work in pat across. Ch 3, turn.

Row 3: Sc in center of next shell, work in pat across, end dc in last sc. Ch 3, turn.

For Size 2 Only: Next Row: Sc in center dc of next shell, dc in last sc. End off.

For Sizes 4, 6 and 8 Only: Next Row: Sc in center dc of next shell, shell in next sc, sc in center of next shell, dc in next sc. End off.

Sk next 1 (1-6-1) sts on last row made before neck and shoulder shaping, join A in next dc, sc in same dc and complete to correspond to opposite side, reversing shaping.

Right Back: Sk next sc on foundation row, join A in center dc on next shell, ch 1, sc in same st, complete row in pat, end ½ shell of 3 dc in last sc. Ch 1, turn. Work

same as for left back, reversing shaping.

Sew shoulder seams.

SKIRT: Beg at lower edge of back and front, with A, ch 152 (182-212-242) loosely.

Row 1: Work same as for foundation row of yoke—25 (30-35-40)

shells. Check gauge; row should measure 38″ (45″-52½″-60″) wide. Turn.

Row 2: Ch 3, 2 dc in first sc (½ shell), * sc in center dc of next shell, shell in next sc, repeat from * across, end ½ shell of 3 dc in last sc. Ch 1, turn.

SMOCK DRESS

Row 3: Sc in first dc, * shell in next sc, sc in center dc of next shell, repeat from * across, end sc in top of ch 3. Turn. Repeat last 2 rows until piece measures 13″ (14″-15″-16″) from start or ½″ less than desired length to underarm. End off.

Gather top of skirt to fit lower edge of yoke. Weave skirt to lower edge of yoke. Sew back seam from lower edge to 1″ above lower edge of yoke.

SLEEVES: Cuff: Beg at lower edge with B, ch 21 (23-26-29).

Row 1: Sc in 2nd ch from hook and in each ch across—20 (22-25-28) sc. Ch 1, turn.

Rows 2-5: Sc in each sc across. Ch 1, turn.

Row 6 (inc row): Sc in first sc, * 2 sc in next sc, sc in next sc, repeat from * across, end 1 (2-1-1) sc in last sc—29 (33-37-41) sc. Ch 1, turn.

Pattern: Row 1: Sc in first sc, * ch 1, sk next sc, (dc, ch 1) 3 times in next sc (open shell made), sk next sc, sc in next sc, repeat from * across—7 (8-9-10) open shells. Turn.

Row 2: Ch 4, dc in first sc (½ open shell), * ch 1, sc in center dc of next shell, ch 1, open shell in next sc, repeat from * across, end ch 1, sc in center dc of last shell, ch 1, (dc, ch 1, dc) in last sc (½ shell made). Ch 1, turn.

Row 3: Sc in first dc, * ch 1, sk next dc, open shell in next sc, ch 1, sc in center dc of next shell, repeat from * across, end ch 1, open shell in last sc, ch 1, sc in 2nd ch of ch 4. Turn. Repeat last 2 rows until piece measures 9″ (10″-11½″-13″) above end of cuff, end pat row 3. Ch 3, turn.

Shape Cap: Row 1: * Sc in center of next shell, ch 1, open shell in next sc, ch 1, repeat from * across, end sc in center dc of last shell. Ch 3, turn. Repeat this row 5 (6-7-8) times. End off.

FINISHING: Sew sleeve seams. Sew in sleeves, easing in extra fullness of sleeve across shoulder.

Collar: Left Half: Beg at neck edge, with B, ch 20 (26-26-32).

Row 1 (mark for right side): Sc in 2nd ch from hook, * ch 1, sk next 2 ch, open shell in next ch, ch 1, sk next 2 ch, sc in next ch, repeat from * across—3 (4-4-5) open shells. Ch 4, turn.

Row 2: Open shell in first sc, * ch 1, sc in center dc of next open shell, ch 1, open shell in next sc, repeat from * across, end ch 1, (dc, ch 1) 3 times in last sc, dc in same sc. Ch 4, turn.

Row 3: Dc in first dc, ch 1, sk next dc, sc in next dc, work in open shell pat, end sc in center dc of last shell, ch 1, ½ shell of dc, ch 1, dc in 2nd ch of ch 4. Ch 1, turn.

Row 4: Sc in first dc, work in open shell pat across, end sc in 3rd ch of ch 4. Ch 4, turn.

Row 5: Dc in first sc, work in open shell pat across, end ½ shell in last sc. End off. Work 2nd half of collar in same manner. Mark first row for wrong side; pat is reversible. Sew collar pieces to neck edge. With A, work 1 row sc around neck opening. Sew buttons evenly spaced on left back edge of opening; spaces between sts on right side of opening form buttonholes. With rustproof pins, pin dress to measurements on padded surface; cover with a damp cloth and allow to dry; do not press.

YELLOW-YOKED SKIMMER

Shown at left on page 192

Two little girls in yellow and white love party clothes! Yoked skimmer is side-buttoned and has a crossed-stitch pattern yoke in front with more crossed stitches accenting the long waist and hem.

SIZES: Directions for size 2. Changes for sizes 4, 6 and 8 are in parentheses.

Body Chest Size: 21″ (23″-24″-26″).

Blocked Chest Size (closed): 23″ (25″-27″-29″).

MATERIALS: Fingering yarn, 6 (6-7-8) 1-oz. skeins white (W); 2 (3-3-4) skeins yellow (Y). Aluminum crochet hook size H. Four (5-5-6) buttons.

GAUGE: 4 sts = 1″; 2 rows (1 row dc, 1 row sc) = ¾″.

Note: Dress is worked with 2

strands of yarn held tog throughout.

DRESS: TORSO: Beg at lower edge, with 2 strands W (see Note), ch 96 (104-112-120).

Row 1 (right side): Dc in 4th ch from hook and in each ch across—94 (102-110-118) dc, counting turning ch as 1 dc. Check gauge; row should measure 23½″ (25½″-27½″-29½″) wide. Ch 1, turn.

Row 2: Sc in each dc across, sc in top of turning ch—94 (102-110-118) sc. Turn.

Row 3: Ch 3, sk first 2 sc, * dc in each of next 3 sc; working over dc's just made insert hook in last sk sc, draw up a lp ¾″ high, yo hook and through 2 lps on hook (crossed st or cr-st made), sk next sc, repeat from * across, end dc in last sc—23 (25-27-29) cr-sts. Ch 1, turn.

Row 4: Sc in each st across, sc in top of ch 3—94 (102-110-118) sc. Turn.

Row 5: Ch 3 (counts as 1 dc), sk first sc, dc in each sc across—94 (102-110-118) dc. Ch 1, turn.

Rows 6-8: Repeat rows 2-4. Piece should measure about 3¾″ from start. Turn. Repeat rows 5 and 4 alternately 3 (4-4-5) times, end row 4. Turn.

Shape Armholes: Back Yoke: Row 1: Sl st in 4 (4-5-6) sc, sc in each of next 38 (42-44-46) sc. Ch 1, turn.

Row 2: Sk first sc, sc in each sc to within last 2 sc, sk next sc, sc in last sc—36 (40-42-44) sc. Ch 1, turn.

Row 3: Repeat last row—34 (38-40-42) sc. Ch 1, turn.

Row 4: Sc in each sc across. Turn.

Row 5: Ch 3 (counts as 1 dc), sk first sc, dc in each sc across. Ch 1, turn.

Row 6: Sc in each dc across, sc in top of turning ch. Turn. Repeat last 2 rows until armholes measure about 4½″ (5″-5½″-6″) above first row of armhole shaping, end row 5. Ch 1, turn.

Shape Left Shoulder (Left-handed crocheters: This will be your right shoulder): **Row 1:** Sc in each of 9 (10-10-11) dc. Turn.

Row 2: Ch 3, sk first sc, dc in each of next 2 (3-3-4) sc, hdc in next 2 sc, sc in next sc, sl st in next sc. End off. Sk next 16 (18-20-20) dc on last long row, attach 2 strands W in next dc, sc in same dc as joining, sc in each of next 7 (8-8-9) dc, sc in top of ch 3. Turn.

YELLOW-YOKED SKIMMER AND YELLOW BUTTERCUP DRESS

Next Row: Sl st in each of next 3 (4-4-5) sc, sc in next sc, hdc in each of next 2 sc, dc in each of next 3 (4-4-5) sc. End off.

Front Yoke: Sk 9 (9-13-13) sc on last long row for underarm, join 2 strands W in next sc, ch 1, sc in same st, sc in each of next 37 (41-41-45) sc. Ch 1, turn.

Row 2: Repeat row 2 on back yoke—36 (40-40-44) sc. Ch 1, turn. Cut W; join 2 strands Y.

Row 3: With Y, repeat row 3 on back yoke—34 (38-38-42) sc. Ch 1, turn.

Row 4: Repeat row 3 on torso—8 (9-9-10) cr-sts. **Note:** Wrong side of this row is right side of dress. Ch 1, turn.

Row 5: Sc in each st across, sc in top of ch 3—34 (38-38-42) sc. Turn. Repeat last 2 rows 2 (2-2-3) times, then repeat row 4. Ch 1, turn.

Shape Neck and Shoulder: Row 1: Sc in each of first 10 sts. Turn. Work even in pat on these 10 sts until armhole measures same as back, end with sc row. Turn.

Next Row: Repeat 2nd row of back left shoulder. End off. Sk center 14 (18-18-22) sts on last long row, attach 2 strands Y in next st, sc in same st and in each of next 9 sts. Complete as for first shoulder, reversing shaping.

SKIRT: From right side, attach double strand Y in first ch at lower edge of front torso.

Row 1: Ch 1, working along opposite side of starting ch, sc in each ch across—94 (102-110-118) sc. Turn.

Row 2: Repeat row 3 of torso—23 (25-27-29) cr-sts. Ch 1, turn.

Row 3: Repeat row 4 of torso. End off. Do not turn. From right side, attach 2 strands W in first sc at beg of last row.

Row 4: Ch 3, sk first sc, dc in each of next 4 (4-5-6) sc, * 2 dc in next sc, put a marker on the 2 dc just made, dc in each of next 11 (12-13-14) sc, repeat from * 6 times, 2 dc in next sc, put a marker on 2 dc just made, dc in each remaining sc—8 markers, 8 sts inc. Turn.

Row 5: Sk first dc, * dc in each dc to marker, 2 dc in each of next 2 dc, repeat from * 7 times, dc in each remaining dc, dc in top of ch 3—16 sts inc.

Row 6: Ch 3, sk first dc, dc in each dc across, dc in top of ch 3—118 (126-134-142) dc. Turn. Repeat row 6 until dress measures about 11½" (12¾"-13½"-14½") from underarm. End off. Sew shoulder seams.

RIGHT ARMHOLE BORDER (Left-handed crocheters: This will be your left armhole border): **Row 1:** From right side, with 2 strands Y, sc around right armhole edge. Ch 1, turn.

Row 2: Sc in each sc around. Ch 1, turn.

Row 3: Sc in each sc around, 3 sc in front underarm corner, sc down front side edge, 3 sc in lower front corner, sc around lower edge of skirt, 3 sc in lower back corner, sc up back side edge, end right back underarm corner. Ch 1, turn.

Side Border: Row 1: Sc in each sc down back side edge, being careful to have multiple of 4 sc, plus 2. Ch 1, turn.

Row 2: Sc in each sc up back side edge. Turn.

Row 3: Work same as for row 3 on torso. Ch 1, turn.

Row 4: Work same as for row 4 on torso.

With pins, mark position of 4 (5-5-6) buttonholes evenly spaced along last row, first pin 2 sts below armhole edge, last pin 2 sts above lower edge.

Row 5: * Sc in each sc to within 1 st of pin, dc in each of next 2 sc, repeat from * across, end sc in last sc. Do not end off; work same as for row 3 on torso across lower edge. End off.

SCALLOP EDGING: From right side, join 2 strands W in first st at lower front edge, ch 1, sc in same st, * sk next st, 5 dc in next st, sk next st, sc in next st, repeat from * across lower edge, up back side edge, around armhole edge, end sc in corner sc. End off.

LEFT ARMHOLE BORDER: From right side, attach 2 strands Y in center of left underarm. **(Left-handed crocheters:** This is your right armhole.)

Rnd 1: Ch 1, sc around armhole edge, having a multiple of 5 sc. Join with sl st in first sc. Ch 1, turn.

Rnd 2: Sc in each sc around. Join with sl st in first sc. Ch 1, turn.

Rnd 3: Repeat rnd 2. Cut Y; join 2 strands W. Do not turn.

Rnd 4 (right side): Sc in first sc, * sk next sc, 5 dc in next sc, sk next 2 sc, sc in next sc, repeat from * around, end sk next 2 sc, sl st in first sc. End off.

NECK EDGING: From right side, join 2 strands W in shoulder seam. Work same as rnd 4 on armhole edge, having 2 (2-3-3) scallops on each side neck edge, 3 (3-4-4) scallops across front neck edge, and 5 (5-6-6) scallops across back neck edge. Join with a sl st in first sc. End off.

Sew buttons on front side edge; spaces between dc form buttonholes. Do not press; to block, pin dress on padded surface with rust-proof pins to desired measurements. Cover with damp cloth; dry.

YELLOW BUTTERCUP DRESS

Shown at right on page 192

Buttercup dress is puff-sleeved and has lacy pattern on top, graceful scalloped skirt.

SIZES: Directions for size 2. Changes for sizes 4, 6 and 8 are in parentheses.

Body Chest Size: 21″ (23″-24″-26″).

Blocked Chest Size (closed): 23″ (25″-27″-29″).

MATERIALS: Fingering yarn, 7 (9-10-11) 1-oz. skeins yellow, main color (MC); 1 skein white, contrasting color (CC). Aluminum crochet hooks sizes H and I. Three buttons.

GAUGE: 3 dc and 1 ch-1 sp = 1″; 2 rows = 1½″ (bodice, size H hook).

Note: Dress is worked with 2 strands of yarn held tog throughout.

DRESS: BODICE: Beg at lower edge of back and front, with 2 strands of MC (see Note) and size H hook, ch 101 (109-117-125).

Row 1: Dc in 4th ch from hook and in each of next 2 ch (center border), * ch 1, sk next 3 ch, 3 dc in next ch, repeat from * across to within last 7 ch, end ch 1, sk next 3 ch, dc in each of last 4 ch (center border). Turn each row. Check gauge; row should measure 23½″ (25½″-27½″-29½″).

Row 2: Ch 3 (counts as 1 dc), sk first dc, * dc in each of next 3 dc, ch 1, repeat from * across, end ch 1, dc in each of last 3 dc, dc in top of turning ch.

Row 3: Ch 3, sk first dc, dc in each of next 3 dc (center border), ch 1, dc in next dc, ch 1, sk next 2 dc, * (dc, ch 1, dc) in next ch-1 sp (V-st made), ch 1, sk next 3 dc, repeat from * across until 21 (23-25-27) V-sts are completed, end ch 1, sk next 2 dc, dc in next dc, ch 1, dc in each of next 3 dc, dc in top of ch 3 (center border).

Row 4: Work center border; ch 1, sk next dc, 3 dc in next ch-1 sp, * ch 1, sk next V-st, 3 dc in next ch-1 sp, repeat from * across, end ch 1, sk last ch-1 sp, work center border.

Row 5: Repeat row 2.

For Sizes 6 and 8 Only: Next Row: Repeat row 2.

For All Sizes: Repeat rows 3 and 4.

Front Yoke: Row 1: Work same as row 2 until 4 (5-5-6) 3-dc groups are completed; end dc in next dc (arm side). Turn.

Row 2: Ch 3, sk first 4 dc, V-st in next ch-1 sp, ch 1, complete row as for row 3 on bodice.

Row 3: Work same as for row 4 on bodice until 3 (4-4-5) 3-dc groups are completed; end ch 1, sk next V-st, dc in top of ch 3.

Row 4: Ch 3, sk first dc, * dc in each of next 3 dc, ch 1, repeat from * 1 (2-2-3) times, dc in each of next 2 dc.

Row 5: Ch 4, (V-st in next sp, ch 1) 2 (3-3-4) times, V-st in top of turning ch.

Row 6: Ch 3, (sk V-st, 3 dc in next sp, ch 1) 2 (2-2-3) times, sk V-st, dc in next sp.

Row 7: Ch 3, sk first dc, dc in each dc and ch 1 over each ch-1 sp across, end dc in top of ch 3. Repeat last row 0 (1-1-2) times. End off.

Back Yoke: Sk next 4 dc for underarm on last long row, attach double strand of MC in next dc.

Row 1: Ch 3, dc in each of next 3 dc, ch 1, work same as for row 2 on bodice until 10 (10-12-12) 3-dc groups are completed, end dc in next dc. Turn.

Row 2: Ch 4, sk first 4 dc, V-st in next ch-1 sp, ch 1, work in V-st pat across, end ch 1, sk next 2 dc, dc in next dc.

Row 3: Ch 3, dc in first ch-1 sp, * ch 1, sk next V-st, 3 dc in next sp, repeat from * across, end ch 1, 2 dc in ch-4 sp.

Row 4: Ch 3, sk first dc, dc in next dc, * ch 1, dc in each of next 3 dc, repeat from * across, end ch 1, dc in last dc, dc in top of ch 3.

Row 5: Ch 4, sk first 2 dc, V-st in next ch-1 sp, work in V-st pat across, end ch 1, sk last dc, dc in top of ch 3. Repeat rows 3-5 until armholes measure same as front armhole. End off.

Second Front Yoke: Sk next 4 dc for underarm on last long row, attach double strand MC in next dc.

Row 1: Ch 3, dc in next 3 dc, ch 1, finish row same as for row 2 on bodice, working center border. Turn. Complete as for left front yoke, reversing shaping.

SLEEVES: Beg at lower edge, with double strand of MC and size H hook, ch 31 (34-34-37).

Row 1: 2 dc in 4th ch from hook, * ch 1, sk next 2 ch, 3 dc in next ch, repeat from * across—10 (11-11-12) groups of 3 dc. Turn each row.

Row 2: Ch 3, sk first dc, dc in each of next 2 dc, * ch 1, dc in each of next 3 dc, repeat from * across, end ch 1, dc in each of last 2 dc, dc in top of ch 3.

Shape Cap: Row 1: Sl st in each st to first ch-1 sp, sl st in ch-1 sp, ch

4, * V-st in next ch-1 sp, ch 1, repeat from * across, end ch 1, dc in last ch-1 sp—7 (8-8-9) V-sts.

Row 2: Ch 3, 2 dc in first ch-1 sp, * ch 1, sk V-st, 3 dc in next ch-1 sp, repeat from * across, end ch 1, 3 dc in ch-4 sp.

Row 3: Ch 3, sk first dc, dc in each of next 2 dc, * ch 1, dc in each of next 3 dc, repeat from * across, end ch 1, dc in each of last 2 dc, dc in top of ch 3.

Row 4: Ch 3, sk first 3 dc, work V-st, ch 1 in each ch-1 sp across, end dc in top of ch 3.

Row 5: Ch 3, sk first V-st, * 3 dc in next ch-1 sp, ch 1, repeat from * across, end dc in top of ch-3—6 (7-7-8) groups of 3 dc.

Row 6: Ch 3, sk first group of 3 dc, * dc in each of next 3 dc, ch 1, repeat from * to within last group of 3 dc, sk last 3 dc, dc in top of ch 3—4 (5-5-6) groups of 3 dc.

For Sizes 4, 6 and 8 Only: Row 7: Ch 3, repeat row 4.

For Sizes 6 and 8 Only: Row 8: Ch 3, repeat row 5. End off all sizes.

Weave sleeve seams; weave shoulder seams. Sew in sleeves, easing in fullness across upper armhole.

Sleeve Edging: Join 2 strands CC at sleeve seam. With size H hook, work 1 rnd sc around lower edge of sleeve, easing in to desired fit; do not join.

Rnd 2: Sc in each sc around.

Rnd 3: * Sc in each of next 3 sc, ch 3, sc in last sc (picot made), repeat from * around. Join with sl st in first sc. End off. Work same edging on 2nd sleeve.

Front and Neck Edging: Join double strand CC at lower edge of right front border.

Row 1: With size H hook, sc up right front edge, around neck edge, easing in to desired fit; do not work down left front edge. Ch 1, turn.

Row 2: Sc in each sc around neck edge only. Ch 1, turn.

Row 3: Sc in first sc, ch 3, sc in last sc (picot made), * sc in each of next 3 sc, picot in last sc made, repeat from * around neck. End off. Lap right front border over left front border; sew 4 sts tog at lower edge.

SKIRT: Join 2 strands MC in center of lower front border. With size I hook, working along opposite side of starting ch of bodice, ch 3, 4 dc in same st where yarn was

attached, make 5 dc in each sp between dc groups around. Join with sl st in top of ch 3—24 (26-28-30) 5-dc scallops.

Rnd 2: Sl st in next dc, ch 1, sc in next dc, * ch 5, sc in center dc of next scallop, repeat from * around, end ch 5, join with sl st in first sc.

Rnd 3: Sl st in next lp, ch 3, (3 dc, ch 1, 4 dc) in same lp, * 4 dc, ch 1, 4 dc in next lp, repeat from * around. Join with a sl st in top of ch 3. End off.

Rnd 4: Join double strand MC in ch-1 sp of any scallop, ch 1, sc in same ch-1 sp, * ch 5, sc in ch-1 sp of next scallop, repeat from * around, end ch 5, join with sl st in first sc. Repeat rnds 3 and 4 until skirt is about 8" (10½"-11"-12") from start or desired length, end rnd 3. End off.

Sew three buttons, evenly spaced on left front edge of center border. Spaces between sts on right front border form buttonholes.

Do not press; to block, pin dress on padded surface with rustproof pins to desired measurements. Cover with damp cloth. When piece is dry, remove pins.

SPRING VIOLET SET

Shown on page 196

Lacy cardigan for little girls is worked in an easy pattern stitch. Borders of single crochet have a touch of soft shell pink to match the pencil-thin stripe on the skirt.

SIZES: Directions for size 4. Changes for sizes 6, 8 and 10 are in parentheses.

Body Chest Size: 23" (24"-27"-28½").

Blocked Chest Size: 24" (26"-28"-30").

MATERIALS: Sport yarn, 5 (5-6-7) 2-oz. balls main color (MC); ½ oz. contrasting color (CC). Crochet hook size H. Five buttons. One yd. 1"-wide elastic.

GAUGE: 4 sc = 1"; 7 rows = 1". 1 shell = 1"; 6 rows = 5".

SKIRT: BACK: Beg at lower edge, with MC, ch 65 (69-73-77).

Row 1 (right side): Sc in 2nd ch from hook and in each ch across—64 (68-72-76) sc. Ch 1, turn each row.

Row 2: Working in front lp, sc in each sc across.

Row 3: Working in back lp, sc in each sc across. Cut MC; join CC.

FOR INFANTS, TODDLERS AND CHILDREN

With CC, repeat row 2. Cut CC; join MC. With MC, repeat row 3. With MC, repeat rows 2 and 3 for pat until piece measures 3″ (4″-5″-6″) from start or 9″ less than desired skirt length. Check gauge; piece should measure 16″ (17″-

18″-19″) wide. Dec 1 sc **(to dec 1 sc,** pull up a lp in each of 2 sc, yo and through 3 lps on hook) each side of next row, then every 2″ 3 times more—56 (60-64-68) sc. Work even until piece measures 11½″ (12½″-13½″-14½″) from start or

½″ less than desired skirt length. Work 2 rows sc, working in both lps. End off.

FRONT: Work same as for back.

FINISHING: Steam-press pieces. Weave side seams. With MC, work casing around upper edge of skirt: With wrong side facing you, join yarn at top edge, * ch ¾″, sl st in st ½″ to left in row ½″ below, ch ¾″, sl st at top edge ½″ to left of last st, repeat from * around. Cut elastic to waist measurement; weave elastic through casing. Sew ends tog securely.

CARDIGAN: BACK: Beg at lower edge, with MC, ch 41 (41-47-47).

Row 1 (wrong side): Sc in 2nd ch from hook, * ch 3, sk next 2 ch, sc in next ch, repeat from * across—13 (13-15-15) ch-3 lps. Turn.

Row 2 (right side): Ch 3 (counts as 1 dc), dc in first sc (½ shell made), * sc in next ch-3 lp, 3 dc in next sc (shell made), repeat from * across, end last repeat ½ shell of 2 dc in last sc—12 (12-14-14) shells plus ½ shell each side. Ch 1, turn.

Row 3: Sc in first dc, * ch 3, sc in center dc of next shell, repeat from * across, end ch 3, sc in top of turning ch. Turn. Repeat rows 2 and 3 for pat until piece measures 10″ (10½″-11″-12″) from start, end pat row 3. Check gauge; piece should measure 13″ (13″-15″-15″) wide.

Shape Armholes: Row 1: Sl st across first ch-3 lp, sl st in sc, work ½ shell of ch 3, dc in same sc, work in pat to within last ch-3 lp, end last repeat ½ shell of 2 dc in next sc. Ch 1, turn—10 (10-12-12) shells plus ½ shell each side. Work even until armhole measures 4¾″ (5″-5½″-6″) above first row of armhole shaping, end pat row 2.

Shape Shoulders: Work 3 (3-4-4) ch-3 lps. Turn. Work 1 row even. End off. Sk 4 shells for back

SPRING VIOLET SET

of neck. Join yarn in center dc of next shell, work 3 (3-4-4) ch-3 lps. Turn. Work 1 row even. End off.

LEFT FRONT (Left-handed crocheters: This will be your right front): Beg at lower edge, with MC, ch 20 (23-23-26). Work as for back having 6 (7-7-8) ch-3 lps on pat row 1, 5 (6-6-7) shells plus ½ shell each side on pat row 2 until piece measures same as back to underarm, end pat row 3. Check gauge; piece should measure 6″ (7″-7″-8″) wide.

Shape Armhole: Sl st across first ch-3 lp, sl st in sc; work ½ shell of ch 3, dc in same sc, work in pat across—4 (5-5-6) shells plus ½ shell each side. Work even until armhole measures 2¾″ (3″-3½″-4″) above armhole shaping row, end pat row 2 (center edge).

Shape Neck: Sl st across to center dc of 2nd full shell, ch 1, sc in same dc, * ch 3, sc in center dc of next shell, finish row—3 (4-4-5) ch-3 lps.

On Sizes 6 and 10 Only: Sl st across to center dc of first full shell, ch 1, sc in same dc, * ch 3, sc in center dc of next shell, finish row.

On All Sizes: Working on 3 (3-4-4) ch-3 lps, work even until armhole measures same as back. End off.

RIGHT FRONT: Work same as left front, reversing shaping. Arm side is at end of pat row 2, neck edge is at beg of pat row 2.

SLEEVES: Beg at lower edge, with MC, ch 29 (32-35-35). Work in pat on 9 (10-11-11) ch-3 lps for 7 (7-7-9) rows, end pat row 3. Check gauge; piece should measure 9″ (10″-11″-11″) wide.

Shape Cap: Row 1: Work row 1 of back armhole shaping—6 (7-8-8) shells plus ½ shell on each side. Ch 1, turn.

Row 2: Work 1 row even—7 (8-9-9) ch-3 lps.

Row 3: Sl st to center of first ch-3 lp, ch 1, sc in same ch-3 lp, 3 dc in next sc, work in pat across, end sc in last ch-3 lp—6 (7-8-8) shells.

Row 4: Sl st to center dc of first shell, ch 1, sc in same dc, ch 3, sc in center dc of next shell, work in pat across, end sc in center dc of last shell—5 (6-7-7) ch-3 lps. Repeat rows 3 and 4 1 (1-2-2) times—3 (4-3-3) ch-3 lps. Repeat row 3 once. End off.

FINISHING: Steam-press pieces. Sew shoulder seams; sew in sleeves. Sew side and sleeve seams. From right side, with MC, work 1 row sc around each sleeve edge.

Border: Join MC in lower edge at side seam. From right side, work 1 rnd sc around entire outer edge of cardigan, working 2 sc in each front corner, easing in neck to desired fit and keeping work flat. Join with a sl st in first sc. Drop MC; join CC. Ch 1, turn.

Rnd 2: With CC, from wrong side, sc in front lp of each sc around, working 3 sc in each corner sc. Join with a sl st in first sc. Cut CC. With MC, ch 1, turn.

Rnd 3: With MC, sc in back lp of each sc around, working 2 sc in each corner. Join with a sl st in first sc. Ch 1, turn.

With pins, mark position of 5 buttonholes evenly spaced on right front edge, first pin 1½″ above lower edge, last pin in 3rd sc below start of neck shaping.

Rnd 4 (buttonholes): * Working in front lp, sc in each sc to within 1 sc of pin, ch 2, sk 2 sc, repeat from * 4 times, sc in next sc, complete rnd, working 2 sc in each corner. Join with a sl st in first sc. Ch 1, turn.

Rnd 5: Working in back lp, sc in each sc and ch around. Join with a sl st in first sc. End off.

Sew on buttons.

PARTY PANTS SET

Shown at left on page 198

Two little girls in blue love the look of lace! Shell-patterned top ends in a flounce over bell-bottomed pants worked in alternate rows of single and double crochet.

SIZES: Directions for size 2. Changes for sizes 4, 6 and 8 are in parentheses.

Body Chest Size: 21″ (23″-24″-26″).

Blocked Chest Size: 23″ (25″-26½″-28″).

Body Hip Size: 22″ (24″-26″-28″).

Blocked Hip Size: 23″ (25″-27″-30″).

MATERIALS: Sport yarn, 5 (6-7-8) 2-oz. skeins. Aluminum crochet hooks sizes F and H. Three-quarter yard 1″-wide elastic.

GAUGE: Pants: 11 sts = 2″; 6 rows = 2″. Top: 2 shells = 1¾″; 2 rows = 1″.

PARTY SET: PANTS: Beg at waistline of front and back below waistband, with size F hook, ch 114 (124-132-144). Being careful not to twist ch, join with sl st in first ch, forming circle.

Rnd 1 (right side): Ch 1, sc in same ch as joining, sc in next ch and in each ch around—114 (124-132-144) sc. Do not turn.

Rnd 2: Ch 3 (counts as 1 dc), dc in next sc and in each sc around—114 (124-132-144) dc. Join with sl st in top of ch 3. Check gauge; piece should measure 21″ (22½″-24″-26″) around.

Rnd 3: Ch 1, sc in same st as joining, sc in next dc and in each dc around. Join with sl st in first sc. Repeat rnds 2 and 3 for pat 2 (3-3-2) times.

Shape Hips: Rnd 1: Ch 3 (counts as 1 dc), dc in same st as joining (1 dc inc), dc in each sc around, end dc in same st as joining (1 dc inc)—116 (126-134-146) dc. Mark last dc for center back. Join with sl st in top of ch 3. Work even in pat for 3 rnds.

Rnd 5: Ch 3, dc in same st as joining (1 dc inc), dc in each of next 57 (62-66-72) sc, 3 dc in next sc (2 dc inc), mark center dc of 3-dc group for center front; dc in each of 57 (62-66-72) sc, end dc in same st as joining (1 dc inc)—120 (130-138-150) dc. Join with sl st in top of ch 3. Work even in pat for 3 rnds.

Rnd 9: Ch 3, dc in same st as joining, dc in each sc to marked dc, 3 dc in sc over marked dc, move marker to center dc of 3-dc group, dc in each dc around, end dc in same st as joining—4 dc inc. Repeat last 4 rnds 1 (1-2-3) times—128 (138-150-166) dc.

Shape Crotch: At end of last row, ch 3 (5-7-7) for crotch, join with sl st in center front marked dc. End off.

Leg: Rnd 1: From right side, join yarn in center ch at crotch, ch 1, sc in same ch, sc in next 1 (2-3-3) ch, sc in same dc as sl st, sc in each

PARTY PANTS SET AND LITTLE GIRL'S EMPIRE DRESS

of next 63 (68-74-82) dc, sc in each of next 1 (2-3-3) ch of crotch—67 (74-82-90) sc. Join with sl st in first sc. Work around in pat until leg measures about 8″ (8½″-9″-9½″) from crotch ch, end sc rnd.

Shape Flare Leg: Rnd 1: Ch 3, dc in each of next 32 (35-40-44) sc, 3 dc in next sc, mark center dc of 3-dc group, dc in each remaining sc—69 (76-84-92) dc. Join with sl st in top of ch 3.

Rnd 2: Ch 1, sc in same st as joining, sc in each dc around. Join with sl st in first sc.

Rnd 3: Ch 3, dc in each dc around, working 3 dc in sc over marked dc—2 dc inc. Repeat last 2 rnds 4 (5-6-7) times—79 (88-98-108) sts. Work even if necessary until leg measures 12½″ (13½″-14½″-16″) from crotch or desired length, end dc rnd. End off. Working on opposite side of crotch ch, from right side, work other leg in same manner.

Waistband: From right side, join yarn at upper center back.

Rnd 1: Ch 3, working around starting ch, dc in each ch around—114 (124-132-144) dc. Join each rnd. Work in pat for 6 rnds, end dc rnd. End off.

FINISHING: Cut elastic to waist measurement; sew ends securely. Fold waistband to wrong side over elastic; sew in place.

TOP: BACK: Beg at lower edge, above peplum, with size H hook, ch 55 (59-63-67).

Row 1: (3 dc, ch 1, dc) in 5th ch from hook (shell made), * sk next 3 ch, shell of 3 dc, ch 1, dc in next ch, repeat from * to within last 2 ch, sk next ch, dc in last ch—13 (14-15-16) shells. Ch 3, turn.

Row 2: * Shell of 3 dc, ch 1, dc in ch-1 sp of next shell, repeat from * across, end shell in ch-1 sp of last shell, sk next 3 dc in same shell, dc in top of turning ch 3—13

(14-15-16) shells. Ch 3, turn. Repeat row 2 for pat until piece measures 6″ (7″-8″-9″) from start. Check gauge; piece should measure 11½″ (12¼″-13″-14″). Turn.

Shape Armholes: Row 1: Sl st in each of first 2 dc, ch and next 3 dc; work ch 3, * shell in ch-1 sp of next shell, repeat from * across until 11 (12-13-14) shells are completed; sk next 3 dc, dc in next dc. Ch 3, turn. Work even in pat until armholes measure 4″ (4½″-5″-5½″) above first row of armhole shaping. Ch 3, turn.

Shape Neck and Shoulders: Row 1: Work in pat until 3 (3-4-4) shells are completed, sk next 3 dc, dc in next sp between shells. Ch 3, turn.

Row 2: Work in pat until 2 shells are completed, sk next 2 dc, hdc in next dc, sc in next dc, sl st in next ch. End off. Sk next 5 (6-5-6) shells on last long row, join yarn in sp before next shell, ch 3, work in pat across remaining 3 (3-4-4) shells, dc in top of ch 3. Turn.

Next Row: Sl st in each st to within ch-1 sp of first (first-2nd-2nd) shell, sc in next ch-1 sp, sc in next dc, hdc in next dc, shell in ch-1 sp of same shell and in ch-1 sp of last shell, dc in top of ch 3. End off.

FRONT: Work same as for back until armholes measure 1½″ (2″-2½″-2½″) above first row of armhole shaping—11 (12-13-14) shells.

Shape Neck: Row 1: Work same as for row 1 on back neck shaping—3 (3-4-4) shells. Turn. Work even until armhole measures same as back, end neck edge.

Shape Shoulders: Work same as for row 2 on back neck shaping. End off. Sk next 5 (6-5-6) shells on last long row, join yarn in sp before next shell, ch 3, work in pat across remaining 3 (3-4-4) shells,

dc in top of ch 3. Turn. Work even until armhole measures same as back, end arm side. Complete as for 2nd shoulder on back.

FINISHING: Sew side and shoulder seams. From right side, work 1 rnd sc around each armhole edge. Join with sl st in first sc. End off. From right side, work 1 rnd sc around neck edge. Join; end off.

Peplum: From right side, with size H hook, join yarn in lower side seam.

Rnd 1: Ch 3, dc in same st as joining, working along opposite side of starting ch, * ch 1, 2 dc in same ch where next shell on rnd 1 was made, (ch 1, 2 dc in center ch of skipped ch between shells) 4 times, repeat from * around lower edge, end ch 1; join with sl st in top of ch 3.

Rnd 2: Sl st in next dc, ch 3, make shell of 3 dc, ch 1, dc in same dc, * sk next dc, make shell in next dc, repeat from * around. Join in top of ch 3.

Rnd 3: Sl st in each dc to first ch-1 sp, (sl st, ch 3, 3 dc, ch 1, dc) in first ch-1 sp, * 4 dc, ch 1, dc in ch-1 sp of next shell, repeat from * around. Join. Repeat last rnd 4 (4-5-6) times. End.

DRAWSTRING: With size F hook, make ch 60″ (62″-64″-66″) long. Put a marker 9″ in from each end of ch.

Row 1: 3 sc in 2nd ch from hook, * 2 sc in next ch, 3 sc in next ch, repeat from * to first marker (9″ from start), sc in each ch to next marker, work from first * across remaining 9″ of ch. End off. Beg at center front, weave drawstring through first rnd of peplum.

Do not press; to block, pin pieces on padded surface with rustproof pins to desired measurements. Cover with damp cloth; dry.

LITTLE GIRL'S EMPIRE DRESS

Shown at right on page 198

*Empire-waisted skimmer has single-button closing, easy-fit drawstring waist,
picot edges.*

SIZES: Directions for size 2. Changes for sizes 4, 6 and 8 are in parentheses.

Body Chest Size: 21″ (23″-24″-26″).

Blocked Chest Size: 23″ (25″-27″-29″).

MATERIALS: Sport yarn, 3 (4-4-5) 2-oz. skeins. Crochet hooks sizes G and I.

GAUGE: 5 hdc = 1″; 3 rows = 1″ (size G hook).

DRESS: BODICE: Beg at lower edge of back and fronts, with size G hook, ch 116 (128-134-146).

Row 1 (right side): Hdc in 3rd ch from hook and in each ch across—114 (126-132-144) hdc. Do not count turning ch as st. Ch 2, turn. Check gauge; row should measure 23″ (25″-26½″-29″) wide.

Divide Work: Left Front Bodice: Row 1: Hdc in first hdc and in each of next 23 (25-26-28) hdc. Ch 2, turn each row.

Row 2: Sk first hdc (1 st dec at armhole edge), hdc in next hdc and in each hdc across—23 (25-26-28) hdc.

Row 3: Hdc in each hdc to within last 2 hdc, end sk next hdc, hdc in last hdc—1 hdc dec at armhole edge.

Row 4: Repeat row 3—1 hdc dec at front edge.

Row 5: Repeat row 2—1 hdc dec at front edge. Repeat rows 4 and 5, decreasing 1 st at neck edge every row until 11 (12-12-13) hdc remain. Work even if necessary until armhole measures 4½″ (5″-5½″-6″) above first row of armhole shaping. End off.

Back Bodice: Sk next 10 (12-12-14) hdc on row 1 for left underarm, join yarn in next st.

Row 1: Ch 2, hdc in same st as joining, hdc in each of next 45 (49-53-57) hdc. Ch 2, turn each row.

Row 2: Hdc in each hdc across—46 (50-54-58) hdc. Work even until armholes measure same as front armhole. End off.

Right Front Bodice: Sk next 10 (12-12-14) hdc on row 1 for right underarm, join yarn in next st.

Row 1: Ch 2, hdc in same st as joining, hdc in each of remaining 23 (25-26-28) hdc. Ch 2, turn each row. Work same as for left front bodice, reversing shaping.

SKIRT: From right side, with size G hook, join yarn in first ch on starting ch.

Rnd 1: Ch 1, sc in same ch as joining; working along opposite side of starting ch, sc in each ch across—114 (126-132-144) sc. Join with sl st in first sc, forming circle.

Rnd 2: Ch 5, * sk next sc, tr in next sc, ch 1, repeat from * around, end sl st in 4th ch of ch 5—57 (63-66-72) sps.

Rnd 3: Ch 1, sc in same ch as sl st, * sc in next ch-1 sp, sc in next tr, repeat from * around, end sc in last ch-1 sp. Join with sl st in first sc—114 (126-132-144) sc.

Rnd 4: Ch 2, hdc in next sc, * ch 3, sk next sc, sc in next sc, ch 3, sk next 2 sc, hdc in each of next 2 sc, repeat from * around, end last repeat ch 3, sk last 2 sc, join with sl st to top of ch 2—19 (21-22-24) pats.

Rnd 5: Ch 2, hdc in next hdc, * ch 3, (sc, ch 3, sc) in next sc (picot lp made), ch 3, sk next ch-3 lp, hdc in each of next 2 hdc, repeat from * around, end last repeat ch 3, join with sl st in top of ch 2.

Rnd 6: Ch 1, sc in same st as joining, sc in next hdc, sc in ch-3 sp, * ch 5, sk picot lp, sc in next ch-3 sp, sc in each of next 2 hdc, sc in next ch-3 sp, repeat from * around, end ch 5, sc in last ch-3 sp, join with sl st in first sc.

Rnd 7: Ch 1, sc in same sc as joining, sc in next sc, * sk next sc, 7 sc in next ch-5 lp, sk next sc, sc in each of next 2 sc, repeat from * around, end 7 sc in last ch-5 lp, join with sl st in first sc—171 (189-198-216) sc.

Rnd 8: Ch 3 (counts as 1 dc), dc in next sc and in each sc around—171 (189-198-216) dc. Join with sl st in top of ch 3.

Rnd 9: Ch 1, sc in same st as joining, sc in each dc around. Join with sl st in first sc. Change to size I hook.

Rnd 10: Ch 3, dc in next sc, * ch 3, sk next 3 sc, sc in next sc, ch 3, sk next 3 sc, dc in each of next 2 sc, repeat from * around, end ch 3, sk next 3 sc, sc in next sc, ch 3, join with sl st in top of ch 3.

Rnd 11: Ch 3; working dc instead of hdc, work same as rnd 5.

Rnd 12: Repeat rnd 6.

Rnd 13: Repeat rnd 7.

Rnds 14 and 15: Repeat rnds 10 and 11.

Rnds 16 and 17: Repeat rnds 6 and 7.

Rnds 18-21: Repeat rnds 8-11.

Rnd 22: Working ch 7 instead of ch 5, repeat rnd 6.

Rnd 23: Working 9 sc instead of 7 sc in each lp, repeat rnd 7.

Rnd 24: Ch 3, dc in next sc, * ch 4, sk next 4 sc, sc in next sc, ch 4, sk next 4 sc, dc in each of next 2 sc, repeat from * around, end ch 4, sk next 4 sc, sc in next sc, ch 4, join with sl st in top of ch 3.

Rnd 25: Ch 3, dc in next st, * ch 4, picot lp in next sc, ch 4, sk next ch-4 lp, dc in each of next 2 dc, repeat from * around, end ch 4, join with sl st in top of ch 3.

Rnd 26: Working ch 7 instead of ch 5, repeat rnd 6.

Rnd 27: Working 9 sc instead of 7 sc in each lp, repeat rnd 7. Repeat rnds 24-27 1 (2-3-4) times.

Next 2 Rnds: Repeat rnds 8 and 9. End off.

FINISHING: With backstitch, sew shoulder seams.

Armhole Edging: From right side, join yarn in center of underarm.

Rnd 1: With size G hook, sc around armhole edge. Join with sl st in first sc.

Rnd 2: Ch 1, sc in same sc as joining, sc in each of next 2 sc, * ch 3, sc in last sc made (picot made), sc in each of next 3 sc, repeat from * around, join with sl st in first sc. End off.

Front and Neck Edging: From right side, join yarn in lower edge of center front.

Row 1: With size G hook, sc evenly up front edge, around neck and down other front edge. End off.

Row 2: From right side, join yarn in first sc, work from * on rnd 2 of armhole edging. Do not join; end off.

Sew button to left front neck edge; spaces between sts on right front edge form buttonhole.

DRAWSTRING: With size G hook, ch 5.

Row 1: Dc in 4th ch from hook, dc in next ch. Ch 3, turn.

Row 2: Sk first dc, dc in next dc, dc in top of turning ch. Ch 3, turn. Repeat last row until drawstring measures 60″ (62″-64″-66″) or desired length. End off. Beg at center front, run drawstring under 2 tr, over next 2 tr around 2nd row on skirt. Tie ends into bow.

Do not press; to block, pin dress on padded surface with rustproof pins to desired measurements. Cover with damp cloth; dry.

YOKED DRESS

Shown at left on page 202

The coral yoke of the toddler's dress is worked from side to side in single crochet, with a stripy skirt in rows of double crochet. The rippled-brim hat is cued to match.

SIZES: Directions for toddlers' size 1. Changes for sizes 2 and 3 are in parentheses.

Fits Body Chest Size: 20″ (21″-22″).

MATERIALS: Yarn of knitting worsted weight, 2 4-oz. skeins each of coral (A) and white (B). Crochet hooks sizes F and I.

GAUGE: 3 sc = 1″; 3 rows sc = 1″; 3 dc = 1″; 2 rows = 1″ (size I hook).

Note: When changing colors, pull new color through last 2 lps to complete dc.

DRESS: YOKE (worked vertically from side seam to side seam): Beg at side edge, with A and size I hook, ch 9 (10-11).

Row 1: Sc in 2nd ch from hook and in each ch across—8 (9-10) sc. Ch 1, turn each row.

Rows 2-4 (6-6): Sc in each sc across. Ch 10 (11-12) at end of last row for strap.

Next Row: Sc in 2nd sc from hook and in each ch and sc across—17 (19-21) sc. Work in sc for 2 (2-4) rows, end lower edge.

Next Row: Sc in each of 12 (13-14) sc. Ch 1, turn. Work in sc for 12 rows, ch 6 (7-8) at end of last row for strap.

Next Row: Sc in 2nd ch from hook and in each ch and sc across—17 (19-21) sc. Work in sc for 2 (2-4) rows, end lower edge.

Next Row: Sc in each of 8 (9-10) sc. Ch 1, turn. Work in sc for 6 (8-8) rows, ch 10 (11-12) for strap at end of last row.

Next Row: Sc in 2nd ch from hook and in each ch and sc across—17 (19-21) sc. Work in sc for 2 (2-4) rows, end lower edge.

Next Row: Sc in each of 12 (13-14) sc. Ch 1, turn. Work in sc for 12 rows, ch 6 (7-8) at end of last row for strap.

Next Row: Sc in 2nd ch from hook and in each ch and sc

across—17 (19-21) sc. Work in sc for 2 (2-4) rows, end lower edge.

Next Row: Sc in each of 8 (9-10) sc. Ch 1, turn. Work in sc for 2 rows. End off.

FINISHING: Sew side seam; sew shoulder straps. From right side, with B and size F hook, work 1 rnd sc around armholes and neck edge, easing in to desired fit.

SKIRT: Join B in lower side seam. With size I hook, ch 3 (counts as 1 dc), dc in same st as joining; work 2 dc in edge of each row around lower edge of yoke, work off last 2 lps with A (see Note). Join with sl st in top of ch 3.

Rnd 2: With A, dc in each dc around; work off last dc with B. Join with sl st in top of ch 3. Repeat rnd 2, working 1 rnd B, 1 rnd A until skirt measures 8″ (9″-10½″) from start or desired skirt length, end A row. End off.

Run in yarn ends on wrong side. Steam lightly.

HAT: Beg at center, with B and I hook, ch 4. Sl st in first ch to form ring.

Rnd 1: Ch 3 (counts as 1 dc), 11 dc in ring—12 dc. Sl st in top of ch 3.

Rnd 2: Ch 3, dc in same ch with sl st, 2 dc in each of next 11 dc—24 dc. Sl st in top of ch 3.

Rnd 3: Ch 3, dc in same ch with sl st, dc in next dc, * 2 dc in next dc, dc in next dc, repeat from * around—36 dc. Sl st in top of ch 3.

Rnd 4: Ch 3, dc in same ch with sl st, dc in each of next 2 dc, * 2 dc in next dc, dc in each of next 2 dc, repeat from * around—48 dc. Sl st in top of ch 3.

Rnd 5: Ch 3, dc in same ch with sl st, dc in each of next 3 dc, * 2 dc in next dc, dc in each of next 3 dc, repeat from * around—60 dc. Sl st in top of ch 3.

Rnds 6-11: Ch 3, dc in each dc

YOKED DRESS AND BLUE JUMPER SET

around—60 dc. Sl st in top of ch 3. If deeper hat is desired repeat last row for desired depth. Cut B.

Brim: With A, make lp on hook, 3 dc in same ch with sl st, 3 dc in each dc around—180 dc. Sl st in first dc. Cut A.

Next Rnd: With B, make lp on hook, dc in same ch with sl st, dc in each dc around. Sl st in first dc. End off.

TIES: Cut 4 24″ lengths of A. Knot 2 strands through row before brim on each side of hat.

BLUE JUMPER SET

Shown at right on page 202

This sea blue jumper, with mated panties, is crocheted in a pretty pattern stitch. Back has small button opening; squared armholes will make it over a blouse, too.

SIZES: Directions for size 4. Changes for sizes 6, 8 and 10 are in parentheses.

Body Chest Size: 23″ (24″-27″-28½″).

Blocked Chest Size: 24″ (26″-28″-29¾″).

MATERIALS: Yarn of fingering yarn weight, 4 (4-5-6) 2-oz. skeins. Crochet hook size F. Three-quarter yd. round elastic for panties. Two small buttons for jumper.

GAUGE: 2 shells = 1¾″; 2 rows = 1″ (pat).

JUMPER: BACK: Beg at lower edge, ch 84 (88-92-96).

Row 1 (wrong side): Sc in 2nd ch from hook and in each ch across—83 (87-91-95) sc. Ch 1, turn.

Row 2: Sc in each sc across. Ch 1, turn.

Row 3: Repeat row 2. Ch 3, turn.

Row 4: Sk first 3 sc, 5 dc in next sc (shell made), * sk next 3 sc, 5 dc in next sc (shell made), repeat from * across, end sk next 2 sc, dc in last sc—20 (21-22-23) shells. Ch 6, turn.

Row 5: Sk first dc, * keeping last lp of each st on hook, work dc in each of 5 dc, yo hook and through 6 lps on hook (cluster st or cl-st made), ch 3, repeat from * across, end last repeat ch 3, dc in top of turning ch. Ch 3, turn.

Row 6: Sk first dc, * 5 dc in top of next cl-st, ch 3, repeat from * across, end 5 dc in top of last cl-st, sk next 3 ch, dc in next ch. Ch 6, turn. Repeat rows 5 and 6 for pat 2 (3-5-6) times, then repeat row 5. Ch 3, turn.

Shape Sides: Row 1: Sk first dc, 3 dc in top of next cl-st (½ shell made), shell of 5 dc in top of each cl-st across, end ½ shell of 3 dc in top of last cl-st, dc in 4th ch of turning ch—½ shell dec each side. Ch 6, turn.

Row 2: Sk first dc; keeping last lp of each st on hook, work dc in each of next 3 dc, yo and through 4 lps on hook (½ cl-st made), ch 3, cl-st over next shell, work in pat across, end ch 3, ½ cl-st over last ½ shell, ch 3, dc in top of ch 3. Ch 3, turn.

Row 3: Sk first dc, 2 dc in top of next cl-st, shell of 5 dc in top of each cl-st across, end 2 dc in top of last ½ cl-st, dc in 4th ch of turning ch. Ch 6, turn.

Row 4: Sk first 3 dc, cl-st over next shell, ch 3, work in pat across, end ch 3, sk next 2 dc, dc in top of ch 3—18 (19-20-21) cl-sts. Ch 3, turn. Repeat last 4 rows twice—14 (15-16-17) cl-sts. Ch 3, turn. Work even until piece measures about 13″ (14½″-16″-18″) from start or desired length to underarm, end pat row 5. Ch 1, turn.

Shape Armholes: Row 1: Sl st in each of first 10 (10-12-12) sts, ch 3, ½ shell of 3 dc in next cl-st, work in pat across next 8 (9-10-11) cl-sts, end ½ shell of 3 dc in next cl-st, sk next 2 (2-0-0) ch, dc in next st. Ch 6, turn.

Row 2: Sk first dc, ½ cl-st over next 3 dc, * ch 3, cl-st over next shell, repeat from * across, end ch 3, ½ cl-st over next 3 dc, ch 3, dc in top of ch 3. Ch 3, turn.

Row 3: Sk first dc, ½ shell of 3 dc in next ½ cl-st, shell in each of next 8 (9-10-11) cl-sts, ½ shell of 3 dc in last ½ cl-st, dc in 4th ch of ch 6. Ch 6, turn.

Row 4: Repeat row 2 of armhole shaping.

Back Opening: Row 1: Half shell of 3 dc in first ½ cl-st, shell in each of next 4 (4-5-5) cl-sts, 0 (3-0-3) dc in top of next cl-st; **on sizes 4 and 8 only,** dc in center of next ch-3 sp. Ch 3 (6-3-6), turn.

Row 2: Work in pat across, working cl-st, ch 3 over each shell and ½ shell, ch 3 over each ½ shell. Work in pat as established until armhole measures about 4½″ (5″-5½″-6″) above first row of armhole shaping, end armhole edge with a cl-st row. Ch 3, turn.

Shape Neck and Shoulders: Row 1: 3 dc in first cl-st, shell in next cl-st, 3 dc in next cl-st, dc in center ch of next ch 3. Ch 6, turn.

Row 2: Sk first dc, ½ cl-st over next 3 dc, ch 3, cl-st over next shell, ch 3, ½ cl-st over last 3 dc, ch 3, dc in top of ch 3. End off. Join yarn in same st with last st worked in on last long row, ch 6 (3-6-3), complete same as other side, reversing shaping.

FRONT: Work same as for back to end of armhole shaping row 4. Work even until armholes measure about 4″ (4″-5″-5″) above first row of armhole shaping, end pat row 5.

Shape Neck and Shoulders: Rows 1 and 2: Work same as rows 1 and 2 on back neck and shoulder shaping. Work even until armhole measures same as back. End off.

Sk 4 (5-6-7) cl-sts on last long row, join yarn in next sp, ch 3, complete same for other side.

FINISHING: Pin pieces to measurements on a padded surface; cover with a damp cloth and allow to dry; do not press. Sew side and shoulder seams.

Armhole Border: From right side, join yarn in underarm seam.

Rnd 1: Sc around armhole edge, easing in to desired fit. Join with a sl st in first sc. Ch 1, turn.

Rnd 2: Sc in each sc around. Join; end off. Work same border around other armhole.

Neck Border: Join yarn in base of back opening.

Rnd 1: From right side, work 1 rnd sc around back opening and neck edge, working 3 sc in each neck corner. Sl st in first sc. Ch 1, turn.

With pins, mark position of 2 button loops on right back opening edge, first pin 1 st below neck edge, 2nd pin about 2″ below first pin.

Rnd 2: Working 3 sc in each neck corner, * sc in each sc to pin, ch 3, sk next 2 sc, sc in next sc, repeat from * once, sc in each re-

maining sc. Join in first sc. End off. Sew on buttons.

PANTIES: FIRST HALF: Beg at lower edge of leg, ch 80 (84-88-92).

Row 1: Sc in 2nd ch from hook and in each ch across—79 (83-87-91) sc. Ch 1, turn.

Rows 2 and 3: Sc in each sc across. Ch 3, turn at end of last row.

Rows 4-6: Work in pat as for back on 19 (20-21-22) shells and cl-sts. Do not ch at end of last row. Turn.

Shape Crotch: Row 1: Sl st in each of first 5 dc, sk next dc, * ch 3, cl-st over next shell, repeat from * to within last shell, sk next dc, dc in next dc. Ch 3, turn.

Row 2: Dc in first cl-st, shell in next cl-st and in each cl-st to within last cl-st, end dc in last cl-st, dc in top of ch 3. Ch 6, turn.

Row 3: Sk first 3 dc, ½ cl-st of 3 dc in center 3 dc of next shell, ch 3,

work in pat to within last shell, ½ cl-st of 3 dc in center 3 dc of last shell, ch 3, sk next 2 dc, dc in top of ch 3. Ch 3, turn.

Row 4: Half shell of 3 dc in first ½ cl-st, work in pat across, end ½ shell of 3 dc in last ½ cl-st, dc in 4th ch of ch 6—13 (14-15-16) shells, plus ½ shell each side. Ch 6, turn. Work in pat until piece measures about 7½″ (8″-8½″-9″) above first row of crotch shaping. End off.

2ND HALF: Work same as for first half.

FINISHING: Pin pieces to measurements on a padded surface; cover with a damp cloth and allow to dry thoroughly; do not press. Sew back and front seams; sew leg seam.

Waist Edging: Cut elastic to waist measurement; fasten ends securely. Working over elastic, work 1 rnd sc around upper edge of panties.

STRIPED SUNSUIT SET

Paint-box stripes go ring-around a sunsuit and cloche worked in easy double crochet. The bib back-ties at the neck.

SIZES: Directions for toddlers' size 1. Changes for sizes 2 and 3 are in parentheses.

Fits Body Waist Size: 19½″ (20″-20½″).

Blocked Hip Size: 21″ (22″-23″).

MATERIALS: Knitting worsted, 6 (7-8) ozs. of desired colors. Crochet hook size I. Round elastic.

GAUGE: 7 dc = 2″; 2 rows = 1″.

Note: Change colors as desired. When changing colors, pull new color through last 2 lps to complete dc.

SUNSUIT: BIB: Beg at upper edge, with any desired color, ch 23 (24-25).

Row 1: Dc in 4th ch from hook and in each ch across—21 (22-23) dc. Always count ch 3 at beg of row as first dc. Turn each row.

Row 2: Ch 3, sk first dc, dc in each dc across, dc in top of turning ch.

Rows 3-12: Repeat row 2. Check gauge; bib should measure 6″ (6¼″-6½″) wide.

PANTIES: Ch 53 (55-57); being

careful not to twist chain, join with a sl st in top of turning ch at beg of last row on bib, forming circle.

Rnd 1: Ch 3, dc in each dc and ch around—74 (77-80) dc. Join with a sl st in top of ch 3.

Rnd 2: Ch 3, dc in each dc around—74 (77-80) dc. Join.

Rnds 3-15 (15-17): Changing colors as desired, repeat rnd 2. End off.

Crotch: With any desired color, dc in each of 8 (8-9) dc across center front and back of pants.

FINISHING: Weave crotch tog. Work 1 rnd dc around each leg opening. Join yarn with a sc in lower edge of bib; work 1 rnd sc around bib; working over elastic, work in sc around top of pants. Join with a sl st in first sc. End off. Adjust elastic to desired fit; fasten ends securely.

STRAPS: Join yarn in top corner of bib; ch 3, dc in each of next 3 sc. Ch 3, turn.

Row 2: Sk first dc, dc in each of next 2 dc, dc in top of ch 3. Ch 3, turn. Repeat last row until strap measures 11″ or desired length. End off. Work 2nd strap on other side of bib in same manner.

HAT: Beg at center with any desired color, ch 4. Sl st in first ch to form ring.

Rnd 1: Ch 3 (counts as 1 dc), 11 dc in ring—12 dc. Sl st in top of ch 3. **Note:** Change colors every rnd or when desired.

Rnd 2: Ch 3, dc in same ch with sl st, 2 dc in each of next 11 dc—24 dc. Sl st in top of ch 3.

Rnd 3: Ch 3, dc in same ch with sl st, dc in next dc, * 2 dc in next dc, dc in next dc, repeat from * around—36 dc. Sl st in top of ch 3.

Rnd 4: Ch 3, dc in same ch with sl st, dc in each of next 2 dc, * 2 dc in next dc, dc in each of next 2 dc,

repeat from * around—48 dc. Sl st in top of ch 3.

Rnd 5: Ch 3, dc in same ch with sl st, dc in each of next 3 dc, * 2 dc in next dc, dc in each of next 3 dc, repeat from * around—60 dc. Sl st in top ch 3.

Rnds 6-11: Ch 3, dc in each dc around —60 dc. Sl st in top of ch 3. If deeper hat is desired, repeat last row for desired depth.

Brim: With any desired color, make lp on hook, 3 dc in same ch with sl st, 3 dc in each dc around— 180 dc. Sl st in first dc.

Next Rnd: With next color, make lp on hook, dc in same ch with sl st, dc in each dc around. Sl st in first dc. End off.

TIES: Cut 4 24″ lengths of yarn. Knot 2 strands through row before brim on each side of hat.

GOLD WRAP-DRESS

This allover-gold wrap-dress has solid bodice, lacy skirt, puff sleeves. The patterns are in crochet, including companion panties and flowers.

SIZES: Directions for size 4. Changes for sizes 6, 8 and 10 are in parentheses.

Body Chest Size: 23″ (24″-27″-28½″).

Blocked Chest Size (closed): 24″ (25″-27″-29″).

MATERIALS: Yarn of fingering yarn weight, 5 (6-7-8) 2-oz. skeins. Trim: Pearl cotton, size 5,

1 ball each of pink, blue, rose and green. Crochet hook size F. Elastic thread. Two snap fasteners. Large-eyed tapestry needle.

GAUGE: 5 sts = 1″; 2 sc and 1

dc rows = ¾″ (skirt pat). 5 sts = 1″; 11 rows = 2″ (bodice pat).

DRESS: SKIRT: Beg at lower edge of back and fronts, ch 232 (242-252-262).

Row 1: Sc in 2nd ch from hook and in each ch across—231 (241-251-261) sc. Check gauge; row should measure 46″ (48″-50″-52″) wide. Ch 1, turn.

Row 2: Sc in each sc across. Ch 1, turn.

Row 3: Sc in each sc across. Ch 4, turn.

Row 4: Sk first 2 sc, dc in next sc, * ch 1, sk next sc, dc in next sc, repeat from * across—115 (120-125-130) sps. Ch 1, turn.

Row 5: Sc in first dc, 2 sc in next ch-1 sp and in each ch-1 sp across, end 2 sc in turning ch sp—231 (241-251-261) sc. Ch 1, turn. Repeat rows 3-5 for pat until piece measures 12″ (12½″-13½″-15″), end pat row 3 or 5. End off.

BODICE: BACK: Beg at lower edge, ch 61 (63-69-73).

Row 1 (right side): Sc in 2nd ch from hook and in each ch across—60 (62-68-72) sc. Ch 1, turn.

Row 2: Sc in each sc across. Turn.

Row 3: Ch 3, sk first sc, sc in next sc, * ch 1, sk next sc, sc in next sc, repeat from * across—30 (31-34-36) sps. Ch 1, turn.

Row 4: 2 sc in each ch-1 sp across, end 2 sc in turning ch sp—60 (62-68-72) sc. Turn. Repeat rows 3 and 4 for pat until piece measures 2″ (2½″-3″-3½″), end pat row 4. Turn.

Shape Armholes: Row 1: Sl st in each of first 4 (4-6-6) sc, * ch 1, sk next sc, sc in next sc, repeat from * to within last 6 (6-8-8) sc, ch 1, sk next sc, sl st in next sc. Ch 1, turn.

Row 2: Sc in first ch-1 sp, 2 sc in each ch-1 sp, end sc in last sp—50 (52-54-58) sc. Turn.

Row 3: Ch 3, sk first 2 sc, sc in next sc, work in pat across, end ch 1, sk next 2 sc, sc in last sc—24 (25-

26-28) ch-1 sps. Ch 1, turn. Work even until armholes measure 5″ (5½″-6″-6½″) above first row of armhole shaping, end pat row 4. Turn.

Shape Shoulders and Neck: Sl st in each of first 4 sc, (ch 1, sk next sc, sc in next sc) 6 (6-6-7) times. Ch 1, turn.

Row 2: 2 sc in each of 3 (3-3-4) ch-1 sps, sl st in next sp. End off. Sk next 16 (18-18-20) sc on last long row, join yarn in next sc, sc in same st as joining, * ch 1, sk next sc, sc in next sc, repeat from * to within last 4 sts. Turn.

Next Row: Sl st in each of 6 sts, finish row. End off.

LEFT FRONT: Beg at lower edge, ch 39 (41-45-49).

Rows 1-4: Work same as for back bodice, having 38 (40-44-48) sc on row 1 and 19 (20-22-24) sps on row 3. Ch 3, turn. Check gauge; piece should measure 7½″ (8″-8¾″-9½″) wide. Mark beg of last row for center edge.

Shape Front Edge: Row 5: Sk first sc, sc in next sc, * ch 1, sk next sc, sc in next sc, repeat from * to within last 2 sc (do not ch 1), sk next sc, sc in last sc—1 st dec. Ch 1, turn.

Row 6: Sk first sc, sc in next sc, 2 sc in each ch-1 sp across. Ch 3, turn.

Row 7: Work in pat to within last 3 sc, end ch 1, sk next 2 sc, sc in last sc—1 st dec. Ch 1, turn.

Row 8: Work in pat across. Ch 3, turn. Working in pat, continue to dec 1 st at center edge of next row, then every other row until piece measures same as back to underarm, end pat row 4 (sc row).

Shape Armhole: Row 1: Sl st in each of first 4 (4-6-6) sc, work in pat across, dec 1 st at center edge. Ch 1, turn.

Row 2: Sk first sc, sc in next sc, work in pat across, end sc in last ch-1 sp. Ch 3, turn.

Row 3: Sk first 2 sc, sc in next sc,

work in pat across, dec 1 st at center edge. Ch 1, turn. Working in pat as established, continue to dec 1 st at front edge every other row until 16 (16-18-18) sc remain on sc row. Work even until armhole measures same as back, end arm side.

Shape Shoulder: Row 1: Sl st in each of first 4 sc, ch 1, sk next sc, sc in next sc, finish row. Ch 1, turn.

Row 2: 2 sc in each of first 3 (3-3-4) ch-1 sps, sl st in next sp. End off.

RIGHT FRONT: Work same as for left front for 4 rows. Mark end of last row for center edge. Ch 1, turn.

Shape Front Edge: Row 5: Sc in first sc, sk next sc, sc in next sc, ch 1, sk next sc, sc in next sc, work in pat across—1 st dec.

Row 6: Work in pat across, work 2 sc in last ch-1 sp, sk next sc, sc in last sc. Ch 1, turn.

Row 7: Sc in first sc, ch 1, sk next 2 sc, sc in next sc, work in pat across—1 st dec. Ch 1, turn.

Row 8: Work in pat across. Continue to dec 1 st at front edge every other row; complete same as for left front, reversing shaping.

SLEEVES: Beg at lower edge, ch 62 (64-68-74).

Row 1: Sc in 2nd ch from hook and in each ch across—61 (63-67-73) sc. Beg with pat row 3, work in pat as for skirt until piece measures 2″ (2″-2¾″-2¾″), end pat row 5. Turn. Check gauge; piece should measure 12¼″ (12½″-13½″-14½″) wide.

Shape Cap: Row 1: Sl st in each of first 4 (4-6-6) sts, sc in each sc to within last 4 (4-6-6) sc. Ch 4, turn.

Row 2: Sk first 3 sc, dc in next sc, * ch 1, sk next sc, dc in next sc, repeat from * to within last 3 sc, end ch 1, sk next 2 sc, dc in last sc. Ch 1, turn.

Row 3: Sc in first dc, sc in next sp, 2 sc in each ch-1 sp across, end sc in turning ch. Ch 1, turn.

Row 4: Sk first sc, sc in each sc to within last 2 sc, sk next sc, sc in last sc. Ch 4, turn. Repeat rows 2-4 until piece measures 4″ (4½″-5″-5½″) above first bound-off sts. End off.

BELT: Make chain 54″ (56″-58″-60″) long, having an odd number of ch.

Row 1: Sc in 2nd ch from hook and in each ch across—even number of sc. Ch 3, turn.

Rows 2 and 3: Work same as rows 3 and 4 on bodice back. End off.

FINISHING: Run in the yarn ends on wrong side. Smooth pieces out wrong side up on a padded surface. Place rustproof pins at top, bottom and sides of each piece, measuring to insure correct length and width. Steam pieces carefully, making sure steam penetrates crochet. When pieces are thoroughly dry, remove pins. With backstitch, sew shoulder seams; gathering extra fullness at shoulder, sew in sleeves. Sew side and sleeve seams. Gather upper edge of skirt to fit lower edge of bodice. Weave bodice and skirt tog. From wrong side, with large-eyed tapestry needle, run double strand of elastic thread along row 5 on each sleeve. Adjust to desired fit; fasten ends securely.

Front Edging: From right side, beg at lower right front edge of skirt, sc along right front edge, across back of neck, down left front edge, end at lower left front edge of skirt. Ch 1, turn. Work 2 rows sc. End off.

Sleeve Edging: From right side, join yarn in sleeve seam. Working along foundation ch, * sc in each of next 2 ch, (sc, ch 2, 4 dc) in next ch, sk next 2 ch, repeat from * around lower edge of sleeve; join with a sl st in first sc. End off. Lap right front over left front; adjust to desired fit; sew 2 snap fasteners at lower edge of bodice.

Belt Loops; Make two 10-st chains; attach to lower edge of each side seam on bodice. Slip belt through loops, adjusting to desired fit.

FLOWER TRIM: FLOWER: With blue, ch 5, join with a sl st to form ring.

Rnd 1: (Sc, ch 2, 4 dc, ch 2) 5 times in ring. Join with a sl st in first sc. End off. Make 1 pink and rose flower in same manner.

LEAF CLUSTER: With green, * ch 12, sc in 2nd ch from hook and in each ch across, repeat from * once, ch 9, sc in 2nd ch from hook and in each ch across; join with a sl st in first ch of starting ch. End off. With green, embroider a French knot at center of each flower. Sew flowers and leaf cluster tog and tack to belt.

PANTIES: FIRST HALF: Beg at lower edge of leg, ch 77 (81-87-91).

Row 1: Sc in 2nd ch from hook and in each ch across—76 (80-86-90) sc. Ch 3, turn. Repeat rows 3 and 4 of back of bodice, having 38 (40-43-45) sps on pat row 3 until piece measures about 1″ (1½″-2″-2″), end row 4.

Shape Crotch: Rows 1-3: Work same as for back armhole shaping rows 1-3. Ch 1, turn.

Row 4: 2 sc in each ch-1 sp across. Ch 1, turn.

Row 5: Sc in each of first 2 sc, * ch 1, sk next sc, sc in next sc, repeat from * across to within last 2 sc, sk next sc, sc in last sc. Ch 1, turn.

Row 6: Sk first sc, sc in next sc, 2 sc in each sp across, end sk next sc, sc in last sc. Ch 3, turn.

Row 7: Sk first 2 sc, sc in next sc, work in pat to within last 3 sc, ch 1, sk next 2 sc, sc in last sc. Ch 1, turn.

Row 8: 2 sc in each ch-1 sp across—60 (64-70-74) sc. Work even until piece measures 7½″ (8″-8½″-9″) above first bound-off sts, end pat row 4. End off.

2ND HALF: Work same as for first half.

FINISHING: Block pieces. Sew front and back seams from crotch to upper edge; sew leg seams.

Waist Edging: Cut double strand of elastic to waist measurement; join ends. Join yarn in top of center back seam; from right side, working over elastic, sc in each st around. Join with a sl st in first sc; end off.

Leg Edging: Cut double strand of elastic to leg measurement; join ends. Join yarn in leg seam.

Rnd 1: From right side, working over elastic, sc around one leg edge, having number of sts divisible by 5. Join with a sl st in first sc. Ch 1, do not turn.

Rnd 2: * Sc in each of next 2 sc, (sc, ch 2, 4 dc) in next sc, sk next 2 sc, repeat from * around; join. End off.

SUNSUIT AND NEWSBOY CAP

A peaked newsboy cap matches a suspendered sunsuit for the beach. Varie-gated yarn creates the design; front and back are the same. Both cap and sunsuit are worked in an easy single crochet, chain-one pattern.

SIZES: Directions for small size (1-2). Changes for medium size (3-4) are in parentheses.
Fits Body Waist Size: 19½"-20" (20½"-21").

MATERIALS: Ombré knitting worsted, 2 4-oz. skeins. Crochet hook size I.
GAUGE: 7 sts = 2"; 3 rows = 1".
SUNSUIT: PANTS: BACK: Beg at crotch, ch 10.
Row 1: Sc in 2nd ch from hook, * ch 1, sk next ch, sc in next ch, repeat from * across—5 sc. Ch 5, turn.
Row 2: Sc in 2nd ch from hook, ch 1, sk next ch, sc in next ch, * ch 1, sc in next sc, repeat from *

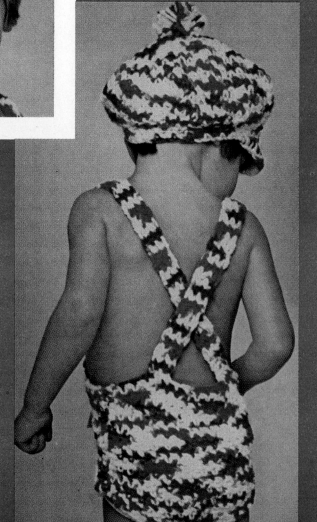

across—7 sc. Ch 5, turn. Repeat last row 4 times, ch 5 (7) at end of last row—15 sc. Turn.
Row 7: Sc in 2nd ch from hook, (ch 1, sk next ch, sc in next ch) 1 (2) times, * ch 1, sc in next sc, repeat from * across—17 (18) sc. Ch 5 (7), turn.
Row 8: Repeat row 7, ch 1, turn at end of row—19 (21) sc.
Row 9: Sc in first sc, * ch 1, sc in next sc, repeat from * across—19 (21) sc. Ch 1, turn. Repeat last row until piece measures 8" (9") from start or desired length from crotch to waistline. Check gauge; piece above last inc row should measure 10½" (11½") wide. End off.
FRONT: Work same as for back.
STRAPS (make 2): Ch 6.
Row 1: Sc in 2nd ch from hook, (ch 1, sk next ch, sc in next ch) twice—3 sc. Ch 1, turn.
Row 2: Sc in sc, (ch 1, sc in next sc) twice. Repeat this row until strap measures 16" (18") or desired length. End off.
FINISHING: Sew crotch and side seams. Sew straps to upper front edge, 2½" (3") from side edges. Cross straps and sew ends to back edge, 2½" (3") in from side edges. Steam lightly.
CAP: Beg at center of crown, ch 2.
Rnd 1: 6 sc in 2nd ch from hook. Do not join rnds; mark end of rnds.
Rnd 2: * Ch 1, sc in next sc, ch 1, sc in same sc, repeat from * around—12 sc and ch-1 sps.
Rnd 3: * Ch 1, sc in next sc, repeat from * around.
Rnds 4 and 5: Repeat rnds 2 and 3—24 sc.

Rnd 6: * (Ch 1, sc in next sc) 4 times, ch 1, sc in sc just worked in, repeat from * 5 times—30 sc.

Rnd 7: * (Ch 1, sc in next sc) 5 times, ch 1, sc in sc just worked in, repeat from * 5 times—36 sc.

Rnd 8: * (Ch 1, sc in next sc) 6 times, ch 1, sc in sc just worked in, repeat from * 5 times—42 sc.

Rnd 9: * (Ch 1, sc in next sc) 7 times, ch 1, sc in sc just worked in, repeat from * 5 times—48 sc.

Rnd 10: * (Ch 1, sc in next sc) 8 times, ch 1, sc in sc just worked in, repeat from * 5 times—54 sc.

Rnd 11: * (Ch 1, sc in next sc) 9 times, ch 1, sc in sc just worked in, repeat from * 5 times—60 sc.

Rnd 12: Repeat rnd 3.

Rnd 13: * Ch 1, pull up a lp in each of next 2 sc, yo and through 3 lps on hook (ch-1, sc dec), (ch 1, sc in next sc) 8 times, repeat from * 5 times—54 sc.

Rnd 14: * Ch 1, pull up a lp in each of next 2 sc, yo and through 3 lps on hook (ch-1, sc dec), (ch 1, sc in next sc) 7 times, repeat from * 5 times— 48 sc. Continue to dec 6 sc and ch-1 sps evenly spaced every rnd 4 times more—24 sc and ch-1 sps. Join with a sl st in next ch-1 sp. Ch 1, turn.

Rnd 19: * Sc in next sc, ch 1, repeat from * around. Do not join or turn.

Rnd 20: Repeat rnd 19, end 3 sc in last sc, sc in next ch-1 sp, sl st in next sc. Ch 1, turn.

Peak: Row 1: Sc in sl st, sc in each of next 7 sts, sl st in next sc. Ch 1, turn.

Row 2: Sc in sl st, sc in each of next 10 sts, sl st in next st. Ch 1, turn.

Row 3: Sc in sl st, sc in each of next 13 sts, sl st in next st. Ch 1, turn.

Row 4: Sc in sl st, sc in each of next 16 sts, sl st in next st. Ch 1, turn.

Row 5: Working over sc, sc in base of each sc of previous row, sl st in next st. End off.

POMPON: Wind yarn 50 times around 1½" cardboard. Tie all windings securely tog at one edge with several strands of yarn. Cut lps at other edge. Trim pompon. Tie to top of cap.

COLOR-RINGED BATHING SUIT

Shown on page 210

A soft rainbow of colors stripes this two-piece beach suit. The suit is simple to make in half double crochet stitch. The pants are slightly pouffed, gathered in at the legs with elastic. The top is a little vest, laced up in front with a twisted cord.

SIZES: Directions for girls' size 4. Changes for sizes 6, 8 and 10 are in parentheses.

Body Chest Size: 23" (24"-27"-28½").

Blocked Chest Size (closed): 23" (24"-27"-28½").

MATERIALS: Mercerized knitting and crochet cotton, 175-yd. balls, 1 (2-2-2) each of royal blue (RB), purple (P), watermelon (W), rose (R), turquoise (T) and aqua (A). Steel crochet hook No. 1. One and a half yds. round or oval elastic.

GAUGE: 11 hdc = 2"; 4 rows = 1".

Notes: Suit is worked with double strand of each color throughout. Cut and join colors as needed.

STRIPED PATTERN: With 2 strands, work 1 row each of P, A, T, RB, R, W. Repeat these 6 rows for striped pat.

BATHING SUIT: TOP: BACK: Beg at lower edge, with 2 strands P, ch 62 (65-73-78).

Row 1: Hdc in 3rd ch from hook and in each ch across—60 (63-71-76) hdc. End off; join 2 strands A in last hdc. Ch 2, turn. Check gauge; row should measure 11" (11½"-13"-14") wide.

Row 2: With 2 strands A, hdc in each hdc across—60 (63-71-76) hdc. End off; join 2 strands T. Ch 2, turn. Repeat last row, working in striped pat until piece measures 2½" (2¾"-3"-3½") from start. Note last color used. End off; turn.

Shape Armholes: Row 1: Keeping to striped pat, sk first 3 (3-4-4) hdc, join next color in next hdc, ch 2, hdc in same hdc, hdc in each

COLOR-RINGED BATHING SUIT

hdc to within last 3 (3-4-4) hdc. End off; turn.

Row 2: Sk first hdc, join next color in next hdc, ch 2, hdc in same hdc, work to within last st—1 hdc dec each side. End off; turn.

Repeat last row 1 (1-3-4) times—50 (53-55-58) hdc. Work even until armholes measure 2″ (2½″-2¾″-3″) above first row of armhole shaping. End off; join next color. Ch 2, turn.

Shape Neck: Row 1: Hdc in each of 18 (19-20-21) hdc. End off; turn.

Row 2: Sk first 3 sts (neck edge), join next color in next st, hdc in same hdc and in each hdc across—15 (16-17-18) hdc. End off; join next color. Ch 2, turn.

Row 3: Hdc in each hdc to within last 2 hdc—13 (14-15-16) hdc. End off; turn.

Row 4: Sk first st, join next color in next st, hdc in same hdc and in each hdc across—12 (13-14-15) hdc. Work even until armhole measures 4½″ (5¼″-5½″-6″) above first row of armhole shaping. End off. Sk center 14 (15-15-16) hdc on last long row, join double strand of color to be used in next st, ch 2, hdc in same hdc, finish row—18 (19-20-21) hdc. Complete same as for first shoulder, reversing shaping.

LEFT FRONT: Beg at lower edge, with double strand of P, ch 32 (34-38-40). Working in striped pat on 30 (32-36-38) hdc same as for back, work even until piece measures same as back to underarm, end same color row. Check gauge; piece should measure 5½″ (6″-6½″-6¾″) wide. End off; turn.

Shape Armhole: Row 1: Keeping to striped pat, sk first 3 (3-4-4) hdc, join next color in next hdc, ch 2, hdc in same st, hdc in each hdc across. End off; join next color. Ch 2, turn.

Row 2: Work in pat to within last st—1 hdc dec. End off; turn.

Row 3: Sk first hdc, join next color in next hdc, work across—25 (27-30-32) hdc.

For Size 8 Only: Repeat rows 2 and 3—28 hdc.

For Size 10 Only: Repeat rows 2, 3, 2—29 hdc.

For All Sizes: Work even until armhole measures 1½″ (2″-2¼″-2½″) above first row of armhole shaping, end arm side. End off; join next color. Ch 2, turn.

Shape Neck: Work as for neck shaping of back until armhole measures same as back, end same color row—12 (13-14-15) hdc. End off.

RIGHT FRONT: Work same as for left front, reversing shaping.

FINISHING: Run in thread ends. Block to measurements. With backstitch, sew side and shoulder seams.

With pins, mark position of 6 (6-7-7) loops evenly spaced on each front edge, having first pin 2 rows above lower edge of each front, last pin at each neck corner.

Edging: From right side, join 2 strands T at lower front edge, sc in edge of first row, * ch 5 for loop, sc in end of each row to next pin, repeat from * 5 (5-6-6) times, sc around neck edge, work from * to lower front edge, end ch 5, sc in last row on lower front edge. End off.

Armhole Edging: From right side, with double strand T, sc around each armhole edge. Join with a sl st in first sc. End off.

CORD: Cut two 3 (3-3½-3½) yard lengths of each color. Make twisted cord. Knot each end. Beg at lower front edge, lace cord through loops up front edges. With all colors make 2 pompons; attach to ends of cord. Tie ends into bow.

PANTS: BACK: Left Leg: Beg at lower edge, with 2 strands RB, ch 47 (51-56-60).

Row 1: Hdc in 3rd ch from hook and in each ch across—45 (49-54-58) hdc. End off; join R. Ch 2, turn. Work 1 row R, 1 row W. Check gauge; piece should measure 8" (9"-10"-10½") wide.

For Sizes 8 and 10 Only: Work 1 row P. End off.

For All Sizes: Right Leg: Work same as for left leg. Working in same color sequence as striped pat, join double strand of next color in last st. Ch 2, turn.

Join Legs: Row 1: Hdc in each hdc across right leg to within last 6 (7-9-10) hdc; from wrong side, sk first 6 (7-9-10) hdc on left leg, hdc in each remaining hdc—78 (84-90-96) hdc. Put a marker between last hdc made on right leg and first hdc on left leg for center back.

End off; join 2 strands of next color. Ch 2, turn.

Row 2: Work in hdc to within 2 sts of center marker, dec 1 hdc **(to dec 1 hdc,** yo hook, pull up a lp in each of next 2 hdc, yo hook and through 4 lps on hook), move up center marker, dec 1 hdc, finish row—1 hdc dec each side of marker. Work 1 row even.

Row 4: Repeat row 2. Repeat last 2 rows 1 (2-2-2) times—72 (76-82-88) hdc. Remove marker. Work in striped pat until legs measure 7" (7"-7½"-8") from start. End off.

FRONT: Work same as for back.

FINISHING: Run in yarn ends. Block pieces. Sew side seams. Sew legs and crotch seams.

Leg Edging: Cut elastic to leg measurement; fasten ends securely. From right side, with double strand T, working over elastic, sc around each leg edge, end sl st in first sc. End off.

Top Edging: Work as for leg edging with double strand of next color in sequence.

Steam-press seams and edgings.

CHECKED BEACH QUARTET

Shown on page 212

Checkerboard squares in fresh green and white pattern a four-piece beach outfit. The free-swinging cover-up ties on over a front-buttoned swimsuit crocheted in the same pattern. Beach bag is the same on both sides.

SIZES: Directions for small size (4-6). Changes for medium size (8-10) and large size (12-14) are in parentheses.

Body Chest Size: 23"-24" (27"-28½"; 30"-32").

Blocked Chest Size: Robe: 27" (31"-35"). Swimsuit: 24" (28"-32").

Robe is loosely fitted; swimsuit is fitted.

MATERIALS: Sport yarn, 6 (6-7) 2-oz. balls green, main color (MC); 4 (5-6) balls white, contrasting color (CC). Aluminum or plastic crochet hook size F. Five buttons. One yd. ½" elastic.

GAUGE: 9 sts = 2"; 2 dc rows = 1"; 5 tr rows = 3".

Note: Always count turning ch as 1 dc or tr. Carry yarn not used loosely across top of sts and work over it.

CHECKED PATTERN FOR SWIMSUIT AND BAG: Row 1:

With MC, dc in 4th ch from hook (counts as 2 dc; see Note), dc in each of next 2 ch, working off last 2 lps of last dc with CC; * with CC, dc in each of next 4 ch, working off last 2 lps with MC; with MC, dc in each of next 4 ch, working off last 2 lps with CC, repeat from * across, changing color in last st as before. Turn.

Row 2: Ch 3 (counts as 1 dc), sk first dc, dc in each of next 3 dc, changing color in last st, * dc in each of next 4 dc, changing color in last st, repeat from * across. Turn. Repeat row 2 for checked pat, being sure to reverse colors each row to form checked pat.

To Bind Off: At beg of a row, sl st loosely across specified sts; **at end of a row,** leave specified sts unworked.

To Dec 1 St: At beg of a row, ch 3, sk first st, * yo over hook, draw up a lp in each of next 2 sts, yo and through 3 lps on hook, yo and through remaining 2 lps on hook *; **at end of a row,** work to last 3 sts, work from first * to 2nd *, dc in last st, working off last 2 lps in alternate color.

BEACH BAG: PANELS (make 2): Beg at lower edge, with MC, ch 42. Work in pat on 40 sts for 18 rows. Check gauge; piece should measure about 9" high. End off.

SIDE INSERT: With MC, ch 121 (should measure long enough to fit around sides and lower edge of panel).

Row 1: Sc in 2nd ch from hook and in each ch across—120 sc. Ch 1, turn each row.

Rows 2-10: Sc in each sc across. End off.

HANDLE: With MC, ch 101. Work same as for side insert for 6 rows. End off.

FINISHING: Steam-press pieces. With MC work 1 row sc around each checked piece. From right side, sl st insert to sides and lower edge of panels. Sew handle in place. Line if desired.

SWIMSUIT: PANTS: FRONT: Beg at upper edge, with MC, ch 58 (66-74). Work in pat on 56 (64-72) sts for 5" (6"-7"). Check gauge; piece should measure 12½" (14½"-16½") wide.

Shape Legs and Crotch: Bind off (see To Bind Off) 12 sts each side of next row, then bind off 4 sts each side every row 2 (3-4) times—16 sts.

On Small Size Only: Bind off 2 sts each side of next row—12 sts.

For All Sizes: Work even for 1 (2-3) rows. End off.

BACK: Work same as for front until 12 (16-16) sts remain. Work 2 (3-4) rows even instead of 1 (2-3) rows. End off.

CHECKED BEACH QUARTET

FINISHING: Steam-press pieces. Matching rows, sew side seams tog. Weave crotch. From right side, with MC, work 2 rnds sc around each leg edge, easing in to desired fit. From right side, with MC, work 3 rnds sc around waistline. Work casing on inside of waistline: With wrong side facing you, join yarn at top edge, * ch ¾″, sl st in st ½″ to left in row ½″ below, ch ¾″, sl st at top edge ½″ to left of last st, repeat from * around. Cut elastic same as waist measurement; insert in casing. Sew ends securely.

TOP: BACK: Beg at lower edge, with MC, ch 54 (62-70). Work in pat on 52 (60-68) sts for 2½″ (2½″-3″) or desired length to underarm. Check gauge; piece should measure 11½″ (13½″-15″) wide.

Shape Raglan Armholes: Bind off 4 sts each side of next row. Dec 1 st (see To Dec 1 St) each side every row 6 (7-8) times—32 (38-44) sts. Working with MC only, dec 1 st each side of next row—30 (36-42) sts.

Shape Neck: Ch 3, dec 1 dc across next 2 sts, dc in each of next 4 (6-8) sts, dec 1 dc, dc in next st, drop MC, sk center 10 (12-14) sts, join another ball of MC in next st, ch 3, dec 1 dc across next 2 sts, dc in each of next 4 (6-8) sts, dec 1 dc, dc in last st—8 (10-12) sts each side. Working on both sides at once, dec 1 st at arm and neck edge every row twice more—4 (6-8) sts. End off.

LEFT FRONT (Left-handed crocheters: This will be your right front): Beg at lower edge, with MC, ch 30 (34-38). Beg with CC, work in pat on 28 (32-36) sts until piece measures same as back to underarm. Mark end of last row for arm side. Check gauge; piece should measure 6¼″ (7″-8″) wide.

Shape Raglan Armhole: Keeping to pat, bind off 4 sts at arm side of next row. Dec 1 st st arm side every row 6 (7-8) times—18 (21-24) sts. Working with MC only, dec 1 st at arm side on next row—17 (20-23) sts.

Shape Neck and Armhole: Bind off 8 (9-10) sts at center edge once, then dec 1 st at center edge every row twice; **at the same time,** dec 1 st at arm side 3 times—4 (6-8) sts remain. End off.

RIGHT FRONT: Work as for left front; mark beg of first row for arm side.

FINISHING: Steam-press pieces. Weave shoulder and side seams. From right side, with MC, work 2 rnds sc around each armhole edge.

Beg at lower edge of front, from right side, with MC, work 1 rnd sc up front edge, around neck (holding in to desired fit), down other front edge and around lower edge of fronts and back, working 3 sc in each corner. Do not turn.

With pins mark position of 5 buttonholes evenly spaced on right center edge, first one ½″ above lower edge, last one ¼″ below neck edge.

Next Rnd: * Sc in each sc to within 1 sc of pin, ch 2, sk 2 sc, repeat from * 4 times, finish rnd, work 2 sc in each corner.

Next Row: Sc in each st on right front only, working 2 sc in ch-2 sps. End off.

Steam-press edges lightly. Sew on buttons opposite buttonholes.

CHECKED PATTERN FOR ROBE: Row 1: With MC, tr in 5th ch from hook (counts as 2 tr; see Note), tr in each of next 2 ch, working off last 2 lps of last tr with CC; * with CC, tr in each of next 4 ch, working off last 2 lps with MC; with MC, tr in each of next 4 ch, working off last 2 lps with CC, repeat from * across, changing color as before in last st. Turn.

Row 2: Ch 4 (counts as 1 tr), sk first tr, tr in each of next 3 tr, changing color in last st, * tr in each of next 4 tr, changing color in last st, repeat from * across. Turn. Repeat row 2 for checked pat, being sure to reverse colors each row to form checked pat.

To Dec 1 St: At beg of a row, ch 4, sk first st, * yo hook, draw up a lp in each of next 2 sts, (yo and through 2 lps on hook) 3 times *; **at end of a row,** work to last 3 sts, work from first * to 2nd *, tr in last st, working off last 2 lps in alternate color.

ROBE: BACK: Beg at lower edge with MC, ch 79 (87-95). Work in pat on 76 (84-92) sts, dec 1 st (see To Dec 1 St) each side every 1½″ (1½″-2″) 8 times—60 (68-76) sts. Work even until piece measures 14″ (16″-18″) from start or desired length to underarm. Check gauge; piece above last dec row should measure 13″ (15″-17″) wide.

Shape Armholes: Keeping to pat, bind off (see To Bind Off) 4 sts each side of next row—52 (60-68) sts. Work even until armholes measure 5″ (6″-6½″) above first bound-off sts. End off.

RIGHT FRONT: Beg at lower edge, with MC, ch 43 (47-51). Mark beg of first row for front edge. Work in pat on 40 (44-48) sts, dec 1 st at side edge every 1½″ (1½″-2″) 8 times—32 (36-40) sts. Work even until piece measures same as back to underarm. Check gauge; piece above last dec row should measure 7″ (8″-9″) wide.

Shape Armhole: Bind off 4 sts at arm side once—28 (32-36) sts. Work even until armhole measures 3½″ (4½″-5″) above first bound-off sts.

Shape Neck: Bind off 12 (16-16) sts at neck edge on next row—16 (16-20) sts. Work even for 1½″. End off.

LEFT FRONT: Work same as for right front; pat is reversible.

FINISHING: Steam-press

pieces. Weave shoulder and side seams. From right side, with MC, work 1 row sc around each armhole edge. Beg at front neck edge, with MC, work 1 row sc around neck, fronts and lower edges. Work 2nd row sc around neck edge.

TIES (make 2): With MC, make a ch 9″ long. Sl st in each ch. End off leaving a 10″ end. Use end for sewing each tie to front neck edge.

ZIP-UP JACKET

A "real" denim jacket, worked in double crochet, has crocheted ribs and flowers! Thick brim on hat made to match turns up to show off more blooms.

SIZES: Directions for size 4. Changes for sizes 6, 8 and 10 are in parentheses.
Body Chest Size: 23″ (24″-27″-28½″).
Blocked Chest Size (closed): 24″ (25″-27½″-30″).
MATERIALS: Knitting worsted weight yarn, 3 (3-4-4) 4-oz. skeins denim color. Trim: Small amounts of scarlet (A), yellow (B) and green (C). Crochet hooks sizes E and G. Separating zipper.
GAUGE: 7 dc = 2″; 2 rows = 1″ (size G hook).
To Bind Off: At beg of a row, ch 1, sl st loosely across specified number of sts; **at end of a row,** leave specified number of sts unworked.
To Dec 1 St: At beg of a row, ch 3 (counts as 1 dc), sk first dc, yo hook, draw up a lp in each of next 2 sts, yo hook and through 2 lps, yo and through 3 lps, work in pat across; **at end of a row,** work to last 2 sts, yo hook, draw up a lp in each of next 2 sts, yo and through 2 lps, yo and through 3 lps.
To Inc 1 St: At beg of a row, ch 3, dc in first st; **at end of a row,** work 2 dc in top of turning ch.
JACKET: BACK: Ribbing (worked from side seam to side seam): With size E hook, ch 13 (13-15-15).
Row 1: Sc in 2nd ch from hook and in each ch across—12 (12-14-14) sc. Ch 1, turn.

Row 2: Sc in back lp of each sc across. Ch 1, turn. Repeat row 2 until 42 (44-48-52) rows from start. Change to size G hook. Ch 3, do not turn.

Pattern: Row 1: Working across side edge of ribbing, sk first row, dc in next row and in each row across—42 (44-48-52) dc, counting ch 3 as 1 dc. Turn.

Row 2: Ch 3 (always counts as 1 dc), sk first dc, dc in next dc and in each dc across—42 (44-48-52) dc. Turn. Repeat last row until piece measures 6½″ (7″-7½″-8″) from start or desired length to underarm. Check gauge; piece above ribbing should measure 12″ (12½″-13¾″-14¾″) wide.

Shape Armholes: Bind off 2 sts each side of next row. Dec 1 st (see To Bind Off and To Dec 1 St) each side every row 2 (2-3-4) times—34 (36-38-40) dc. Work even until armholes measure 4½″ (5″-5½″-6″) above first bound-off sts.

Shape Shoulder: Bind off 5 sts each side of next row, 5 (5-6-6) sts next row—14 (16-16-18) sts. End off.

RIGHT FRONT: Ribbing: Work same as for back ribbing for 21 (22-24-26) rows. Change to size G hook. Ch 3, do not turn.

Pattern: Row 1: Working across side edge of ribbing, sk first row, dc in next row and in each row across—21 (22-24-26) dc, counting ch 3 as 1 dc. Work same as for back until piece measures same as back to underarm. Mark end of last row for side edge. (On left front, mark beg of last row for side edge.)

Shape Armhole: Bind off 2 dc at side edge of next row. Dec 1 dc at same edge every row 2 (2-3-4) times—17 (18-19-20) dc. Work even until armhole measures 3″ (3½″-4″-4½″) above first bound-off sts.

Shape Neck: Bind off 5 (6-6-7) sts at center edge of next row. Dec 1 st at same edge every row twice.

Next Row: Bind off 5 sts at arm side—5 (5-6-6) sts. End off.

LEFT FRONT: Work same as for right front, reversing shaping.

SLEEVES: Ribbing: Work same as for back for 22 (24-26-26) rows. Change to size G hook. Ch 3, do not turn.

Pattern: Work same as for back on 22 (24-26-26) sts for 2 rows. Inc 1 st (see To Inc 1 St) each side of next row, then every 3rd row 4 (4-4-5) times more—32 (34-36-38) dc. Work even until piece measures 10½″ (11½″-13″-14½″) from start or desired length to underarm. Check gauge; piece above last inc row should measure 9¼″ (9¾″-10¼″-10¾″) wide.

Shape Cap: Bind off 2 sts each side of next row. Dec 1 st each side every row 2 (2-3-4) times—24 (26-26-26) sts. Work 1 row even.

Next Row: Sl st across first st, ch 3, sk next st, dec 1 st over next 2 sts, work to within last 3 sts, dec 1 st over next 2 sts, do not work in turning ch—2 sts dec each side. Repeat last row 3 (4-4-4) times—8 (6-6-6) sts. End off.

COLLAR: Beg at neck edge, with size G hook, ch 44 (46-46-48).

Row 1: Dc in 4th ch from hook and in each ch across. Turn. Working in dc, inc 1 st each side of next row, then every other row 2 (2-3-3) times—48 (50-52-54) dc. End.

FINISHING: Smooth pieces out wrong side up on a padded surface. Place rustproof pins at top, bottom and sides of each piece. Do not pin ribbings. Steam pieces carefully, making sure steam penetrates crocheting. Let dry. With backstitch, sew shoulder seams; sew in sleeves. Sew side and sleeve seams. Sew foundation ch of collar to neck edge of jacket. Beg at lower left front edge, work 1 row sc up left front edge, around collar, down right front edge, working 3 sc in each collar corner. Sew in zipper.

APPLIQUÉS: FLOWER: With size G hook and B, ch 2.

Rnd 1: 6 sc in 2nd ch from hook; join with a sl st in first sc. End off.

Rnd 2: Join A in any sc; work 2 sc in each sc around—12 sc. Join with a sl st in first sc.

Rnd 3 (petals): * Ch 4, sc in 2nd ch from hook and in each of next 2 ch, sl st in each of next 2 sc, repeat from * 5 times.

STEM: With C and size G hook, ch 14, sc in 2nd ch from hook and in each ch across. End off.

LEAVES (make 2): With C and size G hook, ch 5, sc in 2nd ch from hook and in each ch across. End off. Make 2 appliqués and sew, wrong side up, with matching color yarn to fronts as pictured.

HAT: With size G hook, ch 4, sl st in first ch to form ring.

Rnd 1: Ch 3 (counts as 1 dc), 11 dc in ring—12 dc. Sl st in top of ch 3.

Rnd 2: Ch 3, dc in same ch with sl st, 2 dc in each of next 11 dc—24 dc. Sl st in top of ch 3.

Rnd 3: Ch 3, dc in same ch with sl st, dc in each of next 2 dc, * 2 dc in next dc, dc in each of next 2 dc, repeat from * around—32 dc. Sl st in top of ch 3.

Rnd 4: Ch 3, dc in same ch with sl st, dc in next dc, * 2 dc in next dc, dc in next dc, repeat from * around—48 dc. Sl st in top of ch 3.

Rnd 5: Ch 3, dc in same ch with sl st, dc in each of next 5 dc, * 2 dc in next dc, dc in each of next 5 dc, repeat from * around—56 dc. Sl st in top of ch 3.

Rnds 6-12: Ch 3, dc in next dc and in each dc around—56 dc. Sl st in top of ch 3. End off. (Ends of rnds are back of hat.)

Brim: Turn work so that wrong side faces you.

Rnd 13: Join double strand of yarn in front lp of dc at back of hat. Sc in front lp of each dc around. Sl st in first sc.

Rnd 14: Ch 1, sc in same sc with sl st and in each of next 11 sc, 2 sc in next sc, * sc in each of next 12 sc, 2 sc in next sc, repeat from * twice—60 sc. Join.

Rnd 15: Ch 1, sc in joining and in each of next 4 sc, 2 sc in next sc, * sc in each of next 5 sc, 2 sc in next sc, repeat from * around—70 sc. Join.

Rnd 16: Ch 1, sc in joining and in each of next 5 sc, 2 sc in next sc, * sc in each of next 6 sc, 2 sc in next sc, repeat from * around—80 sc. Join.

Rnds 17 and 18: Working in sc, continue to inc 10 sc evenly spaced around—100 sc.

Rnds 19-22: Sc in each sc around. End off. Join 1 strand of yarn in free lp of any dc on rnd 12. With inside of crown facing you (right side of dc rnds is inside of crown), ch 1, sc in free lp of each dc on rnd 12 around. Join.

Next Rnd: Sc in each sc around. Join; end off.

FINISHING: Steam-press brim lightly. Make 2 appliqués same as for jacket. Sew to brim as pictured.

SWEATER TWINS

This sweater twosome is a bright addition to any little girl's wardrobe. Cardigan is worked in an easy-to-crochet blue-and-yellow-stripe pattern. Matching sleeveless shell is bordered top and bottom with the same striping.

SIZES: Directions for size 6. Changes for sizes 8, 10 and 12 are in parentheses.

Body Chest Size: 24″ (27″-28½″-30″).

Blocked Chest Size: Pullover: 26″ (28″-30″-32″). Cardigan: 27″ (29″-31″-33″).

MATERIALS: Sport yarn, 4 (5-6-7) 2-oz. balls white, main color (MC); 1 ball each of yellow (A) and blue (B). Crochet hook size H. Five buttons. Neck zipper. Large-eyed needle.

GAUGE: 2 cl-dc and ch 1 = 1″; 9 rows = 5″.

Note: Cut and join colors as needed.

PULLOVER: BACK: Beg at lower edge, with B, ch 51 (55-59-63).

Row 1 (mark for right side): Holding back last lp of each dc, work 2 dc in 3rd ch from hook, yo and through 3 lps on hook (cluster dc or cl-dc made), * ch 1, sk next ch, cl-dc of 2 dc in next ch, repeat from * to last 2 ch, end ch 1, sk next ch, dc in last ch—24 (26-28-30) cl-dc. Cut B; with A, ch 3, turn.

Row 2: * Cl-dc in next ch-1 sp, ch 1, repeat from * across, working last cl-dc in last ch-1 sp, ch 1, dc in top of turning ch—24 (26-28-30) cl-dc. Cut A; with B, ch 3, turn.

Row 3: With B, repeat row 2. Cut B. With MC, ch 3, turn. With MC, repeat row 2 for pat until piece measures 10″ (10½″-11″-12″) from start or desired length to underarm. Check gauge; piece should measure 13″ (14″-15″-16″) wide. Ch 1, turn at end of last row.

Shape Armholes: Sl st loosely across 2 cl-dc, ch 3, cl-dc in ch-1 sp after 2nd cl-dc, ch 1, work in pat to within last 3 cl-dc, end ch 1, dc in next ch-1 sp—20 (22-24-26) cl-dc. Work in pat until armholes measure 1½″ (2″-2½″-3″) above armhole shaping row.

Divide Work: Work 10 (11-12-13) cl-dc, ch 1, dc in same ch-1 sp, drop yarn; join another strand MC in next ch-1 sp, ch 3, cl-dc in same ch-1 sp, finish row—10 (11-12-13) cl-dc each side. Working on both sides at once, with separate strands of MC, work even until armhole measures 4½″ (5″-5½″-6″) above armhole shaping row.

Shape Shoulders: Sl st across 3 (4-4-5) cl-dc, ch 3, work to center opening. Working on other shoulder, work across 7 (7-8-8) cl-dc. End off both sides.

FRONT: Work same as for back, omitting back opening, until armholes measure 3½″ (3½″-4″-4″) above armhole shaping row—20 (22-24-26) cl-dc. Ch 3, turn.

Shape Neck: Work 7 (8-8-9) cl-dc, dc in next cl-dc. Ch 3, turn.

Next Row: Sk first cl-dc, cl-dc in next ch-1 sp, work in pat across, end dc in top of turning ch—6 (7-7-8) cl-dc. Ch 3, turn. Work even until armhole measures same as back. Shape shoulder same as for back. End off.

Sk 5 (5-7-7) cl-dc, join MC in next cl-dc, ch 3, cl-dc in next ch-1 sp, work in pat across, end dc in top of turning ch—7 (8-8-9) cl-dc. Ch 3, turn.

Next Row: Work 6 (7-7-8) cl-dc, dc in next cl-dc. Ch 3, turn. Complete same as for first shoulder.

FINISHING: Run in yarn ends on wrong side. Steam-press pieces lightly. Sew shoulder and side seams. From right side, with B, work 1 row sc around lower edge.

Neckband: Row 1: Join B at upper edge of back opening. Ch 3, work in pat around neck edge, working cl-dc in each ch-1 sp and edge of each row. Cut B; with A, ch 3, turn.

Row 2: With A, work in pat around neck edge. Cut A; with B, ch 3, turn.

Row 3: With B, repeat row 2. End off.

From right side, with matching colors, work 1 row sc around back opening. With MC, work 1 row sc around each armhole. Press seams and borders. Sew in zipper.

CARDIGAN: STRIPED PATTERN: Work pat as for back of pullover, working 1 row B, 1 row A, 1 row B, 3 rows MC. Repeat these 6 rows for striped pat. Cut and join colors as needed.

BACK: Beg at lower edge, with B, ch 51 (55-59-63). Work same as for back of pullover keeping to striped pat, omitting back opening, and working armholes 5″ (5½″-6″-6½″) above armhole shaping row.

Shape Shoulders: Sl st across 3 (4-4-5) cl-dc, work in pat to within last 3 (4-4-5) cl-dc. End off.

LEFT FRONT (Left-handed crocheters: This will be your right front): Beg at lower edge, with B, ch 27 (29-31-33). Work in striped pat, having 12 (13-14-15) cl-dc until piece measures 1″ less than back to underarm, end right side (center edge). Check gauge; piece should measure 6½″ (7″-7½″-8″) wide. Ch 3, turn.

Shape Neck: Next Row: Sk first ch-1 sp, cl-dc in next ch-1 sp, finish row—11 (12-13-14) cl-dc. Continue to dec 1 cl-dc at neck edge every other row 3 (3-4-4) times more; **at the same time,** shape armhole as for right back armhole **(left-handed crocheters:** left back armhole) when piece measures same as back to underarm—6 (7-7-8) cl-dc. Work even until armhole measures same as back. Shape shoulder as for right back shoulder **(left-handed crocheters:** left back shoulder). End off.

RIGHT FRONT (Left-handed crocheters: Substitute "left" for "right" and "right" for "left"): Work same as for left front until piece measures same as left front to start of neck shaping. Work 1 row more, end wrong side (center edge). Complete same as for left front, shaping armhole as for left back armhole and shoulder as for left back shoulder.

SLEEVES: Beg at lower edge, with B, ch 27 (29-31-33). Work in striped pat on 12 (13-14-15) cl-dc for 4 rows.

Next Row: Keeping to pat, work 2 cl-dc in first and last ch-1 sp (1 cl-dc pat inc each side)—14 (15-

16-17) cl-dc pats. Inc 1 cl-dc each side every 6th row twice—18 (19-20-21) cl-dc. Work even until piece measures about 13″ (13½″-14″-15″) from start, end same striped pat row as back at underarm. Check gauge; piece above last inc row should measure 10″ (10½″-11″-12″) wide.

Shape Cap: Sl st across 2 cl-dc, ch 3, cl-dc in ch-1 sp after 2nd cl-dc, work in pat to within last 3 cl-dc, end ch 1, dc in next ch-1 sp—14 (15-16-17) cl-dc. Ch 3, turn.

Next Row: Sk first ch-1 sp, cl-dc in next ch-1 sp, finish row—13 (14-15-16) cl-dc. Ch 3, turn. Continue

to dec 1 cl-dc at beg of every row 5 (6-7-8) times—8 cl-dc. End off.

FINISHING: Run in yarn ends on wrong side. Steam-press pieces. Sew shoulder seams; sew in sleeves. Matching pat rows, sew side and sleeve seams. With B, work 1 row sc around lower edge of sleeves and body of cardigan.

Border: From right side, beg at lower right front edge **(left-handed crocheters:** left front edge), with MC, sc up front edge, around neck edge, down other front edge, keeping work flat and having same number of sc on each front edge. Ch 1, turn.

Rows 2 and 3: Sc in each sc. Ch 1, turn each row.

With pins, mark position of 5 buttonholes evenly spaced on last row of right front edge, first pin in 3rd sc above lower edge, 5th pin in 2nd sc below start of neck shaping.

Row 4 (buttonhole row): From wrong side, * work sc to within 1 sc of pin, ch 2, sk 2 sc, repeat from * 4 times, sc in next sc, finish row.

Row 5: Sc in each sc and ch around.

Row 6: Sc in each sc. End off.

Steam-press seams and border lightly. Sew on buttons.

BANDED PASTELS SWEATER SET

Summer's pastels—mint, lilac and ice blue—encircle bright-pink sweater twins worked in double crochet. Sleeveless shell and brief-sleeve cardigan are banded with a crochet stitch that looks like a knitted rib.

SIZES: Directions for girls' size 8. Changes for sizes 10, 12 and 14 are in parentheses.

Body Bust Size: 27″ (28½″-30″-32″).

Blocked Bust Size: Shell: 29″ (31″-32″-34″). Cardigan (closed): 29½″ (31½″-32½″-34½″).

MATERIALS: Sport yarn, 9 (10-10-11) 1-oz. skeins pink, main color (MC); 2 (2-3-3) skeins each of blue (A), lilac (B) and green (C). Crochet hooks sizes D and E. Seven buttons.

GAUGE: 9 sts = 2″; 4 rows = 2¼″ (dc striped pat, size E hook).

Note: When changing colors, pull new color through last 2 lps to complete dc. Cut and join colors as needed.

To Bind Off: At beg of a row, ch

1, sl st loosely across specified number of sts; **at end of a row,** leave specified number of sts unworked.

To Dec 1 Dc: At beg of a row, ch 3 (counts as 1 dc), sk first dc, * (yo hook, pull up a lp in next st, yo hook and through 2 lps) twice, yo hook and through remaining 3 lps *, work in pat across; **at end of a row,** work to last 2 sts, work from first * to 2nd * once.

To Inc 1 Dc: Work 2 dc in same st.

STRIPED PATTERN: Work in dc, work 5 (5-6-6) rows each of A, MC, B, MC, C; then complete with MC only.

SHELL: BACK: Ribbing (worked from side seam to side seam): With MC and size E hook, ch 11.

Row 1: Sc in 2nd ch from hook and in each ch across—10 sc. Ch 1, turn.

Row 2: Sc in back lp of each sc across, ch 1, turn. Repeat row 2 until 42 (44-46-48) rows from start. Ch 1, do not turn. Continue along side edge of ribbing, work 3 sc in every 2 rows—63 (66-69-72) sc. Work off last sc with A. Turn.

Pattern: Row 1: With A, ch 2 (counts as 1 dc), sk first sc, dc in next sc and in each sc across, inc 2 (4-4-4) dc (see To Inc 1 Dc) evenly spaced—65 (70-73-76) dc. Turn each row.

Row 2: Ch 2 (counts as 1 sc), sk first dc, dc in next dc and in each dc across. Working in striped pat, repeat row 2 until piece measures 12″ (13″-14″-14″) from start. Check gauge; piece above ribbing should be 14½″ (15½″-16″-17″) wide.

Shape Armholes: Bind off (see To Bind Off) 5 dc each side of next row. Dec 1 st (see To Dec 1 Dc) each side every row 2 (3-3-3) times—51 (54-57-60) dc. Work even until armholes measure 4½″ (5″-5½″-6″) above bound-off sts.

Shape Neck: Ch 2, sk first dc, dc in each of next 11 (12-13-14) dc, dec 1 dc over next 2 dc, drop MC; sk next 23 (24-25-26) dc, join another strand of MC in next dc, ch 2, dec 1 dc over next 2 dc, finish row. Working on both sides at once, with separate strands of MC, dec 1 dc at each neck edge of next row. End off.

FRONT: Work same as back until armholes measure 2½″ above bound-off sts.

Shape Neck: Ch 2, sk first dc, dc in each of next 14 (15-16-17) dc, dec 1 dc over next 2 dc, drop MC; sk next 17 (18-19-20) dc, join another strand of MC in next dc, ch 2, dec 1 dc over next 2 dc, finish row. Working on both sides at once, with separate strands of MC, dec 1 dc each neck edge every row 4 times—12 (13-14-15) dc each side. Work even until armhole measures same as back. End off.

FINISHING: Run in yarn ends on wrong side. Steam-press lightly. Weave shoulder and side seams tog. From right side, with MC and size D hook, work 1 rnd sc around each armhole edge, 3 rnds around neck edge, easing in to desired fit.

CARDIGAN: BACK: Ribbing: Work same as for shell for 44 (46-48-50) rows. Ch 1, do not turn. Continuing along side edge of ribbing, work 3 sc in every 2 rows—66 (69-72-75) sc.

Pattern: Row 1: With A, ch 2 (counts as 1 dc), sk first sc, dc in next sc and in each sc across, inc 1 (3-3-3) dc evenly spaced—67 (72-75-78) dc. Work in striped pat until piece measures 12½″ (13½″-

14½″-14½″) from start. Check gauge; piece above inc row should measure 15″ (16″-16¾″-17¼″) wide.

Shape Armholes: Bind off 6 dc each side of next row. Dec 1 st each side every row 2 (3-3-3) times—51 (54-57-60) dc. Complete same as for back of shell.

RIGHT FRONT: Ribbing: Work same as for shell for 22 (22-24-24) rows. Ch 1, do not turn. Continuing along side edge of ribbing, work 3 sc in every 2 rows—33 (33-36-36) sc. Turn.

Pattern: Row 1: With A, ch 2 (counts as 1 dc), sk first sc, dc in

next sc and in each sc across, inc 0 (2-1-3) dc evenly spaced—33 (35-37-39) dc. Work same as for back to start of armhole shaping. End of last row is arm side. Check gauge; piece above inc row should measure 7¼″ (7¾″-8¼″-8¾″) wide.

Shape Armhole: Bind off 6 dc at beg of next row. Dec 1 dc at same edge every row 2 (3-3-3) times—25 (26-28-30) dc. Work even until armhole measures 3½″ (3¾″-4″-4¼″) above first row of armhole shaping.

Shaping Neck and Shoulder: Bind off 9 (9-10-11) dc at center edge of next row. Dec 1 dc at neck edge every row 4 times—12 (13-14-15) dc. Work even if necessary until armhole measures same as back. Bind off 4 (4-5-5) dc at arm side once.

LEFT FRONT: Work same as right front; pat is reversible.

SLEEVES: Ribbing: Work same as for back for 32 (34-36-38) rows. Ch 1, do not turn. Continuing along side edge of ribbing, work 50 (54-56-60) sc evenly spaced. With MC, work even in dc until piece is 7" (7¼"-7½"-8") from start.

Shape Cap: Bind off 6 sts each

side of next row. Dec 1 dc each side every row 5 (6-7-8) times. Bind off 5 dc each side of next row—18 (20-20-22) dc. End off.

FINISHING: Run in yarn ends on wrong side. Steam-press lightly. Weave shoulder seams; sew in sleeves. Sew side and sleeve seams.

Neck Border: From right side, join MC in front corner. With size D hook, work in sc around neck edge, easing in to desired fit. Ch 1, turn. Work 4 more rows sc around neck edge.

Left Front Border: Work 6 rows of sc on left front edge.

Right Front Border: Work 3 rows of sc on right front edge. With pins, mark position of 7 buttonholes evenly spaced on right front edge, first pin in 3rd sc from lower edge, last pin in 3rd sc below neck edge.

Row 4: * Work sc to within 1 sc of pin, ch 2, sk 2 sc, repeat from * 6 times, sc in next sc, sc in last sc. Ch 1, turn.

Row 5: Sc in each sc and in each ch of buttonholes. Ch 1, turn. Work 1 more row in sc. End off.

Steam-press crocheted borders. Sew on buttons.

TYROLEAN CAP AND VEST SET

This charming Tyrolean set, crocheted in an unusual pattern stitch, is reversible. The vest, worked in one piece to the underarms, has borders to match the bright pattern stripes. The cap is in rounds of pattern, topped with a long chain.

SIZES: Directions for girls' medium size (8-10). Changes for large size (12-14) are in parentheses.

Body Chest Size: 27"-28½" (30"-32").

Blocked Chest Size: 28½" (32").

MATERIALS: Knitting worsted, 6 ozs. each of white (W) and gray (G); 4 ozs. each of kelly green (KG), blue (B) and red (R). Plastic or aluminum crochet hook size H.

GAUGE: 6 pats (24 sts) = 6½".

VEST: BODY: Beg at lower edge of fronts and back, with W, ch 99 (115). Sc in 2nd ch from hook and in each ch across—98 (114) sc. Turn.

Pattern: Row 1: With W, ch 1, sk first sc, sc in next sc, * ch 1, sk next sc, sc in next sc, repeat from * across—49 (57) sc. Turn.

Row 2: Ch 3 (counts as 1 tr), sk first st, tr over ch-1 sp into sc below, * ch 2, sk next 2 sts, tr in next sc, tr over ch-1 sp into sc below, repeat from * across. Drop W. Turn.

Row 3: With G, make lp on hook, * sk 2 tr, work tr over ch-2 sp and ch-1 sp below into sc below, tr over ch-2 sp into sc, ch 2, repeat from * across, do not ch 2 at end of row. Drop G; do not turn.

Row 4: Pick up W; with W, ch 3 (counts as 1 tr), sk first W tr, tr in

next W tr, * ch 2, sk next 2 G tr, work tr over ch-2 sp into each next 2 W tr, repeat from * across, end tr in each of last 2 W tr. Drop W. Put G lp on hook; turn.

Row 5: With G, ch 2, * work tr over ch-2 sp into each of next 2 G tr, ch 2, repeat from * across. End off G; do not turn.

Row 6: With W, ch 2 (counts as 1 hdc), hdc in each of next 2 W tr, * sc in each of next 2 G tr, work hdc over ch-2 sp into each of next 2 W tr, repeat from * across, end hdc in each of last 2 W tr. Turn.

Row 7: * Ch 1, sk next st, sc in next st, repeat from * across—49 (57) sc. End off W; join KG. Turn.

Row 8: With KG, * ch 1, sc over ch-1 sp into st on row 6, repeat from * across. Cut KG; join B. Turn.

Row 9: With B, * ch 1, sc over ch-1 sp into st on row 7, repeat from * across. Cut B; join R.

Row 10: With R, * ch 1, sc over ch-1 sp into st on row 8, repeat from * across. Cut R; join KG.

Rows 11-16: Working in sc, ch 1 pat as established, work 1 row KG, 1 row B, 1 row R, 1 row KG, 2 rows W. Repeat rows 2-16 once, then rows 2-14. Check gauge; piece should measure 26½″ (30½″) wide.

Divide Work: Front Yoke: Keeping to pat, work across 18 (22) sts. Turn. Work in pat on these sts for 7″ (7½″). End off.

Back: Sk 6 sts on last long row for underarm. Work in pat across 50 (58) sts. Work in pat on these sts for 7″ (7½″). End off.

Front Yoke: Sk 6 sts on last long row for underarm. Work in pat across last 18 (22) sts. Work even for 7″ (7½″). End off.

FINISHING: Weave shoulder seams. Beg at neck edge of shoulder, with KG, work sc, ch 1 around entire front, neck and lower edges of vest, working (sc, ch 1, sc) in each lower corner (inc). Join with a sl st in first sc. Work around in sc, ch 1 pat, working 1 row each of B, R, KG, B, R, KG. Working in same pat and color sequence, work 4 rows around each armhole edge.

Steam-press vest and edgings lightly, being careful not to stretch garment.

TIES (make 2): With 1 strand each of R, KG, and B, make chain 18″ long. End off. Knot one end; sew other end to front edge as pictured.

CAP: Beg at top, with KG, ch 3, join with a sl st forming ring.

Rnd 1: 8 sc in ring. Do not join; mark end of rnd.

Rnd 2: 2 sc in each sc around, finish last sc with B. Drop KG.

Rnd 3: With B, * ch 1, sc in base of next sc, repeat from * around, finish last sc with R. Drop B.

Rnd 4: With R, * ch 1, sc over ch-1 sp into sc on rnd 2, repeat from * around, finish last sc with KG. Drop R.

Rnd 5: With KG, * ch 1, sc over

ch-1 sp into sc on rnd 3, ch 1, sc in same sc (inc make), (ch 1, sc over ch-1 sp into next sc on rnd 3) 3 times, repeat from * around, finish last sc with B—4 incs. Drop KG.

Rnd 6: With B, work in pat as established, inc 4 sc during rnd, finish last sc with R—24 sc. Drop B.

Rnd 7: With R, work 1 rnd even, finish last sc with KG. Drop R.

Rnd 8: With KG, * ch 1, sc over ch-1 sp into sc on rnd 6, ch 1, sc in same sc (inc made), (ch 1, sc over ch-1 sp into next sc on rnd 6) 3 times, repeat from * around, finish last sc with B—30 sc. Drop KG.

Rnd 9: With B, work 1 rnd even, finish last sc with R. Cut B.

Rnd 10: With R, work 1 rnd even, finish last sc with KG. Cut R.

Rnd 11: With KG, work in pat, inc 4 sc during rnd, finish last sc with W—34 sc. Cut KG.

Rnds 12 and 13: With W, work 2 rnds even.

Rnd 14: With W, ch 3 (counts as 1 tr), tr in next ch-1 sp, * ch 2, sk sc and ch-1 sp, tr in next sc, tr in next ch-1 sp, repeat from * around, end ch 2, join to top of ch 3—17 pats. Drop W.

Rnd 15: With G, make lp on hook, * sk 2 tr, work tr over ch-2 sp into sc below, tr over ch-2 sp into ch-1 sp below, ch 2, repeat from * around, sl st in top of first tr. Drop G.

Rnd 16: Pick up W in front of work; with W, ch 2, then ch 2 over the ch-2 sp (counts as 1 tr), tr over ch-2 sp into next W tr, * ch 2, sk next 2 G tr, work tr over ch-2 sp into each of next 2 W tr, repeat from * around, end ch 2, sl st in top of ch 4. Drop W. Pick up G lp in front of work.

Rnd 17: With G, ch 2, then ch 2 over the ch-2 sp (counts as 1 tr), tr over ch-2 sp into next G tr, * ch 2, work tr over ch-2 sp into each of next 2 G tr, repeat from * around, end ch 2, sl st in top of ch 4. End off G.

Rnd 18: Pick up W lp in front of work, ch 2 over ch-2 sp (counts as 1 hdc), hdc over ch-2 sp into next W tr, * sc in each of next 2 G tr, hdc over ch-2 sp into each of next 2 W tr, repeat from * around, end sc in each of last 2 G tr, sl st in first hdc.

Rnd 19: * Ch 1, sk next st, sc in next st, repeat from * around, end ch 1, sc in first ch 1, changing to KG in last st. Cut W.

Rnd 20: With KG, * ch 1, sc over next ch-1 sp into st on rnd 18, repeat from * around, change to B in last sc.

Rnds 21-29: Work in ch 1, sc pat, working B, R and KG in order.

Rnd 30: With KG, work in ch 1, sc pat.

Rnd 31: With KG, sc in each st around. End off.

FINISHING: With 1 strand each of R, B and KG, make ch 36″ long. Join ends; fold into 4 loops. Sew to top of cap.

EASY-STITCH VARIEGATED VEST

Boy's V-necked vest in bonfire colors is very easy to make in the simplest crochet stitch—single crochet. Color changes in the yarn form the intricate-looking pattern, so every row is different!

SIZES: Directions for size 4. Changes for sizes 6, 8 and 10 are in parentheses.

Body Chest Size: 23″ (24″-26″-28″).

Blocked Chest Size: 25″ (26″-28″-30″).

MATERIALS: Sport yarn, 3 (4-4-5) 1¾-oz. skeins variegated colors, or 3 (3-4-4) 2-oz. skeins solid colors. Aluminum crochet hook size F.

GAUGE: 5 sc = 1″; 13 rows = 2″.

To Bind Off: At beg of a row, sl st loosely across specified number of sts, ch 1, work in sc across; **at end of a row,** leave specified number of sts unworked. Ch 1, turn.

To Dec 1 Sc: Pull up a lp in each of 2 sc, yo and through 3 lps on hook.

To Inc 1 Sc: Work 2 sc in same sc.

VEST: BACK: Beg at lower edge, ch loosely 56 (58-61-66).

Row 1: Sc in 2nd ch from hook and in each ch across—55 (57-60-65) sc. Ch 1, turn.

Row 2: Sc in each sc across. Ch

1, turn each row. Repeat last row twice. Check gauge; piece should measure 11″ (11½″-12″-13″) wide. Inc 1 sc (see To Inc 1 Sc) each side of next row, then every 12th row 3 (3-4-4) times—63 (65-70-75) sc. Work even until piece measures 12″ (12″-12½″-13″) from start or desired length to underarm.

Shape Armholes: Bind off (see To Bind Off) 3 (3-4-4) sc each side of next row. Dec 1 sc (see To Dec 1

Sc) each side every other row 4 (4-5-6) times—49 (51-52-55) sc. Work even until armholes measure 4″ (4½″-5¼″-5½″) above first bound-off sts. * Inc 1 st each side of next row. Work 2 rows even. Repeat from * once—53 (55-56-59) sc.

Shape Shoulders and Neck: Bind off first 5 (6-6-7) sc, sc in each of next 10 sc, dec 1 sc, drop yarn, sk next 19 (19-20-21) sc; with another strand of yarn, make lp on

hook, pull up a lp in each of next 2 sc, yo hook and through 3 lps on hook, sc in each of next 10 sc. Ch 1, turn. Working on both sides at once, bind off 5 sc at each arm side and dec 1 sc at each neck edge of next row. End off.

FRONT: Work same as for back until armhole shaping is completed—49 (51-52-55) sc. Ch 1, turn.

Shape V-Neck: Sc in each of next 24 (25-26-27) sc, drop yarn, sk 1 (1-0-1) sc; with another strand of yarn, sc in each remaining sc—24 (25-26-27) sc each side. Working on both sides at once, with separate strands of yarn, dec 1 sc at each neck edge every 3rd row 4 times, then every other row 5 (5-6-6) times—15 (16-16-17) sc. Work even if necessary until armholes measure 4″ (4½″-5″-5½″) above first bound-off sts. * Inc 1 st each arm side of next row. Work 2 rows even. Repeat from * once—17 (18-18-19) sc each side.

Shape Shoulders: Bind off 5 (6-6-7) sts at each arm side of next row, then 5 sc next row. End off.

FINISHING: With rustproof pins, pin pieces to measurements on padded surface; cover with damp cloth and allow to dry; do not press. With backstitch, sew shoulder and side seams.

Lower Edging: From right side, work 1 rnd sc around lower edge; join with a sl st in first sc. Do not turn.

Rnd 2: Ch 1, sc in back lp of each sc around. Join. Repeat rnd 2 once. End off.

Work same edging around each armhole.

Neck Edging: Join yarn in shoulder seam; from right side, work 1 rnd sc around neck edge, easing in to desired fit. Join.

Rnds 2 and 3: Work same as rnd 2 of lower edging, sk 1 sc at center front. End off.

PATCHWORK DOG

*A many-hued dog is crocheted in afghan stitch with an unusual method.
The yarn (knitting worsted) is put on bobbins; work is one piece from head to
tail. Follow the illustration for colors.*

SIZE: 8″ wide; 9″ high.

MATERIALS: Knitting worsted, small amounts of 5 to 10 colors. Afghan hook size H. Two plastic rings and few yds. black yarn for eyes. Cotton batting or 1″-thick foam rubber, 1 piece 8″ x 9″. Bobbins.

GAUGE: 5 sts = 1″.

AFGHAN STITCH: Work with afghan hook.

Row 1: Keeping all lps on hook, sk first ch from hook at beg of row, pull up a lp in each ch across.

To Work Lps Off: Yo hook, pull through first lp, * yo hook, pull through next 2 lps, repeat from * across until 1 lp remains. Lp that remains on hook always counts as first st on next row.

Row 2: Keeping all lps on hook, sk first vertical bar at beg of row, pull up a lp under next vertical bar and under each vertical bar across. Work lps off as before. Repeat row 2 for afghan st.

To Bind Off: At beg of a row, start with 2nd vertical bar, work first part of st, pull lp through lp on hook thus making a sl st (1 st bound off), continue in this manner for specified number of sts; **at end of a row,** leave specified number of sts unworked. Work lps off as before. When piece is completed, work sl st across unworked bound-off sts, keeping to color as established.

Note: When changing colors, always change colors on wrong side, picking up new color from under dropped color. Cut and join colors as necessary.

DOG: Wind bobbins with colors to be used.

FRONT: Beg at back edge, with A (color at back edge of back foot), ch 30.

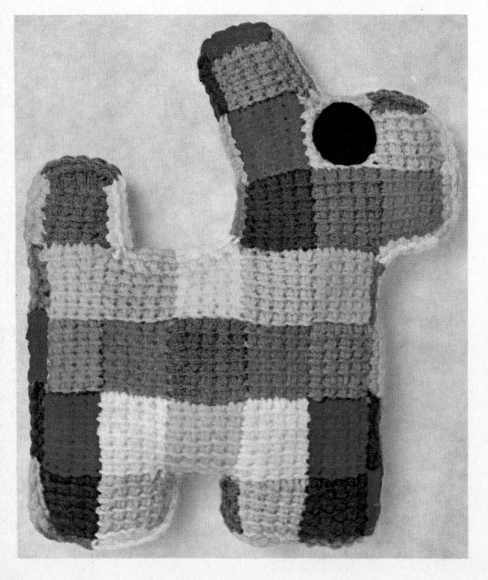

Row 1: Work in afghan st until there are 6 A lps on hook, drop A; with B, work 6 lps, drop B; with C, work 6 lps, drop C; with D, work 6 lps, drop D; with E (color of tail), work 6 lps—30 lps. Work lps off in colors as established.

Rows 2-5: Work in afghan st keeping to colors as established.

Row 6: Following illustration, change to different colors on first 4 blocks; do not work last 6 sts (tail).

Rows 7-10: Work in colors as es- tablished. Following illustration, changing colors every 6th row (blocks are 6 sts wide, 5 rows deep), add and bind off (see To Bind Off) blocks as shown. When adding blocks, work 6 ch for each block.

BACK: Work same as for front, reversing shaping (begin with tail color).

BOXING STRIP: With any color, ch 6. Work in afghan st on 6 sts, changing colors in any desired sequence every 6th row until 150 rows are completed (30 color squares).

FINISHING: With invisible sts, matching squares, weave boxing strip to front and back, leaving seam open at bottom for stuffing. Stuff dog; close opening.

EYES (make 2): With black, work sc closely around plastic ring. Join with a sl st in first sc. End off, leaving a 10″ end; thread needle. Turn sc to center of ring, gather sts tog at center. Sew an eye to each side.

BUNNY TWINS

Bunny twins, carrying fresh "yarn" vegetables, are easy to make in rows of single crochet. Their little white tails are in loopy stitches; yellow outfits are double crochet.

SIZE: About 18″ high.

MATERIALS: Yarn of knitting worsted weight, 6 ozs. gray, 1½ ozs. yellow, ½ oz. white, for both bunnies and clothes; small amounts of brown, green, lime, or- ange, red and natural for vege- table basket. Crochet hook size F. Stuffing. Scraps of gray and pink felt. Two black ball buttons, ⅜″ di- ameter. Four flat round black shank buttons, ⅝″ diameter.

GAUGE: 9 sc = 2″.

BUNNY: HEAD AND BODY (make 2 pieces for each bunny): Beg at top of head, with gray, ch 11.

Row 1: Sc in 2nd ch from hook and in each ch across—10 sc. Ch 1, turn each row.

Row 2: Inc 1 sc each side (**to inc,** work 2 sc in 1 st)—12 sc.

Row 3: Sc in each sc across.

Rows 4-7: Repeat rows 2 and 3 twice.

Row 8: Repeat row 2—18 sc.

Rows 9-17: Repeat row 3.

Row 18: Dec 1 sc each side (**to dec,** pull up a lp in each of 2 sts, yo and through 3 lps on hook).

Row 19: Repeat row 3.

Rows 20-22: Dec 1 sc each side—10 sc.

Row 23: Repeat row 3.

Row 24: Sc in each of 10 sc, ch 23 for arm.

Row 25: Sc in 2nd ch from hook and in each remaining ch, sc in each sc across, ch 23 for arm.

Row 26: Sc in 2nd ch from hook and in each ch and sc across—54 sc.

Rows 27-31: Sc in each sc across.

Row 32: Sc in 36 sc. Ch 1, turn.

Row 33: Sc in 18 sc. Ch 1, turn.

Row 34: Sc in each sc across.

Row 35: Inc 1 sc each side—20 sc.

Rows 36 and 37: Repeat rows 34 and 35.

Rows 38-47: Sc in each sc across—22 sc.

Row 48: Dec 1 sc each side.

Row 49: Sc in each sc across—20 sc.

Row 50: Repeat row 48—18 sc.

Rows 51-55: Sc in each sc across.

Row 56: Sc in 9 sc (leg). Ch 1, turn.

Row 57: Dec 1 sc each side of leg—7 sc.

Rows 58-68: Sc in each sc across.

Row 69: Sc in 7 sc, ch 13 for foot.

Row 70: Sc in 2nd ch from hook and in each ch, sc in 7 sc—19 sc.

Rows 71-74: Sc in each sc across.

Row 75: Sc in 17 sc, dec 1 sc. End off. Work 2nd leg to correspond.

EARS: Row 1: Join gray at top of head 3 sts in from side edge; sc in these 3 sts, sc in 2 sts down side of head. Ch 1, turn.

Row 2: Sc in 5 sc.

Row 3: Inc 1 sc at center of row.

Rows 4-18: Sc in each sc—6 sc.

Row 19: Dec 1 sc at center of row.

Row 20: Sc in each sc—5 sc.

Row 21: Dec 1 sc at each side.

Rows 22 and 23: Sc in each sc.

Row 24: Dec 1 sc, sc in last sc.

Row 25: Dec 1 sc. End off. Work 2nd ear to correspond.

FINISHING: Sew pieces tog around edges, stuffing as you go.

Paw Pads (make 2): With white, ch 2.

Rnd 1: 6 sc in 2nd ch from hook.

Rnd 2: 2 sc in each sc around.

Rnd 3: (Sc in next sc, 2 sc in next sc) 6 times—18 sc. End off. Sew to arm ends.

Cheeks (make 2): Work as for

paw pads, then work 1 rnd even. Stuff; press into shape; sew to face.

Cut a quarter-circle from pink felt, trim to fit in space between cheeks for mouth. Glue or sew in place. Sew on ball button for nose; sew on flat buttons for eyes. Be sure to sew them on securely. Cut 2 gray felt circles 1″ diameter for eyelids. For boy, trim circle to crescent shape; glue or sew in place. For girl, fringe eyelids. Put a line of glue at inner edge of fringe; press fringe back. Glue or sew in place.

Tail: With white, ch 4.

Row 1: Loop st in 2nd ch from hook and in next 2 ch (**to make loop st,** insert hook in st, loop yarn around right index finger, catch strand under finger and pull through st, drop loop from finger, finish sc). Ch 1, turn each row.

Row 2: Sc in each st, inc 1 each end—5 sc.

Row 3: Loop st in each sc. Repeat rows 2 and 3 twice—9 loop sts.

Row 8: Sc in each st, dec 1 sc each end—7 sc.

Row 9: Loop st in each sc. Repeat rows 8 and 9 twice. End off. Stuff and sew tail to back 1″ above crotch with loops down.

DRESS: SKIRT: With yellow, ch 45.

Row 1: Sc in 2nd ch from hook and in each ch across. Ch 1, turn.

Row 2: Sc in each sc across. Ch 3, turn.

Row 3: * Dc in next sc, 2 dc in next sc; repeat from * across—66 dc. Ch 3, turn.

Row 4: Dc in each dc across. End off.

TOP: Sk 17 ch on starting ch at top of skirt; join yellow in next ch, work sc in each of 10 ch. Ch 3, turn.

Row 2: Sk first st, dc in each of next 9 sts. Ch 3, turn.

Row 3: Repeat row 2.

Row 4: Dc in first dc (an inc), dc in each of next 8 dc, 2 dc in top of ch 3. Ch 3, turn.

Rows 5-7: Work even in dc. At end of row 7, ch 1, turn.

STRAP: Sc in each of first 2 dc. Work even on 2 sc until strap is long enough to fit around neck to opposite edge of top. Sew end in place. Sew back of skirt tog at top edge.

EDGING: Join white to first st at bottom edge of skirt; * sc in next dc, ch 2, sc in same dc, ch 1, sk 1 dc, repeat from * around. Work same edging at top of dress.

PANTS: FRONT: With yellow, ch 23.

Row 1: Sc in 2nd ch from hook and in each ch across. Ch 1, turn.

Row 2: Sc in each sc. Ch 3, turn.

Row 3: Sk first sc (ch 3, counts as first dc), dc in each sc across. Ch 3, turn.

Row 4: Sk first dc, dc in each dc across, dc in top of turning ch. Ch 3 turn.

Row 5: Sk first dc, (yo hook, pull up a lp in next st, yo and through 2 lps on hook) twice, yo and through 3 lps on hook (1 dec made), dc in each st across to last dc and turning ch, dec 1 dc—20 dc. Ch 3, turn.

Rows 6 and 7: Work even in dc. Ch 3, turn each row.

Row 8: Sk first dc, dc in each of next 9 dc—10 dc for leg. Ch 3, turn.

Row 9: Work even on 10 dc. End off.

Work other leg to correspond.

BACK (make 2): With yellow, ch 13.

Rows 1 and 2: Repeat rows 1 and 2 of front—12 sc. Ch 3, turn.

Row 3: Sk first sc, dc in each of next 7 sc. Ch 3, turn. Work 1 row even in dc.

Row 5: Dec 1 dc, dc across—7 dc.

Row 6: Work even in dc.

Row 7: Work even in dc, ch 5.

Row 8: Dc in 3rd ch from hook and in each of next 2 ch, dc across—10 dc. Work 2 rows even on 10 dc. End off.

Sew side seams of pants. Sew inside leg seams. Make edging around top edge same as for dress. Put pants on bunny. Leaving back opening for tail, sew top edges tog.

STRAPS (make 2): With yellow, ch 4. Work even on 3 sc until strap is long enough to fit from top of pants in front to top of pants in back, crossing to opposite side in back. Sew straps in place.

BASKET: With brown, ch 2.

Rnd 1: 6 sc in 2nd ch from hook.

Rnd 2: 2 sc in each sc—12 sc.

Rnd 3: (Sc in next sc, 2 sc in next sc) 6 times—18 sc.

Rnd 4: Sc in each sc around.

Rnd 5: 2 sc in each sc—36 sc.

Rnd 6: Sc in each sc around.

Rnd 7: Dc in each sc around.

Rnd 8: Dc in each dc around. Hdc in next dc, sc in each of next 2 dc. Ch 1, turn.

Handle: Sc in each of 3 sts. Ch 1, turn. Work even on 3 sc for 5″. End off. Sew end of handle to opposite side of basket.

CARROT (make 2 pieces): With orange, ch 6.

Row 1: Sc in 2nd ch from hook and in next 4 ch. Ch 1, turn each row.

Rows 2-4: Work even on 5 sc.

Row 5: Dec 1 sc at center of row.

Rows 6-12: Work even on 4 sc.

Row 13: Dec 1 sc at center of row.

Rows 14-19: Work even on 3 sc.

Row 20: Dec 1 sc on row.

Rows 21-24: Work even on 2 sc.

Row 25: Work 2 sc tog. Work 1

row of 1 sc. End off, leaving long end. Sew 2 pieces tog, stuffing as you go. Cut 6″ lengths of lime yarn; sew to top of carrot across center of strands.

ONION (make 2 pieces): Beg at bottom, with natural, ch 7.

Row 1: Sc in 2nd ch from hook and in next 5 ch. Ch 1, turn each row.

Row 2: Work even on 6 sc.

Rows 3 and 4: Inc 1 sc at center of each row.

Row 5: Work even on 8 sc.

Row 6: Dec 1 sc at center of row.

Row 7: Work even on 7 sc.

Row 8: Dec 1 sc each side.

Row 9: Work 2 sc tog twice. End

off. Sew 2 pieces tog, stuffing as you go. At bottom, add a few strands of yarn; brush out to make roots. At top, add 2 chains of green, sewing at center to onion.

RADISH (make 2 pieces): With red, ch 6.

Row 1: Sc in 2nd ch from hook and in next 4 ch. Ch 1, turn each row.

Row 2: Work even on 5 sc.

Rows 3-5: Dec 1 sc each row. End off; leave end. Sew 2 pieces tog, stuffing as you go. Let short end hang at bottom.

LEAF (make 3): With green, leave 6″ end of yarn, ch 7.

Row 1: Dc in 3rd ch from hook and in next 4 ch; leave 6″ end, cut yarn. Ch 4 with 2 ends tog. Sew to radish.

PEAS (make 3): With lime, ch 2.

Rnd 1: 4 sc in 2nd ch from hook.

Rnds 2 and 3: Work even. End off. Stuff and sew into ball.

POD (make 2 pieces): With green, ch 13.

Row 1: Sc in 2nd ch from hook and in next 11 ch. Ch 1, turn each row.

Rows 2 and 3: Dec 1 sc each side. End off. Sew 2 pieces tog, leaving widest part open. Sew peas to bottom seam.

JOLLY BEANBAGS

These smiling beanbags are worked in the round with single crochet. Hat, head and body are one piece filled with beans. Arms and legs are made separately and sewn on.

SIZE: About 7″ high.
MATERIALS: Sport yarn, about ½ oz. of main color for each beanbag, smaller amounts of other colors. Small amounts of knitting worsted for hair and pompons. Steel crochet hook No. 00. Beans. Scraps of felt. All-purpose glue. Yarn needle.
GAUGE: 7 sc = 1″.
Note: All beanbags are worked in sc throughout.
CLOWN: HEAD AND BODY: Beg at tip of hat, with blue, ch 4, sl st in first ch to form ring.

Rnd 1: 5 sc in ring. Do not join rnds; mark ends of rnds.
Rnds 2-4: Work even.
Rnd 5: Inc 3 sc in rnd—8 sc.
Rnds 6-10: Work even.
Rnd 11: Inc 3 sc in rnd—11 sc.
Rnds 12-16: Work even.
Rnd 17: Inc 3 sc in rnd—14 sc.
Rnds 18-20: Work even.
Rnd 21: Inc 4 sc in rnd—18 sc.
Rnds 22 and 23: Work even.
Rnd 24: Inc 6 sc in rnd—24 sc.
Rnds 25 and 26: Work even.
Rnd 27: Inc 6 sc in rnd—30 sc.
Rnds 28 and 29: Work even.

Rnd 30: Inc 6 sc in rnd—36 sc.
Rnds 31 and 32: Work even. Cut blue; join white.
Rnds 33-37: With white, work even.
Rnd 38: Dec 6 sc evenly around—30 sc.
Rnds 39 and 40: Work even.
Rnd 41: Dec 6 sc evenly around—24 sc.
Rnd 42: Work even. Cut white; join blue.
Rnd 43: Inc 12 sc evenly around—36 sc.
Rnds 44 and 45: Work even.

Rnd 46: Inc 12 sc evenly around—48 sc.

Rnds 47-52: Work even.

Rnd 53: Inc 6 sc in rnd—54 sc.

Rnds 54-64: Work even.

Rnd 65: Dec 6 sc evenly around—48 sc.

Rnds 66 and 67: Work even. End off.

BASE: With blue, ch 2.

Rnd 1: 6 sc in 2nd ch from hook.

Rnd 2: 2 sc in each sc—12 sc.

Rnds 3-5: Inc 6 sc in each rnd—30 sc.

Rnds 6-8: Inc 10 sc in each rnd—60 sc.

Rnd 9: Work even. End off.

ARM (make 2): With white, ch 4, sl st in first ch to form ring.

Rnd 1: 6 sc in ring.

Rnd 2: Inc 1 sc in rnd—7 sc.

Rnds 3-5: Work even. Cut white; join blue.

Rnds 6-13: With blue, work even. End off.

LEG (make 2): With white, ch 4, sl st in first ch to form ring.

Rnd 1: 6 sc in ring.

Rnd 2: Inc 2 sc in rnd—8 sc.

Rnds 3-13: Work even. Cut white, join blue on rnd 8.

Rnd 14: Inc 2 sc in rnd—10 sc.

Rnds 15-21: Work even. End off.

FINISHING: Sew base to body, filling bag with beans before closing. (When figure is sitting, beans should come to neck.) Sew arms and legs shut flat; sew in place. Form feet by folding up bottom of leg and sewing through all thicknesses of "heel." Flatten face and make yellow loops of hair at each side of face. Trim cap and front of body with bright pompons. Glue on felt features: blue eyes, black pupils, red nose and mouth, green and red cheek patches.

ELF: Work as for clown with following changes: Beg with green,

work through rnd 32, making stripes of green, white, red, white, green, red, white, green, white, red, and green. Join pink and work through rnd 42. Join green and work in stripes of green, red, white, green, red, white, red, green, white, and green to end of rnd 67. Make base in green. Work arms with pink, changing to green

at end of rnd 5. Work legs in green only.

FINISHING: Finish as for clown with following changes: Sew on beard of red loops. Glue on felt features: green eyes, black pupils, red nose and mouth. Attach white pompon to tip of cap. Tack down top of cap to one side.

BOY: HEAD AND BODY: Beg at top of head, with pink, ch 4, sl st in first ch to form ring.

Rnd 1: 2 sc in each ch around—8 sc.

Rnd 2: Inc in every other st—12 sc.

Rnd 3: Inc in every other st—18 sc.

Rnds 4-6: Inc 6 sc each rnd—36 sc.

Rnds 7-17: Work even on 36 sc.

Rnd 18: Dec 6 sc evenly around—30 sc.

Rnds 19 and 20: Work even.

Rnd 21: Dec 6 sc evenly around—24 sc.

Rnd 22: Work even. Cut pink; join white.

Rnd 23: Inc in every other st—36 sc.

Rnds 24 and 25: Work even.

Rnd 26: Inc in every 3rd st—48 sc.

Rnds 27-32: Work even.

Rnd 33: Inc 6 sc in rnd—54 sc.

Rnds 34-44: Work even, changing to blue in rnd 40.

Rnd 45: Dec 6 sc evenly around—48 sc.

Rnds 46 and 47: Work even. End off.

Base: Make blue base as for clown.

ARM (make 2): Make as for clown's, beg with pink and changing to white at end of rnd 5.

LEG (make 2): With black, ch 4, sl st in first ch to form ring.

Rnd 1: 2 sc in each ch around—8 sc.

Rnds 2-7: Work even. Change to blue at end of rnd 7.

Rnds 8-20: Work even. End off.

FINISHING: Sew base to body, filling bag with beans before closing. Sew arms and legs shut flat; sew in place. Form feet by folding up bottom of leg and sewing through all thicknesses of "heel." Flatten out face and glue on felt features: blue eyes, deeper blue pupils, red mouth, pink ears. For boy's hair, sew orange yarn in loops to top of head; glue loops down on forehead and some strands over ear fronts.

HUMPTY DUMPTY: HEAD AND BODY: Beg at top, with white, ch 4, sl st in first ch to form ring.

Rnd 1: 2 sc in each ch—8 sc.

Rnd 2: Work even.

Rnd 3: Inc 1 sc in every other sc—12 sc.

Rnd 4: Inc 1 sc in every other sc—18 sc.

Rnd 5: Work even.

Rnd 6: Inc 1 sc in every 3rd sc—24 sc.

Rnd 7: Work even.

Rnd 8: Inc 1 sc in every other sc—36 sc.

Rnds 9 and 10: Work even.

Rnd 11: Inc 1 sc in every 3rd sc—48 sc.

Rnds 12-17: Work even.

Rnd 18: Inc 6 sc evenly around—54 sc.

Rnds 19 and 20: Work even. Change to green at end of rnd 20.

Rnds 21-30: Work even.

Rnd 31: Dec 6 sc evenly around—48 sc.

Rnds 32 and 33: Work even.

Rnd 34: Dec 6 sc evenly around—42 sc.

Rnd 35: Work even. End off.

BASE: With green, ch 2.

Rnd 1: 6 sc in 2nd ch from hook.

Rnd 2: 2 sc in each sc—12 sc.

Rnds 3-5: Inc 6 sc each rnd—30 sc.

Rnds 6 and 7: Inc 10 sc each rnd—50 sc.

Rnd 8: Work even. End off.

ARM (make 2): With white, ch 4, sl st in first ch to form ring.

Rnd 1: 6 sc in ring.

Rnd 2: Inc 1 sc in rnd—7 sc.

Rnds 3-5: Work even. Cut white; join green.

Rnds 6-11: Work even. End off.

LEG (make 2): With green, ch 4, sl st in first ch to form ring.

Rnd 1: 2 sc in each ch—8 sc.

Rnds 2-20: Work even. End off at end of rnd 20.

FINISHING: Sew base to body, filling with beans before closing. Sew arms and legs shut flat; sew in place. Form feet by folding up bottom of leg and sewing through all thicknesses of "heel." Sew loops of yellow yarn to top of head; glue down loops. Glue on felt features and trimming: green eyes, black pupils, red cheeks and mouth, white collar, green bow tie.

WALL: FRONT: With red, ch 25.

Row 1: Sc in 2nd ch from hook and in each ch across—24 sc. Ch 1, turn each row.

Rows 2-19: Sc in each sc across. End off.

BACK: Work as for front.

SIDE (make 2): With red, ch 13. Work as for front on 12 sc.

TOP: With white, work as for front on 24 sc until top is same depth as width (12 sc) of side.

BOTTOM: Work as for top.

FINISHING: With white, embroider "bricks" on front and two sides of wall with horizontal rows of running backstitch every 2 rows of crochet; make vertical straight stitches. Sew pieces tog, filling with beans before closing last seam.

THREE PILLOW PETS

Fantastic and friendly pillow pets to toss on a bed or pull up for a seat are easy to make in single crochet. Choose snail, turtle or mouse—or crochet all three.

TURTLE: SIZE: About 18″ long.

MATERIALS: Washable rug yarn, 1¾-oz. skeins: 7 skeins orange (O), 4 skeins green (G), 2 skeins yellow (Y) and 1 skein white (W). Aluminum crochet hook J/9. Scraps of pink, blue, yellow, black and red felt. Black buttonhole or rug thread. Cotton batting for stuffing. All-purpose glue. Rug needle.

GAUGE: 5 sc = 2″.

TURTLE: HEAD: Beg at top of head, with G, ch 9.

Rnd 1: Sc in 2nd ch from hook and in each of next 6 ch, 3 sc in last ch; working on opposite side of ch, sc in each of next 7 ch, 3 sc in next ch—20 sc. Do not join rnds; mark end of each rnd. Mark last st for back of head.

Rnd 2: (Sc in each of next 7 sc, 2 sc in each of next 3 sc) twice—26 sc.

Rnd 3: Sc in each of next 9 sc, 2 sc in each of next 3 sc, sc in each of next 10 sc, 2 sc in each of next 3 sc, sc in next sc—32 sc.

Rnd 4: Sc in each of next 11 sc, 2 sc in each of next 3 sc, sc in each of next 13 sc, 2 sc in each of next 3 sc, sc in each of next 2 sc—38 sc.

Rnds 5 and 6: Sc in each sc around.

Rnd 7: Sc in each of next 11 sc, (2 sc in next sc, sc in next sc) 3 times, sc in each of next 21 sc—41 sc.

Rnd 8: Repeat rnd 5.

Rnd 9: Sc in each of next 13 sc, (2 sc in next sc, sc in next sc) 3 times, sc in each of next 22 sc—44 sc.

Rnds 10-12: Repeat rnd 5.

Rnd 13: Sc in each of next 4 sc, ch 6 for front of neck, sk next 24 sc for front of head, sc in each of next 16 sc.

Rnd 14: Sc in each ch and sc around, inc 3 sc across back of head—29 sc.

Rnd 15: Sc in each sc around.

Rnds 16 and 17: Sc in each sc around, inc 3 sc across back of neck and dec 2 sc (**to dec 1 sc,** pull up a lp in each of 2 sc, yo hook and through 3 lps on hook) across front of neck—31 sc. End off.

NECK BASE: Beg at bottom, with G, ch 7.

Rnd 1: Sc in 2nd ch from hook and in each of next 4 ch, 3 sc in last ch; working on opposite side of ch, sc in each of next 4 sc, 3 sc in next ch—15 sc. Do not join rnds; mark end of each rnd.

Rnd 2: (Sc in each of next 5 sc, 2 sc in each of next 3 sc) twice—21 sc.

Rnd 3: (Sc in each of next 7 sc, 2 sc in each of next 3 sc) twice—27 sc.

Rnd 4: (Sc in each of next 9 sc, 2 sc in each of next 3 sc) twice—33 sc. End off. Weave neck base to head. Stuff firmly through chin opening.

UNDERCHIN: With G, ch 9. Sc in 2nd ch from hook and in each of next 7 ch—8 sc. Ch 1, turn.

Row 2: Sc in each sc across, 3 sc

in ch-1 turning; working on other side of starting ch, sc in each ch—19 sc. Ch 1, turn.

Row 3: Sc in each of 8 sc, 2 sc in each of next 3 sc, sc in each of next 8 sc—22 sc. End off. Weave under-chin into front opening, placing inc edge at front of head.

HIND LEGS (make 2): With G, ch 4, join with a sl st to form ring.

Rnd 1: 6 sc in ring. Do not join rnds; mark end of rnds.

Rnd 2: 2 sc in each sc around—12 sc.

Rnd 3: * Sc in next sc, 2 sc in next sc, repeat from * around—18 sc.

Rnd 4: * Sc in each of next 8 sc, 2 sc in next sc, repeat from * once—20 sc.

Rnds 5 and 6: Sc in each sc around.

Rnd 7: * Sc in each of next 2 sc, dec 1 sc, repeat from * around—15 sc.

Rnds 8 and 9: Sc in each sc around.

Rnd 10: * Sc in next sc, dec 1 sc, repeat from * around—10 sc.

Rnd 11: Sc in each sc around. End off.

FRONT LEGS (make 2): Work same as for hind legs to end of rnd 2—12 sc.

Rnd 3: * Sc in each of next 2 sc, 2 sc in next sc, repeat from * around—16 sc.

Rnds 4 and 5: Sc in each sc around.

Rnd 6: * Sc in each of next 2 sc, dec 1 sc, repeat from * around—12 sc.

Rnds 7 and 8: Sc in each sc around.

Rnd 9: * Sc in next sc, dec 1 sc, repeat from * around—8 sc.

Rnd 10: Sc in each sc around. End off.

TAIL: Beg at tip, with G, ch 4, join with a sl st to form ring.

Rnd 1: 5 sc in ring. Do not join rnds.

Rnds 2-4: Sc in each sc, inc 1 sc—8 sc.

Rnd 5: Sc in each sc around. End off.

BODY: Beg at center top, with O, ch 4, join with a sl st to form ring. Do not join rnds; mark end of rnds.

Rnd 1: 6 sc in ring.

Rnd 2: 2 sc in each sc around—12 sc.

Rnd 3: * Sc in next sc, 2 sc in next sc, repeat from * around—18 sc.

Rnd 4: * Sc in each of next 2 sc, 2 sc in next sc, repeat from * around—24 sc.

Rnd 5: * Sc in each of next 3 sc, 2 sc in next sc, repeat from * around—30 sc. Drop O; join W.

Rnd 6: With W, * sc in each of 4 sc, 2 sc in next sc, repeat from * around—36 sc. Cut W.

Rnd 7: With O, repeat rnd 6, end sc in last sc—43 sc.

Rnd 8: Repeat rnd 7, end sc in each of last 3 sc—51 sc.

Rnd 9: Repeat rnd 7, end sc in last sc—61 sc.

Rnd 10: * Sc in each of next 7 sc, 2 sc in next sc, repeat from * around, end sc in each of last 5 sc—68 sc. Drop O; join W.

Rnd 11: With W, repeat rnd 10, end sc in each of last 4 sc—76 sc. Cut W.

Rnd 12: With O, * sc in each of 8 sc, 2 sc in next sc, repeat from * around, end sc in each of last 4 sc—84 sc.

Rnds 13-15: With O, sc in each sc around. With W, work 1 rnd even. With O, work 4 rnds even. With W, work 1 rnd even. Repeat last 5 rnds twice. End off.

UNDERBODY: Beg at center, with Y, ch 4, join with a sl st to form ring. Do not join rnds; mark end of rnds.

Rnd 1: 7 sc in ring.

Rnd 2: 2 sc in each sc around—14 sc.

Rnd 3: * Sc in next sc, 2 sc in next sc, repeat from * around—21 sc.

Rnds 4-12: Continue to inc 7 sc evenly spaced every rnd—84 sc.

Rnd 13: Sc in each sc around. End off.

CHAIN TRIM (make 30): With W, leaving a 6″ end, ch 5. End off.

FINISHING: Join 6 chains, evenly spaced around, across each O stripe on body. Stuff body, legs and tail. Weave top of body to underbody, leaving opening for head. Insert neck in opening; sew in place. Tack back of head to body. Weave legs and tail to body. From felt, cut 12 pink toes, black nostrils and pupils, yellow outer eyes, blue eyelids and red mouth (see patterns). Glue in place. With black thread, work two long stitches between each toe.

SNAIL: SIZE: About 18″ long.

MATERIALS: Washable rug yarn, 1¾-oz. skeins: 5 skeins blue (B), 3 skeins green (G), 1 skein raspberry (R). Crochet hook size J/9. Scraps of lilac, white, black and pink felt. Cotton batting for stuffing. All-purpose glue. Rug needle.

GAUGE: 5 sc = 2″.

SNAIL: BODY: Beg at upper center with B, ch 4, join with a sl st to form ring.

Rnd 1: 7 sc in ring.

Rnd 2: 2 sc in each sc—14 sc.

Rnd 3: * Sc in next sc, 2 sc in next sc, repeat from * around—21 sc.

Rnd 4: * Sc in each of 2 sc, 2 sc in next sc, repeat from * around—28 sc.

Rnd 5: * Sc in each of 3 sc, 2 sc in next sc, repeat from * around—35 sc.

Rnd 6: * Sc in each of 4 sc, 2 sc in next sc, repeat from * around—42 sc.

Rnds 7-9: Sc in each sc around, inc 4 sc evenly spaced—54 sc.

Rnd 10: Sc in each sc around, inc 5 sc evenly spaced—59 sc.

Rnds 11-13: Repeat rnd 7—71 sc.

Rnds 14-16: Sc in each sc around, inc 3 sc evenly spaced—80 sc.

Rnds 17-22: Sc in each sc.

Rnds 23 and 24: Sc in each sc around, inc 6 sc evenly spaced—92 sc.

Rnds 25 and 26: Sc in each sc. End off. Mark last st for center back.

Shape Neck and Tail: Row 1: Sk 5 sts from marked st, sc in each of next 37 sts. End off.

Row 2: Beg at start of last row, from right side, sk 1 st, sc in each of next 35 sc. End off.

Row 3: Beg at start of last row, sk 1 st, sc in each of next 33 sc. End off.

Rows 4-6: Repeat last row, having 2 sc less each row—27 sc.

Sk 9 sc on last rnd for neck; with B, sc in each of next 37 sc, leaving 9 sts free for back. End off. Work same as for other side. From right side, with B, work 2 rnds sc around entire body. End off.

UNDERBODY: Beg at center, with B, ch 4. Join with a sl st to form ring. Do not join rnds; mark end of rnds.

Rnd 1: 7 sc in ring.

Rnd 2: 2 sc in each sc—14 sc.

Rnd 3: * Sc in next sc, 2 sc in next sc, repeat from * around—21 sc.

Rnd 4: * Sc in each of next 2 sc, 2 sc in next sc, repeat from * around—28 sc. Continue to inc 7 sc each rnd, having 1 more sc between incs each rnd, until there are 11 sc between incs—91 sc. End off. Weave top of body to underbody, leaving opening for head and tail.

HEAD: Beg at center top, with G, ch 4, join with a sl st to form ring.

Rnd 1: 6 sc in ring.

Rnd 2: 2 sc in each sc—12 sc.

Rnd 3: * Sc in next sc, 2 sc in next sc, repeat from * around—18 sc.

Rnd 4: * Sc in each of next 2 sc, 2 sc in next sc, repeat from * around—24 sc.

Rnds 5-9: Continue to inc 6 sc, evenly spaced, around—54 sc.

Rnds 10-20: Sc in each sc around.

Shape Neck: Next Rnds: * Sc in each of next 4 sc, dec 1 sc, repeat from * 25 times—28 sc remain.

Shape Back of Neck: Ch 5, sc in 2nd ch from hook and in each of next 3 ch, * sc in each of next 3 sc, 2 sc in next sc, repeat from * 6 times; working on other side of ch, work sc in each of 4 ch, mark next st for back of neck, work 3 sc in end of ch—46 sc. Work even until 35 rnds from start (center top of head). End off.

HEAD BASE: With G, ch 8.

Rnd 1: Sc in 2nd ch from hook and in each of next 5 ch, 3 sc in last ch; working on other side of ch, sc in each of next 6 ch, 3 sc in next st—18 sc.

Rnds 2-5: Work around, inc 3 sc on each end every rnd—42 sc.

Stuff head firmly. Weave head to base.

TAIL: With G, ch 4, join with a sl st to form ring.

Rnd 1: 4 sc in ring.

Rnd 2: 2 sc in each sc—8 sc.

Rnd 3: * Sc in next sc, 2 sc in next sc, repeat from * around—12 sc.

Rnds 4-13: Continue to inc 4 sc evenly spaced each rnd—52 sc.

Stuff body firmly. Insert base of head into front opening; sew in place. Stuff tail lightly; sew over back opening, keeping bottom of tail flat and rounding upper tail.

CHAIN: With R, make ch 3 yds. long; make another ch 14″ long.

HORNS (make 2): With G, ch 6.

Row 1: Sc in 2nd ch from hook and in each ch across. Ch 1, turn.

Rows 2 and 3: Sc in each sc across. End off, leaving a 10″ end. Thread needle with end; weave last row to starting ch. Sew a horn to each side of head as pictured.

ARMS (make 2): Beg at center, with G, ch 4, join with a sl st to form ring.

Rnd 1: 6 sc in ring.

Rnd 2: 2 sc in each sc—12 sc.

Rnds 3 and 4: Work same as for head—24 sc.

Rnd 5: Inc 2 sc around—26 sc. Work 3 rnds even. End off. Stuff lightly and sew to side of body, next to head.

Coil long chain around top of body as pictured: sew in place. Sew 14″ chain across back of body near bottom. From felt, cut black pupils, white inner eyes, lilac outer eyes and pink mouth (see patterns). Glue in place.

MOUSE: SIZE: About 20″ long, plus 25″ tail.

MATERIALS: Washable rug yarn, 1¾-oz. skeins: 8 skeins turquoise (T) and 2 skeins lavender (L). Aluminum crochet hook size J/9. Scraps of pink, black, white, red, yellow, green, blue and brown felt or any assorted colors. Cotton batting for stuffing. All-purpose glue. Rug needle. One yd. black round elastic.

GAUGE: 5 sc = 2″.

MOUSE: BODY: Beg at front, with T, ch 4, join with a sl st to form ring.

Rnd 1: 6 sc in ring. Do not join rnds; mark end of each rnd.

Rnd 2: 2 sc in each of 5 sc, sc in next sc—11 sc.

Rnd 3: 2 sc in each of 7 sc, sc in each of next 4 sc—18 sc.

Rnd 4: (2 sc in each of next 2 sc, sc in next sc) 3 times, sc in each of next 9 sc—24 sc.

Rnd 5: (Sc in next sc, 2 sc in next sc) 6 times, finish rnd—30 sc.

Rnds 6 and 7: Sc in each sc around.

Rnd 8: 2 sc in next sc, sc in each of next 8 sc, 2 sc in next sc, finish rnd—32 sc.

Rnd 9: (2 sc in next sc, sc in each of next 4 sc) 3 times, finish rnd—35 sc.

Rnd 10: Repeat rnd 9—38 sc.

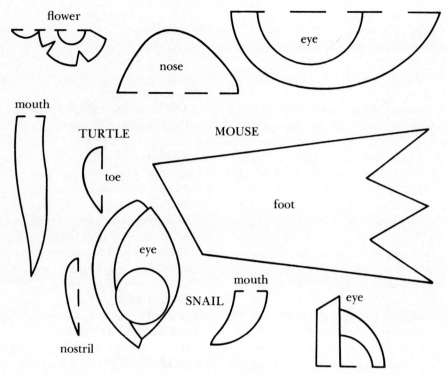

Complete half-patterns indicated by dash lines.

Patterns for Pillow Pets.

Rnd 11: (2 sc in next sc, sc in each of next 5 sc) 4 times, 2 sc in next sc, sc in each of next 13 sc—43 sc.

Rnd 12: (2 sc in next sc, sc in each of next 6 sc) 4 times, 2 sc in next sc, sc in each of next 14 sc—48 sc.

Rnd 13: (2 sc in next sc, sc in each of next 7 sc) 4 times, 2 sc in next sc, sc in each of next 15 sc—53 sc.

Rnds 14-18: Continue to inc 5 sc each rnd, having 1 sc more between incs each rnd (**note:** incs are at top of body)—78 sc.

Rnds 19-22: Sc in each sc around.

Rnd 23: (2 sc in next sc, sc in each of next 38 sc) twice—80 sc.

Rnds 24-55: Sc in each sc around.

Rnd 56: (Dec 1 sc, sc in each of next 8 sc) 8 times—72 sc.

Rnd 57: (Dec 1 sc, sc in each of next 7 sc) 8 times—64 sc.

Rnds 58-61: Continue to dec 8 sts evenly spaced each rnd having 1 sc less between decs—32 sc. Stuff body firmly.

Rnd 62: Sc in each sc around.

Rnd 63: (Dec 1 sc, sc in each of next 2 sc) 8 times—24 sc. Continue to stuff body.

Rnd 64: (Dec 1 sc, sc in next sc) 8 times—16 sc.

Rnd 65: (Dec 1 sc) 8 times—8 sc. End off.

TAIL: Beg at tip, with T, ch 4, join with a sl st to form ring.

Rnd 1: 5 sc in ring.

Rnds 2-20: Stuffing tail as you work, sc in each sc around.

Rnd 21: Inc 1 sc, sc in each sc—6 sc.

Rnds 22-40: Sc in each sc around.

Rnd 41: Repeat rnd 21—7 sc.

Rnds 42-70: Sc in each sc around. End off. Sew to body.

EARS: Make 2 L ears and 2 T ears as follows: Ch 4, join with a sl st to form ring.

Rnd 1: 7 sc in ring.

Rnd 2: 2 sc in each sc around—14 sc.

Rnd 3: * Sc in next sc, 2 sc in next sc, repeat from * around—21 sc.

Rnd 4: * Sc in each of next 2 sc, 2 sc in next sc, repeat from * around—28 sc.

Rnds 5-11: Continue to inc 7 sc evenly spaced around—77 sc. End off.

With wrong sides facing, weave 1 L and 1 T ear tog for each ear. Sew ears to sides of body from rnds 20-28. From felt, cut black nose and pupils, white eyes, pink feet and assorted colored flowers (see patterns). Glue in place as shown; sew feet to bottom of body. Pull three 10″ pieces of round elastic through nose for whiskers; knot ends.

PUPPET TRIO

Shown at bottom on page 236

All ready for a show—three hand puppets are fun to make in a bulky yarn. Rainbow clown is of single and long single crochet stitches; owl is all loop stitch; lion's loopy mane offsets a single crochet body. Each, 12" tall.

SIZE: 12" high.

MATERIALS: Acrylic rug yarn, 4 ozs. orange for lion; 4 ozs. brown for owl; small amounts of rainbow colors, black, peach and white for clown. Crochet hook size I or J. Scraps of felt: tan, brown, white, blue, red. Two buttons for owl's eyes.

GAUGE: 3 sc = 1".

LION: BACK: Beg at lower edge, with orange, ch 16. Sc in 2nd ch from hook and in next 14 ch. Ch 1, turn each row. Work 18 rows of 15 sc. End off.

Shape Arms: Ch 5, sc across 15 sc, ch 6. Sc in 2nd ch from hook and in 4 ch, sc in 15 sc, sc in 5 ch. Work 6 rows of 25 sc. End off.

Shape Head: Sc in 9th sc of last row and in each of next 8 sc. Ch 1, turn. Inc 4 sc evenly spaced across next row. Work 9 rows even. Dec 1 sc each side of next 2 rows. End off.

FRONT: Work as for back through arms.

Shape Head: Cut a 4" strip of cardboard 1" wide. Sc in 9th sc of last row. Insert hook in next sc, wind yarn around cardboard strip held at back of work, yo hook and through st; wind yarn around strip again, yo and through 2 lps on hook—double loop st made. Work double loop st in each of next 7 sc. Ch 1, turn. Inc 4 sc evenly spaced across next row. Complete head as for back. From wrong side, work double loop st around sides and top of head. Sew front and back tog; leave open at bottom.

EAR (make 2): Ch 8. Sc in 2nd ch from hook and in each ch. Ch 1; turn each row. Inc 1 sc at each side of next row. Work 2 rows even.

End off. Sew last row to head, drawing in at bottom of ear to shape ear as you sew.

TAIL: With double yarn, ch 20 loosely. Sl st in each ch. Sew tail to center of back about 7 rows up. Attach loops at other end.

FINISHING: From felt, cut tan eyes, brown pupils and nose. With thin yarn or embroidery cotton, embroider 3 white whiskers each side of nose. With brown, embroider mouth in outline st with French knots above mouth.

OWL: BACK: With brown, beg at lower edge, ch 16. Sc in 2nd ch from hook and in next 14 ch. Ch 1, turn each row.

Row 2: Cut a 4" strip of cardboard 1" wide. Insert hook in first sc, wind yarn around cardboard strip held at back of work, yo hook, draw lp through st, yo and through 2 lps—loop st made. Work loop st in each sc across.

Row 3: Sc in each loop st.

Rows 4-18: Alternate 1 row of loop st and 1 row of sc, end with loop st row. End off.

Shape Arms: Ch 5, sc across 15 sts, ch 6. Work long loop st in 2nd ch from hook (wind yarn twice around strip before finishing st) and in each of next 4 ch, plain loop st in each of 15 sc, long loop st in each of 5 ch.

Work 1 row sc, 1 row loop st (with 5 long loop sts each end), 1 row sc, 1 row loop st. End off.

Shape Head: Sk first 8 sts, sc in each of 9 sts. Ch 1, turn. Work in loop st across. On next row, inc 4 sc evenly across. Alternating 1 row loop st and 1 row sc, work even for 8 rows. Working in loop st, make first 3 and last 3 loops in long loop st. End off.

FRONT: Work as for back, working 7 rows for arms instead of 5.

Shape Head: Work as for back through row 3—13 sc.

Row 4: Work 5 loop sts, 3 sc, 5 loop sts.

Row 5: Work even in sc.

Row 6: Work 2 loop sts, 3 sc, 3 loop sts, 3 sc, 2 loop sts.

Rows 7 and 8: Repeat rows 5 and 6.

Row 9: Work even in sc.

Row 10: Work even in loop st.

Rows 11 and 12: Repeat rows 9 and 10.

Row 13: Work even in sc.

Row 14: Work in loop st, making 3 long loop sts each end. End off.

FINISHING: Sew front and back tog; leave open at bottom. Sew on button eyes. For beak, with orange, ch 4. Sc in 2nd ch from hook, hdc in next ch, dc in last ch. Sew to face.

CLOWN: BACK: Beg at lower edge, with purple, ch 16.

Row 1: Sc in 2nd ch from hook and in next 14 ch. Ch 1, turn each row.

Row 2: Sc in each sc. Change to blue.

Row 3: Sc in first sc, * long sc in next sc (**to make long sc,** work sc in row below you are working on), sc in next sc, repeat from * across.

Row 4: Sc in each sc. Change to green. Work 2 rows of sc. Change to yellow.

Row 7: Repeat row 3. Work 1 row of sc. Change to orange. Work 2 rows sc. Change to red.

Rows 11 and 12: Repeat rows 3 and 4. Change to purple. Work 2 rows sc. Change to blue.

Rows 15-18: Repeat rows 3-6. End off green.

Shape Arms: Row 19: With yellow, ch 5, work row 3 across 15 sc, ch 6. Sc in 2nd ch from hook and in 4 ch, sc in 15 sc, sc in 5 ch—25 sc. Continue in striped pat for 5 more rows, working first red row in long sc pat. End off. Turn.

Shape Head: With peach, sc in 9th sc of last row and in each of next 8 sc. Ch 1, turn. Inc 4 sc evenly spaced across next row. End off peach. Turn.

From wrong side, with orange, work in loop st across. **(To make loop st,** see Owl: Back: Row 2.) Ch 1, turn. Sc in each lp st. Alternate 1 row loop st, 1 row sc until there are 6 rows of loop st. Dec 1 sc each side of next row. End off.

FRONT: Work as for back through 2nd row of head. Do not

cut peach. Work even in sc for 3 more rows.

Row 6 (right side): Sc in 6 sc, finishing 6th sc with red; with red, 4 dc in next sc, drop lp from hook; insert hook in first dc, draw dropped lp through, draw peach through red lp, finish row. Work 5 more rows even. Change to orange. Dec 1 sc each side of next row. From wrong side, work 1 row of loop st. End off.

HANDS: With white, work 5 sc across end of arm piece. Ch 1, turn. Work sc in each sc. End off. Work hand on each arm end.

Sew back and front tog; leave open at bottom.

EAR (make 2): With peach, ch 6. Sc in 2nd ch from hook and in

each of 4 ch. Work 1 more row of 5 sc. End off. Sew to side of head.

FEATURES: From felt, cut white eyes, blue pupils, red mouth. Sew in place.

CAP: With black, ch 4. Sc in 2nd ch from hook and in next 2 ch. Ch 1, turn each row. Working in back lps only, work 24 rows of 3 sc. Working across one long side of piece, work sc in each row—24 sc. Work 4 more rows of sc. Dec 8 sc evenly spaced across next row. Work 1 row even —16 sc. Dec 6 sc across next row. End off. Sew back seam. Draw top of cap tog. Sew on 2″ pompon made of rainbow colors.

GOLDILOCKS AND BEARS

Shown at top on pages 236–237

Goldilocks and the Three Bears are all ready for dinner. Single crochet bodies are sewn together, then dressed in double crochet clothes, all of knitting worsted. Papa Bear stands a tall 18″.

SIZES: Goldilocks: 13″ high. Bears: 14″, 16″ and 18″ high.

MATERIALS: Knitting-worsted-weight yarn, 9 ozs. brown (makes all 3 bears); 2 ozs. each of pink, green and red; 1 oz. each of natural, yellow, white, black, royal blue and light blue. Crochet hook size E. Stuffing. Two clear shank buttons with black center for Goldilocks. Five small black shank buttons. Four large black shank buttons.

GAUGE: 5 sc = 1″; 7 dc = 2″.

GOLDILOCKS: HEAD AND BODY (make 2 pieces): Beg at top of head, with pink, ch 9. Sc in 2nd ch from hook and in each ch across—8 sc. Ch 1, turn each row. Inc 1 sc each side of next 4 rows —16 sc. Work 8 rows even. Dec 1 sc each side of next 5 rows—6 sc.

Shape Arms: Sc in each of 6 sc, ch 26. Sc in 2nd ch from hook and in each ch across, sc in each sc; ch 26 for 2nd arm. Sc in 2nd ch from hook and in each ch and sc across—56 sc. Work even for 3 rows.

Next Row: Sc in 36 sc. Ch 1, turn. Sc in 16 sc. Ch 1, turn. Work even for 8 rows. Cut pink. With white, work even for 8 rows.

Next Row: Dec 1 sc each side— 14 sc.

Shape Leg: Sc in 7 sc. Ch 1, turn.

Next Row: Dec 1 sc, sc in 5 sc.

Next Row: Work even on 6 sc. Cut white. With pink, work even for 20 rows. Cut pink.

Shape Foot: With black, sc in 6 sc, ch 7. Sc in 2nd ch from hook and in each ch and sc across—12 sc. Work even for 4 rows. End off. Work 2nd leg to correspond.

HAND: With pink, work 4 sc on side of arm end, 5 sc across end of arm, 4 sc on other side of arm end.

Sew body pieces tog, right side out, stuffing as you go.

DRESS (make 2 pieces): With light blue, beg at top, ch 18.

Row 1: Dc in 4th ch from hook (counts as 2 dc), dc in each ch across—16 dc. Turn each row.

Rows 2-5: Ch 3, sk first dc, dc in each dc across.

Row 6: Work in dc, inc 1 dc in every 4th st—20 dc.

Rows 7-11: Work even. End off. Sew 2 pieces tog from row 6 to lower edge each side. Join 2 sts of back and front at each shoulder.

SLEEVES: With light blue, work 22 dc around armhole. On next rnd, work 2 sts tog around (yo hook, draw up a lp in each of 2 dc, yo and through all lps on hook).

EDGING: Join white in seam at lower edge, * sc in next dc, 2 sc in next dc, repeat from * around.

Next Rnd: Sl st in first sc, * sl st, ch 2, sl st in next sc, sl st in next sc, repeat from * around. End off.

SASH: With white, make a ch 24″ long. Sc in 2nd ch from hook and in each ch across. End off. Tie sash into a bow at back.

HAIR: For long side and back curls, tie yellow yarn around a pencil. Wind yarn around pencil to desired length, being careful not to overlap yarn. Cut yarn, leaving 6″ end. Thread end in yarn needle, run needle through each twist of yarn from last winding to top. Slip off pencil, pull up a bit and twist into shape. Sew to head. Sew long curls to head part way down. For curls on crown of head, wind loops of yarn around finger and sew on.

Embroider red mouth in satin stitch, red French knot nose. Sew on button eyes. Embroider yellow lashes.

BEARS: Note: Directions are for Baby Bear. Changes for Mama Bear and Papa Bear are in parentheses.

HEAD AND BODY (make 2 pieces): Beg at top of head, with brown, ch 11 (13-15). Sc in 2nd ch from hook and in each ch across—10 (12-14) sc. Working in sc, inc 1 sc each side of next 4 rows. Ch 1, turn each row. Work 4 (5-7) rows even. Inc 1 sc each side of next row—20 (22-24) sc. Work 3 (4-5) rows even. Dec 1 sc each side of next 5 rows—10 (12-14) sc. Work 1 row even.

Shape Arms: Sc in 10 (12-14) sc, ch 23 (24-26); turn. Sc in 2nd ch from hook and in each ch, sc in 10 (12-14) sc, ch 23 (24-26). Sc in 2nd ch from hook and in each ch, sc in 32 (35-39) sc. Work 5 (5-7) rows even. On next row, sc in 37 (40-44) sc; ch 1, turn. Sc in 20 (22-24) sc; ch 1, turn.

Work 14 (16-19) rows even. Dec 1 sc each side of next row.

Form Leg: Sc in 9 (10-11) sc; ch 1, turn. Dec 1 sc, sc in 7 (8-9) sc. Work 10 (9-11) rows even. Dec 1 sc in center of next row. Work 4 (9-9) rows even.

Shape Foot: Sc in 7 (8-9) sc, ch 8 (9-10). Sc in 2nd ch from hook and in each ch, sc in 7 (8-9) sc—14 (16-18) sc. Work 4 (5-6) rows even. End off. Make other leg to correspond.

EAR: With brown, sc in 3 (3-4) end sts on top of head, make 3 (4-

4) sc on side of head—6 (7-8) sc. Ch 1, turn. Inc 1 sc each side of next row. Work 2 (2-4) rows even. Dec 1 sc each side of next 3 rows. End off. Work other ear to correspond. Work ears on both body pieces.

PAW PADS (make 2): With natural, ch 2.

Rnd 1: 6 sc in 2nd ch from hook.

Rnd 2: 2 sc in each sc—12 sc. For Baby and Mama Bear, ch 1, turn. Sc in 4 sc. End off. For Papa Bear, work 1 rnd even, ch 1, turn. Sc in 5 sc. End off.

Sew body pieces tog around edges, right side out, stuffing as you go. Sew pads to arm ends.

BABY BEAR: NOSE: With natural, ch 2.

Rnd 1: 6 sc in 2nd ch from hook.

Rnd 2: 2 sc in each sc—12 sc.

Rnd 3: Work even.

Rnd 4: * Sc in next sc, 2 sc in next sc, repeat from * around—18 sc.

Rnd 5: Sc in next 13 sc. End off. Stuff and sew to face.

Make mouth of red straight sts. Sew on small buttons for eyes and tip of nose.

SWEATER: FRONT: With royal blue, ch 20. Dc in 4th ch from hook (counts as 2 dc), dc in each ch across—18 dc. Turn each row. Ch 3, sk first dc, dc in each dc across, dc in top of turning ch. Repeat last row 4 times more.

Next Row: Dc in 9 dc, ch 2, turn. Work 4 more rows, dec 1 dc at inside (neck) edge every row. End off. Work 2nd half of front to correspond.

BACK: Work 11 rows of 18 dc. Sew back and front tog on bear.

MAMA BEAR: NOSE: Work as for Baby Bear but complete last

rnd. Make mouth of red straight sts. Sew on small button at tip of nose. Sew on large buttons for eyes. For eyelids, take 3 sts across top of eyes with brown; tack sts tog.

DRESS: SKIRT (make 2): With red, ch 23. Sc in 2nd ch from hook and in each ch across. Work 1 row even. Ch 3; sk first sc, dc across.

Next Row: Ch 3, sk first dc, * 2 dc in next dc, dc in next dc, repeat from * across, end 2 dc in top of ch 3—33 dc.

Next Row: Inc in every 3rd st—44 dc. Work 2 rows even. End off.

BIB (make 1): With red, ch 12. Work even on 10 dc for 6 rows. End off.

STRAPS (make 2): With red, ch 3. Work in rows of 2 sc until strap is long enough to go from top of bib to top of skirt, crossing in back. Sew skirt tog.

PAPA BEAR: NOSE: Work as for Baby Bear through rnd 2.

Rnd 3: * Sc in next sc, 2 sc in next sc, repeat from * around—18 sc. Work 1 rnd even.

Rnd 5: Repeat rnd 3—27 sc. Work 1 rnd even. End off. Stuff and sew to face.

Make mouth of red straight sts. Sew on small button at top of nose. Sew on large buttons for eyes.

PANTS (make 2): With green, ch 25. Sc in 2nd ch from hook and in each ch across. Work 1 row even—24 sc. Work 6 rows of dc.

Next Row: Work 12 dc, turn. Working on one leg only, dec 1 dc at inside edge on next 2 rows. Work 7 rows even. End off. Make other leg to correspond.

SUSPENDERS (make 2): With green, ch 6. Work in rows of 4 dc until straps are long enough to cross in back. Sew side seams of pants together.

CAMPFIRE PALS

Shown at bottom on page 237

*Campfire pals, an Indian girl and boy, in easy single crochet rows, have
"clothes" that are embroidered details and yarn fringes; boy's apron ties on.*

SIZES: Girl: 13" high. Boy: 14" high.

MATERIALS: Knitting-worsted-weight yarn, 3 ozs. dark brown; 2 ozs. each of rust and black; small amounts of yellow and red. Crochet hook size E. Four black shank buttons. Two yellow feathers. Scrap of brown felt. Stuffing.

GAUGE: 5 sc = 1".

GIRL: HEAD AND BODY (make 2 pieces): Beg at top of head with rust, ch 10. Sc in 2nd ch from hook and in each ch across. Ch 1, turn each row. Inc 1 sc each side of next 4 rows—17 sc. Work even for 9 rows. Dec 1 sc each side of next 5 rows—7 sc. Work 1 row even. Change to brown. Ch 22 for arm. Sc in 2nd ch from hook and in each ch across, sc in each sc; ch 22 for 2nd arm. Sc in 2nd ch from hook and in each ch and sc across—49 sc. Work even for 5 rows.

Next Row: Sc in 34 sc. Ch 1, turn.

Next Row: Sc in 19 sc. Ch 1, turn. Work even on 19 sc for 25 rows. End off.

LEGS: With brown, sc in 4th sc from side edge and in each of next 4 sc. Ch 1, turn. Work 10 more rows even.

Next Row: Sc across, ch 6. Sc in 2nd ch from hook and in each ch and sc—10 sc. Work 4 rows even. End off. Work other leg to correspond.

HAND: Beg at top of sleeve end, with rust, work 6 sc across wrist edge, leaving 2 rows free at bottom. Work 4 more rows. Dec 1 sc each side of next row. Work 1 row even. End off. Work other hand to correspond.

FINISHING: Sew 2 pieces tog, right side out, stuffing as you go. Knot strands of brown through sts at bottom of arms and around "skirt" 3 rows above start of legs. Embroider dress with cross-stitch, French knots and straight stitch in red and yellow (see illustration, page 237 and stitch details, page 320). Outline top of moccasins with chain stitch.

FACE: With rust, ch 2. Work 6 sc in 2nd ch from hook. Pull into a ball and sew to face for nose. Sew on button eyes. Cut felt crescent mouth; glue on.

HAIR: Cut 30 strands of black yarn about 24" long. With needle threaded with black yarn, fasten yarn at center of first strand, run yarn through center of each strand, keeping strands in single layer. Now cut 20 strands 6" long, run same threaded yarn through center of these strands. Sew to head along center "part," long hair in front. Tie a short piece of yarn tightly around front hair at each side of lower face; sew to face. Braid hair below tie. Wind ends with red yarn. Bring short ends of back hair under long hair at sides; sew ends in place.

HEADBAND: With yellow, ch 40. Work 1 row sc. End off. Sew or tie ends tog. Trim with red running st.

BOY: HEAD AND BODY (make 2 pieces): Work as for girl to end of neck; do not change to brown. Ch 28 for arm. Sc in 2nd ch from hook and in each ch and sc across; ch 28 for 2nd arm. Sc in 2nd ch from hook and in each ch and sc across—61 sc. Work 3 rows even.

Next Row: Sc in 41 sc. Ch 1, turn.

Next Row: Sc in 21 sc. Ch 1, turn. Work 1 row even. Dec 1 sc each side of next row. Work 3 rows even. Dec 1 sc each side of next row. Work 7 rows even. Dec 1 sc each side of next row. Work 1 row even. Change to brown, work 10 rows even.

Legs: Sc in 7 sc. Ch 1, turn. Work 18 more rows of 7 sc.

Next Row: Sc in 7 sc, ch 8.

Next Row: Sc in 2nd ch from hook and in each ch across, sc in 5 sc. Ch 1, turn.

Next Row: Sc in 12 sc. Work 3 more rows even. End off. Work other leg to correspond.

HAND: Working on arm end, with rust, sc in 4 sc on one edge, work 2 sc in corner, 4 sc across end, 2 sc in corner, 4 sc on other edge.

FINISHING: Sew 2 pieces tog, right side out, stuffing as you go. Knot strands of brown through sts down side of legs. Make face and hair same as girl's. Outline top of moccasins with red chain st; decorate with yellow straight sts.

BREECHCLOTH (make 2): With brown, ch 14. Work 7 rows of 13 sc. With yellow, work 1 row sc around 2 long and 1 short edge. Embroider as desired. Tie tog on doll at sides.

Necklaces are single chains in red and yellow.

HEADBAND: With red, ch 40. Work 1 row sc. With yellow, work 1 rnd sc around band. Tie or sew ends tog. Add two feathers at back.

INDIAN PONY

Shown at bottom on page 237

Pony, with body pieces made in the round, is 10" high.

SIZE: 10" high.

MATERIALS: Knitting-worsted-weight yarn, 2 ozs. brown; ½ oz. natural; small amounts of black, orange and gold. Crochet hook size E. Two black shank buttons. Stuffing.

GAUGE: 5 sc = 1".

PONY: BODY: Beg at back, with brown, ch 2.

Rnd 1: 6 sc in 2nd ch from hook.

Rnd 2: Sc in each sc—12 sc.

Rnd 3: (Sc in next sc, 2 sc in next sc) 6 times—18 sc.

Rnd 4: (Sc in next sc, 2 sc in next sc) 9 times—27 sc.

Rnd 5: (2 sc in next sc, sc in each of next 2 sc) 9 times—36 sc.

Rnds 6-30: Work even.

Rnd 31: (Dec 1 sc over next 2 sc, sc in each of next 2 sc) 9 times—27 sc.

Rnd 32: (Dec 1 sc over next 2 sc, sc in next sc) 9 times—18 sc.

Rnd 33: (Sc in next sc, dec 1 sc over next 2 sc) 6 times—12 sc. Stuff body. Dec to 6 sc in next rnd. Sew up hole.

NECK: With brown, ch 25; sl st in first ch to form ring. Work 10 rnds of 25 sc. End off. Stuff and sew to body.

HEAD: Work as for body through rnd 4. Work 10 rnds even.

Next Rnd: (Dec 1 sc over next 2 sc) 3 times, sc in next 21 sc. Work 1 rnd even.

Next Rnd: Sc in 9 sc, (dec 1 sc over next 2 sc) 3 times, sc in 9 sc—21 sc. Work 1 rnd even.

Next Rnd: (Dec 1 sc over next 2 sc, sc in next sc) 7 times. Work 1 rnd even. (Dec 1 sc over next 2 sc) 7 times. End off. Stuff; sew up hole. Sew to neck.

FRONT LEG (make 2): With brown, ch 10; sl st in first ch to form ring. Work 18 rnds of 10 sc. Change to black and dec 1 sc in next rnd. Work 2 rnds even. End off. For bottom, with black, ch 2. Work 6 sc in 2nd ch. Stuff leg and sew on bottom piece. Sew legs to body.

BACK LEG (make 2): With brown, ch 12; sl st in first ch to form ring. Work 10 rnds of 12 sc. On next rnd, dec 2 sc. Work 9 rnds even. Change to black and dec 1 sc in rnd. Work 2 rnds even. End off. Finish same as front leg. Bind a bit at first dec rnd.

EAR (make 2): With brown, ch 6. Sc in 2nd ch from hook and in each ch. Ch 2; working back on other side of starting ch, sc in each of 5 ch. Sew on.

FINISHING: Sew buttons to face for eyes. For tail, cut 12 strands of natural about 12" long. Sew to pony at center of strands. For mane, cut 50 to 60 strands about 6" long. Sew to back of head and neck through center of strands. For forelock, sew a small bunch of yarn to head between ears.

SADDLE BLANKET: With orange, ch 4; sl st in first ch to form ring. Ch 3, 11 dc in ring. Sl st in top of ch 3. End off. With gold, (2 dc in each of 2 dc, 2 dc, ch 2, 2 dc in next dc) 4 times. Join. End off. With orange, sc in each dc around, 2 sc in each corner sp. Work 1 row of sc along one side of square. Change to gold; work 1 more row of sc along same side. End off. Work 1 row of orange sc and 1 row of gold sc across opposite side of square. Loop gold fringe in every other sc on gold rows. Make orange ch long enough to fit under pony to hold blanket on. Work 1 row sc. Sew ends to blanket each side.

JACK AND JILL

Shown on page 242

Jack and Jill, 14" tall, are worked in the same easy crochet. Jack wears green shortalls; Jill's ruffled pinafore has a barrette to match. In knitting worsted with yarn hair, felt features.

SIZE: 14" high.

MATERIALS: Knitting-worsted-weight yarn, 2 ozs. each of pink, white and green; small amounts of black, light brown and dark brown. Crochet hook size F. Stuffing. Scraps of black and bright-pink felt. Glue. Top of spray can. Eight inches of No. 20 wire.

GAUGE: 9 sc = 2".

JACK AND JILL: HEAD AND BODY (make 2 pieces for each doll): Beg at top, with pink, ch 9.

Row 1: Sc in 2nd ch from hook

and in each of next 7 ch. Ch 1, turn each row.

Rows 2-5: Inc 1 sc each side each row.

Rows 6-13: Work even on 16 sc.

Rows 14-18: Dec 1 sc each side each row.

Row 19: Work even on 6 sc. Change to white, ch 18.

Row 20: Sc in 2nd ch from hook and in each of next 16 ch, sc in 6 sc, ch 18.

Row 21: Sc in 2nd ch from hook and in each of next 16 ch, sc in each sc across—40 sc.

Rows 22-24: Work even.

Row 25: Sc in 28 sc. Ch 1, turn.

Row 26: Sc in 16 sc. Ch 1, turn.

Rows 27-42: Work even.

Row 43: Dec 1 sc each side—14 sc.

LEG: Row 44: Sc in 7 sc. Ch 1, turn.

Row 45: Sc 2 sc tog, sc in 5 sc.

Row 46: Work even on 6 sc. Change to pink.

Rows 47-58: With pink, work even. Change to white.

Rows 59-66: With white, work even. Change to black.

Row 67: With black, sc in 6 sc, ch 7.

Row 68: Sc in 2nd ch from hook and in each of next 5 ch, sc in 6 sc.

Rows 69-72: Work even on 12 sc. End off. Beg with row 44, make other leg to correspond.

CUFF AND HAND: With white, work 5 sc across end of arm. Work 2 rows even. Change to pink, work 5 rows even. Dec 1 sc each side of next row. End off.

FINISHING: Sew 2 body pieces tog, stuffing as you go.

JILL'S HAIR: Cut 14 strands of light-brown yarn. Fold strands in half and arrange as bangs. Glue loops across top back of head; sew bangs down along seam at top of head. Cut 45 strands of same yarn 15″ long. Arrange across top of bangs and back of head; sew down center of head. Trim to even length. Glue to sides and back of head.

JACK'S EARS: With pink, ch 4, 2 sc in 2nd ch from hook, sc in next ch, 2 sc in last ch. End off. Sew an ear to each side of head.

JACK'S HAIR: Thread light-brown yarn in tapestry needle. Take long straight sts across head for hair. Sew down from front to back at one side of center. Have a few loose strands at front and at back for cowlick.

FEATURES: Make ½″ black felt circles for eyes, tiny pink circles for nose, pink crescent for mouth. Glue on.

CLOTHES: JUMPER: SKIRT: With green, ch 35.

Row 1: Sc in 2nd ch from hook and in each remaining ch. Ch 1, turn.

Row 2: Work even on 34 sc. Ch 3, turn.

Row 3: * 2 dc in next sc, dc in next sc, repeat from * across, end 2 dc in last sc. Ch 3, turn.

Rows 4 and 5: Work even in dc. End off. Sew back seam.

For suspenders, work 2 strips 2 sc wide and 7″ long. Make cross-strap 2 sc wide and 1¼″ long. Sew suspenders to skirt, crossing in back. Sew cross-strap in place.

For shoulder ruffle, work 3 dc in each of 7 rows of suspenders, centered on shoulder. Edge each ruffle with white; sl st in first dc, * sl st, ch 2, sl st in next dc, sl st in next dc, repeat from * across. Work same edging on skirt. For edging on panties, with white, ch 13. Work on ch as for skirt ruffle. Sew on.

HAIRBOW: With green, ch 6. Work in rows of 5 sc for 1½″. Work white edging on each end as for skirt ruffle. Gather bow at center; sew on.

JACK'S PANTS: Make suspenders same as for Jill, but 8″ long. For pants, with green, ch 17.

Row 1: Sc in 2nd ch from hook and in each remaining ch. Ch 1, turn.

Row 2: Work even on 16 sc. Ch 3, turn.

Row 3: Dc in each sc. Ch 3, turn.

Row 4: Dc in each dc. Ch 3, turn.

Row 5: Dc in 8 dc. Ch 3, turn.

Row 6: Work even. End off. Work 2 rows of dc on remaining 8 dc of row 4. Make another piece the same. Sew side seams and leg seams. With white, work 1 row sc around each pants leg.

PAIL: Make 2 holes in plastic cover for spray can with a needle (held with pliers) heated over stove burner. Bend wire in place through holes for pail handle. With brown, work ch over wire, in front, then in back alternately. Work a round piece for bottom of pail and a straight piece in rows of sc for sides. Sew tog. Slip on pail.

4
CROCHET FOR THE HOME

ROSETTE BEDSPREAD

This elegant bedspread is equally beautiful in white or any pastel color, shown over contrasting fabric. Square motifs, joined in the making, have raised flower centers on round medallion patterns and picot-loop outlines to form the squares. Crisscross edging and fringe add an unusual border.

SIZE: 56" x 77", excluding fringe.

MATERIALS: Mercerized knitting and crochet cotton, 26 250-yd. balls of white or ecru for motifs, 12 balls for edging and fringe. Or 37 175-yd. balls of color for motifs, 17 balls for edging and fringe. Steel crochet hook No. 7.

GAUGE: Motif = 7" square.

FIRST MOTIF: Ch 12; sl st in first ch to form ring.

Rnd 1: 24 sc in ring; sl st in first sc.

Rnd 2: Ch 11, * tr in next sc, sk 1 sc, tr in next sc, ch 7, repeat from * around, end ch 7, tr in next sc, sl st in 4th ch of ch 11.

Rnd 3: Sl st in first lp, ch 3, 8 dc in same lp, * 7 dc over upright bar

of next tr, sk next sc on rnd 1, 7 dc over upright bar of next tr, 9 dc in next lp, repeat from * around, end 7 dc over ch 4, sl st in top of ch 3—8 petals.

Rnd 4: Sc in same ch as sl st, sc in each dc around, sl st in first sc. End off.

Rnd 5: Join thread in sp between 2 petals (sp formed by 2 tr

of rnd 2); working in back of petals, sc in same sp, * ch 7, sc in next sp, repeat from * 6 times, ch 2, dtr in first sc for last lp—8 lps.

Rnd 6: 3 sc in lp just made, * ch 7, 3 sc in next lp, repeat from * 6 times, ch 3, tr in first sc.

Rnd 7: Ch 4, 2 tr and 3 dc in lp just made, * sk 1 sc, sc in next sc, 3 dc, 5 tr and 3 dc in next lp, repeat from * 6 times, sk 1 sc, sc in next sc, 3 dc, 2 tr in first lp, sl st in top of ch 4.

Rnd 8: Ch 4, 2 tr in same place as sl st, * dc in each of next 3 sts; leaving the last lp of each dc on hook, work dc in next st, sk 3 sts, dc in next st, yo hook and through all lps on hook, dc in each of next 3 sts, 5 tr in next st, repeat from * around, end 2 tr in same place as first tr, sl st in top of ch 4.

Rnd 9: Sc in same place as sl st, * ch 12, sk 11 sts, sc in next st (center

tr of 5 tr), ch 19, sc in same st, ch 12, sk 11 sts, sc in next st, ch 8, sc in same st, repeat from * around, end ch 12, sc in same place as first sc, ch 4, tr in first sc.

Rnd 10: Ch 3, 6 dc in lp just made, * 9 sc in next sp, 29 dc in next lp, 9 sc in next sp, 13 dc in next lp, repeat from * around, end 6 dc in first lp, sl st in top of ch 3.

Rnd 11: Ch 6, dc in same place as sl st, * ch 9, sk 9 dc on next lp, tr in next dc, ch 5, tr in same dc, sk 4 dc, tr in next dc, ch 7, tr in same dc, sk 4 tr, tr in next dc, ch 5, tr in same dc, ch 9, sk 6 dc on next lp, dc in next dc, ch 3, dc in same dc, repeat from * around, end ch 9, sl st in 3rd ch of ch 6.

Rnd 12: Sl st in next lp, 2 sc in same lp, ch 3, sl st in last sc (picot made), sc in same lp, * ch 7, (2 sc in next lp, ch-3 picot, sc in same lp, ch 7) twice, tr in center ch of next

lp, ch 7, tr in same ch, (ch 7, 2 sc in next lp, ch-3 picot, sc in same lp) 3 times, repeat from * around, end ch 2 instead of ch 7, dtr in first sc.

Rnd 13: 2 sc, picot and sc in lp just made, * (ch 7, 2 sc, picot and sc in next lp) 3 times, ch 7, tr, ch 7, tr in center ch of next lp, (ch 7, 2 sc, picot and sc in next lp) 3 times, repeat from * around, end ch 7, sl st in first sc. End off.

SECOND MOTIF: Work as for first motif until first tr has been completed at corner on row 13, ch 3, sl st in corner lp on first motif, ch 3, tr in same ch as last tr on second motif, (ch 3, sl st in next lp on first motif, ch 3—joining lp made —2 sc, picot and sc in next lp on second motif) 6 times, a joining lp, tr in center ch of next lp on second motif, a joining lp, tr in same ch, complete as for first motif.

Make 8 rows of 11 motifs, joining each to previous one as second motif was joined to first. Where 4 corners meet, join 3rd and 4th corners to joining of previous motifs.

EDGING: With wrong side facing, join thread in first corner lp on either long side of bedspread, 2 sc in corner lp, * (ch 39, sk next picot, 3 sc in next picot) 3 times **, ch 39, sk joining between motifs, 3 sc in next picot, (ch 39, sk next picot, 3 sc in next picot) twice, ch 39, 3 sc in next joining between motifs, repeat from * along side ending last repeat at **, ch 39, sk next corner lp, 3 sc in next picot, continue in this manner along next 2 sides, end 2 sc in last corner lp on second long side. Ch 1, turn.

Row 2: Sc in first sc, * dc in each of 19 ch, dc, ch 9 and dc in next ch, dc in each of next 19 ch, sk 1 sc, sc in next sc, repeat from * to end. End off.

Row 3: With wrong side facing, working in front of previous row, join thread in first free picot skipped on row 1, 2 sc in same picot, ch 39; working in back of previous row, make 3 sc in next free picot, ch 39; working in front of previous row, make 3 sc in next free picot, ch 39; working in back of previous row, make 3 sc in next

joining between motifs; continue in this manner along 3 sides, working in corner lps to correspond and ending with 2 sc in last free picot. Ch 1, turn.

Row 4: Repeat row 2.

FRINGE: Wind thread 20 times around a 9″ cardboard. Remove from cardboard, knot lps through ch-9 lp on edging. Cut ends and trim. Repeat fringe in each ch-9 lp.

POPCORN SQUARES

A solid crochet coverlet is made of squares, worked from a chart for the placement of the raised popcorns, and joined together for a single or double bed.

SIZES: Directions for single size, 84″ x 96″, plus edging. Changes for double size, 96″ x 96″ plus edging, are in parentheses.

MATERIALS: Knitting and cro-

chet cotton, 75 (85) 250-yd. balls of white or ecru. Steel crochet hook No. 7.

GAUGE: 10 sts = 1″; 8 rows = 1″.

BEDSPREAD: POPCORN

SQUARE (make 56 (64) squares): Beg at center, ch 5, sl st in first ch to form ring.

Rnd 1: Ch 3; 7 dc in ring, sl st in top of ch 3 forming a "button."

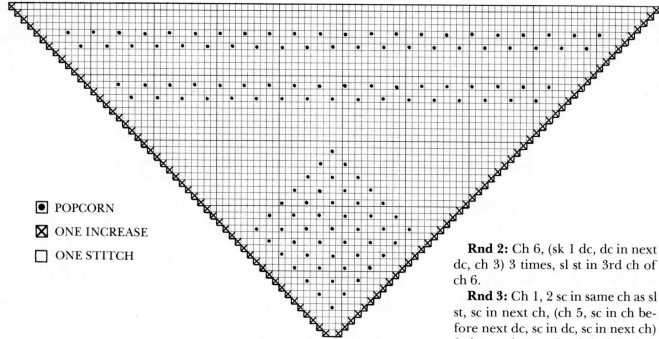

- ◉ POPCORN
- ⊠ ONE INCREASE
- ☐ ONE STITCH

Rnd 2: Ch 6, (sk 1 dc, dc in next dc, ch 3) 3 times, sl st in 3rd ch of ch 6.

Rnd 3: Ch 1, 2 sc in same ch as sl st, sc in next ch, (ch 5, sc in ch before next dc, sc in dc, sc in next ch) 3 times, ch 5, sc in ch before first sc.

Rnd 4: Sc in back lp of 3 sc, sc in next ch, (ch 5, sc in ch before next sc, sc in back lp of 3 sc, sc in next ch) 3 times, ch 5, sc in ch before first sc.

Rnd 5: Sc in back lp of 5 sc, sc in next ch, (ch 5, sc in ch before next sc, sc in back lp of 5 sc, sc in next ch) 3 times, ch 5, sc in ch before first sc.

Rnd 6: Work as for rnd 5, inc 2 sc each side.

Rnd 7: Sc in back lp of next 4 sc, popcorn in next sc (**to make popcorn,** 5 dc in st, drop lp from hook; insert hook in first dc, pull dropped lp through), sc in back lp of next 4 sc, sc in next ch, (ch 5, sc in ch before next sc, sc in back lp of 4 sc, popcorn in next sc, sc in back lp of next 4 sc, sc in next ch) 3 times, ch 5, sc in ch before first sc.

Rnd 8: (Sc in back lp of 5 sc, sc in popcorn, sc in back lp of 5 sc, sc in next ch, ch 5, sc in ch before next sc) 4 times.

Working from chart, complete 53 rnds of square. Sl st in first sc of rnd 53. End off.

Sew squares tog through back lps of sc: 7 x 8 squares for single size, 8 x 8 squares for double size. Work rnd of sc around bedspread.

BORDER: Ch 76.

Row 1: Dc in 4th ch from hook, dc in each of next 3 ch, (ch 2, sk 2 ch, dc in next ch) 3 times, dc in each of next 3 ch, (ch 5, sk 5 ch, sc in each of next 5 ch, ch 5, sk 5 ch, dc in each of next 4 ch) 3 times. Ch 3, turn.

Row 2: 4 dc in first dc, (ch 2, sk 2 dc, dc in next dc, dc in each of next 3 ch, ch 5, sk 1 sc, sc in each of next 3 sc, ch 5, sk 2 ch, dc in each of next 3 ch, dc in next dc) 3 times, ch 2, sk 2 dc, dc in next dc, (ch 2, dc in next dc) 3 times, dc in each of next 3 dc, dc in top of turning ch. Ch 3, turn.

Row 3: Sk first dc, dc in each of next 4 dc, (ch 2, dc in next dc) 4 times, ch 2, sk 2 dc, dc in next dc, (dc in each of next 3 ch, ch 5, sk 1 sc, dc in next sc, ch 5, sk 2 ch, dc in each of next 3 ch, dc in next dc, ch 5, dc in next ch-2 sp, ch 5, sk 3 dc, dc in next dc) 3 times, end last repeat 5 dc in last dc. Ch 3, turn.

Row 4: 4 dc in first dc, (ch 4, sk 4 ch, sc in next ch, sc in dc, sc in next ch, ch 4, sk ch and 3 dc, dc in next dc, dc in each of next 3 ch, ch 2, sk 2 ch of next ch 5, dc in each of last 3 ch, dc in next dc) 3 times, ch 2, sk 2 dc, dc in next dc, (ch 2, dc in next dc) 5 times, dc in each of next 3 dc, dc in top of ch 3. Ch 3, turn.

Row 5: Sk first dc, dc in each of 4 dc, (ch 2, dc in next dc) 6 times, ch 2, sk 2 dc, dc in next dc, (dc in each of 2 ch, dc in next dc, ch 5, sc in ch before next sc, sc in each of 3 sc, sc in next ch, ch 5, sk ch and 3 dc, dc in next dc) 3 times, end last repeat 5 dc in last dc. Ch 3, turn.

Row 6: 4 dc in first dc, ch 2, sk 3 dc, dc in next dc, (dc in each of next 3 ch, ch 5, sc in each of 3 center sc, ch 5, sk 2 ch, dc in each of 3 ch, dc in next dc, ch 2, sk 2 dc, dc in next dc) 3 times, (ch 2, dc in next dc) 7 times, dc in each of next 3 dc, dc in top of ch 3. Ch 3, turn.

Row 7: Sk first dc, dc in each of 4 dc, (ch 2, dc in next dc) 8 times, ch 2, sk 2 dc, dc in next dc, (dc in each of next 3 ch, ch 5, dc in center sc, ch 5, sk 2 ch, dc in each of next 3 ch, dc in next dc, ch 5, dc in ch-2 sp, ch 5, sk 3 dc, dc in next dc) 3 times, end last repeat ch 5, 5 dc in last dc. Ch 3, turn.

Row 8: 4 dc in first dc, (ch 5, sk 4 ch of next ch 5, sc in next ch, sc in dc, sc in next ch, ch 5, sk ch and 3 dc, dc in next dc, dc in next 3 ch, ch 2, sk 2 ch of next ch 5, dc in next 3 ch, dc in next dc) 3 times, ch 2, sk 2 dc, dc in next dc, (ch 2, dc in next dc) 9 times, dc in each of next 3 dc, dc in top of ch 3. Ch 3, turn.

Row 9: Sk first dc, dc in each of 4 dc, (ch 2, dc in next dc) 10 times, ch 2, sk 2 dc, dc in next dc, (dc in each of 2 ch, dc in next dc, ch 5, sk 4 ch of next ch 5, sc in next ch, sc in 3 sc, sc in next ch, ch 5, sk 3 dc, dc in next dc) 3 times, end last repeat 5 dc in last dc. Ch 3, turn.

Row 10: Sk 4 dc, dc in next dc, (dc in each of 3 ch, ch 5, sc in each of 3 center sc, ch 5, sk 2 ch of next ch 5, dc in each of 3 ch, dc in next dc, ch 2, sk 2 dc, dc in next dc) 3 times, dc in each of next 2 ch, dc in next dc, (ch 2, dc in next dc) 10 times, dc in each of next 3 dc, dc in top of ch 3. Ch 3, turn.

Row 11: Sk first dc, dc in each of 4 dc, (ch 2, dc in next dc) 9 times, dc in each of 2 ch, (dc in next dc, ch 4, dc in next ch-2 sp, ch 4, sk 3 dc, dc in next dc, dc in each of next 3 ch, ch 5, dc in center sc of 3 sc, ch 5, sk 2 ch of ch 5, dc in each of next 3 ch) 3 times, dc in next dc. Ch 3, turn.

Row 12: Sk first 3 dc, dc in next dc, (dc in each of next 3 ch, ch 2, sk 2 ch of next ch 5, dc in each of next 3 ch, dc in next dc, ch 5, sc in last ch of next ch 5, sc in dc, sc in first ch of next ch 5, ch 5, sk 3 dc, dc in next dc) 3 times, dc in each of 2 ch, dc in next dc, (ch 2, dc in next dc) 8 times, dc in each of 3 dc, dc in top of ch 3. Ch 3, turn.

Row 13: Sk first dc, dc in each of 4 dc, (ch 2, dc in next dc) 7 times, (dc in each of 2 ch, dc in next dc, ch 5, sc in last ch of next ch 5, sc in each of 3 sc, sc in next ch, ch 5, sk 3 dc, dc in next dc) 3 times, dc in each of 2 ch, dc in next dc. Ch 3, turn.

Row 14: Sk first 3 dc, dc in next dc, (dc in each of next 3 ch, ch 5, sk 1 sc, sc in each of next 3 sc, ch 5, sk 2 ch of ch 5, dc in each of next 3 ch, dc in next dc, ch 2, sk 2 dc, dc in next dc) 3 times; dc in each of next 2 ch, dc in next dc, (ch 2, dc in next dc) 6 times, dc in each of 3 dc, dc in top of ch 3. Ch 3, turn.

Row 15: Sk first dc, dc in each of 4 dc, (ch 2, dc in next dc) 5 times, dc in each of 2 ch, (dc in next dc, ch 4, dc in ch-2 sp, ch 4, sk 3 dc, dc in next dc, dc in each of 3 ch, ch 5, dc in center sc of 3 sc, ch 5, sk 2 ch, dc in each of next 3 ch) 3 times, dc in next dc. Ch 3, turn.

Row 16: Sk first 3 dc, dc in next dc, (dc in each of next 3 ch, ch 2, sk 2 ch of next ch 5, dc in each of next 3 ch, dc in next dc, ch 4, sk 3 dc and 4 ch, sc in next ch, sc in dc, sc in next ch, ch 4, sk 3 dc, dc in next dc) 3 times, dc in each of 2 ch, dc in dc, (ch 2, dc in next dc) 4 times, dc in each of 3 dc, dc in top of ch 3. Ch 3, turn.

Row 17: Sk first dc, dc in each of 4 dc, (ch 2, dc in next dc) 3 times, dc in each of 2 ch, dc in next dc, (ch 5, sc in ch before 3 sc, sc in 3 sc, sc in next ch, ch 5, sk 3 dc, dc in next dc, dc in each of 2 ch, dc in next dc) 3 times. Ch 3, turn.

Repeat rows 2-17 for border. Make border long enough to fit three sides of bedspread with slight gathering at corners. Sew border in place.

NANTUCKET BEDSPREAD

Charming filet mesh bedspread is made all in one piece in a diamond pattern of spider webs outlined with popcorns. Directions are for single or double size, but coverlet can be made any length or width divisible by 10".
Light starching helps Nantucket Bedspread retain its shape, look crisper.

SIZES: Directions for single size, 80″ x 100″. Changes for double size, 90″ x 100″, are in parentheses.

MATERIALS: Mercerized knitting and crochet cotton, 44 (50) 250-yd. balls of white, ecru or cream. Or 63 (72) 175-yd. balls of any color. Steel crochet hook No. 7.

GAUGE: 3 sps or 3 popcorn (pc) bls = 1″; 3 rows = 1″.

BEDSPREAD: Beg at bottom edge, make a ch 8 (9) feet long, having 9 ch to 1″.

Row 1 (wrong side): Dc in 8th ch from hook for first sp, (ch 2, sk 2 ch, dc in next ch) 3 times (3 more sps made), make 3 dc in each of next 2 ch, drop lp from hook, insert hook from back to front in first dc of 6-dc group, draw dropped lp through (reverse popcorn or pc made), dc in next ch (reverse pc bl completed); * make 7 sps, reverse pc bl, repeat from * across until there are 33 (37) reverse pc bls in all, make 4 sps. Cut off remaining ch. Ch 5, turn.

Row 2: Sk first dc, dc in next dc, (ch 2, dc in next dc) twice (3 sps made), 6 dc in next sp, drop lp from hook, insert hook from front to back in first dc of 6-dc group, draw dropped lp through, dc in next dc (pc bl made), ch 9, dc in next dc, * pc bl over next sp, 5 sps, pc bl over next sp, ch-9 lp over next pc bl, repeat from * across, end pc bl, 2 sps, ch 2, sk 2 ch of turning ch, dc in next ch. Ch 5, turn.

Row 3: Make 2 sps; 6 dc in next sp, drop lp from hook, insert hook from back to front in first dc of 6-dc group, draw lp through, dc in next dc (reverse pc bl made); ch 5,

sc in ch-9 lp, ch 5, sk next pc, dc in next dc, * reverse pc bl over next sp, 3 sps, reverse pc bl over next sp, ch 5, sc in ch-9 lp, ch 5, sk pc, dc in next dc, repeat from * across, end reverse pc bl, 2 sps. Ch 5, turn.

Row 4: Make 1 sp, * pc bl, ch 5, sc in next ch-5 lp, ch 1, sc in next ch-5 lp, ch 5, sk pc, dc in next dc, pc bl, 1 sp, repeat from * across. Ch 3, turn.

Row 5: Reverse pc over first sp, * ch 7, sc in next lp, ch 1, sc in ch-1 sp, ch 1, sc in next lp, ch 7, dc in dc after next pc, reverse pc bl over next sp, repeat from * across. Ch 5, turn.

Row 6: Make 1 sp, * pc in next lp, dc in 3rd ch of lp, ch 7, sc in next ch-1 sp, ch 1, sc in next ch-1 sp, ch 7, dc in 5th ch of ch-7 lp, pc in same lp, dc in next dc, ch 2, sk pc, dc in next dc, repeat from * across, end dc in top of ch 3. Ch 5, turn.

Row 7: Make 2 sps, * reverse pc bl over next lp, ch 7, sc in ch-1 sp, ch 7, dc in 5th ch of next lp, reverse pc bl over same lp, 3 sps, repeat from * across, end 2 sps. Ch 5, turn.

Row 8: Make 3 sps, * pc bl over next lp, ch 2, dc in 5th ch of next ch-7 lp, pc bl over same lp, 5 sps, repeat from * across, end 3 sps. Ch 5, turn.

Row 9: Make 4 sps, * reverse pc bl over next sp, 7 sps, repeat from * across, end 4 sps. Ch 5, turn.

Note: Hereafter, continue to make pc bls on every right-side row and reverse pc bls on every wrong-side row.

Row 10: 3 sps, pc bl, ch 9, sk pc, dc in next dc, pc bl in next sp, * 29 sps, pc bl, ch 9, dc in next dc, pc bl, repeat from * across, end 3 sps. Ch 5, turn.

Row 11: 2 sps, pc bl, ch 5, sc in ch-9 lp, ch 5, sk pc, dc in next dc, pc bl, * 27 sps, pc bl, ch 5, sc in ch-9 lp, ch 5, sk pc, dc in next dc, pc bl, repeat from * across, end 2 sps. Ch 5, turn.

Row 12: 1 sp, pc bl, ch 5, sc in next lp, ch 1, sc in next lp, ch 5, dc in dc after next pc, pc bl, * 25 sps, pc bl, ch 5, sc in next lp, ch 1, sc in next lp, ch 5, dc in dc after pc, pc bl, repeat from * across, end 1 sp. Ch 3, turn.

Row 13: Pc bl, ch 7, sc in next lp, ch 1, sc in ch-1 sp, ch 1, sc in next lp, ch 7, dc in dc after pc, pc bl, * 7 sps, pc bl, (3 sps, pc bl) twice, 7 sps, pc bl, ch 7, sc in next lp, ch 1, sc in ch-1 sp, ch 1, sc in next lp, ch 7, dc in dc after pc, pc bl, repeat from * across. Ch 5, turn.

Row 14: 1 sp, pc bl over next lp, ch 7, sc in next ch-1 sp, ch 1, sc in next ch-1 sp, ch 7, dc in 5th ch of next lp, pc bl in same ch-7 lp, * 7 sps, pc bl, ch 9, sk pc, dc in next dc, pc bl, 1 sp, pc bl, ch 7, sk pc, dc in next dc, pc bl, 1 sp, pc bl, ch 9, sk pc, dc in next dc, pc bl, 7 sps, pc bl over next lp, ch 7, sc in next ch-1 sp, ch 1, sc in next ch-1 sp, ch 7, dc in 5th ch of next ch-7 lp, pc bl in same lp, repeat from * across, end 1 sp. Ch 5, turn.

Row 15: 2 sps, pc bl over next lp, ch 7, sc in ch-1 sp, ch 7, dc in 5th ch of next lp, pc bl in same lp, * 7 sps, pc bl, (ch 5, sc in next lp, ch 5, dc in dc after next pc, pc bl) 3 times, 7 sps, pc bl over next lp, ch 7, sc in ch-1 sp, ch 7, dc and pc bl over next lp, repeat from * across, end 2 sps. Ch 5, turn.

Row 16: 3 sps, pc bl over lp, ch 2, dc and pc bl over next lp, * 7 sps, pc bl, ch 5, sc in next lp, ch 1, sc in next lp, ch 5, dc in dc after pc, pc bl over next lp, ch 2, dc and pc

bl over next lp, ch 5, sc in next lp, ch 1, sc in next lp, ch 5, dc in dc after pc, pc bl, 7 sps, pc bl over ch-7 lp, ch 2, dc and pc bl over next ch-7 lp, repeat from * across, end 3 sps. Ch 5, turn.

Row 17: 4 sps, pc bl, * 7 sps, pc bl, (ch 7, sc in next lp, ch 1, sc in ch-1 sp, ch 1, sc in next lp, ch 7, dc in dc after pc, pc bl) twice, 7 sps, pc bl, repeat from * across, end 4 sps, Ch 5, turn.

Row 18: 3 sps, pc bl, ch-9 lp, pc bl, * 7 sps, pc bl over next lp, ch 7, sc in next ch-1 sp, ch 1, sc in next

ch-1 sp, ch 7, dc and pc bl over next ch-7 lp, ch-9 lp, pc bl over next lp, ch 7, sc in next ch-1 sp, ch 1, sc in next ch-1 sp, ch 7, dc and pc bl over next ch-7 lp, 7 sps, pc bl, ch-9 lp, pc bl, repeat from * across, end 3 sps. Ch 5, turn.

Row 19: 2 sps, pc bl, ch 5, sc in ch-9 lp, ch 5, sk pc, dc in next dc, pc bl, * 7 sps, pc bl over next lp, ch 7, sc in ch-1 sp, ch 7, dc and pc bl over next ch-7 lp, ch 5, sc in next lp, ch 5, sk next pc, dc in next dc, pc bl over next lp, ch 7, sc in ch-1 sp, ch 7, dc and pc bl over ch-7 lp,

7 sps, pc bl, ch 5, sc in ch-9 lp, ch 5, dc in dc after next pc, pc bl, repeat from * across, end 2 sps. Ch 5, turn.

Row 20: 1 sp, pc bl, ch 5, sc in next lp, ch 1, sc in next lp, ch 5, dc in dc after pc, pc bl, * 5 sps, pc bl, ch 5, sk pc, dc in next dc, pc bl over ch-7 lp, ch 2, dc and pc bl over next ch-7 lp, ch 5, sc in next lp, ch 1, sc in next lp, ch 5, sk pc, dc in next dc, pc bl over ch-7 lp, ch 2, dc and pc bl over ch-7 lp, ch 5, sk pc, dc in next dc, pc bl, 5 sps, pc bl, ch 5, sc in next lp, ch 1, sc in next lp, ch 5, sk pc, dc in next dc, pc bl, repeat from * across, end 1 sp. Ch 3, turn.

Row 21: Pc bl, ch 7, sc in next lp, ch 1, sc in ch-1 sp, ch 1, sc in next lp, ch 7, sk pc, dc in next dc, pc bl, * 3 sps, pc bl, ch 5, sc in next lp, ch 5, sk pc, dc in next dc, pc bl, ch 7, sc in next lp, ch 1, sc in ch-1 sp, ch 1, sc in next lp, ch 7, sk pc, dc in next dc, pc bl, ch 5, sc in next lp, ch 5, sk pc, dc in next dc, pc bl, 3 sps, pc bl, ch 7, sc in next lp, ch 1, sc in ch-1 sp, ch 1, sc in next lp, ch 7, sk pc, dc in next dc, pc bl, repeat from * across. Ch 5, turn.

Row 22: 1 sp, pc bl over lp, ch 7, sc in next ch-1 sp, ch 1, sc in next ch-1 sp, ch 7, dc and pc bl over next ch-7 lp, * 5 sps, pc bl over next lp, ch 2, dc and pc bl over next lp, ch-9 lp, pc bl over next lp, ch 7, sc in next ch-1 sp, ch 1, sc in next ch-1 sp, ch 7, dc and pc bl over ch-7 lp, ch-9 lp, pc bl over next lp, ch 2, dc and pc bl over next lp, 5 sps, pc bl over next lp, ch 7, sc in next ch-1 sp, ch 1, sc in next ch-1 sp, ch 7, dc and pc bl over next ch-7 lp, repeat from * across, end 1 sp. Ch 5, turn.

Row 23: 2 sps, pc bl over next lp, ch 7, sc in ch-1 sp, ch 7, dc and pc bl over next lp, * 7 sps, pc bl, ch 5, sc in next lp, ch 5, sk next pc, dc in next dc, pc bl over next lp, ch 7,

sc in ch-1 sp, ch 7, dc and pc bl over next ch-7 lp, ch 5, sc in next lp, ch 5, dc in dc after next pc, pc bl, 7 sps, pc bl over next lp, ch 7, sc in ch-1 sp, ch 7, dc and pc bl over next ch-7 lp, repeat from * across, end 2 sps. Ch 5, turn.

Row 24: Repeat row 16.

Row 25: Repeat row 17.

Row 26: 3 sps, pc bl, ch-9 lp, pc bl, * 7 sps, pc bl over next lp, ch 7, sc in next ch-1 sp, ch 1, sc in next ch-1 sp, ch 7, dc and pc bl over next lp, ch 5, dc in dc after next pc, pc bl over next lp, ch 7, sc in next ch-1 sp, ch 1, sc in next ch-1 sp, ch 7, dc and pc bl over next ch-7 lp, 7 sps, pc bl, ch-9 lp, pc bl, repeat from * across, end 3 sps. Ch 5, turn.

Row 27: Repeat row 19.

Row 28: 1 sp, pc bl, ch 5, sc in next lp, ch 1, sc in next lp, ch 5, dc in dc after pc, pc bl, * 7 sps, (pc bl over next lp, ch 2, dc and pc bl over next lp, 1 sp) 3 times, 6 more sps, pc bl, ch 5, sc in next lp, ch 1, sc in next lp, ch 5, dc in dc after pc, pc bl, repeat from * across, end 1 sp. Ch 3, turn.

Row 29: Repeat row 13.

Row 30: 1 sp, * pc bl over next lp, ch 7, sc in next ch-1 sp, ch 1, sc in next ch-1 sp, ch 7, dc and pc bl over next ch-7 lp, 25 sps, repeat from * across, end 1 sp. Ch 5, turn.

Row 31: 2 sps, * pc bl over next lp, ch 7, sc in ch-1 sp, ch 7, dc and pc bl over next lp, 27 sps, repeat from * across, end 2 sps. Ch 5, turn.

Row 32: 3 sps, * pc bl over ch-7 lp, ch 2, dc and pc bl over next ch-7 lp, 29 sps, repeat from * across, end 3 sps. Ch 5, turn.

Row 33: Repeat row 9.

Row 34: Repeat row 2.

Rows 35-41: Repeat rows 3-9.

Repeat rows 10-41, 9 times more. At end of last row, ch 1, turn.

EDGING: From right side, working along top edge, sc in corner sp, ch 3; holding back last lp on hook, make 1 dc in same sp, yo hook, draw up a lp in same sp, yo hook and through all lps on hook (shell made in corner sp), * shell in each sp to next pc bl; placing sts in top of pc, make shell over pc bl, repeat from * across to next corner sp, make 2 shells in corner sp; working along ends of rows, make shell in end sp or end st of each row to next corner sp, make 2 shells in corner sp. Continue in this way to make shell edging along remaining sides of bedspread, end 1 shell in first corner sp. Join with sl st to first sc. End off.

Block to measurements. Starch lightly, if desired.

FILET CROCHET AFGHAN

Five identical strips of filet crochet make this lacy and lightweight coverlet especially easy to make. Each panel is edged round with double crochet, then panels are sewn together.

SIZE: 50″ x 68″.

MATERIALS: Knitting worsted, 11 4-oz. skeins. Crochet hook size F.

GAUGE: 7 sps = 4½″; 2 rows = 1″.

AFGHAN STRIP (make 5): Ch 47 for lower edge.

Row 1 (wrong side): Work 1 dc in 8th ch from hook, * ch 2, sk 2 ch, dc in next ch, repeat from * to end—14 sps.

Row 2: Ch 5, turn, sk first sp, dc in next dc, * ch 2, dc in next dc, repeat from *, end with dc in 3rd ch—14 sps. Repeat row 2 until there are 8 rows.

Row 9: Ch 5, turn, sk first sp, dc in next dc, ch 2; dc in next dc, ch 2, dc in next dc (3 sps made), * 2 dc in next sp, dc in next dc (1 block), repeat from * 7 times, ch 2, dc in next dc, ch 2, dc in next dc, ch 2, dc in 3rd ch (last 3 sps made)—6 sps and 8 blocks.

Row 10: Ch 5, turn, work first 3 sps as before, dc in each of next 24 dc, work last 3 sps.

Row 11: Ch 5, turn, work first 3 sps, dc in each of next 3 dc, * ch 2, sk 2 dc, dc in next dc, repeat from * 5 times, dc in each of next 3 dc, work last 3 sps.

Row 12: Ch 5, turn, work first 3 sps, dc in each of next 3 dc, ch 2, dc in next dc, * 2 dc in next sp, dc in next dc, repeat from * 3 times, ch 2, dc in each of next 4 dc, work last 3 sps.

Row 13: Ch 5, turn, work first 3 sps, dc in each of next 3 dc, ch 2, dc in each of next 13 dc, ch 2, dc in each of next 4 dc, work last 3 sps.

Repeat row 13, 4 times.

Row 18: Ch 5, turn, work first 3 sps, dc in each of next 3 dc, ch 2, dc in next dc, * ch 2, sk 2 dc, dc in next dc, repeat from * 3 times, ch 2, dc in each of next 4 dc, work last 3 sps.

Row 19: Ch 5, turn, work first 3 sps, dc in each of next 3 dc, * 2 dc in next sp, dc in next dc, repeat from * 5 times, dc in each of next 3 dc, work last 3 sps.

Row 20: Repeat row 10.

Row 21: Ch 5, turn, work first 3 sps, * ch 2, sk 2 dc, dc in next dc, repeat from * 7 times, work last 3 sps.

Rows 22-28: Repeat row 2. Repeat rows 9-28 5 times, end on right side. End off. Mark last row for upper edge of afghan.

EDGING: With lp of yarn on hook, from right side, beg in st at upper right corner, ch 3, 4 dc in same st for corner; with care to keep work flat, working along upper edge, dc in first sp, * dc in dc, 2 dc in next sp, dc in dc, dc in next sp, repeat from *, end with 2 dc, in last sp, 5 dc in corner st; along side edge work dc in each sp and dc in base of end st of each row; continue around, working 5 dc in each corner, lower edge same as upper edge and 2nd side edge same as first side edge, join with sl st in top of ch 3. End off.

FINISHING: Block each strip to 10″ x 68″.

Having marked edges of strips at same end, matching rows and keeping seams elastic, from right side sew strips tog, through top lps only. Steam lightly.

RAINBOW AFGHAN

Rainbow tints, soft as a cloud, are formed in rows of broomstick lace for a luxurious afghan in lightweight mohair. Loops are made on a giant knitting needle; a crochet hook works them together.

SIZE: 52″ x 68″, plus fringe.
MATERIALS: Lightweight mohair, 2 40-gram balls each of 11 colors: lavender, pink, pale green, pale orange, aqua, peach, nile green, rose, white, light blue and pale yellow. One knitting needle size 35 (¾″ diameter). Steel crochet hook No. 1.
GAUGE: 6 pats = 7″.

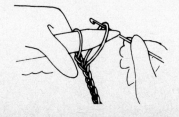

AFGHAN: With lavender and crochet hook No. 1, ch 271. Sc in 2nd ch from hook and in each ch across—270 sc. Do not turn.
PATTERN: Row 1: Pull up lp on hook and place on knitting needle. Holding knitting needle in left hand and working from left to right, sk last sc made, pull up a lp in each sc across, placing lps on needle—270 lps. Do not turn.

Row 2: * Insert hook from left to right through first 6 lps on needle, slip these lps off needle; holding tog as 1 lp, work 6 sc in lp, repeat from * across—45 pats.

End off lavender; tie on pink. Do not turn.

Row 3: Holding knitting needle in left hand and working from left to right, pull up a lp in each sc across, placing lps on needle—270 lps. Do not turn.

Row 4: Insert hook from left to right through first 3 lps, slip these lps off needle; holding tog as 1 lp, work 3 sc in lp; repeat from * to * of row 2 across to last 3 lps, work 3 sc in last 3 lps. End off pink; tie on pale green. Do not turn.

Row 5: Repeat row 3. Repeat rows 2-5 for pat, changing colors every other row in order of listing in Materials. Repeat colors 5 times in all, end row 2. Work 1 row sc across last row.

FINISHING: Weave in all yarn ends. Cut 6 strands of each color 12″ long for each fringe * (Sk 1 st, knot 2 strands of one color in next st) 3 times, knot 12 ends of one color tog to form 1 fringe; repeat from * across each end of afghan, keeping to color sequence of afghan.

COLOR WHEELS

Color wheels offer you a great way to use up odds and ends of knitting worsted. Make strips in slipper stitch crochet using five colors repeated once. Form strips into wheels, gathering in center with black, then work around outer edges of wheels, shaping into squares.

SIZE: 50″ x 70″.

MATERIALS: Knitting worsted, about 42 ozs. of assorted colors and 10 4-oz. skeins of black (background color). For a color scheme of 5 colors, plus background color, 3 4-oz. skeins of first color, 2 skeins each of 4 other colors and 10 4-oz. skeins of background color. Crochet hook size G or 6.

GAUGE: Each square = 10″.

Note: If leftover yarns are used, use a different color for each section of wheel, having as many colors as desired. Make squares either all the same or in different arrangements of colors. Always have same background color for all squares. If five colors only are used for wheels, make all squares in the same color arrangement.

AFGHAN: SQUARE (make 35): **CENTER SECTION** (center section is worked in rows into a straight strip about 17″ long, then gathered into a round shape): **Row 1:** With first color, ch 11. Sc in 2nd ch from hook, sc in each remaining 9 ch. Ch 1, turn.

Row 2: Working in back lp only of each st, sc in each of 10 sc. Ch 1, turn.

Rows 3-6: Repeat row 2. End off. This completes first section. Turn.

Row 7: Join 2nd color with sc in back lp of first sc, sc in back lp of each remaining 9 sc. Ch 1, turn.

Rows 8-12: Repeat row 2. End off.

Rows 13-18: With 3rd color, repeat rows 7-12.

Rows 19-24: With 4th color, repeat rows 7-12.

Rows 25-30: With 5th color, repeat rows 7-12. Repeating 5 colors in same order or using a different color for each section, work 5 more 6-row sections in same way —10 sections; 60 rows.

CENTER RING: Rnd 1: With background color, join yarn with sl st in end sc of row 1 of center section. Ch 3; working tightly over end of rows, work a 3-dc cl over first section as follows: yo hook, draw up a lp in same end st as sl st, yo and through 2 lps, (yo hook, sk next row, draw up a lp in end sc of next row, yo and through 2 lps) twice, yo and through all 4 lps on hook (3-dc cl made), * sk next row (last row of section), work a 3-dc cl in next section, repeat from * across, end sl st in top of first 3-dc cl—10 cls.

Rnd 2: (Sk next cl, sl st in next cl) 5 times. End off.

With first color, overcast last row of strip to ch at beg of strip.

OUTER SECTION: Rnd 1: Working around outer edge of center section, join background color with sc in end sc of row 1, * 2 sc in end st of next row, sc in end st of next row, repeat from * around, end 2 sc in end st of last row, sl st in first sc at beg of rnd— 90 sc.

Rnd 2: Ch 1, sc in same sc as sl st, sc in each of next 7 sc, * 2 sc in next sc, sc in each of next 8 sc, repeat from * around, end with 2 sc in last sc, sl st in first sc—100 sc.

Rnd 3: Ch 1, sc in same sc as sl st, sc in each of next 9 sc, * ch 1, sk next sc, 2-dc cl in next sc **(to make 2-dc cl,** yo hook, draw up a lp in next sc, yo and through 2 lps, yo hook, draw up a lp in same sc, yo and through 2 lps, yo and through all 3 lps on hook), ch 1, sk next sc, work a 2-tr cl in next sc **(to make 2-tr cl,** holding back on hook last lp of each tr, make 2 tr in next sc, yo and through all 3 lps on hook), ch 1, sk next sc, work a 2-dtr cl in next sc (work as for 2-tr cl, but yo hook 3 times for each dtr), ch 1, sk next sc, work a 2-tr tr cl in next sc (yo hook 4 times), ch 5 2-tr tr cl in same sc as last cl, ch 1, sk next sc, 2-dtr cl in next sc, ch 1, sk next sc, 2-tr cl in next sc, ch 1, sk next sc, 2-dc cl in next sc, ch 1, sk next sc, sc in each of next 10 sc, repeat from * around, end last repeat with ch 1, sk last sc, sl st in first sc. End off.

Rnd 4: With first color, join yarn with sc in same sc as last sl st, sc in each of next 9 sc, * (sc in next ch-1 sp, sc in next cl) 4 times, 5 sc in corner ch-5 sp, (sc in next cl, sc in next ch-1 sp) 4 times, sc in each of next 10 sc, repeat from * around, end last repeat with sl st in first sc. End off.

Rnd 5: Join background color with sc in same sc as last sl st, * sc in each sc to center st of next 5-sc group at corner, 3 sc in center st, repeat from * around, end sc in each remaining sc, sl st in first sc. End off.

FINISHING: Pin out each square to correct size on padded surface; cover with a damp cloth; steam, do not press, with a warm iron. Let dry.

With background color, overcast squares tog from corner st to corner st, matching sts. Join squares in 5 rows of 7 squares each, then sew rows tog.

Border: Join background color with sc in center sc at corner of afghan; 2 more sc in same st, * sc in each sc to center st at next corner, 3 sc in corner st, repeat from * around, end sl st in first sc.

Rnd 2: See Note below. Sl st in next sc, ch 1, 3 sc in same sc as sl st, * sc in each sc to center st at next corner, 3 sc in corner sc, repeat from * around, end sl st in first sc.

Rnd 3: Repeat rnd 2. End off.

Note: If desired, rnd 2 may be worked in first color.

IRISH AFGHAN

The rich textures of Irish knits are borrowed for this afghan, all in crochet and worked in one piece.

SIZE: About 45″ x 61″, plus fringe.

MATERIALS: Knitting worsted, 17 4-oz. skeins. Aluminum crochet hooks sizes I and J.

GAUGE: 19 sc = 5″; 1 panel = 4″; 24 rows = 5″ (size I hook).

STITCH PATTERNS: Note: Do not work in stitch directly behind raised dc or double raised dc, or in eye of a cluster.

CLUSTER: (Yo hook, draw up a lp in st) 4 times, yo and draw through all 9 lps on hook. Ch 1 tightly to form eye. (Cluster is worked from wrong side but appears on right side.)

RAISED DC: Dc around upright bar of dc 1 row below, inserting hook behind dc from front to back to front, for ridge on right side.

DOUBLE RAISED DC: Holding back last lp of each dc on hook, make 2 dc around upright bar of st 1 row below, yo and through all 3 lps on hook.

POPCORN: 4 dc in st, drop lp off hook, insert hook in top of first dc, pick up dropped lp and pull through.

Note: This afghan is difficult to start. Once you have completed row 3 and "set" your stitches correctly, the work becomes relatively easy. Before starting afghan, make a swatch of one pattern to familiarize yourself with the stitches. Ch 28 and work row 1—27 sc.

Row 2: Sc in each of first 5 sts, cl in next st, sc in each of next 15 sts, cl in next st, sc in each of last 5 sts.

Row 3: Sc in each of first 3 sc, count off 3 sts on row 1 and work dc around next post, sk the sc on row 2 behind the dc just made and make 1 sc in each of next 3 sts (be sure to work in the cl st only once;

do not work in the eye of the cl), sk 3 sc on row 1 from last raised dc and work a raised dc around next st, sk the sc on row 2 behind the dc just made, sc in each of next 4 sc; sk 4 sc on row 1 from last raised dc and make double raised dc around next sc, sk the sc behind it and work 1 sc, sk 1 sc on row 1 and make another double raised dc, sk the sc behind it and work 4 sc; sk 4 sc on row 1 and work a raised dc around the next sc, sk the sc behind it, work 3 sc (the cl st is the center st of these 3 sc), sk 3 sc on row 1 and work another raised dc around the next sc, sk the sc behind it, work sc in each of last 3 sts.

Beginning with row 4 of the afghan, work pattern without repeats on 27 sts. On all right-side rows from row 3 on, the raised dc's are worked around the previous raised dc's and the double raised dc's are worked around the double raised dc's.

AFGHAN: With I hook, ch 172 loosely.

Row 1: Sc in 2nd ch from hook and in each ch across—171 sc. Ch 1, turn each row.

Row 2 (wrong side): Sc in each of first 5 sts, (cl in next st, sc in each of next 15 sts) 10 times; end cl in next st, sc in each of last 5 sts.

Row 3 (right side): Sc in each of first 3 sc, * work dc around post of next sc 1 row below (row 1), sk next sc on row 2 (see Stitch Patterns: Note), sc in each of next 3 sts, dc around post of next sc 1 row below, sk next sc on row 2, sc in each of next 4 sc; holding back last lp of each dc on hook, make 2 dc around next sc 1 row below, yo

and through 3 lps on hook, sk next sc on row 2, sc in next sc, sk 1 sc on row 1, make 2 dc around next sc as before, sk next sc on row 2, sc in each of next 4 sc, repeat from * across, end dc around post of next sc 1 row below, sc in each of next 3 sts, dc around post of next sc 1 row below, sc in each of last 3 sc.

Row 4: Sc in each of first 4 sts, (cl in next sc, sc in next sc, cl in next sc, sc in each of next 13 sts) 10 times, end cl in next sc, sc in next sc, cl in next sc, sc in each of last 4 sts.

Row 5: Sc in each of first 3 sc, * (raised dc in raised dc, sc in each of next 3 sts) twice, (double raised dc in double raised dc, sc in each of next 3 sc) twice, repeat from * across, end (raised dc in raised dc, sc in each of next 3 sts) twice.

Row 6: Repeat row 2.

Row 7: Sc in each of first 3 sc, * raised dc in raised dc, sc in each of next 3 sts, raised dc in raised dc, sc in each of next 2 sc, double raised dc in double raised dc, sc in each of next 5 sc, double raised dc in double raised dc, sc in each of next 2 sc, repeat from * across, end raised dc in raised dc, sc in each of next 3 sts, raised dc in raised dc, sc in each of last 3 sc.

Row 8: Repeat row 4.

Row 9: Sc in each of first 3 sc, * raised dc in raised dc, sc in each of next 3 sts, raised dc in raised dc, sc in next sc, double raised dc in double raised dc, sc in each of next 3 sc, popcorn in next sc, sc in each of next 3 sc, double raised dc in double raised dc, sc in next sc, repeat from * across, end raised dc

in raised dc, sc in each of next 3 sts, raised dc in raised dc, sc in each of last 3 sc.

Row 10: Repeat row 2.
Row 11: Repeat row 7.
Row 12: Repeat row 4.
Row 13: Repeat row 5.
Row 14: Repeat row 2.
Row 15: Sc in each of first 3 sc, * raised dc in raised dc, sc in next 3 sts, raised dc in raised dc, sc in each of next 4 sc, double raised dc in double raised dc, sc in next sc, double raised dc in double raised dc, sc in each of next 4 sc, repeat from * across, end (raised dc in raised dc, sc in next 3 sts) twice.

Repeat rows 4-15 until 24 diamond patterns have been completed. End off. From right side, work 1 row sc across last row, end 2 sc in last st. Do not end off.

EDGING: Rnd 1: Working down side of afghan, from right side, * sc in end st of next 2 rows, sk 1 row, repeat from * to corner, 3 sc in corner st, sc in each st across end to corner, 3 sc in corner; working up side, repeat from first * to beg of rnd, sl st in first sc.

Rnd 2: Join another strand of yarn. Using double strand and J hook, working from left to right, work sc in every other sc, inc at corners to keep work flat. Join; end off.

FRINGE: Cut strands 14" long. Hold 10 strands tog, fold in half. With hook, pull fold through edge of afghan, pull ends through loop; tighten knot. Knot a fringe in center of each diamond and cluster panel at each end and in each corner. Trim fringe.

BABY AFGHAN

This baby afghan is formed of fifteen blocks in five different arrangements of white, red and shades of blue. Each block is made of granny squares at center and corners of the solid single crochet sections. Border is a scalloped edge of shells.

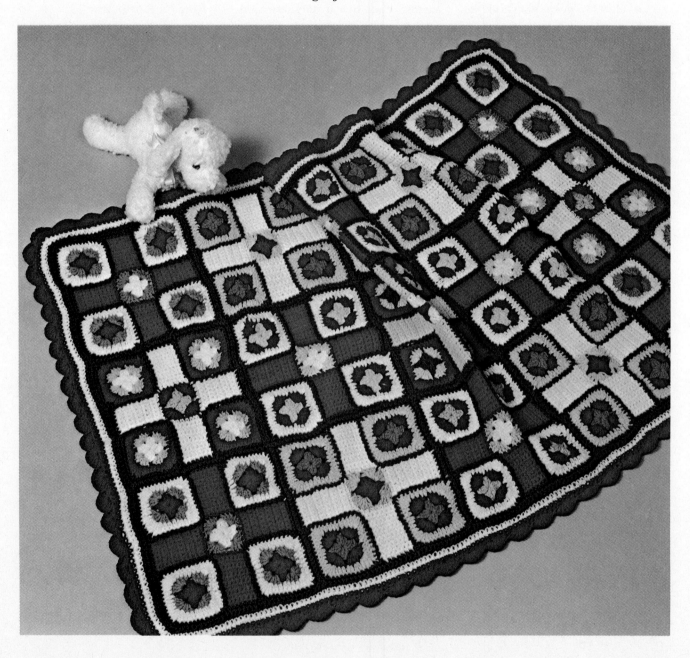

SIZE: 34" x 54".

MATERIALS: Knitting worsted weight yarn, 4 ply, 3 4-oz. skeins each of vermilion and white; 2 skeins royal blue; 1 skein each of medium blue and baby blue; about 24 yds. of aqua. Crochet hook size H.

GAUGE: 4 sc = 1"; 4 sc rows = 1". Each square is 10" square.

Note: Afghan is made of separate squares joined together. Squares are all worked in same manner, using different color arrangements.

AFGHAN: SQUARE NO. 1 (make 4): **CENTER:** Beg at center with white, ch 4. Sl st in first ch to form ring.

Rnd 1 (right side): Ch 3, 2 dc in ring, ch 3, (3 dc in ring, ch 3) 3 times. Join with sl st to top of ch 3 at beg of rnd. End off.

Rnd 2: Join medium blue in any ch-3 sp, ch 3, 2 dc, ch 3, 3 dc in same sp, (ch 1, 3 dc, ch 3, 3 dc in next sp) 3 times, ch 1, sl st in top of ch 3. End off.

FIRST SC SECTION: Row 1: Join vermilion in any ch-3 sp, ch 1, sc in same sp, sc in each of next 3 dc, sc in next ch-1 sp, sc in each of next 3 dc, sc in next sp—9 sc. Ch 1, turn.

Row 2: Sc in each sc across. Ch 1, turn. Repeat row 2, 11 more times. End off.

2ND, 3RD AND 4TH SC SECTIONS: With right side facing, join vermilion in same ch-3 sp with last sc of row 1 of previous sc section, work as for first sc section.

CORNER MOTIF (make 4): With vermilion, work as for center through rnd 1. With medium blue, work as for rnd 2.

Rnd 3: Join white in any ch-3 sp, ch 3, 2 dc in same sp, ch 3, 3 dc in same sp, * sk next dc, dc in each of next 2 dc, dc in ch-1 sp, dc in each of next 2 dc, sk next dc, 3 dc, ch 3, 3 dc in next ch-3 sp, repeat from * twice, sk next dc, dc in next 2 dc, dc in ch-1 sp, dc in next 2 dc. Sl st in top of ch 3. End off.

JOIN CORNER MOTIFS: Place corner motifs in corner spaces of square. Baste 2 sides of each motif loosely to side edges of sc rows. Join royal blue to end of basting seam, ch 1. Working through both thicknesses, from right side, sl st in same place where yarn was joined, * ch 1, sl st loosely through next st on both pieces, repeat from * along basted edges, matching inner corner of motif

with corner sp of center. End off. Join other 3 motifs in same way.

EDGING: From right side, join same color used for joining to any corner sp of square, ch 1, 3 sc in same sp, sc in each st and in each joining around, making 3 sc in each corner sp. End off.

SQUARE NO. 2 (make 4): Work as for Square No. 1 using colors as follows:

Rnd 1: White.

Rnd 2: Aqua.

Sc Sections: Vermilion.

Corner Motifs: Rnd 1: Baby blue.

Rnd 2: Vermilion.

Rnd 3: White.

Joining and Edging: Royal blue.

SQUARE NO. 3 (make 4): Work as for Square No. 1 using colors as follows:

Rnd 1: Vermilion.

Rnd 2: Baby blue.

Sc Sections: White.

Corner Motifs: Rnd 1: Medium blue.

Rnd 2: Vermilion.

Rnd 3: Baby blue.

Joining and Edging: Royal blue.

SQUARE NO. 4 (make 2): Work as for Square No. 1 using colors as follows:

Rnd 1: Aqua.

Rnd 2: Vermilion.

Sc Sections: White.

Corner Motifs: Rnd 1: White.

Rnd 2: Baby blue.

Rnd 3: Vermilion.

Joining and Edging: Royal blue.

SQUARE NO. 5 (make 1): Work as for Square No. 1 using colors as follows:

Rnd 1: Vermilion.

Rnd 2: White.

Sc Sections: Baby blue.

Corner Motifs: Rnd 1: Royal blue.

Rnd 2: Baby blue.

Rnd 3: Vermilion.

Joining and Edging: Royal blue.

Pin squares to measurement on

a padded surface; cover with a damp cloth and allow to dry. Do not press.

TO JOIN SQUARES: Following chart for placement of squares, baste squares tog, matching sts and corners. Join 2 top rows tog with royal blue, working through both thicknesses as before, making sl st and ch 1 in each st across. Join bottom row to center row in same way. Join motifs across short rows in same way.

BORDER: Rnd 1: From right side, join royal blue in center sc of any corner 3-sc group, ch 1, 3 sc in same st, * sc evenly across squares, making 35 sc in each square, to next corner, 3 sc in corner st, repeat from * twice, sc evenly across last side. Sl st in first sc. Ch 1, turn.

Rnd 2: Sc in each sc around, 3 sc in each corner st. Sl st in first sc. End off. Turn.

Rnd 3: Join white to same sc as joining, ch 1, repeat rnd 2. Ch 1, turn.

Rnd 4: Repeat rnd 2. End off. Turn.

Rnd 5: Join vermilion to same sc as joining, ch 1, repeat rnd 2. Ch 1, turn.

Rnd 6: Repeat rnd 2. End off. Turn.

Rnd 7: From right side, join vermilion in center sc of any corner 3-sc group, ch 3, make 5 dc in same sc (shell), sk 2 sc, sc in next sc, * sk 2 sc, 6 dc in next sc (shell), sk 2 sc, sc in next sc, repeat from * around, skipping as necessary at corners to have a shell in each corner. Sl st in top of ch 3. End off.

1	3	2	3	1
4	2	5	2	4
1	3	2	3	1

GREEK FRET PILLOW

Shown below at left

Greek Fret Pillow is crocheted from the center out in rows of flat and raised stitches; the second half repeats the patterns.

SIZE: 14″ x 18″.

MATERIALS: Knitting worsted, 1 4-oz. skein beige (includes back in solid beige); 1 2-oz. skein each of brown, red and pale green. Crochet hook size F or 5. Pillow form.

GAUGE: 7 sts = 2″; 4 rows = 1″.

PILLOW TOP: Beg at center, with brown, ch 46.

Row 1: Sc in 2nd ch from hook and in each remaining ch—45 sc. Ch 1, turn.

Row 2: Sc in each sc across. Ch 1, turn.

Row 3: Sc in first 3 sc, draw up a lp in next sc, drop brown, finish sc with red; with red, 4 dc in next sc, finishing last 2 lps of last dc with brown, drop lp off hook, insert hook in first dc, draw lp through

(popcorn made); * with brown, sc in next 3 sc changing to red; with red, popcorn in next sc changing to brown, repeat from * across, end sc in last 4 sc. Cut red. Ch 1, turn.

Rows 4-6: With brown, sc in each st across. Ch 1, turn each row. Cut brown.

Row 7: With green, sc in first 2 sc; make a chain bar as follows: insert hook in hole of 3rd st on 4th row below (popcorn row), catch yarn and pull a lp through to front; keeping this lp on hook, insert hook in hole 1 row above, pull a lp through hole and through first lp on hook forming a ch; insert hook in hole 1 row above, pull a lp through hole and first lp on hook forming 2nd ch; insert hook

in hole 1 row above, pull a lp through hole and first lp on hook forming 3rd ch, yo and through 2 lps on hook (chain bar made), * sc in next 3 sc, chain bar in next st (between popcorns), repeat from * across, end chain bar, sc in last 2 sc. Ch 1, turn.

Rows 8-10: Sc in each st across. Ch 1, turn each row. Cut green.

Triangles: With red, ch 4. Sl st around post of st at top of first green chain bar on row 7, * ch 8, sl st around post of st at top of next chain bar, repeat from * across, end ch 4. End off.

Row 11: With red, make lp on hook; from right side, insert hook through first ch of triangles, sc in first sc of row 10, * sc in each of next 3 sc, put hook under next ch-

8 lp, sc in next sc, repeat from * across, catching in all ch-8 lps, end sc in each of 3 sc, sc in last sc catching in last ch of triangles. Ch 1, turn.

Row 12: Sc in each sc across. Cut red. Turn.

Row 13: With beige, sc in first sc, sc in next sc 2 rows below (row 11), * sc in next sc, sc in next sc 2 rows below, repeat from * across,

end sc in last sc. Ch 1, turn.

Row 14: Sc in each sc across. Cut beige. Turn.

Rows 15 and 16: With green, work even in sc. Cut green.

Row 17: With brown, sc in each sc across. Ch 1, turn. Repeat rows 2-16 once.

Working along opposite side of starting ch, work 2nd half of pillow same as first half.

EDGING: With beige, sc around all 4 sides of pillow top, working 3 sc in each corner. End off. With brown, working from left to right, work sc in front lp of each sc around.

BACK: With beige, make back in rows of sc, same size as pillow top. Sew top and back tog on 3 sides, insert pillow form, close opening.

GREEK GEOMETRICS PILLOW

Shown at center on page 262

This rectangle of color is crocheted in the same way as the Greek Fret Pillow—from the center out—and uses some of the same stitches.

SIZE: 14″ x 22″.

MATERIALS: Knitting worsted, 1 4-oz. skein brown (includes back in solid brown); 1 2-oz. skein each of orange, pale green and lavender. Crochet hook size F or 5. Pillow form.

GAUGE: 7 sts = 2″; 4 rows = 1″.

PILLOW TOP: Beg at center, with brown, ch 46.

Row 1: Sc in 2nd ch from hook and in each remaining ch—45 sc. Ch 1, turn.

Row 2: Sc in each sc across. Ch 1, turn.

Row 3: Sc in first 3 sc, draw up a lp in next sc, drop brown, finish sc with orange; with orange, 4 dc in next sc finishing last 2 lps of last dc with brown, drop lp off hook, insert hook in first dc, draw lp through (popcorn made); * with brown, sc in next 3 sc changing to orange; with orange, popcorn in next sc changing to brown, repeat from * across, end sc in last 4 sc. Cut orange. Ch 1, turn.

Rows 4-6: With brown, sc in each st across. Ch 1, turn each row.

Row 7: With green, sc in first 2 sc; make a chain bar as follows: insert hook in hole of 3rd st on 4th row below (popcorn row), catch yarn and pull a lp through to front; keeping this lp on hook, insert hook in hole 1 row above, pull a lp through hole and through first lp on hook forming a ch; insert hook in hole 1 row above, pull a lp through hole and through first lp on hook forming 2nd ch; insert hook in hole 1 row above, pull a lp through hole and first lp on hook forming 3rd ch, yo and through 2 lps on hook (chain bar made), * sc in next 3 sc, chain bar in next st (between popcorns), repeat from * across, end chain bar, sc in last 2 sc. Ch 1, turn.

Rows 8-10: Sc in each st across. Ch 1, turn each row. Cut green.

Triangles: With orange, ch 4. Sl st around post of st at top of first green chain bar on row 7, * ch 8, sl

st around post of st at top of next chain bar, repeat from * across, end ch 4. End off.

Row 11: With lavender, make lp on hook; from right side, insert hook through first ch of triangles, sc in first sc of row 10, * sc in each of next 3 sc, put hook under next ch-8 lp, sc in next sc, repeat from * across, catching in all ch-8 lps, end sc in each of 3 sc, sc in last sc catching in last ch of triangles. Ch 1, turn.

Row 12: Sc in first sc; yo hook, pull up a lp in next sc, (yo hook, pull up a lp in same sc) twice, yo and through all 7 lps on hook (cluster made), * sc in next sc, cl in next sc, repeat from * across, end sc in last sc. Ch 1, turn.

Row 13: Sc in each st across. Ch 1, turn.

Row 14: Sc in each sc. Cut lavender. Turn.

Row 15: With brown, sc in each sc across. Ch 1, turn.

Rows 16-28: Repeat rows 2-14.

Row 29: With brown, sc in each sc across. Ch 1, turn.

Row 30: Sc in each sc across. Ch 1, turn.

Row 31: Repeat row 3.

Rows 32-36: Work even in sc.

Row 37: Sc in first 6 sc, * orange popcorn in next sc; with brown, sc in next 3 sc changing to orange, repeat from ·* across, end orange popcorn; with brown, sc in last 6 sc. Ch 1, turn. Cut orange.

Rows 38-40: With brown, sc in each st across. Ch 1, turn each row.

Row 41 and 42: With green, work 2 rows of sc. End off.

Working along opposite side of starting ch, work 2nd half of pillow same as first half.

EDGING: With green, sc around all 4 sides of pillow top, working 3 sc in each corner. End off. With orange, working from left to right, work sc in front lp of each sc around.

BACK: With brown, make back in rows of sc, same size as pillow top. Sew top and back tog on 3 sides, insert pillow form, close opening.

ROUND PILLOW

Shown at right on page 262

A round pillow, striped in two colors, has a radiating popcorn pattern.

SIZE: 16″ diameter.

MATERIALS: Knitting worsted, 5 ozs. of green (includes enough for crocheted back); 3 ozs. of red. Crochet hook size F or 5.

GAUGE: 4 sc = 1″; 4 rnds = 1″.

PILLOW TOP: With green, ch 2.

Rnd 1: 6 sc in 2nd ch from hook.

Rnd 2: 2 sc in each sc around—12 sc.

Rnd 3: (Sc in next sc, 2 sc in next sc) 6 times—18 sc.

Rnd 4: (Sc in each of 2 sc, 2 sc in next sc) 6 times—24 sc.

Rnd 5: (Sc in each of 3 sc, 2 sc in next sc) 6 times—30 sc.

Rnd 6: (Sc in each of 4 sc, 2 sc in next sc) 6 times—36 sc.

Rnd 7: Sc in first sc, pull up a lp in next sc, drop green, complete sc with red; with red, 4 dc in next sc, changing to green to complete last dc; drop lp off hook; insert hook in first dc, draw dropped lp through (popcorn made), * sc in next 2 sc changing to red to complete last sc; with red, make 4 dc in next sc, changing to green to complete last dc and complete popcorn, repeat from * around—12 popcorns. Drop red.

Rnd 8: With green, (sc in 2 sc, 2 sc in popcorn) 12 times—48 sc.

Rnd 9: Sc in each sc around, changing to red in last sc.

Rnd 10: With red, (sc in 3 sc, 2 sc in next sc) 12 times—60 sc.

Rnd 11: (Sc in 4 sc changing to green in last sc, popcorn in next sc changing to red to complete popcorn) 12 times.

Rnd 12: With red, (sc in 4 sc, 2 sc in popcorn) 12 times—72 sc.

Rnd 13: Sc in each sc around, changing to green in last sc.

Rnd 14: With green, (sc in 5 sc, 2 sc in next sc) 12 times—84 sc.

Rnd 15: (Sc in 6 sc changing to red in last sc, popcorn in next sc, changing to green to complete popcorn) 12 times.

Rnd 16: With green, (sc in 6 sc, 2 sc in popcorn) 12 times—96 sc.

Rnd 17: Sc in each sc around, changing to red in last sc.

Continue in this manner, increasing 12 sts every other rnd, changing colors every 4th rnd, and working popcorns on 2nd rnd of every stripe until 3 red stripes have been completed. Sl st in first sc; cut red.

EDGING: With green, working from left to right, sc in front lp of each sc around. Sl st in first st; end off.

For pillow back, make a green disk in sc same size as pillow top. Sew pieces tog halfway around. Insert pillow form. Close opening with a zipper, or sew edges tog.

FOUR-COLOR PILLOW

Shown at top on page 267

Color changes and the placement of long overlay stitches create this gaily striped pillow top.

SIZE: 12″ diameter.

MATERIALS: Knitting worsted or Orlon yarn of knitting worsted weight, 1 oz. pale yellow (A); 2 ozs. light orange (B); 3 ozs. purple or brown (C); 4 ozs. aqua or green (D). Plastic or aluminum crochet hook size H. Pillow form. Felt.

PILLOW TOP: With A, ch 2.

Rnd 1: 6 sc in 2nd ch from hook. Sl st in first sc, ch 1 each rnd.

Rnd 2: 2 sc in each sc around.

Rnd 3: * Sc in next sc, 2 sc in next sc, repeat from * around—18 sc. Sl st in first sc; end off.

Rnd 4: With B, make lp on hook; sc in each of 3 sc, long sc in next sc of rnd 2, * sc in each of next 3 sc, sk 1 sc on rnd 2, long sc in next sc of rnd 2, repeat from * around.

Rnd 5: * Sc in each of 3 sc, 2 sc in next sc, repeat from * around—30 sc.

Rnd 6: * Sc in each of 4 sc, 2 sc in next sc, repeat from * around—36 sc. Sl st in first sc; end off.

Rnd 7: With C, make lp on hook, sc in each of 4 sc (have 4 sc directly over 3 sc of rnd 4), long sc in next sc of rnd 5, long sc in center of long sc of rnd 4, long sc in next sc of rnd 5, * sc in each of next 4 sc, long sc in next sc of rnd 5, long sc in center of long sc of rnd 4, long sc in next sc of rnd 5, repeat from * around—42 sts.

Rnd 8: * Sc in each of 6 sc, 2 sc in next sc, repeat from * around.

Rnd 9: * Sc in each of 7 sc, 2 sc in next sc, repeat from * around—54 sc. Sl st in first sc; end off.

Rnd 10: With D, make lp on hook, sc in each of 5 sc (have 5 sc directly over 4 sc of rnd 7), long sc in next sc of rnd 8, long sc in center of each of 3 long sc of rnd 7, long sc in next sc of rnd 8, * sc in each of next 5 sc, long sc in next sc in rnd 8, long sc in center of each of 3 long sc of rnd 7, long sc in next sc of rnd 8, repeat from * around—60 sts.

Rnd 11: * Sc in each of 9 sc, 2 sc in next sc, repeat from * around.

Rnd 12: Sc around, inc 6 sc evenly spaced around—72 sc. Sl st in first sc; end off.

Rnd 13: With A, make lp on hook, sc in each of 8 sc (have 8 sc directly over 5 sc of rnd 10), long sc in next sc of rnd 11, long sc in center of each of 3 long sc of rnd 10, long sc in next sc of rnd 11, * sc in each of next 8 sc, long sc in next sc of rnd 11, long sc in center of each of 3 long sc of rnd 10, long sc in next sc of rnd 11, repeat from * around—78 sts.

Rnd 14: Sc around, inc 6 sc evenly spaced around—84 sc.

Rnd 15: Sc around, inc 6 sc evenly spaced around—90 sc. Sl st in first sc. End off.

Rnd 16: With B, make lp on hook, sc in each of 10 sc (have 10 sc directly over 8 sc of rnd 13), long sc in next sc of rnd 14, long sc in center of each of 3 long sc of rnd 13, long sc in next sc of rnd 14, * sc in each of next 10 sc, long sc in next sc of rnd 14, long sc in center of each of 3 long sc of rnd 13, long sc in next sc of rnd 14, repeat from * around—90 sts.

Rnd 17: Sc in each of first 5 sc, * long sc in next sc of rnd 14, sc in each of next 15 sc, repeat from * around, end last repeat sc in each of last 10 sc—96 sc.

Rnd 18: * Sc in each of 15 sc, 2 sc in next sc, repeat from * around—102 sc. Sl st in first sc; end off.

Rnd 19: With C, make lp on hook, sc in each of 5 sc (have 5 sc directly over 5 sc before single long sc of rnd 17), * long sc in next sc of rnd 17, long sc in center of long sc of rnd 17, long sc in next sc of rnd 17, sc in each of next 5 sc, long sc in next sc of rnd 17, long sc in center of each of 3 long sc of rnd 16, long sc in next sc of rnd 17, sc in each of next 5 sc, repeat from * around, end long sc in center of each of 3 long sc of rnd 16, long sc in next sc of rnd 17—108 sts.

Rnd 20: * Sc in each of 17 sc, 2 sc in next sc, repeat from * around—114 sc.

Rnd 21: Sc in each sc around—114 sc. Sl st in first sc; end off.

Rnd 22: With D, make lp on hook, * sc in each of 5 sc (have 5 sc directly over 5 sc of rnd 19), long sc in next sc of rnd 20, long sc in center of each of 3 long sc of rnd 19, long sc in next sc of rnd 20, repeat from * around—120 sts.

Rnds 23 and 24: Sc in each st around.

Rnd 25: Working from **left** to **right**, work 1 sc in each sc around—120 reverse sc. End off.

FINISHING: Weave in yarn ends. Steam-press piece. For pillow with boxing strip, work a strip of sc rows as wide as boxing and long enough to fit around pillow. Cut felt same size as pillow top. Sew pieces tog over pillow form.

THREE-COLOR PILLOW

Shown second from top on page 267

This three-color pillow top uses long single crochet stitches to spark its design.

SIZE: 11″ diameter.

MATERIALS: Knitting worsted or Orlon yarn of knitting worsted weight, ½ oz. pale yellow (A); 1 oz. each of orange (B) and green (C). Plastic or aluminum crochet hook size G. Pillow form. Felt.

PILLOW TOP: With A, ch 2.

Rnd 1: 6 sc in first ch. Do not join rnds. Mark end of rnds.

Rnd 2: 2 sc in each sc—12 sc.

Rnd 3: * Sc in next sc, 2 sc in next sc, repeat from * around.

Rnd 4: * 2 sc in next sc, sc in each of next 2 sc, repeat from * around—24 sc.

Rnd 5: * Sc in each of next 3 sc, 2 sc in next sc, repeat from * around—30 sc.

Rnd 6: * 2 sc in next sc, sc in each of next 2 sc, repeat from * around—40 sc.

Rnd 7: * Sc in each of next 3 sc, 2 sc in next sc, repeat from * around—50 sc.

Rnd 8: * 2 sc in next sc, sc in each of next 4 sc, repeat from * around—60 sc.

Rnd 9: * Sc in each of next 11 sc, 2 sc in next sc, repeat from * around—65 sc. Sl st in next st. End off.

Rnd 10: With B, make lp on hook. Sk 2 sts from last sl st made, * sc in each of next 6 sc, long sc in next sc of rnd 8, long sc in next sc of rnd 7, long sc in next sc of rnd 6, long sc in next sc of rnd 5, long sc in next sc of rnd 6, long sc in next sc of rnd 7, long sc in next sc of rnd 8, repeat from * around, skipping 5 sts on rnd 5 between longest sc's. Sl st in first sc, ch 1 each rnd.

Rnds 11-13: Sc in each st, inc 5 sc evenly spaced around—80 sc. At end of rnd 13, end off B.

Rnd 14: With C, make lp on hook. * Sc in each of 10 sc (have 10 sc over 6 regular sc on rnd 10), long sc in next st of rnd 12, long sc in next st of rnd 11, long sc in next st of rnd 10, long sc in center of longest sc of rnd 10, long sc in next st of rnd 10, long sc in next st of rnd 11, long sc in next st of rnd 12, repeat from * around.

Rnds 15-17: Sc in each st, inc 5 sc evenly spaced around—100 sc. At end of rnd 17, end off C.

Rnd 18: With B, make lp on hook. * Sc in each of 13 sc (have 13 sc over 10 regular sc on rnd 14), make 7 long sc as before, repeat from * around—100 sts.

Rnds 19-21: Sc in each st, inc 5 sc evenly spaced around—115 sc. At end of rnd 21, end off B.

Rnd 22: With C, make lp on hook. * Sc in each of 17 sc (have 17 sc over 13 regular sc on rnd 18), make 7 long sc as before, repeat from * around—120 sts.

Rnds 23-25: Sc in each st around. End off.

FINISHING: Steam-press piece. Cut felt same size; sew tog over pillow form.

YELLOW PILLOW

Shown third from top on page 267

Colors and design give this pillow top a sunburst effect.

SIZE: 11″ diameter.

MATERIALS: Knitting worsted or Orlon yarn of knitting worsted weight, 1 oz. each of dark yellow (A) and light yellow (B). Plastic or aluminum crochet hook size G. Pillow form. Felt.

PILLOW TOP: With A, ch 2.

Rnd 1: 4 sc in first ch. Sl st in first sc, ch 1 each rnd.

Rnd 2: 2 sc in each sc around.

Rnd 3: * Sc in next sc, 2 sc in next sc, repeat from * around.

Rnd 4: * 2 sc in next sc, sc in each of next 2 sc, repeat from * around—16 sc.

Rnd 5: Repeat rnd 3—24 sc.

Rnd 6: Repeat rnd 4—32 sc.

Rnd 7: * Sc in each of 3 sc, 2 sc in next sc, repeat from * around.

Rnd 8: * Sc in each of 4 sc, 2 sc in next sc, repeat from * around.

Rnd 9: * Sc in each of 5 sc, 2 sc in next sc, repeat from * around.

Rnd 10: * Sc in each of 6 sc, 2 sc in next sc, repeat from * around— 64 sc. End off A.

Rnd 11: With B, make lp on hook; sc in sc at any of the 8 "points" of rnd 10, long sc in next sc of rnd 9, long sc in next sc of rnd 8, long sc in next sc of rnd 7, long sc in next sc of rnd 6, long sc in next sc of rnd 7, long sc in next sc of rnd 8, long sc in next sc of rnd 9, sc in sc at next "point" of rnd 10, repeat from * around, skipping 3 sc on rnd 6 between longest sc, end sl st in first sc, ch 1.

Rnds 12-15: Sc in each sc around, inc 8 sc evenly each rnd— 96 sc. End off B at end of rnd 15.

Rnd 16: With A, make lp on hook, sc in each of 2 sc at any "point," * long sc in next sc of rnd 14, long sc in next sc of rnd 13, long sc in next sc of rnd 12, long sc in each of next 2 sc of rnd 11, long sc in center of longest sc of rnd 11 (put hook through rnd 9), long sc in each of next 2 sc of rnd 11, long sc in next sc of rnd 12, long sc in next sc of rnd 13, long sc in next sc of rnd 14, sc in each of 2 sc at next "point," repeat from * around, end sl st in first sc, ch 1—104 sts.

Rnds 17-19: Sc in each sc around—104 sc. End off A at end of rnd 19.

Rnd 20: With B, make lp on hook, * work 3 long sc in rnd 15 between patterns of long sc, sc in each of next 11 sc, repeat from * around, end sl st in first long sc, ch 1.

Rnd 21: Sc in each sc around, inc 8 sc in rnd—120 sc.

Rnds 22 and 23: Sc in each sc around. End off.

Rnd 24: With A, make lp on hook; working from **left** to **right,** work sc in each sc around—120 reverse sc. End off.

FINISHING: Steam-press piece. Cut felt same size; sew tog over pillow form.

GREEN PILLOW

Shown at bottom on page 267

Long single crochet stitches are used here to blend rings of green.

SIZE: 14″ diameter.

MATERIALS: Knitting worsted or Orlon yarn of knitting worsted weight, 2 ozs. each of two greens, A and B. Plastic or aluminum crochet hook size G. Pillow form. Felt.

PILLOW TOP: With A, ch 4. Sl st in first ch to form ring.

Rnd 1: Ch 1, 8 sc in ring. Join in first sc, ch 1 each rnd.

Rnd 2: 2 sc in each sc around—16 sc.

Rnd 3: * Sc in next sc, 2 sc in next sc, repeat from * around—24 sc.

Rnd 4: * 2 sc in next sc, sc in each of next 2 sc, repeat from * around—32 sc.

Rnd 5: * Sc in each of next 3 sc, 2 sc in next sc, repeat from * around—40 sc. Sl st in first sc. End off.

Rnd 6: With B, make lp on hook. Working over rnd 5 into rnd 4, long sc in any sc on rnd 4, long sc in each of next 2 sc on rnd 4, (long sc in next sc on rnd 3) twice, * long sc in each of next 3 sc on rnd 4, sk 1 sc on rnd 3, (long sc in next sc on rnd 3) twice, repeat from * around—40 long sc.

Rnd 7: Sc in each st around.

Rnd 8: * Sc in each of next 4 sc, 2 sc in next sc, repeat from * around—48 sc.

Rnd 9: * 2 sc in next sc, sc in each of next 5 sc, repeat from * around—56 sc.

Rnd 10: * Sc in each of next 6 sc, 2 sc in next sc, repeat from * around—64 sc. Sl st in first sc. End off.

Rnd 11: With A, make lp on hook. Sc in each of 5 sc (place these 5 sc so that they come above the 3 shorter sc of rnd 6), long sc in next sc of rnd 9, (long sc in next sc of rnd 8) twice, long sc in next sc of rnd 9, * sc in each of next 5 sc, long sc in next sc of rnd 9, sk 4 sc of rnd 8, (long sc in next sc of rnd 8) twice, long sc in next sc of rnd 9, repeat from * around—72 sts.

Rnd 12: 2 sc in next sc, sc in each of next 8 sc, repeat from * around—80 sc.

Rnd 13: Sc in each sc around.

Rnd 14: * Sc in each of 9 sc, 2 sc in next sc, repeat from * around.

Rnd 15: Sc in each sc around—88 sc. Sl st in first sc. End off.

Rnd 16: With B, make lp on hook. Sc in each of 2 sc, long sc in next sc of rnd 14, (long sc in next sc of rnd 13) twice, long sc in next sc of rnd 14, * sc in each of 2 sc, long sc in next sc of rnd 14, sk 3 sc of rnd 13, (long sc in next sc of rnd 13) twice, long sc in next sc on rnd 14, repeat from * around—96 sts.

Rnd 17: Sc in each st around—96 sc.

Rnd 18: Sc in each sc around.

Rnd 19: * 2 sc in next sc, sc in each of next 11 sc, repeat from * around—104 sc.

Rnd 20: Sc in each sc around—104 sc. Sl st in first sc. End off.

Rnd 21: With A, make lp on hook. Sc in each of 3 sc (place these 3 sc so that they come above the 2 regular sc of rnd 16), long sc in next sc of rnd 19, (long sc in next sc of rnd 18) twice, long sc in next sc of rnd 19, * sc in each of 3 sc, long sc in next sc of rnd 19, sk 4 sc of rnd 18, (long sc in next sc of rnd 18) twice, long sc in next sc of rnd 19, repeat from * around—112 sts.

Rnd 22: * Sc in each of next 13 sc, 2 sc in next sc, repeat from * around—120 sc.

Rnd 23: Sc in each sc around.

Rnd 24: * 2 sc in next sc, sc in each of next 14 sc, repeat from * around—128 sc.

Rnd 25: Sc in each sc around. Sl st in first sc. End off.

Rnd 26: With B, make lp on hook. Sc in each of 5 sc (place these 5 sc so that they come above the 3 sc of rnd 21), long sc in next sc of rnd 24, (long sc in next sc of rnd 23) twice, long sc in next sc of rnd 24, * sc in each of 5 sc, long sc in next sc of rnd 24, sk 5 sc of rnd 23, (long sc in next sc of rnd 23) twice, long sc in next sc of rnd 24, sc in each of next 5 sc, long sc in next sc of rnd 24, sk 6 sc of rnd 23, (long sc in next sc of round 23) twice, long sc in next sc of rnd 24, repeat from * around—144 sts.

Rnd 27: Sc in each st around.

Rnd 28: Working from **left** to **right,** work sc in each st around—144 reverse sc. End off.

FINISHING: Steam-press pieces. Cut felt same size; sew tog over pillow form.

PATCH PILLOW

Charming patch pillow is formed with 25 motifs, no two alike, joined with herringbone stitch to create a rectangular shape, somewhat irregular around the four sides. Indentations on the edges are filled in with stitches of varying lengths.

SIZE: 14" x 18".

MATERIALS: Knitting worsted, about 8 ozs. altogether of various colors, including variegated and tweeds (2 ozs. of one color needed for border and some motifs). If crocheted back is desired, use 2 4-oz. skeins of one color for back, border and some motifs. Crochet hook size H. Small amount of lighter-weight wool in pastel colors for joining motifs. Tapestry needle. Pillow form. Fabric for pillow cover, ½ yd.

GAUGE: 4 sts = 1".

PILLOW TOP: MOTIF 1 (made with 4 colors): With first color, ch 4, sl st in first ch to form ring.

Rnd 1: Ch 3, 2 dc in ring, (ch 2, 3 dc in ring) 3 times, ch 2, sl st in top of ch 3. End off.

Rnd 2: Join 2nd color in any ch-2 sp, ch 3, 3 dc in sp, (ch 5, 4 dc in next sp) 3 times, ch 5, sl st in top of ch 3. End off.

Rnd 3: Join 3rd color in any ch-5 sp, ch 3, 2 dc in sp, ch 3, 3 dc in same sp, (ch 3, 3 dc, ch 3, 3 dc in next sp) 3 times, ch 3, sl st in top of ch 3. End off.

Rnd 4: Join 4th color in any corner sp, ch 3, 4 dc in sp, (ch 3, 3 dc in next sp, ch 3, 5 dc in corner sp) 3 times, ch 3, 3 dc in next sp, ch 3, sl st in top of ch 3. End off.

MOTIF 2 (made with 2 colors): Work as for motif 1 through rnd 1.

Rnd 2: Join 2nd color in any ch-2 sp, ch 3, 2 dc in sp, ch 1, 3 dc in same sp, (ch 1, 3 dc, ch 1, 3 dc in next sp) 3 times, ch 1, sl st in top of ch 3. End off.

MOTIF 3 (made with 2 colors): With first color, ch 4, sl st in first ch to form ring.

Rnd 1: Ch 3, 2 dc in ring, (ch 3, 3 dc in ring) twice, ch 3, sl st in top of ch 3. End off.

Rnd 2: Join 2nd color in any ch-3 sp, ch 3, 2 dc in sp, ch 1, 3 dc in same sp, (ch 2, 3 dc, ch 1, 3 dc in next sp) twice, ch 2, sl st in top of ch 3.

Rnd 3: Sc in each dc, 2 sc in each ch-1 sp, 4 sc in each ch-2 sp around. End off.

MOTIF 4 (made with 4 colors): With first color, ch 4, sl st in first ch to form ring.

Rnd 1: Ch 4, (dc, ch 1) 9 times in ring, sl st in 3rd ch of ch 4. End off.

Rnd 2: Join 2nd color in any ch-1 sp, ch 3, dc in same sp, ch 1, (2 dc in next sp, ch 1) 9 times, sl st in top of ch 3. End off.

Rnd 3: Join 3rd color in any ch-1 sp, ch 3, 2 dc in same sp, ch 2, (3 dc in next sp, ch 2) 9 times, sl st in top of ch 3. End off.

Rnd 4: Join 4th color in any ch-2 sp, ch 3, 4 dc in same sp, ch 2, (2 dc in next sp, ch 2, 5 dc in next sp, ch 2) 4 times, 2 dc in last sp, ch 2, sl st in top of ch 3. End off.

MOTIF 5: Work as for motif 1.

MOTIF 6 (made with 3 colors): With first color, ch 5, sl st in first ch to form ring.

Rnd 1: Ch 3, 2 dc in ring, (ch 2, 3 dc in ring) 4 times, ch 2, sl st in top of ch 3. End off.

Rnd 2: Join 2nd color in any ch-2 sp, ch 3, 2 dc in same sp, ch 2, 3 dc in same sp, (ch 1, 3 dc, ch 2, 3 dc in next sp) 4 times, ch 1, sl st in top of ch 3. End off.

Rnd 3: Join 3rd color in any sp, ch 3, 2 dc, ch 1, 3 dc in same sp, (ch 1, 3 dc, ch 1, 3 dc in next sp) 9 times, ch 1, sl st in top of ch 3. End off.

MOTIF 7 (made with 3 colors): With first color, ch 6, sl st in first ch to form ring.

Rnd 1: Ch 3, 2 dc in ring, (ch 3, 3 dc in ring) 3 times, ch 3, sl st in top of ch 3. End off.

Rnd 2: Join 2nd color in any sp, ch 3, 2 dc in same sp, ch 3, 3 dc in same sp, (ch 2, 3 dc, ch 3, 3 dc in next sp) 3 times, ch 2, sl st in top of ch 3. End off.

Rnd 3: Join 3rd color in any ch-3 sp, ch 3, 2 dc in same sp, ch 2, 3 dc in same sp, (ch 2, 3 dc in next sp, ch 2, 3 dc, ch 2, 3 dc in next sp) 3 times, ch 2, 3 dc in next sp, ch 2, sl st in top of ch 3. End off.

MOTIF 8 (made with 1 color): Ch 5, sl st in first ch to form ring. Ch 3, work 13 dc in ring. Sl st in top of ch 3. End off.

MOTIF 9 (made with 2 colors): With first color, ch 10. Work afghan st square as follows:

Row 1: Pull up a lp in 2nd ch from hook and in each ch across— 10 lps on hook. Yo hook, pull through first lp, * yo hook, pull through next 2 lps, repeat from * until 1 lp remains on hook. This lp counts as first st of next row.

Row 2: Sk first vertical bar, pull up a lp in each of next 9 vertical bars—10 lps on hook. Work lps off as on row 1.

Rows 3-7: Repeat row 2. End off.

Join 2nd color in first sp of row 7 (between first and 2nd vertical bars), ch 3, 2 dc in same sp, (ch 1, sk 1 sp, 3 dc in next sp) 4 times; working down side of square, (ch 1, sk 1 row, 3 dc in edge of next row) twice, ch 1, 3 dc in corner; working across ch edge of square, (ch 1, sk 2 ch, 3 dc in next ch) 3 times; working up side of square, (ch 1, sk 1 row, 3 dc in next row)

twice, ch 1, sl st in top of ch 3. End off. Use last side for top edge of motif.

MOTIF 10 (made with 2 colors): With first color, ch 8, sl st in first ch to form ring.

Rnd 1: Ch 3, 14 dc in ring. Sl st in top of ch 3.

Rnd 2: Ch 5, (dc in next dc, ch 2) 14 times, sl st in 3rd ch of ch 5. End off.

Rnd 3: Join 2nd color in any sp, ch 3, 2 dc in same sp, 3 dc in each sp around, sl st in top of ch 3. End off.

Rnd 4: Join first color with sc in sp between any 2 dc, sc in each sp between dc's around, sl st in first sc. End off.

MOTIF 11: Work as for motif 8.

MOTIF 12: Work as for motif 8.

MOTIF 13 (made with 1 color): Ch 5, sl st in first ch to form ring. Ch 4, 16 tr in ring. Sl st in top of ch 4. End off.

MOTIF 14 (made with 2 colors): With first color, ch 4, sl st in first ch to form ring.

Rnd 1: Ch 4, 2 tr in ring, (ch 3, 3 tr in ring) 3 times, ch 3, sl st in top of ch 4. End off.

Rnd 2: Join 2nd color in any ch-3 sp, ch 3, 2 dc in same sp, ch 1, 3 dc in same sp, (ch 3, 3 dc, ch 1, 3 dc in next sp) 3 times, ch 3, sl st in top of ch 3. End off.

MOTIF 15 (made with 5 colors): With first color, ch 4, sl st in first ch to form ring.

Rnd 1: Ch 3, 2 dc in ring, (ch 3, 3 dc in ring) 3 times, ch 3, sl st in top of ch 3. End off.

Rnd 2: Join 2nd color in any ch-3 sp, ch 3, 2 dc in same sp, ch 3, 3 dc in same sp, (ch 4, 3 dc, ch 3, 3 dc in next sp) 3 times, ch 4, sl st in top of ch 3. End off.

Rnd 3: Join 3rd color in any ch-3 sp, ch 3, dc in same sp, ch 1, 2 dc in same sp, (ch 3, 4 dc in next sp, ch 3, 2 dc, ch 1, 2 dc in next sp) 3 times, ch 3, 4 dc in next sp, ch 3, sl st in top of ch 3. End off.

Rnd 4: Join 4th color in any ch-1 sp, ch 3, 2 dc in same sp, * (ch 1, 5 dc in next sp) twice, ch 1, 3 dc in next sp, repeat from * around, end ch 1, sl st in top of ch 3. End off.

Rnd 5: Join 5th color with sc in any dc, sc in each dc, 2 sc in each ch-1 sp around. End off.

MOTIF 16 (made with 3 colors): Work as for motif 3 through rnd 2. End off.

Rnd 3: Join 3rd color in any ch-1 sp, ch 3, 2 dc in same sp, ch 1, 3 dc in same sp, (ch 1, 6 dc in next sp, ch 1, 3 dc, ch 1, 3 dc in next sp) twice, ch 1, 6 dc in next sp, ch 1, sl st in top of ch 3. End off.

MOTIF 17 (made with 3 colors): With first color, ch 8, sl st in first ch to form ring.

Rnd 1: Ch 2, 15 hdc in ring. Sl st in top of ch 2.

Rnd 2: Ch 3; holding back last lp of each dc, 2 dc in same st with sl st, yo and through all lps on hook (cluster), (ch 3, sk 1 hdc, 3 dc cl in next hdc) 7 times, ch 3, sl st in top of first cl. End off.

Rnd 3: Join 2nd color in any sp, ch 3, 4 dc in same sp, (ch 3, 4 dc in next sp, ch 3, 5 dc in next sp) 3 times, ch 3, 4 dc in next sp, ch 3, sl st in top of ch 3. End off.

Rnd 4: Join 3rd color in any sp before 5-dc group, ch 3, 3 dc in same sp, ch 1, 4 dc in same sp, (ch 1, 3 dc, ch 1, 3 dc in next sp, ch 1, 4 dc, ch 1, 4 dc in next sp) 3 times, ch 1, 3 dc, ch 1, 3 dc in next sp, ch 1, sl st in top of ch 3. End off.

MOTIF 18: Work as for motif 7, beg with ch 4 instead of ch 6.

MOTIF 19: Work as for motif 3 through rnd 2. End off.

MOTIF 20 (made with 2 colors): With first color, ch 4, sl st in first ch to form ring.

Rnd 1: Ch 3, 2 dc in ring, (ch 1, 3 dc in ring) twice, ch 1, sl st in top of ch 3. End off.

Rnd 2: Join 2nd color in any ch-1 sp, ch 3, 2 dc in same sp, (ch 4, 3 dc in next sp) twice, ch 4, sl st in top of ch 3. End off.

MOTIF 21: Work as for motif 20.

MOTIF 22: Work as for motif 20.

MOTIF 23: Work as for motif 18 through rnd 2. End off.

MOTIF 24 (made with one color): Ch 4, sl st in first ch to form ring. Ch 3, 5 dc in ring. End off.

MOTIF 25: Work as for motif 24.

FINISHING: See diagram for placement of motifs. Join motifs with herringbone stitch, working through back lps only on edge of motifs and using lightweight yarn. With border color, work around pillow top in sc, filling in uneven sections and indentations around edge with longer sts as necessary.

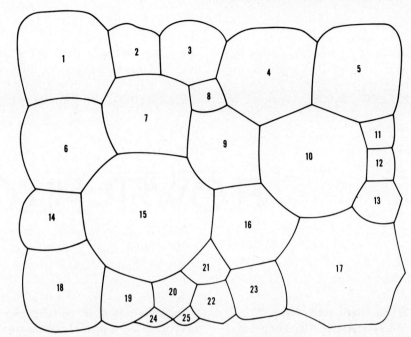

Work 3 or 4 rnds of sc, working 3 sc in each corner each rnd. Crochet a back for pillow same size as top, or cut fabric back. If back is crocheted, join top and back with sc. If back is fabric, stitch back to top through next to last rnd of crochet.

SUNBURST PILLOW

Shown at lower left on page 272

Popcorns center a fluted pillow made in sunny yellows, oranges, browns.

SIZE: 12″ in diameter.

MATERIALS: Knitting worsted, 1 oz. each of yellow (A), light orange (B), medium orange (C), dark orange (D), beige (E), light brown (F), medium brown (G), dark brown (H). Steel crochet hook No. 0. Plastic crochet hook size 5. Foam rubber pillow, 12″ in diameter, 2½″ thick. Tapestry needle.

GAUGE: 5 sc = 1″ (crochet hook size 5).

PILLOW TOP: Beg at center with A and No. 0 hook, ch 4. Sl st in first ch to form ring.

Rnd 1: 10 sc in ring, sl st in first sc.

Rnd 2: Ch 4 (counts as 1 dc), 3 dc in first sc, drop lp off hook, insert hook from front to back in first dc, draw lp through (popcorn made), ch 1, * 4 dc in next sc, drop lp off hook, insert hook from front to back in first dc, draw lp through (popcorn made), ch 1, repeat from * around—10 popcorns. Join with a sl st in first popcorn.

Rnd 3: Work a popcorn, ch 1, in each st around—20 popcorns. Join in first popcorn.

Rnd 4: Ch 1, (sc in each of next 3 sts, 2 sc in next st) 10 times—50 sc. Join in first sc.

Rnd 5: * Ch 7, sc in 2nd ch from hook and in each of next 5 ch, sl st in next sc, sc in next sc, repeat from * 24 times—25 points. Join in next st. Turn. Work with size 5 hook hereafter.

Row 6: * Sk sc and sl st; sc in back lp of each of next 6 sc; work sc, ch 1, sc in top of point, work 6 sc on side of ch, repeat from * around, end sl st in joining sl st. Turn.

Row 7: Sk first sc; * sc in back lp of each of 6 sc; work sc, ch 2, sc in ch 1, sc in back lp of each of 6 sc, sk next 2 sc, repeat from * around, end last repeat sk next sc, sl st in sl st. Cut A; join B. Turn.

Rows 8-10: With B, sk first sc, * sc in back lp of each of 6 sc; work sc, ch 2, sc in ch-2 sp, sc in back lp of each of 6 sc, sk next 2 sc, repeat from * around, end last repeat sk next sc, sl st in sl st. Turn. Repeat row 8 for pat.

Rows 11-36: Work 4 rows C, 4 rows D, 2 rows H, 2 rows G, 2 rows

F, 2 rows E, 2 rows A, 2 rows B, 2 rows C, 2 rows D, 2 rows H. End off.

PILLOW BACK: Work as for pillow top working rows 1-7 with E, then 3 rows F, 4 rows G, 2 rows H. End off; leave end for sewing.

FINISHING: Run in all yarn ends on wrong side. Working through back lps, with H, weave edges of pillow top and back tog over pillow.

FLOWER PILLOW

Double crochet clusters and spaces form one side of Flower Pillow; the other side is "rose."

SIZE: 12″ in diameter.

MATERIALS: Knitting worsted, 4 ply, 1 2-oz. skein each of white (A), green (B), yellow (C), orange (D) and light brown (E). Plastic crochet hook size H. Foam rubber pillow, 12″ in diameter, 2½″ or 3″ thick. One-half yd. white fabric. Matching sewing thread. Tapestry needle.

GAUGE: 5 dc = 1″.

PILLOW TOP: Beg at center with A, ch 7. Join with sl st in first ch to form ring.

Rnd 1: Ch 3 (counts as 1 dc), 19 dc in ring. Do not join.

Rnd 2: * Ch 7, sk 4 dc, sl st in back of work around bar of next dc, repeat from * twice, end ch 7, sl st in first ch of ch-7 lp at beg of rnd—4 lps.

Rnd 3: Work sc, hdc, 8 dc, hdc, sc in each ch-7 lp, end sl st in first sc—4 petals.

Rnd 4: * Ch 5, sl st in back of work around bar of 4th dc of same petal, ch 5, sl st in first sc of next

BACK OF FLOWER PILLOW, TOP LEFT; SUNBURST PILLOW, LOWER LEFT

Front of Flower Pillow

petal, repeat from * 3 times, end sl st in first ch of rnd—8 ch-5 lps.

Rnd 5: Work sc, hdc, 7 dc, hdc, sc in each ch-5 lp, end sl st in first sc—8 petals.

Rnd 6: Ch 3, * sl st in back of work around bar of 4th dc of next petal, ch 7, repeat from * 7 times, end sl st in first sl st—8 ch-7 lps.

Rnd 7: Work sc, hdc, 10 dc, hdc, sc in each ch-7 lp, end sl st in first sc—8 petals.

Rnd 8: * Ch 5, sl st in back of work around bar of 5th dc of same petal, ch 5, sl st in first sc of next petal, repeat from * 7 times—16 ch-5 lps.

Rnd 9: Work sl st, ch 2, 7 dc, ch 2, sl st in each ch-5 lp, end with sl st in first st—16 petals. End off.

Rnd 10: Join B with a sl st in 4th dc of next petal, work ch 3, 2 dc in same dc, ch 3, work tr between sl sts at end of petal, * ch 3, work 3 dc in 4th dc in next petal, ch 3, tr between sl sts at end of petal, repeat from * around, end ch 3, sl st in top of ch 3.

Rnd 11: Sl st in next dc, ch 5, * (dc in next ch-3 sp) twice, ch 2, dc in center dc of 3-dc group, ch 2, repeat from * around, end ch 2, sl st in 3rd ch of ch 5. End off.

Rnd 12: Join C with a sl st in center of 2-dc group, ch 5, * (dc in next ch-2 sp) twice, ch 2, dc between 2 dc of next 2-dc group, ch 2, repeat from * around, end ch 2, sl st in 3rd ch of ch 5. End off.

Rnd 13: Join D in ch-2 sp after 2 dc, ch 3, 2 dc in same ch-2 sp, * ch 1, 3 dc in next ch-2 sp, ch 1, dc between 2 dc, ch 1, 3 dc in next ch-2 sp, repeat from * around, end ch 1, dc between next 2 dc, ch 1, sl st in 3rd ch of starting ch. End off.

Rnd 14: Join C in next ch-1 sp between 3-dc groups, ch 5, * 2 dc in next ch-1 sp, 2 dc in next ch-1 sp, ch 2, dc in next ch-1 sp, ch 2, repeat from * around, end last repeat ch 2, sl st in 3rd ch of starting ch. End off.

Rnd 15: Join A in last ch-2 sp made before sl st, ch 2, 2 hdc in same sp, * ch 1, 3 hdc in next ch-2 sp, ch 1, sk 2 dc, work 2 hdc between 2-dc groups, ch 1, sk 2 dc, work 3 hdc in next ch-2 sp, repeat from * around, end last repeat ch 1, sl st in top of starting ch.

Rnd 16: Ch 5, 2 hdc in next ch-1 sp, * ch 3, 2 hdc in next sp, ch 2, 2 hdc in next sp, ch 3, 2 hdc in next sp, repeat from * around, end last repeat ch 2, hdc in last sp, sl st in 2nd ch of starting ch. End off.

Rnd 17: Join E with sl st in next sp, ch 3, 2 dc in same sp, * ch 1, 3 dc in next sp, repeat from * around, end ch 1, sl st in top of starting ch.

Rnd 18: Sl st in next 2 dc, sl st in ch-1 sp, ch 3, dc in same sp, * ch 1, 2 dc in next sp, repeat from * around, end ch 1, sl st in top of ch 3. End off.

Rnd 19: Join A with sl st in any sp, ch 2, hdc in same sp, * ch 1, 2 hdc in next sp, repeat from * around, end ch 1, sl st in top of ch 2.

Rnd 20: Sl st in next hdc, sl st in ch-1 sp, ch 2, hdc in same sp, * ch 1, 2 hdc in next sp, repeat from * around, end ch 1, sl st in top of ch 2. End off.

Rnd 21: Join E with sl st in any sp, ch 3, dc in same sp, * ch 1, 2 dc in next sp, repeat from * around, end ch 1, sl st in top of ch 3.

Rnd 22: Sl st in dc, sl st in ch-1 sp, ch 3, dc in same sp, * ch 1, 2 dc in next sp, repeat from * around, end ch 1, sl st in top of ch 3. End off.

PILLOW BACK: Beg at center with A, ch 7. Sl st in first ch to form ring.

Rnd 1: Ch 3, 21 dc in ring. Join with a sl st in top of ch 3.

Rnd 2: Ch 5, sk next dc, * dc in next dc, ch 2, sk next dc, repeat from * around, end ch 2, sl st in 3rd ch of starting ch 5—11 sps.

Rnd 3: Sl st in sp, ch 3, 2 dc in same sp, * ch 2, 3 dc in next sp, repeat from * around, end ch 2, sl st in top of ch 3. End off.

Rnd 4: Join A in next ch-2 sp, ch 3, 3 dc in same sp, * ch 2, 4 dc in next sp, repeat from * around, end ch 2, sl st in top of ch 3. End off.

Rnd 5: Join C in 3rd dc of 4-dc group, ch 5, * 3 dc in next ch-2 sp, ch 2, dc in 3rd dc of next 4-dc group, ch 2, repeat from * around, end ch 2, sl st in 3rd ch of starting ch. End off.

Rnd 6: Join D in center dc of 3-dc group, ch 5, * 2 dc in next sp, ch 1, 2 dc in next sp, ch 2, dc in center dc of 3-dc group, ch 2, repeat from * around, end last repeat ch 2, sl st in 3rd ch of starting ch. End off.

Rnd 7: Join C in ch-2 sp after 2-dc group, work ch 3, 2 dc in same sp, * ch 1, 3 dc in next ch-2 sp, ch 1, dc in next ch-1 sp, ch 1, 3 dc in next ch-2 sp, repeat from * around, end last repeat ch 1, sl st in top of starting ch. End off.

Rnd 8: Join A in ch-1 sp between 3-dc groups, ch 6, * 2 dc in next sp, ch 1, 2 dc in next sp, ch 3, dc in next sp, ch 3, repeat from * around, end last repeat ch 3, sl st in 3rd ch of starting ch. End off.

Rnd 9: Join E in next ch-1 sp, ch 5, * 4 dc in ch-3 sp, ch 1, 4 dc in next sp, ch 2, dc in next sp, ch 2, repeat from * around, end last repeat ch 2, sl st in 3rd ch of starting ch.

Rnd 10: Ch 3, 2 dc in sp, ch 1, * dc in 3rd dc of 4-dc group, ch 1, dc in ch-1 sp, ch 1, dc in 3rd dc of next 4-dc group, ch 1, 3 dc in ch-2 sp, ch 1, 3 dc in next ch-2 sp, ch 1, repeat from * around, end last repeat ch 1, sl st in top of starting ch. End off.

FINISHING: Run in all yarn ends on wrong side. Cover pillow form tightly with fabric. With A, sc edges of pillow top and back tog over pillow.

BARGELLO CROCHET PILLOW

Stripes of single crochet and long single crochet in graduated lengths pattern a 14" pillow top in four colors to resemble the flamelike designs of bargello needlepoint.

MATERIALS: Orlon yarn of knitting worsted weight, 1 oz. each of 4 colors: natural (A), turquoise (B), rust (C) and peach (D). Crochet hook size G. Fifteen-inch square of fabric for pillow back. Fourteen-inch pillow form.

GAUGE: 3 sts = 1".

PILLOW TOP: With A, ch 44.

Row 1: Sc in 2nd ch from hook and in each ch across—43 sc. Ch 1, turn.

Rows 2-4: Sc in each sc across. Ch 1, turn each row. At end of row 4, end off A; turn.

Row 5: With B, make lp on hook. Working over ends of A and B to hide them, sc in first sc, * long sc in next st 2 rows below (in row 3), long sc in next st 3 rows below (in row 2), long sc in next st 4 rows below (in row 1), long sc in next st 3 rows below, long sc in next st 2 rows below, sc in next sc, repeat from * across. Ch 1, turn.

Rows 6-8: Sc in each sc across. Ch 1, turn each row. At end of row 8, end off B; turn.

Rows 9-12: With C, repeat rows 5-8.

Rows 13-16: With D, repeat rows 5-8. Alternating 4 rows each of A, B, C, D, work in pat through row 64 (4 repeats of each color), then work 4 rows of A in pat. End off.

FINISHING: Block piece to 14½" square. Place pillow top and pillow back together, wrong sides out. Stitch together on 3 sides, taking ½" seam allowance on pillow back and ¼" seam allowance on pillow top. Turn right side out. Insert pillow form; sew open side closed.

TABLECLOTHS, PLACE MATS AND A LACY CURTAIN

HARVEST TABLECLOTH

Four exquisite tablecloths, shown in this section, herald a return to the love of heirloom designs. The Harvest Tablecloth, made entirely of square motifs, suggests spikes of wheat on a filmy background. Chain loops and picots form the cloth's edging.

SIZE: 63″ x 83″.

MATERIALS: Mercerized crochet cotton, size 30, 27 400-yd. balls of white or ecru, or 19 550-yd. balls of white or ecru. Steel crochet hook No. 10.

GAUGE: Each motif = 4¼″ square.

TABLECLOTH: FIRST MOTIF: Beg at center, ch 6. Sl st in first ch to form ring.

Rnd 1: Ch 3, 23 dc in ring. Sl st in top of ch 3.

Rnd 2: Ch 6, dc in same place as sl st, * ch 3, sk 2 dc, dc in next dc, ch 3, sk 2 dc; in next dc make dc, ch 3 and dc (corner sp), repeat from * around, end ch 3, sl st in 3rd ch of ch 6.

Rnd 3: Ch 4; in next sp make 4 tr, ch 3 and 5 tr; * ch 2, sk 1 sp; in next dc make dc, ch 3 and dc; ch 2; in corner sp make 5 tr, ch 3 and 5 tr, repeat from * around, end ch 2, sl st in top of ch 4.

Rnd 4: Ch 5; holding back on hook last lp of each dtr, make dtr in next 4 tr, yo hook and through all lps on hook (cluster made); * ch 3; in next sp make (5 dtr, ch 3) twice, 5 dtr cl over next 5 tr, ch 3, sk 1 sp; in next sp make tr, ch 3 and tr; ch 3, cl over next 5 tr, repeat from * around, sl st in tip of cl.

Rnd 5: Sl st to next dtr, ch 5, 4 dtr cl over next 4 dtr, * ch 3; in next sp make (5 dtr, ch 3) twice, cl over next 5 dtr, ch 3, sk 2 sps; in next sp make (tr, ch 3) 4 times, sk 2 sps, cl over next 5 dtr, repeat from * around; join.

Rnd 6: Sl st to next dtr, ch 5, complete a cl, * ch 3; in next sp make (5 dtr, ch 3) twice, cl over 5 dtr, ch 3, sk 2 sps; in each of next 3 sps make (tr, ch 3) twice, sk 2 sps, cl over 5 dtr, repeat from * around; join.

Rnd 7: Sl st to next dtr, ch 5, complete a cl, * ch 3, 5 dtr in next sp, ch 3, cl over 5 dtr, ch 3, sk 2 sps; in each of next 5 sps make (tr, ch 3) twice; sk 2 sps, cl over 5 dtr, repeat from * around; join.

Rnd 8: Sc in same place as sl st, * ch 9, cl over 5 dtr, ch 5, sc in tip of same cl, ch 9, sc in next cl, ch 7, sk 1 sp, sc in next sp, ch 5, sc in next sp, (ch 3, sc in next sp) 6 times, ch 5, sc in next sp, ch 7, sc in next cl, repeat from * around; join to first sc. End off.

2ND MOTIF: Work as for first motif until 7 rnds have been completed.

Rnd 8: Sc in same place as sl st, ch 9, cl over 5 dtr, ch 2, sl st in

corner lp of first motif, ch 2, sc in same cl on 2nd motif, ch 4, sl st in next lp on first motif, ch 4, sc in next cl on 2nd motif, ch 3, sl st in next lp on first motif, ch 3, sk 1 sp on 2nd motif, sc in next sp, ch 2, sl st in next lp on first motif, ch 2, sc in next sp on 2nd motif, (ch 1, sl st in next lp on first motif, ch 1, sc in next sp on 2nd motif) 6 times, ch 2, sl st in next lp on first motif, ch 2, sc in next sp on 2nd motif, ch 3, sl st in next lp on first motif, ch 3, sc in cl on 2nd motif, ch 4, sl st in next lp on first motif, ch 4, cl over 5 dtr on 2nd motif, ch 2, sl st in corner lp on first motif, ch 2, sc in

tip of same cl on 2nd motif. Complete rnd as for first motif. There are no more joinings.

Make 14 x 19 motifs, joining as 2nd motif was joined to first motif. Where 4 corners meet, join 3rd and 4th corners to joining of previous 2 corners.

EDGING: Rnd 1: Join thread to a free corner lp, sc in lp, * (ch 7, sc in next lp) twice, (ch 5, sc in next lp) 9 times, ch 7, sc in next lp, ch 7, sc in joining, repeat from * across, ending with sc in corner lp. Continue around, working other sides to correspond, end with sc in last lp, ch 3, tr in first sc.

Rnd 2: Sc in lp just formed, ch 7, sc in same lp, ch 7; in next lp make sc, ch 7 and sc, * ch 5, sc in next lp, repeat from * around, making 3 ch-7 lps over the 2 lps at each corner and ending with ch 3, tr in the tr.

Rnd 3: Sc in lp just formed, (ch 7, sc in next lp) 3 times; * ch 5, sc in next lp, repeat from * around, making 3 ch-7 lps at each corner and ending as before.

Rnd 4: Sc in lp just formed, * ch 7, dc in 5th ch from hook, ch 2, sc in next lp, repeat from * around; join to first sc. End off. Starch lightly and press.

SHADOW SQUARES

Small squares with cobwebby centers are joined in the crochet to make this pretty tablecloth. Work goes quickly with cotton heavier than usual for tablecloths.

SIZES: Small cloth: 65" square. Large cloth: 65" x 84".

MATERIALS: Knitting and crochet cotton, 18 250-yd. balls of white or ecru for small cloth, 24 balls for large cloth; or 26 175-yd. balls of cream or other color for small cloth, 35 balls for large cloth. Steel crochet hook No. 7.

GAUGE: Each motif = 2¾" square.

TABLECLOTH: FIRST MOTIF: Beg at corner, ch 5.

Row 1: In 5th ch from hook make tr, ch 7 and 2 tr. Ch 3, turn.

Row 2: Sk first tr, dc in next tr, ch 5, sc in next lp, ch 5, dc in next tr, dc in top of starting ch. Ch 3, turn.

Row 3: Sk first dc, dc in next dc, ch 5, sc in next lp, sc in next sc, sc in next lp, ch 5, dc in next dc, dc in top of turning ch. Ch 4, turn.

Row 4: Sk first dc, tr in next dc,

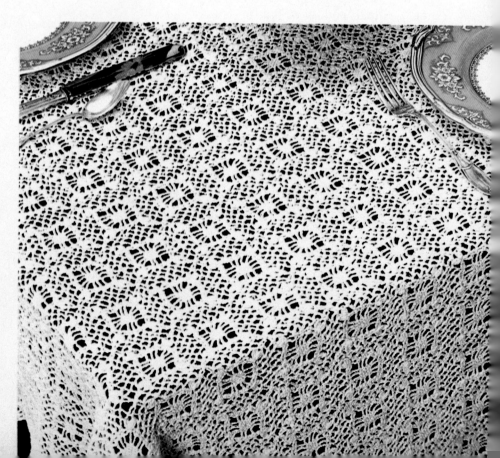

ch 5, sc in next lp, sc in next 3 sc, sc in next lp, ch 5, tr in next dc, tr in top of turning ch. Ch 4, turn.

Row 5: Sk first tr, tr in next tr, ch 4, sc in next 5 sc, ch 4, tr in next tr, tr in top of turning ch. Ch 3, turn.

Row 6: Sk first tr, dc in next tr, ch 4, sk next sc, sc in next 3 sc, ch 4, dc in next tr, dc in top of turning ch. Ch 3, turn.

Row 7: Sk first dc, dc in next dc, ch 3, sk next sc, sc in next sc, ch 3, dc in next dc, dc in top of turning ch. Ch 4, turn.

Row 8: Sk first dc; holding back on hook the last lp of each tr, tr in next dc, sk next 2 lps, tr in next dc, tr in top of turning ch, yo hook and through all lps on hook—**joint tr made.** Ch 3; do not turn.

Work in rnds as follows:

Rnd 1: Holding back on hook the last lp of each dc, make 2 dc in tip of first joint tr, yo hook and through all lps on hook—**2-dc cluster made;** ch 3, 3-dc cl in same place; working along the 4 sides of motif, ch 4, sc in top of turning ch made at end of row 6, ch 5, sc in top of last dc of row 6, ch 5, sc in top of turning ch made at end of row 4, ch 4, 3-dc cl in top of last tr of row 4, ch 3, 3-dc cl in same tr; ch 4, sc in top of turning ch made at end of row 2, ch 5, sc in top of last dc of row 2, ch 5, sc in top of starting ch, ch 4, 3-dc cl in first ch of starting ch, ch 3, 3-dc cl in same ch; ch 4, sc in top of last tr of row 1, ch 5, sc in top of turning ch made at end of row 1, ch 5, sc in top of last dc of row 3, ch 4, 3-dc cl in top of turning ch made at end of row 3, ch 3, 3-dc cl in same ch; ch 4, sc in top of last tr of row 5, ch 5, sc in top of turning ch made at end of row 5, ch 5, sc in top of last dc of row 7, ch 1, dc in tip of first cl to form last lp.

Rnd 2: Ch 1, sc in lp just formed, * ch 5; in next ch-3 corner lp make sc, ch 7 and sc, (ch 5, sc in

next lp) 4 times, repeat from * around, end (ch 5, sc in next lp) 3 times, ch 5, sl st to first sc. End off.

2ND MOTIF: Work as for first motif until rnd 1 has been completed.

Rnd 2: Ch 1, sc in lp just formed, ch 5, sc in next ch-3 corner lp, ch 3; now join 2 motifs along one side as follows: Sl st in 4th corner lp made on first motif, ch 3, sc in same corner lp on 2nd motif, (ch 2, sl st in next lp on first motif, ch 2, sc in next lp on 2nd motif) 4 times, ch 2, sl st in next lp on first motif, ch 2, sc in next corner lp on 2nd motif, ch 3, sl st in next corner lp on first motif, ch 3, sc in same corner lp on 2nd motif; working on 2nd motif only, (ch 5, sc in next lp) 4 times; beg at * on rnd 2 of first motif, complete 2nd motif as for first motif.

Make 23 x 23 motifs for small cloth, or 23 x 30 motifs for large cloth, joining motifs as 2nd motif was joined to first motif. Where 4 corners meet, join corners to previous joinings.

BORDER: Rnd 1: Join thread in last lp preceding any corner lp, sc in same lp, * ch 5; in corner lp

make sc, ch 5 and sc; ** (ch 5, sc in next lp) 5 times; ch 5, sc in joining between motifs, repeat from ** to within next corner lp; repeat from * around, end ch 2, dc in first sc to form last lp.

Rnd 2: Ch 1, sc in lp just formed, ch 5, sc in next lp, * ch 5; in next corner lp make sc, ch 5 and sc; ** ch 5, sc in next lp, repeat from ** across to within next corner lp; repeat from * around, end as on rnd 1.

Rnd 3: Ch 1, sc in lp just formed, (ch 5, sc in next lp) twice; beg at * on rnd 2, complete rnd.

Rnd 4: Ch 1, sc in joining, ch 4, sc in next lp, ch 4; in next lp make sc, ch 3 and 2 dc; ch 3, sl st in last dc made; in next lp make 2 dc, ch 3 and sc; * ch 4; in next corner lp make 3 dc, ch 5 and 3 dc; ** ch 4; in next lp make sc, ch 3 and 2 dc; ch 3, sl st in last dc made; in next lp make 2 dc, ch 3 and sc; ch 4, sc in next lp, repeat from ** across to within next corner lp, end 2 dc, ch 3 and sc in last lp, repeat from * around, end 2 dc in first lp used at beg of rnd, ch 3, sl st to first sc. End off.

Block to measurements.

QUEEN ANNE'S LACE

The most treasured pattern of all, Queen Anne's Lace, combines lovely flowerlike motifs of two sizes. A simple scalloped border finishes the edges.

SIZE: 60″ x 80″.

MATERIALS: Mercerized crochet cotton, size 20, 25 325-yd. balls of white or ecru. Steel crochet hook No. 9.

GAUGE: Each motif = 4¾″ diameter.

TABLECLOTH: FIRST MOTIF: Beg at center, ch 6. Join with sl st to form ring.

Rnd 1: Ch 6, (tr in ring, ch 2) 7 times; join to 4th ch of ch 6—8 sps.

Rnd 2: Sl st in next sp, ch 4, 4 tr in same sp, (ch 2, 5 tr in next sp) 7 times, ch 2; join to top of ch 4.

Rnd 3: Ch 4, tr in same place as sl st was made, tr in next 4 tr, * tr in next ch, ch 3, tr in next ch and in next 5 tr; repeat from * around, end ch 3, join to top of ch 4.

Rnd 4: Sl st in next tr, ch 4; holding back on hook the last lp of each tr, tr in next 4 tr, yo hook and through all lps on hook (cluster made), * ch 4, 5 tr in next sp, ch 4, sk next tr, 5-tr cl over next 5 tr; repeat from * around, end ch 4, join to tip of first cl.

Rnd 5: Ch 8, sk next 3 ch, * tr in next ch, tr in next 5 tr, tr in next ch, ch 4, tr in tip of next cl, ch 4, sk next 3 ch; repeat from * around, end ch 4, join to 4th ch of ch 8.

Rnd 6: Ch 1, sc in same place as sl st, * ch 12, sk next tr, 5-tr cl over next 5 tr, ch 12, sk next tr, sc in next tr; repeat from * around, end ch 12, join to first sc—16 lps. End off.

2ND MOTIF: Work as for first motif until first cl on rnd 6 has been completed. Join 2nd and 3rd lps on 2nd motif to first motif as follows: ch 6, sl st in center of 3rd lp on first motif, ch 6, sk next tr on 2nd motif and sc in next tr, ch 6, sl st in center of 2nd lp on first motif, ch 6, sk next tr, 5-tr cl over next 5 tr on 2nd motif and complete rnd as for first motif (no more joinings).

Make 13 rows of 17 motifs, joining 2 corresponding lps to adjacent motifs and leaving 2 lps free between joinings.

FILL-IN MOTIF: Beg at center, ch 8.

Rnd 1: In 8th ch from hook make (tr, ch 4) 3 times; join to 4th ch of ch 8.

Rnd 2: Sl st in next sp, ch 4, 6 tr in same sp, (ch 5, 7 tr in next sp) 3 times, ch 5, join to top of ch 4.

Rnd 3: Sl st in next tr, ch 4, 4-tr cl over next 4 tr; now join fill-in motif to the 8 free ch-12 lps on motifs as follows: * ch 5, sl st in center of ch-12 lp on motif, ch 5, sc in next lp on fill-in motif, ch 5, sl st in center of next ch-12 lp on motif, ch 5; on fill-in motif, sk next tr, 5-tr cl over next 5 tr; repeat from * around, end ch 5, join to tip of first cl on fill-in motif. End off.

EDGING: Join thread in joining sl st between 2 motifs, * 7 sc in next small lp; (sc, hdc, 5 dc, 4 tr, 5 dc, hdc, sc) in each large lp to next small lp, 7 sc in small lp; repeat from * around. Join; end off.

TEA CLOTH

Completely feminine tea cloth, 41" square, combines lacy crochet with fabric. Pattern can be used for larger cloths; center motif can be appliquéd to curtains or other linens.

SIZE: 41" square.

MATERIALS: Mercerized crochet cotton, size 30, 8 skeins white. Steel crochet hook No. 13. White sewing thread. Seven-eighths yd. colored linen.

GAUGE: Block = 5½" square.

Note: Work tightly for best results.

TEA CLOTH: CENTER MOTIF: Beg at center, ch 8, join with sl st to form ring.

Rnd 1: Ch 1, 12 sc in ring. Join with sl st in first sc.

Rnd 2: Ch 8, tr in same sc as sl st, * ch 10, sk 2 sc, (tr, ch 3, tr) in next sc, repeat from * twice, ch 5, join with tr in 5th ch of ch 8—4 ch-3 sps and 4 ch-10 lps.

Rnd 3: * 3 tr in next ch-3 sp, ch 4, sl st in last tr (p made); in ch-3 sp last worked in make (4 tr, p) twice and 3 tr, sc in next ch-10 lp, repeat from * twice, join with sl st in first tr of rnd—4 petals.

Rnd 4: * Ch 7, (tr, ch 5, dtr) in 3rd tr after next p, ch 7, (dtr, ch 5, tr) in 2nd tr after next p, ch 7, sc in sc between petals, repeat from * 3 times, end rnd with sl st.

Rnd 5: Ch 3; holding back on hook last lp of each dc, make 2 dc in next sp, yo and draw tightly through 3 lps on hook (½ cl made), * 4 dc in balance of sp, dc in next tr, 5 dc in next sp, dc in next dtr, 3 dc in next sp, (2 dc, p, 2 dc) in center ch of same sp (corner), 3 dc in balance of same sp, dc in next dtr, 5 dc in next sp, dc in next tr, 4 dc in next sp; holding back on hook last lp of each dc, make tight cl of (2 dc in same sp, dc in sc between petals and 2 dc in next sp, yo and draw tightly through 6 lps on hook), repeat from * 3 times, ending last repeat with first 2 dc of cl, insert hook in first ½ cl of rnd, yo and draw tightly through cl and 3 lps on hook. End off.

BLOCK: Border: Beg with inner 4 sides of block, (ch 6, dc in 6th ch from hook) 48 times. Join with sl st in starting st of border, forming a ring with ch lps on inside edge and straight dc sps on outside edge of border.

First Corner Section: Ch 3, 2 dc in same place as sl st, ** (3 dc in next dc sp, dc in st between dc sps) 6 times, 2 dc in next dc sp, ch 7, turn. Sk 4 dc, sl st in next dc, ch 1, turn. 9 sc in lp just made, sl st in top side of last dc, dc in balance of sp on border, dc between dc sps, 3 dc in next dc sp, dc between dc sps, 2 dc in next dc sp, ch 5, turn. Tr in 2nd sc over lp, ch 5, sk 2 sc, (3 tr, ch 5, 3 tr) in next (center) sc, ch 5, sk 2 sc, tr in next sc, ch 5, sk 7 dc over border, sl st in next dc, ch 1, turn, (3 sc, p, 3 sc) in first sp, sc in next tr, (3 sc, p, 3 sc) in next sp, sc in each of 3 tr, 5 sc in next sp, sc in each of 3 tr, (3 sc, p, 3 sc) in next sp, sc in next tr, (3 sc, p, 3 sc) in end sp, sl st in top side of last dc, dc in balance of dc sp on border, dc between dc sps, 3 dc in next dc sp, dc between dc sps, 2 dc in next dc sp, ch 5, turn. Sk 7 dc, dtr in next dc, (ch 5, tr in sc over next tr) twice, ch 5, (3 tr, ch 5, 3 tr) in center sc over next sp between 3-tr groups (center sp), ch 5, sk 4 sc, tr in next sc, ch 5, tr in sc over next tr, ch 5, dtr in same dc at base of last row, ch 5, sk 7 dc on border, sl st in next dc, ch 1, turn. (3 sc, p, 3 sc) in each of next 4 sps, sc in each of next 3 tr, 5 sc in next sp (center sp), sc in each of next 3 tr, (3 sc, p, 3 sc) in each of last 4 sps, sl st in top side of last dc on border, dc in balance of dc sp, dc in st between dc sps, 3 dc in next dc sp, 3 dc in st between dc sps (first half-corner made), ch 5, turn. Sk 7 dc, tr in next dc, (ch 5, dc in center sc between next 2 p) 3 times, ch 5, tr in

sc over next tr, ch 5, (3 dtr, ch 7, 3 dtr) in center sc over next sp, ch 5, sk 4 sc, tr in next sc, (ch 5, dc in center sc between next 2 p) 3 times, ch 5, tr in same dc at base of last row, ch 5, sk 7 dc over border, sl st in top of ch 3, ch 1, turn. (3 sc, p, 3 sc in next sp, sc in next st) 6 times, sc in each of 3 dtr, in next sp (center sp) make (sc, a ch-4 p, 4 sc, a ch-7 p, 4 sc, a ch-4 p, sc), sc in each of 3 dtr, (3 sc, p, 3 sc in next sp, sc in next st) 6 times, sl st in top side of last dc of corner 3-dc group made over border, make 3 more dc at base of same corner 3-dc group (2nd half-corner made) **. Make 3 more corner sections, working from first ** to 2nd **, omitting 2nd half-corner at end of last repeat, join with sl st to top of ch 3 at beg of first section. End off.

Stretch the 4 inner sides of dc border of block to form a true square. Cut a square of linen 1/16″ larger all around than outside edge of dc border that forms inner square of block. Pin or baste dc borders around edge of linen. Hem down inner edge of dc border and tack down center of each ch-5 lp. Working on back of work, turn edge of linen under against back of dc border and hem down.

Stretch and pin center motif right side down on ironing board. Steam through a doubled wet cloth, then press motif dry through a doubled dry cloth. Pin motif in center of linen and hem down around outside edge. On back of work, cut out linen ¼″ inside stitching; turn this ¼″ edge under against dc border and hem down.

Make 49 blocks. Join blocks 7 x 7 as follows:

Joining-Edge First Block: Join thread with sc in 3rd sc to right of a corner p on first bl (block), * (4 dc, ch 7, 4 dc) in corner p, sk 2 sc, sc in next sc, (ch 10, sc midway between next 2 p) 13 times, ch 10, sc in 2nd sc to left of next p, repeat

from * around, joining final ch 10 with sl st to first sc. End off.

Joining-Edge 2nd Block: Join thread with sc in 3rd sc to right of a corner p on 2nd bl, 4 dc in corner p, ch 3, join with sl st in 1 lp of center st of a corner ch-7 lp on first bl, ch 3, 4 dc back in same corner p on 2nd bl, sk 2 sc, sc in next sc, (ch 5, join with sl st under next ch 10 of first bl, ch 5, sc back midway between next 2 p on 2nd bl) 13 times, ch 5, sl st in next ch-10 lp on first bl, ch 5, sc back in 2nd sc to left of next p on 2nd bl, 4 dc in next corner p, ch 3, join with sl st in 1 lp of center ch of next corner lp on first bl, ch 3, 4 dc back in same p on 2nd bl, sk 2 sc, sc in next sc. Complete edge as for first bl. Forming square, join 3rd bl to 2nd bl, then join a 4th bl to first and 3rd bls in same way. **Note:** Where 4 corners meet, always join to same st where first 2 corners were joined. Continue in this way until all bls are joined.

EDGE: Rnd 1: Join thread with sc in right-hand end of ch-7 lp at one corner of cloth, ** ch 13, sc in left end of same lp, (ch 10, sc in next ch-10 lp) 14 times, * ch 10, sk 4 dc, sc in right end of next joined corner sp, ch 10, sc in left end of next joined corner sp, (ch 10, sc in next ch-10 lp) 14 times *, repeat from first * to 2nd * across side, ch 10, sc in right end of corner ch-7 lp, repeat from ** around. Omit last ch-10 lp, make ch 5 and join with tr in first sc of rnd.

Rnd 2: ** Ch 4, 3 dtr in 5th ch of corner ch-13 lp, (ch 5, sk next ch of same lp, 3 dtr in next ch) twice, ch 4, sc in next ch-10 lp, * (ch 4, 3 dtr in 5th ch of next ch-10 lp, ch 5, 3 dtr in next ch of same lp, ch 4, sc in next lp) *, repeat from first * to 2nd * across side, repeat from ** around, end with sl st instead of sc.

Rnd 3: Sl st in each of 4 sts of next ch, sl st in next 3 dtr, sl st in next sp, ch 7, (2 dtr, ch 5, 3 dtr) in same sp, ** ch 5, sk next dtr, 3 dtr in next dtr, (ch 5, 3 dtr) twice in next sp, * in center sp of next shell make (3 dtr, ch 5, 3 dtr, ch 5, 3 dtr) *, repeat from first * to 2nd * across side, sk first 3 dtr at corner, (3 dtr, ch 5, 3 dtr) in next sp, repeat from ** to end of rnd, end rnd at 2nd *, join with sl st in top of ch 7 at beg of rnd.

Rnd 4: Sc in each of next 2 dtr, 5 sc in next sp, * sc in each of next 2 dtr, make ch-4 p, sc in next dtr, 2

sc in next sp, ch 10 lp, turn, sk p, sl st in 2nd sc over next sp, ch 1, turn, (6 sc, p, 6 sc, 1 sl st) in ch-10 lp just made, ch 1, 3 sc in balance of ch-5 sp, repeat from * twice, sc in each of next 2 dtr, sk 2 dtr (1 each side of angle), ** sc in each of next 2 dtr, 5 sc in next sp, sc in each of next 2 dtr, make p, sc in next dtr, 2 sc in next sp, ch 10 lp, turn, sk p, sl st in 2nd sc over next sp, ch 1, turn, (6 sc, p, 6 sc, sl st) in ch-10 lp just made, ch 1, 3 sc in balance of ch-5 sp, sc in each of next 2

dtr, sk next 2 dtr (1 each side of angle), repeat from ** across side, repeat from beg of rnd, join with sl st in first sc. End off edge.

Placing a rustproof pin in each scallop around edge, pin tea cloth right side down on a large padded board, stretching cloth several inches each way so that it will measure 41″ x 41″.

Steam through a wet cloth, then press dry through a doubled dry cloth. Do not remove pins until cloth is completely dry.

PINK PLACE MATS

Pastel mats are for special occasions. Crocheted of size 30 cotton, with solid centers for table protection, lacy borders for eye appeal, these lovely pink mats are yours for the making.

SIZE: 11″ x 18″.

MATERIALS: Mercerized crochet cotton, size 30, 2 250-yd. balls for each mat. Steel crochet hook No. 10.

GAUGE: 12 sts = 1″; 7 rows = 1″; motif = 2¼″.

MAT: MAIN SECTION: Ch 135.

Row 1: Sc in 2nd ch from hook and in each ch across—134 sc. Ch 3, turn.

Row 2 (right side): Sk first sc, dc in each sc across—134 dc, counting turning ch 3 as 1 dc. Ch 1, turn.

Row 3: Sc in first dc, * ch 3, sk 3 dc, sc in sp between dc's, repeat from * across, end sc in top of ch 3—44 lps. Ch 3, turn.

Row 4: 3 dc in each lp, dc in last sc. Ch 1, turn.

Rows 5-14: Repeat rows 3 and 4, 5 times. At end of row 14, ch 3, turn.

Row 15: Sk first dc, dc in each

dc across, dc in top of turning ch 3. Ch 3, turn.

Row 16: Sk first dc, dc in each dc across, dc in top of turning ch 3. Ch 1, turn.

Repeat rows 3-16, 3 times more, then repeat rows 3-15. At end of row 15, ch 1, turn.

Last Row: Sc in each dc across, sc in top of turning ch. End off.

SINGLE STRIP: First Motif: Ch 8, sl st in first ch to form ring.

Rnd 1: Ch 1, 16 sc in ring. Sl st in first sc.

Rnd 2: Sc in same place as sl st, * ch 7, sc in 2nd ch from hook, hdc in next ch, dc in each of next 3 ch, ch 1, sk next sc, sc in next sc (petal made), repeat from * around, end sk last sc, sl st in first sc.

Rnd 3: Sl st to top of first petal, ch 7, dc in same place as last sl st, * ch 4, dc, ch 4, dc in top of next petal, repeat from * around, end ch 4, sl st in 3rd ch of ch 7.

Rnd 4: Sc in same place as sl st, * 5 sc in next lp, sc in next dc, 4 sc in next lp, sc in next dc, repeat from * around, end 4 sc in last lp, sl st in first sc.

Rnd 5: Sc in same place as sl st, sc in each of next 3 sc, drop lp from hook, insert hook in first foundation ch of main section and draw dropped lp through (joining st made), sc in same sc on motif, ** joining st in next ch on main section, sc in same sc on motif, (joining st in next ch on main section, sc in next sc on motif) 11 times, joining st in next ch on main section, 2 sc in same sc on motif, * sc in each of next 10 sc, 3 sc in next sc, repeat from * around, end sc in each of last 7 sc, sl st in first sc. End off.

2ND MOTIF: Work as for first motif for 4 rnds.

Rnd 5: Sc in same place as sl st, sc in each of next 3 sc, sk 26 sc after last joining st on first motif, joining st in next sc on first motif, sc in same sc on 2nd motif; working along sc just skipped, work a joining st in next sc on first motif, sc in same sc on 2nd motif, (joining st in next sc on first motif, sc in next sc on 2nd motif) 11 times, joining st in next sc on first motif, 2 sc in same sc on 2nd motif, sc in each of next 11 sc, sk 16 ch on foundation ch of main section, joining st in next ch, sc in same sc on 2nd motif, repeat from ** on rnd 5 of first motif.

Make and join 3 more motifs in same manner.

DOUBLE STRIP: First Strip: Work as for single strip, joining motifs to last row of main section.

Second Strip: Make and join one more strip of 5 motifs, joining to previous strip to correspond.

Dampen mat and pin out to measurements.

YELLOW TRAY MAT

Here a versatile pattern of 3" motifs is shown as a tray mat, but a different design will make pretty place mats, tablecloths or curtains. Very lacy fill-in motifs between the main motifs lend a mosaiclike quality to the pattern.

SIZE: 15" x 21".

MATERIALS: Mercerized crochet cotton, size 30, 3 250-yd. balls. Steel crochet hook No. 10.

GAUGE: Each motif is 3".

MAT: FIRST MOTIF: Ch 10.

Rnd 1: In 9th ch from hook work (dtr, ch 4) 7 times, sl st in 6th ch of ch 10—8 sps.

Rnd 2: Sc in same ch as sl st, * 4 sc in next sp, 3 sc in next dtr (corner), 4 sc in next sp, sc in next dtr, repeat from * around, end 4 sc in last sp, sl st in first sc.

Rnds 3-5: Sc in same place as sl st, * sc in each st to center corner st, 3 sc in center sc, repeat from * around, sl st in first sc.

Rnd 6: Ch 5, sk 2 sc, dc in next sc, * ch 2, sk 2 sc, dc in next sc, (ch 5, sk 2 sc, dc in next sc) twice, (ch 2, sk 2 sc, dc in next sc) 3 times, repeat from * around, end ch 2, sk 2 sc, dc in next sc, ch 2, sl st in 3rd ch of ch 5.

Rnd 7: Ch 5, * dc in next dc, ch 2, dc in next dc, ch 5, sc in next sp, sc in next dc, sc in next sp, ch 5, (dc in next dc, ch 2) 3 times, repeat from * around, end (dc in next dc, ch 2) twice, sl st in 3rd ch of ch 5.

Rnd 8: Ch 5, * dc in next dc, ch 2, dc in next dc, ch 5, sc in next sp, sc in each of next 3 sc, sc in next sp, ch 5, (dc in next dc, ch 2) 3 times, repeat from * around, end as for rnd 7.

Rnd 9: Sc in same ch as sl st, (3 sc in next sp, sc in next dc) twice, * 2 sc in next ch-5 sp, ch 5, drop lp from hook, insert hook in 5th last st made before last ch 5 and draw

2ND MOTIF: Work as for first motif to within first picot on rnd 9, ch 5, drop lp from hook, insert hook in 5th last st made before last ch 5 and draw dropped lp through, 2 sc in lp just made, drop lp from hook, insert hook in center sc on corresponding picot of first motif and draw dropped lp through 3 sc in same lp on 2nd motif, sl st in last sc before lp (a joining picot made), work to within next picot, make a joining picot, sc in same lp on 2nd motif, complete as for first motif.

Make 5 rows of 7 motifs, joining adjacent sides as 2nd motif was joined to first, leaving one picot free on each motif between joinings.

FILL-IN-MOTIF: Ch 9, sl st in center sc of any free picot, ch 3, dtr in first ch of ch 9, (ch 5, sl st in next joining between motifs, ch 5, dtr in same ch as last dtr, ch 3, sl st in center sc of next picot, ch 3, dtr in same ch as last dtr) 3 times, ch 5, sl st in next joining between motifs, ch 5, sl st in 6th ch of ch 9. End off.

Fill in all spaces between motifs in same way.

dropped lp through, 5 sc in lp just made, sl st in last sc before lp (picot made), 3 sc in same ch-5 sp, sc in each of next 5 sc, 5 sc in next ch-5 sp, sc in next dc, 2 sc in next sp, 1 picot, sc in same sp, sc in next dc, 3 sc in next sp, ** sc in next dc, 2 sc in next sp, 1 picot, sc in same sp, sc in next dc, 3 sc in next sp, sc in next dc, repeat from * around, end last repeat at **, sl st in each of first 3 sc, 1 picot, working last sl st in same place as last sl st before picot. End off.

ORANGE-AND-GREEN MAT

This orange-and-green place mat of heavy cotton is crocheted in a unique way—a row of shells forms half-disks from bottom to top of mat, then shells complete the little circles from top to bottom. Working from one side of mat to the other, the joined disks form the pattern.

SIZE: 12″ x 18″.
MATERIALS: Quick crochet cotton, 3 100-yd. balls orange, 1 ball green. Steel crochet hook No. 1.

MAT: Row 1: Beg at side edge with orange, (ch 5, 5 dc in 4th ch from hook) 11 times—11 shells. Do not turn.
Row 2: Work 5 more dc in same ch as last shell was made, ch 3, sl st in same ch (top disk made), * sl st in next ch (between the shells), 5 dc in same ch as next shell was made, ch 3, sl st in same ch, repeat

from * to bottom shell—11 disks. Do not turn.

Row 3: Ch 10, 3 dc in 4th ch from hook; drop lp off hook; insert hook in 3rd dc on side of last disk, pick up dropped lp and draw it through st, ch 1, 2 dc in same ch as 3 dc, * ch 5, 3 dc in 4th ch from hook; drop lp off hook; insert hook in 3rd dc on side of next disk above, pick up dropped lp and draw it through st, ch 1, 2 dc in same ch as 3 dc, repeat from * to top. Do not turn.

Row 4: Repeat row 2.

Repeat rows 3 and 2 until there are 14 rows of disks, end row 2. Turn work to wrong side.

BORDER: Rnd 1 (wrong side): Ch 5, sc in 2nd dc of disk just worked, (ch 5, sc in 2nd dc of next disk) 10 times, ch 5, sc in center top of corner disk, (ch 5, sc in center top of next disk) 13 times, ch 5, sc in 2nd dc from end of corner disk, (ch 5, sc in 2nd dc from end of next disk) 10 times, ch 5, sl st in center bottom of corner disk. End off. Turn mat to right side.

Rnd 2: Join green in back lp of sl st just made; ch 3, dc in each of next 2 ch, 3 dc in next ch (corner), dc in each of next 2 ch, dc in back lp of next sc, (dc in each of next 5 ch, dc in back lp of next sc) 10 times, dc in each of next 2 ch, 3 dc in next ch (corner), dc in each of next 2 ch, dc in back lp of next sc, (dc in each of next 5 ch, dc in back lp of next sc) 13 times, dc in each of next 2 ch, 3 dc in next ch (corner), dc in each of next 2 ch, dc in back lp of next sc, (dc in each of next 5 ch, dc in back lp of next sc) 10 times, dc in each of next 2 ch, 3 dc in next ch (corner), dc in each of next 2 ch, (dc in each of next 6 ch) 13 times, sl st in top of ch 3 at beg of rnd. End off.

Rnd 3: Join orange in any dc, ch 3, dc in st before ch 3, * sk next free dc, dc in next dc, dc in skipped dc, repeat from * around, sl st in top of ch 3 at beg of rnd. End off.

Rnd 4: Join green in any dc, ch 3, dc in each st around, working 3 dc in each corner dc, sl st in top of ch 3 at beg of rnd. End off.

Rnd 5: Join orange in any dc, ch 1; working from left to right, sc in each st around. Join; end off.

STRAW TABLE SETTING

This straw table setting includes striped place mats, glass jackets, covers for tin cans to hold flowers, napkin rings, as well as a place card corsage, a grape cluster and coasters.

SIZES: Place mat 11″ x 17″. Glass jacket: 2½″ diameter, 3″ high. Large flower container: 4″ diameter, 4½″ high. Small flower container: 2¾″ diameter, 3″ high.

MATERIALS: Swistraw, matte finish. Four mats: 36 24-yd. skeins beige, main color (MC); 4 skeins each taffy (T) and chartreuse (C); 2 skeins blue (B). One glass jacket: 2 skeins. Large flower container: 4 skeins. Small flower container: 2 skeins. Four napkin rings: 2 skeins MC; 1 skein each C and B. Steel crochet hook No. 0. Tin can No. 2½ for large flower container, 8-oz. size for small flower container.

GAUGE: 5 sts =1″; 5 rows =1″.

Note: To join a new skein of same color, lightly moisten about 6″ of both joining ends and spread to full width. Cut each 6″ end to half width. Touch ½″ at each end with all-purpose glue and glue each end over opposite piece. Leave center split.

PATTERN STITCH: Row 1: Picking up 2 lps of each ch, sc in 3rd ch from hook, * ch 1, sk 1 ch, sc in next ch, repeat from * across. Ch 1, turn. Always turn edge toward you.

Row 2: Sk first sc, * sc over next ch 1 into 2 lps of skipped ch of starting ch, ch 1, repeat from * aross, end ch 1, sc in ch-2 sp of starting ch. Ch 1, turn.

Row 3: Sk first sc, * sc over ch 1 into top (back) lp of sc of previous row, ch 1, repeat from * across, end with sc in ch-1 sp of turning ch. Ch 1, turn. Repeat row 3 for pat.

Finishing Row (right side): When work is desired length and starting end of piece is at the left edge, ch 1, turn. * Sc over ch-1 sp as usual, sc in both lps of next sc, repeat from * across, end with sc in ch-1 sp of turning ch. End off.

MAT: With T, ch 55 to measure 11½". Work in pat for 10 rows. Change to MC. **To change colors,** work last sc until there are 2 lps on hook, drop working color; finish sc with new color, ch 1. Cut dropped strand leaving 2" end. With smaller hook, pull end through to top of sc. On next row, work over this end. On following row, work over end of new color as you approach it.

With MC, work in pat for 7 rows. Change to B. With B, work in pat for 3 rows. Change to C. With C, work in pat for 9 rows. Change to MC. With MC, work in pat until mat is 17"; work finishing row.

GLASS JACKET: BASE: With any mat color, ch 4, join with sl st in first ch to form ring.

Rnd 1: Ch 1, 2 sc in back lp only of each ch—8 sc.

Rnd 2: Working in back lp of each sc, 2 sc in each sc around—16 sc.

Rnd 3: Working in back lp of each sc, * sc in next sc, 2 sc in next sc, repeat from * around—24 sc.

Rnd 4: Working in back lp of each sc, * sc in each of next 2 sc, 2 sc in next sc, repeat from * around—32 sc.

Rnd 5: Working in back lp of each sc, * sc in each of next 3 sc, 2 sc in next sc, repeat from * around to last st, sc in last sc—39 sc. Sl st in next st, ch 2, turn.

SIDES: Rnd 6: * Sk 1 sc, sc in both lps of next sc, ch 1, repeat from * around, end ch 1, sl st in first ch of ch 2—20 ch-1 sps. Ch 1, turn.

Rnd 7: * Sc over next ch 1 into top (back) lp of sc of previous rnd, ch 1, repeat from * around, omit ch 1 after last sc, sl st in ch-1 sp. Ch 1, turn.

Rnds 8-20: Sk first sc, * sc over next ch 1 into top (back) lp of sc of previous rnd, ch 1, repeat from * around, omit ch 1 after last sc, sl st in ch-1 sp. Ch 1, turn.

Rnd 21 (right side): * Sc in both lps of next sc, sc over next ch 1 into top lp of sc of previous rnd, repeat from * around. End off.

LARGE FLOWER CONTAINER: With C or any desired color, ch 61 or any uneven number to fit around can. Work in pat st for 27 rows or until piece almost reaches top of can. Work finishing row; leave end for sewing. Weave edges tog row by row to form snugly fitting tube.

SMALL FLOWER CONTAINER: With B or any desired color, ch 43 or any uneven number to fit around can. Work in pat st for 17 rows or until piece almost reaches top of can. Work finishing row; leave end for sewing. Weave edges tog row by row to form snugly fitting tube.

NAPKIN RING: With MC, ch 7. Work in pat st for 31 rows. Work finishing row; do not end off, turn. Sl st in 2nd st, ch 6 for button loop, sk 2 sts, sl st in next st, 6 sl st in ch 1 at edge. End off.

BUTTON: Leaving 4" end of MC, ch 4, join with sl st in first ch to form ring, ch 1.

Rnd 1: 10 sc in ring, sl st in ch 1. Ch 1.

Rnd 2: Sc in each sc around; join. Ch 1, turn.

Rnd 3: * Sk next sc, sl st in next sc, repeat from * around. End off leaving 4" end. With hook, weave end through last rnd; pull starting end through work; tie ends tog. Tie button to napkin ring opposite loop with the ends.

FLOWER (make 2): Leaving 4" end of B, ch 4, join with sl st in first ch to form ring. * Ch 3, dc in 3rd ch from hook, sc in same ch, sl st in ring, repeat from * 4 times—5 petals. End off; leave 4" end.

Weave end through ring so that it is opposite starting end.

LEAF: Leaving 4" end of C, ch 5. Sc in 2nd ch from hook and in each of next 2 ch, 4 sc in last ch; working back on other side of ch, sc in each of next 2 ch, 2 sc in same ch as first sc of rnd. Sl st in back lp of each of next 5 sc. End off; leave 4" end.

STEMS: Cut 4 lengths of C 6" long. Tie 2 ends of leaf around stems at mid-point; fold 8 stems down.

FINISHING: Place leaf on napkin ring 1½" from button loop. Cross leaf ends over folded stems and pull ends, 1 st apart, through napkin ring to wrong side; tie tightly. Tie flowers in place in same way, one each side of leaf.

PLACE CARD CORSAGE: MATERIALS: Swistraw, 2 yds. each of 3 flower colors and green. Steel crochet hook No. 1. Stamens. Floratape. Green covered wire.

CORSAGE: FLOWER (make 1 of each color): Make as napkin-ring flower above.

LEAF: Cut 6" length of wire. With green, ch 5. Working over wire, sc in 2nd ch from hook and in each of next 2 ch, 4 sc in last ch; working back on other side of ch and over wire, sc in each of next 2 sc, 2 sc in same ch as first sc of rnd. Sl st in first sc. End off.

FINISHING: Insert small bunch of stamens through each flower center. Wind stamen stems and leaf wire with tape. Arrange flowers and leaf; tape stems tog. Glue to place card or sew to napkin ring.

GRAPE CLUSTER: SIZE: About 7" long.

MATERIALS: Swistraw, 2 24-yd. skeins each of 2 blues; 1 skein of green. Steel crochet hook No. 1. Cotton for stuffing. Plastic ring.

GAUGE: 5 sc=1".

CLUSTER: GRAPE (make 8

dark blue, 7 medium blue): Ch 4, sl st in 4th ch from hook to form ring. Ch 1.

Rnd 1: 2 sc in each ch around, 2 sc in ch 1—10 sc.

Rnd 2: Working in back lp of each sc throughout, * sc in next sc, 2 sc in next sc, repeat from * around—15 sc.

Rnd 3: * Sc in each of next 2 sc, 2 sc in next sc, repeat from * around—20 sc.

Rnds 4 and 5: Sc in each sc around.

Rnd 6: * Sc in each of next 2 sc, sk 1 sc, repeat from * around, end sc in each of last 2 sc—14 sc. Stuff ball.

Rnds 7 and 8: * Sk next sc, sc in next sc, repeat from * around. Sl st in next st. End off; leave end for sewing.

SMALL LEAF (make 2): With green, ch 8.

Row 1: Sc in 2nd ch from hook and in each ch to end ch, 2 sc in end ch, ch 1, 2 sc in same ch; work-ing back on opposite side of start-ing ch, sc in each ch, sc in end sp. Ch 1, turn.

Row 2: Working in back lp of each st throughout, sc in each sc to ch 1, sc, ch 1 and sc in back lp of ch 1, sc in each sc to within 3 sc of end. Ch 1, turn.

Rows 3-5: Repeat row 2.

Row 6: Sc in back lp of each sc to ch 1, sl st in both lps of ch 1. End off; leave end for sewing.

LARGE LEAF: With green, ch 12.

Row 1: Work as for row 1 of small leaf.

Rows 2-7: Work as for row 2 of small leaf.

Row 8: Work as for row 6 of small leaf.

FINISHING: Arrange grapes as illustrated. Tie some together in pairs. Join grapes by tacking them loosely tog. Tack leaves to cluster, large leaf between small leaves. Sew ring to top of cluster.

CROCHETED COASTERS:

SIZE: 3¾″ diameter.
MATERIALS: Swistraw, 1 24-yd. skein for each coaster (3 skeins will make 2 coasters).
GAUGE: 6 sts = 1″; 3 rnds = 1″.
COASTER: Ch 3, join with sl st in first ch to form ring.

Rnd 1: Ch 1, 8 sc in ring. Join with sl st in ch 1. Ch 2, turn.

Rnd 2: Dc and sc in front lp of each sc around—8 pats. Join in top of turning ch. Ch 2, turn.

Rnd 3: Dc and sc in front lp of each st round—16 pats. Join. Ch 2, turn.

Rnd 4: * Dc in front lp of next st, sc in front lp of next st, dc and sc in front lp of each of next 2 sts, repeat from * around—24 pats. Join. Ch 2, turn.

Rnd 5: * (Dc in front lp of next st, sc in front lp of next st) 3 times, dc and sc in front lp of each of next 2 sts, repeat from * around—30 pats. Join. Ch 1, turn.

Rnd 6: Sc in front lp of each st around. Join. End off.

CLUSTER STITCH MAT

A brightly colored hot mat alternates nine colors in a pleasing variety of stitch patterns. Made of knitting and crochet cotton, used double, the mat design offers you the perfect opportunity to use up your leftover cottons from other projects.

SIZE: 10″ diameter.
MATERIALS: Knitting and cro-chet cotton, 1 175-yd. ball each of yellow, orange, dark orange, red, rose, pale green, aqua, lavender and purple. Steel crochet hook No. 0.
GAUGE: 6 sts = 1″ (double strand).
Note: Use double strand of cot-ton throughout.

MAT: With 2 strands of yellow held tog, ch 5, sl st in first ch to form ring.

Rnd 1: 8 sc in ring. Sl st in first sc.

Rnd 2: Ch 1, 2 sc in each sc around—16 sc. Sl st in first sc. End off.

Rnd 3: Join orange in any sc, ch 3 (counts as 1 dc), * 2 dc in next sc, dc in next sc, repeat from * around, end 2 dc in last sc, sl st in top of ch 3—24 dc. End off.

Rnd 4: With lavender, make lp on hook, (sc in each of 3 dc, 2 sc in next dc) 6 times—30 sc. Join; end off.

Rnd 5: Turn piece to wrong side. With purple, make lp on hook, * sc in each of 2 sc, yo, pull up a lp in next sc, (yo, pull up a lp in same sc) 4 times, yo and

CLUSTER STITCH MAT

through all 11 lps on hook, ch 1 for eye of cluster (cl st made), repeat from * around, sl st in first sc—10 cl sts. End off.

Rnd 6: Turn piece to right side. With red, make lp on hook, sc in each st around (do not work in eye of cl), inc in every other st—45 sc. Join; end off.

Rnd 7: With yellow, sc around, inc in every 3rd st—60 sc. Join; end off.

Rnd 8: Join dark orange in any sc, ch 3, dc in each of next 3 sc, 2 dc in next sc, * dc in each of next 4 sc, 2 dc in next sc, repeat from * around—72 dc. Join; end off.

Rnd 9: Turn piece to wrong side. With orange, repeat rnd 5—24 cl sts. End off.

Rnd 10: Turn piece to right side. With yellow, sc around, inc in every 9th st—80 sc.

Rnd 11: Join aqua in any sc, ch 3, for first dc, dc around, inc in every 8th st—90 dc.

Rnd 12: Turn to wrong side. With rose, repeat rnd 5—30 cl sts.

Rnd 13: Turn to right side. With green, sc around, inc 6 sts in rnd—96 sc.

Rnd 14: With orange, work in dc around, inc 6 sts in rnd—102 dc.

Rnd 15: With lavender, work in sc around, inc 6 sts in rnd—108 sc.

Rnd 16: Turn piece to wrong side. With purple, repeat rnd 5—36 cl sts.

Rnd 17: Turn piece to right side. With red, work in sc around, inc 6 sts in rnd—114 sc.

Rnd 18: With yellow, work in sc around, inc 6 sts in rnd—120 sc.

Rnd 19: With dark orange, work in dc around, inc 6 sts in rnd—126 dc.

Rnd 20: Turn to wrong side. With orange, repeat rnd 5—42 cl sts.

Rnd 21: Turn to right side. With green, sc in any st after a cl, * sk 1 st, work sc, dc, ch 2, dc, sc in cl st, sc in next st, repeat from * around. End off.

YELLOW MAT

Shown on page 290

This little round mat of clusters and chain loops can be used in many ways and made in many sizes, by changing the size of the cotton or adding more rounds of loops at the edge. For smaller mats, use size 30 crochet cotton; for larger mats, use knitting and crochet cotton double.

SIZE: 9″ diameter.

MATERIALS: Mercerized knitting and crochet cotton, 1 175-yd. ball. Steel crochet hook No. 6.

MAT: Ch 3, sl st in first ch to form ring.

Rnd 1: Ch 1, 8 sc in ring. Sl st in first sc.

Rnd 2: Ch 3; holding back last lp of each dc, work 2 dc in same st as sl st, yo hook and through 3 lps on hook (cluster), * ch 7; holding back last lp of each dc, work 3 dc in next sc, yo hook and through 4 lps on hook, repeat from * 6 times, ch 7, sl st in top of first cl—8 cls.

Rnd 3: Sl st in each of first 4 ch, * ch 4, sl st in same ch as last sl st (picot), ch 7, sl st in center ch of next lp, repeat from * around, end sl st in bottom of first picot.

Rnd 4: Sl st in each of 2 ch of first picot, ch 3, 2-dc cl in picot, * ch 7, 3-dc cl in center ch of next lp, ch 7, 3-dc cl in next picot, repeat from * around, end ch 7, 3-dc cl in center ch of last lp, ch 7, sl st in top of first cl—16 cls.

Rnd 5: Sl st in each of next 4 ch, ch 3, sl st in same ch as last sl st (picot), * ch 13, sl st in center ch of next lp, sl st in same ch, re-

ch 3, dc, ch 5, dc in center ch of last lp, ch 3, sl st in top of first cl.

Rnd 8: Ch 3, sl st in sl st at end of rnd 7 (picot), * ch 4, sk next ch-3 lp, dc, ch 7 and dc in center ch of ch-5 lp, ch 4, sl st, ch 3 and sl st in top of next cl (picot), repeat from * around, end ch 4, sl st in bottom of first picot. End off.

Rnd 9: Join thread in center of any ch-7 lp, ch 3, sl st in same ch (picot), ch 5, 2-tr cl in same ch, * 2-tr cl in center of next ch-7 lp, ch 5, sl st in same ch with 2-tr cl, ch 3, sl st in same ch (picot), ch 5, 2-tr cl in same ch, repeat from * around, end 2-tr cl in same ch as joining, ch 5, sl st in same ch.

Rnd 10: Ch 1, sc in picot, * ch 9, sc between next cls, ch 9, sc in next picot, repeat from * around, end ch 9, sl st in first sc—32 lps.

Rnd 11: Ch 1, sc in sc with sl st, * ch 5, sc in next lp, ch 5, sc in next sc, repeat from * around, end ch 5, sl st in first sc—64 lps.

Rnd 12: Sl st to center of first lp, sc in lp, * ch 5, sc in next lp, repeat from * around, end ch 5, sl st in first sc.

Rnds 13 and 14: Repeat rnd 12. End off.

Weave in ends on wrong side.

peat from * around, end ch 13, sl st at bottom of first picot. End off.

Rnd 6: Join yarn with sl st in center ch of any ch-13 lp, ch 3, 2-dc cl in same ch as sl st, ch 5, 3-dc cl in same ch, * ch 5, 3-dc cl, ch 5, 3-dc cl in center ch of next lp, repeat

from * around, end ch 5, sl st in top of first cl.

Rnd 7: Sl st in each of first 3 ch, ch 3, 2-dc cl in same ch as last sl st, * ch 3, dc, ch 5, dc in center ch of next lp, ch 3, 3-dc cl in center ch of next lp, repeat from * around, end

ORANGE HOT MAT

A big slice of orange is rendered in crochet to be used as a kitchen hot mat or place mat. In quick crochet cotton and easy stitches, the mat is simple to make. Segments of the orange are embroidered in chain stitch, seeds in satin stitch. Green leaves, crocheted separately and attached, are optional.

SIZE: 15″ diameter.
MATERIALS: Quick crochet cotton, 3 100-yd. balls of orange; 1 ball each of white and green. Steel crochet hook No. 00. Large-eyed embroidery needle.

GAUGE: 9 hdc =2″; 3 rnds =1″.
Note: Use cotton double throughout.
MAT: With double strand of white, ch 6. Sl st in first ch to form ring.

Rnd 1: 12 sc in ring. Sl st in first sc. End off.
Rnd 2: With double strand of orange, sc in any sc, * 2 sc in next sc, sc in next sc, repeat from * around, 2 sc in last sc—18 sc.

Rnd 3: * 2 sc in next sc, sc in each of next 2 sc, repeat from * around—24 sc.

Rnd 4: * Sc in each of next 3 sc, 2 sc in next sc, repeat from * around—30 sc. Sl st in next sc.

Rnd 5: Ch 2 (counts as 1 hdc), hdc in next sc, 2 hdc in next sc, * hdc in each of next 2 sc, 2 hdc in next sc, repeat from * around—40 hdc. Sl st in top of ch 2.

Rnd 6: Ch 2, 2 hdc in next st, * hdc in next st, 2 hdc in next st, repeat from ·* around—60 hdc. Join.

Rnd 7: Ch 2, work in hdc around, inc in every 6th st—70 hdc. Join.

Rnd 8: Ch 2, work in hdc around, inc in every 7th st—80 hdc. Join.

Rnd 9: Ch 2, work in hdc, inc 10 sts in rnd—90 hdc. Join.

Rnds 10-15: Repeat rnd 9—150 hdc.

Rnd 16: Ch 2, work in hdc, inc 4 sts in rnd—154 hdc.

Rnd 17: (Sc in each of next 2 sts,

hdc in each of next 2 sts, dc in each of next 2 sts, 2 tr in next st, dc in each of next 2 sts, hdc in each of next 2 sts, 2 sc in each of next 2 sts, sl st in next st) 11 times, ending with sl st in joining sl st of previous rnd.

Rnd 18: (Sc in each of 4 sts, hdc in each of 6 sts, sc in each of 4 sts, sl st in sl st) 11 times. End off.

Rnd 19: Join white in sl st, ch 4, (dc in each of 4 sts, sc in each of 6 sts, dc in each of 4 sts, tr in sl st) 11 times, end dc in each of last 4 sts, sl st in top of ch 4.

Rnd 20: Sc in each st around. End off.

Rnd 21: With orange, sc in each st around. End off.

With white, embroider lines between segments in chain stitch; embroider seeds in satin stitch.

LEAF (make 2): With double strand of green, ch 20.

Row 1: Sc in 2nd ch from hook and in each remaining ch. Ch 1, turn.

Row 2: Sk first sc, sl st in next sc,

sc in next 8 sts, dc in next 7 sts, sc in next st, sl st in last st. Ch 1, turn.

Row 3: Sk first st, sc in next st and in each of next 7 sts, dc in next 4 sts, sc in next 2 sts, sl st in each st to end.

Row 4: Working on other side of original ch, sl st in first 3 ch, sc in next 14 ch, sl st in last 2 ch. Ch 1, turn.

Row 5: Sk 2 sl sts, sc in next 4 sts, dc in next 6 sts, sc in next 3 sts, sl st in next 2 sts. Ch 1, turn.

Row 6: Sk first st, sc in next 2 sts, dc in next 10 sts, sc in next 2 sts, sl st to point. End off.

Sew one leaf over mat with invisible stitches; attach other leaf along edge with a few stitches.

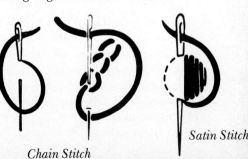

Chain Stitch   *Satin Stitch*

FLOWER-AND-FERN MAT

Exceptionally beautiful mat has an eight-petaled "flower" at center surrounded by fernlike "fronds" in varying shapes and sizes. For a small doily, crochet only the center section. For a larger centerpiece, make the Flower-and-Fern Mat in knitting and crochet cotton.

SIZE: 16″ diameter.

MATERIALS: Mercerized crochet cotton, size 30, 2 balls. Steel crochet hook No. 12.

CLUSTERS: 3-Dc Clusters (cls): At beg of a rnd, ch 3 (counts as first dc), holding back on hook last lp of each dc, make 2 dc in same sp, yo and through 3 lps on hook; **on rnd,** holding back on hook last lp of each dc, make 3 dc in same sp, yo and through 4 lps on hook.

3-Tr Cls: At beg of a rnd, ch 4 (counts as first tr), holding back on hook last lp of each tr, make 2 tr in same sp, yo and through 3 lps on hook; **on rnd,** holding back last lp of each tr, make 3 tr in same sp, yo and through 4 lps on hook.

MAT: Beg at center, ch 9, join with sl st to form ring.

Rnd 1: In ring, make 8 3-dc cls with ch-4 sp between each cl, ch 4, join in top of first cl.

Rnd 2: Sl st in first sp, make 2 3-dc cls with ch-3 sp between in same sp, * ch 3, 2 3-dc cls with ch-3 sp between in next sp, repeat from * around, end ch 3, join in top of first cl—16 cls.

Rnd 3: 3-dc cl in first cl, * ch 3, 3-dc cl in next sp, ch 3, 3-dc cl with ch-3 sp between in each of next 2 cls, repeat from * around, end last repeat with 1 cl, ch 3, join in first cl—24 cls.

Rnd 4: 3-dc cl in first cl, * ch 3, 2 3-dc cls with ch-3 sp between in next cl, ch 3, 3-dc cl with ch-3 sp between in each of next 2 cls, repeat from * around, end last repeat with 1 cl, ch 3, join in first cl—32 cls.

Rnd 5: 3-dc cl in first cl, ch 3, 3-dc cl in next cl, * ch 3, 3-dc cl in next sp, ch 3, 3-dc cl with ch-3 sp between in each of next 4 cls, repeat from * around, end last repeat with 2 cls, ch 3, join—40 cls.

Rnd 6: * 3-dc cl with ch-3 sp between in each of 5 cls, ch 5, repeat from * around, join ch in first cl—40 cls.

Rnd 7: * 3-dc cl with ch-3 sp between in each of 5 cls, ch 9, repeat from * around, join ch 9 in first cl—40 cls.

Rnd 8: 3-dc cl in first cl, * ch 3, 3-dc cl with ch-1 sp between in each of next 3 cls, ch 3, 3-dc cl in next cl, ch 6, dc in 5th ch of ch 9, ch 6, 3-dc cl in next cl, repeat from * around, omit last cl, join ch 6 in first cl—40 cls.

Rnd 9: 3-dc cl in first cl, * ch 3, 3-dc cl in next cl, ch 1, sk next cl, cl in next cl, ch 3, cl in next cl, ch 6, (dc, ch 7, dc) in next dc, ch 6, cl in next cl, repeat from * around, omit last cl, join ch 6 in first cl—32 cls.

Rnd 10: 3-dc cl in first cl, * ch 1, sk next cl, cl in next ch-1 sp, ch 1, cl in next cl, ch 7, dc in next dc, ch 7, dc in 4th ch of next ch 7, ch 7, dc in next dc, ch 7, cl in next cl, repeat from * around, omit last cl, join ch 7 in first cl—24 cls.

Rnd 11: 3-dc cl in first cl, * ch 1, sk next cl, 3-dc cl in next cl, ch 7, dc in next dc, ch 7, (dc, ch 5, dc) in next dc, ch 7, dc in next dc, ch 7, 3-dc cl in next cl, repeat from * around, omit last cl, join ch 7 in first cl—16 cls.

Rnd 12: Sl st in first ch-1 sp, 3-dc cl in first sp, * ch 12, sc in next dc, ch 12, sk next sp, sc in next ch-5 sp, ch 12, sk next dc, sc in next dc, ch 12, 3-dc cl in next ch-1 sp between cls, repeat from * around, omit last cl, join ch 12 in first cl—8 cls.

Rnd 13: Sl st to 5th ch of first ch-12 sp, 3-tr cl in next ch of same sp, * ch 11, 2 tr in 6th ch of next ch-12 sp, ch 11, 3-tr cl in 6th ch of next ch-12 sp, repeat from * around, omit last cl, join ch 11 in first cl—16 cls and 16 groups of tr.

Rnd 14: 3-tr cl in first cl, * ch 5, 5 tr in next tr, ch 2, tr in same tr, tr in next tr, ch 2, 5 tr in same tr (shell made), ch 5, 3-tr cl in next cl, repeat from * around, omit last cl, join ch 5 in first cl—16 shells, 16 cls.

Rnd 15: 3-tr in first cl, * ch 1, 3-tr cl in same cl, ch 4; holding back on hook last lp of each tr, make 1 tr in each of first 5 tr of shell, yo and through 6 lps on hook (5-tr cl st made); ch 5, 3 tr in next tr, 2 tr in next tr, ch 5, 5-tr cl st over last 5 tr of same shell, ch 4, 3-tr cl in next cl, repeat from * around, omit last cl, join ch 4 in first cl.

Rnd 16: 3-tr cl in first cl, ch 4, tr in next ch-1 sp, ch 4, 3-tr cl in next cl, ch 7, sk first 5-tr cl st of shell, sc in each of next 5 tr, ch 7, sk last 5-tr cl st of same shell, 3-tr cl in next 3-tr cl, repeat from * around, omit last 3-tr cl, join ch 7 in first cl.

Rnd 17: 3-tr cl in first cl, * ch 6, tr in next tr, ch 6, 3-tr cl in next cl, ch 7, 5-tr cl st over next 5 sc, ch 7, 3-tr cl in next cl, repeat from * around, omit last 3-tr cl, join ch 7 in first cl.

Rnd 18: 3-tr cl in first cl, * ch 8, (tr, ch 3, tr) in next tr, ch 8, 3-tr cl in next cl, ch 6, sc in next 5-tr cl st, ch 6, 3-tr cl in next cl, repeat from * around, omit last cl, join ch 6 in first cl.

Rnd 19: 3-tr cl in first cl, * ch 8; 5 tr in next tr, ch 2, 2 tr in next ch-3 sp, ch 2, 5 tr in next tr (shell); ch 8, 3-tr cl in next cl, ch 6, sc in next sc, ch 6, 3-tr cl in next cl, repeat from * around, omit last cl, join ch 6 in first cl.

Rnd 20: 3-tr cl in first cl, ch 8, sl st in top of cl just made (p), * ch 8, 5-tr cl st over first 5 tr of shell, ch 5, 5 tr in next tr, ch 2, tr in same tr, tr in next tr, ch 2, 5 tr in same tr, ch 5, 5-tr cl st over last 5 tr of same shell, ch 8, 3-tr cl in next cl, ch 8, sl st in top of last cl made (p), 3-tr cl in next cl, repeat from * around, omit last ch-8 p and 3-tr cl, join in first cl.

Rnd 21: Sl st in first p, (3-tr cl, ch 7, 3-tr cl) in first p, * ch 8, sk first 5-tr cl st of shell, 5-tr cl st over next 5 tr, ch 5, 5 tr in next tr, ch 2, tr in same tr, tr in next tr, ch 2, 5 tr in same tr, ch 5, 5-tr cl st over next 5 tr, ch 8, sk last 5-tr cl st of same shell, (3-tr cl, ch 7, 3-tr cl) in next p, repeat from * around, omit last 2 cls, join ch 8 in first cl.

Rnd 22: 3-tr cl in first cl, * ch 5, 3-tr cl in next sp, ch 5, 3-tr cl in next cl, ch 7, sk first 5-tr cl st of shell, 5-tr cl st over next 5 tr, ch 7, 3 tr in next tr, 2 tr in next tr, ch 7, 5-tr cl st over next 5 tr, ch 7, sk last 5-tr cl st of same shell, 3-tr cl in next cl, repeat from * around, omit last 3-tr cl, join ch 7 in first cl.

Rnd 23: 2 3-tr cls with ch 3 between in first cl, * (ch 4, 2 3-tr cls with ch 3 between in next cl) twice, ch 10, sk first 5-tr cl st of shell, sc in each of next 5 tr, ch 10, sk last 5-tr cl st of same shell, 2 3-tr cls with ch 3 between in next cl, repeat from * around, omit last 2 cls, join ch 10 in first cl.

Rnd 24: 3-tr cl in first cl, * (ch 3, 3-tr cl in next sp, ch 3, 3-tr cl in next cl, ch 4, 3-tr cl in next cl) twice, ch 3, 3-tr cl in next sp, ch 3, 3-tr cl in next cl, ch 9, 5-tr cl over next 5 sc, ch 9, 3-tr cl in next cl, repeat from * around, omit last 3-tr cl, join ch 9 in first cl.

Rnd 25: 3-tr cl in first cl, * (ch 3, 3-tr cl in next cl) twice, (ch 4, 3-tr cl with ch 3 between in each of next 3 cls) twice, ch 8, sc in next 5-tr cl, ch 8, 3-tr cl in next cl, repeat from * around, omit last cl, join ch 8 in first cl.

Rnd 26: 3-tr cl in first cl, * (ch 2, 3-tr cl in next cl) twice, (ch 4, tr in next sp, ch 3, tr in same sp, ch 4, 3-tr cl in next cl, ch 2, 3-tr cl in next cl, ch 2, 3-tr cl in next cl) twice, ch 8, sc in next sc, ch 8, 3-tr cl in next cl, repeat from * around, omit last cl, join ch 8 in first cl.

Rnd 27: 3-tr cl in first cl, * (sk next cl, 3-tr cl in next cl, ch 4, tr in next tr, ch 4, tr in next sp, ch 4, tr in next tr, ch 4, 3-tr cl in next cl) twice, sk next cl, 3-tr cl in next cl, ch 4, tr in cl last worked in, tr in next cl, ch 4, 3-tr cl in cl last worked in, repeat from * around, ending with last tr in same place as first cl, ch 4, join in first cl.

Rnd 28: Sl st between first 2 cls, ch 11, sl st in 6th ch from hook (p), ch 7, sl st in same ch as before (2nd p), ch 6, sl st in same ch as before (3rd p), tr between first 2 cls, * (ch 6, sc in next tr, ch 6, tr in next tr; **make 3-p group:** ch 6, sl st in top of last tr worked for first p, ch 7, sl st in same place for 2nd p, ch 6, sl st in same place for 3rd p; tr in same tr as last tr was worked in, ch 6, sc in next tr, ch 6, tr between next 2 cls, make 3-p group, tr in same sp as last tr was worked in) twice, ch 6, sc between next 2 single tr, ch 6, tr between next 2 cls, make 3-p group, tr in same sp as last tr was worked in, repeat from * around, ending last repeat with ch 6, sc between next 2 single tr, ch 6, join in first tr of rnd. End off. Block mat.

LACY CURTAINS

Lacy curtains, made of two motifs, let in light yet give privacy, and may be made to any size.

SIZE: Any desired size.

MATERIALS: Mercerized crochet cotton, size 30, about 12 yds. for each motif plus fill-in motif. Steel crochet hook size 10.

GAUGE: Each motif = 2½".

CURTAIN: FIRST MOTIF: Ch 12, sl st in first ch to form ring.

Rnd 1: Ch 1, 24 sc in ring. Sl st in first sc.

Rnd 2: Ch 8, * sk next st, tr in next st, ch 3, repeat from * around, end ch 3, sl st in 5th ch of ch 8—12 sps.

Rnd 3: Ch 1, sc in same ch with sl st, * 3 sc in next sp, sc in next tr, repeat from * around, end 3 sc in last sp, sl st in first sc.

Rnd 4: Ch 5 (counts as 1 dtr), dtr in each of next 3 sc, * ch 6, dtr in each of next 4 sc, repeat from * around, end ch 6, sl st in top of ch 5.

Rnd 5: Ch 1, sc in same ch with sl st, sc in each of next 3 dtr, * 7 sc in next sp, sc in each of next 4 dtr, repeat from * around, end 7 sc in last sp, sl st in first sc. End off.

2ND MOTIF: Work as for first motif through rnd 4.

Rnd 5: Ch 1, sc in same ch with sl st, sc in each of next 3 dtr, 3 sc in next sp, drop lp from hook; insert hook in center sc of 7 sc in sp of previous motif, draw dropped lp through; 3 sc in same sp of 2nd motif, sc in each of next 4 dtr, 3 sc in next sp, join as before to next sp of previous motif, 3 sc in same sp, * sc in each of next 4 dtr, 7 sc in next sp, repeat from * around, sl st in first sc. End off.

Join all motifs in this way, leaving 1 sp free between joinings on all motifs. Work fill-in motif in space formed by 4 motifs.

FILL-IN MOTIF: Ch 10; sl st in first ch to form ring.

Rnd 1: Ch 1, 24 sc in ring. Sl st in first sc.

Rnd 2: Ch 1, sc in first sc, * ch 4, drop lp from hook; insert hook in center sc of free sp on a motif, draw dropped lp through, ch 4, sk 2 sc on fill-in motif, sc in next sc, ch 5, drop lp from hook; insert hook in joining st between motifs, draw dropped lp through, ch 5, sk 2 sc on fill-in motif, sc in next sc, repeat from * 3 times, sl st in next sc. End off.

CROCHET FOR THE KITCHEN
PICTURE POT HOLDERS

Picture Pot Holders make bright accents for a kitchen, best sellers at bazaars, inexpensive gifts. Designs include pine tree, star flower, sailboat, tulip, butterfly, country cottage.

SIZE: 6½" square.

MATERIALS: Rayon and cotton rug yarn, 1 70-yd. skein each of the following colors: white, evergreen and medium green for pine tree pot holder; medium blue, white, yellow and evergreen for star flower pot holder; national blue, medium blue, red and white for sailboat pot holder; white, cerise and dark green for tulip pot holder; light yellow, turquoise and black for butterfly pot holder; white, black, dark green, medium blue and national blue for cottage pot holder. Aluminum crochet hook size G or H. Large-eyed sewing needle.

GAUGE: 4 sts = 1"; 7 rows = 2".

GENERAL DIRECTIONS: Design Note: When a row has more than one color, start extra color or colors at beginning of row. Work over color or colors not being used.

When changing colors, work last sc or reverse sc of one color until there are 2 lps on hook, drop strand to wrong side. Pick up new color and finish sc.

POT HOLDER: See chart for desired pot holder. With color of first row of chart, ch 24.

Row 1 (right side): Sc in 2nd ch from hook and in each ch across—23 sc. Ch 1, turn.

Row 2: Following next row of chart from left to right, work in reverse sc as follows: Insert hook from back to front in first sc, yarn around hook from back to front, pull lp through and complete sc; work reverse sc in each sc across. Ch 1, turn.

Row 3: Following next row of chart from right to left, sc in each

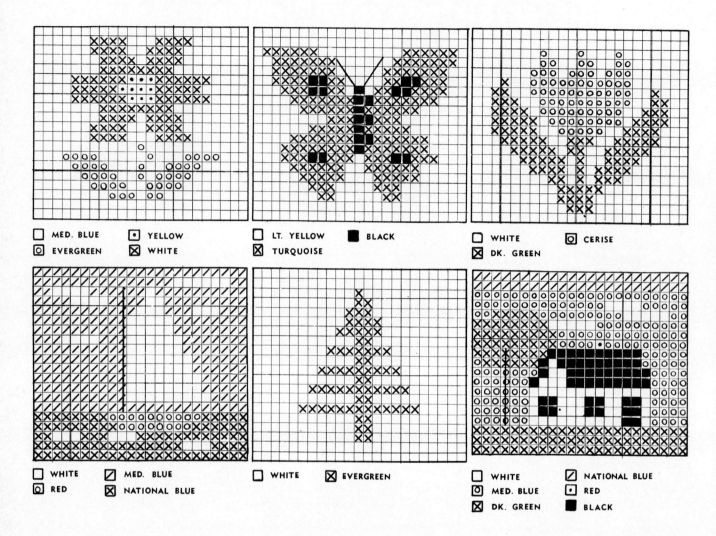

| MED. BLUE | • YELLOW |
| EVERGREEN | WHITE |

| LT. YELLOW | BLACK |
| TURQUOISE | |

| WHITE | CERISE |
| DK. GREEN | |

| WHITE | MED. BLUE |
| RED | NATIONAL BLUE |

| WHITE | EVERGREEN |

WHITE	NATIONAL BLUE
MED. BLUE	RED
DK. GREEN	BLACK

sc. Ch 1, turn. Repeat rows 2 and 3 to top of chart, changing colors as directed above. End off.

BORDER: Rnd 1: With border color (see illustration), from right side, work in sc around edge of pot holder, making 3 sc in each corner. Join with sl st in first sc.

Rnd 2: Working in back lp of sts, work sl st in each sc around. Join in first sl st. End off.

RING HANGER: Ch 8, join with sl st in first ch. Cut yarn, leaving an end for sewing. Sew ring to top of pot holder.

EMBROIDERY DETAILS: Untwist a piece of black rug yarn and, with 2 strands, embroider mast of sailboat, antennae of butterfly, and tree trunk of cottage pot holder in outline st. If red chimney of cottage was not crocheted in, embroider chimney in satin st with red cotton.

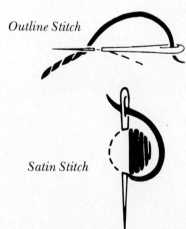

Outline Stitch

Satin Stitch

GIANT POT HOLDERS

Colorful pot holders in generous sizes are made of rayon and cotton rug yarn in an interesting technique. All in single crochet, some stitches are worked into holes one, two or three rows below to create overlay patterns. Square and white-edged holders have three colors; design at bottom has four.

SIZES: 9"-10" diameter; 8" square.

MATERIALS: Rayon and cotton rug yarn, 1 70-yd. skein each of 3 or 4 colors (will make 2 or more pot holders). Aluminum crochet hook size 8 or I. Yarn needle for weaving ends.

GAUGE: 3 sts = 1".

FOUR-COLOR POT HOLDER: Made with white (W), yellow (Y), green (G) and coral (C). With W, ch 2.

Rnd 1: 6 sc in 2nd ch from hook.

Rnd 2: 2 sc in each sc around— 12 sc. Sl st in first sc. End off.

Rnd 3: With Y, make lp on hook, * 2 sc in next sc, long sc in next sc of rnd 1, repeat from * around—18 sts.

Rnd 4: * 2 sc in next sc, sc in each of next 2 sc, repeat from * around—24 sc. Sl st in first sc. End off.

Rnd 5: With C, make lp on hook, * long sc in center of Y long sc of rnd 3, sc in next sc, sk 1 sc of rnd 3, 2 long sc in next sc of rnd 3, sc in next sc, repeat from * around—30 sts.

Rnd 6: * 2 sc in next st, sc in each of next 4 sts, repeat from * around—36 sc. Sl st in first sc. End off.

Rnd 7: With G, make lp on hook, * long sc in center of C long sc of rnd 5, sc in each of next 2 sts, 2 long sc in hole between 2 long sc of rnd 5, sc in each of next 2 sts, repeat from * around—42 sts.

Rnd 8: * 2 sc in next st, sc in each of next 6 sts, repeat from * around—48 sc. Sl st in first sc. End off.

Rnd 9: With W, make lp on hook, * long sc in center of G long sc of rnd 7, sc in each of next 3 sts, 2 long sc in hole between 2 long sc of rnd 7, sc in each of next 3 sts, repeat from * around—54 sts.

Rnd 10: * 2 sc in next st, sc in each of next 8 sts, repeat from *

around—60 sts. Sl st in first sc. End off.

Rnd 11: With Y, make lp on hook, * long sc in center of W long sc of rnd 9, sc in next sc, sk 1 W sc of rnd 9, long sc in each of next 2 sts of rnd 9, sc in next sc, 2 long sc in hole between 2 long sc of rnd 9, sc in next sc, sk 1 W sc of rnd 9, long sc in each of next 2 sts of rnd 9, sc in next sc, repeat from * around—66 sts.

Rnd 12: * 2 sc in next st, sc in each of next 10 sts, repeat from * around—72 sc. Sl st in first sc. End off.

Rnd 13: With C, make lp on hook, * long sc in center of Y long sc of rnd 11, sc in each of next 2 sc, long sc in center of each of next 2 long Y sc of rnd 11, sc in each of next 2 sc, 2 long sc in hole between 2 long sc of rnd 11, sc in each of next 2 sc, long sc in center of each of next 2 long Y sc of rnd 11, sc in each of next 2 sc, repeat from * around—90 sts.

Rnd 14: Sl st in each st around. Ch 12 for hanger; end off. Sew end in place. Weave in ends. Steam-press pot holder.

WHITE-EDGED POT HOLDER: Made with green (G), white (W) and coral (C). With G, ch 3, sl st in first ch to form ring.

Rnd 1: Ch 1, 6 sc in ring, sl st in first sc.

Rnd 2: Ch 1, 2 sc in each sc—12 sc. Sl st in first sc. End off.

Rnd 3: With W, make lp on hook, * long sc in rnd 1, 2 sc in next sc of rnd 2, repeat from * 5 times—6 long sc, 12 sc.

Rnd 4: * 2 sc in next st, sc in each of next 2 sts, repeat from * around—24 sc.

Rnd 5: * 2 sc in next sc, sc in each of next 3 sc, repeat from *

around—30 sc. Sl st in first sc. End off.

Rnd 6: With C, make lp on hook, * long sc in center of long sc of rnd 3, sc in each of next 2 sc, long sc in rnd 4, sc in each of next 2 sc, repeat from * around—36 sts.

Rnd 7: * Sc in each of next 5 sts, 2 sc in next st, repeat from * around—42 sc.

Rnd 8: * Sc in each of next 6 sc, 2 sc in next sc, repeat from * around—48 sc. Sl st in first sc. End off.

Rnd 9: With G, make lp on hook, * long sc in center of long sc of rnd 6, sc in next sc, long sc in rnd 7, sc in next sc, repeat from * around—48 sts.

Rnd 10: * Sc in each of next 7 sts, 2 sc in next st, repeat from * around—54 sc.

Rnd 11: * Sc in each of next 8 sc, 2 sc in next sc, repeat from * around—60 sc. Sl st in first sc. End off.

Rnd 12: With W, make lp on hook, * long sc in center of long sc of rnd 9, sc in next sc, (long sc in rnd 10, sc in next sc) twice, repeat from * around—72 sts.

Rnd 13: Sc in each st around.

Rnd 14: Sl st loosely in each sc around. Ch 12 for hanger. Sew end in place. Weave in ends. Steam-press pot holder.

SQUARE POT HOLDER: Made with green (G), white (W) and coral (C). With G, ch 3, sl st in first ch to form ring.

Rnd 1: Ch 1, 8 sc in ring.

Rnd 2: * Sc, ch 1 and sc in next sc (corner), sc in next sc, repeat from * 3 times. Sl st in first sc. End off.

Rnd 3: With W, make lp on hook, * sc, ch 1 and sc in ch-1 sp at corner, sc in next sc, long sc in rnd

1, sc in next sc, repeat from * 3 times.

Rnd 4: Sc in first sc, * sc, ch 1 and sc in ch-1 sp at corner, sc in each st to next corner, repeat from * around, end sl st in first sc. End off.

Rnd 5: With C, make lp on hook, * sc, ch 1 and sc in ch-1 sp at corner, sc in each of next 2 sc, long sc in center of long sc of rnd 3, sc in each of next 2 sc, repeat from * 3 times.

Rnd 6: Repeat rnd 4.

Rnd 7: With G, make lp on hook, * sc, ch 1 and sc in ch-1 sp at corner, sc in next sc, long sc in W sc of rnd 4, sc in each of next 2 sc, long sc in center of long sc of rnd 5, sc in each of next 2 sc, long sc in W sc of rnd 4, sc in next sc, repeat from * 3 times.

Rnd 8: Repeat rnd 4.

Rnd 9: With W, make lp on hook, * sc, ch 1 and sc in ch-1 sp at corner, sc in next sc, long sc in G sc of rnd 7, (sc in each of next 2 sc, long sc in center of long sc of rnd 7) 3 times, sc in each of next 2 sc, long sc in G sc of rnd 7, sc in next sc, repeat from * 3 times.

Rnd 10: Repeat rnd 4.

Rnd 11: With C, make lp on hook, * sc, ch 1 and sc in ch-1 sp at corner, sc in next sc, long sc in W sc of rnd 9, (sc in each of next 2 sc, long sc in center of long sc of rnd 9) 5 times, sc in each of next 2 sc, long sc in W sc of rnd 9, sc in next sc, repeat from * 3 times.

Rnd 12: Repeat rnd 4. Do not end off.

Rnd 13: Sl st loosely in each sc around. End off. Ch 12 for hanger; sew ends to point of pot holder. Weave in ends. Steam-press pot holder.

VEGETABLE POT HOLDERS

Cross-stitch vegetables decorate pot holders, 10″ square, worked in afghan stitch crochet. Green "frames" and hangers are crocheted, making "pictures" of pot holders.

SIZE: 10″ square.

MATERIALS: Rayon and cotton rug yarn, 6 70-yd. skeins white (W); 1 skein each of dark green (DG), light green (LG), olive green (OG), dark red (DR) and scarlet (S). Aluminum afghan hook size 10. Large-eyed yarn needle.

GAUGE: 7 sts = 2″; 3 rows = 1″.

POT HOLDER (make 4): With W and afghan hook, ch 30.

AFGHAN STITCH: Row 1: Keeping all lps on hook, pull up a lp in 2nd ch from hook and in each ch across—30 lps.

To Work Lps Off: Yo hook, pull through first lp, * yo hook, pull through next 2 lps, repeat from * across until 1 lp remains. (Lp that remains always counts as first st of next row.)

Row 2: Keeping all lps on hook, sk first vertical bar, pull up a lp under next vertical bar and under

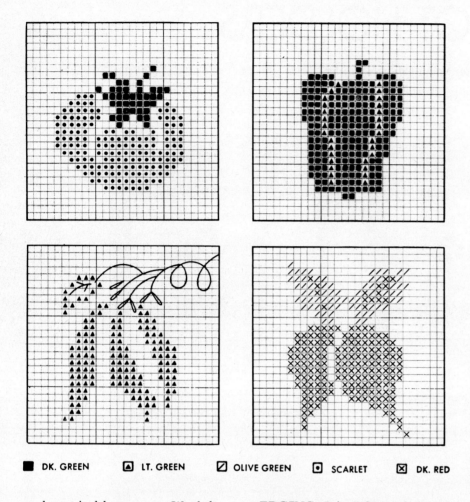

Outline Stitch

Lazy Daisy Stitch

■ DK. GREEN   ▲ LT. GREEN   ⊘ OLIVE GREEN   ⊡ SCARLET   ⊠ DK. RED

each vertical bar across. Work lps off as before.

Rows 3-28: Repeat row 2. End off W.

EDGING: Join DG, work 1 rnd sc around pot holder, working 1 sc in each st, 3 sc in each corner. Sl st in each sc around.

HANGER: Join DG in one top corner of pot holder, ch 33, join with sl st to top corner opposite. Ch 1, turn; sl st in each ch across. End off. Weave in ends.

FINISHING: Pin out to square shape. Block, using wet cloth and hot iron. Let dry. Embroider designs in cross-stitch (see diagram on facing page), working 1 cross-stitch over 1 vertical bar, following charts. To finish bean embroidery, split a length of DG in half. With split strand, embroider stems and leaf veins in outline st; make two lazy daisy sts at top of each bean.

HOT MITTS

Three chunky hot mitts are all worked the same in afghan stitch, but the backs are embroidered in three different ways. White mitt, at left, has a cross-stitch "gingham" design. Yellow mitt, center, is woven to resemble smocking. Cerise mitt, at right, has yellow-and-white checkerboard pattern.

MATERIALS: Rayon and cotton rug yarn, 2 70-yd. skeins of white, yellow, or cerise, main color (MC); 1 skein cerise, contrasting color (CC), for white and yellow mitts; 1 skein each of yellow and white for cerise mitt. Aluminum afghan hook size 9. Rug needle.

GAUGE: 7 sts = 2"; 3 rows = 1".

MITT: FIRST HALF: With MC, ch 20. Work in afghan st as follows:

Row 1: Sk first ch (lp on hook is first st), pull up a lp in each ch across, keeping all lps on hook.

To Work Lps Off: Yo hook, pull through first lp, * yo hook, pull through next 2 lps, repeat from * across until 1 lp remains. Lp that remains on hook always counts as first st of next row.

Row 2: Sk first vertical bar, pull up a lp under next vertical bar and under each vertical bar across, keeping all lps on hook. Work lps off as before. Repeat row 2 for afghan st.

Rows 3-5: Work even—20 sts.

Row 6: Insert hook under 2nd and 3rd vertical bars, pull up a lp (1 st dec), work to 3rd st from end, insert hook under 3rd and 2nd vertical bars from end, pull up a lp (1 st dec), pull up a lp in last vertical bar. Work lps off—18 sts.

Rows 7 and 8: Work even.

Row 9: Work across to last st, insert hook under top strand of horizontal bar between last 2 sts, pull up a lp (1 st inc), work last st—19 sts. Work lps off.

Row 10: Work even.

Rows 11-16: Repeat rows 9 and 10.

Row 17: Repeat row 9—23 sts.

Divide for Thumb: Row 18: Work across 16 sts. Working on these sts only, work even until there are 25 rows from start. Dec 1 st each side every other row 3 times—10 sts. Sl st in each st across. End off.

Thumb: Row 1: Join yarn in 17th st of last long row, work across—7 sts. Work lps off.

Row 2: Dec 1 st at beg of row, inc 1 st at end of row.

Row 3: Work even.

Row 4: Repeat row 2.

Row 5: Dec 1 st at beg of row, work across—6 sts. Sl st in each st across. End off.

2ND HALF: Work as for first half through row 8.

Row 9: Inc 1 st at beg of row—19 sts.

Row 10: Work even.

Rows 11-16: Repeat rows 9 and 10.

Row 17: Repeat row 9.

Divide for Thumb: Row 1: Work first 7 sts.

Row 2: Inc 1 st at beg of row, dec 1 st at end of row.

Row 3: Work even.

Row 4: Repeat row 2.

Row 5: Dec 1 st at end of row—6 sts. Sl st in each st across. End off.

Join yarn in next free st of row 17, work as for first half from row 18.

EMBROIDERY: White Mitt: Thread strand of CC in rug needle. Beg in row 1 on back of mitt, following chart, embroider cross-stitch design (see illustrations below), working 1 cross-stitch over each afghan st except first and last sts of row.

Yellow Mitt: First Row: Thread strand of CC in rug needle; make knot in end. Bring needle up from wrong side through back of mitt between first and 2nd sts, between rows 2 and 3. Weave under 3rd st of row 1, 5th st of row 3, 7th st of row 1, 9th st of row 3, 11th st of

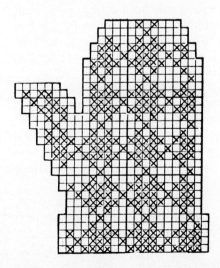

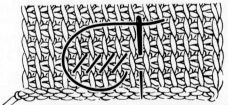

Half Cross-Stitch on Afghan Stitch

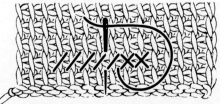

Cross-Stitch on Afghan Stitch

row 1, 13th st of row 3, 15th st of row 1, 17th st of row 3, 19th st of row 1. Bring needle down to wrong side before last st in sp between rows 2 and 3.

2nd Row: Bring needle up between rows 4 and 5, between 20th and 19th sts. Weave under 17th st of row 3, 15th st of row 5, 13th st of row 3, etc., end in same sp with knot. Continue in this manner, always weaving through last row woven through and 2 rows above.

Cerise Mitt: Working half cross-stitch over each afghan st except first and last sts of each row, embroider first 2 sts at right edge in white for 4 rows, * next 4 sts in yellow for 4 rows, next 4 sts in white for 4 rows, repeat from * once. On next 4 rows above, reverse colors for checkerboard design and continue reversing colors every 4 rows.

EDGING: With CC, make lp on hook. From right side, beg at outer edge of mitt, sc pieces tog along sides and top, working 2 sc at each top corner of palm and thumb, and 1 sl st at inner corner of thumb. When bottom of mitt is reached, sc around bottom edge. End off.

BOTTLE COVERS

Unique "slips" cover a trio of tinted wine bottles. The designs are worked in the round in easy crochet stitches and are adapted to fit each shape. The base and neck are in single crochet, the cover in double crochet, wrong side out. For fun, top a cork with a cover.

SIZE: Quart, half-gallon and gallon sizes.

MATERIALS: No. 21 seine twine, 8 ozs. for quart size, 16 ozs. for half-gallon size, 24 ozs. for gallon size. For cork trim, small amount of lighter-weight cord. Aluminum crochet hook size H. Steel crochet hook No. 00.

GAUGE: 2 sts = 1″. Be sure to check your gauge.

COVERS: FOR QUART SIZE: With size H hook, ch 5. Sl st in first ch to form ring.

Rnd 1: Ch 1, 8 sc in ring. Do not join rnds.

Rnd 2: 2 sc in each sc around— 16 sc.

Rnd 3: * Sc in next sc, 2 sc in next sc, repeat from * around— 24 sc.

Rnd 4: * 2 sc in next sc, sc in each of next 2 sc, repeat from * around—32 sc.

Rnd 5: * Hdc in each of next 2 sc, 2 hdc in next sc, repeat from * around, hdc in each of last 2 sc— 42 hdc.

Rnd 6: Ch 4 (counts as 1 tr), * sk 1 hdc, tr in next hdc, repeat from * around—21 tr. Sl st in top of ch 4.

Rnd 7: Ch 4, tr in each tr around. Sl st in top of ch 4. Try piece on bottle. Work tighter or looser as needed.

Rnds 8-11: Repeat rnd 7.

Rnd 12: Place cover on bottle, wrong side out (or right side out, if crocheting is too difficult). Ch 4, tr in next tr, * sk 1 tr, tr in next tr, repeat from * around—11 tr. Sl st in top of ch 4.

Rnd 13: Ch 4, tr in next tr, * sk 1 tr, tr in next tr, repeat from * around—6 tr. Sl st in top of ch 4.

Rnd 14: Ch 1, sc in same tr as sl st (2 sc in next tr, sc in next tr) twice, 2 sc in last tr—9 sc. Do not join.

Work even in sc until cover reaches top of bottle. Sl st in next sc. End off.

FOR HALF-GALLON SIZE (oval bottom): With size H hook, ch 9.

Rnd 1: Sc in 2nd ch from hook and in each of next 6 ch, 3 sc in last ch. Working back on opposite side of ch, sc in each of next 6 ch, 2 sc in ch with first sc of rnd—18 sc.

Rnds 2-4: Sc in each sc around, inc 3 sc evenly around each end— 36 sc.

Rnd 5: Work sc in each st around ends and dc in each st on sides—36 sts. Sl st in first st.

Rnd 6: Ch 3 (counts as 1 dc), dc in each st around. Sl st in top of ch 3.

Rnds 7-12: Ch 3, dc in next dc and in each dc around. Sl st in top of ch 3. While working, try cover on bottle. Work tighter or looser as needed.

Rnd 13: Working with cover on bottle, work in dc, sk 6 sts evenly spaced around—30 dc.

Rnds 14 and 15: Working in dc,

sk 5 sts evenly spaced around—20 dc.

Rnd 16: Working in dc, sk 6 sts around—14 dc.

Rnd 17: Working in dc, sk 2 sts in rnd—12 dc.

Rnd 18: Sc in each dc around. Work even in sc for 9 rnds or until cover reaches top of bottle. Sl st in next st. End off.

Trim cork with a coil of twine, glue on.

FOR GALLON SIZE: With size H hook, ch 5. Sl st in first ch to form ring.

Rnd 1: Ch 3 (counts as 1 dc), 9 dc in ring—10 dc. Sl st in top of ch 3.

Rnd 2: Ch 3, dc in same st as sl st, 2 dc in each st around—20 dc. Sl st in top of ch 3.

Rnd 3: Repeat rnd 2—40 dc.

Rnd 4: Ch 3, dc in same st as sl st, * dc in next dc, 2 dc in next dc, repeat from * around, end dc in last dc—60 dc.

Rnd 5: Work in dc, inc 4 dc evenly spaced around—64 dc.

Rnds 6-14: Work even in dc. While working, try cover on bottle. Work tighter or looser as needed.

Rnd 15: Work in dc, sk 8 sts evenly spaced around—56 dc. Place cover on bottle, wrong side out (or right side out, if crocheting is too difficult).

Rnds 16-18: Work in dc, sk 8 sts evenly spaced around—32 dc.

Rnd 19: Ch 3, dc in next dc, (sk next dc, dc in next dc) 7 times, dc in each of next 2 dc, (sk next dc, dc in next dc) 7 times—18 dc.

Rnd 20: Sc in each dc around—18 sc. Work even in sc for 8 rnds or until cover reaches top of bottle. Sl st in next st. End off.

CORK TRIM: With lighter-weight cord and No. 00 hook, ch 6, sl st in first ch to form ring. Ch 3, work 15 dc in ring. Sl st in top of ch 3. End off.

For knob, leaving end for sewing, ch 4, sl st in first ch to form ring. Ch 1, 6 sc in ring. End off; leave end for sewing. Bring ends through hole in center of trim, sew ends to trim. Glue trim in place on top of cork.

CROCHETED BASKET

Shown at left on page 303

Rows of openwork encircle a sturdy basket crocheted in basic stitches with a double strand of twine. A perfect holder for dried flowers, it is 10" high.

SIZE: 10" high, 9" diameter.

MATERIALS: 4 8-oz. balls No. 24 seine twine. Crochet hook size J.

GAUGE: 2 sc = 1" (double strand).

Note 1: Do not join each rnd with sl st, but mark beg of each rnd.

Note 2: Work with 2 strands of twine held tog throughout.

BASKET: Beg at bottom, ch 4, sl st in first ch to form ring.

Rnd 1 (right side): Ch 3 (counts as 1 dc), work 9 dc in ring—10 dc.

Rnd 2: 2 sc in each st around—20 sc.

Rnds 3-7: Working in sc, inc 8 sc evenly spaced each rnd—60 sc. Turn work so that wrong side is facing you.

Rnd 8: Working in back lp only, sc in each sc around.

Rnd 9: Working in both lps, sc in each sc around.

Rnds 10-13: Repeat rnd 9.

Rnd 14: Sl st in first sc, ch 3, * sk next sc, hdc in next sc, ch 1, repeat from * around, end ch 1, sk last sc, sl st in 2nd ch of ch 3.

Rnd 15: Ch 1, sc in same place as sl st, sc in each ch and hdc around—60 sts.

Rnds 16-18: Sc in each sc around.

Rnds 19-23: Repeat rnds 14-18.

Rnds 24-28: Repeat rnds 14-18.

Rnd 29: Sc in each sc around.

Rnd 30: Sl st in each sc around. End off.

VEGETABLE STORER

Shown at right on page 303

Handles and cover distinguish an unusual vegetable storer. Made in a half double crochet pattern stitch of natural stiff twine, basket measures 10" in diameter.

SIZE: 5" high, 10" diameter.

MATERIALS: About 3 lbs. of natural stiff jute twine. Crochet hook size J. Rug needle.

GAUGE: 2 sc = 1".

BASKET: Beg at center, ch 6, sl st in first ch to form ring.

Rnd 1: Ch 1, 12 sc in ring. Sl st in first sc.

Rnd 2: Ch 2 (counts as first hdc), hdc in same place as sl st, * 2 hdc in next sc, repeat from * around—24 hdc. Sl st in top of ch 2.

Rnd 3: Ch 2, 2 hdc in same place as sl st, * sk next hdc, 3 hdc in next hdc, repeat from * around, sl st in top of ch 2—36 hdc.

Rnd 4: Ch 2, * 3 hdc in next hdc, sk 1 st, hdc in next st, repeat from * around, end 3 hdc in next to last st, sl st in top of ch 2—48 hdc.

Rnd 5: Ch 2, 2 hdc in same place as sl st, * sc in each of next 2 sts, sk 1 st, 3 hdc in next st, repeat from * around, end sc in next 2 sts, sl st in top of ch 2—60 sts.

Rnd 6: * Sc in each of next 2 sts, sk 1 st, 3 hdc in next st, sk 1 st, repeat from * around, end sl st in first sc—60 sts.

Rnds 7-13: Ch 1, sc in each st around. Sl st in first sc. End off at end of rnd 13.

HANDLES (make 2): Make a ch 10" long; leave end for sewing. Sl st in 2nd ch from hook and in each ch across. Sl st in each ch along opposite side of ch. End off; leave end for sewing. Sew a handle to each side of basket along top edge.

COVER: Beg at center, ch 4. Sl st in first ch to form ring.

Rnd 1: Ch 3, 9 dc in ring, sl st in top of ch 3—10 dc.

Rnd 2: Ch 3, dc in same place as sl st, * 2 dc in next dc, repeat from * around, sl st in top of ch 3—20 dc.

Rnd 3: Ch 1, 2 sc in each dc around, sl st in first sc—40 sc.

Rnd 4: Ch 1, sc around, inc 10 sc evenly spaced around, sl st in first sc—50 sc.

Rnd 5: Repeat rnd 4—60 sc.

Rnds 6-8: Work even in sc.

Rnd 9: Sl st in each sc around. End off.

KNOB: Ch 3; sc in 2nd ch from hook and in last ch. Sew knob to cover. Sew cover to basket through 1 st on side edge.

5

COMPLETE INSTRUCTIONS FOR CROCHET

STEP-BY-STEP LESSON
FOR RIGHT-HANDED CROCHETERS

If you have never learned to crochet, you can teach yourself from this step-by-step lesson. On these pages, we show, in a series of photographs, basic information on crochet—how to hold your yarn and hook, how to make chain stitch, single crochet, double crochet, half double crochet, and slip stitch, how to turn your work at the end of a row, how to increase and decrease, how to end off. After you have finished the lesson, turn to page 317 for additional crochet instructions. We include abbreviations used in our crochet directions, other information you will need to follow directions, and the importance of gauge in making any crocheted fashion.

Lessons for Left-handed Crocheters, page 312.

HOW TO CROCHET

GETTING READY TO CROCHET

Use a ball of knitting worsted for practicing your stitches when learning to crochet and a plastic crochet hook size H or 6 in a contrasting color.

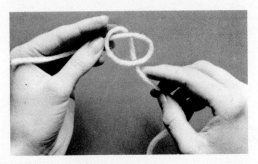

Grasp the yarn about 2″ from the end between your thumb and forefinger. With your right hand, lap the long strand over the short, forming a loop.

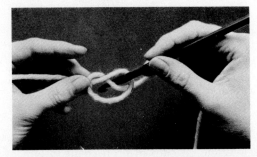

Hold this loop in place between your left thumb and forefinger. Grasp the hook in your right hand like a pencil. Insert the hook through the loop.

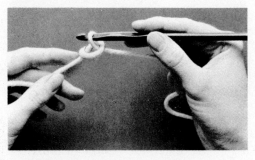

CHAIN STITCH (ch)

Catch the strand with the hook and draw it through loop. Pull end of yarn and strand coming from ball in opposite directions to close loop around hook.

Loop yarn coming from ball around base of little finger of your left hand. Bring this yarn across front of three fingers and back under forefinger.

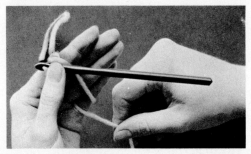

To adjust the tension of your yarn, grasp the hook and loop in your left hand as shown. Pull strand from ball firmly down to tighten around fingers.

COMPLETE INSTRUCTIONS FOR CROCHET

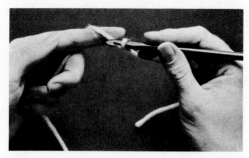

Hold the hook in your right hand as shown. Bend the little finger, ring finger, and middle finger of your left hand to control the strand of yarn.

Pass hook under yarn on index finger and catch yarn with hook as you did for chain stitch. Draw yarn through chain. There are now two loops on hook.

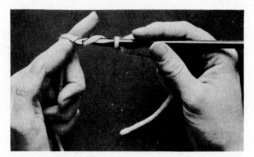

Pass the hook under the strand of yarn on index finger. Catch yarn with hook and draw it through loop on hook. This makes one chain stitch (1 ch).

Yarn over hook again and draw it through the two loops on hook. This completes one single crochet (1 sc). One loop is left on the hook, as shown.

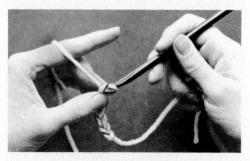

Make as many chains as needed. (One loop always remains on hook, but does not count as a chain.) Practice until you can make chains even in size.

Insert hook under two top threads of next chain as shown and repeat single crochet: yarn over hook, draw loop through, yarn over and through two loops.

SINGLE CROCHET (sc)

Chain about 20 stitches for your practice piece. Hold chain with right side toward you. Insert hook under the two top threads of 2nd chain from hook.

TO TURN SINGLE CROCHET

Work a single crochet in each chain to end of row. You will have one single crochet less than number of original chains. At end of the row, chain one.

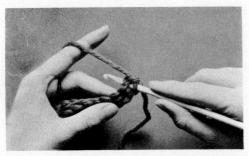

Turn work so that reverse side faces you. Insert hook under two top threads of first stitch. Work single crochet as before in each stitch across.

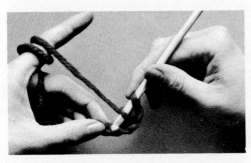

DOUBLE CROCHET (dc)

Chain about 20 stitches for your practice piece. Yarn over hook, insert hook under two top threads of 4th chain from hook (do not count loop on hook).

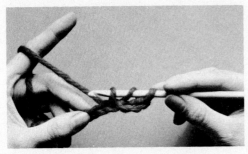

Pass the hook under the strand of yarn on index finger. Catch yarn with hook and draw it through the chain stitch. There are three loops on hook.

Pass hook under yarn on index finger again, catch yarn with hook and draw it through two loops on hook. There are now two loops remaining on hook.

Yarn over hook again and draw through the last two loops on hook. This completes one double crochet (1 dc). Work double crochet in each chain across.

HALF DOUBLE CROCHET (hdc)

Yarn over hook, insert hook under two top threads of 3rd chain from hook, catch yarn with hook, draw it through chain. There are three loops on hook.

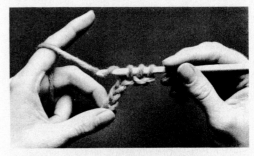

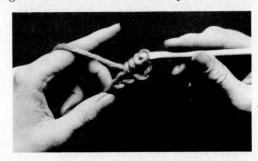

Pass hook under yarn on index finger again, catch yarn with hook and, with one motion, draw through all three loops on hook—one half double crochet.

SLIP STITCH (sl st)

Slip stitch is often used as an edge stitch on crochet and knitting. Insert the hook in stitch, yarn over, pull through stitch and loop in one motion.

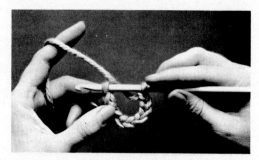

SLIP STITCH FOR JOINING

Slip stitch is also used for joining chains into rings and joining rounds of crochet. For joining ring, insert the hook in the last chain from hook.

Pass the hook under strand of yarn on index finger, draw yarn through chain and through loop on hook with one motion—ring is joined with slip stitch.

TO INCREASE 1 STITCH (inc 1 st)

When directions say "increase one stitch," make two stitches in one stitch. In working hats and other round pieces, increases are made every round.

TO DECREASE 1 SINGLE CROCHET (dec 1 sc)

When directions say "decrease one single crochet," work one single crochet until there are two loops on hook. Begin next single crochet—three loops.

Yarn over hook and draw through all three loops on hook with one motion. There is now only one stitch to work in on the next row instead of two stitches.

TO DECREASE 1 DOUBLE CROCHET (dec 1 dc)

Work one double crochet until there are two loops on hook. Begin next double crochet in next stitch: yarn over hook, insert in stitch, draw loop through.

With four loops on hook, pass hook under strand of yarn on index finger, catch yarn with hook, draw it through two loops, leaving three loops on hook.

Yarn over hook and draw through all three loops on hook with one motion. There is now only one stitch to work in on the next row instead of two stitches.

TO END OFF

When directions say "end off," cut the yarn 3″ or more from your last stitch. Insert hook in final loop, yarn over hook and draw through last loop.

Pull yarn end to tighten stitch. This fastens the end of your work. To hide yarn end, thread it in a yarn needle and weave it into the back of work.

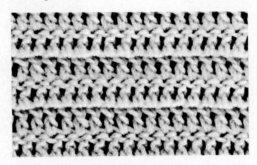

ROWS OF DOUBLE CROCHET

Photograph shows double crochet worked back and forth in rows. When turning work at end of row, ch 3 to count as first double crochet of next row.

STEP-BY-STEP LESSON
FOR LEFT-HANDED CROCHETERS

If you are left-handed, you can learn to crochet, too, from this step-by-step lesson. On these pages, we show, in a series of photographs, basic information on crochet—how to hold your yarn and hook, how to make chain stitch, single crochet, double crochet, half double crochet, and slip stitch, how to turn your work at the end of a row, how to increase and decrease, how to end off. After you have finished the lesson, turn to page 317 for additional crochet instructions. We include abbreviations used in our crochet directions, other information you will need to follow directions, and the importance of gauge in making any crocheted fashion. In all our directions, wherever there is a change necessary for left-handed crocheters, we indicate the change.

HOW TO CROCHET

GETTING READY TO CROCHET

Use a ball of knitting worsted for practicing your stitches when learning to crochet and a plastic crochet hook size H or 6 in a contrasting color.

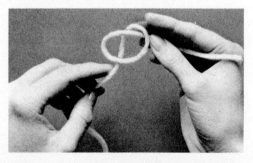

Grasp the yarn about 2″ from the end between your thumb and forefinger. With your left hand, lap the long strand over the short, forming a loop.

Hold this loop in place between your right thumb and forefinger. Grasp the hook in your left hand like a pencil. Insert the hook through the loop.

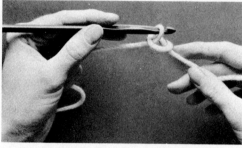

CHAIN STITCH (ch)

Catch the strand with the hook and draw it through loop. Pull end of yarn and strand coming from ball in opposite directions to close loop around hook.

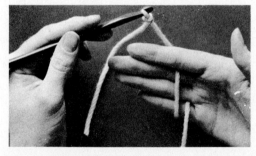

Loop yarn coming from ball around base of little finger of your right hand. Bring this yarn across front of three fingers and back under forefinger.

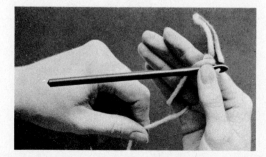

To adjust tension of your yarn, grasp the hook and loop in your right hand as shown. Pull strand from ball firmly down to tighten around fingers.

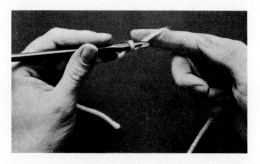

Hold the hook in your left hand as shown. Bend the little finger, ring finger, and middle finger of your right hand to control the strand of yarn.

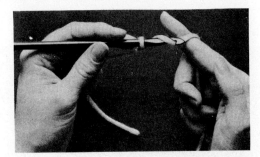

Pass the hook under the strand of yarn on index finger. Catch yarn with hook and draw it through loop on hook. This makes one chain stitch (1 ch).

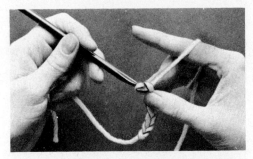

Make as many chains as needed. (One loop always remains on hook, but does not count as a chain.) Practice until you can make chains even in size.

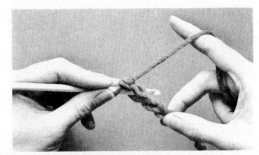

SINGLE CROCHET (sc)

Chain about 20 stitches for your practice piece. Hold chain with right side toward you. Insert hook under the two top threads of 2nd chain from hook.

Pass hook under yarn on index finger and catch yarn with hook as you did for chain stitch. Draw yarn through chain. There are now two loops on hook.

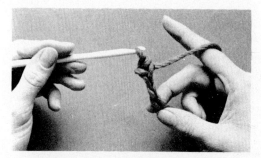

Yarn over hook again and draw it through the two loops on hook. This completes one single crochet (1 sc). One loop is left on the hook, as shown.

Insert hook under two top threads of next chain as shown and repeat single crochet: yarn over hook, draw loop through, yarn over and through two loops.

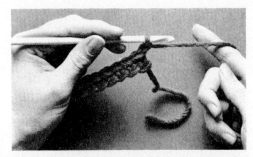

TO TURN SINGLE CROCHET

Work a single crochet in each chain to end of row. You will have one single crochet less than number of original chains. At end of the row, chain one.

Turn work so that reverse side faces you. Insert hook under two top threads of first stitch. Work single crochet as before in each stitch across.

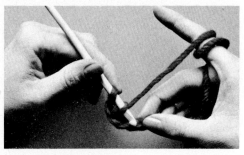

DOUBLE CROCHET (dc)

Chain about 20 stitches for your practice piece. Yarn over hook, insert hook under two top threads of 4th chain from hook (do not count loop on hook).

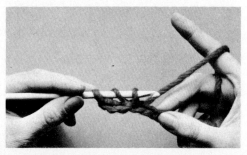

Pass the hook under the strand of yarn on index finger. Catch yarn with hook and draw it through the chain stitch. There are three loops on hook.

Pass hook under yarn on index finger again, catch yarn with hook and draw it through two loops on hook. There are now two loops remaining on hook.

Yarn over hook again and draw through the last two loops on hook. This completes one double crochet (1 dc). Work double crochet in each chain across.

HALF DOUBLE CROCHET (hdc)

Yarn over hook, insert hook under two top threads of 3rd chain from hook, catch yarn with hook, draw it through chain. There are three loops on hook.

Pass hook under yarn on index finger again, catch yarn with hook and, with one motion, draw through all three loops on hook—one half double crochet.

SLIP STITCH (sl st)

Slip stitch is often used as an edge stitch on crochet and knitting. Insert the hook in stitch, yarn over, pull through stitch and loop in one motion.

SLIP STITCH FOR JOINING

Slip stitch is also used for joining chains into rings and joining rounds of crochet. For joining ring, insert the hook in the last chain from hook.

Pass the hook under strand of yarn on index finger, draw yarn through chain and through loop on hook with one motion—ring is joined with slip stitch.

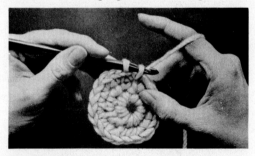

TO INCREASE 1 STITCH (inc 1 st)

When directions say "increase one stitch," make two stitches in one stitch. In working hats and other round pieces, increases are made every round.

TO DECREASE 1 SINGLE CROCHET (dec 1 sc)

When directions say "decrease one single crochet," work one single crochet until there are two loops on hook. Begin next single crochet—three loops.

Yarn over hook and draw through all three loops on hook with one motion. There is now only one stitch to work in on the next row instead of two stitches.

TO DECREASE 1 DOUBLE CROCHET (dec 1 dc)

Work one double crochet until there are two loops on hook. Begin next double crochet in next stitch: yarn over hook, insert in stitch, draw loop through.

With four loops on hook, pass hook under strand of yarn on index finger, catch yarn with hook, draw it through two loops, leaving three loops on hook.

Yarn over hook and draw through all three loops on hook with one motion. There is now only one stitch to work in on the next row instead of two stitches.

TO END OFF

When directions say "end off," cut the yarn 3" or more from your last stitch. Insert hook in final loop, yarn over hook and draw through last loop.

Pull yarn end to tighten stitch. This fastens the end of your work. To hide yarn end, thread it in a yarn needle and weave it into the back of work.

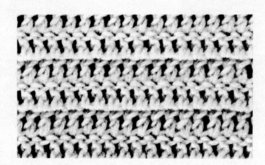

ROWS OF DOUBLE CROCHET

Photograph shows double crochet worked back and forth in rows. When turning work at end of row, ch 3 to count as first double crochet of next row.

CROCHET ABBREVIATIONS

ch—chain stitch
st—stitch
sts—stitches
lp—loop
inc—increase
dec—decrease
rnd—round
beg—beginning
sk—skip
p—picot
tog—together
sc—single crochet

sl st—slip stitch
dc—double crochet
hdc—half double crochet
tr—treble or triple crochet
dtr—double treble crochet
tr tr—treble treble crochet
bl—block
sp—space
cl—cluster
pat—pattern
yo—yarn over hook

HOW TO FOLLOW DIRECTIONS

An asterisk (*) is often used in crochet directions to indicate repetition. For example, when directions read "* 2 dc in next st, 1 dc in next st, repeat from * 4 times" this means to work directions after first * until second * is reached, then go back to first * 4 times more. Work 5 times in all.

When () (parentheses) are used to show repetition, work directions within parentheses as many times as specified. For example, "(dc, ch 1) 3 times" means to do what is within () 3 times altogether.

"Work even" in directions means to work in same stitch without increasing or decreasing.

THE IMPORTANCE OF GAUGE IN CROCHET

Before crocheting a garment, make a swatch to check your gauge using the yarn and hook called for in the directions.

Start with a chain about four inches long and work the swatch in the pattern stitch of the garment until piece is about three inches deep. Block swatch by smoothing it out, pinning it down along edges and steam-pressing it. Measure across two inches, counting the number of stitches to the inch. If you have *more* stitches to the inch than directions call for, you are working too tightly; try a new swatch with a larger hook or work more loosely. If you have *fewer* stitches to the inch, you are working too loosely; try a smaller hook or work more tightly.

If you wish to substitute one yarn for another, be sure the substitute yarn produces the proper gauge. By crocheting a swatch you will be able to check your gauge and determine the texture of the substitute yarn in the pattern stitch.

In crocheting household designs, you may wish to alter the appearance of the design by choosing a different thread from the one recommended. In this case be sure to work a small sample first, then check the appearance and gauge to be sure you will obtain the result you wish.

Actual-size photograph of box stitch shell pattern worked very tightly with steel crochet hook No. 0.

Same yarn and stitch were used for this swatch, worked very loosely with plastic hook size H or 8.

ADJUSTING TO LARGER OR SMALLER SIZES

To determine what size to make, take body measurements. Find the column of measurements in the tables which approximates those measurements. The size at the top of the column is the size to make. If one body measurement differs from the measurement given for that size, adjustments can be made in the blocking and finishing.

Usually, there is a 2″ difference in bust, waist and hip between each misses' and each women's size and a 2″ difference in chest and waist between men's sizes. To make a garment one size larger than given in directions, add the number of stitches equaling 1″ to both back and front of a pullover or dress, 1″ to back and ½″ to each front for a cardigan or jacket, 2″ to a skirt. Subtract same amounts for smaller size. For sizes that do not vary 2″, such as 6, 8 and 10, subtract the amounts they vary from the larger size given in directions. When the stitch is a repeat pattern, add or subtract the number of stitches equal to one or more multiples.

There is ½″ difference across back and front at shoulders for each misses' and each women's size, 1″ for each men's size. To obtain desired width at shoulders, decrease more or fewer stitches at armhole shaping, dividing evenly between armholes. For sleeves, there is a ¼″ difference in width at wrist and ½″ at underarm for each size.

BODY MEASUREMENTS

MISSES' BODY MEASUREMENTS

SIZE	6	8	10	12	14	16	18
BUST	30½	31½	32½	34	36	38	40 ins.
WAIST	22	23	24	25½	27	29	31 ″
HIP	32½	33½	34½	36	38	40	42 ″

YOUNG JUNIORS/TEENS

SIZE	7/8	9/10	11/12	13/14
BUST	29	30½	32	33½ ins.
WAIST	23	24	25	26 ″
HIP	32	33½	35	36½ ″

MEN'S BODY MEASUREMENTS

SIZE	34	36	38	40	42	44
CHEST	34	36	38	40	42	44 ins.
WAIST	30	32	34	36	38	40 ″

WOMEN'S BODY MEASUREMENTS

SIZE	38	40	42	44	46	48
BUST	42	44	46	48	50	52 ″
WAIST	34	36	38	40½	43	45½ ″
HIP	44	46	48	50	52	54 ″

INFANTS' AND GIRLS' BODY MEASUREMENTS

SIZE	6 mos.	1	2	3	4	6	8	10	12	14
CHEST	19	20	21	22	23	24	27	28½	30	32 ins.
WAIST	19	19½	20	20½	21	22	23½	24½	25½	26½ ″
HIP	20	21	22	23	24	26	28	30	32	34 ″
HEIGHT*	22	25	29	31	33	37	41	45	49	53 ″

BOYS' BODY MEASUREMENTS

SIZE	1	2	3	4	6	8	10	12	14	16
CHEST	20	21	22	23	24	26	28	30	32	34 ins.
WAIST	19½	20	20½	21	22	23	24	25½	27	29 ″
NECK					11	11½	12	12½	13½	14 ″
HIP	20	21	22	23	25	27	29	31	33	35½ ″
HEIGHT*	25	29	31	33	37	41	45	49	53	55 ″

* Height for girls and boys (with shoes) is measured from socket bone at back of neck to floor.

FINISHING TECHNIQUES

STITCHES

Treble or Triple Crochet (tr): With 1 loop on hook put yarn over hook twice, insert in 5th chain from hook, pull loop through. Yarn over and draw through 2 loops at a time 3 times. At end of a row, chain 4 and turn. Chain 4 counts as first treble of next row.

Double Treble (dtr): Put yarn over hook 3 times and work off 2 loops at a time as for treble.

Treble Treble (tr tr): Put yarn over hook 4 times and work off 2 loops at a time as for treble.

SEAMS

Most seams are sewn with running backstitch, especially seams on curved, slanted or loose edges. Pin right sides of pieces together, keeping edges even and matching rows or patterns. Thread matching yarn in tapestry needle. Run end of yarn through several stitches along edge to secure; backstitch pieces together close to edge. Do not draw yarn too tight; keep seam elastic. Experiment with different kinds of seams on your crocheted pieces—use overhand stitch, weaving stitch, or sewing machine—to find the best seam for each article.

BLOCKING

Smooth pieces out, wrong side up, on a padded surface. Using rustproof pins, place pins at top and bottom of each piece, measuring to insure correct length. Pin sides of piece to correct width. Place pins all around outer edges, keeping patterns straight.

For flat pressing technique (flat rows of crochet, smooth yarns): Cover with damp cloth. Lower iron gently, allowing steam to penetrate piece. Do not press down hard or hold iron in one place long enough to dry out pressing cloth. Do not slide iron over surface.

For steaming technique (raised pattern stitches, fluffy yarns): Support weight of iron in your hand; hold as close as possible to piece without touching it and move slowly over entire piece, making sure steam penetrates piece. If yarn is extra heavy, use a spray iron or wet pressing cloth to provide extra steam.

When blocked pieces are dry, remove pins and sew pieces together. Steam-press seams from wrong side, using a steam iron; a damp cloth and dry iron may also be used.

BOX STITCH SHELL PATTERN

Shown on page 317

Row 1: Dc in 3rd ch from hook, dc in each of next 2 ch, sk 2 ch, sl st in next ch, * ch 2, dc in each of next 3 ch, sk 2 ch, sl st in next ch; repeat from * across, ending last shell with dc in last 3 ch. Turn.

Row 2: Sl st across top of 3 dc, sl st under ch-2 lp of shell, * ch 2, 3 dc under same ch-2 lp, sl st under ch-2 lp of next shell; repeat from * across to last shell, make shell in ch-2 lp of last shell. Turn.

Repeat row 2 for pat, having same number of shells in each row.

CASING

On Skirt or Pants: With wrong side facing you, join yarn at top edge, * ch ¾", sl st in st ½" to left in row ½" below, ch ¾", sl st at top edge ½" to left of last st, repeat from * around.

CHANGING COLORS

When changing colors in crochet, work last st of old color until 2 lps remain on hook, finish st with new color. Work over yarn ends, or weave them into wrong side of work later.

HOW TO MAKE A TWISTED CORD

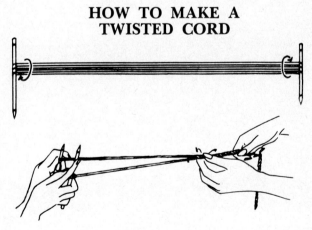

Twisted Cord

Method requires two people. Tie one end of yarn around pencil. Loop yarn over center of second pencil, back to and around first, and back to second, making as many strands between pencils as needed for thickness of cord; knot end to pencil. Length of yarn between pencils should be three times length of cord desired. Each person holds yarn just below pencil with one hand and twists pencil with other hand, keeping yarn taut. When yarn begins to kink, catch center over doorknob or hook. Bring pencils together for one person to hold, while other grasps the center of the yarn, sliding hand down yarn and releasing yarn at short intervals, and letting the yarn twist.

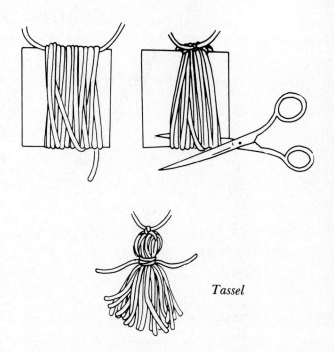

HOW TO MAKE A TASSEL

Wind yarn around a cardboard cut to size of tassel desired, winding it 25 to 40 times around, depending on thickness of yarn and plumpness of tassel required. Tie strands tightly together around top as shown, leaving at least 3″ ends on ties; clip other end of strands. Wrap a piece of yarn tightly around strands a few times about ½″ or 1″ below top tie and knot. Trim ends.

Tassel

EMBROIDERY STITCH DETAILS

Running Backstitch

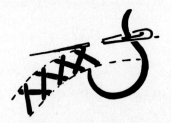

Herringbone Stitch

Cross-stitch

Chain Stitch

French Knot